ENCYCLOPEDIA OF
EDUCATION

SECOND EDITION

EDITORIAL BOARD

ENCYCLOPEDIA OF EDUCATION

SECOND EDITION

James W. Guthrie, Editor in Chief

VOLUME

2

Common–Expertise

MACMILLAN REFERENCE USA™

New York • Detroit • San Diego • San Francisco • Cleveland • New Haven, Conn. • Waterville, Maine • London • Munich

Encyclopedia of Education, Second Edition

James W. Guthrie, Editor in Chief

For permission to use material from this product, submit your request via Web at http://www.gale-edit.com/permissions, or you may download our Permissions Request form and submit your request by fax or mail to:

Permissions Department
The Gale Group, Inc.
27500 Drake Road
Farmington Hills, MI 48331-3535
Permissions Hotline: 248-699-8006 or
800-877-4253 ext. 8006
Fax: 248-699-8074 or 800-762-4058

LIBRARY OF CONGRESS CATALOGING-IN-PUBLICATION DATA

Encyclopedia of education / edited by James W. Guthrie.—2nd ed.
　　p. cm.
Includes bibliographical references and index.
　　ISBN 0-02-865594-X (hardcover : set : alk. paper)
1. Education—Encyclopedias. I. Guthrie, James W.
　　LB15 .E47 2003
　　370'.3—dc21
　　　　　　　　　　　　　　　　　　　　　　2002008205

ISBNs
Volume 1: 0-02-865595-8
Volume 2: 0-02-865596-6
Volume 3: 0-02-865597-4
Volume 4: 0-02-865598-2
Volume 5: 0-02-865599-0
Volume 6: 0-02-865600-8
Volume 7: 0-02-865601-6
Volume 8: 0-02-865602-4

Printed in the United States of America
10 9 8 7 6 5 4 3 2 1

CONTINUED

COMMON SCHOOL MOVEMENT

The ubiquity of "common" schools in the United States belies both the long effort to establish a system of publicly supported elementary and secondary schools and the many controversies that have attended public schools before and since their creation. The belief that *public,* or *free,* schools and *pauper* schools were synonymous terms, and that such schools were only for children of the poor, long hampered the acceptance of the idea that publicly supported schools could and should exist for all children, regardless of social class, gender, religion, ethnicity, or country of origin. Moreover, the European and colonial insistence that responsible parents need concern themselves only with the education of their own children through the avenues of the family, church, or the voluntary efforts of like-minded citizens only slowly gave way to the conviction that publicly supported common schools might serve all children equally, and in so doing advance the moral, social, and economic interests so vital to the nation.

The common school movement took hold in the 1830s, and by the time of the Civil War organized systems of common schools had become commonplace throughout most of northern and midwestern states. Expansion of common school systems into the southern and far-western states progressed at a slower rate, but by the opening years of the twentieth century publicly supported systems of common schools had become a cornerstone of the American way of life. However, the emergence of a system of public schools across the nation was neither an inevitable nor an uncontested movement. Moreover, its survival into the future may prove to be as problematic as was its development in the past.

Colonial and Republican Schooling

From the earliest days of American settlement, education has been a concern. Colonists up and down the Atlantic seaboard established local varieties of both *fee* and *free* schools as community conditions, benevolence, and population increase seemed to warrant. However, the Puritans who established the New England colonies displayed a special eagerness to provide for education and literacy as bulwarks against religious and cultural decline. In 1635 Boston town officials saw the need to hire a schoolmaster "for the teaching and nurturing of children with us" (Cremin 1970, p. 180). The Boston Latin Grammar School opened the next year, along with the founding of Harvard College.

Other New England towns moved haltingly toward providing support and encouragement for formal schooling in the same period. The famous Old Deluder Satan Act of 1647 reflected the urgency felt by some Puritan leaders. While not requiring school attendance, this pronouncement by the Massachusetts General Court mandated that towns with fifty or more families were to make provision for instruction in reading and writing, and that in communities of a hundred households or more, grammar schools should be established that would prepare boys for entry into Harvard College. Although noncompliance could result in a fine levied against a town, not all towns adhered to the requirements of the enactment. Throughout the colonial period, provisions for schooling remained very much a matter of local, and somewhat haphazard, arrangements.

Town schools in New England had their parallel in the form of local schools set up by transient schoolmasters and various denominational groups who filtered into the Middle Atlantic colonies and the southern regions of the country. The general attitude in many parts of the American colonies was framed by Virginia's governor, Sir William Berkeley, who in 1671 wrote that in his colony, education was basically a private matter. Virginians, he said, were following "the same course that is taken in England out of towns; every man according to his own ability in instructing his children" (Urban and Wagoner, p. 22–23).

The coming of the American Revolution and the influence of Enlightenment ideas began to challenge the laissez-faire doctrines of the colonial period, however. Recognizing that the dictum of "every man according to his own ability" might work rather nicely for the economic elite but not for the mass of the population (or for the health and survival of the emerging nation), another Virginia governor, Thomas Jefferson, took the lead in setting forth plans calling for more systematic and encompassing educational arrangements in his native state. As part of a massive reform package, In 1779 Jefferson proposed *A Bill for the More General Diffusion of Knowledge.* Jefferson's general plan envisioned public support for secondary schools and scholarships for the best and brightest students to attend the College of William and Mary. But the foundation of his system was basic education for the mass of the population.

Jefferson called for the division of each county into wards, or "little republics," and the creation therein of elementary schools into which "all the free children, male and female," would be admitted without charge. These publicly supported elementary schools would equip all citizens with the basic literacy and computational skills they would need in order to manage their own affairs.

Civic literacy was an essential component of Jefferson's plan. He recommended the study of history as a means of improving citizens' moral and civic virtues and enabling them to know and exercise their rights and duties. Projecting a theme that would echo throughout the common school movement in the next century, Jefferson conceived of elementary schooling as basic education for citizenship; it was to be a public investment in the possibility of self-government and human happiness at both the individual and social levels. In the words of Jefferson: "If a nation expects to be ignorant and free in a state of civilization, it expects what never was and never will be" (Ford, pp. 1–4). In a letter to George Washington in 1786, Jefferson declared: "It is an axiom in my mind that our liberty can never be safe but in the hands of the people themselves. This it is the business of the state to effect, and on a general plan" (Boyd, pp. 150–152).

Jefferson was by no means alone in his concern over the educational requirements of the new nation. A number of other prominent Americans, some of whom differed quite sharply with Jefferson (and each other) on certain political, religious, and educational particulars, nonetheless shared his general sense of urgency regarding the necessity of new approaches to education for the new nation. A decade after Benjamin Rush signed his name to the Declaration of Independence, he declared that the war for independence was only "the first act of the great drama. We have changed our forms of government, but it yet remains to effect a revolution in principles, opinions, and manners so as to accommodate them to the forms of government we have adopted" (Butterfield, pp. 388–389). Rush called for a system of schools in his native state of Pennsylvania, and he then expanded his plan into one for a national system of education. Directly attacking the argument that any system of publicly supported schools would require a repressive taxation system, Rush set forth an argument that, like Jefferson's political rationale, would become a vital part of the movement that led to the establishment of common schools. Rush argued that the schools he was advocating were "designed to *lessen* our taxes." His argument merits quotation:

> But, shall the estates of orphans, bachelors, and persons who have no children be taxed to pay for the support of schools from which they can derive no benefit? I answer in the affirmative to the first part of the objection, and I deny the truth of the latter part of it. . . . The bachelor will in time save his tax for this purpose by being able to sleep with fewer bolts and locks on his doors, the estates of orphans will in time be benefited by being protected from the vantages of unprincipled and idle boys, and the children of wealthy parents will be less tempted, by bad company, to extravagance. Fewer pillories and whipping posts and smaller jails, with their usual expenses and taxes, will be necessary when our youth are more properly educated than at present. (Rudolph, p. 6–7)

Noah Webster, whose "blue-backed" *American Spelling Book* and *American Dictionary of the English Language* did much to help define the new nation, agreed with Jefferson and Rush on the educational needs of the fragile American republic. A schoolmaster and later a founder of Amherst College, Webster considered the role of education so central to the working of a free government that he flatly asserted it to be the most important business of civil society.

However, in spite of the pleas and schemes of these and other "founding fathers," the new nation ended the eighteenth century with a patchwork pattern of schools, most of which were conducted under the auspices of private schoolmasters or sectarian religious groups. Schools essentially served private purposes and educational attainment reflected the religious, racial, class, and gender differences in society. Even so, the educational requirements for work and a productive life for most people in the latter half of the eighteenth century and the early nineteenth century were modest, regardless of one's background. Skills and knowledge were often learned through one's labor within the family or through apprenticeship. However, the economic realties and social conditions that ushered in the nineteenth century prompted renewed calls for expanded and better organized approaches to the education of the public.

Changes in the Antebellum Era

Although the American mode of education in 1800 bore remarkable resemblance to that of the pre-Revolutionary era, by 1900 public education was so radically different and far-reaching that the common school movement of the 1800s is widely regarded as the most significant change or reform in nineteenth century American education. This dramatic change was precipitated by a number of factors, including industrialization and the rise of the factory system; labor unrest; the spread of merchant capitalism; the expansion and economic influence of banks and insurance companies; transportation advances brought on by steam travel on inland and coastal waterways and by railroad; burgeoning population growth (including the arrival of large numbers of Roman Catholic immigrants who challenged the social and cultural norms of the mostly Protestant citizenry); and the westward migration of settlers, many of whom sought to establish the eastern tradition of town schools on the frontier.

To a large extent, the spread of common schools was an institutional response to the threat of social fragmentation and to a fear of moral and cultural decay. Reformers of various types—ministers, politicians, Utopians, Transcendentalists, workingmen, and early feminists—saw in schools, or at least in education, a way to ameliorate the disturbing social vices that were increasingly associated with swelling urban centers. Schools were seen as a means of turning Americans—whether "native" or "foreign born," rural or urban—into patriotic and law-abiding citizens, thereby achieving the Jeffersonian goal of securing the republic.

Protestant denominations began putting some of their sectarian differences aside and joined forces to establish charitable schools for poor children in cities like Philadelphia and New York. These charity schools were precursors of nonsectarian public common schools in the sense that they became organized into centralized bureaucracies that received public subsidies. Interdenominational cooperation among Protestant denominations became a key ingredient in, and an essential feature of, the gradual acceptance of the common school ideal.

The Rise of the Common School

The common school movement began in earnest in the 1830s in New England as reformers, often from the Whig party (which promoted greater public endeavors than the comparatively laissez-faire Democrats), began to argue successfully for a greater government role in the schooling of all children. Horace Mann, often referred to as the Father of the Common School, left his career as a Massachusetts lawyer and legislator to assume the mantle and duties of secretary to the newly established state board of education in 1837.

Mann's commitment to common schools stemmed from his belief that political stability and social harmony depended on universal education. He stumped the state arguing for common schools that would be open to all children, and he preached that support for nonsectarian common schools was a religious as well as a civic duty. His message to the working classes was the promise that "education . . . is the great equalizer of the conditions of men, the balance wheel of the social machinery" (Cremin 1957, p. 65). To men of property he asserted that their security and prosperity depended upon having literate and law-abiding neighbors who were competent workers and who would, via the common school, learn of the sanctity of private property. To all he proclaimed that Providence had decreed that education was the "*absolute right of every human being that comes into the world*" (Cremin 1957, p. 87).

Mann was joined in his crusade for common schools by like-minded reformers in other states. In his own state, James G. Carter played an important role in pushing Massachusetts to establish normal schools to prepare teachers for the emerging "profession" of education. Henry Barnard played a leading role in Connecticut and Rhode Island, as did Samuel Lewis and Calvin Stowe in Ohio, along with numerous others across the country. Catharine Beecher, sister of abolitionist author Harriet Beecher Stowe, is noteworthy among the women who took up the cause of educational reform and the promotion of women as teachers and exemplars of self-improvement. Graduates of Beecher's Hartford Female Seminary, founded in 1823, were in the forefront of generations of "schoolmarms" who staffed the nation's rapidly growing supply of public schools.

Resistance to Common Schools

Historian Carl Kaestle has maintained that the eventual acceptance of state common school systems was based upon American's commitment to republican government, the dominance of native Protestant culture, and the development of capitalism. While the convergence of these forces can be credited with the emergence and endurance of America's common schools, the arguments and fears of opponents of public education were not easily overcome. The hegemonic Pan-Protestant common school system may have had general popular support, but many Roman Catholics (and some Protestant sects) strenuously objected to the supposedly "nonsectarian" schools. Many Catholics agreed with New York City Bishop John Hughes, who argued that the public schools were anti-Catholic and unacceptable to his flock. When repeated pleas for a share of public funds dedicated to the support of religious schools failed to win legislative approval in New York and elsewhere, many Catholics rejected the nondenominational public school compromise, a situation that eventually led to the creation of a separate and parallel system of parochial schools.

Religious division was not the only obstacle to universal acceptance of the doctrine of universal public education. A desire to maintain strict local control over schools put many advocates of statewide organization on the defensive. Intermixed with class, race, and ethnic tensions, demands for local control of schools was—and remains—a hotly contested issue. Opposition to taxation, raised as an objection to publicly financed schemes of education during the colonial period, continued to provoke resistance. Related to issues of control and taxation were charges that government involvement in education was a repudiation of liberalism and parental rights. Advocates of this position championed the right of individuals to be left alone and responsible for their own lives.

Finally, if some of the more conservative members of society feared that public schools and democratic rhetoric might unsettle relations between capital and labor and lead to increased clamoring over "rights" on the part of the working classes, some of the more radical labor leaders contended that public day schools, while useful, did not go far enough toward creating a society of equals. Among the most extreme positions was that put forward by the workingmen's party in New York, of which Robert Dale Owen, social reformer and son of Robert Owen (founder of the utopian New Harmony Community in Indiana) was a member. In 1830 that body called for public support of common *boarding schools* in which all children would not only live together and study the same subjects, but would dress in the same manner and eschew all reminders of "the pride of riches, or the contempt of poverty" (Carlton, p. 58). Few reformers were willing to endorse so radical a proposal, however.

The Survival and Spread of Common Schools

Political consensus and compromise led state after state to adopt systems of common or public schools by the latter half of the nineteenth century. Although a few southern states had made progress in this direction before the Civil War, it was not until after that conflict that the states that had been in rebellion adopted legally mandated—but racially segregated—systems of public education. In 1855 Massachusetts had become the first state to abolish legal segregation; it took yet another full century for the United States Supreme Court to extend that practice to the entire nation by declaring in the famous *Brown v. Board of Education* decision of 1954 that the practice of "separate but equal" was unconstitutional. Other twentieth-century court decisions ended religious practices such as Bible reading and prayer in public schools.

Competing educational philosophies, as well as political and social divisions in society, have made the issue of what should be "common" about common schooling one that is continually under review. If, as one historian has observed, the "the American public school is a gigantic standardized compromise most of us have learned to live with" (Kaestle 1976, p. 396), it is a compromise that has been, and must continue to be, constantly renegotiated.

See also: ELEMENTARY EDUCATION, *subentry on* HISTORY OF; MANN, HORACE.

BIBLIOGRAPHY

BOYD, JULIAN P., ed. 1950. *The Papers of Thomas Jefferson,* Vol. I. Princeton, NJ: Princeton University Press.

BUTTERFIELD, L. H., ed. 1951. *Letters of Benjamin Rush.* Princeton, NJ: Princeton University Press.

BUTTS, R. FREEMAN. 1978. *Public Education in the United States: From Revolution to Reform.* New York: Holt, Rinehart and Winston.

CARLTON, FRANK TRACY. 1965. *Economic Influences upon Educational Progress in the United States, 1820–1850* (1908). Madison: University of Wisconsin.

CREMIN, LAWRENCE A. 1957. *The Republic and the School: Horace Mann on the Education of Free Men.* New York: Teachers College Press.

CREMIN, LAWRENCE A. 1970. *American Education: The Colonial Experience, 1607–1783.* New York: Harper and Row.

CREMIN, LAWRENCE A. 1980. *American Education: The National Experience, 1783–1876.* New York: Harper and Row.

FORD, PAUL L., ed. 1892–1899. *The Writings of Thomas Jefferson,* Vol. 10. New York: G. P. Putnam's Sons.

FRASER, JAMES W. 1999. *Between Church and State: Religion and Public Education in a Multicultural America.* New York: St. Martin's.

KAESTLE, CARL F. 1973. *The Evolution of an Urban School System: New York City, 1750–1850.* Cambridge, MA: Harvard University Press.

KAESTLE, CARL F. 1976. "Conflict and Consensus Revisited: Notes Toward a Reinterpretation of American Educational History." *Harvard Education Review* 46:390–396.

KAESTLE, CARL F. 1983. *Pillars of the Republic: Common Schools and American Society, 1780–1860.* New York: Hill and Wang.

KATZ, MICHAEL B. 1971. *Class, Bureaucracy, and Schools: The Illusion of Educational Change in America.* New York: Praeger.

LANNIE, VINCENT P. 1968. *Public Money and Parochial Educational: Bishop Hughes, Governor Seward, and the New York School Controversy.* Cleveland, OH: Case Western Reserve University Press.

LOCKRIDGE, KENNETH A. 1974. *Literacy in Colonial New England: An Enquiry into the Social Context of Literacy in the Early Modern West.* New York: W. W. Norton.

MEDLER, KEITH E. 1972. "Woman's High Calling: The Teaching Profession in America." *American Studies* 13:19–32.

MONDALE, SARAH, and PATTON, SARAH, eds. 2001. *School: The Story of American Public Education.* Boston: Beacon.

PESSEN, EDWARD. 1967. *Most Uncommon Jacksonians: The Radical Leaders of the Early Labor Movement.* Albany: State University of New York Press.

RUDOLPH, FREDERICK, ed. 1965. *Essays on Education in the Early Republic.* Cambridge, MA: Harvard University Press.

SCHRAG, PETER. 1970. "End of the Impossible Dream." *Saturday Review* 53:68–70; 92–96.

TYACK, DAVID. 1974. *The One Best System: A History of American Urban Education.* Cambridge, MA: Harvard University Press.

URBAN, WAYNE J., and WAGONER, JENNINGS L., JR. 2000. *American Education: A History,* 2nd edition. New York: McGraw-Hill.

WELTER, RUSH. 1962. *Popular Education and Democratic Thought in America.* New York: Columbia University Press.

JENNINGS L. WAGONER
WILLIAM N. HAARLOW

COMMUNITY-BASED ORGANIZATIONS, AGENCIES, AND GROUPS

Child and youth development are influenced not only by families and schools, but by a wide variety of formal and informal community organizations; some of which involve youth directly, while others effect neighborhood changes that affect youth and families.

Community Organization versus Community Organizing

It is important to distinguish community organization from community organizing. *Community organization* may be thought of from a broader, community perspective. Such a structural orientation considers a community's social ecology (the number and variety of organizations throughout a community, and the relationships among these organizations). Community organizations are most often nonprofit organizations—particularly service agencies—that are located in, and provide services to, neighborhoods and communities. Community organizations include parent-teacher organizations, sports clubs, church groups, block or neighborhood associations, 4-H clubs, and many others.

In contrast, *community organizing* is conceptualized more as a process aimed at creating change. This may be done either through developing leadership among individuals or by building power for collectives. Community organizing is best described as seeking empowerment, both as a process and an outcome. Community organizing, as a process, is practiced in community organizations, though not all community organizations practice community organizing. However, many community organizations whose main function is service provision have expanded the services they provide to include community organizing. So, while some organizations exist exclusively to practice the process of organizing, other organizations engage in some organizing, and still others practice no organizing.

The distinction between community organization and community organizing is made because the terms are sometimes used interchangeably. While the junction of these terms is sometimes appropriate and sometimes not, it is important to understand the historical relationship between these two terms, the fact that this relationship has changed dramatically over time, and that both have relevance for children and teenagers.

The History of Community Organization

Following the American Civil War, there was a rapid rise in the number of charitable agencies designed to lend assistance to those displaced, disabled, or im-poverished by the war. Many of these organizations were progressive in philosophy, even by the standards of the early twenty-first century, and they provided services to, or activities for, children and teens. The late 1800s also saw an expansion of the public school system, along with the creation of hundreds of orphanages, hospitals, settlement houses, and other charity services. Due to the rapid rise of such organizations, and a lack of government oversight, the distribution and coordination of services soon became problematic. The term *community organization* was coined by social workers in this era to address the problem of coordinating charity-based services, thus reflecting the structural perspective of community.

The next phase in the evolution of community organization stressed cooperative planning among privately run community-service agencies. Efforts were geared toward specialization of services and centralization of decisions regarding these services. By the late 1940s, community organization became professionalized in the field of social work. Community organization theory stressed organizing as a process where a professional organizer worked with communities to help develop leadership within a community.

In the 1960s, new realizations about the context of American communities—particularly the vast social and economic underclass and the inability of the welfare bureaucracy to adequately address the needs of the poor—influenced the orientation of community organization efforts to deal more closely with community organizing. It was during this period that the concepts of community organization and community organizing became more interconnected. The emphasis on organizing, rather than organization, led to an emphasis on citizen participation and empowerment.

During the 1980s and 1990s, community organizations expanded to the point of being referred to as a movement, and the process of community organizing expanded into many community organizations. One struggle that emerged in this period was the awareness of power shifting from local communities to regions, nations, and international corporations. The process of globalization has raised new questions about the efficacy of local organizations in addressing problems caused by large-scale economic forces.

Types of Community Organization

Categorizing community organizations is difficult, because they may range from voluntary organizations to professional service agencies to informal groups. These organizations are often considered to include churches, unions, schools, health care agencies, social-service groups, fraternities, and clubs. Community organizations are predominantly conceptualized as nonprofit, but broader conceptions of community sometimes include all organizations, including for-profit enterprises. Service agencies are frequently termed *community-based* agencies because their service has shifted from centralized institutional settings to dispersed geographical locations providing greater access to residents. Social-service agencies have received criticism because, although their geographic placement has improved resident access, their hierarchical social practices retain social- and cultural-access barriers.

There is a further distinction to be made, between volunteer and professional organizations. Volunteer organizations often have professional or paid staff, but volunteers perform the vast majority of these organizations' efforts. These organizations are frequently advocacy-oriented, and they apply community-organizing strategies to accomplish their goals. In contrast, professional organizations are usually staffed by experts who provide services with little or no volunteer input. These service-oriented organizations usually have greater resources than volunteer organizations, and they interface with residents based on professional norms and standards, whereas volunteer organizations have a more egalitarian orientation.

Another type of community organization is the informal group. These groups are represented by informal networks of friends and neighbors that exist throughout communities. The growth or decline in the number of these groups has been debated. While some argue that informal groups, such as bowling leagues, are declining, there is also evidence that other groups, such as self-help groups or small support groups, have proliferated.

Ecological Perspectives on Community Organizations

To understand the role of community organization in the lives of children and teens, it is important to understand these organizations from the perspective of the ecology of community life. There are numerous perspectives that may be considered ecological or structural, and a number of these will be looked at here.

Sociologist Robert Park, working in the 1960s in Chicago, was among the first to study ecological aspects of community. His ecological orientation viewed community not as a collection of streets and buildings, but as a psychological and sociological orientation based on customs, traditions, and organized attitudes. Park understood that community organizations, agencies, and groups are critical in the shaping of this psychological and sociological orientation.

Extending this work to the functional patterns of community, sociologist Norton Long viewed community as the product of interactions among powerful entities. For Long, community functioning is the result of competing and complementary interactions by those with power—usually groups and organizations operating in their own self-interest. He conceptualized this dynamic pattern of interactions as an ecology of games. The community's social structure is a by-product of sets of "players" who compete to achieve their goals and "win." Each "player" (a group or organization with power), defines their own "game" (the goals and objectives of that particular entity). A community's social structure, then, is composed of multiple groups and organizations geared toward reaching their organizational objectives. As different issues arise for "players" in the community, different allies and enemies are generated among the "players." Alliances and oppositions are based on the objectives of each player regarding that particular issue. From this perspective, patterns of community functioning are the product of powerful entities interacting, not the result of functional necessity or rational decisions.

In an application of this ecological orientation to the life of children, the psychologist Roger Barker (also in the 1960s) studied the diverse settings embedded in communities, and the constraints and opportunities those settings provide for children's development. His research established that different children in the same place behaved more similarly than the same children in different places. He concluded that settings exert a great deal of control over behavior—more so than personality or intrapsychic variables.

Barker's subsequent research focused more on settings, organizations, and schools, and less on individuals in those settings. He came to scrutinize *behavior settings* as units of analysis. Behavior settings are small-scale social systems composed of individuals and their immediate environments, which are configured such that they shape a pattern of behaviors, or what is called a *routine program of actions,* including specific time and place boundaries. Barker delineated three components to a behavior setting: (1) physical properties (e.g., size of a room, arrangement of chairs); (2) human components (roles or niches within an environment that individuals can fill, such as chairperson or observer); and (3) the setting program (the patterned sequence of transactions among actors in a specific environment).

In a 1964 study of two high schools, one large and one small, Roger Barker and Paul Gump compared the number of behavioral settings and the number of students in the each school. They found that the ratio of settings to students was much higher in the small school than in the big school. The result was that students in small high schools participated in a broader range of settings. They were also more likely to be involved participants than passive spectators and they had greater competence and cooperation when working with peers.

An explicit examination of the role of a community's ecology on human development was made by developmental psychologist Urie Bronfenbrenner in the 1970s. His work examined the successive ecologies that youth are embedded in, and the influence of these ecologies on development. At the most minute level, *microsystems* are the settings in which an individual participates (they are comparable to Barker's behavior settings). *Mesosystems* are the interactions and relations between microsystems. For example, the relationship between the education and law enforcement systems will impact the opportunities and constraints an individual encounters, which will have an impact on both the individual's behavior and personal safety. These two ecologies, the microsystem and mesosystem, play an important role in the development of children and teens. Bronfenbrenner articulates other ecologies, but these two are the most relevant in a discussion of community organizations.

The organizations that are part of a community have been termed *mediating structures.* Local community organizations provide a common ground for residents to share problems and resources. Organizations thus serve to mediate between seemingly powerless individuals or families and the large institutions of mass society. They include PTAs, school-community partnerships, churches, and voluntary associations. Mediating structures are *people-sized;* that is, they are small enough to reflect the values and realities of individual life, yet large enough to empower individuals to influence the broader social structures (e.g., large schools or school systems, government bureaucracies, large local corporations or chain enterprises, mass media) that may be the target of social-change efforts. Additionally, mediating structures represent contexts through which an empowerment process unfolds for individuals, organizations, and communities. Community organizations are one type of mediating structure. They function as mechanisms through which individuals can express their collective self-interests, particularly regarding the issues and problems affecting their families and communities.

As a field, community psychology has been at the forefront of research on supportive and empowering community settings for human development, and on the prevention of social and mental health problems. Much of this work has been done in religious, self-help/mutual aid, or block and neighborhood organizations. However, small-scale voluntary associations such as these are often suspicious of professionals and researchers, and therefore are difficult to study or evaluate, despite their importance.

The literature suggests that the assemblage of local organizations, agencies, and groups serve as a critical determinant of behavior and development. The implication for children and teens is that they will be assisted in their development to the extent that the organizational landscape is composed of numerous settings that involve and engage youth in healthy and appropriate developmental challenges.

Finally, *social capital* is a concept that has become very popular in discussions about community organization. Social capital is most commonly understood as the accumulation of trust embedded in the norms and networks that exist in a community. Some authors have emphasized informal networks, whether inside or outside organizations. Others have emphasized formally organized networks, or both formal and informal ones. Yet community organizations are, by definition, networks of civic engagement. Agencies that serve residents without developing relationships or building enduring activity and participation are not accumulating social capital. Community organizations, however, such as block groups, neighborhood associations, sports clubs, and school-based organizations, often embody the associational glue that creates social capital. When the norms and dynamics of these organizations include trust and reciprocity, the capacity for individuals within such groups to act for mutual benefit is great. Social capital may be therefore be understood as the norms of trust and reciprocity that exist both within and between the organizations, agencies, and groups that form the social ecology of a community.

Approaches to Community Organizing

It is important to examine community organizing—the process of empowering individuals and collectives. As noted previously, some community organizations exist to exclusively conduct community organizing, while some engage only partially in organizing, and some do no community organizing at all.

Bases of organizing. Community and labor organizer Si Kahn has identified four bases, or origins, of organizing: union, community, constituency, and issue organizing. Union organizing is based in the workplace; community organizing is based on location or geography; constituency organizing is based on common individual characteristics (e.g., gender, language, ethnic background); and issue organizing is based on issues rather than common individual characteristics (e.g., taxes, schools, war, health care). These bases of organization, like all typologies of organizations, are not mutually exclusive, and there is no common agreement about dividing typologies.

Types of organizing. There is a great diversity in community organizing typology. The most commonly cited approaches are social-planning, social-action, community-development, civic-agency, electoral, and pressure-group organizing. Again, this typology is not composed of mutually exclusive categories, and the differences between types are often minimal. Political scientist Janice Perlman reduces these multiple categories into three types: self-help or alternative institutions, electoral groups, and pressure groups.

Self-help community organizing includes three specific classifications of organizing: social planning, civic agency, and community development. Social planning is geared toward technical problem solving, especially with regard to the delivery of goods and services to people in need. Civic agency is a process characterized as providing services for those in need. Social change is not an issue for a civic agen-

cy—in fact, the civic agency approach sometimes must avoid social change, as change is politically difficult due to the support for this approach that exists within the existing social structure. Community development organizations most often emphasize the development of the built environment, and only secondarily stress social change. This approach uses consensus-building techniques to achieve improved community environments, and conflict is avoided. All three classifications of organizing incorporate professionals or experts in a variety of fields who work together to develop ideas and plans for specific programs. Historically, these approaches have involved very little community input, but the engagement and participation of citizens has increased throughout the 1990s.

Electoral organizing, often called *political participation*, involves the attainment of power through the electoral process. The activities of the electoral approach include voting, campaigning for candidates, and supporting or opposing specific issues. Involvement in the political process, while requiring the participation of many people, reflects the value of leadership in that the social problem or issue being campaigned for is ultimately placed in the hands of the elected official. From the perspective of this approach, the elected official, it is believed, can quickly and effectively deal with the issue.

Pressure groups are referred to by many names, including social-action organizations, social-influence associations, instrumental voluntary associations, power-transfer organizations, and empowerment-based organizations. The goal of social-action organizations is to develop power in an effort to pressure social systems and institutions to respond to the needs of disadvantaged communities. Any differences among pressure-group typologies are more a matter of degree than substance; all share the value of citizen participation. Inherent in the pressure-group approach is the belief that citizens are best able to know what their communities need, and that the community organization is a mechanism that enables citizens to address those needs.

The key issue in community organizing is the development of power in both individuals and organizations. Different approaches vary in the directness with which they address issues of power. For example, some organizing efforts settle for the empowerment of individual members and do not seek to build a power base capable of creating community change. Nevertheless, the power issue is usually at the base of any understanding in community organizing efforts.

Process of Community Organization

The process of building a community capable of acting to improve its circumstances is called *community organizing*. Organizing involves building relationships across networks of people who identify with common values and ideals, and who can participate in sustained social action on the basis of those values. Community organizing represents the entire process of organizing relationships, identifying issues, moving to action on identified issues, evaluating the efficacy of those actions, and maintaining a sustained organization capable of continuing to act on issues and concerns.

Tension can arise between the process of empowering individuals who participate in organizing and the process of building power for organizations where organizing is practiced. This tension is, in effect, between organizing as a process and as an outcome. For some organizations, efforts that develop the skills, consciousness, knowledge, and confidence of individuals are sufficient to be labeled *empowerment*. Others emphasize the need to address the causes of human suffering in the broader community and society through empowering communities of people capable of changing their circumstances.

Applications for Children and Teens

Community organizations that focus on youth have existed for a long time. Church-based activities for youth have existed at least since the mid-nineteenth century, and the early-twentieth century saw the creation of the Boy Scouts, Girl Scouts, 4-H clubs, Junior Achievement, and the Junior Red Cross. By the middle of the twentieth century, education became more dominant than work as the major activity for young people. As school operated for a shorter duration than work, this resulted in more time after school and, relatedly, more organizations to serve youth.

Of the many community organizations that provide services and activities for youth, few have worked to engage youth in active, participatory ways. Service-oriented efforts, such as traditional recreation and education efforts, rather than the participatory and empowering activities represented in the principles of community organizing, have been the norm. However, this interest in altering the standard or traditional pattern of interacting with youth is changing. Increasingly, organizations and agencies are incorporating organizing principles and strategies into youth work. Additionally, youth organizations are considering ways to alter the community ecology to be more supportive of youth.

Historically, organizations that involved youth in participatory activities consistent with organizing emerged in the 1960s. One such example is the Mobilization for Youth (MFY) Program in New York City. This program, run in a settlement house on the Lower East Side of Manhattan, was funded by the National Institute for Mental Health and has been acknowledged as a precursor to community action programs in the War on Poverty. MFY is an important effort historically because it demonstrated many of the challenges in bringing organizing processes to youth in settings that had traditionally provided only services such as education, recreation, or job training.

MFY was designed as a program to address juvenile delinquency and was based on the premise that the lack of constructive opportunities in a young person's environment can lead to delinquency. Specific delinquency prevention efforts targeted jobs for teenagers, local neighborhood service centers, employment programs for neighborhood residents, and mobilizing residents to take action on issues of common concern. Mobilizing residents for organizing activities became the locus of bitter controversy when groups organized by MFY attempted to alter their local ecology by protesting against the police, schools, and welfare department. Local politicians and established institutions retaliated against MFY, but because MFY had federal funding it was able to survive organizationally. However, the tremendous pressure applied by the local establishment caused MFY to abandon its organizing efforts and return to the service-oriented agency it had been prior to their organizing efforts.

This experience parallels that of many organizations throughout the United States that have attempted to bring community-organizing processes to traditional service-oriented agencies. Despite these experiences, both organizing processes and the ecological understandings of community have been accepted by many organizations as guides in working to improve outcomes for youth.

Current Trends in Community Organizing for Youth

Since about 1980, there has been an increased interest in bringing community-organizing principles and understandings of community ecology to organizations and agencies that work with youth. Often, the links to community organizing and community ecology are implicit, but the emphasis on the active participation of youth and the attempts to reshape the community ecology to be supportive of youth are the hallmarks of many current efforts.

Many of the efforts linking children and teens to communities stems from concerns about the quality of public education. These approaches use schools as the base of community support for youth. Most popular among these approaches are collaborations between community agencies and schools that bring agency services to the schools. However, some have argued against service provision in schools, urging instead an integration of community services in multiple neighborhood locations. While school-based services make the location of service delivery centralized and easy for providers, the school as locus of service provision is often removed from the context of community problems and controlled by the professionals recognized in school settings. The placement of integrated services in diverse locations throughout a community is believed to allow for greater resident involvement in shaping service planning and tailoring service delivery to diverse population needs.

The most popular framework around which these activities take place is called *youth development.* Youth development programs are guided by several principles. First, the emphasis is on assets or strengths inherent in all youth, rather than a traditional approach that focuses on deficits. Second, the level of intervention is often the community rather than individuals. With this orientation, youth development is aligned with a community organization or ecological approach—it emphasizes the breadth of organizations and the connections between organizations that compose a community. Third, youth development approaches seek the active participation of youth in program design and implementation. This participatory element parallels the process of community organizing.

Organizations and agencies that apply a youth development approach are numerous. They include, for example, the National Crime Prevention Council, 4-H clubs, the United Way, and federal agencies such as the Office of Juvenile Justice and Delinquency Prevention.

As noted, youth development efforts incorporate both community organization and community organizing approaches. However, other activities also fall under the rubric of youth development, including community service, mentoring, and social services.

Learning in community settings. Since the 1990s, there has been special attention paid to learning that occurs in communities and community organizations. The formal and informal networks of community, in all their social and organizational complexity, are essential, yet often overlooked, vehicles of learning. Such learning includes intergroup and intragroup learning of cultural norms and displays; civic learning and the adaptation of people and populations; information, referral, and mutual assistance within groups and organizations; and social change in individuals, families, organizations, and society. These processes are part and parcel of what may be called *learning communities.*

Community service-learning, which is the testing and illumination of curriculum through participatory student projects that address local needs, has become an extremely popular pedagogy. Service-learning is more than simply experiential or vocational learning. By explicitly focusing on a local community's social problems and getting involved in their solution, it links classroom learning to the development of a sense of community, civic responsibility, and greater understanding and awareness of political, economic, and other root causes of the problems observed. Service-learning takes the idea of a *learning community* literally in exploring concrete ways to bring students, local government officials, community-development practitioners and researchers, and community residents and leaders together to learn and benefit from each other. It adds reality and relevance to the curriculum by bringing to life dry classroom materials; by showing how social processes really work; by giving students the skills, experience, and connections that often lead to employment opportunities; and by providing tangible effects of students' efforts (whether planting trees, cleaning a park, building a playground or house, or simply seeing improvement and joy in a tutored child).

Service-learning is thought to be a "win-win-win-win" situation. The winners are: (1) the instructor, whose teaching is brought to life and made more relevant through application to the "real world"; (2) the students, who almost unanimously report getting more out of the course, not only in terms of practical skills and experience, but also in terms of theory application and testing; (3) the community residents or clients of the host community or organization, who usually get more personal attention and energetic bodies to help with their problems; and (4) the host organizations, who get unskilled, semiskilled, and even skilled labor—and a chance to test the performance of possible future workers, both at little to no cost.

How effective is service-learning? Its salutary effect on students' social development is well established, but its impact on learning and cognitive development has been debated for years. Similar to many of the community programs in which they volunteer, service-learning tends to be very popular among the students, instructors, and agency staff who participate. What may be least known about service-learning is its actual impact on community organizations and conditions.

Strengths-based youth interventions. This attention to the role of community organizations in child and youth development is consistent with several national trends, many of which are loosely coalescing into a growing movement to promote a *strengths-based* approach to psychological theory, educational and social-service practice, and public policy, rather than more traditional deficit and victim-blaming models. This movement favors a variety of positive psychological and intervention concepts that are thought to operate on both the individual and community levels (and often the family and organizational levels as well). These include empowerment, development, resilience, competency-based prevention, health (and mental health) promotion, community psychology, positive psychology, ecological theory, asset-based community development, social capital, networks, diversity, and multiculturalism. The American Psychological Association (APA) has commissioned a group of scholars to explore the implications of this strengths orientation for policies affecting children, youth, families, and communities.

The APA volume compiles a range of policy recommendations, many of which aim to support particular strengths-based youth and community-development programs. These community-based programs address such adversities as divorce, child or adult domestic violence, parents' alcoholism or mental illness, pediatric illnesses, teen pregnancy and parenthood, school transitions, school failure, negative peer influences, minority status, community violence, and other community-level economic, social, environmental, and political adversities. (Ironically, it is testament to the pull of deficit thinking that even this volume on strengths approaches was organized around problems.) Most of the recommended programs may be locally planned to be culture and context specific. Some are necessarily government run, some are nonprofit, more and more represent public-private partnerships, and all recognize the key role of both public support and community involvement.

Four strategic goals, in line with the APA group, appear fundamental to strengths-based research and social policy: (1) to recognize and build upon existing strengths in individuals, families, and communities; (2) to build new strengths at each level; (3) to strengthen the larger social environments in which individuals, families, and communities are embedded; and (4) to engage individuals, families, and communities in a strengths-based process of designing, implementing, and evaluating interventions that are collaborative, participatory, and empowering.

Conclusion

These examples make it clear that education and human development do not stop at the schoolhouse door or the end of the family driveway. The integration of community organizing and community organization approaches, along with community learning and more traditional service-oriented activities, appears to hold promise for children and teens. Fundamental to the movement toward community organizing and community organization has been a shift away from viewing youths as objects to be served, and toward a view of youths as participants with assets and skills. In addition to a new perspective on youths themselves, a broader analysis entailing an ecological understanding of community has altered the nature of many youth-focused organizations to develop new partnerships and innovations that seek to modify communities to become youth-enhancing environments.

See also: COMMUNITY EDUCATION; FAMILY, SCHOOL, AND COMMUNITY CONNECTIONS; NEIGHBORHOODS; SERVICE LEARNING.

BIBLIOGRAPHY

AUGUST, GERALD J.; REALMUTO, GEORGE M.; HEKTNER, JOEL M.; and BLOOMQUIST, MICHAEL L. 2001. "An Integrated Components Preventive Intervention for Aggressive Elementary School Children: The Early Risers Program." *Journal of Consulting and Clinical Psychology* 69:614–626.

BARKER, ROGER G. 1968. *Ecological Psychology: Concepts and Methods for Studying the Environment of Human Behavior.* Stanford, CA: Stanford University Press.

BARKER, ROGER G., and GUMP, PAUL V. 1964. *Big School, Small School: High School Size and Student Behavior.* Stanford, CA: Stanford University Press.

BERGER, PETER L., and NEUHAUS, RICHARD J. 1977. *To Empower People: The Role of Mediating Structures in Public Policy.* Washington, DC: American Enterprise Institute for Public Policy Research.

BOYTE, HARRY C. 1989. *Commonwealth: A Return to Citizen Politics.* New York: Free Press.

BRAGER, GEORGE; SPECHT, HARRY; and TORCZYNER, JAMES L. 1987. *Community Organizing.* New York: Columbia University Press.

BRONFENBRENNER, URIE. 1979. *The Ecology of Human Development: Experiments by Nature and Design.* Cambridge, MA: Harvard University Press.

BROWN, B. BRADFORD, and THEOBALD, WENDY. 1998. "Learning Contexts Beyond the Classroom: Extracurricular Activities, Community Organizations, and Peer Groups." In *The Adolescent Years: Social Influences and Educational Challenges,* ed. Kathryn Borman and Barbara Schneider. Chicago: The University of Chicago Press.

CAZENAVE, NOBEL A. 1999. "Ironies of Urban Reform: Professional Turf Battles in the Planning of the Mobilization for Youth Program Precursor to the War on Poverty." *Journal of Urban History* 26:22–43.

CHASKIN, ROBERT J., and RICHMAN, HICHMAN A. 1992. "Concerns about School-Linked Services: Institution-Based versus Community-Based Models." *The Future of Children* 2:107–117.

CLOWARD, RICHARD A., and OHLIN, LLOYD. 1960. *Delinquency and Opportunity: A Theory of Delinquent Gangs.* New York: Free Press.

CRUZ, NADINNE I., and GILES, DWIGHT E. 2000. "Where's the Community in Service-Learning Research?" *Michigan Journal of Community Service Learning* 7:28–34.

CUNNINGHAM, JAMES V., and KOTLER, MILTON. 1983. *Building Neighborhood Organizations.* Notre Dame, IN: University of Notre Dame Press.

DRYFOOS, JOY G. 1994. *Full-Service Schools: A Revolution in Health and Social Services for Children, Youth, and Families.* San Francisco: Jossey-Bass.

EYLER, JANET S. 2000. "What Do We Most Need to Know about the Impact of Service-Learning on Student Learning?" *Michigan Journal of Community Service Learning* 7:11–17.

FERRARI, JOSEPH R., and WORRALL, LAURIE. 2000. "Assessments by Community Agencies: How 'the Other Side' Sees Service-Learning." *Michigan Journal of Community Service Learning* 7:35–40.

FISHER, ROBERT. 2002. *Bridging Social Movement and Community Organization Activism: Rethinking Theoretical and Organizational Barriers.* Presentation at the 32nd Annual Meeting of the Urban Affairs Association. Boston, MA: Urban Affairs Association.

GITTELL, ROSS, and VIDAL, AVIS. 1998. *Community Organizing: Building Social Capital as a Development Strategy.* Thousand Oaks, CA: Sage.

JACOBY, ARTHUR P., and BABCHUK, NICHOLAS. 1963. "Instrumental and Expressive Voluntary Associations." *Sociology and Social Research* 47:461–471.

JARVIS, SARA V.; SHEAR, LIZ; and HUGHES, DELLA M. 1997. "Community Youth Development: Learning the New Story." *Child Welfare* 76:719–741.

KAHN, SI. 1982. *Organizing.* New York: McGraw-Hill.

KNOKE, DAVID, and WOOD, JAMES R. 1981. *Organized for Action.* New Brunswick, NJ: Rutgers University Press.

LEVINE, MURRAY, and LEVINE, ADELINE. 1970. *A Social History of the Helping Services: Clinic, Court, School, and Community.* New York: Appleton-Century-Crofts.

LONG, NORTON E. 1958. "The Local Community As an Ecology of Games." *American Journal of Sociology* 64:251–261.

MATON, KENNETH I. 1989. "Community Settings As Buffers of Life Stress? Highly Supportive Churches, Mutual Help Groups, and Senior Centers." *American Journal of Community Psychology* 17: 203–232.

MATON, KENNETH I., and RAPPAPORT, JULIAN. 1984. "Empowerment in a Religious Setting: A Multivariate Investigation." *Prevention in Human Services* 3:37–72.

MATON, KENNETH I., and SALEM, DEBORAH. A. 1995. "Organizational Characteristics of Empowering Community Settings: A Multiple Case Study Approach." *American Journal of Community Psychology* 23:631–656.

MCKNIGHT, JOHN. 1996. *The Careless Society: Community and Its Counterfeits.* New York: Basic Books.

MONDROS, JACQUELINE B., and WILSON, SCOTT M. 1994. *Organizing for Power and Empowerment.* New York: Columbia University Press.

ORFIELD, MYRON. 1997. *Metropolitics: A Regional Agenda for Community and Stability.* Washington, DC: Brookings Institution Press.

PARK, ROBERT E.; BURGESS, ERNEST W.; and MCKENZIE, RODERICK D. 1967. *The City.* Chicago: University of Chicago Press.

PERKINS, DOUGLAS D.; BROWN, BARBARA B.; and TAYLOR, RALPH B. 1996. "The Ecology of Empowerment: Predicting Participation in Community Organizations." *Journal of Social Issues* 52:85–110.

PERKINS, DOUGLAS D., and LONG, D. ADAM. 2002. "Neighborhood Sense of Community and Social Capital: A Multi-Level Analysis." In *Psychological Sense of Community: Research, Applications, and Implications,* ed. Adrian Fisher, Christopher Sonn, and Brian Bishop. New York: Putnam.

PERLMAN, JANICE E. 1979. "Grassroots Empowerment and Government Response." *Social Policy* 10:16–21.

PITTMAN, KAREN J., and WRIGHT, MARLENE. 1991. *Bridging the Gap. A Rationale for Enhancing the Role of Community Organizations Promoting Youth Development.* Washington, DC: Center for Youth Development and Policy Research, Academy for Educational Development.

PUTNAM, ROBERT D. 2000. *Bowling Alone: The Collapse and Revival of American Community.* New York: Touchstone.

RAPPAPORT, JULIAN. 1987. "Terms of Empowerment/Exemplars of Prevention: Toward a Theory for Community Psychology." *American Journal of Community Psychology* 15:121–144.

REITZES, DONALD C., and REITZES, DIETRICH C. 1987. "The Alinsky Legacy: Alive and Kicking." In *Social Movements, Conflicts and Change,* ed. Louis Kriesberg. Greenwich, CN: Jai Press.

RIGER, STEPHANIE. 1993. "What's Wrong with Empowerment." *American Journal of Community Psychology* 21:279–292.

ROBINSON, BUDDY, and HANNA, MARK G. 1994. "Lessons for Academics from Grassroots Community Organizing: A Case Study—the Industrial Areas Foundation." *Journal of Community Practice* 1:63–94.

RUBIN, HERBERT J., and RUBIN, IRENE S. 2001. *Community Organizing and Development,* 3rd edition. Needham Heights, MA: Allyn and Bacon.

SCHALLER, LYLE E. 1966. *Community Organization: Conflict and Resolution.* Nashville, TN: Abingdon Press.

SPEER, PAUL W., and HUGHEY, JOSEPH. 1995. "Community Organizing: An Ecological Route to Empowerment and Power." *American Journal of Community Psychology* 23:729–748.

SWIFT, CAROLYN, and LEVIN, GLORIA. 1987. "Empowerment: An Emerging Mental Health Technology." *Journal of Primary Prevention* 8:71–94.

WANDERSMAN, ABE. 1984. "Citizen Participation." In *Psychology and Community Change,* ed. Kenneth Heller. Chicago: Dorsey.

WUTHNOW, ROBERT. 1994. *Sharing the Journey: Support Groups and America's New Quest for Community.* New York: Free Press.

WYNN, JOAN R.; MERRY, SHEILA M.; and BERG, PATRICIA G. 1995. *Children, Families, and Communities: Early Lessons from a New Approach to Social Services.* Washington, DC: American Youth Policy Forum of the Institute for Educational Leadership, Education and Human Services Consortium.

YATES, MIRANDA, and YOUNISS, JAMES. 1998. "Community Service and Political Identity Development in Adolescence." *Journal of Social Issues* 54:495–512.

YOUNISS, JAMES, and YATES, MIRANDA. 1999. "Youth Service and Moral-Civic Identity: A Case for Everyday Morality." *Educational Psychology Review* 11:361–376.

ZIMMERMAN, MARC A. 1995. "Psychological Empowerment: Issues and Illustrations." *American Journal of Community Psychology* 23:581–599.

PAUL W. SPEER
DOUGLAS D. PERKINS

COMMUNITY COLLEGES

The community college is largely a phenomenon of twentieth-century American higher education. The label applies to an array of institutions that offer six-month vocational diplomas; one- and two-year vocational, technical, and pre-professional certificates; and two-year programs of general and liberal education leading to an associate degree. Two-year colleges may be public, private, proprietary, or special purpose, although public institutions represent the majority of community colleges in the twentieth-first century. States, counties, municipalities, school districts, universities, and religious denominations have all organized community colleges. Some were designed for specific racial and ethnic groups, for women, or for specific purposes such as business, art, or military training. At the close of the twentieth century, two-year colleges enrolled 5,743,000 students, 96 percent of whom attended public community colleges. Nearly 40 percent of all undergraduate students attended community and junior colleges. Between 1900 and 2000 the significance of this sector of higher education grew enormously as its predominantly public character evolved from a much wider variety of origins.

The multiple forces fueling community college development contributed to confusion over the name and mission of these institutions. The terms *community college, junior college, technical college,* and *technical institute* encompass a wide array of institutions.

Two-year college refers to all institutions where the highest degree awarded is a two-year degree (i.e., associate of arts, associate of science, associate of general studies, associate of applied arts, associate of applied science). Generally, community colleges are comprehensive institutions that provide: (a) general and liberal education, (b) career and vocational education, and (c) adult and continuing education. Yet many two-year colleges do not offer the comprehensive curriculum just outlined, and therefore are not truly community colleges in this comprehensive use of the term.

Junior college refers to an institution whose primary mission is to provide a general and liberal education leading to transfer and completion of the baccalaureate degree. Junior colleges often also provide applied science and adult and continuing education programs as well.

Technical college and *technical institute* refer only to those institutions awarding no higher than a two-year degree or diploma in a vocational, technical, or career field. Technical colleges often offer degrees in applied sciences and in adult and continuing education. Also, there are technical institutes with curricula that extend to the baccalaureate, master's, and doctorate (i.e., Massachusetts Institute of Technology, Rensselaer Polytechnic Institute), but these are not community colleges. There are also proprietary (for-profit) two-year colleges that refer to themselves as technical colleges, technical institutes, or community colleges. Adding to the confusion of labeling is the fact that *community college* has become used generically in higher-education literature to refer to all colleges awarding no higher than a two-year degree.

The United States has been able to adapt and capitalize on its diversity of peoples, regions, and economics, in part due to the pragmatic and adaptive nature of its educational system. At the postsecondary level, the comprehensive community college has made a singular contribution to this adaptiveness and pragmatism. While many countries possess binary divisions of their higher-education system (universities and polytechnic colleges or institutes), these are accessible only to individuals with an acceptable performance on government-sponsored high-school graduation examinations. In contrast, American postsecondary education has remained steadfastly committed to inventing courses of study, educational programs, or even whole institutions dedicated to the needs and expectations of its society, peoples, and cultures.

As a distinctively American invention, the comprehensive community college stands between secondary and higher education, between adult and higher education, and between industrial training and formal technical education. Community colleges have provided educational programs and services to people who otherwise would not have enrolled in a college or university. For the most part community colleges offer admission to all who possess a high school education; in addition, many provide assistance to adults in completing their secondary education. They attract students who live in geographic proximity and who seek low-cost postsecondary education.

The History of Community Colleges

The community college evolved from at least seven sources of educational innovation. Two began in the 1880s and 1890s: (1) community boosterism and (2) the rise of the research university. Three came from the educational reforms of the Progressive Era (1900–1916): (3) the advent of universal secondary education, (4) the professionalization of teacher education, and (5) the vocational education movement. The final two, (6) open access to higher education, and (7) the rise of adult and continuing education and community services, were primarily post–World War II phenomena. The seeds of all seven of these innovations can be found even in the earliest junior colleges.

Boosterism. The development of community colleges generally mirrored that of American higher education in that it was not guided by national controls or policy. In colonial times, while colleges required a charter from the king of England to operate, many began in the absence of one. Similarly, many towns, groups, and denominations began early junior colleges without legal authority, and enabling legislation often followed, rather than preceded, a college's founding.

Along with the museum, library, opera house, and symphony band shell, municipalities established colleges to provide evidence of their cultural stature relative to neighboring towns and cities. Religious denominations that favored a lay ministry established their own colleges as well. In the nineteenth century the distinction between public and private colleges was not so marked as it is at the beginning of the twenty-first. Communities would band together to found the local college, with the citizens laying the bricks and mortar and raising funds through bake sales. If the community was predominantly Lutheran, then the college might well be affiliated with area Lutheran congregations. If the community had no prevailing religious denomination, then the college might be public. Whether public or private, communities generally had more enthusiasm for founding colleges than providing ongoing support for them, and many of these nine-

teenth-century colleges failed. With no clear sources of students or finance, economic downturns were particularly difficult to survive. These booster colleges offered programs of varying duration and purpose, but those that survived into the twentieth century became junior colleges.

The Panic of 1893—a major economic downturn in the late nineteenth century—led to the first formal thinking about two-year colleges. Reverend J. M. Carroll, president of Baylor University, convened the Baptist colleges in Texas and Louisiana the next year. The assembly recognized that there were insufficient finances and students to support the numerous small Baptist institutions in the two states. Carroll pragmatically proposed that the smaller colleges reduce their curriculum to the first two years of study and rely on Baylor to provide their students with the third and fourth years of the baccalaureate degree. Thus, the two-year college was born. By limiting the curriculum to the first two years, the colleges required fewer teachers, fewer resources, and fewer students to operate.

The junior college and the research university. Two years after Carroll proposed the two-year Baptist college as a solution to the financial and enrollment crises in Texas and Louisiana, two northern Baptists gave this invention a name and a place within the broader context of higher education. William Rainey Harper, president of the University of Chicago, believed that the American liberal arts college provided inadequate rigor and quality, thinking their programs akin to the German gymnasium (or high school) rather than true university-grade work. He isolated and strengthened the first two years of undergraduate study in an organizational unit of the university labeled *The Junior College*. Further, he urged denominational colleges in the area to reduce their curriculum to two years and send their students on to the university, indicating that formal arrangements could be made for the acceptance of their students' work toward the baccalaureate degree. He also advocated that high schools extend their curriculum to include the first two years of college. Two fellow members of Harper's congregation, S. V. Hedgepeth and J. Stanley Brown, were superintendents of local high schools (Goshen, Indiana and Joliet, Illinois respectively). Accepting Harper's offer, they developed junior colleges within their high schools. Joliet Junior College, established in 1901, is generally recognized as the oldest continuously operating community college.

During the latter half of the nineteenth century, American university presidents educated in Germany advocated greater purpose, organization, and eminence for higher education. Leaders like Henry Tappan of the University of Michigan, Alexis Lange of the University of California, David Starr Jordan of Stanford University, William Watts Folwell of the University of Minnesota, and Harper distinguished between university and collegiate grades of work. Collegiate work provided breadth of education in the arts and sciences, and also developed the student's abilities to study and inquire. Junior colleges offered collegiate study, while a university education was devoted to the advancement of knowledge and scientific inquiry. These leaders believed that the general education of undergraduates could be supplied by high schools or small liberal arts colleges and should be limited to the first two years of the baccalaureate program.

National associations were founded and grew around the debate regarding the role of the junior college, the research university, and the liberal arts college, and the organization and sequence of the American baccalaureate degree. The Association of American Universities (AAU), founded in 1900, advanced the agenda of the research institutions. The Association of American Colleges (AAC), founded in 1914, defended the role of the small four-year college and advanced the cause of liberal learning as the primary aim for higher education. The American Association of Junior Colleges (AAJC), begun in 1921, provided a forum for the motley assemblage of emerging institutions, including high schools providing two-year collegiate programs, women's colleges, military institutes, private junior colleges, and technical institutes.

The advancement of the research university and the junior college was abetted by the growth of high schools and compulsory secondary education. In 1907 legislation was passed in California permitting high schools to offer the thirteenth and fourteenth grades—at the time, the state had less than one high school per county. Also that year, President Jordan of Stanford urged the university to abandon teaching the first two years, arguing they were the proper concern of liberal arts colleges; he made no mention then of the upward extension of the high school. Once the 1907 legislation passed and the Los Angeles Polytechnic High School began a two-year post–high school curriculum, Jordan also advocated high schools as providers of collegiate studies. For Jordan,

Harper, and other prominent university presidents of the era, the municipal junior college fit their plans for the reform of the university.

Junior colleges and educational reform. The first great growth period of junior colleges—1910 to 1920—coincided with the growth of kindergartens and junior high schools. Many school districts constructed junior high schools to relieve the overcrowding in elementary and high schools. Junior highs, like junior colleges, often began as pragmatic solutions. When junior highs opened, the four-year high school became a three-year institution. The restructuring of K–12 education freed high school facilities for the operation of junior colleges. This school expansion and restructuring, along with the passage of mandatory secondary education, also created a shortage of teachers. Teacher-training programs provided through normal schools and junior colleges alleviated staffing shortages in the elementary and secondary grades. Educational leaders of the Progressive Era came to portray these reforms holistically as a system stemming from kindergarten and continuing through high school to "terminal" vocational and general education, or continuing on to the baccalaureate degree, and perhaps to graduate and professional education conferred by the research universities.

Contemporary community colleges hold the collegiate function central to their mission. In addition to the traditional-age student seeking the first years of a baccalaureate degree, collegiate (also know as *transfer*) courses enroll (1) career preparation students, such as nursing students seeking knowledge in the basic life sciences; (2) reverse transfer students (who begin at a university and later choose to continue at a community college); and (3) part-time casual students (who enroll for personal rather than degree-completion reasons). Collegiate courses may involve core courses or distribution requirements in general education, articulated technical programs in the sciences and mathematics, dual-credit programs in high schools where talented juniors and seniors can earn college credits, and alternative delivery programs—such as evening and weekend courses, televised courses, and courses delivered over the Internet.

Junior colleges and the normal school movement. Many junior colleges first began as normal schools. The professional preparation of teachers began in three normal schools of Massachusetts (the first in the nation) that were founded on the pedagogical principles of Horace Greeley. During the 1880s normal schools were a form of alternative secondary education for those students (mostly women) who wished to teach as a profession. As the number of high schools grew, pedagogy became a post–high school subject. As states adopted compulsory secondary education laws and teacher certification standards, the demand for qualified teachers grew.

Local high schools developed normal-school programs for their graduates, employing teachers with master's degrees as instructors of pedagogy. For example, the Joplin (Missouri) Central High School added a normal-school program in 1913 to meet the need for qualified teachers in the area. Local citizens interested in collegiate level education urged the school superintendent to inquire of the University of Missouri as to whether general and liberal education courses taken in the postgraduate high school program could be applied to the baccalaureate degree. University president Albert Ross Hill had been one of the university leaders within the AAU calling for the establishment of junior colleges to provide the first two years of college.

In several ways, the last two decades of the twentieth century mirror the first two in terms of public policy issues. In the 1980s and 1990s the quality of elementary and secondary educational programs reemerged in public discourse. As part of their efforts to reform education, lawmakers in various states proposed that community colleges help to prepare qualified teachers and provide teachers with continuing education and professional development. Similar trends occurred in workforce development. The American Association of Community and Junior Colleges (AACJC—formerly the AAJC, and now the American Association of Community Colleges [AACC]), advocated that community colleges work with area high schools to develop new, intensive, technical-education programs. These programs consisted of two years of science and technology preparatory work in the high school, followed by specialized technical training in the community college. The focus on student performance resulting from the educational reforms of the 1980s and 1990s stimulated examination of the transparency of programs among higher education institutions. The American Association for Higher Education (AAHE) promoted the creation of two-year and four-year college partnerships with high schools to strengthen the articulation of curriculum and students between the cultures of secondary and higher

education. During the 1910s and 1920s, and again in the 1980s and 1990s, community colleges advanced as an integral part of the rethinking and restructuring of elementary, secondary, and higher education.

The vocational education movement. Many of the first two-year colleges were primarily or exclusively technical institutes. Lewis Institute, established in 1896, and Bradley Polytechnic Institute (now Bradley University), established in 1897, were founded with the guiding influence of William Rainey Harper. Frederick Pratt converted the Pratt Institute, a vocational high school, into a two-year curriculum for adults "age thirty or so" (Ratcliff 1986, p. 16). In 1891 the Detroit Young Men's Christian Association (YMCA) consolidated the evening and day classes it offered adults with the professional curricula of the Detroit College of Pharmacy to form the Detroit Institute of Technology. Chartered in 1909, it provided collegiate instruction in mechanical, technical, industrial, professional, and semiprofessional fields, and in the literary and musical arts. The vocational education movement of the late nineteenth century, the emphasis on technical education during the years of the Great Depression and World War II, the career education initiatives of the 1970s and 1980s, and contemporary workforce-development programs of states and the federal government have insured that vocational, technical, pre-professional, and para-professional programs are mainstays of the community college.

Students pursuing vocational and career-education programs include: (1) traditional-age students preparing for their first job, (2) working adults seeking the upgrading and retraining of knowledge and skills, (3) students employed by local business or industry in internship or cooperative-education programs, (4) members of labor organizations, (5) the underemployed and unemployed, and (6) older adults and retirees seeking to develop a skill or technical knowledge for personal reasons. The programs they select may include specialized degree programs (such as accounting or occupational therapy), career-ladder programs (e.g., moving from engineering technology to engineering), contract training provided to workers of a local company, apprenticeship training programs operated in cooperation with trade organizations, *two-plus-two* programs articulating high-school and college vocational education, and international training programs. Certain states have separate systems of two-year vocational institutions, such as the Wisconsin Area Vocational Technical Institutes, while other states, such as Iowa, converted their vocational-technical institutes to comprehensive community colleges in the 1990s.

Open access to higher education. In the United States many colleges and universities were established before a system of secondary education was developed. Harvard, America's first college, was founded much earlier than college preparatory programs. Land-grant colleges and universities were established many years prior to the provision of secondary education in rural areas—in their first years, more than half of their students enrolled in precollegiate studies. Women's colleges, colleges and institutes for American Indians, and historically black colleges and universities were established before there were secondary educational programs to prepare these groups for collegiate level studies. This curious American phenomenon required higher education to judge the merits of the students admitted, rather than relying on secondary diplomas and exit exams, as was the case in many countries at the time. Inadvertently, this placed higher education in the position of articulating academic standards for college preparatory and secondary education.

The flood of immigrants coming to the United States between 1900 and 1920 also fueled the growth of community colleges. The educational needs and backgrounds of junior college students diversified as enrollments grew. The suffrage movement and women's educational expectations augmented enrollment as well. In 1920 less than 4 percent of the American population (238,000 students) went to college. By the end of the 1920s, 12 percent of high school graduates were attending college.

A new wave of immigration began in the 1980s, a wave that continued into the twenty-first century. Once again the United States is expanding and extending higher education to new segments of the population. Some come with little or no formal education or language skills, others come with extensive education but few language skills, while a third group consist of those with English language skills but little formal education. English-as-a-second-language instruction represents as much as one-third of all humanities instruction at community colleges.

Community colleges, as open admissions institutions, hold a unique position in this juxtaposition of secondary and postsecondary education. For not only did higher education assume the role of setting college preparatory standards, but also of providing precollegiate instruction for those able but insufficiently educated to succeed in the rigors of a regular collegiate program. Community colleges increasingly have been called upon to provide remedial and developmental programs and services to those students without adequate levels of academic preparation to succeed in college. Several states and higher education systems, including Colorado, Florida, and California, have prescribed or sought to place developmental and remedial courses in the community colleges.

Community colleges play a significant role in meeting immediate and short-cycle needs of the immigrant, the disabled, and the unemployed with a wide range of courses and programs. Community colleges expanded the scope of higher-education offerings by adding to the curriculum practical and pragmatic courses of study that meet the educational needs of an advanced, complex, and technological society. The federal government has encouraged this expansion through incentives to colleges that serve such groups as displaced homemakers, students with disabilities, those needing adult basic education, and the unemployed seeking job retraining. Programs targeted for these students have broadened the curriculum, subsidized enrollment growth, and provided access to college for those who otherwise could not afford it, thereby widening the demographic profile of students served. The demand for higher education has risen as the value of a high school education has declined in the marketplace of jobs and careers.

Adult and continuing education and community services. Programs and services for adults, for the continuing education of workers in the skilled trades, technical occupations, and the allied professions, and courses and programs of general interest and value to personal and corporate development in the local community have always been a distinguishing feature of community and junior colleges. Early junior and technical colleges (e.g., Pratt Institute, St. Joseph Junior College, Oklahoma Institute of Technology) also provided adult education and community services programs. After World War II, and particularly during the presidency of Edmund Gleazer at the AACJC, this function grew in prominence. Gleazer's vision was that community colleges would render educational services to the entire local community, not just to traditional college-age groups.

Providing credit and noncredit courses and nonacademic educational services (e.g., films, lecture series, fine art exhibits, musical performances) to the area served became a priority for community colleges in the 1970s and 1980s. Nevertheless, adult and continuing education and community services have been regarded in two ways. One holds them ancillary to general and liberal education and vocational and technical education in the community college. The second views community services not so much as a separate function of the college, but as an intrinsic quality that distinguishes community colleges from the rest of higher education. From this perspective, the role of service to the surrounding community has become fundamental to the definition of the public community college mission.

The Community College Mission

Contemporary discussions regarding the mission, role, and function of the community college rely on historical notions of the evolution of the institution. If one chooses to emphasize the vocational education stream, one may reach the conclusion that community colleges are post-high school, but not higher education. If one examines the success of students who otherwise would not have attended college, then one may conclude that community colleges track students into certain social strata or advance their station in society. Examining the adult education and community services function leads one to conclude that the institutions' roots are to be found there. In short, a comprehensive community college incorporates an eclectic set of educational philosophies and purposes into its mission.

The contemporary and prevalent normative view of the American community college is as a local, public institution understood by its commitment and connection to the community it serves. While exceptions and variations abound, the evolution of this view from that of junior college, booster college, normal school, technical institute, or private preparatory college was galvanized largely by the 1947 President's Commission on Higher Education (the Truman Commission), which suggested "the name 'community college' to be applied to the institution designed to serve chiefly local community educational needs. It may have various forms of organization and may have curricula of various lengths. Its dominant feature is its intimate relations to the life of the community its serves" (President's Commission, p. 3). Also significant in its develop-

ment was the advocacy of the Carnegie Commission on Higher Education (1970) for the establishment of community colleges within commuting distance of every adult. These commissions, together with the Higher Education Act of 1964 (and the Educational Amendments of 1972 to the act that promoted statewide planning and provision of higher education throughout the nation), enabled community colleges to be rapidly established to meet the swelling demand for higher education among the World War II generation—and among their sons and daughters.

The mission of the community college, like that of other institutions, has evolved in relation to social context. In many cases, the community, junior, or technical college was but one phase in the development of a particular institution. This was especially true of those with origins connected to educating teachers. Brigham Young University, Millersville University, Wayne State University, and Midwestern State University all began as two-year colleges with teacher education programs. As the profession matured, these institutions expanded their programs horizontally, to other fields of study, and vertically, becoming baccalaureate-granting institutions. Liberal arts colleges, comprehensive colleges, and doctorate granting universities, such as Mills College, Bradley University, and the Susquehanna University, also evolved from private junior colleges and technical institutes.

This tendency of two-year colleges to become baccalaureate-granting institutions did not erase from their host communities the need for a community college. California State University-Fresno, the University of Texas at El Paso, and the University of Southern Colorado all began as two-year colleges. When these institutions became baccalaureate-granting institutions, they adopted more selective admissions and broadened their curriculum—both vertically and horizontally. They also left an educational vacuum due to the lack of open admissions, adult education and community services, and two-year vocational and technical programs. A growing social need for an urban regional university did not alleviate local need for a community college, and public demand in these cities led to the establishment of new community colleges: Wayne County Community College, El Paso Community College, and Pueblo Community College. In 2002 the Gates Foundation provided support for seventy small high schools to develop associate degree programs, setting in motion changes similar to those in the 1920s and 1930s that brought about many new two-year colleges. As society changes, so will its institutions of higher learning.

Conclusions

The distinctive contribution of community colleges to American higher education is their adaptive, transmutable mission. They represent education's local, front-line interface with society. To fulfill this transmutable mission, comprehensive community colleges provide (1) general and liberal education, (2) vocational and technical education, (3) adult, continuing, and community education, (4) developmental, remedial, and college-preparatory education, and (5) counseling, placement, and student development services.

In individual institutions, one or more of these five functions may have grown to predominate in response to local needs and expectations. When the small Baptist colleges faced financial exigency in 1894, they restricted their curriculum to two years and sent their students on to Baylor University. In the 1960s and 1970s, when the focus of public educational policy was on accessibility and affordable higher education, community colleges developed outreach programs, personal development and adult education programs grew, and the community dimension of the institution was promoted. In the 1980s and 1990s, when taxpayers sought to curb public spending and to promote economic growth and competitiveness, community colleges dropped personal development courses, and instead defined the needs of adults in terms of employment and economic development. Thus, the demand for the specific functions, programs, and services of community colleges ebb and swell with the social and economic conditions of the municipality, the region, and the nation—and they often may do so more rapidly than at their four-year college and university counterparts.

The community college, in all its various manifestations, is a truly unique component of American higher education. It provides a flexible and adaptive form of higher education tailored to local needs. It helps a complex industrialized society have a full range of education and training—from bookkeepers to accountants to those with an associate degree in business administration—depending on the demands and needs of society and the workplace. Community colleges train the legal aid and legal assistant with general and specialized knowledge to support and complement the work of the lawyer. Community colleges educate numerous allied health professionals who work in support of physicians and surgeons. Career and transfer programs are open largely to all, because the community college also provides the development and remedial coursework necessary for individuals with the capacities, but not the formal education prerequisite, for entry into postsecondary education. These adaptive, flexible, and accessible characteristics are what give community, junior, and technical colleges their unique and singularly important role in American society.

See also: AMERICAN ASSOCIATION OF COMMUNITY COLLEGES; HIGHER EDUCATION IN THE UNITED STATES; STUDENT SERVICES, *subentry on* COMMUNITY COLLEGES.

BIBLIOGRAPHY

BOORSTIN, DANIEL J. 1965. *The Americans: The National Experience.* New York: Random House.

BRINT, STEVEN, and KARABEL, JEROME. 1989. *The Diverted Dream: Community Colleges and the Promise of Educational Opportunity in America, 1900–1985.* New York: Oxford University Press.

CARNEGIE COMMISSION ON HIGHER EDUCATION. 1970. *The Open-Door Colleges: Policies for Community Colleges.* New York: McGraw-Hill.

CHRONICLE OF HIGHER EDUCATION. 2000. "Almanac Issue" 47(1).

CLOWES, DARREL A., and LEVIN, BERNARD H. 1989. "Community, Junior, and Technical Colleges: Are They Leaving Higher Education?" *Journal of Higher Education* 60:349–355.

COHEN, ARTHUR M., and BRAWER, FLORENCE B. 1996. *The American Community College,* 3rd edition. San Francisco: Jossey-Bass.

CROSS, K. PATRICIA. 1971. *Beyond the Open Door: New Students to Higher Education.* San Francisco: Jossey-Bass.

EBY, FREDERICK. 1927. "Shall We Have a System of Public Junior Colleges in Texas?" *Texas Outlook* 20:22–24.

GLEAZER, EDMUND J., JR. 1968. *This Is the Community College.* New York: Houghton Mifflin.

GLEAZER, EDMUND J., JR. 1973. *Project Focus: A Forecast Study of Community Colleges.* New York: McGraw-Hill.

GLEAZER, EDMUND J., JR. 1980. *The Community College: Values, Vision, and Vitality.* Washington,

DC: American Association of Community and Junior Colleges.

KELLEY, ROBERT L. 1940. *The American Colleges and the Social Order.* New York: Macmillan.

PARNELL, DALE. 1982. "Will Bellydancing Be Our Nemesis?" *Community Services Catalyst* 12:45–47.

PARNELL, DALE. 1985. *The Neglected Majority.* Washington, DC: Community College Press.

PRESIDENT'S COMMISSION ON HIGHER EDUCATION. 1947. *A Report of the President's Commission on Higher Education,* Vols. 1, 3, 5. Washington, DC: U.S. Government Printing Office.

RATCLIFF, JAMES L. 1986. "Should We Forget William Rainey Harper?" *Community College Review* 13(4):12–19.

RATCLIFF, JAMES L. 1987. "'First' Public Junior Colleges in an Age of Reform." *Journal of Higher Education* 58:151–180.

RATCLIFF, JAMES L. 1993. "Seven Streams in the Historical Development of the Modern American Community College." In *A Handbook on the Community College in America: Its History, Mission and Management,* ed. George A. Baker III. Boulder, CO: Greenwood Press.

ROARK, DANIEL B. 1926. "The Junior College Movement in Texas." Master's thesis, Baylor University.

RUDOLPH, FREDERICK. 1977. *Curriculum: A History of the American Undergraduate Course of Study Since 1636.* San Francisco: Jossey-Bass.

ZWERLING, L. STEVEN. 1976. *Second Best: The Crisis of the Community College.* New York: McGraw-Hill.

JAMES L. RATCLIFF

COMMUNITY EDUCATION

In numerous polls and surveys, Americans identify education as one of the leading domestic challenges of the twenty-first century. Specifically, the challenge is not just to reform public schools but also to achieve the goal of academic success for all students. Many educational experts agree that reaching that goal will require increased cooperation among the schools themselves and a new kind of collaboration with the families and communities served by the schools.

Community education offers a structured, effective way to respond to the challenge to improve public education because it expands the school's traditional role and creates a mutually interdependent relationship among home, school, and community. Community education has three basic components—lifelong learning opportunities, community involvement in schools, and efficient use of resources—and is based on a set of ten broad principles:

- *Lifelong learning.* Education is a birth-to-death process, and everyone in the community shares in the responsibility of educating all members of the community. Formal and informal learning opportunities should be available to residents of all ages in a wide variety of community settings.
- *Self-determination.* Community residents have a right and a responsibility to be involved in assessing community needs and identifying community resources that can be used to address those needs.
- *Self-help.* People are best served by their leaders when their capacity to help themselves is acknowledged and developed. When people assume responsibility for their own well-being, they achieve some degree of independence.
- *Leadership development.* Training local leaders in problem solving, decision-making, and group-process skills is essential to community improvement efforts.
- *Institutional responsiveness.* Because public institutions exist to serve the public, they are obligated to develop programs and services that address constantly changing public needs and interests.
- *Integrated delivery of services.* Organizations and agencies that operate for the public good can best use their limited resources, meet their own goals, and serve the public by collaborating with organizations and agencies with similar goals and purposes.
- *Localization.* Community services, programs, and volunteer opportunities close to people's homes have the greatest potential for high levels of public participation.
- *Maximum use of resources.* The physical, financial, and human resources of every community should be fully available and rationally interconnected if the diverse needs and interests of the community are to be met.

- *Inclusiveness.* Community programs, activities, and services should involve the broadest possible cross-section of community residents without segregation by age, income, sex, race, ethnicity, religion, or other characteristics.

- *Access to public information.* Public information should be shared across agency and organization lines because an effective community not only has "the facts," but it also knows what those facts mean in the lives of the diverse people who make up the community.

A Comprehensive Plan

The current lack of confidence in public education has been more pervasive and prolonged than the crisis in confidence that followed the launch of *Sputnik* in 1957 by the Soviet Union. Community education has become the approach of choice of many educators who are determined to improve the public confidence in schools and to build partnerships in support of public education.

Community education is a way of looking at public education as a total community enterprise. A community education program is a comprehensive and coordinated plan for providing educational, recreational, social, and cultural services for all people in the community. The following strategies provide a framework for developing such a program. The strategies have overlapping characteristics and functions, but taken together, they outline a comprehensive action plan.

Strategy 1. Encourage increased use of community resources and volunteers to augment the basic educational program. Every community has human, physical, and financial resources that can be used to enrich and expand traditional education programs. Community resources and volunteers have been used to expand curricular options, conduct field and study trips, offer various kinds of tutoring, sponsor student-based enterprises, and support experiential learning.

Strategy 2. Develop educational partnerships between schools and public and private service providers, business and industry, and civic and social service organizations. Complex, often interrelated, social and economic problems create a broad array of service needs in many communities, and meeting them effectively is likely to require more resources than any single agency or organization can provide. The development of partnerships for cooperative use of available resources will help prevent unnecessary duplication in the delivery of such services as child care, after-school programs, drug education and treatment, literacy and remedial programs, internships and work-study programs, and career awareness activities.

Strategy 3. Use public education facilities as community service centers for meeting the educational, social, health, cultural, and recreational needs of all ages and sectors of the community. Since community attitudes and support affect the schools' ability to carry out their mission to educate all children, educators must consider the needs and concerns of nonparents in the community. This strategy encourages keeping school buildings open on a planned, organized basis at hours beyond the regular school day. It takes advantage of the strong support community centers generally receive, as well as the economic benefits to the community of more efficient use of public facilities.

Strategy 4. Develop an environment that fosters lifelong learning. This strategy acknowledges learning as a lifelong process. It recognizes that learning takes place, both inside and outside the school setting, without formal instruction. It encourages the development of education programs to meet learning needs that change over a lifetime, including the need for new skills and knowledge. Lifelong learning programs and activities may include early childhood education, extended-day and enrichment programs for school-age children, adult education, vocational training and retraining programs, leisure activities, and intergenerational programs.

Strategy 5. Establish a process for involving the community in educational planning and decision-making. The total community has a stake in the mission of educating community members. Individual community members, therefore, have a right and a responsibility to participate in determining community needs, setting priorities, and allocating resources. The cyclical process of planning, evaluating, and changing takes advantage of a basic fact of human behavior: Those who participate in planning and decision-making develop feelings of ownership. Encouraging the broadest possible involvement capitalizes on another fact: The greater the number and diversity of people involved, the greater the likelihood that diverse needs will be met. Involvement opportunities should range from participation in ongoing advisory councils to membership on ad hoc task forces and committees.

Strategy 6. Provide a responsive, community-based system for collective action by all educational and community agencies to address community issues. Many community problems are so complex that resolving them requires cooperative use of a broad range of resources. Seeking the involvement of nonschool agencies can help schools address such social, health, and economic issues as substance abuse, housing, child abuse, mental illness, violence, crime, vandalism, teen pregnancy, and various kinds of discrimination.

Strategy 7. Develop a system that facilitates home-school-community communication. Research shows that schools that involve all their publics and keep them well informed have community support, and that those that fail to reach beyond the parents of current students do not. Effective home-school-community communication goes beyond news releases, speeches, newsletters, and open houses; it includes use of the media, home visitations by teachers and administrators, school displays throughout the community, and special community outreach programs conducted both in the schools and at other sites in the community.

Community School

The term *community school* designates a school site where the concept of community education is put into practice. Community education may also be implemented in community agencies and organizations, but the most common site is a public school.

A community school departs from a traditional public school's schedule and curriculum. A community school is open year-round, eighteen hours or more a day, often seven days a week. The school thus becomes not just a place to teach children but a community learning center with multiple uses.

In a community school, the concept of public education is extended beyond the traditional K–12 program to include the provision of learning opportunities for the entire community. The traditional schedule is expanded through extended day programs (including before- and after-school activities and care), and recreational, social, and educational programs for community residents of all ages. Activities and programs may not be limited to the school building, itself, as the school extends itself into the community, turning agencies, factories, businesses, and the surrounding environment into learning laboratories.

By organizing programs and activities that serve all ages and populations, a community school encourages disparate elements of the community to come together to work toward common goals. It provides a physical setting as well as an organizational structure for school-community collaboration.

Impact on Education and Communities

Because many community problems ultimately affect a community's ability to educate all children, educators in some communities are taking a leadership role in the search for solutions to community problems. From a problem-solving point of view, a community school can be a support center for a network of agencies and institutions committed to addressing broad community needs. Using schools as community centers is a cost-effective, practical way to use one of the community's largest investments—its school buildings. The community school reaches out to the community and works as a cooperative partner to address community needs, including educational needs.

The possible benefits to schools and communities from a well-designed and carefully implemented community education program have been described in a variety of studies, including the U.S. Department of Education's *Strong Families, Strong Schools* (1994) and *Safe and Smart,* from the U.S. Departments of Education and Justice (1998). Documented improvements include a better school learning climate, reduced violence and vandalism, more efficient energy use, increased family involvement, and broadened community-wide educational opportunities. Other studies show improved institutional responsiveness to the needs of parents and community members and increased public support for schools and other public agencies.

Community Education in Action

Community education takes advantage of local resources and capabilities and responds to an individual community's particular needs and wishes. Just as no two communities have exactly the same program, no community retains exactly the same program over a period of years. As a community matures, its institutions, population, assets, and problems change, and its community education program must be modified to reflect those changes if it is to remain successful.

Because every community education program is designed to reflect the current needs of a specific community and the resources available to meet those needs, there are literally hundreds of models of programs. The website of the National Center for Community Education has descriptions of exemplary models and case studies of community education programs in three model settings—school, district, or agency. The website of the Coalition for Community Schools profiles nine community schools (four elementary, two middle, two high schools, and one preschool).

See also: RECREATION PROGRAMS IN THE SCHOOLS; RURAL EDUCATION; YEAR-ROUND EDUCATION.

BIBLIOGRAPHY

DECKER, LARRY E., and BOO, MARY R. 2001. *Community Schools: Serving Children, Families, and Communities.* Fairfax, VA: National Community Education Association.

DECKER, LARRY E.; DECKER, VIRGINIA A.; and ASSOCIATES. 2001. *Engaging Families and Communities: Pathways to Educational Success.* Fairfax, VA: National Community Education Association.

PARSON, STEVE R. 1999. *Transforming Schools into Community Learning Centers.* Larchmont, NY: Eye on Education.

U.S. DEPARTMENT OF EDUCATION. 1994. *Strong Families, Strong Schools: A Research Base for Family Involvement in Learning.* Washington, DC: U.S. Department of Education.

INTERNET RESOURCES

COALITION FOR COMMUNITY SCHOOLS. 2001. "What Is a Community School?" <www.communityschool.org>.

NATIONAL CENTER FOR COMMUNITY EDUCATION. 2001. "Models and Case Studies." <www.nccenet.org>.

NATIONAL COMMUNITY EDUCATION ASSOCIATION. 2001. "What Is Community Education?" <www.ncea.com>.

U.S. DEPARTMENT OF EDUCATION. 1998. "Safe and Smart: Making After-School Hours Work for Kids." <www.ed.gov/pubs/SafeandSmart>.

LARRY E. DECKER

COMMUTER STUDENTS

According to Laura J. Horn and Jennifer Berktold, approximately 86 percent of college and university students are defined as *commuter students,* that is, students not living in university-owned housing. The commuter student population is a diverse group, which encompasses full-time students who live with their parents, part-time students who live in off-campus apartments, parents with children at home, and full-time workers. Commuters range in age from the traditional college student (eighteen to twenty-four years old) to the older adult. They attend every type of higher education institution, including two-year and four-year public universities or private colleges. Typically commuter students walk, ride bikes, take public transportation, or drive to campus to go to classes. They often attend classes and then go home or to work, rarely spending additional time outside of the classroom on campus.

Students commute to campus for several reasons. Unlike many full-time residential students, commuter students may have competing responsibilities outside the academic classroom, such as family, home, and work interests. For those students who are working full-time, raising a family, or caring for an elderly parent, campus residency is not a viable option. Also, commuting may be economically beneficial because many commuter students cannot afford to live on campus. Despite residing off-campus, most commuter students have high academic aspirations and a strong commitment to learning.

Commuter Student Challenges

Commuter students encounter many challenges that residential students do not. Commuter students, particularly first-year students, often have a difficult time "fitting in" to the campus community. Commuters often find the task of meeting students challenging because their only point of contact with other students is in the classroom, a small part of the total college experience. Residential students live, eat, study, and socialize together in residence halls, thus having greater opportunities to make friends and to become socially integrated into the campus community. A great amount of socialization for college students also occurs in the cafeteria, student center, recreation center, through extracurricular activities, or during late-night study sessions. Alexander Astin, in his 1993 study, has shown that this peer group interaction positively affects critical thinking skills, cultural awareness, leadership development, and academic development. As a result of not living in residence halls or spending a substantial amount of time on campus, commuter students miss out on these opportunities to "connect" to the university and other students and to enhance their learning and development.

Not only is frequent contact with students outside the classroom difficult to obtain, but commuters often face limited contact opportunities with faculty and staff members as well. Commuters must make additional trips to campus to meet with faculty members during their designated office hours. Unlike residential students, commuter students rarely have the opportunity to observe faculty and staff members on campus involved in nonclassroom activities, such as playing sports in the recreation center or interacting with students in the student center. These informal student-faculty interactions have been linked to academic performance and to personal and intellectual development for students, according to Ernest Pascarella and Patrick Terenzini's 1991 report. The interaction time for commuters with faculty members is often limited to a few minutes between classes or briefly during office hours, leaving commuter students feeling disconnected from the academic system of the university. Commuters often find forming relationships with faculty and administrators difficult because of these limited interactions outside of the classroom.

Transportation issues are a large part of commuter concerns. First, because of limited parking availability on most campuses, commuters have difficulty finding parking spaces and must often allow extra time to do so. Further, commuters often readjust their course schedules to attend classes in large blocks of time, again reducing the hours spent on campus outside of the classroom and the opportunity to become socially and academically integrated into the college community. Some classes may be scheduled at difficult times for commuters to attend, such as early morning or midafternoon. Because of long commutes to school, these students may encounter difficulty attending such classes, which are easily accessible for residential students.

Because of the short amount of time spent on campus each day, commuter students have a limited knowledge of the university itself, including the location of buildings, functions of university departments, campus policies and procedures, and current

events. Residential students become familiar with the university by spending a substantial amount of time on campus, taking part in student forums, and discussing current campus events in the residence hall or in small groups. Therefore, residential students often have a better understanding of the status of the university, because commuter students must wait to receive pertinent information through mailings or newspaper articles. In addition, greater proximity gives residential students more frequent occasions to establish personal relationships with faculty and staff, who serve as resources and mentors. These mentors may provide assistance and information regarding new policies and procedures.

Finally, research indicates that commuter students have lower retention rates than those living on campus. A study by Vincent Tinto in 1987 indicates that students who have high interaction with their university's academic and social systems are more likely to persist in college. Because commuter students spend limited time on campus and limited time creating relationships with other students, faculty, and staff, they have fewer opportunities to engage in quality interactions with these individuals. Therefore they are less likely to make a strong commitment to the university or its programs and are more likely to drop out of school than residential students.

See also: COLLEGE AND ITS EFFECT ON STUDENTS; COLLEGE AND UNIVERSITY RESIDENCE HALLS; COLLEGE STUDENT RETENTION.

BIBLIOGRAPHY

ASTIN, ALEXANDER W. 1975. *Preventing Students from Dropping Out.* San Francisco: Jossey-Bass.

ASTIN, ALEXANDER W. 1993. "What Matters in College?" *Liberal Education* 79:4–15.

HORN, LAURA J., and BERKTOLD, JENNIFER. 1998. *Profile of Undergraduates in U.S. Postsecondary Education Institutions: 1995-96.* Washington, DC: Office of Educational Research and Improvement, U.S. Department of Education (NCES 98-084).

JACOBY, BARBARA. 2000. "Involving Commuter Students in Learning: Moving from Rhetoric to Reality." In *Involving Commuter Students in Learning: New Directions for Higher Education No. 109,* ed. Barbara Jacoby. San Francisco: Jossey-Bass.

Pascarella, Ernest; Bohr, Louise; Amaury, Nora; Zusman, Barbara; Inman, Patricia; and Desler, Mary. 1993. "Cognitive Impacts of Living on Campus Versus Commuting to College." *Journal of College Student Development* 34:216–220.

Pascarella, Ernest T., and Terenzini, Patrick T. 1991. *How College Affects Students.* San Francisco: Jossey-Bass.

Tinto, Vincent. 1987. *Leaving College.* Chicago: University of Chicago Press.

Wolfe, Janice S. 1993. "Institutional Integration, Academic Success, and Persistence of First-Year Commuter and Resident Students." *Journal of College Student Development* 34:321–326.

Amy M. Tenhouse

COMPARATIVE EDUCATION

See: Canada; East Asia and the Pacific; Eastern Europe and Central Asia; Islam; Latin America and the Caribbean; Middle East and North Africa; Small Nations; South Asia; Sub-Saharan Africa; Western Europe.

COMPENSATORY EDUCATION

UNITED STATES
Geoffrey D. Borman
POLICIES AND PROGRAMS IN LATIN AMERICA
Fernando Reimers

UNITED STATES

The detrimental effects of poverty on children's academic outcomes and general well being are well documented. Children who grow up in poverty suffer higher incidences of adverse physical health, developmental delays, and emotional and behavioral problems than children from more affluent families. In school, children and adolescents living in poverty are more likely to repeat a grade, to be expelled or suspended, to achieve low test scores, and to drop out of high school. Though more research is needed to understand many of the dynamics and general effects of poverty, there is also evidence suggesting that the depth, duration, and timing of poverty are im-

portant considerations. Specifically, children who live in extreme poverty or who live below the poverty line for multiple years seem to suffer the worst outcomes. The impact of poverty during the preschool and early school years also appears to be more deleterious than the effects of poverty in later years.

About one in five children in the United States has the misfortune of living in a family whose income is below the official poverty threshold. In general, these families have trouble meeting basic needs for food, clothing, shelter, and health care. Household resources, including engaging toys, books, and computers—important for children's cognitive development—are also limited. Because of the tight connection between neighborhoods and schools in the United States, poor children tend to be served by schools that offer fewer resources for learning, provide fewer and less challenging opportunities to learn, and are less inviting and friendly places than schools serving children from more affluent communities. These individual, family, neighborhood, and school effects that are associated with poverty conspire to place children at considerable risk for failing in school and in life in general.

Purpose

The idea behind compensatory education is to, in a sense, "compensate" for these disadvantages by expanding and improving the educational programs offered to children living in poverty. The largest and most celebrated compensatory education programs grew out of President Lyndon B. Johnson's "War on Poverty" in the early 1960s. During an era in which civil rights and desegregation were of profound national significance, the advent of compensatory education programs served as an unprecedented symbol of the federal commitment to equality of educational opportunity. In the nineteenth century, the educator Horace Mann had expressed the notion that one of the classic American ideals for education was that it be the "great equalizer," or "balance wheel of the social machinery." Similarly, President Johnson, a former school teacher, held the belief that if poor children were provided a higher quality education they could attain the same high levels of educational and occupational outcomes as their more advantaged counterparts and, ultimately, could escape the vicious cycle of poverty.

Although state governments have primary responsibility for elementary and secondary education in the United States, the federal government provides support in a few notable areas. Federal support for compensatory education grew out of two legislative acts: the Elementary and Secondary Education Act of 1965 and the Economic Opportunity Act of 1964. The Elementary and Secondary Education Act established Title I and the Economic Opportunity Act established the Head Start program. Of the total dollar amount spent nationwide on education at all levels, 93 percent comes from state, local, and private sources and about 7 percent comes from federal revenues. That federal investment represents only about 2 percent of the federal government's overall budget. Though this funding level seems slight, a substantial portion of these funds has continued to be targeted on a single mission: ensuring equal access to high-quality education across the nation. President Johnson's War on Poverty surely has lost some of its initial momentum. The federal concern for the education of poor children, though, has remained compelling enough to support the continued funding and commitment to compensatory education policies from the mid-1960s to the early twenty-first century.

Title I of the Elementary and Secondary Education Act of 1965

The central educational component of President Johnson's "Great Society" programs was put into law by Congress as the Elementary and Secondary Education Act (ESEA) of 1965. Title I of the law provided approximately five-sixths of the total funds authorized under the ESEA legislation. Serving more than 10 million children in nearly 50,000 schools, and funded at nearly $9 billion during fiscal year 2001, Title I has remained as the federal government's largest single investment in America's schools. Title I was mandated "to provide financial assistance to . . . local educational agencies serving areas with concentrations of children from low-income families to expand and improve their educational programs by various means . . . which contribute particularly to meeting the special educational needs of educationally deprived children" (Elementary and Secondary Education Act of 1965, 79 Stat. 27, 27). Title I funds may be used to upgrade the educational programs of children from preschool through high school, but most of the students served are from elementary schools. The overall goal of Title I is to help close the achievement gap separating economically disadvantaged children and their more advantaged peers.

In the early twenty-first century, Title I serves eligible schools and students in diverse ways. Indeed, Geoffrey Borman and Jerome D'Agostino pointed out that Title I is better thought of as a funding mechanism rather than a coherent educational program or set of educational practices. Throughout much of the history of Title I, it has operated as a supplemental targeted, or categorical, program. Specifically, the funds allocated under Title I are provided to schools in order to supplement the regular school program and to target the needs of a certain category of students. Although Title I funds are distributed to schools based on the percentage of poor children they serve, the services within schools traditionally have been targeted toward the most "educationally disadvantaged" students. That is, targeted Title I programs must be established to serve low-achieving students (e.g., more than one-half grade equivalent below grade level or below the thirty-fifth national percentile) attending schools with a significant percentage of children whose families are below the poverty line.

Early years. The early years of Title I, during the late 1960s, resulted in poor implementation and large-scale violations in the operation of the program. These outcomes were due to several factors. First, the original program mandates were ambiguous concerning the proper and improper uses of the federal money, and the guidelines and intent of the law were open to varying interpretations. Some local school system officials originally thought of Title I as a general aid fund, which was labeled as a program for the disadvantaged for diplomatic and political reasons only. Second, in 1965 the educational knowledge base for developing effective compensatory education programs was extremely limited. The vast majority of local administrators and teachers had no experience developing, implementing, or teaching compensatory programs. Third, although the federal money provided localities an incentive to improve education for the disadvantaged, a viable intergovernmental compliance system was not in place. Without effective regulation, the receipt of funds did not depend on meeting the letter or the spirit of the law. Responding to local self-interests, and utilizing Title I dollars for established general aid policies, was an easier option than the new and more complicated task of implementing effective educational programs for poor, low-achieving students.

Although federal policymakers were hesitant to restrict local control, these early results, combined with growing pressures exerted by local poverty and community action groups, prompted the U.S. Office of Education to reconsider the legislative and administrative structure of Title I. During the 1970s, Congress and the U.S. Office of Education established more prescriptive regulations related to how schools and students should be selected to receive services, the specific content of programs, and program evaluation, among other things. In addition, the Office of Education made efforts to recover misallocated funds from several states, and warned all states and localities that future mismanagement would not be tolerated. Funded in part by federal dollars, larger and more specialized state and district bureaucracies emerged to monitor local compliance. In turn, state and local compliance was confirmed through periodic site visits and program audits by the U.S. Office of Education and by the Department of Health, Education, and Welfare.

Delivering Title I to local schools. One of the most important regulations affecting program delivery has been the provision that the compensatory services provided through Title I must supplement, not supplant, the regular educational programs provided to eligible students. In case of program audits, and to clearly account for the federal money, educators and administrators must be able to show that the targeted Title I program is actually providing something "extra," and that it is not merely replacing services that the students would have received through the regular school program. This regulation led to widespread use of the "pullout model" as a means for delivering supplemental compensatory services to eligible Title I students. Most often, the students who qualify for services are removed, or "pulled out," from their regular classrooms for thirty to forty minutes of remedial instruction in reading and math. This arrangement has the advantage of making it clear that the funds are providing something separate from the regular school program, as special teachers, books, and other materials are clearly allocated only to the pulled-out Title I students and not their regular classroom peers. Through the 1970s, 1980s, and much of the 1990s, about three of four Title I schools used the pullout model to deliver supplemental services.

After the initial problems with implementation in the 1960s and early 1970s, the tighter regulations began to have their desired effect. As the 1970s progressed, the services were delivered to the children targeted by the law. The implementation of Title I became a cooperative concern and professional responsibility of local, state, and federal administrators. In addition, Paul Peterson and his colleagues noted that Title I had inspired greater local concern for, and attention to, the educational needs of the children of poverty. In marked contrast to the first decade of the program, during the later half of the 1970s and throughout the 1980s the specific legislative intents, and the desired hortatory effects, were achieved on a far more consistent basis.

After this basic standard of implementation was achieved, during the late 1980s and throughout the 1990s, new legislation contained in the Hawkins-Stafford Amendments of 1988, the Improving America's Schools Act (IASA) of 1994, and other laws focused on reforming and improving the educational services offered in Title I schools. This new legislation granted schools greater freedom in designing and implementing effective programs, but also included new provisions that held them accountable for improved student outcomes and designated a program improvement process for those schools with poor or declining performance. Rather than the popular but fragmented pullout programs, the law encouraged educators to establish more frequent and regular coordination between the Title I program and the regular school program. Also, rather than targeting only low-achieving students, all schools serving very high proportions of poor children became eligible to use their Title I funds for schoolwide projects designed to upgrade the school as a whole. Instead of developing fiscal and procedural accountability, Title I policymakers have attempted to develop laws encouraging, and to some degree mandating, accountability for educational reform and improvement.

The Title I of the twenty-first century offers great promise for upgrading the educational opportunities of the nation's poor children. The emphasis is on high academic standards with aligned curriculum, assessment, and professional development. Title I's focus is on helping disadvantaged students meet the same high standards expected of all children. As part of its emphasis on high standards, the new law requires Title I funds to be used in new ways. For instance, schools are encouraged to extend learning time—before school, after school, and during the summer months—rather than pulling children out of their regular classrooms. Instructional programs support higher-order thinking skills rather than rote learning, accelerated curricula rather than remediation, and the use of research-proven strategies rather than services designed to satisfy program audits. These new policies, along with the federal government's increasing support of whole-school reform, are designed to transform Title I from a separate system of remedial teachers, materials, and assessments to an integral component of standards-based, whole-school reform and improvement.

Head Start

In 1964 the federal government convened a panel of child development experts to develop a program that would help communities meet the special needs of preschool children living in poverty. The recommendations of that panel became the blueprint for project Head Start. The Economic Opportunity Act of 1964 helped initiate the War on Poverty on three fronts by introducing: the Job Corps program to provide education and training for employment; Volunteers in Service to America (VISTA), a domestic Peace Corps program; and Community Action Programs to empower community planning and administration of their own assistance programs for the poor. As part of the Community Action Programs initiative, Head Start was born as an eight-week summer program in 1965, but was quickly converted to the more comprehensive nine-month program that it is in the early twenty-first century.

Recruiting preschoolers, primarily aged three and four, Head Start was designed to help break the "cycle of poverty" by providing young children of low-income families with a comprehensive program to meet their emotional, social, health, nutritional, and psychological needs. Similar to Title I, the educational services provided through Head Start are diverse. There is no single, standardized educational curriculum that every program uses. From the beginning, Head Start program providers have been granted considerable flexibility in planning educational offerings that meet the specific needs of the children and parents within the community. The curricula are designed to improve not only the cognitive abilities of young children, but also their physical well being, social skills, and self-image. In addition to services focused on education and early childhood development, Head Start grantee and delegate agencies offer a broad array of medical, dental, mental health, nutritional, and parent involvement programs.

Goals. As noted by Edward Zigler and Jeanette Valentine, the following seven goals set forth by the founders of Head Start in 1965 have remained as the basis for the program's mission and values.

- Improving the child's physical health and physical abilities

- Helping the emotional and social development of the child by encouraging self-confidence, spontaneity, curiosity, and self-discipline

- Improving the child's mental processes and skills, with particular attention to conceptual and verbal skills

- Establishing patterns and expectations of success for the child that will create a climate of confidence for future learning efforts

- Increasing the child's capacity to relate positively to family members and others, while at the same time strengthening the family's ability to relate positively to the child and his problems

- Developing in the child and his family a responsible attitude toward society, and encouraging society to work with the poor in solving their problems

- Increasing the sense of dignity and self-worth within the child and his family

In addition to the strong focus on comprehensive services for preschoolers, Head Start has served as a community empowerment initiative for the parents and community members who live in the impoverished areas that are served by programs. Believing that children develop in the context of their families, culture, and communities, Head Start services are family centered and community based. Rather than passive recipients of services, Head Start casts economically disadvantaged families as active, respected participants and decision makers who help plan and run their own programs. In contrast to Title I, which allocates nearly all of its resources to state and local school systems, Head Start programs are operated by a diverse collection of approximately 2,000 community-based organizations. Grantees include universities, community health centers, tribal governments, city and county governments, school districts, community action agencies, and other for-profit and nonprofit organizations.

During fiscal year 2000, the program served more than 800,000 low-income children and their families at over 18,000 centers with an average per-child cost of nearly $6,000. During fiscal year 2001,

Head Start allocations exceeded $6 billion. Although these funding levels still do not provide services for all eligible children and families, the level and quality of services clearly compare favorably to those offered during the hasty beginnings of Head Start in 1965.

Performance Standards. Starting the program so quickly and ambitiously may have led the program managers to ignore quality controls during Head Start's early years. Indeed, it was not until 1975 that the Head Start Program Performance Standards were fully implemented. During the 1970s and 1980s, funding cutbacks and inflation, combined with increasing demands for services, further exacerbated problems regarding the quality of services. In 1990 Congress passed the Head Start Expansion and Quality Improvement Act, which, for the first time in the program's history, made a significant commitment to addressing issues of program quality. The act mandated that 10 percent of all appropriations for 1991 be devoted to program improvement rather than expansion and that 25 percent of all new funding in subsequent years be set aside for the same purpose.

Since the 1990s, Head Start programs have placed more emphasis on helping children meet specific academic performance standards, employing well-prepared teachers, and improving the overall quality of the interactions between staff and children and parents. This progress is similar to the story of Title I. In both cases, during the early years of the program the primary concern was simply ensuring eligible children's access to the services. As the years have gone by, though, new legislation and new efforts by those who actually implement and operate the programs have stressed the overall reform and improvement of compensatory education.

Evaluation of Effectiveness

The Title I and Head Start compensatory education programs have come a long way, but neither has reached its full potential. Title I has evolved from an ineffectual, poorly implemented program to one that is relatively well implemented, modestly effective, but in need of further improvement. Intergovernmental conflict, poor implementation, and a lack of an achievement effect marked the first stage of the program. A second stage, during the 1970s and 1980s, was marked by the development of increasingly specific program implementation and accountability standards, federal and local cooperation, improved implementation, and growing, but modest, program effects. During the late 1980s and during the 1990s, changes in the Title I legislation stressed reform and improvement but, aside from some tinkering around the edges, the administration and operation of Title I remained fairly stable, and the program's effects remained essentially unchanged. In the twenty-first century, a new stage of the program's evolution has emerged; one in which widespread implementation of research-proven programs and practices is increasingly regarded as the key to improving the effectiveness of Title I.

Borman, Samuel Stringfield, and Robert Slavin pointed out that researchers, policymakers, and politicians have disagreed about the effectiveness and overall merits of Title I. Most seem to agree, though, that Title I has not fulfilled its original expectation: to close the achievement gap between disadvantaged students and their more advantaged peers. Given the rather modest level of funding the program provides, though, it may have been naive to have ever thought that Title I, alone, could close the gap. The results from Title I research also appear to show that without the program the children served since 1965 would have fallen further behind academically.

Some of the most exciting research evidence related to Head Start has suggested that if early childhood programs begin early enough, during the preschool years or even during infancy, children may realize lasting benefits through school and into adulthood. Indeed, a long-term experimental research project conducted by Lawrence Schweinhart and colleagues on the Perry Preschool program, which operated during the early 1960s in Ypsilanti, Michigan, has documented sustained effects on the participants through the age of 27 on diverse outcomes including: arrest rates; earnings and economic status; and educational performance. Though Perry Preschool was not a Head Start program, and was funded at a level that was approximately twice as high as a typical Head Start program, the results from this study have been held up as examples of the effects that high-quality early childhood programs can have on participants' outcomes.

The results from Head Start evaluations have been less compelling, but a review of the well-designed evaluations showed that the program has been successful in meeting many of its objectives, including strong short-term effects on participants' cognitive outcomes. Contrary to the findings for Perry Preschool, most long-term studies of Head Start participants have shown a "fade-out" of the initial program effects. Craig Ramey and Sharon Ramey (1998) indicated, though, that no developmental theory is based on the assumption that positive early learning experiences are alone sufficient to ensure that children perform well throughout their lives. Despite the early optimism of some researchers and policymakers, it is not likely that Head Start, or any other preschool program, could be the educational equivalent to an early inoculation, which provides a child with protection for a lifetime all in one early dose.

Indeed, neither Title I or Head Start may ever serve as the "great equalizer" that President Johnson had envisioned. To compensate for poor schools, suboptimal health care, poverty, and a variety of other contextual conditions known to have adverse effects on students' development, more of a commitment than one or two isolated federal compensatory educational programs is needed. In the history of both programs, neither has had sufficient funding to provide services to all eligible children. To the millions of children that Title I and Head Start have served, though, it has made important differences in their lives, their families' lives, and in their schools.

See also: FEDERAL EDUCATION ACTIVITIES, *subentry on* HISTORY; FINANCIAL SUPPORT OF SCHOOLS, *subentry on* HISTORY; POVERTY AND EDUCATION.

BIBLIOGRAPHY

BORMAN, GEOFFREY D. 2000. "Title I: The Evolving Research Base." *Journal of Education for Students Placed at Risk* 5:27–45.

BORMAN, GEOFFREY D., and D'AGOSTINO, JEROME V. 1996. "Title I and Student Achievement: A Meta-Analysis of Federal Evaluation Results." *Educational Evaluation and Policy Analysis* 18:309–326.

BORMAN, GEOFFREY D.; STRINGFIELD, SAMUEL C.; and SLAVIN, ROBERT E., eds. 2001. *Title I: Compensatory Education at the Crossroads.* Mahwah, NJ: Erlbaum.

BROOKS-GUNN, JEANNE, and DUNCAN, GREG J. 1997. "The Effects of Poverty on Children." *The Future of Children* 7(2):55–71.

McKEY, RUTH H., et al. 1985. *The Impact of Head Start on Children, Family, and Communities: Final Report of the Head Start Evaluation, Synthesis, and Utilization Report.* Washington, DC: U.S. Government Printing Office.

PETERSON, PAUL E.; RABE, BARRY G.; and WONG, KENNETH W. 1986. *When Federalism Works.* Washington, DC: Brookings Institution.

RAMEY, CRAIG T., and RAMEY, SHARON L. 1998. "Early Intervention and Early Experience." *American Psychologist* 53:109–120.

SCHWEINHART, LAWRENCE J.; BARNES, HELEN V.; and WEIKART, DAVID P. 1993. *Significant Benefits: The High/Scope Perry Preschool Study through Age 27.* Ypsilanti, MI: High/Scope.

ZIGLER, EDWARD, and VALENTINE, JEANNETE, eds. 1979. *Project Head Start: A Legacy of the War on Poverty.* New York: Free Press/Macmillan.

GEOFFREY D. BORMAN

POLICIES AND PROGRAMS IN LATIN AMERICA

Questions that have puzzled education scholars, policymakers, and social reformers since the 1960s are the following: Do schools reproduce social stratification? Do they enable social mobility? Can schools help poor children learn at hight levels? Do deliberate attempts to reform education policy influence school life?

Theoretical and Historical Context

Whether education policy can change the distribution of educational opportunity depends on the context of schools and of the students they serve. Comparative analysis shows that school quality is more significant in helping disadvantaged children learn. More privileged children, whose parents have higher levels of schooling, often learn much from them. Hence, the potential of education policy to influence schools is greater in marginalized schools. This entry discusses the results of policies aimed at expanding the learning chances of poor and marginalized children in Latin America during the 1990s.

It is fitting to study the potential of policies aimed at improving educational opportunity for the poor in Latin America. During the twentieth century, Latin America experienced a dramatic educational expansion, as did most developing regions. This expansion allowed for intergenerational education mobility: social differences were no longer expressed in terms of access to only the lower levels of schooling, but rather as social differences in the quality of education, as most of the expansion was possible in fragile institutions of insufficient quality to enable the newly incorporated groups to succeed academically. This in turn transferred preexisting social differences to differences in the likelihood to successfully complete the lower levels of education and therefore to access secondary and tertiary education. With the expansion of public education many of the dominant groups transferred their children to private institutions, hence contributing to further differentiation and stratification of schools.

In spite of the significant educational expansion of the twentieth century much inequality is still reproduced across generations in terms of the lower-education chances for the children of the poor. Low-income groups are the last to access education at any given level, are largely excluded from higher education, and also to a great extent from secondary education and preschool education. Most of those who are still excluded from primary education come from the poorest families. For children of a given education level, disparities exist among schools in per pupil expenditures, in the levels of education of their teachers, in the amount of instructional time they receive, and in the instructional resources to which they have access. These disparities also mirror the inequalities of origin between the children of the poor and the affluent. Low-income children are more likely to be assigned to poorly endowed schools, with less-experienced teachers who are in school fewer hours with the consequent less time on task than their higher-income counterparts.

During the 1980s the region faced a series of economic shocks resulting from a debt crisis and ensuing programs of economic adjustment that negatively affected the already fragile public education systems. These and related changes in the delivery of social services and in economic conditions increased poverty and inequality. In the early 1990s political elites focused on the need to reduce poverty as a way to reduce and prevent social conflict and violence, and to enhance the ability to govern increasingly unstable societies. One of the strategies to reduce poverty was to target resources to improve educational opportunity for the children of the poor.

Three Types of Compensatory Policies in Latin America

Compensatory policies seek to close the gaps in learning opportunities between children of the poor and the affluent. According to the way compensation is interpreted, policies and programs that seek

to foster equal educational opportunity are of three kinds. A first group of compensatory policies includes those that aim to equalize the distribution of educational inputs financed publicly. The objective is to close the input gap between the school environments attended by the poor and the affluent. These include the following: (1) more equitable funding of schools such as the financing reforms implemented in the 1990s in Brazil that sought to close the gap in per pupil spending across schools; (2) those that aim to increase access to a given education level by building more schools, hiring more teachers, or developing alternative modalities to more effectively reach particular groups such as the use of TV-based secondary education in rural areas in Mexico (*telesecundaria*), the use of community-based modalities of education to offer education to multiage groups in remote rural communities in Mexico (*postprimaria rural*), or the program to expand access to preschool and primary education in rural areas in El Salvador (EDUCO); and (3) those that try to provide schools attended by low-income children with minimum instructional resources commonly available to the affluent such as textbooks, school libraries, and training for teachers. Examples include the program to overcome educational backwardness in Mexico (Pare); the Escuela Nueva program in Colombia to enhance the quality of rural schools; and the program to enhance the quality of the schools with lowest levels of student achievement, the P900 program in Chile (which took its name from targeting the 900 poorest primary schools, representing 10% of the total).

The policies to equalize the distribution of inputs followed in Chile included a new teaching statute that gave salary incentives to teachers working in marginalized areas; instituting programs to improve the quality of the most vulnerable schools at the primary and secondary level, and programs for at-risk children (e.g., the school health program and summer camp programs); and teacher incentives for after-school programs.

In Mexico compensatory programs expanded from a small program that targeted 100 schools in the early 1990s, to coverage of 46 percent of all public schools in 1999. The objective of the programs was to improve the quality of primary education and expand access to preprimary and primary education through the provision of infrastructure, training, materials, and incentives to teachers and supervisors. Starting in 1998, coverage of the programs included lower secondary education.

A second group of compensatory policies includes those that aim to reorient the utilization of public resources to equalize the distribution of educational opportunities understood as outputs. Some call these policies positive discrimination. These policies recognize that the outcomes of schools reflect the contributions of school and family resources; therefore, the purpose of compensation is to offset the greater opportunities some children receive from home resources. For example, success in the first grade of primary school is a function both of what goes on during that year, but also of the conditions of health and nutrition of children prior to entering first grade, and of the cognitive, emotional, and social stimulation received in early childhood. Consequently equality of treatment in school during the first grade would most likely not lead to equality of learning outcomes for children from different social backgrounds. Equality of outcomes would require extra resources and attention to low-income children both during early childhood and in first grade. Similarly, the "opportunity cost" of staying in school varies for children of different social backgrounds; therefore, achieving equal opportunity to attain the same levels of schooling requires interventions that appropriately cover those opportunity costs (e.g., scholarships for low-income students that cover the direct and indirect costs of participation in school). An example of this policy is the scholarship program to support school attendance of low-income children in Mexico (Progresa) or a scholarship program for similar purposes in Brazil (Bolsa Escola). Programs of full-day school sessions for low-income children in Chile, Uruguay, and Venezuela (when the affluent attend half-day sessions) are examples of positive discrimination focused on enhancing the quality or intensity of inputs. Given the stark discrepancies between the conditions of the targeted schools and the nontargeted schools, and the relatively low level of funding of these policies, much of the so-called policies of positive discrimination in Latin America are in fact attempts to equalize the distribution of inputs. At best they are designed to close the resource gap—the levels of initial input inequality among schools—and not to endow schools of low-income children with greater resources to achieve equality of output. For example, the program of the 900 schools in Chile, and the Programa para Abatir el Rezago Educativo in Mexi-

co, target resources and attention to schools attended by disadvantaged children to try to redress previous neglect and gaps in resources between these schools and the schools of the affluent. The same is true of the Escuela Nueva program in Colombia, which attempts to improve the quality of rural multigrade schools through teacher training and provision of instructional materials.

A third group of compensatory policies are those that support differentiated forms of treatment for low-income children in recognition of their unique needs and characteristics. The main objective of these policies is to support opportunities for relevant and meaningful learning for low-income children. The goal is not to achieve equality of learning outputs, but equality of life chances. The assumption is that the school curriculum contributes only a fraction of the cultural and social capital that the affluent acquire in life; the rest attained as a result of experiences facilitated by family, neighbors, and community. In order for the poor to have comparable opportunities to live a life that is consistent with their choices, schools need to provide more cultural and social capital and be capable of associating and accessing vertical and horizontal social networks such as personal effectiveness, and political and negotiation skills. Although equality of inputs and equality of outputs assume the equivalency of the relevance of curricular objectives for all children, this particular group of efforts does not make that assumption, and attempts instead to support curricular goals and pedagogical approaches that specifically allow low-income children to move out of poverty through individual or collective action. The purpose of these policies is to help children learn skills whose significance is contextually situated, "preparing all students to live in and contribute to a diverse society but also preparing them to recognize and work to alter the economic and social inequities of that society" (Cochran-Smith, p. 931). Examples of this approach include various forms of popular education as described by Paulo Freire and his colleagues and followers, the various modalities of education designed and supported by Fe y Alegria, the network of publicly funded schools managed by the Society of Jesus in thirteen Latin American countries, and the early-twenty-first century modality of community-based post-primary education developed in Mexico.

Effects of Compensatory Policies

Extant evaluations of compensatory policies tend to be descriptive, mostly emphasizing intended policy and short-term effects. When these reports are analytical, they focus on outcomes such as access or achievement on curriculum-based tests and adopt a "black box" approach to policy implementation, often assuming that policy output is implemented as intended. The designs employed rely on pre-postcomparisons—often inappropriately disaggregating the effects of the policies being evaluated with those of other policies or changes—or on comparisons between target populations and some quasi-control groups—often assuming learning from differences between groups, inappropriately accounting for the nonrandom selection of students to treatment schools.

Limited studies indicate that some desired outcomes (more typically access, but also achievement levels) improve with the implementation of a compensatory policy, but say nothing about whether the distance separating the beneficiaries of the policy from the rest of the children shortens or widens as a result of the policy. It is unknown whether these policies, embedded in process of general education improvement, represent marginal improvements in the educational opportunities of the poor or real reductions in the equity gaps existing in each country. Most studies concentrate on the effects of the policies, rather than on their costs. Little is known about the practical consequence of some of the effects (many of which are discussed as a percentage increase in student achievement in a test or a percentage change in access). In particular almost nothing is known about the long term effects of compensatory policies, whether they are sustained or interact with further interventions and what kinds of other long-term outcomes they have, such as access to higher levels of schooling, acquisition of skills or life chances.

Education reforms in Brazil, which through a constitutional amendment reduced the gaps in per pupil spending across schools and regions and provided scholarships to children in low-income families to attend school at least 85 percent of the school year, contributed to making access to primary school universal. By 2002, 97 percent of the children in the relevant age group were enrolled in primary school; the gains in access were significantly greater for the children from the lower income families. For the poorest income quintile primary school attendance increased from 75 percent in 1992 to 93 percent in 1999. Promotion and completion rates increased, as repetition rates declined. There is less conclusive evidence regarding the impact of these reforms on the learning outcomes of students.

Compensatory policies in Mexico expanded coverage significantly in disadvantaged areas, mostly as a result of concentrating the hiring of teachers in indigenous schools and in new modalities of primary and secondary schooling adaptable to small rural communities. Compensatory policies in Mexico have succeeded in distributing inputs (textbooks, pedagogical materials, improving infrastructure) and in providing opportunities for teacher professional development, hence improving the minimum resource base in marginalized schools.

With this improvement in basic conditions, completion rates have improved considerably more in areas targeted by compensatory policies than in other regions of the country. Teachers provide good reports of the training courses, but there is no evidence of impact of the training in teacher practice or on student achievement. Several studies consistently point out that implementation significantly transformed the programs, with negative consequences for learning opportunity.

To sum up, Mexico's experience with compensatory programs during the 1990s shows that it is possible to provide basic inputs to the most disadvantaged schools, therefore reducing inequality in inputs. Because initial inequalities are so significant, this alone is an important accomplishment of policy. Important gains can be achieved in expanding access and primary school completion by supporting the basic functioning of schools in this way. Achieving changes in learning, and therefore contributing to reduce inequality in learning outcomes, is more complicated. In part this reflects the challenges of changing teacher capacity from very low initial levels. Helping teachers become effective is much harder than providing them or their students with textbooks and notebooks. The simple program theory underlying compensatory policies is more appropriate to achieve the latter than the former. Program theory aside, the implementation challenges to developing new teaching practices are greater than to providing financial incentives for teachers to show up to school or for parents to fix up schools.

Research on the impact of compensatory policies in Chile confirms the results of the few studies available for Mexico. Most of the research follows a black box approach and fails to identify significant changes in learning outcomes, and there is limited information about program implementation. Only short-term effects are affected in a narrow set of cognitive domains, as measured by multiple option tests. Ernesto Schiefelbein and Paulina Schiefelbein question the predictive validity of these tests of the skills that matter to obtain high-paying jobs in the labor market. As in the case of Mexico the greatest challenge appears to be in documenting changes in teacher capabilities. Also as in Mexico, the existing studies document relatively short-term effects of these policies, spanning six to seven years.

A study of the impact of compensatory programs in Chile documented sustained improvement in levels of student achievement in mathematics and Spanish since 1990. The achievement gap between the highest-performing and lowest-performing schools has narrowed in fourth grade (but not in eighth grade), in line with the emphasis of the programs in the lower cycle of education. An external evaluation conducted by a Chilean center of educational research (CIDE) in 1991 confirmed the greater levels of learning for students in the program than in comparable schools (though the actual learning gains are small, only 3%). The evaluation also documented that for schools involved in the P900 program teachers became more active and provided more opportunities for student participation.

Chile's recent policies to improve equity in education, like Mexico's, suggest that it is possible to provide inputs to the most disadvantaged schools, hence reducing inequality. In spite of the emphasis of Chilean policy on positive discrimination, and its emphasis on assessing inequality in learning outcomes as a starting point for policy, there are conflicting accounts on whether the achievement gaps between the poor and the affluent had narrowed. The conflict stems in part from the kind of adjustment made to student achievement scores to make them comparable over time. It should be pointed out that these reforms were implemented in a context where total expenditures in education increased significantly, and other social policies and the results of significant economic growth resulted in reduction of the incidence of poverty, the existing studies do not discuss this context nor do they attempt to parcel out the contributions of compensatory policies from the effects of these other policy-induced changes. Judging from differences in raw student

achievement scores, the gains over time for all schools are greater than the reduction in the gap between the targeted schools and the non-targeted schools: Some potentially promising avenues to enhance student learning are left unexplored in this study.

The studies of this case, as the studies of the Mexican case, highlight the importance of basic school supplies and infrastructural conditions to enable school learning. Children do better when they have textbooks, when their schools are not in disrepair, when there are school libraries, and their teachers have instructional resources. These effects should not be surprising given that these policies are targeting schools and children in great need, where a simple pencil and notebook is a great addition to facilitate learning. What these studies do not answer is how far can the expansion of such basic provision of school inputs go? It is reasonable to expect that the effects of these strategies will level off after a point. None of the existing studies in Mexico, Chile, or elsewhere focus on the question of which skills are more relevant to facilitate intergenerational social mobility and the reduction of inequality.

Although there are other studies of the effects of compensatory and equity policies in Latin America, their results are consistent with those reviewed. Studies of the impact of these policies suggest that it is easier to distribute inputs than to educate teachers, and that changes in student achievement levels are modest. In Colombia the equity policies emphasized reorienting education expenditures towards rural areas and supporting Escuela Nueva, a program to strengthen the quality of rural schools. The reorientation of expenditures has effects in expanding access to different levels. Escuela Nueva has been assessed by various studies that document children's improved performance in rural multigrade schools where teachers are appropriately trained and where learning materials are available than those students in less-endowed rural schools. The basic story of these studies is similar: it is possible to improve the learning conditions of poor children through policies that enhance learning inputs. There are great challenges in implementation, particularly when the policies involve altering instructional practices. Although effects in terms of student achievement and completion rates can be documented, the social significance of those and the long-term correlates of those effects has not been assessed. Studies are biased toward short-term effects, probably because sponsors of research are more interested in recent policies than in assessing effects over fairly long periods.

On the whole more is known about policies that attempt to reduce disparities in inputs than about policies that aim true positive discrimination or enhancement of the social and cultural capital of poor students. Regarding whether education fosters social reproduction or mobility in a context of rapid expansion and deliberate affirmative policy, the studies of compensatory policies in Mexico and Chile pose more questions than they answer. What is the practical significance of student achievement in the tests used to measure curriculum coverage? How does performance on these tests relate to life chances? How well does performance on those tests predict performance in higher levels of education? What is the influence of the compensatory programs on other social and attitudinal outcomes? What is the impact of these programs in building social capital in the communities? What are the perspectives of the intended beneficiaries of these programs? What do they think they get out of them? What do they think about how these programs should be run? Existing evaluations document relatively the short-term impact of these programs, which does not describe how effects change as the inputs they support in schools consolidate.

The high levels of social exclusion characteristic of Latin America are indicative of politics and history that have produced and maintained such inequities. Compensatory policies are formulated and implemented in a context and through mechanisms that reflect the very inequalities of origin at the root of the problem they try to correct. In what they changed and in what they failed to alter they express the tensions between the role of schools as levers of social change and as mechanisms to reproduce social stratification.

See also: LATIN AMERICA AND THE CARIBBEAN.

BIBLIOGRAPHY

AGUERRONDO, INES. 2000. "Can Education Measure Up to Poverty in Argentina?" In *Unequal Schools, Unequal Chances,* ed. Fernando Reimers. Cambridge, MA: Harvard University Press.

BOURDIEU, PIERRE, and PASSERON, JEAN CLAUDE. 1977. *Reproduction.* Beverly Hills, CA: Sage.

BRAZILIAN GOVERNMENT. MINISTRY OF EDUCATION. 2001. *Encouraging Citizenship: Progress in Brazilian Education.* Brasilia, Brazil: Ministry of Education.

BRAZILIAN GOVERNMENT. MINISTRY OF EDUCATION. 2002. *Facts Concerning Education in Brazil 1994–2001.* Brasilia, Brazil: Ministry of Education.

CAMARA, GABRIEL, and LOPEZ, DALILA. 2001. *Tres anos de posprimaria comunitaria rural.* Mexico City, Mexico: Secretaria de Educacion Publica.

CEPAL. 1999. *Panorama social.* Santiago, Chile: United Nations.

COCHRAN-SMITH, MARY. 1998. "Teacher Development and Educational Reform." In *International Handbook of Educational Change,* ed. Andrew Hargreaves et al. London: Kluwer.

COLEMAN, JAMES, et al. 1966. *Equality of Educational Opportunity.* Washington, DC: Government Printing Office.

CONSEJO NACIONAL DE FOMENTO EDUCATIVO. 1999. *Programas compensatorios.* Mexico City, Mexico: Consejo Nacional de Fomento Educativo.

ELMORE, RICHARD. 1982. "Backward Mapping: Implementation Research and Policy Decisions." In *Studying Implementation. Methodological and Administrative Issues,* ed. Walter Williams et al. New Jersey: Chatham House.

EZPELETA, JUSTA, and WEISS, EDUARDO. 1994. *Programa para abatir el rezago educativo.* Guanajuato, Mexico: Centro de Investigacion y Estudios Avanzados del Instituto Politecnico Nacional. Departamento de Investigaciones Educativas.

FREIRE, PAULO. 1970. *Pedagogy of the Oppressed.* New York: Continuum.

GARCIA-HUIDOBRO, JUAN EDUARDO. 2000. "Education Policy and Equity in Chile." In *Unequal Schools, Unequal Chances,* ed. Fernando Reimers. Cambridge, MA: Harvard University Press.

GORDON, EDMUND, and MILLER, LaMAR P. 1974. *Equality of Educational Opportunity: A Handbook for Research and Compensatory Education for the Disadvantaged.* New York: AMS Press.

HEYNEMAN, STEPHEN, and LOXLEY, WILLIAM. 1983. "The Effect of Primary School Quality on Academic Achievement across Twenty-Nine High- and Low-Income Countries." *American Journal of Sociology* 88:1162–1194.

LOERA, ARMANDO. 2000. *Las escuelas primarias rurales y los apoyos de los programas compensatorios.* Mexico City, Mexico: Mimeo.

McEwan, Patrick. 1995. *Primary School Reform for Rural Development: An Evaluation of Colombian New Schools.* Washington, DC: InterAmerican Development Bank.

Munoz-Izquierdo, Carlos, et al. 1995. "Valoracion del impacto educativo de un programa compensatorio, orientado a abatir el rezago escolar en la educacion primaria." *Revista Latinoamericana de Estudios Educativos* 25(4):11–58.

Munoz-Izquierdo, Carlos, and Ahuja, Raquel. 2000. "Function and Evaluation of a Compensatory Program Directed at the Poorest Mexican States." In *Unequal Schools, Unequal Chances,* ed. Fernando Reimers. Cambridge, MA: Harvard University Press.

Reimers, Fernando. 1991. "The Impact of Economic Stabilization and Adjustment on Education in Latin America." *Comparative Education Review* 35(2):319–353.

Reimers, Fernando, ed. 2000. *Unequal Schools, Unequal Chances.* Cambridge, MA: Harvard University Press.

Sarmiento, Alfredo. 2000. "Education Policy and Equity in Colombia." In *Unequal Schools, Unequal Chances,* ed. Fernando Reimers. Cambridge, MA: Harvard University Press.

Schiefelbein, Ernesto, and Schiefelbein, Paulina. 2000. "Education and Poverty in Chile." In *Unequal Schools, Unequal Chances,* ed. Fernando Reimers. Cambridge, MA: Harvard University Press.

Secretaria de Educacion Publica. 1999. *Informe de labores 1998–1999.* Mexico City, Mexico: Secretaria de Educacion Publica.

Swope, John y Marcela Latorre. 1999. *Comunidades educativas donde termina el asfalto.* Santiago, Chile: Centro de Investigación y Desarrollo de la Educación.

World Bank. 1997. *Implementation Completion Report: Mexico Primary Education Project.* Washington, DC: World Bank.

Fernando Reimers

COMPULSORY SCHOOL ATTENDANCE

The term *compulsory attendance* refers to state legislative mandates for attendance in public schools (or authorized alternatives) by children within certain age ranges for specific periods of time within the year. Components of compulsory attendance laws include admission and exit ages, length of the school year, enrollment requirements, alternatives, waivers and exemptions, enforcement, and truancy provisions.

Compulsory age requirements vary by state. Data collected by the Education Commission of the States in March 2000 indicate that the earliest age for compulsory attendance is five, with a range to seven, and the upper age limit varies from sixteen to eighteen. Withdrawal from school prior to the age limit is permissible in some states, provided certain conditions are met. State policies setting the length of the school year differ as well. The 2000 Council of Chief State School Officers Policies and Practices Survey indicates that state requirements for the number of school days range from 175 to 186, with variations on exceptions, minimum hours, and start dates.

Enforcement of compulsory attendance laws is usually accomplished through local school attendance officers, superintendents, law enforcement officers, and municipal or juvenile domestic relations courts. Parents, or those persons with legal custody, are held responsible for school attendance in every state. Penalties for noncompliance can include fines and jail sentences, but these are not usually imposed until administrative measures prove unsuccessful. Consequences for students vary but include removal from regular classrooms and placement in alternative programs and denial of driving privileges. In some states, criminal penalties exist for contributing to truancy.

The authority for compulsory attendance laws has been defined through courts of law as a valid use of the police power of the state provided by the U.S. Constitution. The U.S. Supreme Court opinion in *Meyer v. Nebraska* (1923) describes the police power of states as "founded on the right of the State to protect its citizens, to provide for their welfare and progress and to insure the good of society" (Gee and Sperry, p. C-19).

Development of Compulsory School Attendance Philosophy and Laws

The authority of a state to mandate that parents send children to school has not always been endorsed or recognized in the United States. Parental provision of instruction for children originated with the English poor laws of the sixteenth century, which required vocational training for destitute youth. Schools were organized in connection with poorhouses and workhouses for training the inhabitants' children.

In colonial America, the earliest educational laws required training in skills and trades through apprenticeships for orphans and needy children—a large population due to the immigration of youth as indentured servants. By the mid-eighteenth century, laws had been expanded to include training in reading and writing. Teaching children the fundamental skill of reading enabled religious instruction and reading of the Bible.

The first compulsory education law in America was enacted in 1642 by the Massachusetts Bay Colony. This law required parents to provide an understanding of the principles of religion to children under their care, as well as an education in reading, writing, and a trade. Other New England colonies adopted similar laws between 1642 and 1671, but the southern colonies did not enact laws for appriced children until 1705.

Early laws were driven by the need for individuals to understand religious principles and moral concepts and to meet the expectations of their station as citizens. They provided the foundation for governmental action to require education, even if it was seen as more of a private responsibility than a public one. The concept of freedom of children from work while attending school was not included, and would not be until the nineteenth century.

Interest and support for compulsory education declined during the seventeenth and eighteenth centuries due to several factors, including movement from towns into the frontier, the need for children to work at home, difficulty in enforcement, and less emphasis on religion. After the American Revolution, new reasons for interest in an educated citizenry appeared, based on democratic ideals, religious tolerance, and the integration of immigrants into the mainstream of American society.

In 1852 the state of Massachusetts passed a weak law to require attendance in schools. The Massachusetts School Attendance Act of 1852 specified that children between the ages of eight and fourteen had to attend school for twelve weeks per year, six of which had to be consecutive if the school remained open for that time. Although unclear and ill-defined, exemptions were included in the law, as were penalties for enforcement.

Early compulsory attendance laws provided for a minimum time that children had to attend school before they could be lawfully employed, usually three months, but enforcement was lax. The South lagged behind, and many of the laws of the southern states left enforcement and practice to localities. The early laws were vague, and parents who needed children at home to help earn a living resisted.

By 1900 court cases had affirmed state enforcement of compulsory attendance laws based on the benefit to the child and the welfare and safety of the state and community. In 1901 the authority to mandate school attendance was expressed in the Indiana Supreme Court opinion for *State v. Bailey*. The finding stated that "the welfare of the child and the best interests of society require that the state shall exert its sovereign authority to secure to the child the opportunity to acquire an education" (Hudgins and Vacca, p. 275). In the 1944 case of *Prince v. Massachusetts*, the U.S. Supreme Court declared: "Acting to guard the general interest in youth's well being, the state as *parens patriae* may restrict the parent's control by requiring school attendance, regulating or prohibiting the child's labor, and in many other ways" (Gee and Sperry, p C-20).

Lawrence Kotin and William Aiken, in their book *Legal Foundations of Compulsory School Attendance* (1980), cite several conditions in the labor sector that reinforced the sentiment for compulsory attendance in schools. The need for a general education for children was reinforced by the need to protect children from abuse in the workplace (as expressed through child labor laws). In addition, the need for skilled and literate workers increased as the industrial age unfolded. Working children provided competition for employment in unskilled jobs that adults needed, providing another factor for wanting children to be in school. An alignment of labor leaders and advocates of self-sufficiency and improvement in the human condition created a demand for longer years in school and school attendance.

A National Bureau of Economic Research study found that school attendance rates in 1900 were significantly raised in those states that combined compulsory school attendance with child labor laws. By the second decade of the twentieth century, a majority of states had specific child labor laws that set the minimum age for employment at fourteen and included specification of the completion of school grades and other educational requirements.

Exemptions and Alternatives

The expansion of learning arrangements recognized by state law as alternatives to attendance in public schools has evolved through case law. According to Gee and Sperry, compulsory attendance laws must meet the demands of reasonableness. This term was defined in the U.S. Supreme Court case *Pierce v. Society of Sisters* (1925). In this case, the state of Oregon required that children within the age ranges of the compulsory attendance law attend public school only, or their parents would be guilty of a misdemeanor. The Court ruled in favor of the operators of a private school that challenged the state law, finding the statute unconstitutional on the basis of violating the fourteenth amendment rights of the parents and the property rights of schools. The court supported compulsory attendance but not the concept that compliance could only be achieved through public schools. Private schools were an alternative.

The right of parents to provide an alternative to public or private schooling to honor and preserve religious convictions was established through the case of *Wisconsin v. Yoder* (1972). Members of the Old Order Amish Religions objected to formal public schooling beyond the eighth grade because it presented and reinforced values that were in opposition to beliefs of the Amish community. The Amish had experienced conflict with state authorities over compulsory school attendance over the years, but, instead of litigation, would pay fines, be subjected to short-term jailings, or move.

Amish parents Jonas Yoder and Adin Yutzy appealed the decision of the Wisconsin Circuit Court that convicted them for violating Wisconsin's mandate for school attendance until the age of sixteen. The state of Wisconsin justified the conviction based on the need to preserve the political system, ensure economic survival, and provide for the socialization of children. A basic education, the state declared, included the ability to read and reason in order to evaluate issues and exercise citizens' rights such as voting. The Wisconsin Supreme Court, however, reversed the lower court ruling. The court found that

the Amish alternative to formal secondary school education could convey "the social and political responsibilities of citizenship without compelled attendance beyond the eighth grade at the price of jeopardizing their free exercise of religious belief" (Gee and Sperry, p. 23).

The United States Supreme Court upheld this decision in 1972, with Chief Justice Warren Burger ruling: "A State's interest in universal education is not totally free from a balancing process when it impinges on other fundamental rights and interests, such as those specifically protected by the Free Exercise clause of the First Amendment and the traditional interest of parents with respect to the religious upbringing of their children" (Keim, p. 98).

State compulsory attendance statutes have been amended to provide for students attending alternative education programs, as well as for various waivers and exemptions. For example, the Code of Virginia states that requirements for compulsory attendance may be satisfied by sending a child to an alternative program of study or work-study offered through a public, private, denominational, or parochial school, or by a public or private degree-granting institution of higher education. A local school board must excuse from school attendance any pupil who, with his or her parents, is conscientiously opposed to attendance due to religious training or belief. Also mandated is release from attendance by local school boards for verified medical reasons or for personal safety as determined by a juvenile and domestic-relations district court.

Virginia law recognizes home instruction by parents or instruction by tutors, provided that specified conditions are met, and provisions for some form of home schooling are provided in the majority of the fifty states. Other exemptions and delays for attendance are made for children with medical, physical, or emotional problems. Exceptions to compulsory attendance laws may be made if children within certain ages do not have public transportation provided within certain distances from their homes. Information provided by the Education Commission of the States in 2000 shows that, in several states, students sixteen years old may be eligible for withdrawal from the regular classroom if fully employed or enrolled in alternative education programs, with approval by parents and principals.

Issues Associated with Compulsory Attendance

Despite the changes in state laws to increase flexibility, there are some critics who maintain that compulsory school attendance should be ended. The National Center for Policy Analysis provides some of the arguments to lower the compulsory school upper age limit, or to limit hours. Opponents claim that compulsory school attendance does not necessarily result in better education for students, but could subject them to social engineering. Others claim that compulsory attendance results in prolonged adolescence and suggest that forced attendance in high school could contribute to violence and discipline problems. Compulsory attendance laws have been said to limit innovation and be burdensome for parents who home-school their children. Yet the National Center for Policy Analysis cites statistics indicating that students who attend school a greater percentage of time than their counterparts with lesser attendance records score higher on state knowledge and skills tests.

Respondents to the thirty-third annual Phi Delta Kappa/Gallup Poll of the public's attitudes toward the public schools, conducted in January 2001, support reforming the existing public school system by almost two-to-one, rather than creating alternatives to the existing system. Seventy-five percent of the respondents prefer to improve the existing public school system rather than provide vouchers to pay for private or church-related schools.

Not only is an argument made for attendance at schools in order to prepare children for employment and economic success, but also for the development of values and the character traits needed for citizenship. The Center on Education Policy makes the case that public education is essential not only in teaching the principles of democracy and the role of government, but also in promoting civic values and the philosophy of tolerance for diversity and respect for differences in race and religion.

Whether the basis is economic self-sufficiency, educational reform, preparation for work or further study, character development, or promotion of the citizenry and the democratic way of life, the reasons for compulsory attendance of some kind reinforce the continued existence of state statutes. However, changing circumstances, flexibility for parents and students, and the needs of various student populations continue to shape these laws and contribute to their evolution.

See also: CONSTITUTIONAL REQUIREMENTS GOVERNING AMERICAN EDUCATION; ELEMENTARY EDUCATION, *subentry on* HISTORY OF; SECONDARY EDUCATION, *subentry on* HISTORY OF.

BIBLIOGRAPHY

COUNCIL OF CHIEF STATE SCHOOL OFFICERS. 2000. *Key State Education Policies on K–12 Education: 2000.* Washington, DC: Council of Chief State School Officers.

DUCKWORTH, KENNETH. 1992. "Attendance Policy." In *Encyclopedia of Educational Research,* Vol. 1, ed. Marvin C. Alkin. New York: Macmillan.

ENSIGN, FOREST CHESTER. 1921. *Compulsory School Attendance and Child Labor.* Iowa City, IA: Athens Press.

GEE, GORDON E., and SPERRY, DAVID J. 1978. *Education Law and the Public Schools: A Compendium.* Boston: Allyn and Bacon.

GOOD, HARRY GEHMAN. 1956. *A History of American Education.* New York: Macmillan.

GOODLAD, JOHN I., and MCMANNON, TIMOTHY J., eds. 1997. *The Public Purpose of Education and Schooling.* San Francisco: Jossey-Bass.

HUDGINS, H. C., JR., and VACCA, RICHARD S. 1995. *Law and Education, Contemporary Issues and Court Decisions,* 4th edition. Charlottesville, VA: Michie.

KEIM, ALBERT N. 1975. *Compulsory Education and the Amish: The Right Not to Be Modern.* Boston: Beacon Press.

KOTIN, LAWRENCE, and AIKMAN, WILLIAM. 1980. *Legal Foundations of Compulsory School Attendance.* New York: National University Publications, Kennikat Press.

ROSE, LOWELL C., and GALLUP, ALEC M. 2001. "The Thirty-Third Annual Phi Delta Kapppa/Gallup Poll of the Public's Attitudes Toward the Public Schools." *Phi Delta Kappan* 83(1):41–58.

VIRGINIA DEPARTMENT OF EDUCATION. 2000. *Virginia School Laws.* Charlottesville, VA: Michie.

WHITE, PATRICIA. 1996. *Civic Virtues and Public Schooling, Educating Citizens for a Democratic Society.* New York: Teachers College Press.

INTERNET RESOURCES

EDUCATION COMMISSION OF THE STATES. 2000. "Attendance." <www.ecs.org>.

MARGO, ROBERT A., and FINEGAN, ALDRICH T. 1996. "Compulsory Schooling Legislation and School Attendance in Turn-of-the-Century America: A 'Natural Experiment' Approach." National Bureau of Economic Research. <www.nber.org>.

NATIONAL CENTER FOR POLICY ANALYSIS. "Forcing Kids to Learn." 1996. <www.ncpa.org/pi/edu/pdedu/pdedu26.html>.

NATIONAL CENTER FOR POLICY ANALYSIS. 1998. "Compulsory School-Attendance Laws Reconsidered." <www.ncpa.org/pi/edu/pd12298d.html>.

NATIONAL CENTER FOR POLICY ANALYSIS. 2000. "Taking a Second Look at School Attendance." <http://www.ncpa.org/pi/edu/pd062700c.html>.

CYNTHIA A. CAVE

COMPUTER-SUPPORTED COLLABORATIVE LEARNING

The traditional expansion for the acronym CSCL is *computer-supported collaborative learning.* However, many who work in the field find aspects of this title problematic; therefore a convention has developed to use the acronym as a free-standing designation in its own right. The traditional title is controversial in several ways.

As Pierre Dillenbourg points out, the term *collaborative learning* has been used in two different senses. On the one hand, some have treated collaborative learning as a distinctive form of socially based learning that is fundamentally different from prevailing psychological formulations. For example, Kenneth Bruffee defines collaborative learning as "a reculturative process that helps students become members of knowledge communities whose common property is different from the common property of the knowledge communities they already belong to" (p. 3). An alternative way to think about collaborative learning, however, is not as a type of learning at all, but rather as a theory of instruction. Stated simply, the theory of collaborative learning, as noted by Jeremy Roschelle and Stephanie Teasley, asserts that learning is enhanced when learners are placed in situations involving "coordinated, synchronous activity that is the result of a continued attempt to construct and maintain a shared conception of a problem" (p. 70). It has been incorporated into a variety of well-known instructional methods, including problem-based learning, some versions of cooperative learning, and project-based learning. Collaborative learning is not limited to settings of formal instruction, however. Learning in the context of joint activity occurs in workplaces, homes, and informal learning settings as well as in schools.

Other terms have been suggested as replacements for *collaborative*. Roy Pea, for example, observes that what takes place in settings of joint activity is often anything but collaborative, and he has proposed that the word *collective* be used instead. There are also other possibilities to be considered. In 1987 Yrgö Engeström drew upon a set of distinctions originally proposed by Bernd Fictner in 1984 between coordination, cooperation, and reflective communication in learning. The difference between coordination and cooperation has to do with the degree to which a learning task involves a prescribed division of labor among participants. This same distinction, however, is employed by Dillenbourg, and by Roschelle and Teasley, to differentiate between cooperation and collaboration. The critical point is that there has been no consensus with respect to the basic terminology for describing interaction in these settings, and it is probably premature to try to establish definitive labels for the field.

There are also misunderstandings that arise from the first half (computer-supported) of CSCL. Not all uses of technology applied to learning in groups are necessarily representative of CSCL research, and not all CSCL research necessarily involves computer-based instruction. Though there is a lively interest within the CSCL community in the ways that new and emerging computer and telecommunications technologies might foster and transform collaborative learning, this is not the sole, or even the central, object of inquiry. There is, indeed, a widely held recognition that the fundamental processes by which learning takes place in settings of joint activity are not well understood. As a result, a good number of CSCL researchers are engaged in basic research designed to illuminate how mutual understanding is accomplished in collaborative settings, whether augmented with technology or not.

A Brief History of CSCL Research

Precursors to what was to become the field of CSCL can be found in three influential projects, all initiated in the early 1980s. The first was a multi-university project known as ENFL, begun at Gallaudet University to support instruction in composition. Workers in this area developed a set of computer-based applications that have subsequently come to be referred to as CSCWriting programs. A second and highly influential project was undertaken by Marlene Scardamalia, Carl Bereiter, and colleagues at the Ontario Institute for Studies in Education (OISE) at the University of Toronto. This project had its origins in reading research and focused from the outset on student epistemologies and the development of skills for knowledge sharing. It led to the development of programs (CSILE, Knowledge Forum) that have been widely used in instructional settings around the world. A third early influence was the 5th Dimension Project organized by Mike Cole and other researchers at the Laboratory of Comparative Human Cognition (LCHC) at the University of California in San Diego. The 5th Dimension is an international multi-site network of after-school teaching programs initially developed as clinical training sites for pre-service teachers. It was less technologically oriented than the other early projects, but the 5th Dimension Project made considerable contributions toward the development of a theoretical framework for studying learning from a sociocultural perspective.

In 1983 a workshop on the topic of "joint problem solving and microcomputers" was held at LCHC. The organizers of this workshop, Mike Cole, Naomi Miyake, and Denis Newman, were all to assume prominent roles in the CSCL community as it developed. Six years later, a NATO-sponsored workshop was held in Maratea, Italy. Though there was some cross-fertilization between the groups (Denis Newman, for instance, participated in both workshops), the Maratea workshop largely involved participants from European research centers, while the San Diego workshop was attended by researchers from the United States and Japan. The Maratea workshop is considered by many to mark the birth of the field since it was the first public and international gathering to use the term *computer-supported collaborative learning* in its title.

The first full-fledged CSCL conference was organized at Indiana University in the fall of 1995. Subsequent international meetings have taken place biennially, with conferences at the University of Toronto in 1997, Stanford University in 1999, and the University of Colorado in 2002. A European conference was held at the University of Maastricht in the Netherlands in 2001. The fifth international conference in the biennial series will be held in Norway at the University of Bergen in 2003. A specialized literature documenting theory and research in CSCL has developed since the NATO-sponsored workshop in Maratea. Four of the most influential monographs are Kenneth Bruffee's *Collaborative Learning* (1993), Charles Crook's *Computers and the Collaborative Experience of Learning* (1994), Newman, Griffin, and Cole's *The Construction Zone* (1989), and Carl Bereiter's *Education and Mind in the Knowledge Age* (2002). Additionally, there have been a number of edited collections specifically focusing on CSCL research.

A Paradigmatic Example of CSCL Research

A paradigmatic example of CSCL research can be found in an early study reported by Jeremy Roschelle in 1992. Roschelle's data consisted of videotapes of two students, Dana and Carol, working together with a program designed to enable users to visualize and experiment with the trajectories of Newtonian particles. For each of these exchanges he described the "conversation action," capturing not only the lexical components, but also timing, prosodic features, and affiliated gestures; the "conceptual change" evidenced in the exchange; and finally the displayed "shared knowledge."

Rather than attending exclusively to *what* was learned using some sort of outcome measure, Roschelle's study focused instead on *how* learners achieve new conceptual understandings in the presence of computational artifacts. When one examines the actual interaction of learners engaged in such activities it is often unclear what is being accomplished through their discourse or how participants move from their initial levels of understanding to appreciations more closely approximating those of a physicist. Roschelle discussed how convergent change is possible using "only figurative, ambiguous, and imprecise language and physical interactions" (p. 239). He argued that conceptual convergence is made possible by four elements: "(a) the construction of a deep-featured situation at an intermediate level of abstraction from the literal features of the world; (b) the interplay of metaphors in relation to each other and to the constructed situation; (c) an iterative cycle of displaying, confirming, and repairing situated actions; and (d) the applications of progressively higher standards of evidence for convergence" (p. 237).

Roschelle's study illustrates three distinctive features of CSCL research. First, as noted by Shelly Goldman and James Greeno, because CSCL research concerns itself with learning in settings of joint activity, learning is treated not as hidden or occult, but rather as a visible and accountable form of social practice. Second, and closely related to the first point, CSCL research is centrally concerned with the process by which meaning is constructed within such settings. Finally, there is an orientation in CSCL research to learning as a form of mediated activity—mediated not only by designed artifacts such as computer programs, but also by the more basic resources of human concentration, such as language and gesture. It is these features that distinguish work in CSCL from other research on the application of instructional technology to learning in groups.

See also: COOPERATIVE AND COLLABORATIVE LEARNING; PEER RELATIONS AND LEARNING; TECHNOLOGY IN EDUCATION.

BIBLIOGRAPHY

BEREITER, CARL. 2002. *Education and Mind in the Knowledge Age.* Mahwah, NJ: Erlbaum.

BONK, CURTIS JAY, and KING, KIRA, eds. 1998. *Electronic Collaborators: Learner-Centered Technologies for Literacy, Apprenticeship, and Discourse.* Mahwah, NJ: Erlbaum.

BRUFFEE, KENNETH. 1993. *Collaborative Learning.* Baltimore: Johns Hopkins University Press.

COLE, MICHAEL; MIYAKE, NAOMI; and NEWMAN, DENIS, eds. 1983. *Proceedings of the Conference on Joint Problem Solving and Microcomputers* (Technical Report No. 1). La Jolla, CA: University of California, San Diego, Laboratory of Comparative Human Cognition.

CROOK, CHARLES. 1994. *Computers and the Collaborative Experience of Learning.* London: Routledge.

DILLENBOURG, PIERRE, ed. 1999. *Collaboratove Learning: Cognitive and Computational Approaches.* Oxford: Pergamon.

ENGESTRÖM, YRGÖ. 1987. *Learning by Expanding: An Activity-Theoretical Approach to Developmental Research.* Helsinki, Finland: Orienta-Konsultit Oy.

FICTNER, BERND. 1984. "Co-ordination, Cooperation, and Communication in the Formation of Theoretical Concepts in Instruction." In *Learning and Teaching on a Scientific Basis: Methodological and Epistemological Aspects of the Activity Theory of Learning and Teaching,* ed. Mariane Hedegaard, Pentti Hakkarainen, and Yrgö Engeström. Aarhus, Denmark: Aarhus University Psykologisk Institut.

GOLDMAN, SHELLY, and GREENO, JAMES. 1998. "Thinking Practices: Images of Thinking and Learning in Education." In *Thinking Practices in Mathematics and Science Learning,* ed. James Greeno and Shelly Goldman. Mahwah, NJ: Erlbaum.

KOSCHMANN, TIMOTHY, ed. 1996. *CSCL: Theory and Practice of an Emerging Paradigm.* Mahwah, NJ: Erlbaum.

KOSCHMANN, TIMOTHY; HALL, ROGERS; and MIYAKE, NAOMI, eds. 2002. *CSCL 2: Carrying Forward the Conversation.* Mahwah, NJ: Erlbaum.

LITTLETON, KAREN, and LIGHT, PAUL, eds. 1999. *Learning with Computers: Analyzing Productive Interactions.* New York: Routledge.

NEWMAN, DENNIS; GRIFFIN, PEG; and COLE, MICHAEL. 1989. *The Construction Zone: Working for Cognitive Change in Schools.* Cambridge, Eng.: Cambridge University Press.

O'MALLEY, CLAIRE, ed. 1995. *Computer Supported Collaborative Learning.* Berlin: Springer-Verlag.

PEA, ROY. 1996. "Seeing What We Build Together: Distributed Multimedia Learning Environments for Transformative Communications." In *CSCL: Theory and Practice of an Emerging Paradigm,* ed. Timothy Koschmann. Mahwah, NJ: Erlbaum.

ROSCHELLE, JEREMY. 1992. "Learning by Collaboration: Convergent Conceptual Change." *Journal of the Learning Sciences* 2:235–276.

ROSCHELLE, JEREMY, and TEASLEY, STEPHANIE. 1995. "The Construction of Shared Knowledge in Collaborative Problem Solving." In *Computer Supported Collaborative Learning,* ed. Claire O'Malley. Berlin: Springer-Verlag.

SCARDAMALIA, MARLENE, and BEREITER, CARL. 1989. "Intentional Learning as a Goal of Instruction." In *Knowing, Learning, and Instruction: Essays in Honor of Robert Glaser,* ed. Lauren B. Resnick. Hillsdale, NJ: Erlbaum.

SCARDAMALIA, MARLENE, and BEREITER, CARL. 1996. "Computer Support for Knowledge-Building Communities." In *CSCL: Theory and Practice of an Emerging Paradigm*, ed. Timothy Koschmann. Mahwah, NJ: Erlbaum.

SCARDAMALIA, MARLENE; BEREITER, CARL; MCLEAN, ROBERT; SWALLOW, JONATHON; and WOODRUFF, EARL. 1989. "Computer-Supported Intentional Learning Environments." *Journal of Educational Computer Research* 5:51–68.

TIMOTHY KOSCHMANN

CONANT, J. B. (1893–1978)

Twenty-third president of Harvard University, James Bryant Conant witnessed many defining moments of twentieth-century American history. He was intimately involved with transformational events: World War I, as president of Harvard University, the initial formation of federal science policy, the development of the atomic bomb in World War II, the cold war and the postwar atomic energy policy (including opposition to the H-bomb), the reconstruction of Europe, and the reconsideration of public education in the United States. His autobiography is aptly titled *My Several Lives,* and he moved with remarkable ease through lives in academic, scientific, governmental, and diplomatic circles.

Conant was born in Dorchester (Suffolk County), Massachusetts, to James Scott Conant and Jennett Orr Bryant. His father had served the Union in the Civil War, owned an engraving and etching business, and speculated in real estate and residential construction. Conant could trace his lineage back to the ships immediately following the Mayflower on his mother's side and to the founding of Salem on his father's.

In his own words, Conant was raised by "a regiment of women," including his mother, several aunts and cousins, and his two elder sisters. Both parents were members of the Swedenborgian Church, an organization devoted to exploring the entwinement of religion, nature, and life. His mother's interest in the church waned, however, and Conant later referred to himself as a Unitarian.

Education

Conant attended the Roxbury Latin School, a college preparatory school that required a rigorous entrance examination for admission. At home, he nurtured his budding interest in science in general and chemistry in particular by practicing magic tricks and doing experiments in his small laboratory equipped by his father. At Roxbury, his career was solidified by his relationship with science teacher Newton Henry Black. Black guided Conant through the high school science curriculum, and then exposed him to more advanced texts and techniques, including college entrance exams. Conant's performance in high school earned him the Harvard Club Scholarship and graduation in 1910 near the top of his class of twenty-one students.

Conant graduated Phi Beta Kappa from Harvard in three years and managed to find enough time away from the classroom and laboratory to write for the Harvard *Crimson,* join Delta Upsilon, and develop a friendship with his rooming house neighbor, novelist J. P. Marquand. Conant's graduate school plans included study with physical chemist Theodore W. Richards, the first American-born winner of the Nobel Prize in chemistry. In his third year of undergraduate studies, he did some special research with organic chemist E. P. Kohler, a new arrival to Harvard from Johns Hopkins University. This project resulted in Conant's becoming Kohler's graduate assistant in advanced organic chemistry for two years. Ultimately, Conant wrote a double thesis in physical and organic chemistry for his Ph.D. degree in 1916.

War Work

The outbreak of World War I in Europe prevented Conant from realizing his dream of postdoctoral study in Germany. However, in the summer of 1916 Roger Adams left the Harvard faculty, and Conant was selected to fill this vacancy in the chemistry department faculty. At the close of the 1916 through 1917 academic year, Conant joined the United States Bureau of Mines, which was soon absorbed by the Department of Defense as the Chemical Warfare Service. World War I would be remembered as the "chemist's war," primarily due to the use of poison gas warfare initiated by the German army against the French in 1915. Conant worked on gas warfare projects in laboratories at American University in Washington, D.C., the largest federally funded scientific research project to that date.

Newly commissioned Lieutenant Conant immediately went to work on mustard gas and then on a more toxic and easily deliverable gas, lewisite. In July

1918 the Army promoted Conant to the rank of major and placed him in charge of a lewisite production facility at an automobile factory in Cleveland. The gas was a weapon intended to be used offensively, but it was never employed. Significantly, the chemist's war connected chemistry to society through demonstration of its applied uses, and allowed Conant to associate with the leaders of government, the military, business, higher education, and administration who would shape the remainder of his career.

Academic Career

In September 1919, following demobilization of the war effort, Conant returned to Harvard with an appointment as assistant professor of chemistry, and in 1921 married Grace T. (Patty) Richards, daughter of T. W. Richards, his department chair and mentor. Conant's early research focused on the areas of mechanisms of chemical reactions, equilibrium-rate studies, and free radical structure. His later research interests centered on respiratory pigments and the properties of hemoglobin and other natural products, especially chlorophyll. He was promoted to associate professor, granted tenure in 1924, and elevated to full professor in 1927. During this period, he and his wife had two sons.

In 1931, Conant was named the Shelden Emery Professor of Organic Chemistry and accepted the department chairmanship. Awards and honors accumulated as Conant was elected to the American Academy of Arts and Science and the National Academy of Science. His research won him the Nichols Medal of the American Chemical Society and the Chandler Medal of Columbia University, among others. Between 1919 and 1933 he wrote or coauthored five chemistry textbooks, including his first, *Practical Chemistry* (1920), written with his former Roxbury science teacher, Newton H. Black.

The Conants made three significant sabbatical trips, two to California and one to Germany. In 1924 they spent a semester at the University of California, Berkeley, and in 1927 a semester at the California Institute of Technology in Pasadena. There, contacts with western scientific leaders A. A. Noyes and Robert A. Millikan would not only prove valuable later during World War II, they resulted in a lucrative offer to move to Pasadena to join the faculty there. In 1925, Conant, Patty, and their son, Jimmy, spent nine months in Germany, where Conant was exposed to the fast-paced scientific competition

among individuals and institutions alike. Much of what he learned of science and scientific administration in Germany would be applied to his own administrative practices. He and his biographers characterized his persona as science itself, with all the characterization implied: the scientific method, increasing specialization, and reduction of a problem to its simplest elements.

In 1933 Harvard's president, Abbott Lowell Lawrence, announced his expected retirement amid much speculation on his successor's identity. Lowell was the administrative opposite of his predecessor, Charles W. Eliot. Lowell was a close supervisor of faculty, a harsh master of students, and a highly opinionated, socially conservative policymaker. It is said that a list of forty possible candidates existed at that time, and it did not include the name *Conant*. A difference of opinion among the Harvard corporate board led to a visit from a board member to Conant. His recommendation appears to have solidified the corporation; on May 8, 1933, Conant was selected as the twenty-third president of Harvard University and was formally installed on October 9, 1933.

President of Harvard University

Conant was immediately forced to begin thinking not only about campus issues and politics, but also about contemporary world events: the Great Depression, the rise of Nazism in Germany, the eventual establishment of the Third Reich, and the foreboding threat of World War II. Conant's presidency would be broken into three distinct eras: 1933 to 1940 was a period of innovative policies at the institutional level and pleas for military and civilian preparedness at the national level; 1940 to 1946 was marked by long absences from Cambridge as Conant became closely involved with the organization and administration of scientific research funded by the federal government; and 1946 to 1953 as postwar equilibrium was achieved and the debates over atomic energy policy and the manufacture of thermonuclear devices heated up.

As president, Conant began to implement policies, some controversial, to improve faculty quality. Among these were the so-called up or out rule—an assistant professor who was not promoted at the end of the probationary term was terminated as a member of the faculty. In addition, university professorships were established to recognize and retain exceptional scholars. Conant put policies in place to establish a more diversified student body; the Harvard National Scholarships were merit-based awards established with the intent of reducing financial and geographic barriers to a Harvard education. He was elected to the Carnegie Foundation for the Advancement of Teaching board of trustees in 1934 and was an early proponent of standardized testing, including nationwide administration of the Scholastic Aptitude Test as a reliable admissions tool.

As war in Europe seemed imminent, Conant supported the Roosevelt administration's quest for peacetime military conscription legislation, an action that was not warmly received by the undergraduates at Harvard. Following Germany's invasion of her European neighbors, Conant's attitude crystallized; he sought ways that scientists and scholars could mobilize to defeat Hitler.

Vannevar Bush, a contemporary of Conant, had been a professor of engineering at the Massachusetts Institute of Technology and, later, vice president of MIT. Bush moved to Washington, D.C. in 1939 to assume the presidency of the Carnegie Institution with its traditional role of science adviser to the government. Bush convinced President Franklin D. Roosevelt that the military needed to make rapid advances in technology and employ civilian scientists with the necessary expertise to do so. Thus, the new National Defense Research Committee (NDRC) was established almost eighteen months before United States entry into war, and Bush recruited Conant for the committee. The NDRC mobilized civilian scientists for war and let contracts, funded by the federal government, to academic and industrial laboratories.

As 1941 progressed, Conant became chair of the NDRC with direct responsibility for committee-supervised work on uranium fission, and, ultimately, the crash program to build the atomic bomb. He was present at Ground Zero, Alamagordo, New Mexico, for the Trinity atomic device test explosion.

Meanwhile Harvard went about its business without the physical presence of Conant, who took a voluntary twenty-five percent salary reduction from 1942 to 1946. One seminal bit of policymaking that did occur during the war years was the agreement reached with Radcliffe College to merge classroom instruction. As a result of a wartime shortage of faculty, 310 years of all-male Harvard education came to an end.

Presidential Appointments

When Dwight D. Eisenhower, former president of Columbia University, was inaugurated as president of the United States in 1953, one of his first appointments was the choice of Conant to become the U.S. high commissioner to Germany. Conant took this opportunity to return to Germany to aid reconstruction as the ideal time to retire from Harvard following twenty years as president. Following the ratification of the treaty establishing the Federal Republic of Germany, Conant became the U.S. ambassador to Germany.

Publications

Conant served in Germany for Eisenhower's first term, then retired from the diplomatic corps in 1957 to undertake a study of American secondary education for the Carnegie Corporation. Several influential books arose from his research, including the *American High School Today* (1959), an on-site examination of the critical problems facing the public "comprehensive" high school. Although the fieldwork began before the launch of the Soviet satellite *Sputnik*, the timing of the publication to coincide with national fears that the country was falling behind the Soviets in secondary education triggered sales of nearly 200,000 copies and Conant's third *Time* magazine cover story. The book outlines twenty-one recommendations, ranging from an increase in the number of guidance counselors to a call for a twelfth-grade capstone course in American democracy. The volume received much attention from parents, educators, and critics, but little substantive reform resulted.

The controversial look at urban schools, *Slums and Suburbs* (1961) presents a contrasting picture of high schools within "half an hour's drive" of one another in the cities of Philadelphia, New York, Detroit, Chicago, and St. Louis. Conant argued that "we are allowing social dynamite to accumulate in our large cities" (p. 2) as evidenced by racial discrimination, poverty, and violence. Contending that a school is a product of the socioeconomic status of the families it serves, he concluded that, "More money is needed in slum schools" (p. 146) rather than busing pupils to other schools. This opinion was not well received among civil rights leaders, thus dooming the rest of Conant's recommendations to obscurity.

Moving to higher levels of the education system, the final two volumes to emerge from this study were *The Education of American Teachers* (1963), a critique of the curricula and teacher certification of schools of education, and *Shaping Educational Policy* (1964), an examination of state and federal education policy.

Contribution

Conant's career and his life-long educational philosophy should be remembered as one of service—to education, to science, and to the interests of his country. He took a "hands on" approach to his supervisory duties in the laboratory, the president's office, and his national study of secondary education. Upon assuming the Harvard presidency, he undertook the daunting task of attending and presiding over every faculty meeting of every college in the university.

Conant's admiration for the German university system fueled his belief that Harvard could be transformed from a New England university with a national reputation to a world-level institution. He initiated graduate degrees in education, public policy, and history of science. His innovations included faculty appointments unattached to any specific department so as to strongly encourage interdisciplinary thinking and collaboration. At Harvard, as at other institutions, the budgetary effects of the depression were felt, and Conant found it necessary to keep the faculty ranks spare. He managed to do this without sacrificing quality by eliminating many of Harvard's inbred hiring policies and instituting the practice of opening position vacancies internationally.

Student enrollment reforms accompanied those of the faculty. Conant purposefully directed the admissions office to scrutinize legacies more closely, open the doors to more first-generation and ethnic immigrant applicants, and scour the country for the most brilliant students. The goal of a more diverse student body was pursued through these directives and the addition of standardized admission testing. Conant strongly believed that the American system of higher education allowed for sorting by ability, and, therefore, students need not reach beyond their grasp in the choice of a college.

In the introduction to the *American High School Today*, Conant wrote of his regret over the talent wasted in the European system of early preselection of students for the university. He clearly understood that the diversity of American institutions of higher education and their ability to absorb all those who wish to go to college are foundational American ideals that promote equality of opportunity and equality of standing. The public benefits of all forms of education were foremost in Conant's pursuit of excellence in science technology education and federal policy. He wrote in his freshman diary at Harvard, "Education is what is left after all that has been learned is forgotten" (Hershberg, p. 20).

In 1963 Conant was awarded the Presidential Medal of Freedom by President John F. Kennedy. An arrhythmic heart condition that was discovered in 1965 caused Conant to curtail drastically his public life. He and his wife spent most subsequent winters in their Manhattan apartment and summers in the hills and mountains of New Hampshire until his death in Hanover, New Hampshire.

See also: CURRICULUM, SCHOOL; EDUCATION REFORM; GENERAL EDUCATION IN HIGHER EDUCATION; HARVARD UNIVERSITY; HIGHER EDUCATION IN THE UNITED STATES, *subentry on* HISTORICAL DEVELOPMENT; PHILOSOPHY OF EDUCATION.

BIBLIOGRAPHY

CONANT, JAMES B. 1948. *Education in a Divided World: The Function of the Public Schools in our Unique Society.* Cambridge, MA: Harvard University Press.

CONANT, JAMES B. 1952. *Modern Science and Modern Man.* New York: Columbia University Press.

CONANT, JAMES B. 1959. *The American High School Today: A First Report to Interested Citizens.* New York: McGraw-Hill.

CONANT, JAMES B. 1961. *Slums and Suburbs: A Commentary on Schools in Metropolitan Areas.* New York: McGraw-Hill.

CONANT, JAMES B. 1963. *The Education of American Teachers.* New York: McGraw-Hill.

CONANT, JAMES B. 1970. *My Several Lives: Memoirs of a Social Inventor.* New York: Harper and Row.

DAVIS, NUEL P. 1968. *Lawrence and Oppenheimer.* New York: Simon and Schuster.

HERSHBERG, JAMES G. 1993. *James B. Conant: Harvard to Hiroshima and the Making of the Nuclear Age.* New York: Knopf.

DAVID A. CAMPAIGNE

CONSORTIA IN HIGHER EDUCATION

A *consortium* is an association of institutions for the purpose of improved and expanded economic collaboration to achieve mutually beneficial goals. In higher education, this organizational form was originally designed to foster interinstitutional cooperation among a group of colleges and universities for the purpose of enhancing services within a geographic region. More recently, as information and communication technologies have increased the availability of resources for research and development purposes, universities have joined with corporations and government agencies to form national and international consortia.

The parameters of academic cooperation may vary in scope by level of control (public-private), discipline (computer science, engineering, medicine), service provider (libraries, universities, science laboratories), or institutional level (research institute, government agency, corporation). Originating initially in the 1960s at a time of unprecedented expansion in higher education, consortia enabled institutions to share abundant resources. These consortia were voluntary, multi-institutional, multipurpose, and designed to serve their member institutions. By the mid-1970s, as institutions became more dependent on external sources of support, universities and colleges established consortia to sustain high-cost programs and facilities, strengthen constituent services, and penetrate new markets beyond their service area. In some instances, governing boards and funding agencies encouraged consortia development as evidence of economic collaboration among local and regional institutions to eliminate superfluous expenditures and achieve economies of scale and cost savings. Contemporary academic consortia may also be structured as school-university partnerships, business-university alliances, community-university coalitions, and multisystem networks. The current status of the academic consortium as an organizational form demonstrates its potential significance as a manifestation of the entrepreneurial university in a consumerist society.

Types of Consortia

The initial consortium structure consisted of three or more colleges and universities signing an agreement to cooperate in providing joint ventures, such as tuition waivers for cross-registration, faculty exchanges and professional development, interuniversity library privileges, joint purchasing of goods and services, and outreach projects. The success of these activities was heightened by comparability in missions, goals, laws, regulations, resources, and sources of support. More sophisticated and complex structural arrangements are now conceptualized around specialized purposes such as supercomputing, scientific research and development, medical school–teaching hospital collaboration, and cooperative degree programs in low-enrollment, specialized fields. In these cases, consortium objectives may be to reduce duplication and redundancy, gain access to federal agency funding, recruit international students, engage in advanced research, and utilize high-cost facilities.

Since the 1990s increased institutional investments in information and communication technology, with support from business and industry, have added important dimensions to consortia design. This growth has been most evident in multisystems and research universities as well as across national and international boundaries. Factors contributing to their longevity include the leadership and commitment of senior executives; formal agreements on resource sharing; collaboration in agenda setting, issue definition, and problem solving; realistic timelines for project development; continuity in personnel; and complementary strategies for overcoming inequities and cultural differences among disparate partners.

Multipurpose academic consortia. The Association for Consortium Leadership (ACL) has identified 125 member consortia in the United States; these vary in size from 3 to 100 institutions engaged in a variety of collaborative projects. Two successful multipurpose academic consortia are Five Colleges, Inc. (Amherst, Smith, Mount Holyoke, and Hampshire Colleges and the University of Massachusetts–Amherst) and the Claremont Colleges, Inc., in California. Five Colleges is an independent, not-for-profit entity coordinated by an executive director and staff, drawing financial support from its member institutions and foundation grants, and operating collaborative faculty and student projects, including free transit throughout its service area. The Claremont Colleges in California, founded in 1925, brings together five independent but contiguous liberal arts colleges and two graduate institutions for collaborative business and academic services, most recently involving the development of an online cross-registration module in the five undergraduate colleges and better utilization of information technology across all seven institutions. The Western Interstate Commission on Higher Education (WICHE) works with fifteen member states in devising cooperative programs and conducting policy research that addresses the needs of students in its service area. These include a student exchange program at the undergraduate, graduate, and professional levels, a cooperative for educational telecommunications, and the Consortium for North American Higher Education Collaboration (CONA-HEC).

Technology-planning consortia. Other examples of consortia engaged in strategic technology planning across entire regions are the Colleges of Worcester (Massachusetts) Consortium, the New Hampshire College and University Council, and the Consortium of Universities in the Washington Metropolitan Area. The Internet2 Project, a consortium of more than 100 universities, has as its mission cooperative development, operation, and technology transfer of advanced, network-based applications and network services in its member universities as well as internationally. A technology initiative in the greater Chicago area brings together public and private colleges and universities in the North Suburban Higher Education Consortium with museums, school districts, and historical societies. A faculty initiative of twelve of the Pennsylvania State University's academic colleges and its library system, and two historically black institutions, Cheyney and Lincoln Universities, are also engaged in designing and developing standards for quality distance education. Its guiding principles address learning goals and content presentation, teaching-learning interactions, assessment and evaluation criteria, instructional media and software tools, and the development of learner support systems and services. A national initiative, the Community of Agile Partners in Education (CAPE), includes 125 colleges, universities, school districts, medical schools and hospitals, and community-based organizations throughout the United States and abroad, providing training in pedagogical applications of videoconferencing, Internet use, and other technologies, and the sponsorship of interinstitutional cooperative faculty teaching and research projects.

Local business- and industry-linked consortia. Multinational as well as local businesses and industries are another catalyst for consortia development,

often providing resources and expertise to influence university participation. One of the earliest examples is the Alliance for Higher Education, a Dallas, Texas-based consortium of thirty two-year and four-year colleges and research universities, corporations, hospitals, and other nonprofit organizations that link business and higher education through distance-education initiatives. Formed in 1965 as the Association for Graduate Education and Research (TAGER) by the cofounder of Texas Instruments, for the purpose of workforce training and economic development in the Dallas–Fort Worth region, it has enabled several thousand area engineers and other professionals to earn advanced degrees on-site through distance education. An education and information network facilitates interactive audio, video, and high-speed data transmission among member institutions and area employers, also fostering faculty consulting, workshops and seminars on corporate training needs and services, and, in 1994, a state-accredited multi-institutional teaching facility, the Universities Center of Dallas.

Research and academic library consortia. Research and academic libraries constitute another significant growth area in consortia development as library directors seek mechanisms for meeting user demand in gaining access to electronic databases and other sources of information. These consortia now engage in joint purchasing and referral services, online borrowing, high-speed delivery, the digitization of library holdings, and staff development. Evidence of this growth may be seen in the advent of the International Coalition of Library Consortia (ICOLC) in 1997, an informal, self-organized group comprising nearly 150 library consortia worldwide. ICOLC informs consortia about electronic resources and pricing practices of electronic providers and vendors, also providing guidelines for web-based resources and other services. Examples of library consortia include such statewide links as GALILEO in Georgia, PALCI in Pennsylvania, VIVA in Virginia, MIRACL in Missouri, and CLICNet in Minnesota. Multistate networks include SOLINET in the southeastern United States, CIC Virtual Electronic Network in the Midwest, CIRLA in the mid-Atlantic states, and the New England Land-Grant University Libraries. The transformation of library science academic degree programs into information sciences is accelerating with the introduction of high-speed retrieval of online documents, electronic books and journals, specialized databases in all academic fields, digitized manuscripts and photographs, interactive video transmission, and other such advances. As informational boundaries become more porous, libraries find it practical and trouble free to pool information, resources, and materials. Such issues as insurance, space, personnel, network compatibility, and cost sharing play important roles in determining the success of library and related consortia.

Scientific research and development consortia. Consortia for the purpose of scientific research and development bring together universities, research centers, government agencies, and multinational corporations engaged in supercomputing, geoscience, medical research, and other sophisticated research projects. Numerous examples may be found on the U.S. Department of Defense, Department of Energy, National Science Foundation, and National Aeronautic and Space Administration websites. A recent Department of Defense initiative is the Maui High Performance Computing Center, developed and managed by a consortium led by the University of New Mexico under a cooperative agreement with the U.S. Air Force's Phillips Laboratory. Its mission is "to create a world-class, national, high performance computing center, to foster technology exchange among the governmental, academic, and industrial communities . . . ." Its partner organizations include Carnegie Mellon University's Imaging Group, the Cornell Theory Center, the Maui Economic Development Board, and the IBM Corporation. A Coalition of Academic Supercomputing Centers provides another level of cooperation and resource sharing among university-based and autonomous centers for research and development in high-performance communications, enabling businesses and universities to be more cost effective in the allocation of resources and the development of new computer applications.

Conclusions

The consortium can be likened to an interorganizational network in which environmental conditions affect its activities. Numerous examples of informal partnerships and coalitions can be given, but in practice the formalized agreements of consortia offer structural opportunities of another dimension. A basic problem is the inconsistency between cooperation evolving from the inability to compete that runs counter to the free market model it seeks to protect. A study by Judith S. Glazer of consortia development in 1978 to 1980 showed that unrealistic expectations

could make it difficult to sustain cooperative agreements despite presidential support and large infusions of foundation resources. Issues arising in efforts to establish a doctoral-level consortium in New York City included a lack of clarity in goal setting, perceived differences in the quality and commitment of participating programs, faculty resistance to cooperate in planning their own retrenchment, inadequate incentives for developing substantive agreements, and, above all, the fact that informal collegial networks of presidents, deans, or faculty are not easily transformed into a cohesive working group. The experiences of consortia directors and others engaged in the collaborative process indicate that policymakers and planners need to address the following: (1) the conflict between institutional autonomy and interdependence at a time when state regulatory agencies advocate greater accountability in the deployment of resources; (2) the need for incremental long-range planning rather than grandiose or large-scale schemes; (3) the central role of the full-time executive director and staff in administering consortia projects; (4) the need to distinguish between consortia, partnerships, networks, and other interinstitutional alliances; and (5) the importance of cooperating in areas of strength rather than weakness and in addressing the fundamental differences between government-sponsored and independent institutions. Among all else, the ideal consortium will be based on an understanding that organizational change in response to market shifts necessitates flexibility, long-range planning, and adequate resources among equal partners.

BIBLIOGRAPHY

Baus, Frederick, and Ramsbottom, Claire A. 1999. "Starting and Sustaining a Consortium." *New Directions for Higher Education* 106:3–18.

Bridges, David, ed. 1996. *Consorting and Collaborating in the Education Marketplace.* Bristol, PA: Falmer.

Dotolo, Lawrence G., and Strandness, Jean T. 1999. *Best Practices in Higher Education Consortia: How Institutions Can Work Together.* San Francisco: Jossey-Bass.

Glazer, Judith S. 1982. "Designing and Managing an Inter-University Consortium in a Period of Decline." *Journal of Higher Education* 53:177–193.

HANSS, TED. 1997. "Internet2: Building and Deploying Advanced Networked Applications." *Cause/Effect* 20(2):4–7.

MORAN, LOUISE, and MUGRIDGE, IAN. 1999. *Collaboration in Distance Education.* New York: Routledge.

PATTERSON, FRANKLIN. 1974. *Colleges in Consort.* San Francisco: Jossey-Bass.

RAGAN, LAWRENCE C. 1999. "Good Teaching Is Good Teaching: An Emerging Set of Guiding Principles and Practices for the Design and Development of Distance Education." *Cause/Effect* 22(1):20–24.

WATSON, ALLAN, and JORDAN, LINDA. 1999. "Economic Development and Consortia. *New Directions for Higher Education* 106:93–100.

WYLIE, NEIL R., and YEAGER, TAMARA L. 1999. "Library Cooperation." *New Directions for Higher Education* 106:27–36.

INTERNET RESOURCES

ASSOCIATION FOR CONSORTIUM LEADERSHIP. 2002. <www.acl.odu.edu>.

INTERNATIONAL COALITION OF LIBRARY CONSORTIA. 2002. <www.library.yale.edu/consortia>.

JUDITH GLAZER-RAYMO

CONSTITUTIONAL REQUIREMENTS GOVERNING AMERICAN EDUCATION

The right to a free public education is found in the various state constitutions and not in the federal constitution. Every state has a provision in its constitution, commonly called the "education article," that guarantees some form of free public education, usually through the twelfth grade. The federal constitution, on the other hand, contains no such guarantee. In *San Antonio Independent School District v. Rodriquez,* the U.S. Supreme Court in 1973 held that education is not a "fundamental right" under the U.S. Constitution. Thus, as a matter of constitutional law, the founding fathers left it to the states to decide whether to provide an education or not and, if deciding to provide one, determine at what level of quality.

Not only does the federal constitution confer no right to education, it does not even explicitly empower the U.S. Congress to legislate on the subject. Most federal education legislation is therefore enacted under the "spending clause" of the Constitution, which gives Congress the authority to tax and spend for the general welfare. Since federal grants to the states may be conditioned upon the state's adoption of certain legal and regulatory structures, the federal government has been able to exercise substantial authority over K–12 education policy. For example, in *South Dakota v. Dole,* the Supreme Court in 1987 upheld a federal law withholding a percentage of federal highway funds from any state that declined to raise its minimum drinking age to twenty-one. This kind of carrot-and-stick approach underlies much federal education law, from the setting of nationwide achievement standards to the education of students with disabilities to Title I and other federal grants relating to education. That other great source of federal regulatory authority, the Constitution's "commerce clause," however, has not been used to justify federal legislation in these areas. In *United States v. Lopez,* the Supreme Court in 1995 held that a law making it a crime to possess a firearm within a certain distance of a school was an impermissible overextension of Congress's commerce power. Even the justices dissenting in *Lopez* agreed that the content of education was a classic area of state, not federal, authority.

Nevertheless, once a state decides to provide an education to its children, as every state has, the provision of such education must be consistent with other federally guaranteed constitutional rights, such as the Fourteenth Amendment's right to equal protection under the law and the First Amendment's right to the free exercise of, and the nonestablishment of, religion. Therefore, even though the U.S. Constitution does not, in the first instance, require that an education be provided, it nevertheless has had a significant effect on American education.

Any treatment of education and constitutional rights must begin with the Fourteenth Amendment, which guarantees every citizen equal protection under the law. Application of this doctrine has been most profound in the area of school desegregation. In 1954 the U.S. Supreme Court struck down state-sponsored racial segregation of schools in the famous case of *Brown v. Board of Education of Topeka, Kansas.* This decision and hundreds of later court decisions applying it to individual school districts all over the United States have had major ramifications on virtually every facet of school district operations from the mid-1950s into the twenty-first century. This has been true not only in the South, but throughout the rest of the country, as school districts and courts struggled with how to effectively desegregate the nation's schools. In the decades since *Brown,* most school districts have eliminated "vestiges" of state-sponsored segregation, have been declared to be a "unitary" school district (as opposed to a former dual-race system), and have been released from federal court supervision.

Nevertheless, many unitary school districts, now concerned that their schools will become resegregated, are seeking to take steps to preserve racial diversity at their schools. In one of the supreme ironies of American jurisprudence, such efforts may now be illegal under the same Fourteenth Amendment that previously required school districts to employ race-conscious student assignments as a remedial measure but forbids such measures as a means of preserving integrated schools in school districts no longer under court supervision.

Another major constitutional issue facing American education involves public funding of vouchers for private schools. Although several states have enacted limited voucher programs, their legality and continued existence remains in doubt under the First Amendment of the Constitution, which requires the separation of church and state. In June 2002 the Supreme Court ruled that students in the Cleveland, Ohio, area may use state-funded vouchers to pay tuition at private schools, including schools with a religious affiliation. The decision in this case is likely to have a significant impact for decades to come.

As desegregation lawsuits in federal courts wind down, the most important constitutional litigation involving education is increasingly taking place in state courts, as plaintiffs' groups seek to enforce state constitutional guarantees. Beginning in the early 1970s plaintiffs' groups began to make constitutional challenges to the heavy use of local property tax revenues in most states to finance public schools. This system of funding public schools often resulted in large disparities in per-pupil expenditures between property-rich and property-poor districts. As a result of a series of these "equity" suits, which were based on state constitutional guarantees of equal protection and uniformity, most states in the years since the early 1980s have reformed their state education funding formulas to provide a greater degree of equity (although not complete equality) in fund-

ing between school districts. This has been accomplished in many states by providing more state-level funding to property-poor districts to offset their lower local revenues, and less state funding to property-rich districts.

During the same period, plaintiffs' groups also began to challenge the adequacy of state education systems, including the sufficiency of funding of public schools, under the "education articles" of state constitutions. These cases are quite different from "equity" cases, which are based on disparities in funding; "adequacy" cases challenge the sufficiency of the funding to provide the level of educational opportunities required by the particular state constitution, regardless of how such funding is allocated among a state's school districts. It is these state court "adequacy" cases that are likely to be the main source of constitutional litigation in the early twenty-first century.

Federal Constitutional Requirements

Below are discussed the evolution of school desegregation since the landmark 1954 Brown decision and the racial diversity in U.S. schools in the post-desegregation era. This section also reviews the status of school vouchers and their constitutionality under the First Amendment.

School desegregation. There is no question that since the early 1960s school desegregation suits under the Fourteenth Amendment have had a greater impact on American schools than almost any other factor. In its 1954 *Brown v. Board of Education* decision, the Supreme Court declared state-mandated racial segregation of schools illegal. A year later, in *Brown II,* the Court ordered that segregated schools be eliminated with "all deliberate speed." The Court, however, gave little practical guidance as to how school districts and the lower courts were to carry out this major transformation in the social fabric of many regions of the country. As a result, the process of desegregating formerly dual-race school systems lasted for decades and in the early twenty-first century had still not been completed in some school districts.

After *Brown,* little happened until the mid-1960s as many southern states waged a program of massive resistance to school desegregation. In *Stanley v. Darlington School District,* the federal court in South Carolina described the different forms of such resistance. In the mid- to late 1960s, token desegregation occurred, but that was due more to the passage of the Civil Rights Act of 1964, which forced school districts to desegregate as a precondition to receiving federal funds, than it was to court enforcement of constitutional guarantees. In 1968 the situation dramatically changed with the Supreme Court decision of *Green v. School Board of New Kent County.* In *Green,* the Court required that school districts *promptly* take steps to *effectively* desegregate the operations of their schools in the areas of student assignments, faculty and staff assignments, facilities, extracurricular activities, and transportation. Ineffective plans that resulted in only token desegregation were no longer permitted. *Green* was followed by the Court's 1971 *Swann v. Charlotte-Mecklenburg Board of Education* decision, which approved the use of mandatory busing as a desegregation tool. Thus began the real process of desegregating the schools. Mandatory busing, however, was extremely controversial, especially among white parents, and the effect of such desegregation plans was often undermined by what became known as "white flight" (i.e., white parents moving out of the district or placing their children in private schools). Therefore, in the 1980s, the courts began to rely more and more on voluntary desegregation plans that centered on magnet schools and other measures designed to encourage, but not require, students to transfer to racially mixed schools. One of the first such plans was approved by the federal court in 1989 in *Stell v. Savannah-Chatham County Board of Education,* which involved the school district in Savannah, Georgia.

By the 1990s most school districts had accomplished as much faculty and student desegregation as was practical, given "white flight" and the persistence of de facto segregation in housing patterns. Consequently, the courts began to release more and more school districts from court supervision on the grounds that they had eliminated the vestiges of the former segregated school systems "to the extent practicable." Nevertheless, although not discussed in *Green,* some courts also began to examine whether the "achievement gap" between minority and white students in many school districts was also a "vestige" of the former segregated system. Consequently, in deciding whether to dismiss desegregation cases, courts in the 1990s did not focus as much on student or faculty assignments (the main issues from 1954 through the 1980s), but rather on whether poor academic performance of minority pupils is a "vestige"

of the former segregated system that must be eliminated before court supervision is terminated. In 1995 in *Jenkins v. Missouri,* the Supreme Court held that such low performance had to be causally linked to the prior dual school system. Because this is difficult to establish, plaintiffs have had only limited success in convincing courts that low minority performance is sufficiently related to the prior dual school system to serve as a basis for continued court supervision.

Therefore, as the nation entered the new millennium, the constitutional obligation to desegregate, which greatly influenced operations and planning in many school districts for more than forty years, had been satisfied in most districts and was becoming less and less of a factor in those relatively few districts that remained under active federal court supervision.

Diversity. The closing of the desegregation era does not mean, however, that issues of race have disappeared in public education. Many school districts, which successfully desegregated the student populations of their schools and have therefore been declared unitary and released from court supervision, continue the struggle to maintain racial integration or, as it is now more often called, "diversity," in their schools. Nevertheless, the Fourteenth Amendment, which once required race-based student assignments and admissions as a remedial measure, may now prohibit school districts from continuing to use race-conscious plans once such school districts have completed remedial proceedings and been declared unitary. Once the effects of past discrimination have been remedied, as in the case of a school district declared unitary, it is argued that there is no longer a remedial justification for taking student race into account in making student assignments or deciding upon admissions to special programs, such as magnet schools. For example, if student race is considered in admitting students to a magnet school, a student denied admission because her race did not contribute to racial diversity may claim that she was denied admission based on race and that such a decision is discriminatory and a denial of equal protection. School districts often respond that maintaining racial diversity is a compelling governmental interest, and that some use of race in the decision-making process regarding assignment of students should therefore be permitted. The lower courts are split on the issue, although the majority view tends to prohibit race-based admissions and assignment policies unless they serve a remedial purpose. Until the Supreme Court decides the issue, the lower courts are likely to careful scrutinize and in most regions of the country prohibit any consideration of student race in the student assignment and admissions process.

School vouchers. Many school reform advocates believe that public schools suffer from a lack of competition and that states or school districts should provide vouchers to students, especially poor and minority students attending substandard inner-city schools, to enable them to attend a private school. At least three states (Florida, Wisconsin, and Ohio) have passed legislation funding such vouchers. Until spring 2002 one huge unknown factor in the debate over using public funds to support private, parochial schools was whether such use of public funds violates the First Amendment of the Constitution, which prohibits government from unduly supporting religion or favoring one religion over another. In June 2002 the Supreme Court held in the case *Zelman v. Simmons-Harris* that the use of public funds to pay for religious school tuition is constitutional. Under this program, the State of Ohio provides vouchers to some 4,000 students from low-income families. The vouchers can be used to pay tuition at participating private schools, including religiously affiliated schools. Although the Supreme Court's ruling resolved the constitutionality of school vouchers, the policy debates about the vouchers are likely to continue in the years to come.

State Constitutional Issues

As school desegregation issues, which have dominated public education for decades, are finally resolved, lawsuits based on state constitutional requirements have moved to the forefront. These lawsuits have become known as either "equity" or "adequacy" cases.

Equity cases. These cases began with the unsuccessful efforts of plaintiffs in *San Antonio Independent School District v. Rodriquez,* a case brought in the early 1970s in federal court to challenge the method of funding public education in Texas. At the time, Texas, like most states, financed its schools primarily through local property taxes. Because property values differed greatly between districts, this method of funding resulted in significant spending disparities between school districts, with the wealthier districts in Texas spending more than two to three times as much as the poorest districts on a per-pupil basis. In rejecting plaintiffs' equal protection claim under the Fourteenth Amendment, the Supreme Court held

that education was not a fundamental right under the Constitution. It therefore held that disparities in the provision of education services and facilities did not have to be justified by a showing that they served a compelling governmental interest, but could be justified merely by showing that a rational basis existed for such a taxing mechanism. Because the local property tax system had a rational basis, in the view of the Court, it was not unconstitutional.

Notwithstanding this initial defeat in the federal courts, proponents of equity among school districts in education funding continued their fight in the state courts, and they won victories in the mid-1970s in California (*Serrano v. Priest*) and New Jersey (*Robinson v. Cahill*). In these decisions, the courts struck down property tax–based systems based on state constitutional provisions requiring equal protection and uniformity, and they ordered the use of more equitable funding systems in which the resources provided for a child's education did not depend nearly as much on the property wealth in the community in which a child lived and attended school. Since then, "equity cases," as they are often called, have been brought in almost every state, and plaintiffs have been successful in many of them. While local property taxes remain a major source of school revenues, states have modified their education financing formulas to provide more state aid to property-poor districts to offset lower local property tax revenues in such districts and to provide less state aid to property-rich districts. While complete equality in funding has rarely, if ever, been realized, and is not required under most state court decisions, large disparities in funding between school districts have been greatly reduced in many states.

Adequacy cases. Equity cases, while successful in reducing funding disparities between school districts in many states, have fallen short of being the panacea that many school finance reformers believed they would be, for several reasons. First, attaining equity does not necessarily mean increases in education spending. Indeed, while the result of *Serrano v. Priest* was to insure equity in spending among California's school districts, it has at the same time moved California from one of the highest spending states on education to one of the lowest. Moreover, the equity cases did not, in the minds of many plaintiffs' groups, address the claims of many urban school systems. Such school districts and their supporters contend that they need additional funding to address the educational needs of the large numbers of their students who are at risk of academic failure because of the effects of poverty and other socioeconomic problems. Simply obtaining funding equal to other school districts is not sufficient, it is argued, given the extraordinary needs of such districts.

Since the 1970s plaintiffs have brought "adequacy" suits in more than twenty states, alleging that the state has failed to provide an "adequate" education, a right guaranteed by many state constitutions. Generally, such suits allege that educational "inputs," such as facilities, curriculum, textbooks and other instructional materials and equipment, and number and quality of teachers, are insufficient to enable schools and school districts to provide an "adequate" education for their students. Plaintiffs also rely on substandard "outcomes," as evidenced by low scores on standardized tests, low graduation rates, and high dropout rates as proof that the state has failed to provide an adequate education for substantial numbers of its children.

Such suits are normally based on the "education article" contained in most state constitutions that requires the state legislature to provide for some type of a "system" of free public schools. Generally, the education articles are couched in fairly vague terms, such as requiring "a thorough and efficient system of education" or a "system of free common schools." Although the constitutional language rarely gets any more specific than the foregoing examples, the highest courts of many states have interpreted such language to require an "adequate" or "sound, basic" education.

In several states, adequacy suits have been dismissed on the grounds that they involve political questions reserved by the state constitution to the legislature, and therefore that they violate the separation of powers doctrine. In essence, because the terms used both by the courts (e.g., "adequate") and the constitution (e.g., "thorough," "efficient") are ambiguous and capable of many meanings, these courts have held that if the courts decided such cases, they would in effect be substituting themselves for the legislature in determining important policy questions normally reserved by the state constitution to the legislative branch (e.g., what level of education to provide and how much of the state's resources to devote to education).

Notwithstanding pretrial dismissals in several states, plaintiffs have enjoyed success in increasing numbers of states, including most notably New Jersey, Ohio, Kentucky, and Wyoming. The highest courts of these states have struck down the state system for financing public schools and required the legislatures to appropriate significantly increased spending for public education. Other important cases, such as those in Arkansas, New York, and North Carolina, have been decided at the trial court level in plaintiffs' favor, but they have not yet been reviewed by the state's highest court. In still other states, such as Florida, cases have been filed but not yet decided.

In states where plaintiffs have been successful, often after many years or decades of litigation, such lawsuits have led to higher spending for education, including expenditures for school facilities, teacher's salaries, special programs, and technology. Whether these lawsuits have resulted or will result in improved student achievement, however, is another oft-debated question that is beyond the scope of this entry.

Conclusion

Both federal and state constitutional requirements have heavily influenced the organization, funding, and operation of America's schools in the past and are likely to continue to do so in the future.

See also: SUPREME COURT OF THE UNITED STATES AND EDUCATION.

BIBLIOGRAPHY

Abbott v. Burke, 710 A.2d 450 (N.J. 1998).

ARMOR, DAVID J. 1995. *Forced Justice: School Desegregation and the Law.* New York: Oxford University Press.

Brown v. Board of Education of Topeka, Kansas, 347 U.S. 483 (1954).

Brown v. Board of Education of Topeka, Kansas, 349 U.S. 753, 757 (1955) (*Brown II*).

Campbell County Sch. Dist. v. State, 907 P.2d 1238 (Wyo. 1995).

Civil Rights Act of 1964. U.S. Code. Vol. 42, sec. 2000d.

DAYTON, JOHN. 2001. "Serrano and its Progeny: An Analysis of 30 Years of School Funding Litigation." *157 West's Educational Law Reporter* 447.

Green v. School Board of New Kent County, 391 U.S. 430 (1968).

Jenkins v. Missouri, 515 U.S. 70 (1995).

Robinson v. Cahill, 303 A. 2d 273 (N.J. 1973).

Rose v. Council for Better Educ., 790 S.W.2d 186 (Ky. 1989).

San Antonio Independent School District v. Rodriguez, 411 U.S. 1 (1973).

Serrano v. Priest, 557 P. 2d 929 (Cal. 1976).

Stell v. Savannah-Chatham County Board of Education, 888 F. 2d 82 (11th Cir. 1989).

Swann v. Charlotte-Mecklenburg Board of Education, 402 U.S. 1 (1971).

Tuttle v. Arlington County Sch. Bd., 195 F.3d 698 (4th Cir. 1999).

United States v. Lopez, 514 U.S. 549 (1995).

Alfred A. Lindseth

CONTINUING PROFESSIONAL EDUCATION

UNITED STATES
Robert D. Fox

INTERNATIONAL CORPORATIONS
Brian Holland

UNITED STATES

Continuing professional education (CPE) may be thought of as the planned and systematic attempt to introduce, review, or alter the competencies and thereby the professional performance of professionals. Cyril Houle refers to CPE in observing that "whether it designates the improvement of professional competence or any other goal, (it) implies some form of learning that advances from a previously established level of accomplishment to extend and amplify knowledge, sensitiveness or skill" (p. 77). The term *continuing professional education* contains three separate concepts, each worthy of definition as a means to understand the overall concept.

Education is a systematic process that seeks to alter knowledge and skill by engaging learners interactively with teachers or other knowledge resources, using a considered strategy to achieve an effect in the altered knowledge, skill, or attitudes of the learner.

Professional refers to people who engage in work based on a large, complex body of knowledge usually gained in professional schools. Professions include law, medicine, architecture, engineering, education, and other disciplines that codify practice. Professionals are thoughtfully engaged in the development and ongoing review of a body of applied knowledge, control over practices and the practice environment, membership criteria, ethics, and the economics of the delivery of services to clients. Although autonomy is an issue for all professions, it exists on a continuum from those with little self-control to those with expansive self-regulatory authority and autonomy.

In this three-part term, *continuing* refers to the post-preparatory phase of professional development. In this phase the professional is engaged in practice on a regular basis and is learning in ways that adjust practice to correct errors, expand or adjust performance, and introduce new or reformed practices and perspectives on practices. This process is continuous in that learning new or better ways of fulfilling professional roles is an everyday occurrence. Self-directed learning is used by professionals to manage their practice performance, therefore it is also considered to be part of the system of ongoing development that is the object of continuing professional education.

When all who participate in the CPE enterprise are considered, the costs are high. It is estimated that CPE costs approximately $60 billion per year and that when indirect costs are included the annual total may exceed $210 billion. The degree to which society is likely to invest in CPE is based on the extent to which people depend upon the performance of professionals to solve problems and improve the quality of life. As professional services expand, costs for ongoing development and education will likely follow.

Constituents of Continuing Professional Education

Although it would seem self-evident that continuing professional education systems direct their energies to professionals, CPE also serves the needs of a variety of groups and organizations that are concerned with the performance of professionals. For example, some professionals practice in partnership organizations, like clinics or firms. Others practice in large and small businesses where an employer may see CPE as means to alter services and therefore improve the prospects for profit. The quality of CPE may also be a high priority for organizations that do not employ professionals but depend on them and their performance to achieve their organizations' purposes. These organizations are concerned with quality control and coordination of resources. They sponsor or offer CPE in an attempt to influence the performance of the professional in a specific manner. Often these purposes are contrary to the interests of a given profession or reflect an influence that does not necessarily reflect the priorities of the profession in terms of the problems or solutions that are endorsed by the community of practitioners as a whole. This cataract of forces on professional performance creates conflicts that have led to a variety of regulatory and quality control systems to insure that CPE programs sanctioned by a profession are appropriate for the purposes and needs of the practice community.

Sources of Continuing Professional Education

Continuing professional education programs are offered by a variety of organizations, each with a particular set of purposes, some shared and some discreet. Universities, as the homes of most professional training programs, are a major provider of CPE. Often these programs are within the control of the faculty. They may be broadly based updates of an area of practice, or the programs may be designed to introduce new knowledge and skill emanating from research or scholarship in the discipline base of the profession.

Professional associations are also engaged in the planning and delivery of CPE, most often at annual meetings offered over several days at one location or at special sessions, topical in nature, offered nationally or at regional sites. These programs focus on issues the profession has identified as important to the well-being of the profession and the success of its practitioners, or useful in securing desirable outcomes for the profession's client systems.

Practice organizations are the firms, groups, hospitals, or other collections of practitioners who offer professional services in a specific field. Examples of practice organizations include a law office, an architecture or engineering firm, a managed health care organization, or a hospital. The CPE programs offered by these organizations often reflect the problems they encounter in the delivery of services to clients.

There are also private companies that offer CPE as a primary product in an effort to make a profit. These companies are engaged in the production of CPE programs directed toward the perceived needs of the marketplace. Often they work in concert with an industry that supports a particular profession or its client systems. These companies contract with other CPE organizations or directly offer CPE to address the educational needs and interests of the profession when these interests are congruent with the business interests of the industry and the corporation.

Government agencies are also important sponsors and providers of CPE, offering a variety of continuing professional development programs. These programs may be embedded in other initiatives, such as attempts to improve access to services for indigent populations by educating social workers or teachers in the screening and recruitment of clients. They may be offered for the direct purpose of introducing new techniques and methods, such as the efforts of the National Institutes of Health to improve health care worker practices in the area of HIV infections. Or they may be developed in support of new regulations that have changed the nature of professional practices in a particular area, such as new requirements for documentation or delivery of services to a new clientele.

Forms of Continuing Professional Education

Continuing professional education takes a variety of forms, some more common than others and some that are used often in one profession but almost never in another. One of the most common forms of CPE is in-service or on-the-job training. This may be very formal or almost undetectable to the observer but it is always directed toward introducing, updating, or modifying the way the profession is practiced in the work setting. It is characterized by an emphasis on practice and coaching. It may be loosely organized and episodic, arising as practice problems arise and disappearing as the need disappears. It is an important part of the learning community in any profession.

A more common form of CPE is a formal organized program built around definite objectives such as conferences, institutes, workshops, and lectures. Collectively, these methods represent only a small portion of the learning that occurs continuously for professionals. They are usually short-term in duration and may be focused on a general refresher of professional competencies, an overview of a new issue or collection of practices, or an effort to introduce new technique, skill, or practice protocols.

Short courses are similar to these methods of educating professionals but occur over several meetings with time for preparation or practice between sessions.

Distance education has made a serious impact in most professions, but its success has varied according to the way the profession is practiced. In technical and scientific professions, computer assisted and web-based CPE has grown more rapidly than in fields like teaching and social work, where the practice setting is not as friendly to the insertion of computers and technological solutions. Nevertheless, the notion that education can be delivered at the time and in the setting where the work occurs promises a wider application of distance education in most professions.

The most effective strategies at changing professional performance are those that involve multiple methods of CPE and account for the needs of learners. Emphasis on motivation and needs in successful CPE reflects the role of experience in learning and the belief that the acquisition of new knowledge, skills, and professional practices is facilitated and enhanced when learning efforts are based on existing knowledge and skills and existing practices. This emphasis on knowledge of real and perceived needs as a basis for the design of education is widely accepted as essential for success in CPE.

An emphasis on complex strategies for facilitating learning in the professions is based on the complexities of adopting or modifying practices. Professionals develop means of performing their work based on extensive training and the ongoing evaluation of these practices in their work with clients. They grow confident in these practices and are reluctant to change them without evidence that different practices are better. Professionals desire a sense that new ideas are compatible with overall practice patterns and client needs, and sometimes they want to observe new practices before they incorporate them into their own work. They depend on consistency of information from many different sources, including colleagues, literature from their disciplines, and CPE programs. They often need to solicit feedback on their proficiency before they actually incorporate new knowledge or skill in the performance of their professional duties. A professional may require multiple learning opportunities and multiple methods of education to satisfy these expectations for information, practice, and feedback.

By far the most frequent means employed by professionals to enhance their professional growth is self-directed learning. Self-directed learning refers to the projects that professionals engage in to learn without the formal direction or organization of materials, methods, and educational strategies of a formal program of CPE. In this method of learning, the learner identifies his or her needs, sets objectives, develops strategies, and evaluates success. It is self-education and it is at the heart of the concept of the "learned" professional.

Foundations of Continuing Professional Education Practice

The practice of providing CPE programs and services depends on research and scholarship in several areas of adult education. It includes a focus on the theories and principles of planned change, adult learning and development, program and curricular design, applied research, consultation, and of course, the methods and materials of education. Masters and doctoral level programs of study are available to those who want to develop a concentrated knowledge of adult education and curriculum development. However, the majority of practitioners of CPE develop their areas of competency while "on the job" and have little formal preparation in adult education. Nevertheless, the literature and scholarship of CPE in each of the professions is connected to the literature and scholarship of adult education.

Accreditation of Continuing Professional Education Programs

In some fields there is a high level of interest in quality control over the professional educational process. This is manifest in complex systems that have developed for awarding credit to learners and extensive efforts to ensure the quality of CPE through systems of accreditation. In the United States, Canada, and Australia, the American Medical Association, the American Academy of Family Physicians, and the Royal Colleges of Physicians and Surgeons of Canada and Australia are among the many organizations that allow physicians and surgeons to receive documentation of learning from programs intensively reviewed for compliance with minimum standards for assuring quality. These organizations also record and certify participation by physicians in these programs.

Systems for quality assurance apply standards that focus on such attributes as qualifications of faculty, relevance to practice needs, adequacy of educational strategy, and documentation of outcomes. They may certify programs individually, or they may certify the organizations that offer the programs. Many professional practitioners depend on receiving career education credits as evidence of their continuing competence to their professional associations, licensing bodies, or client systems.

Issues and Trends

One of the most important recent trends in CPE has been the growing emphasis on developing a body of knowledge about how professionals learn and how they change their performance. Books and research articles in medicine have focused heavily on this topic as this and other professions struggle with how to make education a more effective tool for influencing the practice of the professions. Related to the need for more research and more effective procedures is the problem of how knowledge is handled across professions. Each profession has developed and implemented a system of CPE without tapping the experience or expertise of other professions. Some have annual research conferences and research journals that report the studies in their field. Most devote attention to the issues of CPE at annual meetings or conferences. It is rare that one profession will cite, or in other ways refer to, the knowledge and experience related to CPE that is gained in another profession. This gap in communication and collaboration on the issues of CPE has resulted in redundancy where coordination of the development of general knowledge and principles of CPE may have been beneficial. This may change as professionals are asked to work in teams more often to solve interdisciplinary societal problems.

Another issue important for the ongoing development of CPE is the growing pressure from society to document and certify professional competence. Two primary approaches have been taken to solve this problem: test on a regular basis or document participation in CPE. Different professions, different political jurisdictions, and even different specialties within professions have adopted one or both of these approaches to assure competence. Both approaches depend upon the continued growth of a competent system of CPE. This encourages research and development of the field as well and accountability from the providers of CPE to clients and client systems.

Continuing professional education is a requirement for professional competence as professionals encounter new problems and professional schools develop new knowledge and new ways of performing professional roles to meet the problems of practice. The practices of disseminating information, correcting errors in professional performance, and renewing the fund of knowledge and skills of professionals are essential if professionals are to maintain a high level of proficiency over thirty or forty years of practice beyond their formal, pre-professional education programs. For CPE to succeed it must continue to focus on providing learning opportunities that meet professional needs and practice problems while promoting the adoption of new knowledge and skills.

See also: CORPORATE COLLEGES; DISTANCE LEARNING IN HIGHER EDUCATION; LIFELONG LEARNING.

BIBLIOGRAPHY

CERVERO, RONALD M. 1988. *Effective Continuing Education for Professionals.* San Francisco: Jossey-Bass.

CERVERO, RONALD M. 2000. "Trends and Issues in Continuing Professional Education." In *Charting a Course for Continuing Professional Education; Reframing Professional Practice,* ed. Vivian W. Mott and Barbara J. Daley.

DAVIS, DAVID A.; THOMSON, MARY A.; OXMAN, ANDREW D.; and HAYNES, ROBERT BRIAN. 1995. "Changing Physician Performance: A Systematic Review of the Effect of Continuing Medical Education Strategies." *Journal of the American Medical Association* 274:700–705.

DAVIS, DAVID, et al. 1999. "Impact of Formal Continuing Medical Education. Do Conferences, Workshops, Rounds, and Other Traditional Continuing Education Activities Change Physician Behavior or Health Care Outcomes?" *Journal of the American Medical Association* 282:867–74.

FOX, ROBERT D., and BENNETT, NANCY L. 1998. "Learning and Change: Implications for Continuing Medical Education." *BMJ* 316:466–468.

HOULE, CYRIL O. 1972. *The Design of Education.* San Francisco: Jossey-Bass.

ROBERT D. FOX

INTERNATIONAL CORPORATIONS

The United States, western Europe, and Japan all face a common set of economic restructuring and demographic changes. Each is in transition away from a manufacturing and industrial-sector base, and moving toward a postindustrial, information-based economy. Each is also encountering labor-market population changes as the overall population is aging and birth rates remain relatively low. The effects of these changes have been felt in labor shortages in some sectors. Yet for all the similarities among America, Europe, and Japan, there are striking differences in the coordination of labor markets for private companies to train employees. To explain why these differences exist, it is helpful to look at the history and structure of workforce training efforts in Europe (particularly Britain and Germany) and Japan designed to bring about public-private cooperation for skills development and human capital investment.

Workforce Training in Britain

Britain has been marked by a more voluntary connection between the public and private sector in workforce development policy. Initially, training policy until 1963 was characterized by a limited state intervention in labor markets—except for occasional efforts during the interwar years and the first decade after World War II to provide training as a means of remedying unemployment. The establishment of industrial training boards (ITBs) in 1963 was the first government recognition that economic growth was slipping in Britain, as compared to other European countries. The ITBs, while developing a compulsory levy/grant system to finance training efforts, did little to raise awareness of the linkage between economic growth and investments in human capital.

The ITBs were weakened by the 1973 Employment and Training Act, which set up the Manpower Services Commission (MSC). Unlike the ITBs, the MSC's main focus (until the rise of Thatcherism in 1981) was on job creation programs, although the legislative intent was to develop a comprehensive manpower strategy. The New Training Initiative (NTI), which was introduced in a 1981 white paper, returned MSC to its adult-training mission and moved to integrate youth into the workforce. The NTI again promoted a volunteer connection between employer training needs and the public sector, but shifted focus to stress portable skills for identified labor shortages and as a bridge for school-to-work connections. But the MSC failed to change the paradigm of employer involvement in training, and

the National Audit Office was critical of the MSC's fiscal accountability and its failure to address the high-level course needs of employers.

Borrowing from the American model of private industry councils, the MSC was replaced by Training and Enterprise Councils (TECs) in 1988. While still being a more voluntarist model of cooperation between the public and private sectors, TECs are designed to be locally based and include private employer representation to set policy direction, although they are publicly funded through the Department of Employment. The charge of TECs, announced in the 1990 white paper *Employment for the 1990s,* was not to deliver training, but rather to transfer responsibility for skills-development investment to employers, who would identify needs and administer public funds. In so doing, Britain embarked on the creation of a true training market, compatible with a limited government role in industrial policy.

Germany

By contrast, the mark of the German training system is the role of strong financial incentives that promote and enhance the coordination of the public and private sectors, primarily through the apprenticeship training initiatives for younger workers. As early as 1908, industrial employers in Germany recognized the need for a systematic training process to meet their shortage of skilled workers. In response to these problems, a committee called DATSCH (*Deutschen Ausschuss für Technisches Schulwesen*) was formed. In 1909 DATSCH recommended that all apprentices in the areas of industry and commerce be trained at an equivalent level. Following World War I, DATSCH worked with companies such as AEG and Siemens to design an apprenticeship program for these employers, and by 1925 a working committee set out to define industrial trades and distinguish between skill requirements in the labor force.

During the 1930s, before the rise to power of the Nazis, the apprenticeship content developed by DATSCH was recognized more globally by industry and chambers of commerce, and the principles of apprenticeship were refined by industry associations. Accordingly, training was geared toward, and reflected the needs of, employers. Following the war, there was concern that industrial apprenticeships would become fragmented and disorganized, and by 1953 the ABB (*Arbeitsstelle für Betriebliche Berufsausbildung*) had been organized to carry out similar functions as DATSCH. In the 1960s apprenticeship training met with criticism, as it was viewed as not meeting the needs of employers, and as being neglectful of an organized, tailored curriculum for industry.

The discontent behind the apprenticeship system eventually led to an expansion of the government's role in training. Passage of the 1969 Vocational Training Act shifted the orientation of the apprenticeship system from macroeconomic concerns, such as reducing unemployment, to a set of standards for testing procedures that would ensure that apprenticeships met employer needs. In fact, the law set up the contemporary vertical system of secondary school education with the design of the *Hauptschule* (general secondary school) and *Realschule* (intermediate secondary school) system. Following the passage of the law, any person age eighteen or younger who completes *Haptschule, Realschule,* or level one of *Gymansium* and does not pursue an *Abitur* (a university education track) is required to attend the apprenticeship system, which combines part-time vocational education with work experience. Accordingly, the German approach is far more interventionist and has been able to achieve higher labor participation rates. These higher labor-force participation rates allow employers to have a stronger labor force with diminished turnover.

Japan

As a hybrid of both the British and German models, the Japanese tradition of hierarchical mentoring is a pattern that seems to have been replicated in industrial and skills training, although with less formal government support. In Japan, two unique features are present in the implementation of workforce preparation. First, there is an extensive level of on-the-job training that is required to be conducted between senior workers and new, less-experienced workers. Indeed, it has been documented that the ability to teach one's coworkers is a key criterion for promotion within a Japanese firm. These new workers are recruited from schools, where employers have established relationships for identifying and selecting high-performing students. New hires receive orientation sessions in safety and corporate culture (*fudo*) and informal on-the-job-training led by a senior worker.

The second critical element of Japan's investment in human capital is that employers engage their workers in a rotation system over their lifetime in employment. By engaging in the rotation system, the employee gains firm-specific skills that are commensurate with a career-ladder approach. Accordingly, the employee is trained in both technical skills and employment relations, and the employer is able to provide some measure of lifetime job security. But while job training is conducted formally in classroom settings to complement existing knowledge, the homogeneity of Japanese labor markets within firms encourages private employers to tailor programs that are more firm-specific than industry-specific in focus.

United States

On the federal government level, a sweeping set of workforce development reforms were implemented with the passage of the Workforce Investment Act (WIA) in 1998. WIA marked a radical departure from past federal workforce/employment policy for adult workers—a patchwork quilt of categorical, tailored responses—to the consolidation of some seventy separate programs under WIA into three funding streams.

In a significant development, policymakers made a conscious decision not to provide WIA with an open-ended authorization as was the case under the Job Training Partnership Act (JTPA). In repealing the JTPA, WIA sought to expand the role of the private sector with a more active voice to ensure that the workforce development system incorporates their input to prepare people for current and future jobs. In addition, WIA recognized that meeting individual needs in the workforce development system was paramount and resulted in a move toward greater decentralized delivery of training services.

Workforce Investment Boards (WIBs) under WIA replace the former Private Industry Councils (PICs) that existed under JTPA and implement the public-funded workforce development strategy of their geography. In so doing, the federal formula dollars are disbursed to WIBs to provide a comprehensive set of services at some 1,500 One Stops across the United States. These services include: a preliminary assessment of skills and support-service needs; information on a full array of employment-related services, including listings of training providers, job search and placement assistance, career counseling, access to up-to-date labor market information (which identifies job vacancies), and skills necessary for in-demand jobs; and information about local, regional, and national employment trends.

By the same token, the American workforce development system is decentralized for employers. Yet there can be connections between employers and potential employees at the One Stop Centers. In fact, One Stops enable employers with a single point of contact to list job openings and to provide information about their particular company's hiring needs and requisite skills for occupational openings. This emphasis on using market forces to enable customers to get the skills and credentials required in their local economies makes accountability among training providers a paramount concern.

In sum, the differences among Britain, Germany, Japan, and the United States fall along a continuum between individual autonomy and compulsory codetermination for employers in the provision of workforce training. The design of a genuine training market that reflects both employer demands and the existing labor supply (or the potential labor supply) is evolving. However, to encourage employers' investment in their employees will require a set of financial incentives and strategic planning to ensure the connection between school, work, and lifelong learning, rather than a policy approach that solely addresses unemployment and job creation.

See also: CORPORATE COLLEGES; LIFELONG LEARNING.

BIBLIOGRAPHY

ADNETT, NICK. 1996. *European Labour Markets: Analysis and Policy.* London: Longman.

BECKER, GARY. 1964. *Human Capital: A Theoretical and Empirical Analysis with Special Reference to Education.* New York: National Bureau of Economic Research.

BLOTEVOGEL, HANS H., and FLEMING, ANTHONY J., eds. 1997. *People, Jobs, and Mobility in the New Europe.* New York: Wiley.

EVANS, BRENDAN. 1992. *The Politics of the Training Market.* London: Routledge.

FREEMAN, RICHARD. 1994. *Working Under Different Rules.* New York: Russell Sage Foundation.

LAYARD, RICHARD; MAYHEW, KEN; and OWEN, GEOFFREY. 1994. *Britain's Training Deficit.* Aldershot, Eng.: Avebury.

LYNCH, LISA M., ed. 1994. *Training and the Private Sector: International Comparisons.* Chicago: University of Chicago Press.

WEIR, MARGARET. 1992. *Politics and Jobs: The Boundaries of Employment Policy in the United States.* Princeton, NJ: Princeton University Press.

BRIAN HOLLAND

COOPERATIVE AND COLLABORATIVE LEARNING

Cooperative and collaborative learning are instructional contexts in which peers work together on a learning task, with the goal of all participants benefiting from the interaction. Cooperation and collaboration can be treated as synonymous, as a truly cooperative context is always collaborative. Varied perspectives on collaboration and their implications for classroom instruction will be described here, and a number of cooperative techniques involving dyads or larger groups will be outlined, including the costs and benefits associated with them in terms of cognitive or affective outcomes. Finally, the relationship between group and individual performance will be addressed.

Theoretical Perspectives on Collaboration

In 1996, Robert Slavin described a variety of perspectives on peer learning, including social-psychological, sociocultural, cognitive-developmental, and cognitive-elaboration approaches. Explanations of how and what peers can learn from one another differ. Angela O'Donnell and James O'Kelly note that classroom decisions a teacher makes in relation to cooperative or collaborative learning depend on the theoretical approach adopted. Social-psychological approaches suggest that the interdependence among group members is the underlying mechanism for effective cooperation. Interdependence is created by using group rewards or by encouraging social cohesion and a norm of caring and helpfulness. From a cognitive-developmental perspective, effective peer learning occurs as a result of processes of cognitive conflict and resolution, or through the modeling of skilled behavior.

A sociocultural perspective would suggest that the joint knowledge of the group members is greater than the individual knowledge of any member and that the group operates as an interacting system. In contrast, a cognitive-elaboration approach suggests that collaboration enhances student learning by providing a context in which individual learning is promoted by the use of more effective learning processes. In other words, an individual learns better with a peer because the peer provides an audience, prompts more metacognition, or maintains an individual's focus on a task. In creating and using collaborative groups for instructional purposes, teachers' decisions about the size and composition of groups, the kinds of tasks on which students will work, whether or not they should use explicit rewards, and the particular stance to take in relation to the collaborative groups will be influenced by the theoretical perspective that the teachers adopt.

Collaborative Learning in Dyads and Groups

Dyads have many advantages as a functional unit for collaborative learning. The likelihood of participation by all students is increased when there are only two individuals involved. The larger the group, the more opportunity there is for diffusion of responsibility among group members or for exclusion of some members. Active participation in the collaborative process is essential for learning to occur.

Among the cooperative techniques that can by used by dyads are *scripted cooperation,* devised by Angela O'Donnell and Donald Dansereau; *reciprocal peer tutoring,* devised by John Fantuzzo and colleagues; and *guided peer questioning,* as outlined by Alison King. In scripted cooperation, partners work together to learn text material. The text is broken down into sections and both partners read the first section. One partner summarizes the material for his or her partner, who in turn provides a critique of the summary. Both partners elaborate on the information, and they then alternate roles for the second section of the text, continuing in this way until they have completed the reading. They then review the material together. The activities in which students engage (oral summarization, elaboration, metacognition, elaboration, review) are known to promote effective learning. The technique works well for acquiring information, and students are typically positive about their learning experiences with their partners.

In reciprocal peer tutoring (RPT), students work together to teach one another, and they alternate between the roles of student and teacher. This

technique combines elements of both motivational and cognitive approaches to collaboration. Motivation is encouraged by the use of group rewards, such as choices of desired activities or acting as the teacher's helper or messenger, which are intended to create interdependence among group members. Rewards are based on team achievement. The technique also promotes cognitive processing by using a structured approach to teaching and learning within a tutoring context. RPT has been used successfully to promote achievement and is also associated with positive social outcomes including an increase in students' self-confidence and better scores on measures of behavior.

In contrast to scripted cooperation and reciprocal peer tutoring, King's guided peer questioning technique is explicitly intended to promote knowledge construction through higher-order thinking. This technique can be used in dyads and with larger groups. It involves a process of question asking and answering, which is guided by the provision of question starters, such as: "Why is . . . important?" Students pick a few of the question starters, generate questions that fit the form of the starter, and then ask questions of their peers and answer their peers' questions. The question starters serve as a scaffold for students' thinking. Different kinds of questions can be used that support comprehension or complex knowledge construction. The provision of starters supports students in constructing high-level questions to which their peers must provide explanations rather than simple responses of a terminal nature. In addition, the students must engage in self-monitoring. Because these questions require complex answers, peers must probe their own understanding of material in order to answer. Positive effects on achievement are associated with the use of guided peer questioning.

One of the advantages associated with the techniques described above is the increased participation in cognitive activities by more students in a classroom than would be possible in whole-group instruction. In whole-group instruction, for example, teachers typically ask questions (often low-level questions such as those that simply require the recall of factual information but do not probe understanding) and a small number of students have the opportunity to construct a response. With the focused activity of guided peer questioning, all students have the opportunity not only to respond to questions, but to generate them as well. The techniques previously described promote active processing of material using activities that are strongly linked to achievement. In all of these techniques, the interactions of students are very structured, and this structure is important to the success of the techniques.

A potential disadvantage to dyadic interaction may emerge on complex tasks, as there may be insufficient resources within a dyad to generate appropriate strategies to complete the task. As group size increases, the likelihood of having someone in the group who can satisfactorily complete a challenging task increases. Larger groups present their own difficulties, however. Although group members can help one another through explanations, reminders, and questions, they can also distract one another from the task at hand. In addition, some students may elect not to participate, while others many be precluded from doing so.

One solution to the problem of differential participation of students is to structure the group interaction to ensure equitable participation. This can be accomplished by assigning specific roles, alternating roles and activities, or requiring that consensus among group members be reached. These strategies can be effective. In a 1999 study, for example, Noreen Webb and Sydney Farivar trained students to both seek and give appropriate help. The collaborative technique used by groups is a more open-ended one than those previously described. By focusing the group norms on helping, Webb and Farivar were successful in ensuring participation by students. Elizabeth Cohen suggests that structuring the interaction of group members may also stifle the spontaneous interaction that may be necessary to effective problem solving in groups. Instead of tightly structuring tasks, Cohen believes that an interest in complex tasks will result in genuine collaboration. Students, however, need to be prepared to work with one another so that patterns of inclusion and exclusion associated with having high or low status in a group are minimized. Cohen and her colleagues have been very successful in promoting achievement among students in collaborative groups using tasks that are interesting, challenging, and that involve higher-order thinking.

Decisions about what size of group to use, whether members of that group should be heterogeneous or homogeneous with respect to ability, and what kind of support students will need to achieve the desired outcomes must be carefully considered. Such decisions will be influenced by the theoretical

perspective one adopts with respect to collaborative learning.

Group and Individual Performance

The relationship between group and individual performance in cooperative or collaborative learning is not well understood. Slavin's work on cooperative learning emphasizes the role of individual accountability. His techniques depend on group rewards that are earned by each student in a team when performance is improved. In Slavin's work, therefore, there is continuity between individual and group performance. However, the question of the relationship between group and individual performance is often unexamined. The issue of what factors transfer from a group to subsequent individual performance is not well understood. Part of the difficulty in addressing this issue comes from the variability of approaches to peer learning, as the importance or relevance of this issue varies across approaches. Nevertheless, because of the prevalent use of cooperative and collaborative techniques in schools, the increases in high-stakes testing, and the concerns of parents in relation to their children's involvement in collaborative experiences, the relationship of individual and group performance warrants consideration.

Teachers who wish to use cooperative and collaborative leaning to promote students' achievement need to be thoughtful in considering the implications of their decisions about group size, rewards, group composition, and their own role in the classroom. The variety of theoretical perspectives available to inform such decisions can be confusing. Fundamentally, cooperative learning that promotes student achievement depends on the quality of student interaction. Such interaction needs to be task oriented, helpful, characterized by deep processing of content that involves organization or restructuring of knowledge, and elaboration of that knowledge. Making decisions about group size, for example, becomes simpler if the teacher focuses on the expected quality of interaction among students. Large groups limit participation while smaller groups provide more opportunities for interaction. Other decisions such as the composition of the group will also be informed by a focus on the quality of interaction. If the group is of mixed ability, other interventions may be needed to maintain the quality of participation (such as the use of question stems or other ways of structuring the interaction to maximize quality) or to guarantee the inclusion of all participants.

See also: COMPUTER-SUPPORTED COLLABORATIVE LEARNING; INSTRUCTIONAL DESIGN; PEER RELATIONS AND LEARNING.

BIBLIOGRAPHY

FANTUZZO, JOHN W.; KING, JUDITH A.; and HELLER, LAUREN R. 1992. "Effects of Reciprocal Peer Tutoring on Mathematics and School Adjustment: A Component Analysis." *Journal of Educational Psychology* 84:331–339.

KING, ALISON. 1999. "Discourse Patterns for Mediating Peer Learning." In *Cognitive Perspectives on Peer Learning,* ed. Angela M. O'Donnell and Alison King. Mahwah, NJ: Erlbaum.

O'DONNELL, ANGELA M., and DANSEREAU, DONALD F. 1992. "Scripted Cooperation in Student Dyads: A Method for Analyzing and Enhancing Academic Learning and Performance." In *Interaction in Cooperative Groups: The Theoretical Anatomy of Group Learning,* ed. Rachel Hertz-Lazarowitz and Norman Miller. New York: Cambridge University Press.

O'DONNELL, ANGELA M., and O'KELLY, JAMES B. 1994. "Learning from Peers: Beyond the Rhetoric of Positive Results." *Educational Psychology Review* 6:321–349.

SLAVIN, ROBERT E. 1996. "Research on Cooperative Learning and Achievement: What We Know, What We Need to Know." *Contemporary Educational Psychology* 21:43–69.

WEBB, NOREEN M., and FARIVAR, S. 1994. "Developing Productive Group Interaction in Middle School Mathematics." In *Cognitive Perspectives on Peer Learning,* ed. Angela M. O'Donnell and Alison King. Mahwah, NJ: Erlbaum.

ANGELA M. O'DONNELL

CORPORATE COLLEGES

Dramatic changes have occurred in the scale of corporate investment in employee education since the end of World War II. Business and industry leaders have recognized that an educated workforce is essential to remaining competitive in a global economy.

It is estimated that organizations in the United States with 100 or more employees spend approximately $60 billion annually for employee education. This estimate does not include the costs of informal on-the-job education, nor does it include indirect costs, such as the wages and benefits paid to employees while they are participating in educational programs.

Some corporations, such as Arthur D. Little and General Motors, have created and sustained their own in-house educational institutions that offer accredited academic degrees just like traditional universities. These are known as *corporate colleges.* Most of these institutions were created to offer accredited degree programs that were not available elsewhere. Indeed some were established because their parent corporations were unsuccessful in their efforts to forge partnerships with established universities and colleges to create programs that met their corporate needs.

How do corporate colleges compare with traditional universities? Corporate colleges offer degrees ranging from the associate to the doctoral levels with most offering graduate degrees. The curricula offered by corporate colleges varies widely, although each corporate college offers a limited range of programs. Examples of the curricula include insurance, architecture, financial services, business management, health sciences, textile technology, policy analysis, and various types of engineering. These institutions are fully accredited by state authorities and regional accrediting bodies. Their governance models, administrative structures, and academic and administrative titles are very similar to those of traditional postsecondary institutions. Tuition fees charged by corporate colleges are similar to those of traditional institutions, but in some cases, such as the New England College of Finance (NECF), the banks that are member institutions of the NECF may offer tuition reimbursement to their employees.

At the same time there are significant differences between corporate colleges and traditional universities. Corporate colleges make far greater use of part-time faculty, mostly practicing professionals, than is common at traditional postsecondary institutions. Even full-time faculty members do not have tenure; limited-term appointments are the norm. Corporate colleges offer a limited number of highly specialized programs and lack the diversity of programs of traditional universities and colleges. This is not surprising since they have typically been established to respond to a particular need.

The Evolution of Corporate Colleges

One of the earliest corporate colleges in the United States was the General Motors Institute (GMI), which was founded in Flint, Michigan, in 1919. In 1945 the Institute's Board of Regents approved a proposal for GMI to award degrees in engineering. Accreditation was received in 1962. GMI changed its name to Kettering University in 1998.

In the 1970s and 1980s there was a significant expansion in the number of corporate colleges. Their rapid growth prompted the prediction that hundreds of corporate colleges might be created in the years to come.

In 2000 a total of twenty-six institutions had been identified as corporate colleges. Their existence was found to be tenuous. A number of these institutions, such as the Wang Institute of Graduate Studies, closed after only a few years in operation: it was created in 1979 and ceased operation in 1987. Others, such as the Arthur D. Little School of Management and Kettering University, evolved into freestanding private institutions that were independent of their original corporate sponsor. Only five of the twenty-six met the definition of a corporate college and continued to exist in 2001 (Clarkson College, the Institute of Paper Science and Technology, the Institute of Textile Technology, the New England College of Finance, and the RAND Graduate School of Policy Studies). No corporate colleges were created in the 1990s. The impetus for corporations to create corporate colleges appears to have passed.

The Decline of Corporate Colleges

The most likely causes of the lack of growth in the number of corporate colleges are corporate outsourcing of training, the demands of accreditation, and an increased willingness by traditional universities to cooperate in corporate education.

Outsourcing. One of the primary corporate strategies for successfully competing in the global economy involves focusing on the core business of the corporation and the core competencies supporting it. Accordingly, many corporations have chosen to rely heavily on outsourcing to meet their educational needs. It is estimated that approximately one-third of corporate training budgets is spent on training products and services supplied by outside providers.

These corporations prefer collaborative arrangements with universities and colleges to creating and sustaining their own corporate colleges.

Accreditation. This process involves at least two, and in some cases three, separate stages of evaluation and approval. The first stage requires state legislative approval to receive authority to grant degrees. The second stage requires acceptance by one of six regional accrediting associations in the United States. In order to be recognized as an accredited degree-granting institution approval must be obtained at both of these levels. Some specialized programs also have national accrediting bodies that constitute a third stage of evaluation. For example, business schools are accredited by the Association to Advance Collegiate Schools of Business (AACSB), and engineering schools are accredited by the Accreditation Board for Engineering and Technology (ABET). Each stage of the accreditation process requires an extensive application that must be thoroughly documented. Moreover, accreditation is not a one-time matter. Accredited institutions are periodically reviewed and reassessed. Applying for, receiving, and maintaining accreditation is costly and time-consuming. The expectations of accrediting bodies are quite demanding with extensive requirements regarding organization and governance, programs and instruction, faculty, student services, library and information resources, physical resources, and financial resources. Establishing a corporate college is a substantial, long-term commitment. Corporations must be prepared to relinquish a high degree of independence and autonomy of operation if they want their programs to be accredited. For many corporations these expectations are sufficient to dissuade them from such a course of action.

Cooperation. One of the primary reasons that led corporations to create corporate colleges was the unwillingness of universities and colleges to accommodate corporate training needs. A number of the corporations that sponsored the creation of corporate colleges did so after unsuccessfully attempting to cooperate with existing universities and colleges. Much has changed since the early 1980s as a growing number of corporations have established strategic partnerships with universities and colleges and jointly develop degree and certificate programs tailored to meet corporate needs.

In summary, the combined effects of these three factors have contributed to a greatly reduced inclination on the part of corporations to establish their own corporate colleges. If universities and colleges continue to be willing partners in meeting corporate education needs there are likely to be few, if any, new corporate colleges created. A related, and relatively recent development, is the emergence of *corporate universities.*

Corporate Universities

One of the major developments in corporate education that emerged in the 1980s and 1990s was the creation of corporate universities. Indeed, the concept of corporate universities may well have its roots in corporate colleges.

Corporate universities are distinguished from corporate colleges in that the latter are accredited degree-granting entities whereas the former are not themselves degree-granting but frequently partner with traditional degree-granting universities and colleges. Corporate universities are essentially refashioned corporate training departments that have adopted some of the superficial characteristics of traditional universities, such as terminology. For example, a "dean" usually administers a corporate university. Corporate universities are similar to traditional universities in that their mandate includes training and the dissemination of knowledge, but unlike traditional universities they are not dedicated to the creation of new knowledge.

Most corporate universities serve the training needs of employees of the parent company but some also provide training to employees of corporate suppliers and corporate clients. They are a rapidly expanding creation. It is estimated that in the United States, there were about 400 corporate universities in 1988 and ten years later their number was estimated to be more than 1,000.

A majority of these corporate universities have created partnerships with accredited universities and colleges that lead to degrees and certificates. Such partnerships are founded on a willingness by the educational institutions to design curricula appropriate to the training needs of the corporations and to continually update those curricula as needed. Typically, the corporate partner will pay some, if not all, of the costs associated with the development and delivery of the training program. While the corporate partner will expect to have some input to the curricula, the instruction is given and the degrees and certificates are awarded by the academic institution. This allows corporations to access training programs relevant to corporate needs while coincidentally allowing their employees to earn university credentials. It also allows corporations interested in offering such training to their employees to avoid the complications associated with accreditation of "in-house" corporate colleges because the university partner is responsible for ensuring that the program is an accredited offering.

Conclusion

Corporate colleges and corporate universities represent major investments by corporations to achieve corporate objectives through education. Corporate colleges evolved on a limited scale but were a highly visible development that peaked at the end of the twentieth century. Corporate universities are the emerging major development in corporate education at the start of the twenty-first century.

Finally, it is important to note the increasing presence of for-profit educational institutions in postsecondary education. These institutions may come to play an increased role as providers of corporate education.

See also: CONTINUING PROFESSIONAL EDUCATION, *subentry on* UNITED STATES; LIFELONG LEARNING.

BIBLIOGRAPHY

EURICH, NELL P. 1985. *Corporate Classrooms: The Learning Business.* Princeton, NJ: The Carnegie Foundation for the Advancement of Teaching.

MEISTER, JEANNE C. 1998. *Corporate Universities: Lessons in Building a World-Class Work Force.* New York: McGraw-Hill.

PRIMARY RESEARCH GROUP. 1998. *Corporate/ Government Partnerships with Higher Education in Training and Human Resource Development.* New York: Primary Research Group.

STAMPS, DAVID. 1998. "The For-Profit Future of Higher Education." *Training* 35(6):23–30.

THOMPSON, GORDON. 2000. "Unfulfilled Prophecy: The Evolution of Corporate Colleges." *The Journal of Higher Education* 71(3):322–341.

GORDON THOMPSON

COST EFFECTIVENESS IN EDUCATION

Cost-effectiveness analysis is an evaluation tool that is designed to assist in choosing among alternative courses of action or policies when resources are limited. Most educational decisions face constraints in the availability of budgetary and other resources. Therefore, limiting evaluation to the educational consequences of alternatives, alone, without considering their costs provides an inadequate basis for decision-making. Some alternatives may be more costly than others for the same results, meaning that society must sacrifice more resources to obtain a given end. It is desirable to choose those alternatives that are least costly for reaching a particular objective or that have the largest impact per unit of cost. This is intuitively obvious because the most cost-effective solution will free up resources for other uses or allow a greater impact for any given investment in comparison to a less cost-effective solution.

Applying this to educational interventions, there are a host of options from which schools, school districts, and higher education institutions can choose to improve educational outcomes. Many have shown at least some evidence of effectiveness, although the standards of evidence vary considerably. Thus, at the very least, consistent standards of evidence are needed to compare the competing alternatives. But estimates of the costs of the alternatives are needed as well. Even if one alternative is 10 percent more effective than another, it will not be preferred if it is twice as costly. Thus, both costs and effectiveness must be known in order to make good public policy choices.

Before reviewing briefly the methodology of cost-effectiveness analysis, it is important to differentiate it from a closely related evaluation tool, cost-benefit analysis. The approach to measuring costs is similar for both techniques, but in contrast to cost-effectiveness analysis where the results are measured in educational terms, cost-benefit analysis uses monetary measures of outcomes. This approach has the advantage of being able to compare the costs and benefits in monetary values for each alternative to see if the benefits exceed the costs. It also enables a comparison among projects with very different goals as long as both costs and benefits can be placed in monetary terms. In education, cost-benefit analysis has been used in cases where the educational outcomes are market-oriented such as in vocational ed-

ucation or in consideration of the higher income produced by more or better education. It has also been used in cases where a variety of benefits can be converted into monetary values such as in the noted study of the Perry Preschool Program discussed in W. Steven Barnett's 1996 book. In most educational interventions, however, the results are measured in educational terms rather than in terms of their monetary values.

Methodology

The method of doing cost-effectiveness can be summarized briefly, but it is best to refer to more extensive treatments of the subject if a study is being contemplated (for example, *Cost-Effectiveness Analysis*, by Henry M. Levin and Patrick J. McEwan). Cost-effectiveness begins with a clear goal and a set of alternatives for reaching that goal. Comparisons can be made only for alternatives that have similar goals such as improvement of achievement in a particular subject or reduction in absenteeism or in dropouts. A straightforward cost-effectiveness analysis cannot compare options with different goals and objectives, any more than a standard type of evaluation could compare results in mathematics with results in creative writing. Alternatives being assessed should be options for addressing a specific goal where attainment of the goal can be measured by a common criterion such as an achievement test. It should be noted that a more complex, but related, form of analysis, cost-utility, can be used to assess multiple objectives.

In almost all respects, measuring the effectiveness of alternatives for purposes of cost-effectiveness analysis is no different than for a traditional evaluation. Experimental or quasi-experimental designs can be used to ascertain effectiveness, and such studies should be of a quality adequate to justify reasonably valid conclusions. If a study of effectiveness does not meet reasonable standards in terms of its validity, there is nothing in the cost-effectiveness method that will rescue the result. What cost-effectiveness analysis adds is the ability to consider the results of different alternatives relative to the costs of achieving those results. It does not change the criteria for what is a good effectiveness study.

The concept of costs that is used in cost-effectiveness studies is one that is drawn from economics, namely, opportunity cost. When a resource is used for one purpose, individuals or society lose the opportunity to use that resource in some alternative use. In general, the concept of opportunity cost is viewed as the value of a resource in its best alternative use. This may differ from the everyday understanding of what a cost is. For example, many school districts will refer to an unused facility as having no cost to the district if it is used for a new program. That facility, however, has value in alternative use in the sense that it could be sold or leased in the market or used for other purposes that have value. In this sense it is not "free." If the school district uses it for a new program, it sacrifices the potential income that the facility could yield in the marketplace or the value to other programs that could use the facility.

There is a standard methodology for measuring the cost of an intervention in cost-effectiveness analysis. The ingredients required to replicate the interventions are specified for all alternatives. Most interventions require personnel, facilities, materials, equipment, and other inputs such as client time. Using these categories as organizing rubrics, the ingredients are listed in terms of both quality and quantity such as, for the personnel category, the number of full-time teachers and their qualifications as well as other staff. Information on ingredients is collected through interviews, reports, and direct observations.

When all of the ingredients are accounted for, their cost values are determined. There are a variety of ways to estimate these costs. In the case where ingredients are purchased in competitive marketplaces, the costs are readily obtainable. Of course, the total costs of personnel include both salaries and the employee benefits. Other approaches are often used to estimate the value of facilities and equipment. In general, the technique for measuring costs is to ascertain their annual value. Because facilities and equipment have a life that is greater than one year, the annual value is derived through determining annual depreciation and interest costs. There are standard methods for ascertaining the annualized value of costs for ingredients.

These costs are summed up to obtain total annual costs, and they are usually divided by the numbers of students to get an average cost per student that can be associated with the effectiveness of each intervention. The ratio of cost per unit of effectiveness can then be compared across projects by combining the effectiveness results with costs. Alternatives with the largest effectiveness relative to cost are usually given highest priority in decision-making, although other factors such as ease of im-

plementation or political resistance need to be considered. The cost analysis can also be used to determine the burden of cost among different government or private entities where each alternative has different possibilities in terms of who provides the ingredients. In this respect it should be noted that the total cost of an intervention must even include volunteers and donated resources, although the cost to the sponsor may be reduced by others sharing the cost burden through providing resources in-kind.

Examples

The application of cost-effectiveness analysis can best be understood by providing examples of its use. In a 1984 study, Bill Quinn, Adrian Van Mondfrans, and Blaine R. Worthen examined the cost-effectiveness of two different mathematics curricula. One approach was based upon a traditional, text-book application. The other was a locally developed curriculum that emphasized highly individualized instruction with special methods for teaching mathematics concepts. With respect to effectiveness, the latter curriculum was found to be more effective in terms of mathematics achievement, on average, than the traditional program. It was also learned that the lower the socioeconomic status (SES) of the student, the greater were the achievement advantages of the innovative program.

But the innovative program had a cost that was about 50 percent higher per student than the traditional one. The question is whether the additional achievement justified the higher cost. The evaluators found that the cost per raw score point on the Iowa Tests of Basic Skills was about 15 percent less for the innovative program than for the traditional one, showing that the higher achievement more than compensated for the higher cost. For low SES students the cost per point of the innovative program was less than 40 percent that of the traditional program. For high SES students, however, the traditional program was slightly more cost-effective. This study demonstrates the value of cost-effectiveness and its usefulness as an evaluation technique among different types of students. In a low SES school or district the innovative program was far superior in terms of its cost-effectiveness. In a high SES school or district, the traditional program might be preferred on cost-effectiveness grounds.

One of the most comprehensive cost-effectiveness studies compared four potential interventions in the elementary grades: reductions in class size in a range between twenty and thirty-five students per class, peer tutoring, computer-assisted instruction, and longer school days. The measures of educational effectiveness included both mathematics and reading achievement. Tutoring costs per student were highest, followed by decreases in class size from thirty-five to twenty, computer-assisted instruction, and longer school days. The high costs for peer tutoring are a result of the cost of adult coordinators who must organize and supervise the tutoring activities of effective programs. Effectiveness measures were taken from evaluation studies that had focused on the achievement gains associated with each type of intervention. Although peer tutoring had a high cost, it also had very high effectiveness and the highest cost-effectiveness. In general, computer-assisted instruction was second in cost-effectiveness with class size and longer school days showing the lowest cost-effectiveness. Results differed somewhat between reading and mathematics, but the cost-effectiveness of reduced class size and of longer school days was consistently lower than those of peer tutoring and computer-assisted instruction.

A study in northeastern Brazil undertook a cost-effectiveness analysis of different approaches to school improvement. A range of potential school improvements was compared to ascertain effects on student achievement. These included teacher-training programs, higher salaries to attract better teaching talent, better facilities, and greater provision of student textbooks and other materials. The authors used statistical models to determine the apparent impact of changes in these inputs on Portuguese language achievement for second graders. Costs were estimated using the ingredients method outlined above. Effectiveness relative to cost was highest for the provision of more instructional materials and lowest for raising teacher salaries. Given the very tight economic resources available for improving schooling in Brazil, this type of study provides valuable guidance for those people making resource decisions.

Use of Cost-Effectiveness Analysis

Studies of the effectiveness of educational interventions are very common. Studies of their cost-effectiveness are rare. What might account for this discrepancy? There may be many reasons. Evaluators of social programs rarely have background in cost analysis. Few programs or textbooks in educa-

tional evaluation provide training in cost-effectiveness analysis. That decision makers are often unfamiliar with cost-effectiveness analysis limits their ability to evaluate and use such studies. Yet, in the early 1980s, the field of health was also limited in terms of both the production and use of cost-effectiveness studies. By the early twenty-first century, the concept had been widely applied to health decisions in response to severe resource stringencies in health care. Because the field of education is pressed with similar resource constraints, there might be increased development and use of cost-effectiveness techniques in educational decision-making.

See also: DECISION-MAKING IN SCHOOLS, APPLYING ECONOMIC ANALYSIS TO; ECONOMIC BENEFITS OF EDUCATION INVESTMENT, MEASUREMENT; PUBLIC SCHOOL BUDGETING, ACCOUNTING, AND AUDITING.

BIBLIOGRAPHY

BARNETT, W. STEVEN. 1996. *Lives in the Balance: Age-27 Benefit-Cost Analysis of the High/Scope Perry Preschool Program.* Ypsilanti, MI: High/Scope Press.

GOLD, MARTHE, ed. 1996. *Cost-Effectiveness in Health and Medicine.* New York: Oxford University Press.

HARBISON, RALPH W., and HANUSHEK, ERIC. 1992. *Educational Performance of the Poor: Lessons from Rural Northeast Brazil.* New York: Oxford University Press.

LEVIN, HENRY M. 2001. "Waiting for Godot: Cost-Effectiveness Analysis in Education." In *Evaluation Findings that Surprise,* ed. Richard Light. San Francisco: Jossey-Bass.

LEVIN, HENRY M.; GLASS, GENE V.; and MEISTER, GAIL. 1987. "Cost-Effectiveness of Computer Assisted Instruction." *Evaluation Review* 11(1):50–72.

LEVIN, HENRY M., and McEWAN, PATRICK J. 2001. *Cost-Effectiveness Analysis,* 2nd edition. Thousand Oaks, CA: Sage.

ORR, LARRY L. 1999. *Social Experiments.* Thousand Oaks, CA: Sage.

QUINN, BILL; VAN MONDFRANS, ADRIAN; and WORTHEN, BLAINE R. 1984. "Cost-Effectiveness of Two Math Programs as Moderated by Pupil SES." *Educational Evaluation and Policy Analysis* 6(1):39–52.

SHADISH, WILLIAM R.; COOK, THOMAS D.; and CAMPBELL, DONALD T. 2002. *Experimental and Quasi-Experimental Designs for Generalized Causal Inference.* New York: Houghton Mifflin.

HENRY M. LEVIN

COUNCIL FOR BASIC EDUCATION

The Council for Basic Education (CBE) was founded in 1956 by a group of distinguished citizens alarmed at the shift in American education from intellectual development to an emphasis on social development. From its inception CBE set out, as it states in its by-laws, to ensure "that all students without exception receive adequate instruction in the basic intellectual disciplines, especially English, mathematics, science, history, and foreign languages." CBE is a nonprofit educational organization whose primary purpose is to strengthen the teaching and learning of the basic liberal arts subjects in American undergraduate schools. A critical voice for education reform, CBE has complemented its strong advocacy by designing and administering practical programs to foster better teaching and learning.

History

CBE, in the belief that there is an intimate relationship between a healthy democracy and the ideal of excellence in education, from its earliest days published monthly and quarterly periodicals to provide a platform for its advocacy, analysis, and programs. Among its early directors, board members, and supporters were Mortimer Smith, Mary Bingham, Admiral Hyman Rickover, Potter Stewart, and Jacques Barzun. In 1959 James D. Koerner's *The Case for Basic Education* articulated CBE's ideals about the goals in education and contained what has become a celebrated essay by one of its founding members, Clifton Fadiman, on what he defined as the "generative" power of what is contained in the basic liberal arts. In 1971 CBE published "Inner-City Children Can Be Taught to Read: Four Successful Schools," an article by George Weber, then a director at CBE, which continues to be read by those who are alarmed at the number of illiterate students in the nation's urban schools.

Activities

In addition to speeches, publications, and conferences, CBE's programmatic activities began when it was invited by the National Endowment for the Humanities to administer a program that would allow school teachers to engage in independent study in the humanities during the summertime. From 1983 until 1997, more than 3,000 teachers participated as CBE Fellows, and from 1985 until 1996, CBE conducted Writing to Learn, which taught effective writing across the curriculum, primarily in urban school districts.

Following the National Education Summit in 1989 in Charlottesville, Virginia, which called for strong national standards for education, CBE's historic commitment for high standards established it as a national leader. CBE provided support for the development and implementation of academic standards in a number of states and school districts, including Alaska, Hawaii, Illinois, Kansas, Maryland, Mississippi, Chicago, Los Angeles, Cleveland (Ohio), Milwaukee (Wisconsin), Montgomery County (Maryland), and Sacramento and Santa Barbara (both California). In 1995, through its project known as Standards for Excellence in Education (SEE), CBE condensed, consolidated, and edited the national standards in the basic subjects to form a single volume, which continues to be used in many school systems. During that same period of time, CBE was asked to convene a panel to review the then controversial national history standards, which produced a report that became the basis for the revised national history standards.

In addition to its standards and fellowship programs, CBE developed a program, Standards-Based Teacher Education (STEP), to promote students' deep understanding of the subjects they will eventually teach and encourage the colleges of the arts and sciences to join forces with the teacher preparation faculties in requiring a strong academic curriculum for future teachers. STEP is operational on campuses in Maryland, Indiana, Kentucky, Georgia, and Delaware. Schools around the World (SAW) is a program that engages teachers from eight nations to compare student work on common science and mathematics topics and trains teachers in the United States to improve instruction.

In 1997 CBE initiated the Humanities Scholars Fellowship program and the Charter School Fellowship program. In 1999 it collaborated with the Laboratory for Student Success and the Maryland State Department of Education to launch the Mid-Atlantic Regional Teachers' Project (MARTP), a coalition of five states that looks at issues of teacher quality and demand in a regional area. CBE is a partner with the George Washington University and the Institute for Educational Leadership to develop a National Clearinghouse for Comprehensive School Reform. CBE also manages American Education Reaches Out (AERO), a project designed to develop a set of voluntary academic-content standards for the American schools overseas that are supported by the U.S. Department of State.

Legal Status, Governance, and Publications

CBE is incorporated as a 501 (c)(3) organization and is governed by an independent board of directors. The council publishes *Basic Education* (monthly) and occasional special reports and books.

Assessment of CBE's Influence and Significance

From its beginning, CBE has been known as an independent voice for educational reform, and it is frequently called upon and quoted in national newspapers, periodicals, and on television and radio. Its publications are read by a diverse audience, including professional educators, members of Congress, the U.S. Department of Education, state legislators, and the media, as well as by members of the general public who seek an understanding of educational policies and trends. Both national and international education officials confer regularly with CBE about education policy. As of 2001, CBE had worked in twenty-five states, twenty-eight districts, and eight countries.

See also: SCHOOL REFORM; STANDARDS FOR STUDENT LEARNING; STANDARDS MOVEMENT IN AMERICAN EDUCATION.

BIBLIOGRAPHY

BARTH, PATTE, and MITCHELL, RUTH. 1992. *Smart Start.* Golden, CO: North American Press.

KOERNER, JAMES D. 1959. *The Case for Basic Education.* Boston: Little, Brown.

MITCHELL, RUTH. 1992. *Testing for Learning.* New York: Maxwell Macmillan International.

PATTON, SUSANNAH, and HOLMES, MADELYN, eds. 1988. *The Keys to Literacy.* Washington, DC: Council for Basic Education.

PRITCHARD, IVOR. 1998. *Good Education: The Virtues of Learning.* Norwalk, CT: Judd.

TYSON, HARRIET. 1994. *Who Will Teach the Children?* San Francisco: Jossey-Bass.

TYSON-BERNSTEIN, HARRIET. 1988. *A Conspiracy of Good Intentions: America's Textbook Fiasco.* Washington, DC: Council for Basic Education.

WEBER, GEORGE. 1971. "Inner-City Children Can Be Taught to Read: Four Successful Schools." Washington, DC: Council for Basic Education.

CHRISTOPHER T. CROSS
M. RENÉ ISLAS

COUNCIL FOR EXCEPTIONAL CHILDREN

The Council for Exceptional Children (CEC) is a professional association dedicated to improving the educational success of children with disabilities and/or gifts and talents. Its members include special education teachers and administrators, professors, related service providers, paraprofessionals, and parents.

Program

CEC focuses on improving the quality of special and general education. To achieve this goal, the council works with state and local education districts, the federal government, and other education organizations to find ways to better identify, teach, and care for children with exceptionalities.

In addition to encouraging the professional growth of its members and other special educators, CEC aids in recruiting personnel and promoting high professional standards. It encourages research in the education of children with exceptionalities and assists in the dissemination of research findings. And it engages in lobbying efforts at all levels of government to promote legislation that supports the education of children with special needs.

Disseminating information about the education of children with exceptionalities is one of CEC's major activities. CEC provides information to members and others who work with children with disabilities and/or gifts and talents through conventions, conferences, the CEC website, and publications. The council publishes two journals, *Teaching Exceptional Children,* a professional, practical-based journal, and

Exceptional Children, a research journal. CEC also publishes *CEC Today,* the organization's newsletter, which covers current trends in special education and CEC activities. In addition, CEC publishes books and videos on special education and instructional strategies, research monographs, reviews of research, and special bulletins.

Another significant aspect of the council's activities is developing standards for the field. To date, CEC has developed standards for what special education teachers, diagnosticians, administrators, and paraeducators must know to provide effective instruction and service. An important aspect of CEC's standards activities is providing recognition for outstanding special educators, which it accomplishes through its professional awards program.

CEC also engages in extensive advocacy activities. The council cooperates with other education organizations to promote legislation that supports education in general, and special and gifted education in particular. CEC focuses its legislative efforts on ensuring that gifted children and children with disabilities receive a high quality education and that special and gifted education programs are adequately funded. The council further works to inform legislators at all levels, as well as the general public, of the benefits society receives when children with exceptionalities reach their educational potential.

In addition, CEC operates four national information centers. The centers provide information on the education of children with disabilities and gifts and talents, the special education profession, and the Individuals with Disabilities Education Act (IDEA).

Organizational Structure

CEC consists of state and provincial federations, which are made up of local chapters, branches, and affiliates, and the Student Council for Exceptional Children. Federations address statewide or provincial issues, hold conferences, publish newsletters, and coordinate the activities of the local chapters. The local chapters hold meetings, engage in projects to advance the education of children with exceptionalities, and publish newsletters. Students in full-time attendance at an accredited college or university are eligible for membership in the Student Council for Exceptional Children.

CEC has seventeen divisions, each of which specializes in a particular area of special education (such as learning disabilities, mental retardation, gifted ed-

ucation). Each division holds conferences on its particular area of special education and produces a journal, website, and newsletter. The divisions also provide networking opportunities and support for their members.

CEC's board of directors, the association's primary governing body, makes internal and external policy for the organization. A representative assembly serves as an advisory body to the board of directors. As such, it identifies, discusses, and makes recommendations to the board of directors on positions CEC should take on issues involving special education; advises CEC on public policy issues and initiatives; and oversees CEC internal governance policies and procedures.

Membership and Financial Support

CEC's approximately 50,000 members are special education teachers, administrators, college professors, related service providers, paraprofessionals, and parents. Although CEC has an international membership, the majority of its members reside in the United States.

Financial support comes primarily from membership dues. Various special projects receive funds from the federal government and foundation grants.

History and Development

CEC was organized in 1922 by a small group of administrators and faculty members at Teachers College, Columbia University. In 1941 it merged with the special education department of the National Education Association (NEA) and became a department of NEA. In 1977 CEC withdrew its affiliation with NEA and became its own association. During its history, CEC has grown substantially in membership, and it has become a leading national voice for special education. CEC's national headquarters are located in Arlington, Virginia.

See also: SPECIAL EDUCATION.

INTERNET RESOURCE

COUNCIL FOR EXCEPTIONAL CHILDREN. 2002. <www.cec.sped.org>.

LYNDA VAN KUREN

COUNCIL OF CHIEF STATE SCHOOL OFFICERS

The Council of Chief State School Officers (CCSSO) is a nationwide, nonprofit organization composed of the public officials who head the departments of elementary and secondary education in the states, five U.S. extra-state jurisdictions, the District of Columbia, and the Department of Defense Education Activity. The council serves these leaders and their state education agencies by:

- Advocating federal education policy that will most effectively increase student achievement before the U.S. Congress and the administration;

- Providing services and assistance to the chief school officers and members of their agencies to help them carry out their leadership responsibilities, including administration of federal programs; and

- Working in partnership with federal agencies and private foundations on research and statistical studies, such as surveys of mathematics and science programs, and managing projects such as the Wallace–Reader's Digest Funds' initiative, Leaders Count, which support state actions to strengthen leadership in schools and districts.

Membership in the council is voluntary. Dues are paid by the state education agencies; each state's dues are based on the total expenditure for elementary and secondary education for that state related to the total expenditures for the nation. In 2001 council dues totaled $1.6 million, which was less than 10 percent of the overall budget of $17.5 million. More than 90 percent of the budget was in grants and contracts from federal agencies and private foundations. The council offices are in Washington, D.C.

History

Council members first convened in Washington in 1908 at the invitation of the U.S. Congress, which was seeking advice on crafting federal policy for vocational education. In 1927 the council was incorporated as a private nonprofit organization. Since then members have conferred regularly with the Congress and representatives of federal agencies. The council has provided a forum for shaping state consensus on federal educational policy, for exchanging practices among states, and for organizing multistate consortia to attain common objectives such as developing testing strategies and administering teacher licensing examinations.

During the 1960s, in addition to advocacy of federal policy on legislation such as the Elementary and Secondary Education Act of 1965, which relied on the states to administer the programs, the council began to link with the U.S. Office of Education, later the U.S. Department of Education (DoE), to help states administer the act. Similar connections have been made for administering other federal acts such as those for vocational education, education of disabled students, civil rights, telecommunications, and teacher education.

The growth of these supportive administrative activities, together with increased assistance to the DoE on data gathering and securing new foundation funds, expanded annual resources from $2.5 million with fifteen staff members in 1986 to $17.5 million and seventy-five staff members in 2001. Major grant projects included support for early childhood and parent education, teacher preparation and licensure, school leadership policies, arts education, and development of student standards and assessments.

Governance and Operations

Because the total maximum membership is fifty-seven persons, the council operates with extensive direct decision-making by the full membership. The entire membership elects officers and board members, sets state dues, approves all position papers and federal legislative positions, and approves the creation of committees and their membership. The council is guided by a board of nine directors, three of whom are officers. The board approves the budget and receipt of all grants and contract funds, sets the council agenda, and appoints the executive director, who in turn appoints all staff. No board members or officers are paid for their services to the council.

The membership meets three times each year: a federal legislative conference in Washington each March; a Summer Institute for professional development on the priority topic of the year in July, each year in a different host state; and a business meeting held in a different host state each November, at which major policy votes are taken and council priorities set.

The board and membership take extensive time to select and prepare each year's priority topic. One year is spent in development; the "priority" year is used for research and preparation of a council policy statement and the design of state implementation activities to be carried out through at least the two following years. Examples of topics include early childhood education, learning technologies, use of standards and assessments in reform strategies, international education, and preparation for employment and leadership for learning.

In addition to providing a network of services to the chiefs, the council offers more than a dozen nationwide networks for specialists in state education agencies. Examples of the network memberships are the deputy leaders of the state education agencies, assessment directors, statistical experts, mathematics and science coordinators, teacher licensing specialists, health education directors, learning technology experts, school reform strategists, and federal legislative representatives. With these networks the council helps to strengthen capacity throughout the state agencies.

The council staff comprises experts in the priority areas as established by the members. Staff strengths are in equity of education opportunity, assessments, standards and improvement strategies, leadership, teacher education, arts education, and federal legislative advocacy.

Accomplishments and Influence

The influence of CCSSO is illustrated by examples of federal legislative success, major policy statements, and significant innovative projects.

Federal legislation. The council is considered one of the top education lobbying forces in Washington. The provisions of the 2001 reauthorization of the Elementary and Secondary Education Act (ESEA) illustrate results on council-supported positions including strengthened emphasis on targeted aid to children of poverty; substantial increase of funding; increased state role in assessment and accountability; improved programs of learning technology, teacher preparation, 21st Century Schools, and accountability—with these programs featuring added flexibility in administration; and continued responsibility of state education agencies for state plans and administration. Proposals to transform targeted programs to federal revenue sharing, to establish vouchers for private school enrollment, and to transfer state administration to governors, which were considered by Congress, were omitted from the final legislation as advocated by the council.

Other major legislative successes in the 1990s include enactment of the Goals 2000: Educate America Act, which provided nearly $2.5 billion for the development of state and local student standards, assessments, and reform strategies, and enactment of the "universal services" funding for learning technology under the Telecommunications Act of 1996, which has provided nearly $2.2 billion of services to schools and libraries each year since enactment.

Policy papers. Among the most influential council statements is the 1984 paper calling for nationwide testing to provide state-by-state comparisons of student achievement. This position has been pivotal for enabling federal legislation authorizing state-by-state reporting of the National Assessment of Education Progress (NAEP), the measurement of progress on the National Goals of 1989, the establishment of state standards and assessments in the 1990s, and the key provisions for measuring progress of schools under the ESEA reauthorizations of 1994 and 2001. A second important CCSSO statement is the 1987 paper "Assuring Education Success for All," which called for a national goal of virtually 100 percent student graduation from high school. A third is a paper on early childhood education advocating universal opportunity for three- and four-year-olds to attend pre-kindergarten without barrier of cost. A fourth is a set of papers advocating comprehensive education reform based on student standards. These papers provided the underpinning for major federal initiatives in the 1990s, including the Goals 2000 legislation and the ESEA reauthorizations of 1994 and 2001, and for the reform strategies of the states during this period.

Exemplary projects. Among the extensive projects of the council, several have made notably unique nationwide contributions. From 1987, the time of authorization for state-by-state NAEP, into the early twenty-first century, the council won the contracts to prepare nearly all of the content frameworks for the subjects of the NAEP. Second, since the early 1960s the council has administered the national and state Teacher of the Year programs, the nation's most prestigious recognition of teaching.

Third, since 1995 the council, together with the National Association of State Arts Agencies, has provided leadership for the nation's most extensive advocacy of arts education. Fourth, to anticipate the increasing pressures of the global economy, worldwide security, and communications and to improve American education and better understand education in other nations, the council has assisted in shaping the system for international comparative studies of education. The council has served as the U.S. representative to the International Association for the Evaluation of Educational Achievement (IEA), which conducts the major studies of mathematics, science, reading, civics education, and technology. The council has assisted in enabling the major breakthrough of direct state participation in these international comparisons. The council has also organized a decade-long exchange of practices with the education leaders of Japan.

Fifth, CCSSO has led formation of several coalitions of public and private education leaders to promote mutual support for legislative initiatives and exchange of practice, rather than antagonism. Sixth, the council has led the creation of a consortium of the major organizations of state officials—governors, legislators, and state education boards and chiefs—as the major partner with the Wallace–Reader's Digest Funds to assist states in strengthening policies and programs to improve school and district leadership. Through the Leaders Count program this project has been granted $8.9 million to help states with policy changes.

Concluding Note

Global communication, competition, and commerce are generating increasing pressures to nationalize education in the United States. In order to realize the advantages of pooling the nation's resources for improving education, centralization of authority is occurring at the national level. To assure such centralization does not drive out diversity and options in education, CCSSO is in a unique position to provide a countervailing force. The organization serves both to organize the state partnership with the federal government and as an independent advocate for state and local authorities to craft policies and govern education according to the particular aspirations of their jurisdictions. Around the globe nations are struggling with the task of finding the best mix of centralized and decentralized power to assure the most effective performance of their students gauged by international benchmarks. In the United States the council is uniquely placed to help fashion the best balance between standardized improvement and experimentation toward realizing new goals of equity and excellence.

See also: STATE DEPARTMENTS OF EDUCATION.

BIBLIOGRAPHY

AMBACH, GORDON M. 1987. *The State of Learning, New York 1977–1987.* Albany: State University of New York, State Education Department.

AMBACH, GORDON M. 1993. "Federal Action Essential for Education Reform." In *National Issues in Education: The Past Is Prologue,* ed. John F. Jennings. Bloomington, IN: Phi Delta Kappa International.

AMBACH, GORDON M. 1995. "Goals 2000: A New Partnership for Student Achievement." In *National Issues in Education: Goals 2000 and School-to-Work,* ed. John F. Jennings. Bloomington, IN: Phi Delta Kappa International.

GORDON M. AMBACH

COUNSELING, CAREER

See: CAREER COUNSELING IN HIGHER EDUCATION.

COUNSELING, PSYCHOLOGICAL

See: PERSONAL AND PSYCHOLOGICAL COUNSELING AT COLLEGES AND UNIVERSITIES.

COUNSELING, SCHOOL

See: GUIDANCE AND COUNSELING, SCHOOL.

COUNTS, GEORGE S. (1889–1974)

Progressive educator, sociologist, and political activist, George S. Counts challenged teachers and teacher educators to use school as a means for critiquing and transforming the social order. Perhaps best known for his controversial pamphlet *Dare the School Build a New Social Order?* (1932), Counts authored scores of scholarly works that advanced the social study of education and emphasized teaching as a moral and political enterprise. His work on schooling and society continue to have relevance to contemporary dilemmas in education.

Counts was born and raised in Baldwin, Kansas. His family was Methodist and, by his own account, imparted strong ideals of fairness and brotherhood. Counts earned his B.A. from Baker University, the local Methodist school, in 1911 with a degree in classical studies. After graduating, he was employed as a high school math and science teacher, an athletic coach, and principal before beginning postgraduate studies in education at the University of Chicago in 1913, at the age of twenty-four. After receiving a Ph.D. degree with honors, Counts taught at Delaware College, now the University of Delaware (1916–1917) as head of the department of education. He taught educational sociology at Harris Teachers College in St. Louis, Missouri (1918–1919), secondary education at the University of Washington (1919–1920), and education at Yale University (1920–1926) and at the University of Chicago (1926–1927). For nearly thirty years, Counts taught at Teachers College, Columbia University in New York (1927–1956). After being required to retire at the age of 65 from Teachers College, Counts taught at the University of Pittsburgh (1959), Michigan State University (1960), and Southern Illinois University (1962–1971).

Sociology and Education

Much of Counts's scholarship derives from his pioneering work in the sociology of education. His adviser as a doctoral student at the University of Chicago was the chairman of the department of education, psychologist Charles H. Judd. Significantly, Counts insisted on fashioning for himself a minor in sociology and social science at a time when professors of education wholly embraced psychology as the mediating discipline through which to study educational practice and problems. Although his contemporaries were fascinated with the "science of education" and its psychological underpinnings, Counts was interested in the study of social conditions and problems and their relationship to education. Heavily influenced by Albion Small and other Chicago sociologists, Counts saw in sociology the opportunity to examine and reshape schools by considering the impact of social forces and varied political and social interests on educational practice. For example, in the Selective Character of American Secondary Education (1922), Counts demonstrated a close relationship between students' perseverance in school and their parents' occupations. In the Social Composition of Boards of Education: A Study in the Social Control of Public Education (1927) and School and Society in Chicago (1928), he asserted that dominant social classes control American boards of education and school practices respectively. Because schools were run by the capitalist class who wielded social and economic power, Counts argued, school practices tended towards the status quo, including the preservation of an unjust distribution of wealth and power.

Counts's educational philosophy was also an outgrowth of John Dewey's philosophy. Both men believed in the enormous potential of education to improve society and that schools should reflect life rather than be isolated from it. But unlike Dewey's Public and Its Problems, much of Counts's writing suggests a plan of action in the use of schools to fashion a new social order.

Social Reform

From 1927 to the early 1930s Counts became fascinated with the Soviet Union precisely for its willingness to employ schools in the inculcation of a new social order. Although he later became disillusioned with mounting evidence of Soviet totalitarianism and an outspoken critic of the Communist Party (he was elected as president of the American Federation of Teachers in 1939 having run as the anti-Communist candidate), Counts—like twenty-first century criticalists—believed that schools always indoctrinated students. What interested Counts was the schools' orientation: what kind of society did the schools favor and to what degree. As he put it, the word indoctrination "does not frighten me" (1978, p. 263). This position, in particular, later brought Counts fierce critics like Franklin Bobbit, a leader of the social efficiency movement, who countered that the schools were not to be used as agents of social reform.

Counts was accordingly critical of the child-centered Progressives for their failure to articulate any conception of a good society. He chided their preoccupation with individual growth at the expense of democratic solidarity and social justice. In his speech to the Progressive Education Association (PEA), "Dare Progressive Education be Progressive?" which later became the pamphlet Dare the School Build a New Social Order?, he argued that Progressive education had "elaborated no theory of social welfare" (1978, p. 258), and that it must "emancipate itself from the influence of class" (p. 259).

Political Activism

Counts was also a political activist. He was chairman of the American Labor Party (1942–1944), a founder of the Liberal Party, and a candidate for New York's city council, lieutenant governor, and the U.S. Senate. He was president of the American Federation of Teachers (AFT) and a member of the Commission on the Social Studies of the American Historical Association. He was the first editor of the Progressive journal *Social Frontier* which, at its peak, boasted a circulation of 6,000, and advocated enlisting teachers in the reconstruction of society.

Contribution

Counts's importance to and impact on American education remain a matter of debate. His contributions to the evolving discourse on democracy and education are evident in a great deal of his writing, specifically in his conviction that schools could be the lever of radical social change. Highly critical of economic and social norms of selfishness, individualism, and inattention to human suffering, Counts wanted educators to "engage in the positive task of creating a new tradition in American life" (1978, p. 262). He wanted teachers to go beyond abstract, philosophical conceptions of democracy and teach explicitly about power and injustice. He wanted teachers and students to count among their primary goals the building of a better social order.

See also: PHILOSOPHY OF EDUCATION; PROGRESSIVE EDUCATION.

BIBLIOGRAPHY

COUNTS, GEORGE S. 1922. *The Selective Character of American Secondary Education.* Chicago: University of Chicago Press.

COUNTS, GEORGE S. 1927. *The Social Composition of Boards of Education: A Study in the Social Control of Public Education.* Chicago: University of Chicago Press.

COUNTS, GEORGE S. 1928. *School and Society in Chicago.* New York: Harcourt Brace.

COUNTS, GEORGE S. 1931. *The Soviet Challenge to America.* New York: Day.

COUNTS, GEORGE S. 1934. *The Social Foundations of Education: Report of the Commission on the Social Studies.* New York: Scribners.

COUNTS, GEORGE S. 1952. *Education and American Civilization.* New York: Teachers College, Columbia University.

COUNTS, GEORGE S. 1971. "A Humble Autobiography." In *Leaders in American Education, The Seventieth Yearbook of the National Society for the Study of Education,* ed. Robert J. Havighurst. Chicago: University of Chicago Press.

COUNTS, GEORGE S. 1978. *Dare the School Build a New Social Order?* (1932). Carbondale: Southern Illinois University Press.

CURTI, MERLE. 1966. *The Social Ideas of American Educators.* Totawa, NJ: Littlefield, Adams.

GUTEK, GERALD L. 1970. *The Educational Theory of George S. Counts.* Columbus: Ohio State University Press.

GUTEK, GERALD L. 1984. *George S. Counts and American Civilization: The Educator as Social Theorist.* Macon, GA: Mercer University Press.

LAGEMANN, ELLEN C. 1992. "Prophecy or Profession? George S. Counts and the Social Study of Education." *American Journal of Education.* 100(2):137–165.

JOEL WESTHEIMER

CREATIVITY

Creativity is the ability and disposition to produce novelty. Children's play and high accomplishments in art, science, and technology are traditionally called creative, but any type of activity or product, whether ideational, physical, or social, can be creative.

Characteristics

Creativity has been associated with a wide range of behavioral and mental characteristics, including associations between semantically remote ideas and contexts, application of multiple perspectives, curiosity, flexibility in thought and action, rapid generation of multiple, qualitatively different solutions and answers to problems and questions, tolerance for ambiguity and uncertainty, and unusual uses of familiar objects.

Biographical studies of exceptionally creative individuals have uncovered recurring features. Creative individuals typically master a practice or tradition before they transform it. They organize their lives around a network of interrelated and mutually supporting enterprises. They are prolific. There is no evidence for an inverse relation between quantity and quality; instead, the two appear to be correlated. Exceptionally creative accomplishments are complex, evolving outcomes of long-term efforts sustained by high levels of intrinsic motivation, often in the absence of societal rewards.

There are many examples of exceptionally creative individuals who led troubled and turbulent lives and there is widespread belief in a relation between creativity and mental disorder, but it has not been conclusively shown that the more frequent such disorders are, the higher the level of creativity.

The rate of professional productivity in art, science, and other creative endeavors increases rapidly at the beginning of a career, reaches a peak in midlife, and then slowly declines. It is not known whether the decline is necessary or a side effect of other factors, for example, health problems. That some individuals begin creative careers late in life is evidence against an inevitable decline.

Creativity as Ability

All individuals with healthy brains have some degree of creative potential, but individuals vary in how much novelty they in fact produce. Psychometric measures of creativity are based on the hypothesis that the ability to create is general across domains of activity (art, business, music, technology, etc.) and stable over time. This view implies that a person whose creativity is above average in one domain can be expected to be above average in other domains also.

The Remote Associations Test (RAT) developed by Sarnoff A. Mednick measures how easily a person can find a link between semantically different concepts. E. Paul Torrance's Tests of Creative Thinking (TTCT) measures divergent production, that is, how many different answers to a question a person can provide within a time limit. For example, a person might be asked to propose alternative titles to a well-known movie. More recent tests developed by Robert J. Sternberg uses complex test items from realistic contexts. Creativity tests correlate modestly with each other. Critics point out that there are no objective criteria for scoring the responses and that test performance might not be indicative of a creative mind.

Relation to Intelligence

Correlations between creativity tests and IQ tests vary in magnitude from study to study and depend on which tests are used. Some correlations are no smaller than correlations among creativity tests, so they do not provide strong evidence that IQ and creativity are distinct dimensions. The findings can be understood in terms of a so-called triangular correlation (also known as the threshold hypothesis): Individuals in the lower half of the IQ distribution lack the requisite cognitive capacity to create and hence necessarily exhibit low creativity; individuals in the upper half of the IQ distribution have the requisite capacity but may or may not develop a disposition to create. Consequently, creativity and IQ are highly correlated at low IQ levels but weakly correlated at high IQ levels. Alternative interpretations of the relation between creativity and intelligence have been proposed, including that they are two aspects of the same ability, that they are unrelated, and that they are mutually exclusive.

Creativity as Process

The fact that the human mind can generate novel concepts and ideas requires explanation. Cognitive psychologists aim to infer the relevant mental processes from observations of how individuals solve problems that require creativity. One hypothesis states that creation is a process of variation and selection, analogous to biological evolution. The mind of a creative person spontaneously generates a large number of random combinations of ideas, and a few chosen combinations become expressed in behavior. An alternative hypothesis is that a creative person is able to override the constraining influence of past experiences and hence consider a wide range of actions and possibilities. The moment at which a previously unheeded but promising option comes to mind is often referred to as insight. A closely related hypothesis is that creative individuals are more able to break free from mental ruts—trains of thought that recur over and over again even though they do not lead to the desired goal or solution. It has also been suggested that people create by making analogies between current and past problems and situations, and by applying abstractions—cognitive schemas—acquired in one domain to another domain.

These process hypotheses are not mutually exclusive. Each has received support in research studies. Due to the separation within psychology of the cognitive and psychometric traditions, there is little or no interaction between process hypotheses and test development.

Relation to Imagery

There is widespread belief that highly creative individuals think holistically, in visual images, as opposed to the step-by-step process that supposedly characterizes logical thinking. Although consistent with often quoted autobiographical comments by Albert Einstein, Wolfgang Amadeus Mozart, F. A. Kekulé and others, systematic support for this belief is lacking. There is strong research support for a function for visual imagery in memory recall, but its relevance for creativity is unclear.

Relation to Knowledge

Cognitive and biographical studies have shown that creative problem solutions require thorough knowledge of the relevant domain and domain-specific strategies. For example, scientific discovery depends, in part, on knowing what the current theory predicts, plus the strategy of paying close attention to data that deviate from those predictions; creativity in other domains requires other strategies. It is possible that creativity is not a general ability or process, but that creative behaviors and products emerge when a competent and knowledgeable person is motivated to engage in a cumulative effort over a long period of time. If so, a person who is unusually creative in one domain of activity is not necessarily unusually creative in other domains.

Creativity and Education

It is not known to what extent an individual's ability to create can be enhanced. The popular press produces a steady stream of books that advocate particular techniques and training programs; most have not been evaluated, so it is not known whether they work. The small number of training techniques that have been evaluated systematically produce modest effects. It is possible that more effective training techniques exist but have yet to be invented. Most training programs implicitly assume that creativity is a general ability or process.

Although it is unclear whether the ability to create can be enhanced, there is consensus that the disposition to create can be suppressed. Creativity and discipline are not antithetical—creative individuals practice much and work hard—but extensive reliance on overly structured activities can thwart the impulse to create, with negative effects on students' well-being. Students with high ability will perform better than others in activities that require design, imagination, or invention, but participation in such activities encourages the disposition to create in students at any level of ability.

Creative individuals often elicit negative reactions from others by violating social norms and expectations. In a school setting, care should be taken to distinguish creative students from students who cause disturbances due to emotional or social problems. Creative students who find ways to engage others in their projects are likely to become outgoing and adopt leadership roles. Creative students who experience difficulties in this regard are likely to engage in individual projects. In short, high creativity is compatible with both social and individualistic life styles; either outcome is healthy.

There is widespread concern among educators in Western countries that the trend to define the goals of schooling in terms of standardized tests forces teachers to prioritize fact learning and analytical ability over creativity. Participation in creative activities is emphasized in schools that implement particular pedagogical theories, for example, the Montessori and Waldorf schools.

Broader View

Creativity is a historical force. Art and science transform people's ideas and worldviews, and technological innovation continuously transforms social practices. Toward the end of the twentieth century, the importance of innovation for economic production was widely recognized among business leaders.

See also: INTELLIGENCE, *subentry on* TRIARCHIC THEORY OF INTELLIGENCE; LEARNING THEORY, *subentries on* CONSTRUCTIVIST APPROACH, HISTORICAL OVERVIEW, SCHEMA THEORY.

BIBLIOGRAPHY

STERNBERG, ROBERT J., ed. 1999. *Handbook of Creativity.* Cambridge, Eng: Cambridge University Press.

STELLAN OHLSSON
TRINA C. KERSHAW

CUBBERLEY, ELLWOOD (1868–1941)

An influential educator in the field of educational administration, Ellwood Patterson Cubberley helped guide the teacher education curriculum in the early twentieth century through his edited textbook series. His account of educational history set the historiographical tone for the first half of the twentieth century.

Education and Career

Cubberley was born in 1868 in Antioch (later to be named Andrews), Indiana. He graduated from Indiana University in 1891 and showed special promise in science and mathematics. His ambition was to become a geologist, but teaching eventually overcame that early goal. Before graduation, he spent a year teaching in a tiny country school in Rock Hill, Indiana. After graduation he taught briefly at Ridgeville College (Ridgeville, Indiana), before moving to Vincennes University (Vincennes, Indiana), where he soon became president. During this period, he married his second cousin Erla Little.

In 1896 he moved to California and became superintendent of the San Diego Board of Education. There he battled local politicians over the appointment of qualified applicants.

In 1898 he left San Diego and took a severe pay cut to accept a teaching position with Stanford University and its fledgling two-person Department of Education (which would later become the School of Education). He would spend the remainder of his career there. On leave from Stanford, he received his Ph.D. from Columbia University in 1905 and was named full professor at Stanford in 1908. He assumed leadership of Stanford's School of Education in 1917 and proceeded to expand vastly the scope of its activities. Throughout his career, Cubberley remained deeply involved in shaping national policy on issues from teacher certification to textbooks. He retired in 1933.

Contribution

Cubberley was perhaps the most significant educational administrator of his day. At the outset of Cubberley's career, school administration was thought of as a set of general principles without any conception of theoretical or scientific plans. There were no formal textbooks from which to teach educational administration to students. Educational administrators had no place to learn better practices and, as such, learned solely from experience. Indeed, educational administration posts were often political plums requiring little, if any, formal training. Most universities lacked education departments.

In *Changing Concepts of Education* (1909), Cubberley laid the foundation for public schooling in America. He asserted that universal education was indispensable to democracy and was an appropriate exercise of state power. Cubberley refocused school policy to include not just teaching children but also to advance public welfare and democratic institutions. For educational policy to improve, Cubberley sought to free educational administration from technical ignorance and external political pressures. He advocated giving power to technically trained educators. He also urged improved teacher training.

In his landmark *Public School Administration* (1916, followed by second and third editions in 1929 and 1947), Cubberley called for increased social efficiency in schools. He extolled the use of tests and measurements as techniques to measure educational efficiency and to provide scientific accuracy to education. He analogized the educational process to industrial production, in that schools should strive to maximize efficiency and product. Tests and measurements could continually serve as efficiency indicators, providing a basis for reorganization, hiring and firing, and assessing student performance. He further advocated the reorganization of public schools and the appointment of experts as administrators.

Cubberley pioneered the use of the school survey as an instrument to improve education, in his reports on the Baltimore, Maryland; New York City; Oakland, California; Portland, Oregon; and Salt Lake City, Utah schools. In conducting surveys, he applied an integrated theory of organization, administration, and teaching, to assess the strengths and weaknesses of individual schools. He used the latest statistical and quantitative methods. His surveys were significant steps down a new road toward improving school functions.

Additionally, Cubberley edited a series of textbooks for Riverside Press that sold more than 3 million copies. This textbook series helped form education's knowledge base and included seminal works on such important concepts as I.Q. In his textbooks, he advocated autonomy for school administrators. Although school boards might set policy, they lacked expertise to run school systems and Cubberley believed they should give way to the administrator's expertise in day-to-day operations.

Cubberley's *Public Education in the United States* (1919), perhaps his greatest work, set the historiographical tone for educational history for more than forty years. Adopting an instrumentalist approach to education, Cubberley portrayed education as the main tool of America's progress. He saw the rise of universal public schooling as a triumph of democratic forces. Cubberley saw educational systems as continually improving, and he associated the rise and refinement of education with America's continued progress.

Cubberley's legacy has been decidedly mixed. Since his death in 1941, Cubberley's celebrationist historical account has been attacked, perhaps most memorably by Lawrence Cremin's *The Wonderful World of Ellwood Patterson Cubberley* (1965). Historiographically, some academicians have used Cubberley's methodology as a cautionary tale and termed his approach anachronistic and evangelistic. In a similar vein, Cubberley's administration stances have been attacked as sexist and autocratic. Regardless, Cubberley's historical account was a Promethean achievement, in light of the then-existing state of knowledge. And, without a doubt, Cubberley's views on empirical research in education and increased efficiency in public schools have remained dominant paradigms in contemporary public education.

See also: SUPERVISION OF INSTRUCTION; TEACHER EDUCATION.

BIBLIOGRAPHY

CREMIN, LAWRENCE. 1965. *The Wonderful World of Ellwood Patterson Cubberley.* New York: Columbia University.

CUBBERLEY, ELLWOOD P. 1909. *Changing Conceptions of Education.* Cambridge, MA: Riverside Press.

CUBBERLEY, ELLWOOD P. 1919. *Public Education in the United States.* Cambridge, MA: Riverside Press.

CUBBERLEY, ELLWOOD P. 1920. *The History of Education.* Cambridge, MA: Riverside Press.

CUBBERLEY, ELLWOOD P. 1929. *Public School Administration.* Cambridge, MA: Riverside Press.

NEWMAN, JOSEPH W. 1992. "Ellwood P. Cubberley: Architect of the New Educational Hierarchy." *Teaching Education* 4(2):161–168.

SEARS, JESSE B., and HENDERSON, ADIN D. 1957. *Cubberley of Stanford and His Contribution to American Education.* Stanford, CA: Stanford University Press.

J. EAGLE SHUTT

CULTURE AND ETHNICITY

See: AFFIRMATIVE ACTION COMPLIANCE IN HIGHER EDUCATION; AFRICAN-AMERICAN STUDIES; BILINGUALISM, SECOND LANGUAGE LEARNING, AND ENGLISH AS A SECOND LANGUAGE; INDIVIDUAL DIFFERENCES, *subentry on* ETHNICITY; LANGUAGE MINORITY STUDENTS; LITERACY AND CULTURE; MULTICULTURALISM IN HIGHER EDUCATION; RACE, ETHNICITY, AND CULTURE.

CURRICULUM, HIGHER EDUCATION

INNOVATIONS IN THE UNDERGRADUATE CURRICULUM
Deborah DeZure
NATIONAL REPORTS ON THE UNDERGRADUATE CURRICULUM
Lisa R. Lattuca
TRADITIONAL AND CONTEMPORARY PERSPECTIVES
Kathryn Dey Huggett
Nora C. Smith
Clifton F. Conrad

INNOVATIONS IN THE UNDERGRADUATE CURRICULUM

During the last decade of the twentieth century, significant changes occurred in American higher education generally and in the undergraduate curriculum in particular. These changes were propelled by several developments. Together they provided the momentum to enable higher education to make unprecedented strides. Educational leaders debate whether these changes are primarily additive and limited to small scale programmatic innovations or truly transformative for institutions and higher education. Nonetheless, there is widespread agreement that the academy and the undergraduate curriculum have evolved in significant ways.

Defining Curriculum

An undergraduate curriculum is a formal academic plan for the learning experiences of students in pursuit of a college degree. The term *curriculum,* broadly defined, includes goals for student learning (skills, knowledge and attitudes); content (the subject matter in which learning experiences are embedded); sequence (the order in which concepts are presented); learners; instructional methods and activities; instructional resources (materials and settings); evaluation (methods used to assess student learning as a result of these experiences); and adjustments to teaching and learning processes, based on experience and evaluation. Although the term *curriculum* is variably used, this definition is sufficiently inclusive and dynamic to account for the many innovations in the undergraduate curriculum that involve instructional methods, sequencing, and assessments as well as instructional goals and content, all of which have been implemented in order to improve learning.

Forces for Change

During the 1980s critiques of American higher education were increasing in frequency and stridence. Reports such as *A Nation at Risk* (1983) and *Integrity in the College Curriculum* (1985) underscored the need for reform, citing a lack of accessibility, quality, and coherence. Business and industry leaders decried the inadequate skills of graduates who were unable to problem-solve, communicate through writing and speaking, engage in ethical decision-making, work in teams, and interact effectively with diverse others. Citizen groups noted the disengagement from civic life of recent graduates, citing low voter participation.

Calls for increased accountability came from outside the academy, including government agencies, state boards, regional and professional accrediting bodies, and professional associations. Their concerns resulted in mandates for assessment of student learning outcomes and the growth of the assessment movement in higher education. Against a backdrop of fiscal constraints, competition for students from for-profit educational vendors was considered a threat to colleges and universities, further fueling the impetus for reform.

Demographic changes led to increased participation by students with varied academic preparation, declining student enrollments, and falling retention rates. The pool of students pursuing science and math was shrinking, and women and minorities were underrepresented. Scientific literacy was weak among non-science graduates, posing a threat to the economy as well as the future of scientific and technological endeavors.

Concurrently, there were great strides in research on effective college teaching and learning, with shifts in emphasis from what teachers *do* to what students *learn.* New conceptions of learning that emphasize the social construction of knowledge gained advocates. New interdisciplinary fields were burgeoning (e.g., women's studies, ethnic studies). The publication of Ernest Boyer's *Scholarship Reconsidered* in 1990 promoted the re-conceptualization of faculty roles and rewards, giving legitimacy to the scholarship of teaching. From the mid-1980s, faculty development emerged as a field of practice to assist faculty in their instructional efforts; during this time, numerous institutions founded teaching and learning centers. Last but not least, new technologies had implications for new fields of study and their use in instruction and research. Taken together, these forces enabled significant reforms to develop and proliferate in higher education.

Trends

Many of the curricular innovations and reforms during the last decade of the twentieth century reflect three shifts in emphasis: (1) from learning goals that focus on mastery of content and content coverage to demonstration of broad competencies; (2) from learning in disparate disciplines to integrative learning experiences across the curriculum; and (3) from changes in subject matter as the primary means to improve learning to innovations in instructional methods and assessments as integral to curricular reforms. Diversity and global competency have emerged as major undergraduate curriculum issues, as well.

From content to competencies. In the first years of the twenty-first century, the undergraduate curriculum continued to consist of general education or liberal studies (averaging 37.6% of bachelor of arts degree requirements), a major specialization, minors, and electives. The rationale for this configuration has been to ensure breadth through distribution requirements and depth through the major. At the structural level, this model is holding fast at most institutions. What has changed are the goals for learning—from emphasis on knowledge of disciplinary facts and concepts (what students know) to broadly defined competencies (what students are able to do with what they know) to ensure that graduates have the skills needed by citizens in the twenty-first century.

The expanding list of proficiencies commonly identified by colleges and universities include: critical thinking and problem-solving; multiple modes of inquiry in the natural sciences and mathematics, social sciences, humanities, and arts; communication skills, including writing, speaking, and listening; technology and information literacy; sensitivity to diversity, including multicultural and intercultural competencies for participation in a pluralistic democracy; civic, global, and environmental responsibility and engagement; interpersonal skills, including teamwork and collaboration; self-awareness; moral and ethical reasoning, and integration of knowledge from diverse sources.

Integration across the curriculum. The majority of colleges and universities indicate that general education is a high priority among administrators and faculty, and their institutions are actively engaged in reviewing their general education programs. Given the difficulty of learning all the aforementioned competencies within a general education program, many institutions are blurring the boundaries between general education and the major by infusing these competencies throughout the collegiate experience. This can be seen in the adoption of upper division writing requirements and writing-intensive courses in the major; integrative capstone courses that require collaborative teamwork and projects; courses in the major that emphasize ethics and civic engagement; and the integration of technology, information literacy, and multiculturalism throughout the curriculum.

Diversity learning. Diversity learning is a high priority, including multicultural and intercultural understanding. Although variably defined, *diversity learning* often refers to sensitivity to difference, including race, gender, socioeconomic class, ethnicity, religion, sexual orientation, and disability. In Debra Humphreys's report of a national survey in 2000, 62 percent of reporting institutions had a diversity course requirement or were developing one; among these, 58 percent require one course and 42 percent require two or more courses. In the most common model among schools with requirements (68%), students select a course on diversity from a list of options. Increasingly multicultural perspectives are also infused throughout the curriculum, particularly in the humanities and social sciences.

Internationalization. Global competencies are often identified as a valued goal of liberal learning, but currently few American students develop intercultural competence during college. Four elements commonly associated with internationalization include foreign language study, study abroad, global studies, and the presence of international students. Foreign language enrollments comprise 8 percent of total enrollments, concentrated in a few languages (55% Spanish, 17% French, 8% German, 6% Asian languages, and less than 2% Middle Eastern). This is in sharp contrast to other developed countries where language study is emphasized.

Participation in study abroad is equally limited. Despite indications from incoming first-year students that they hope to study abroad, only 3 percent of American students study abroad, and increasingly they select programs shorter than a semester. Although global and intercultural courses are available, fewer than 7 percent of college students meet even basic standards for global competence. International students accounted for 3 percent of undergraduates and 11 percent of graduate students in the United States in 1998–1999. The United States enrolls more international students than any other country—most of them from Asia. American higher education is likely to increase its emphasis on global competencies in order to better prepare students to participate in global issues during the twenty-first century.

Curriculum Coherence and Integration

In response to mounting criticism that the undergraduate curriculum is fragmented, burdened with too many isolated bits of information, and lacking coherence, institutions have developed strategies and structures to help students integrate the disparate elements of their college experiences. One strategy has been to clarify, tighten, and sequence requirements so they provide greater coherence. Requirements and prerequisites increased in the 1990s, reversing the trend toward reduced requirements during the 1970s and 1980s. A second strategy has been to provide educational experiences calibrated to the developmental learning needs of students at different stages of their collegiate lives. The most prevalent model is the first-year program, often comprising orientation programs, orientation courses, cocurricular offerings, developmental courses for underprepared students, access to academic support services, first-year seminars, courses of which many are interdisciplinary, and learning communities.

The goal of these offerings is to ease the transition from high school to college, to teach skills and attitudes to enable students to succeed in college, and to improve retention, particularly among at-risk students. K–16 collaborations also support the transition between high school and college by promoting curricular discussions between K–12 teachers and college faculty and by providing collegiate experiences to motivate younger students.

To ease the transition from college to the work world, institutions offer senior seminars and capstone experiences. These are designed to help students integrate intentionally what they have learned in their major specialization and to relate those insights to other disciplinary perspectives, the community, or the work world. Other variants include experiences designed for sophomores and keystone courses that mark the mid-collegiate transition from general education into the major, providing a supportive environment to assess student readiness to move forward.

Learning communities. Learning communities comprise curricular models that link courses or course work to reinforce their curricular connections, maximize opportunities for students to collaborate with each other and their instructors, and provide interpersonal support. Although often designed for first-year students, learning communities now appear throughout the curriculum. They are designed to build communities of learners, and in many cases, provide the structure to promote interdisciplinary study and integration.

Interdisciplinarity. Interdisciplinary studies, which are considered a major trend in teaching and research, have grown exponentially since 1990. Two widespread innovations are first-year interdisciplinary seminars and courses based on themes or problems, many of which are team-taught. Courses in new interdisciplinary fields are flourishing (e.g., neuroscience, bioengineering) as are courses in multiculturalism, often spurred by diversity requirements. Courses that apply ethics and environmentalism to professional areas, such as undergraduate nursing and engineering, reflect accreditation mandates. In addition, faculty across the disciplines use innovative pedagogies and course structures that promote integration and interdisciplinary perspectives, such as academic-service learning, multidisciplinary group work, internships, fieldwork, and study abroad.

Innovative Instructional Methods

Innovative instructional methods are proliferating in higher education and are integral to curricular reform efforts. Supported by research on how students learn, instructional innovations emphasize active and experiential learning (i.e., learning by doing); inquiry, discovery, and problem-based learning; collaborative and cooperative learning in groups; writing to learn; undergraduate research; academic-service learning; and instructional technology. Although lecture and small group discussions are still the dominant instructional methods, active and collaborative learning is now commonplace in higher education. As reported by George D. Kuh in 2001, 90 percent of seniors polled in a national survey indicated that they had participated in group work in class during college.

Reform efforts in science, math, engineering, and technology (SMET) characterize the integral relationship between innovations in instructional methods and curricular reform in the last decade. In Workshop Physics, for example, lecture and lab sections are integrated. All class instruction is done through hands-on experiments and demonstrations that rely heavily on microcomputers to assist in data analysis. Students work in cooperative learning groups based on the principles of discovery-based learning, emphasizing problem-solving. Similarly, in Calculus Reform, a curricular innovation with roots in the 1980s, students work in groups to problem-solve, often using story problems that relate to the real world, geometric visualization, and instructional technology. A National Science Foundation study published in 1998 indicates that among the most important innovations in SMET since 1990 are (1) Calculus Reform; (2) undergraduate research in which students work on research projects with faculty; and (3) collaborations among institutions, business, industry, and research labs to promote student learning.

Assessment of Student Learning

Widespread efforts to assess student learning are also having an impact on the undergraduate curriculum. While multiple choice tests are still widely used, new evaluation methods provide opportunities to assess and to promote higher-order critical thinking skills and the competencies now valued in higher education. Methods include self-assessments, student portfolios, student journals, case studies, simulations, poster sessions, group projects, and technology-based innovations, among others—all of which reflect the shifts from content to competencies, from fragmentation to integration, and from passive to active modes of learning. Increasingly, assessment results are being used to improve programs and promote the ongoing process of curricular reform.

See also: ACADEMIC CALENDARS; ACADEMIC MAJOR, THE; CAPSTONE COURSES IN HIGHER EDUCATION; COLLEGE SEMINARS FOR FIRST-YEAR STUDENTS; GENERAL EDUCATION IN HIGHER EDUCATION.

BIBLIOGRAPHY

ASSOCIATION OF AMERICAN COLLEGES. 1985. *Integrity in the College Curriculum: A Report to the Academic Community.* Washington, DC: Association of American Colleges.

ASSOCIATION OF AMERICAN COLLEGES. 1990. *The Challenge of Connecting Learning.* Washington, DC: Association of American Colleges.

BOYER COMMISSION ON EDUCATING UNDERGRADUATES IN THE RESEARCH UNIVERSITY. 1998. *Reinventing Undergraduate Education: A Blueprint for America's Research Universities.* Palo Alto, CA: Carnegie Foundation for the Advancement of Teaching.

BOYER, ERNEST. 1990. *Scholarship Reconsidered: Priorities of the Professoriate.* Princeton, NJ: Carnegie Foundation for the Advancement of Teaching.

DAVIS, JAMES R. 1995. *Interdisciplinary Courses and Team Teaching: New Arrangements for Learning.* Phoenix, AZ: American Council on Education/ Oryx Press.

DEZURE, DEBORAH, ed. 2000. *Learning from CHANGE: Landmarks in Teaching and Learning in Higher Education from CHANGE Magazine (1969–1999).* Sterling, VA: Stylus Publications.

EDWARDS, ALAN. 1996. *Interdisciplinary Undergraduate Programs: A Directory,* 2nd edition. Acton, MA: Copley.

GAFF, JERRY G. 1999. *General Education: The Changing Agenda.* Washington, DC: Association of American Colleges and Universities.

GAFF, JERRY G.; RATCLIFF, JAMES L.; and ASSOCIATES. 1997. *Handbook of the Undergraduate Curriculum: A Comprehensive Guide to Purposes, Structures, Practices and Change.* San Francisco: Jossey-Bass.

HAYWARD, FRED M. 2000. *Internationalization of U.S. Higher Education: Preliminary Status Report 2000.* Washington, DC: American Council on Education.

KLEIN, JULIE THOMPSON. 1999. *Mapping Interdisciplinary Studies.* Washington, DC: Association of American Colleges and Universities.

KUH, GEORGE D. 2001. "Assessing What Really Matters to Student Learning: Inside the National Survey of Student Engagement." *Change* 33:10–17, 66.

NATIONAL COMMISSION ON EXCELLENCE IN EDUCATION. 1983. *A Nation at Risk: The Imperative for Educational Reform.* Washington, DC: U.S. Government Printing Office.

NATIONAL SCIENCE FOUNDATION. 1998. *Shaping the Future: Volume II: Perspectives on Undergraduate Education in Science, Mathematics, Engineering and Technology.* NSF 98-128. Washington, DC: National Science Foundation.

RATCLIFF, JAMES L., et al. 2001. *The Status of General Education in the Year 2000: Summary of a National Survey.* Washington, DC: Association of American Colleges and Universities.

SCHNEIDER, CAROL GEARY, and SHOENBERG, ROBERT. 1998. *Contemporary Understandings of Liberal Education.* Washington, DC: Association of American Colleges and Universities.

STARK, JOAN S. and LATTUCA, LISA R. 1997. *Shaping the College Curriculum: Academic Plans in Action.* Boston: Allyn and Bacon.

INTERNET RESOURCES

EVERGREEN STATE COLLEGE. "Learning Community Commons." *National Learning Communities Project.* Washington Center for Improving the Quality of Undergraduate Education. <www.evergreen.edu/washcenter/natlc/home. asp>.

GREEN, KENNETH C. 2000. "The 2000 National Survey of Information Technology in U.S. Higher Education." *The Campus Computing Project.* <www.campuscomputing.net/summaries/ 2000>.

HUMPHREYS, DEBRA. Fall 2000. "National Survey Finds Diversity Requirements Common Around the Country." *Diversity Digest.* <www.diversityweb.org/Digest/f00/survey. html>.

KEZAR, ADRIANNA J. 2000. *Higher Education Trends (1997–1999): Curriculum.* Eric Clearinghouse on Higher Education. <http://eriche.org/trends/curriculum.html>.

NATIONAL CENTER FOR POSTSECONDARY IMPROVEMENT AT THE UNIVERSITY OF MICHIGAN. 2001. "Reform and Innovation in Teaching, Learning, and Assessment." <www.umich.edu/~ncpi/53/describe.html>.

PROJECT KALEIDOSCOPE. 2001. "What Works." <www.pkal.org/whatwork.html>.

DEBORAH DEZURE

NATIONAL REPORTS ON THE UNDERGRADUATE CURRICULUM

During the 1980s and 1990s critics and advocates of U.S. higher education issued numerous reports calling for reform of the college and university curriculum. These reports—from individuals, panels of experts assembled by federal agencies, educational lobbying organizations, and private foundations—responded to changes in postsecondary curricula implemented in the 1960s as the baby boom generation swelled college and university enrollments; and as the civil rights movement, the women's liberation movement, and Vietnam War protests led to demands for more relevant and student-centered curricula.

As the era of economic prosperity that fueled the educational innovations of the 1960s ended, a number of social and political forces converged to produce a climate conducive to calls for reform of the undergraduate curriculum. Then the economic recession of the 1970s focused the attention of businesses, students, and parents on employment prospects for graduates and the marketability of a college degree. A downward trend in college admission test scores and related concerns about a decline in U.S. economic competitiveness resulted in calls for higher educational standards at elementary, secondary, and postsecondary levels. At the same time, a Republican administration decentralized responsibility for educational expenditures in an effort to hold the states more accountable for educational improvements, and legislators committed to cost-effectiveness trimmed allocations to higher education.

In 1983 concerns about the widespread public perception of problems in the U.S. educational sys-

tem were the impetus for the widely read report, *A Nation At Risk* (1983), issued by the National Commission on Excellence in Education. In 1981 Terrel Bell, then U.S. Secretary of Education, directed the commission to examine the quality of education in the United States. Although the commission focused primarily on high school education, selective attention was also paid to higher education, elementary education, and vocational and technical programs. The commission's findings regarding decreases in high school students' preparation for college, declines in standardized college admission test scores and college selectivity, and general concerns about the quality of elementary and secondary education raised concerns about the impact of these problems on undergraduate education. Secretary Bell, and his successor, William Bennett, encouraged further scrutiny of college and university education and prompted calls for accountability at the postsecondary level.

An Emphasis on Curricular Content

The reports on higher education of the 1980s and 1990s often stressed the need to include specific courses or course content in postsecondary curricula, which had recently experienced a period of experimentation. Acceding to student demands for more choice of majors and elective courses, many colleges and universities in the 1960s and 1970s had relaxed requirements for the baccalaureate degree by reducing the number of required courses needed for graduation and permitting more elective courses—or by increasing the number and kinds of courses that would fulfill the requirements. Additional changes had occurred in major concentration programs, allowing students in many institutions to select from an array of courses to fulfill basic requirements or create majors based on their personal interests. Advances in knowledge and the creation of new disciplines, fields of study, and specializations also contributed significantly to changes in the college curriculum. Increased course options, increasing faculty commitment to advancing their disciplines, and growing departmental autonomy led to curricular fragmentation, while the combination of increased disciplinary specialization and student desire for degrees that would lead directly to employment created conditions conducive to the growth and diversification of postsecondary curricula.

In 1984 the National Endowment for the Humanities (NEH), under the leadership of William

Bennett, issued one of the first reports examining higher education. In *To Reclaim a Legacy: A Report on the Humanities in Higher Education,* Bennett, a former humanities professor, maintained that colleges and universities had lost a clear sense of the purpose of education. Defining the primary goal of education as learning about civilization and culture, he contended that students should study Western literature, history, and culture to obtain an understanding of the origins and development of their civilization and culture, as well as a sense of major trends in art, religion, politics, and society. Few college graduates, he argued, received adequate instruction in their own culture because faculty had succumbed to pressure for enrollments and to intellectual relativism, rather than assume "intellectual authority" for what students should learn (p. 20). Bennett also criticized faculty who taught the humanities in a "tendentious, ideological manner" that overtly valued or rejected particular social stances (p. 16). According to advocates of the Western canon such as Bennett, the push for student choice and relevance in the curriculum had backfired, leaving U.S. democracy and society in disarray.

Bennett believed that knowledge of Western civilization and culture should be fostered through careful reading of masterworks of English, American, and European literature. He also recommended that students become familiar with the history, literature, religion, and philosophy of at least one non-Western culture or civilization. Five years later, Bennett's successor at NEH, Lynne Cheney, issued *50 Hours: A Core Curriculum for College Students.* Arguing, as did Bennett, that a common core curriculum was essential to a coherent education, Cheney proposed a required curriculum that stressed the study of Western civilization, but also included the study of additional civilizations, foreign languages, science, mathematics, and social sciences.

From Curricular Content to Educational Processes

At the same time that Bennett issued *To Reclaim a Legacy,* a study group convened by the National Institute of Education (NIE) issued *Involvement in Learning: Realizing the Potential of American Higher Education* (1984). Rather than prescribe the content of the curriculum, the NIE group recommended that institutions emphasize three conditions of excellence in undergraduate education: (1) student involvement, which would result in improvements in stu-

dents' knowledge, skills, capacity, and attitudes; (2) high expectations, which must be clearly established and communicated to students; and (3) assessment and feedback, defined as the efficient and cost-effective use of student and institutional resources to realize improvements.

Whereas the reports of Bennett and Cheney emphasized improvements in programs of study and the quality of teaching, *Involvement in Learning* focused primarily on students and their learning. The report urged faculty and chief academic officers to agree upon and disseminate a statement of the knowledge, skills, and attitudes required for graduation, and to systematically assess whether expectations for student learning were met. It contended that individualized and integrated education, learning communities, and the use of active rather than passive instructional processes would foster greater student involvement. Finally, *Involvement in Learning* called upon undergraduate colleges to expand liberal education requirements to two full years of study, and urged graduate schools to require applicants to have a broad undergraduate education to balance their specialized training.

Higher education associations and other concerned parties issued responses to these federally sponsored calls for reform. All accepted the need to improve liberal or general education and decried the perceived erosion of curricular quality. In 1985 the Association of American Colleges (AAC) published *Integrity in the College Curriculum: A Report to the Academic Community,* which described the work of the AAC Project on Redefining the Meaning and Purpose of a Baccalaureate Degree. The AAC committee responsible for the report argued that contemporary students were less well prepared for collegiate study, were more vocationally oriented, and were more materialistic than those in previous generations. The baccalaureate credential, the committee argued, had become more important than the course of study, and colleges and universities had surrendered to the demands of the marketplace rather than developing creative approaches to a changing environment. The report also chided faculty for abdicating their corporate responsibility for the undergraduate curriculum.

In *Integrity in the College Curriculum,* the AAC claimed that faculty were "more confident about the length of a college education than its content and purpose" and that the major in most institutions was little more than "a gathering of courses taken in one department" (p. 2). The committee identified nine content-related experiences that constitute a "minimum required curriculum." This set of experiences, intended to provide students with the general knowledge, behaviors, and attitudes needed by citizens and workers in the contemporary world, consists of: (1) inquiry (abstract logical thinking and critical analysis); (2) literacy (writing, reading, speaking, and listening skills); (3) understanding numerical data; (4) historical consciousness; (5) the sciences; (6) values; (7) art; (8) international and multicultural experiences; and (9) study in depth (one's major specialization). The AAC urged faculty to take responsibility for designing educational experiences that provided students with a "vision of the good life, a life of responsible citizenship and human decency" (p. 6). The committee also recommended that educational programs help students see the connections among domains of knowledge as well as connections among areas of study, life, and work.

The critique and recommendations that Ernest Boyer, president of the Carnegie Foundation, offered in College: The Undergraduate Experience in America (1987), greatly resemble those of Integrity in the College Curriculum. Boyer noted eight points of tension in the curriculum, including the curriculum itself, the conditions of teaching and learning, and the priorities of the faculty. Boyer argued that vocationalism, intense departmentalism among faculty, the fragmentation of knowledge, and the loss of cultural commonalities and coherence in general, had weakened the undergraduate curriculum.

Boyer asserted that colleges should develop students' proficiencies in reading, writing, and composition, as well as their capacity for social and civic engagement. He recommended a set of general education objectives that emphasized seven areas of inquiry: language, art, heritage, society, nature, ecology, work, and identity. Boyer urged educators to stress the connections among these discipline-driven areas of inquiry, to relate knowledge to life experiences, and to emphasize the application of knowledge beyond college. He discussed the undergraduate major as well, arguing that such specializations should have both an identifiable intellectual content and the capacity to enlarge students' visions of the world. Boyer believed that a coherent educational experience would help students develop as individuals, and would also foster a community of learners.

An emphasis on the quality of student learning experiences in reports issued by AAC, the Carnegie Foundation, and others replaced the focus on programs and good teaching common to the NEH reports. In College, Boyer reasserted the NIE's call for greater student involvement in learning and urged faculty to incorporate active learning techniques in their classrooms. Both Boyer and the AAC included discussions, small group and collaborative projects, out-of-class assignments, and undergraduate research among the active learning strategies that faculty should employ to engage students in the educational process and to convince them to take greater responsibility for their learning. In 1988, in A New Vitality for General Education, a second AAC task force summarized the increasingly shared sentiment that what was taught was likely less important than how it was taught.

The task force responsible for A New Vitality asked faculty to engage students not only as active learners, but to see them as co-inquirers who must become reflective about their own learning. The task group noted that rather than simply suggesting useful teaching techniques, it was redefining teaching: "We propose approaches that make it possible for us to find out not just what our students learn but how they learn it and what motivates them. Informing students about the purposes of our courses and program, obtaining sophisticated feedback from them, and collaborating with them are indispensable activities under this expanded definition of teaching" (p. 39).

Continuing Scrutiny of General Education and the Major

Where Integrity spotlighted the undergraduate course of study in general, A New Vitality examined the rationale, purposes, and scope of general education, as well as issues of implementation. The report eschewed both normative proposals like those of the NEH and the typical distribution requirement system that "sidestepped" important debates about the content of the curriculum and instead offered "a conglomerate of courses conceived along specialized disciplinary lines" (p. 48). A New Vitality argued that general education programs should develop specific competencies and abilities in students, and that these competencies (e.g., critical thinking, problem solving, inquiry in writing) must be grounded in content. The question of what content was suitable for all students, the task group acknowledged, was complicated by the diversity of the student body, which differed by "age, race, sex, social and economic background, abilities, attitudes, ambitions, and goals" (p. 6).

The task group proposed a broad plan for improving general education that included integrating general education throughout the undergraduate years, improving student advising, involving commuter students and improving residential life on campuses, expanding cross-cultural experiences, creating cross-disciplinary seminars for faculty and students, and organizing campus think tanks to explore the issues of undergraduate and general education. The report also called for student involvement in the assessment of general education, and of administrative support for creative efforts toward improvement of general education programs.

The AAC issued a second report on general education in 1994, titled *Strong Foundations: Twelve Principles for Effective General Education Programs.* This report was based on the experiences of seventeen institutions that had revised their general education curricula. Claiming that flawed conceptions of general education as breadth requirements that merely exposed students to different fields of study needed to be replaced with a new understanding, the report outlined twelve principles focused on communicating the value of general education and fostering support for it among students, faculty, and administration.

Concerns about course requirements and the proper content of general education curricula, however, continued. In 1996 the National Association of Scholars (NAS), a group known for conservative educational ideals, published *The Dissolution of General Education: 1914–1993.* Based on a study of fifty elite colleges and universities, the report claimed that since 1964, many of the required basic survey courses that taught students about the historical, cultural, political, and scientific foundations of their society had been purged from the curriculum. Course requirements in foreign languages, the sciences, mathematics, history, literature, and philosophy were reduced or virtually eliminated, and students now chose courses from broad and formless distribution categories. As a result of decreases in general education requirements, students were not learning a common core of knowledge.

Another AAC task force focused specifically on the undergraduate major (or study-in-depth). *The*

Challenge of Connecting Learning (1991) presented the results of a three-year review of liberal arts and sciences majors in the context of liberal education. Members of the AAC national advisory committee developed a set of organizing principles that guided the work of disciplinary task forces appointed by twelve participating learned societies. In its charge to the task forces, the committee asked the learned societies to address (1) faculty responsibility for shaping major programs; (2) organizing principles for study-in-depth; (3) processes for integrating learning; and (4) relations between the major and other parts of the undergraduate curriculum. Students, the committee contended, had a right to expect coherent and integrated curricula that addressed and encouraged relationships among subjects of study. *Integrity in the College Curriculum* urged faculty to help students develop critical perspectives on what they studied and to aid them in connecting what they learned to their lives and to the world of work. Finally, the committee appealed to faculty to create more inclusive communities of learners by reducing barriers to underrepresented students. Abridged reports of the twelve individual task forces were published in *Reports from the Fields* (1991).

In 1988 a report of the Professional Preparation Network, *Strengthening the Ties That Bind: Integrating Undergraduate Liberal and Professional Study,* argued that educators could use different plans to achieve similar purposes. A national task force of instructors from liberal arts and professional fields identified ten student outcomes that were common to both professional and liberal arts education, as well as specific outcomes unique to either type of program. The authors hoped that recognition of common purposes might ease tension in the debate between liberal and professional education and provide opportunities to develop proposals for integration.

General Commentaries on the State of Higher Education

A few reports of this era examined higher education in general rather than the undergraduate curriculum specifically, and these reports often included some recommendations for curricular reform. A 1985 Carnegie Foundation Special Report, *Higher Education and the American Resurgence,* argued that education was essential to the advancement of key national interests. To ensure political, economic, and social health and progress, higher education must produce individuals who can think creatively and act with conviction and concern. A coherent general education program would educate students for civic responsibility. To develop graduates who would think creatively and act responsibly, the report advocated active learning in the classroom and experiences in public service.

In *To Secure the Blessings of Liberty* (1986), the National Commission on the Role and Future of State Colleges and Universities expressed similar concerns about a constellation of social, political, economic, and educational conditions. According to this report, high dropout rates, poor achievement of underrepresented minority students, adult illiteracy, and the growth of the U.S. underclass jeopardized American society. Thus, the report recommended the integration of experiential and service learning into the undergraduate curriculum in order to expand knowledge about the workplace, cultivate a commitment to the public good, develop students' international perspectives and communications skills through the study of foreign languages and cultures, and improve graduates' abilities to understand science and technology so they could contribute knowledgeably to public discussions. The commission also urged state institutions to provide remedial education.

In 1986 the Education Commission of the States, in an attempt to identify how the states might effectively support improvements in postsecondary education, published *Transforming the State Role in Undergraduate Education: Time for a Different View.* Noting the challenges facing higher education (including student preparation for a changing society and workforce, diversity, and student involvement), the report recommended student assessment at all levels. The National Governors Association, in its 1986 report, *Time for Results,* also considered assessment a key to improving undergraduate education, arguing that assessment results should not only be used for improvement but also shared with the public. The recommendations on assessment in *To Secure the Blessings of Liberty* were more cautious, with the authors advising that assessment be used primarily to enhance program quality rather than as a means to ensure accountability.

In January 1993 four leading private foundations convened a working group to examine the question of what society needed from higher education. The resulting report, *An American Imperative: Higher Expectations for Higher Education,* echoed concerns about student dropout rates, low educational standards, and credentialing: "The simple fact is that some faculties and institutions certify for graduation too many students who cannot read and write very well, too many whose intellectual depth and breadth are unimpressive, and too many whose skills are inadequate in the face of the demands of contemporary life" (Wingspread Group on Higher Education, p. 1). The report challenged higher education institutions to model the values they taught, to offer students' educations opportunities to experience and reflect on their society, and to include moral and spiritual development among their goals. Furthermore, institutions needed to recommit themselves to student learning by setting higher expectations for learning and by effectively helping students to meet those expectations. Finally, the report urged institutions to align education with the personal, civic, and workplace needs of the twenty-first century. Many of the specific recommendations of the report focused on setting, communicating, and assessing goals and expectations.

The higher education community has responded in different ways to these various reports. Some colleges and universities have used the reports to stimulate discussion about the curriculum on their campuses, while a number of campuses have revised their major and general education programs. It is unclear, however, which of these actions were directly attributable to the calls for reform. The reports also had their critics. Feminists and pluralists disagreed with the NEH recommendations for assuming that a canon of works that all students should study could be identified, and for insisting on a Western humanities curriculum that excluded ideas from individuals of different classes, ethnicities, nationalities, faiths, and gender. Others challenged the ideas that students should passively accept tradition and that liberal education truly served society. For example, Daniel Rossides (1987) claimed that liberal education masked a conservative social agenda focused on preserving the self-interest and power of social elites. According to Rossides, the humanities were no longer relevant because the world they interpreted had disappeared.

See also: ACADEMIC MAJOR, THE; CURRICULUM, HIGHER EDUCATION, *subentry on* TRADITIONAL AND CONTEMPORARY PERSPECTIVES; GENERAL EDUCATION IN HIGHER EDUCATION.

BIBLIOGRAPHY

AMERICAN ASSOCIATION OF STATE COLLEGES AND UNIVERSITIES. 1986. *To Secure the Blessings of Liberty: Report of the National Commission on the Role and Future of State Colleges and Universities.* Washington, DC: American Association of State Colleges and Universities.

ASSOCIATION OF AMERICAN COLLEGES. 1985. *Integrity in the College Curriculum: A Report to the Academic Community.* Washington, DC: Association of American Colleges.

ASSOCIATION OF AMERICAN COLLEGES. 1988. *A New Vitality in General Education.* Washington, DC: Association of American Colleges.

ASSOCIATION OF AMERICAN COLLEGES. 1991. *The Challenge of Connected Learning.* Washington, DC: Association of American Colleges.

ASSOCIATION OF AMERICAN COLLEGES. 1991. *Reports from the Fields.* Washington, DC: Association of American Colleges.

ASSOCIATION OF AMERICAN COLLEGES. 1994. *Strong Foundations: Twelve Principles for Effective General Education Programs.* Washington, DC: Association of American Colleges.

BENNETT, WILLIAM J. 1984 *To Reclaim a Legacy: A Report on the Humanities in Higher Education.* Washington, DC: National Endowment for the Humanities.

BOYER, ERNEST L. 1987. *College: The Undergraduate Experience in America.* New York: Harper and Row.

CHENEY, LYNNE. 1989. *50 Hours: A Core Curriculum for College Students.* Washington, DC: National Endowment for the Humanities.

EDUCATION COMMISSION OF THE STATES. 1986. *Transforming the State Role in Undergraduate Education: Time for a Different View.* Denver, CO: Education Commission of the States.

EL-KHAWAS, ELAINE. 1992. *Campus Trends, 1992.* Washington, DC: American Council on Education.

NATIONAL ASSOCIATION OF SCHOLARS. 1996. *The Dissolution of General Education: 1914–1993.* Princeton, NJ: National Association of Scholars.

NATIONAL COMMISSION ON EXCELLENCE IN EDUCATION. 1983. *A Nation at Risk: The Imperative for Educational Reform.* Washington, DC: U.S. Government Printing Office.

NATIONAL GOVERNORS ASSOCIATION. 1986. *Time for Results: The Governors' 1991 Report on Education.* Washington, DC: Center for Policy Research and Analysis.

NATIONAL INSTITUTE OF EDUCATION. 1984. *Involvement in Learning: Realizing the Potential of American Higher Education.* Washington, DC: U.S. Government Printing Office.

NEWMAN, FRANK. 1985. *Higher Education and the American Resurgence.* Princeton: Carnegie Foundation for the Advancement of Teaching.

ROSSIDES, DANIEL. 1987. "Knee-Jerk Formalism: The Higher Education Reports." *Journal of Higher Education* 58(4):404–429.

STARK, JOAN S., and LOWTHER, MALCOLM A. 1988. *Strengthening the Ties That Bind: Integrating Undergraduate Liberal and Professional Study.* Ann Arbor: University of Michigan, Professional Preparation Network.

WINGSPREAD GROUP ON HIGHER EDUCATION. 1993. *An American Imperative: Higher Expectations for Higher Education.* Racine, WI: The Johnson Foundation.

LISA R. LATTUCA

TRADITIONAL AND CONTEMPORARY PERSPECTIVES

The term *curriculum* has been associated with academic study and training in higher education since its appearance in vernacular English in the sixteenth century. At several points in its history, the term not only defined an identifiable course or plan of study in a university context, it also referred to the corollary body of scholars engaged in that coursework. As such, curricula refer to both an individual and collective learning experience. In common terminology, a curriculum vitae (literally, the course of one's life) is the accepted form of an academic resume, a brief account of a scholar's education and career.

In the United States, the curriculum designated the form and content of baccalaureate experience in early American colleges beginning with Harvard College in 1636. Because the term lent itself readily to documents in both English and Latin, university administrators and faculty used it frequently, and it appears consistently throughout seventeenth- and eighteenth-century sources. As institutions of higher education expanded rapidly throughout the period preceding the Civil War, the essential curricula forming the core of their instruction continued to follow the academic inheritance of the classical Greek schools and medieval European universities. The quadrivium—the "higher" arts of arithmetic, geometry, astronomy, and music—fortified more basic instruction in the trivium: grammar, rhetoric, and logic. As early American universities matured, national and institutional leaders influenced curricula and advanced new ideas concerning university philosophy and purpose, especially as land-grant institutions and state universities were founded across the country in the nineteenth century. Academic course offerings in higher education typically reflected both federally recognized and funded curricula along with more localized learning needs. In this respect, curricula continue to serve functions recognizable in higher education today.

While most modern academic departments can trace their roots to the historic plans of study described in the quadrivium and trivium, more recent developments reflect the increasing specialization of academic and administrative systems within institutions of higher education in the United States. In the twentieth century, most societal institutions invoked rational principles and a scientific method of development. Just as the Industrial Revolution fueled technological advances in the nineteenth century, technological revolutions have propelled the form and function of educational institutions. In the latter half of the twentieth century, increasing percentages of the adult population in the United States enrolled in increasingly diverse types of colleges, universities, and vocational programs. The national demographic of education has shifted, and the curriculum in higher education has responded to and reflected changing political, socioeconomic, and cultural dynamics. Growing recognition of professional fields and the attendant expansion of professional education has also fostered curricular adaptation and evolution. As these developments have changed expectations for higher education, they have also transformed perspectives on the meaning and development of curricula.

Reflecting on Curriculum in Higher Education in the United States

Curriculum enables people to make sense of our lives and the world around them. Individuals use curriculum with varying degrees of intentionality to interpret events, to deepen their understanding of what they learn and who they are as learners, and to create a shared experience for teaching and learning.

In simplest terms, any curriculum presents an academic plan, a designed progression of coursework framing a student's experience in higher education. Certain curricula or designed plans mandate more rigidity and more refined coursework for the student, but minimum undergraduate requirements commonly include these emphases: inquiry and critical thinking; enhanced literacy; numerical comprehension; historical consciousness; scientific, ethical, and artistic pursuits; some kind of international or multicultural experience; and in-depth study in the student's chosen topic or field.

Consonant with emerging conceptions of curriculum, contemporary perspectives on the curriculum in higher education in the United States consider the necessity of such academic plans and planning as representative of both educational and social experience, as a way of being in, understanding, and assessing a constantly changing world. In turn, researchers and practitioners alike are focusing on learning experiences in general and shared learning experiences in particular. Researchers in curricular studies regularly engage sociological, historical, cultural, psychological, and pedagogical issues in quantitative and qualitative inquiries. Increasing emphasis has been placed on measuring the outcomes of curricular design and implementation, measurements that help students and teachers alike determine the efficacy of curricula, the students' balance between a breadth of knowledge and depth in training, and the continuity of learning and experience.

Developing Shared Learning Experiences: Recurring and Emerging Models of Curricula

Several theorists have described the design, organization, and delivery of curricula in higher education, and scholars and practitioners from all disciplines have suggested approaches to curricular planning. Many of these approaches are anchored in the rationalist tradition underpinning institutions of higher education in the United States and offer rational models to guide contemporary curricular planning.

Ralph Tyler, arguably the first commentator on postsecondary curricula in the United States, published *Basic Principles of Curriculum and Instruction* in 1949. He posited four essential questions that could be used to structure knowledge in educational contexts: (1) What purpose shall the curriculum serve? (2) What experiences should the institution and its faculty provide to meet these expressed purposes? (3) How might the curriculum be organized most effectively? (4) How can one best determine the outcomes of learning—the purposes and attainment of the curriculum?

In her 1962 book *Curriculum Development: Theory and Practice,* Hilda Taba provided, in essence, the first manual for curricular planning for a generation of college and university leaders. Taba furthered Tyler's essential questions by arguing that a change in the curriculum signals a change in the institution and charges teachers to play an active role in establishing goals and objectives for learning. Taba introduced a seven-step model for developing curriculum, and her efforts to create an orderly process spurred educational scholars to develop additional models and approaches.

Paul Dressel (1968) and Clifton Conrad (1978) advanced rational approaches that acknowledged Tyler's and Taba's seminal works but provided a more modern perspective on topics such as decision-making strategies, political influence, and the role of stakeholders in the curricular planning process. In the early 1980s, William H. Bergquist and his colleagues described eight curricular models that encompassed all undergraduate experience in the United States, models that described knowledge structured according to institutional mission and purpose: thematic, competency, career, experience, student, values, future, and heritage. Since the publication of their 1981 book *Designing Undergraduate Education,* other leading curricular scholars have refined and revealed diagnostic and formulaic assessments drawing upon the taxonomy of Bergquist and his colleagues and the curricular dimensions, or elements, essential to organizing curriculum. In a 1983 article Conrad and Anne M. Pratt examined these elements and introduced a model that considered inputs or curricular design variables that influence the process. Joan S. Stark and Lisa R. Lattuca, authors of the 1997 book *Shaping the College Curriculum: Academic Plans in Action,* also considered influences upon the planning process, in particular the characteristics of academic disciplines. They revisited the idea of curriculum as an academic plan and suggested that this can be used to develop a course, a program, or even a comprehensive college curriculum.

Since the 1980s several curricular scholars, including Kenneth A. Bruffee, William G. Tierney, Jennifer Grant Haworth, and Conrad, have advanced a perspective that acknowledges students as active participants in determining and assessing their learning experiences in higher education. Their work, along with that of Marcia Baxter Magolda, Marcia Mentkowski, and Becky Ropers-Huilman, marks a departure from traditional, rational approaches and embraces the view that curriculum is more than a static plan created by faculty to direct the academic progress of students. These scholars contend that curriculum is socially constructed and, as such, reflects the engagement of students, teachers, administrators, and other stakeholders. This perspective is attracting renewed attention as enrollment and hiring patterns continue to shift in higher education. College and university students embody the most culturally diverse segment of the national population in the history of the United States, and they will inherit a complex of social, political, economic, and environmental problems. While the composition of student enrollment has changed, so has the number of students. In the early twenty-first century some 70 percent of high school graduates in the United States matriculated in some form of higher education, and educators have pointed to the need for the curriculum to address more holistically a learner's lifelong experience and the profound variation characterizing these experiences.

Emerging Challenges in Creating Shared Experiences

Arguably the most significant opportunity for leaders of learning communities will be to create enriching shared experiences in healthy tension with diverse individual needs and interests. Existing and emergent perspectives on learning and curricular design, however, are not value-neutral and have engendered unprecedented competition and conflict. Fewer and fewer curricula, too, accommodate comprehensive training for individual learning styles and needs; national trends reflect increasing specialization and fragmentation of subject matter and methodology. Those who wish to create shared learning experiences will face challenges from within and beyond academe, challenges that ask people to understand their roles as teachers and learners, incorporate multiple perspectives on curricular content, and reconsider established curricular features including general education, the liberal arts, and the academic major.

Incorporating multiple perspectives on curricular content. Like any other aspect of an educational institution, the curriculum responds to external and internal forces and reflects the identity, assumptions, and perspectives of decision makers affecting it. Curricular development and practice are not apolitical processes, nor are they static. A flurry of publications in the national media in the early 1980s testified to the importance of curricula in higher education; not only was the curriculum seen as an academic construct, it was also understood to be the repository of cultures, both national and multinational, and the historic medium for the transmission of cultural themes. The conflict of the so-called Culture Wars at the center of the discourse over educational missions and curricula in the 1980s and 1990s reflected a larger and longer shift in the national demographic of education. As more and more women and minorities matriculated in institutions of higher education, the curricula available to them as learners broadened as a result of this development. Some educational leaders and programs balked at more inclusive measures to redesign the curriculum, but the resurgent interest in control of curricula clearly signaled that what students read, and who decides what they will be reading, still shapes the national conversation about higher education and its purpose. Unlike any other single feature of an educational institution, the curriculum represents the core values and shared beliefs of communities. Developing shared learning experiences, then, requires that educational leaders invite and engage the values and beliefs of not one, but many communities.

Balancing the individual and collective experience. Curriculum is the rational conversation between learner and coursework in higher education. It is the students' experience, on any given campus, of any given course; each syllabus represents one sequential or supporting piece of evidence that students have indeed engaged the institution. Curricula are as distinct as learners, and more differentiated than ever before in the history of education, in terms of guiding framework, applications and practices, and enrollments. Just as the term was used to imply both direction and pace in its original context in Latin, curriculum, much like a river, follows both a recognizably fluid and formed course.

In the United States, people in the twenty-first century will likely change careers and jobs several times in the course of their productive years. As the nature of employment changes within society, educational goals likewise shift. Curricula serve as an important measure of learning and student achievement within a shifting landscape, so any institutional assessment of curriculum should provide compelling answers to increasingly demanding questions and needs of the society, the state agencies funding higher education, and the individual learners and participants themselves.

Understanding general education as the formed course. In the typical college and university setting, general education courses structure the core instruction that is provided by and required by the institution, and these courses usually occupy the first two years of coursework, regardless of a student's designated or intended field of study. These courses stress skills rather than specialized intellectual training, and they are usually designed to overlook disciplinary boundaries, to articulate and expand the implications of knowledge for students. Educators have long agreed that the integration of general requirements within curricula should repeatedly emphasize learning how to learn, the common process by which each individual student integrates their advancing knowledge and skills. Students must be able to meaningfully relate their classroom experiences and the insights they gain in less structured environments. Likewise, general education courses, or core requirements, at most institutions of higher education are designed to evoke the analytical and interpretive sensibilities of scholars and of learning communities, while also providing broader frames of reference for students.

The purpose of general education requirements is to provide coherence and unity in an otherwise specialized undergraduate experience, and to promote the social and intellectual integration of the students enrolled in these courses. Many university leaders have also argued that general education requirements provide students with readily accessible strategies for discerning truth, knowledge, and insight, that is, developing the most general and most useful skills and habits of the mind.

General education requirements are intended to provide a common experience but critics contend that such requirements cannot resolve the problems created by fragmentation and specialization. General education must be considered in concert with liberal and disciplinary studies in order to create meaningful, shared learning experiences.

Recognizing liberal arts as a tradition of fluidity. In historical consideration of higher education, the liberal arts have formed a core curriculum since the formation of medieval universities in Europe, and they comprise a tradition of intellectual training that transferred to most American universities. In theory, a liberal education affords educational experience that encourages and sustains lifelong learning—an education defined not necessarily by specific knowledge, as Paul L. Dressel explained in 1968, but instead by the ways in which individuals think and behave. In practice, the curricula of liberal arts balances innovative and imitative subject matter for undergraduates, generating a breadth of knowledge and depth of insight in the course of required readings. The historical emphasis of the liberal arts is tangible and includes the essential courses listed in the quadrivium and trivium; in modern institutions of higher education, however, the subject matter, pedagogy, and consequential learning of a liberal education typically orient students to the broad array of disciplines represented in the humanities in the evolved curriculum of medieval universities. A liberal arts curriculum asserts that certain texts have been proven historically to be most instructive to think with, although all texts might be useful to think about. In closer reading of these selected texts—the canon—learners engage in elemental inquiry, gaining insights into the nature and meaning of life, human purpose and ethos, and societal organization and improvement.

Leading theorists of liberal curricula have suggested that such an education improves students' cultural awareness and supports the education mission with an identifiable moral agency that affords students an appreciation of wisdom gained in the past. The emphasis is on knowledge as its own end—that learning is valuable for its own sake, and that learners engaged in learning on such levels inherently contribute in service to their communities, in the solution of complex problems, or in the creation of more informed public policies.

Understanding the purpose of the academic major. Under the influence of eighteenth- and nineteenth-century European university models, specific academic fields of study began to appear in the United States in the twentieth century, and since the 1950s, majors have become the standard units of curricular organization, the most obvious identifying feature of any student's coursework. Faculty and scholars affiliated with institutions of higher education have rearranged and aligned themselves according to subject matter and specialized areas of interest and research; departments have relocated themselves within institutions in more segmented and narrowly defined components. Learners are asked to organize

and align their own interests and coursework according to these educational constructs. The dominant scientific paradigm mandates increasingly refined focus in order to further inquiry and specify useful study. Rapidly expanding numbers of departments, majors, minors, and subspecialties have occurred throughout American higher education since the 1970s. Recognizably interdisciplinary fields of study (such as the liberal arts) have subsequently receded. This, some critics charge, has encouraged an overemphasis on specialization and denies students the opportunity for a liberal education.

See also: ACADEMIC MAJOR, THE; CURRICULUM, HIGHER EDUCATION, *subentry on* NATIONAL REPORTS ON THE UNDERGRADUATE CURRICULUM; GENERAL EDUCATION IN HIGHER EDUCATION.

BIBLIOGRAPHY

BAXTER MAGOLDA, MARCIA B. 1999. *Creating Contexts for Learning and Self-Authorship: Constructive-Developmental Pedagogy.* Nashville, TN: Vanderbilt University Press.

BERGQUIST, WILLIAM H.; GOULD, RONALD A.; and GREENBERG, ELINOR M. 1981. *Designing Undergraduate Education.* San Francisco: Jossey-Bass.

BRUFFEE, KENNETH A. 1993. *Collaborative Learning: Higher Education, Interdependence, and the Authority of Knowledge.* Baltimore: Johns Hopkins University Press.

CONRAD, CLIFTON F. 1978. *The Undergraduate Curriculum: A Guide to Innovation and Reform.* Boulder, CO: Westview Press.

CONRAD, CLIFTON F., and PRATT, ANNE M. 1983. "Making Decisions about the Curriculum: From Metaphor to Model." *Journal of Higher Education* 54:16–30.

DRESSEL, PAUL L. 1968. *College and University Curriculum.* Berkeley, CA: McCutchan.

HAWORTH, JENNIFER GRANT, and CONRAD, CLIFTON F. 1997. *Emblems of Quality in Higher Education: Developing and Sustaining High-Quality Programs.* Boston: Allyn and Bacon.

MENTKOWSKI, MARCIA, and ASSOCIATES. 2000. *Learning that Lasts: Integrating Learning, Development, and Performance in College and Beyond.* San Francisco: Jossey-Bass.

ROPERS-HUILMAN, BECKY. 1998. *Feminist Teaching in Theory and Practice: Situating Power and*

Knowledge in Poststructural Classrooms. New York: Teachers College Press.

STARK, JOAN S., and LATTUCA, LISA R. 1997. *Shaping the College Curriculum: Academic Plans in Action.* Boston: Allyn and Bacon.

TABA, HILDA. 1962. *Curriculum Development: Theory and Practice.* New York: Harcourt, Brace, and World.

TIERNEY, WILLIAM G. 1989. "Cultural Politics and the Curriculum in Postsecondary Education." *Journal of Education* 171:72–88.

TYLER, RALPH W. 1949. *Basic Principles of Curriculum and Instruction.* Chicago: University of Chicago Press.

KATHRYN DEY HUGGETT
NORA C. SMITH
CLIFTON F. CONRAD

CURRICULUM, INTERNATIONAL

The field of curriculum studies is cluttered by an array of dissimilar definitions of the term *curriculum.* In empirical studies, definitions of curriculum run the gamut from those that would have the term signify everything that takes place in a classroom to others that restrict its meaning to only the topics that are defined as instructional requirements in the official policy of an educational system. There are also those that limit the definition of curriculum to only those topics actually taught by teachers.

In 1979, during the development of the Second International Mathematics Study (SIMS) conducted under the auspices of the International Association for the Evaluation of Educational Achievement (IEA), Curtis C. McKnight proposed a model that subdivides the curriculum into three components: the intended, the implemented, and the attained (see Figure 1). The intended curriculum is understood to be what an official educational agency (most often a ministry, secretariat, or other national or subnational agency responsible for guiding and articulating the educational intent of a system) expects to be taught or holds as learning goals in its educational system. The intended curriculum is thus distinguishable from both the implemented curriculum—the instructional implementation of the intended curriculum—which is therefore embodied in classroom instruction, and the attained curriculum. The attained curriculum is understood to be the skills, knowledge, and dispositions that students effectively acquire as a result of their schooling. This model subdivides the curriculum for purposes of analysis, and the different levels are not considered wholly independent. This discussion makes use of this model, focusing primarily on the intended curriculum.

The intended curriculum acquired special prominence in educational policy in the latter half of the twentieth century. Many of the world's educational systems experienced a shift of focus in education policies during that period. Whereas the stress had traditionally fallen on improving material investments and guaranteeing universal access to public education, the 1980s and 1990s brought a stronger emphasis on the conceptual understandings, procedural knowledge, and other academic objectives to be met by all students in primary and secondary education—and thus a renewed interest in the intended curriculum as a critical policy instrument. The movement toward the development of educational standards in many educational systems reflects this emphasis on the quality of the content of the intended curriculum, as policymakers and educational leaders have favored the development of official curricula and a variety of implementation tools in order to ensure the delivery and attainment of socially significant disciplinary content. Most new curricula stipulate the acquisition of higher-order knowledge by all students, and such prescription tends to be informed by the type and amount of knowledge that is perceived to be critical for students to function effectively in society and in the economy.

A considerable body of work has been contributed to support the use of educational policy programs focused on the quality of the content of schooling in what has been termed content-driven systemic reform. It is stated that ambitious curriculum intentions must be formulated and subsequently appropriate mechanisms must be designed to implement these curricula so that students have the opportunity to attain high levels of achievement. Content-driven reform holds that a core specification of curriculum goals provides the basis for setting up a policy structure designed to enhance the achievement of pupils. Thus, the intended curriculum is intended to directly influence teacher training and certification, school course offerings, instructional resources, and systems of accountability.

Curriculum reform policy, as espoused in these reform theories, assigns to standards documents, curriculum guides, frameworks, programs of study, and the like a primary role in defining potential educational experiences. They are intended to help shape goals and expectations for learning. These visions are anticipated to guide the experiences of students in classrooms.

Certainly high expectations concerning the role of policies regarding curriculum intentions have been held in many countries. In a survey of thirty-eight nations conducted as a part of the Third International Mathematics and Science Study (TIMSS) the majority reported a number of reforms and managed changes in the content, pedagogy, and technology prescribed in national curriculum policy for school mathematics and science.

Authority and Function

At the time TIMSS curriculum data were collected (1990–1992), curriculum guides published by national or subnational governmental bodies existed in all TIMSS countries with the exception of Iran. The guides all carried some degree of official status, although status and authority varied among countries and occasionally within a country in the case of subnational or regional guides. The significance of these documents varied substantially by country. Curriculum guides in Australia, for example, had titles such as "Course Advice," whereas in Japan they were known as "National Courses of Study" and in Norway as "Curriculum Guidelines." These diverse titles suggest different statuses and functions. Some guides specified the courses of study for which teachers were responsible. Others specified how teachers might pursue their goals and what types of instructional methods and assessment strategies might be appropriate. Still others left most implementation details to teachers and attempted to achieve their purpose solely by stating shared objectives.

These documents that set forth the intended curriculum for entire educational systems varied in the type of strategic elements they used to present policy and shape its enactment. Specifically, some strategic elements were more prescriptive than others were; they stated policies, formal objectives for instruction, and so on. Other elements were more facilitative; they included such information as suggested strategies for teachers, examples, and assessment ideas. The TIMSS analysis of intended curricula, however, revealed that there was a high

FIGURE 1

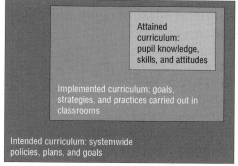

Three-level analytical model of curriculum

Attained curriculum: pupil knowledge, skills, and attitudes

Implemented curriculum: goals, strategies, and practices carried out in classrooms

Intended curriculum: systemwide policies, plans, and goals

SOURCE: Based on McKnight, Curtis C. 1979. "Model for the Second International Mathematics Study." *SIMS Bulletin* 4: 6–39.

level of cross-national agreement on the use of a prescriptive approach to setting forth curriculum policy. Most countries favored the prescription of specific policies, objectives, goals, and contents in their curriculum guides, over the use of material that facilitated implementation through the suggestion of appropriate pedagogy, the use of exemplars of particular curriculum elements, or recommendations regarding appropriate ways to assess whether or not goals have been reached. In fact, the countries that exhibited the highest levels of mean student achievement on the TIMSS mathematics and science tests commonly had intended curricula with the heaviest reliance on the prescription of an inventory of skills and contents to be mastered by pupils, grade by grade, throughout primary and secondary schooling. Policy instruments balancing facilitative and prescriptive approaches were rare. This finding, coupled with earlier secondary analysis of SIMS data—which found that countries with the mostly highly centralized forms of curriculum policy structures were the most effective ones in guaranteeing the enactment of a given intended curriculum—provided evidence contradictory to policies intended to promote decentralized decision-making regarding educational goals or standards.

Curriculum and Globalization

A particularly vexing problem for educational policymakers advocating content-driven reform has been the increasingly international character of discussions on the intended curriculum. Curriculum experts, professional associations, and policymakers became concerned with how standards defined in their own country compared to those in other countries, especially the countries they regarded as their most important economic competitors. Most traditional cross-national research provided little guidance here, as three associated theoretical-methodological perspectives largely guided it. A large amount of theoretical work was done in the 1970s, and this work largely concentrated on the structure of social and economic relationships that curricula were thought to promote or reproduce. This aspect of the intended curriculum was often termed the "hidden" curriculum, and many theoreticians in the Marxist tradition devoted their attention to describing its nature and its function in perpetuating the class struggle in the world's most developed capitalist economies. Other theorists used dependency theory, another variant of the Marxist tradition that arose mostly from work done in political economy and economic history in Latin America and Africa, to develop accounts of the imposition of dominant models of schooling on nations of the economic and social periphery. These authors affirmed that the propagation of curricula from the great economic metropoles to the periphery was a particular instance of cultural domination within the framework of an international division of labor. A third tradition, largely influenced by "world systems" theories, studied aspects of curriculum associated with the worldwide expansion of enrollments in schooling. Theorists within this tradition argued that since the 1950s the "Western" model of schooling has spread throughout the world as part of a pervasive phenomenon of the emergence of an increasingly integrated world economic and social system. This was considered to have resulted, for example, in virtually all of the world's educational systems according similar importance to mathematics and science education in their curricula.

But what of policymakers and curriculum designers who wished to find information to guide their efforts in promoting educational opportunities that would enhance national economic competitiveness? Increasingly, regardless of their specific economic circumstances, many countries developed a consensus in according much importance to prescribing rigorous curricula in academic disciplines, despite a paucity of strong empirical evidence at the time connecting achievement in these disciplines

with economic benefits (subsequently some evidence was advanced in the early 1990s that the character of mathematics courses taken in secondary school affects mean individual income levels, and that increases in hours allocated to elementary instruction in the sciences is associated with increases in national standards of living). Despite the apparent international consensus on the value of teaching mathematics and the sciences, for example, there was clearly considerable cross-national variation in the specific topics that were taught as part of these disciplines and the specific sets of skills and dispositions that were promoted in regard to these topics.

Interest groups in education across the world, such as governments, the business community, professional associations of educators, and many others, began to be concerned with the idea of "world-class standards" and were preoccupied with formulating rigorous and meaningful intended curricula that compare favorably with that elusive standard. But what precisely are "world-class" standards? What expectations do, for example, high-achieving countries have regarding essential knowledge and skills that children must acquire in order to meet the goals held for them by the educational system? As the attention to the intended curriculum increased among educational leaders and policymakers, it thus occasioned an increased interest in the possible educational application of another instrument that—like the idea of "standards" themselves—arose from modern business management strategies: international benchmarking.

Benchmarking. Benchmarking originated in efforts of business firms to identify external points of reference for their business practices in order to achieve continuous improvement. As such, the selection of the "point of reference" is central to determining how benchmarking studies can be used. From the perspective of educational systems, this choice is in effect a selection of the school systems from which they would like to learn. As the concern regarding the "international competitiveness" of intended curricula and the interest in benchmarking has increased, consequently so has interest in cross-national studies of student achievement. These have become of critical importance to policymakers, which explains the high levels of participation in the original TIMSS in the 1990s—and in subsequent endeavors conducted, most notably by the Organisation for Economic Co-operation and Development (the Programme for International Student Assessment—PISA) and the IEA (through the continuation of TIMSS by way of the Trends in Mathematics and Science Study and PIRLS—Progress in International Reading Literacy Study).

The first published reports from the original TIMSS constituted important milestones in curriculum studies. In a pair of companion volumes the U.S. TIMSS research team used the first large-scale cross-national empirical study of the intended curriculum (termed the TIMSS Curriculum Analysis) to identify those curricular standards that are most common to TIMSS countries. These standards were then compared to standards in specific countries—beginning with the United States. Interest in cross-national benchmarking was acute given that on the one hand, a national policy objective was for U.S. schoolchildren to be "first in the world" in mathematics and science—and on the other hand, mean student performance on the TIMSS assessment at the close of the twentieth century proved the nation to be quite distant from that objective. Prior to the TIMSS curriculum analysis, no comprehensive effort to empirically measure and specify intended curricula using a large sample of countries and representative samples of curricular materials had ever been attempted.

These studies uncovered notable differences between the intended curricula of countries exhibiting high levels of mean student achievement in mathematics and science and that of countries with lower mean achievement levels. Focusing on the exhaustive characterization of the disciplinary content and expectations for student performance contained in standards documents and student textbooks, these studies resulted in findings with important implications for the development of curriculum policy.

These findings point to a variety of elements common among most high-achieving countries that are not shared by most low-achieving countries. They make up what appears to be necessary, but not sufficient, conditions for the realization of higher achievement for larger numbers of schoolchildren.

A number of low-achieving countries in the TIMSS had curricula that emphasized the coverage of long lists of topics. Conversely, highest achieving countries intended the teaching and learning of a more focused set of basic contents, to be explored in depth and mastered. The unfocused curriculum of broad-ranging lists of topics to be covered is also typically a curriculum of very little coherence. TIMSS studies reveal that attempting to cover a large number of topics results in textbooks, and teaching methods, that are disjointed and episodic. That is, textbooks and teachers present items from the long lists of topics prescribed by these curricula one after the other, in an attempt to cover them all before the school year runs out with little or no effort invested in exploring the relationships between these topics or in fundamental unifying ideas or themes. Loss of these relationships between ideas appears to encourage students to regard these disciplines as no more than a series of disconnected notions that they are unable to conceive of as belonging to a disciplinary whole.

Learning goals. These benchmarking studies also reveal important differences in how school systems define learning goals. In a number of low-achieving countries—with the most relevant example being the United States—there is an extremely static definition of fundamental goals. That is, goals that are deemed fundamental (often termed "the basics") are considered to be fundamental throughout schooling, requiring repetition in many grades. Arithmetic, for example, is a set of contents and skills prominent in curricula throughout the years of compulsory schooling. Even in eighth grade, when most high-achieving TIMSS countries concentrate their curricular focus on algebra and geometry, arithmetic is a major part of schooling in the United States.

In high-achieving nations, when goals first enter the curriculum they receive concentrated attention with the expectation that they can be mastered and that students can be prepared to attain a new set of different priority goals in ensuing grades. Focused curricula are the motor of a dynamic definition of curricular objectives. In most of the highest achieving countries, each new grade sees a new set of curricular goals receiving concentrated attention to prepare for and build toward mastering more challenging goals yet to come.

The consequence of lack of focus and coherence, and the static approach to defining what is basic, is that these types of curricula are undemanding compared to those of other countries. Materials intended for students in these countries cover a large array of topics, most of which are first introduced in the elementary grades. This cursory treatment does not include much more than the learning of algo-

FIGURE 2

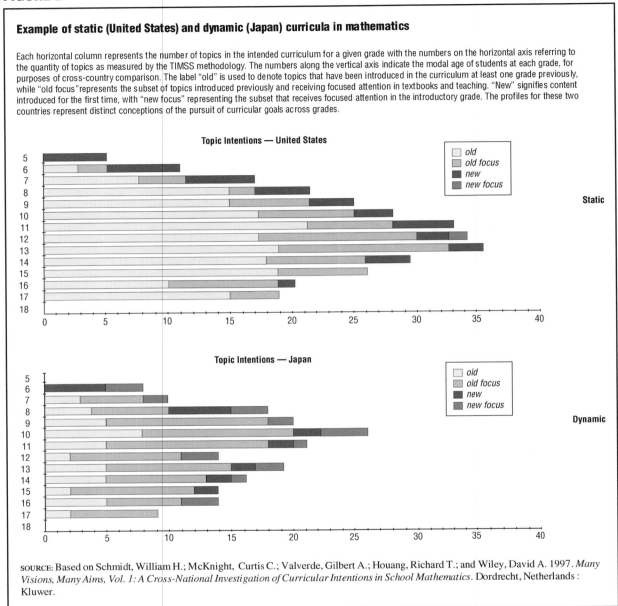

Example of static (United States) and dynamic (Japan) curricula in mathematics

Each horizontal column represents the number of topics in the intended curriculum for a given grade with the numbers on the horizontal axis referring to the quantity of topics as measured by the TIMSS methodology. The numbers along the vertical axis indicate the modal age of students at each grade, for purposes of cross-country comparison. The label "old" is used to denote topics that have been introduced in the curriculum at least one grade previously, while "old focus" represents the subset of topics introduced previously and receiving focused attention in textbooks and teaching. "New" signifies content introduced for the first time, with "new focus" representing the subset that receives focused attention in the introductory grade. The profiles for these two countries represent distinct conceptions of the pursuit of curricular goals across grades.

SOURCE: Based on Schmidt, William H.; McKnight, Curtis C.; Valverde, Gilbert A.; Houang, Richard T.; and Wiley, David A. 1997. *Many Visions, Many Aims, Vol. 1: A Cross-National Investigation of Curricular Intentions in School Mathematics*. Dordrecht, Netherlands : Kluwer.

rithms and simple facts. Demanding standards appear to require more sophisticated content taught in depth, as students progress through the grades. Rigorous standards are a result of a dynamic process of focused and coherent transitions from more simple to increasingly more complex content and skills. Figure 2 presents an illustration of the contrast between the static curriculum of the United States—a country that showed mediocre mean student achievement in TIMSS—and the dynamic curriculum of a significantly higher achieving Japan.

Curriculum and Learning

The fundamental premise of educational reforms that focus on the intended curriculum is that the intended curriculum serves to support the creation of opportunities for students to learn. This is to say that the faith placed in standards—world-class or otherwise—is derived from the assumption that standards are associated with learning. This premise, until recently, had little empirical support. The original TIMSS study, however, by including comprehensive integrated data on all three levels of curriculum, provided an unprecedented opportunity to test this assumption in a number of ways. Results from these tests indicate clearly that the intended curriculum—oftentimes as mediated through textbooks—is significantly related to specific learning opportunities (that is, the pedagogical decisions of teachers) and consequently to the growth in knowledge and skills that students are able to demonstrate in achievement tests. It is also clear from this work that there are identifiable structural relationships among subareas in mathematics and science curricula that intensify their relationship with learning—such that learning one aspect of an academic subject is related not only to the specific opportunities that are provided to learn that aspect but also to opportunities to learn other aspects of the discipline that are structurally related. Further, there is evidence that the enactment of the intended curriculum—to be effective in promoting learning—is not simply a matter of covering the contents specified in the curriculum, nor even simply a matter of the amount of time devoted to teaching them. Clearly there are pedagogies that are more appropriate to achieve the levels of rigor and cognitive demand promoted by many of the world's most ambitious curricula.

Thus, there is evidence that the intended curriculum deserves the intense attention of policymakers that it has enjoyed over the past decades. It is a key instrument in assuring access to rich and meaningful educational experiences. New methods have been developed to characterize and benchmark curricular material. These have resulted in the specification of many of the key features of curricula that would promote high achievement. Much empirical work remains, however, particularly in the area of determining whether it is possible to reconcile these most recent findings with the movement toward decentralized systems of curriculum policy formulation and enactment. Future scholarship must focus on the cultural traditions, policy instruments, and other formal and informal processes that determine how power over the intended curriculum is exercised at various levels in different educational systems; how different educational stakeholders interact in these processes; and how decisions regarding curricular objectives are made—with an eye to gauging their influence on the quality of educational experiences that students are provided.

See also: GLOBALIZATION AND EDUCATION; INTERNATIONAL ASSESSMENTS.

BIBLIOGRAPHY

BENAVOT, AARON. 1992. "Curricular Content, Educational Expansion, and Economic Growth." *Comparative Education Review* 36:150–174.

KAMENS, DAVID H., and BENAVOT, AARON. 1991. "Elite Knowledge for the Masses: The Origins and Spread of Mathematics and Science Education in National Curricula." *American Journal of Education* 99:137–180.

MCKNIGHT, CURTIS C. 1979. "Model for the Second International Mathematics Study." *SIMS Bulletin* 4:6–39.

SCHMIDT, WILLIAM H.; MCKNIGHT, CURTIS C.; HOUANG, RICHARD T.; WANG, HSING CHI; WILEY, DAVID E.; COGAN, LELAND S.; and WOLFE, RICHARD G. 2001. *Why Schools Matter: A Cross-National Comparison of Curriculum and Learning.* San Francisco: Jossey-Bass.

SCHMIDT, WILLIAM H.; MCKNIGHT, CURTIS C.; VALVERDE, GILBERT A.; HOUANG, RICHARD T.; AND WILEY, DAVID A. 1997. *Many Visions, Many Aims,* Vol. 1: *A Cross-National Investigation of Curricular Intentions in School Mathematics.* Dordrecht, Netherlands: Kluwer.

STEVENSON, DAVID LEE, and BAKER, DAVID P. 1991. "State Control of the Curriculum and Classroom Instruction." *Sociology of Education* 64:1–10.

VALVERDE, GILBERT A. 2000. "Strategic Themes in Curriculum Policy Documents: An Exploration of TIMSS Curriculum Analysis Data." *International Journal of Educational Policy Research and Practice* 1:133–152.

VALVERDE, GILBERT A., and SCHMIDT, WILLIAM H. 2000. "Greater Expectations: Learning from Other Nations in the Quest for World-Class Standards in U.S. School Mathematics and Science." *Journal of Curriculum Studies* 32:651–687.

GILBERT A. VALVERDE

CURRICULUM, SCHOOL

OVERVIEW

In its organizational aspect the curriculum is an authoritative prescription for the course of study of a school or system of schools. In their traditional form, such prescriptions set out the content to be covered at a grade level or in a course or sequences of courses, along with recommended or prescribed methods of teaching. In their contemporary form such prescriptions have been re-presented as national and state *standards*, outlining outcomes to be achieved by schools without prescribing the specific bodies of content to be covered or methods of teaching to be used.

Curricula in both of these senses are seen as defining what schools purposefully do. However, most scholars and administrators who work with curricula or evaluate the impact of curriculum prescriptions or reforms do not believe that "curricula-as-documents" direct the work of schools in significant ways. Curricula-as-documents are more often than not developed after the fact, and are based on existing practices of teachers or a simple listing of the content of textbooks being used. Further, many teachers are not familiar with the curriculum their district has mandated.

Nevertheless, curricula and curricular mandates are the objects of persistent and hotly contested debates around schooling, and are widely taken to be important. Interest groups, governments, school districts, and their staffs devote much time and attention to discussions of the curriculum. Why does the idea of the curriculum and curriculum reform assume such importance in educational discourse and policymaking? Is it possible to direct the work of schooling?

Curricula, Education, and Schooling

All curricula emerge from ideas about what should be taught and learned, and how such teaching and learning might best be undertaken and then certified. As a result the fundamental question lying behind the prescription and development of all curricula is often seen as "What knowledge is of most worth?"—because it is the knowledge that is of most worth that education should, seemingly, reflect. In its ideological or philosophical aspect, much curricular thought seeks to articulate reasoned starting points for one or another form of curriculum. Such work can accept the framework of contemporary understanding of the scope and nature of education and schooling. It can be critical, seeking to articulate the hidden assumptions around such categories as race, gender, and class that have driven, and drive, schooling in inappropriate, even morally wrong, directions.

However, looked at more analytically, the curriculum of the school reflects layered cultural understandings of what is considered necessary for young people to know or experience if they are to take their place in the social and cultural order. Thus, as the central component of a pervasive modern institution, the curriculum is necessarily a part of all of the sociological and cultural ambiguities within societies. As such, the scope and nature of the curriculum are viewed as critically important for teachers, parents, cultural critics, interest groups, and the employers of the graduates of the school. As the curriculum as an idea is seen through the eyes of all such groups, it becomes a mirror that reflects different visions of the society and culture, and the tensions within the society around, say, the proper nature of the work of schooling and/or status-attainment and employment possibilities. As a result inevitable and unresolved differences of viewpoint characteristically surface around all discussions of the curriculum as a symbol of both a normative order for education and of the quality and character of what schools are understood as doing.

For these reasons the history of curriculum thinking and practice is marked, on the one hand, by popular and professional conflict and debate about what the curriculum should be and how teaching should be undertaken and, on the other hand, by rationalization of the good and/or bad consequences of one or another curriculum. What, for example, should the curriculum that is most appropriate for young people be based on?

- The needs of the economy for human resources
- National or international ideals
- The need for societal and cultural change or preservation
- Ameliorating pervasive distinctions of gender and race
- The set of perennially "essential" and fundamental forms of knowledge and ways of thinking
- The forms of a life that is most worth living

As a result of the competition between such starting points, there is political, cultural, and policy conflict around what should be authoritatively prescribed in curricula, how teaching should be undertaken, and how schooling should be organized.

The classification of such different conceptions of education and educating has been one of the core approaches used to give both teachers and laypeople a framework for approaching the normative issues that circle around such starting points for education and curriculum building. Often, as with Elliot Eisner and Elizabeth Vallance's 1974 classification, these issues are presented as involving perennial controversies. Thus in their frame there is a web of controversy built around an unresolved conflict among five classical curriculum "conceptions": (1) curriculum as the development of cognitive processes; (2) curriculum as technology; (3) curriculum as self-actualization or consumatory experience; (4) curriculum for social learning; and (5) curriculum for academic rationalization. But Eisner and Vallance also point to other ways of framing such debates: child-centered versus society-centered; futurist, that is, socially reconstructive, versus presentist or adaptive; values-centered education versus skills-training; and humanist or existential versus behaviorist models of education and teaching.

There are, of course, difficulties associated with such controversy-framed conceptions around the curriculum problem. Such overviews of curricular conceptions reflect abstractions about the curriculum rather than the practices of schooling. Most centrally, they do not reflect the complexities of curricular action.

Walter Doyle has sought to clarify the endemic questions around all curriculum thinking by pointing out that curricular action occurs at three distinct levels.

1. Institutional, where the issues center on policies at the intersection between schooling, culture, and society.

2. Programmatic, where the issues center on (1) the specification of subject content for schools, school types and tracks, with their core and elective course requirements or expectations, subject specifications, and so forth; and (2) the construction of appropriate content for classroom coverage within these subjects.

3. Classroom, where the issues center on the elaboration of the programmatic curriculum and its connection to the worlds of schools and classrooms in their real-world contexts.

For instance, all institutional work around either the scope and rationale of an optimal mathematics curriculum or how the teaching of reading should best be undertaken centers on metaphors that reflect idealized norms for an imagined social institution. More often than not the discourse is framed in terms of *reform* and the need for change if a convergence between a normative ideal and the ongoing work of schools is to be achieved. Such discussions rarely, if ever, connect in any immediate way to the central issues around either programmatic or classroom curricula. There the effective delivery of *existing* procedures and practices, and not reform, is the overriding preoccupation. Nevertheless, the image-making that is characteristic of curriculum policy debates within and among interest groups is important. Such debates symbolize and instantiate what communities should value. In this sense curriculum discussion, debate, and planning—and the public and professional processes involved in such work— is a social form for clarifying the role that schooling *as an idea* plays in the social and cultural order.

Programmatic curriculum work has two tasks. On the one hand, it is focused on the sociocultural, political, and organizational processes through which educational visions that are accepted by elites or publics are translated into operational frameworks for schools. Thus a policy language of "excellence" becomes the introduction of gifted programs in elementary schools or Advanced Placement courses in the high school. Programmatic work is also part of the search for solutions to operational problems, such as a mismatch between the capacity of a school system or school and enrollments, and the need to reconfigure a system around, for instance, middle schools. All such programmatic discourse and action seeks to precipitate social, cultural, and educational symbols into a workable and working organizational interpretation and framework. Such organizational frameworks, however, are only indirectly linked to actual classroom teaching. In such discourse and program building, teaching is seen as a passive agency implementing or realizing both an organizationally sanctioned program and its legitimating ideology. Curriculum work in this programmatic sense *frames* the character of schools and classrooms organizationally, as well as the ways in which schools might be seen within their communities. It does not direct the work of schools or teachers in any straightforward way.

At the classroom level the curriculum is a sequence of activities, jointly developed by teachers, students, parents and communities, that reflects their understanding of the potential for them of the programmatic framework or curriculum. At this level teachers, and the schools they work within, are active interpreters, not passive agents, of the mandated or recommended policy, programmatic, or organizational frameworks. Their interpretations may or may not be well articulated with the curriculum as imaged or mandated at the policy and programmatic levels. The educational legitimacy of such local interpretations, however, is not derived from the organizational framework of the curriculum. Instead it derives from the seeming match between what a local school is, and seems to be, doing and the understandings of its community about what its school can and should be doing.

But consistency among what a community's school does, the language and symbols used to describe and project that work, and the dominant ideologies and values is only one component of the framework for the school or district programs and curricula. Financial and/or personnel issues, state-sanctioned or state-funded mandates for programs such as special education or physical and health education, and the incentives for program change offered by governments and/or foundations are, more often than not, the immediate determinants of whether or not a school offers a pre-kindergarten program or upper-level "academic" courses.

In other words, the curriculum is the symbolic center of a loosely coupled system of ideologies, symbols, organizational forms, mandates, and subject and classroom practices that instantiates collective, and often differing, understandings about what is to be valued about the idea and the ongoing practice of education. At the same time the myth of an authoritative and hierarchical framework by which legislative bodies determine classroom work, with the curriculum as the agent of the linkage, is necessary for the legitimacy of a public schooling that is subject to political control. It is this paradox that gives all discussion of the curriculum its emotional force.

Curriculum-Making in the Twentieth Century

In an essay written at the beginning of the twentieth century, John Dewey declared his pessimism about the implications for educational reform of a "settlement" he saw between progressive educational reformers, who controlled educators' ideologies, and conservatives, who controlled actual school conditions, and had little or no interest in reform. The settlement he described has persisted and has controlled most of the conventional historical writing on the twentieth-century curriculum of the American school. The histories of the American curriculum across the twentieth century offer accounts of the absence of real and lasting Progressive curriculum reform in the school, along with a search for explanations of the seemingly persistent failure of reform impulses. But it was fundamental change that marked the history of the curriculum in the twentieth century. This reality is most clearly seen in the history of the secondary school and its curriculum.

In the late nineteenth century the significant curricular questions around the idea of what was later termed *secondary education* centered on the character of the cultures present in secondary schools or academies—the conflict between cultures achieving its force from its interaction with the changing relationships between social groups. Should the curriculum offer as its core the traditional humanistic inculcation into the classical and liberal culture built around the teaching of Latin and Greek, or should it embrace "modern" subjects like science and English literature? Should the ideology of the high-status secondary school be exclusively liberal (i.e., centered on high-status classical or modern academic knowledge), or should it be directly or indirectly vocational in the sense that it might embrace and give educational legitimacy to agriculture, engineering, applied sciences and arts, and so forth?

The late nineteenth- and early twentieth-century programmatic resolution of these policy conflicts centered around the development of several secondary school types (e.g., classical and modern pre-university, technical/prevocational, and vocational schools), with each type seeking legitimacy in terms of a different curricular ideology and a different clientele of parents and students. At this time the high-status pre-university schools were schools for the elite only. Most adolescents who entered secondary schools sought employment well before graduation, or were enrolled in school types, such as normal schools, that did not lead to matriculation to a university.

In the 1920s and 1930s this situation changed dramatically in the United States in a way that was not repeated in western Europe until the 1960s. Schooling began to assume a much greater significance in the pathway to adulthood, with the result that a new form of mass high school emerged as an alternative to apprenticeship as the way to work and adulthood. This new school offered the symbol of a high school diploma, along with a set of tracked four-year courses of study potentially open to the adolescent age cohort. This new school was, in Martin Trow's words, a "mass terminal" secondary school.

This new school required new legitimating ideologies that could serve to make it appear inevitable and desirable to both the range of its external constituencies and to the teachers who would work within it. Schooling as a preparation for work and life, (i.e., life-adjustment; citizenship; Americanization; child-centeredness; and, in the Great Depression, the vision of the school and the curriculum as a seedbed for social and cultural reconstruction) emerged as new educational ideologies to submerge (but not replace) the older public and professional ideology of academic training and mental discipline as the legitimate core tasks of the high school.

Seen in terms of their programs, however, these new schools offered reinterpretations of the modern curricular categories of the traditional high-status pre-university high school in their new, nonuniversity tracks, plus, as appropriate, prevocational or explicitly vocational courses. In other words, the program of the mass terminal high school did not build on the curricular potential of the technical or applied arts curricular traditions, or develop a new curricular form—although its extracurriculum of athletics and music did represent something quite new. It was, of course, the idea of the high school experience that its students and parents were seeking.

The years after World War II saw the second major transformation of the American school as a mass college-preparatory high school emerge from the prewar mass terminal school. This new high school required a rearticulation of the ideology of the high school curriculum with the ideology of the university, creating, in its turn, a need for new ways to frame popular and professional understandings. This required the rejection of the ideological platforms of the very different prewar high school. Thus, the college-preparatory role of the school reemerged into public visibility, a visibility most clearly symbolized by the comprehensive high schools being built in the new suburbs.

The new mission of the high school was presented in terms of academic development and the need to teach the intellectual structure of the now symbolically important sciences of physics and math—a goal that was interpreted as having implications for national defense and the national welfare. Programs embodying the new ideologies were aggressively introduced as symbols of the new mission of the school, although the program-building practices of those years centered overwhelmingly on merely serving the expanding number of students enrolling in the traditional college-prep track.

The high school of the late 1960s and 1970s reflected the political and cultural turbulence, and the rejection of tradition, of those years. These years brought a renewal of the avant-garde ideologies and curricular platforms of the 1930s (often with a countercultural gloss) as well as of a vision of the school as a site for social, cultural, and racial reconstruction, social justice, and the like. Programmatically, noncanonical works appeared in literature courses; environmentalism emerged as a topic in science; courses in film, black studies, and so forth, emerged in many schools. With these changes the ordered institution of the school was being questioned symbolically and, as a result, appeared at risk. The subject categories of the school seemed to lose their clear meaning and significance, and the quality of, for example, urban schools became an issue as the racial and ethnic makeup of their student bodies changed from majority to minority students. Public anxieties around the symbolic meaning and effectiveness of the high school as the way to adulthood became the focus of demands for a restoration of more traditional understandings of the school.

These tensions were symbolized by the National Commission on Excellence in Education's 1983 report *A Nation at Risk,* an endorsement of the symbols of the "traditional" academic model of the preuniversity high school. But most observers of the contemporary school agree that while, programmatically, courses have been renamed and given new rationales, classroom work has continued on its own trajectory. Middle school mathematics courses are renamed *algebra,* but traditional eighth-grade mathematics texts are used. And, to complete the picture of the stable ideological order around the curriculum that Dewey described, constructivism has come to serve as the educators' counterpoint to the symbolic conservative restoration.

Rethinking Curriculum Discussions

Seen historically, it is clear that much, if not most, public discussion of the curriculum should be seen as a rhetorical form that seeks to stake out positions in the ideological space around the concept of the *school*. Such discourse, as Dewey noted, does not directly influence programmatic or classroom practice, which have their own logics. Thus looked at across the twentieth century, the Progressive educational and curriculum philosophies, conceptions, platforms, and developments that journalists' and educators' discussions have taken as significant have had little demonstrable impact on the day-to-day work of the school. They are part of the changing parade of ideologies and platforms that have been invoked to legitimate one or another image of the school as an institution.

When the characteristic forms of normative educational and curriculum philosophy are looked at analytically, it is clear that they cannot have any significant directive force on the complexities of schooling and teaching. Most important, what such discourse also fails to offer is any explanation of the overwhelming success of the school as an institution across the divides of race, class, gender, and so forth, and of the ways in which the curriculum has both contributed to, and responded to, this success. The secondary school as an institution has achieved an increasingly dominant role in the lives of children and youth across all developed nations. This dominance is overwhelmingly accepted by the societies and cultures that host the modern school, despite the tensions that can circle around it.

Elizabeth McEneaney and John Meyer have argued that all thinking and research around the curriculum, and by extension all policymaking and program development, must be grounded in the recognition of the overwhelming success of the school as an institution. For McEneaney and Meyer an understanding of the idea or model of the modern nation, and of the individually empowered citizen in the nation, lies at the heart of any understanding of the success of the school and the curriculum. Access to high-status forms of schooling has come to be seen as both as a right of citizenship and as a way of integrating citizens within the framework of a common national culture. This culture is, in its turn, seen as both inclusive and rational, a self-understanding that must be instilled by way of the curriculum that frames the knowledge and attitudes that are seen to undergird the modern nation and modern society.

As a result of this twofold mission of incorporating the population and teaching an understanding of modernity, both the curriculum and teaching have become, paradoxically, increasingly participatory and expressive, yet increasingly rational in terms of their emphasis on mathematics and science, and tolerance of global and local diversity. Conversely, this modern curriculum has increasingly de-emphasized transcending (and often exclusionary) cultural or religious traditions as well as rigid patterns of allocation of student-citizens across schools or school types.

As the implicit expression of the pervasive modern self-image of the citizen and nation, these changes have not, and do not, take place as a result of planned activity or reform. Instead, they come about as the model of society, and modern models for the curriculum, are incorporated, in routinized ways, in the work of teachers and policymakers. Of course, this instantiation of the model of society in the school and curriculum has not come about as a linear process. There are cycles of reform and resistance, the product of the tensions between older and newer models of society and the school and between the global and the local. Organizational structures, as seen for example in the highly centralized French system, can make change problematic at times. In the U.S. school system, with its loosely coupled, locally based structures, many of the tensions that create the need for major cycles of curriculum reform in other countries can be contained. As McEneaney and Meyer point out, schools can be required at the policy level to teach sexual abstinence and at the same time hand out condoms in the classroom. The policy curriculum can be an object of controversy; but the programmatic curriculum works in stable, deliberate ways at further incorporation of youth into the idea and institution of the school, while the classroom curriculum selectively incorporates a changing model of schoolwork in unplanned and unorganized ways. The evolving, changing classroom curriculum can at times be celebrated symbolically at the programmatic level, and made very visible to local communities. Or it can be concealed by a skillful management of the programmatic models and symbols presented to local communities, with their diverse publics.

In one sense, such an "institutionalist" account of the curriculum can be seen as *Progressive,* in the way that that term has been understood by educators for over a century. But Dewey, in common with most educational reformers of his time and since, bemoaned the absence in American society of what he saw as an appropriately Progressive theory of education, and insistently asked why this was the case in the face of the self-evident claims of the Progressive ideal. The institutional understanding of the curriculum outlined by McEneaney and Meyer, however, suggests that the United States, in common with all developed societies, has in fact institutionalized a normative democratic understanding of the curriculum and the school. It is this understanding that has determined, and is determining, the actual form of both the structures and work of schools.

An institutional understanding of the curriculum, and of the school that gives it agency, presents a major challenge to most of the ways that are used by educators to discuss the school curriculum. It offers a framing context in which their conventional approaches to understanding the curriculum might be placed while at the same time explaining what those approaches cannot explain.

See also: CURRICULUM, SCHOOL, *subentry on* HIDDEN CURRICULUM; ELEMENTARY EDUCATION, *subentries on* CURRENT TRENDS, HISTORY OF; SECONDARY EDUCATION, *subentries on* CURRENT TRENDS, HISTORY OF.

BIBLIOGRAPHY

COHEN, DAVID K. 1988. "Teaching Practice: Plus Ça Change." In *Contributing to Educational Practice: Perspectives on Research and Practice,* ed. Philip W. Jackson. Berkeley, CA: McCutchan.

COHEN, DAVID K., and SPILLANE, JAMES P. 1992. *Policy and Practice: The Relations between Governance and Instruction.* Review of Research in Education 18. Washington, DC: American Educational Research Association.

CUBAN, LARRY. 1996. "Curriculum Stability and Change." In *Handbook of Research on Curriculum,* ed. Philip W. Jackson. New York: Macmillan.

DEWEY, JOHN. 2001. "The Educational Situation: As Concerns the Elementary School" (1902). *Journal of Curriculum Studies* 33:387–403.

DOYLE, WALTER. 1996. "Curriculum and Pedagogy." In *Handbook of Research on Curriculum,* ed. Philip W. Jackson. New York: Macmillan.

EISNER, ELLIOT W., and VALLANCE, ELIZABETH, eds. 1974. *Conflicting Conceptions of Curriculum.* Berkeley, CA: McCutchan.

FUHRMAN, SUSAN H., ed. 2001. *From the Capitol to the Classroom: Standards-Based Reform in the States.* 100th Yearbook of the National Society for the Study of Education, Part 2. Chicago: National Society for the Study of Education.

HOPMANN, STEPHAN. 1999. "The Curriculum as a Standard in Public Education." *Studies in Philosophy and Education* 18:89–105.

KLIEBARD, HERBERT M. 1996. "Constructing a History of the American Curriculum." *Handbook of Research on Curriculum,* ed. Philip W. Jackson. New York: Macmillan.

MCENEANEY, ELIZABETH H., and MEYER, JOHN W. 2000. "The Content of the Curriculum: An Institutionalist Perspective." In *Handbook of the Sociology of Education,* ed. Maureen T. Hallinan. New York: Kluwer.

PINAR, WILLIAM F.; REYNOLDS, WILLIAM M.; SLATTERY, PATRICK; and TAUBMAN, PETER M. 1995. *Understanding Curriculum: An Introduction to the Study of Historical and Contemporary Curriculum Discourses.* New York: Lang.

TROW, MARTIN. 1961. "The Second Transformation of American Secondary Education." *International Journal of Comparative Sociology* 2:144–165.

TYACK, DAVID, and TOBIN, WILLIAM. 1994. "The 'Grammar' of Schooling: Why Has It Been So Hard to Change?" *American Educational Research Journal* 31:453–479.

WESTBURY, IAN. 1988. "Who Can Be Taught What: General Education in the Secondary School." In *Cultural Literacy and the Idea of General Education,* ed. Ian Westbury and Alan C. Purves. 87th Yearbook of the National Society for the Study of Education, Part 2. Chicago: University of Chicago Press.

IAN WESTBURY

CORE KNOWLEDGE CURRICULUM

More properly termed "the Core Knowledge Sequence," Core Knowledge is a grade-by-grade specification of topics in history, geography, literature, visual art, music, language, science, and mathematics for grades pre-kindergarten through eight. These topics are set forth with some specificity in a publication called *The Core Knowledge Sequence,* available from the nonprofit Core Knowledge Foundation.

The following is an example of the sequence in grade two history and geography:

II. Early Civilizations: Asia

  A. Geography of Asia

    1. The largest continent with the most populous countries in the world

    2. Locate: China, India, Japan

  B. India

    1. Indus River and Ganges River

    2. Hinduism

      a. Brahma, Vishnu, Shiva

      b. Many holy books, including the *Rig Veda*

    3. Buddhism

      a. Prince Siddhartha becomes Buddha, "The Enlightened One"

      b. Buddhism begins as an outgrowth of Hinduism in India, then spreads through many countries in Asia

      c. King Asoka (also spelled Ashoka)

This example illustrates the specificity and the selectivity of the sequence, as well as its unique feature of providing solid content in the primary grades.

The selectivity of the sequence is partly a result of expert consensus on the importance of topics within a domain, but is mainly determined by whether or not this knowledge tends to be taken for granted in books addressed to a general reader, and whether or not it tends to be possessed by the top economic tier of U.S. society, but not by the bottom economic tier. The sequence is premised on the belief that if schools teach this enabling knowledge, the knowledge gap and the related income gap between the lowest and highest economic groups would be reduced.

The contents of the sequence have evolved as the result of field testing and consensus building, starting in March 1990, with a conference of some 150 teachers, scholars, and administrators meeting in Charlottesville, Virginia.

The Goals of the Core Knowledge Curriculum

The basic goals of the Core Knowledge Curriculum are congruent with the basic goals of education in a democracy: fostering autonomous and knowledgeable citizens, giving every person an equal chance, and fostering community. These basic goals are intertwined, and all of them depend upon shared knowledge. The acquired abilities that give people an equal chance in life are the same abilities that make for autonomous citizens and a cohesive society. That is because the ability to communicate and to learn is based upon the same foundation of shared knowledge as the ability to earn a living and to vote intelligently, as well as to communicate with fellow citizens. The founding theory of the Core Knowledge Curriculum was that an inventory of this shared knowledge could be taken, and that imparting this knowledge to all rather than a few would foster all the democratic aims (including the equity aims) of public education.

Assessments of Effectiveness

Where Core Knowledge is implemented, the effects on achievement and equity have been highly significant both statistically and from the standpoint of effect size. The most important studies of actual school effects include a three-year study conducted by a team from Johns Hopkins University, and a large-scale study conducted by the Oklahoma City public schools. In the Hopkins report, "the gain difference on standardized tests between low and high implementing schools varied from 8.83 NCEs to 16.28 NCEs. That is an average rise of about 12 NCEs (similar to percentile points) over the controls, more than half a standard deviation—a very significant gain" (p. 26). (NCEs are Normal Curve Equivalents, a way of measuring where students fall along the normal curve when the mean is 50 and the standard deviation is 21.06.) The Oklahoma City study analyzed the effects of implementing one year of Core Knowledge in grades three, four, and five using the well-validated Iowa Test of Basic Skills. The study paired some 300 Core Knowledge students with 300 students not in the Core Knowledge program that had the same characteristics on seven variables:

1. Grade level

2. Pre-score

3. Sex

4. Race/ethnicity

5. Free-lunch eligibility

6. Title I eligibility

7. Special-education eligibility

Given the precise matching of these 300 pairs of students, the expectation would be that the end-of-year results of both groups would continue to be similar on the Iowa Test of Basic Skills. But, in fact, the Core Knowledge students made significantly greater one-year gains in reading comprehension, vocabulary, science, mathematics concepts, and social studies. The greatest gains—in reading, vocabulary, and social studies—were computed to be statistically highly significant. The vocabulary gain was especially notable, because vocabulary is the single best predictor of academic achievement and the area where the gap between ethnic and racial groups has proved to be especially difficult to overcome.

See also: SCHOOL REFORM.

BIBLIOGRAPHY

CUNNINGHAM, ANNE E., and STANOVICH, KEITH E. 1997. "Early Reading Acquisition and Its Relation to Reading Experience and Ability 10 Years Later." *Developmental Psychology* 33(6):934–945.

HOFSTETTER, C. RICHARD; STICHT, THOMAS G.; and HOFSTETTER, CAROLYN HUIE. 1999. "Knowledge Literacy, and Power." *Communication Research* 26(February):58–80.

KOSMOSKI, GEORGIA J.; GAY, GENEVA; and VOCKELL, EDWARD L. 1990. "Cultural Literacy and Academic Achievement." *Journal of Experimental Education* 58(4):265–272.

PENTONY, JOSEPH F. 1992. "Cultural Literacy: A Concurrent Validation." *Educational and Psychological Measurement* 52(4):967–972.

PENTONY, JOSEPH F. 1997. "Cultural Literacy." *Adult Basic Education* 7(1):39–45.

STANOVICH, KEITH E.; WEST, RICHARD F.; and Harrison, Michele R. 1995. "Knowledge Growth and Maintenance across the Life Span." *Developmental Psychology* 31(September):811–826.

INTERNET RESOURCE

CORE KNOWLEDGE FOUNDATION. 1999. *The Core Knowledge Sequence.* Charlottesville, VA: Core Knowledge Foundation. <www.coreknowledge.org>.

E. D. HIRSCH JR.

HIDDEN CURRICULUM

Hidden curriculum refers to messages communicated by the organization and operation of schooling apart from the official or public statements of school mission and subject area curriculum guidelines. In other words, the medium is a key source of messages. The messages of hidden curriculum usually deal with attitudes, values, beliefs, and behavior. There are numerous such messages conveyed indirectly. For example, that reading and mathematics are the most important elementary school subjects is clearly if implicitly communicated by scheduling more time for these subjects than for others, such as science and social studies, scheduling them in morning prime time rather than in the afternoon, and testing them more often than other subjects or skills.

The messages of hidden curriculum may complement or contradict each other as well as the official curriculum. For example, while school social studies curriculum typically emphasizes and even celebrates democratic political systems and principles, such as one person-one vote, majority rule and minority rights, separation of church and state, equality before the law, and due process, these principles are not always practiced in public school classrooms and corridors. Hidden curriculum can support or undermine official curriculum. Prominent displays of athletic trophies in the hallway near the school's main office—but not recognition for debate or music or scholarship—communicates a hierarchy of valued accomplishments that puts sports ahead of academics. It is likely that hidden curriculum has the most impact when there is an aggregate or a pattern of consistent messages. When hidden and explicit curricula conflict, it may be that hidden curriculum, like nonverbal communication, carries more weight.

Much of the organization and culture of schooling now referred to as hidden curriculum was once explicit assertive socialization according to a 1977 study by Elizabeth Vallance. The nineteenth-century McGuffey readers, for example, were intended to inculcate good behavior, such as passivity, punctuality, and respect for authority, through their stories, Protestant Christian prayers, and direct admonitions. Such teachings became implicit, if not hidden, by the early twentieth century because they were seen to be working and could be taken for granted as natural and normal. Students new to U.S. public schools, such as recent immigrants, were expected to adapt and fit in, for example, by looking at the teacher when spoken to, learning and using standard English, waiting (to speak, for the teacher's attention, for permission to use the toilet), and working hard.

Thus, a major purpose of the hidden curriculum of U.S. public schools has been cultural transmission or teaching students the routines for getting along in school and the larger society. In other words, hidden curriculum usually serves to maintain the status quo, specifically the dominant culture and prevailing socioeconomic hierarchy. It is this conservative bias, portrayed in articles by Jean Anyon and Michael Apple, that has been targeted by critics concerned about aspects of hidden curriculum, which work against diversity, equity, and social justice. Nonpublic schools, in contrast, such as Quaker or elite private schools, convey different hidden curriculum messages.

Earlier studies of hidden curriculum were conducted primarily in public elementary schools with a focus on academic classrooms. More recent work also has examined physical and business education and student cultures, with attention to messages about race/ethnicity, disability, and gender/sexual orientation as well as social class, politics, and culture. For example, Annette Hemmings investigated what she calls a "hidden corridor curriculum" that students have to negotiate in one way or another. Played out in hallways, lunchrooms, restrooms, and other nonclassroom spaces in two urban high schools she studied, it was dominated by a hostile, alienated youth culture antagonistic to typically middle-class school and social norms.

Two related aspects of hidden curriculum—or sources of hidden curriculum messages—can be distinguished: the structural or organizational and the cultural. These categories and the illustrative examples that follow can be useful guides to what to look or listen for in examining the nature and extent of hidden curriculum at a particular school.

Structural or organizational aspects of hidden curriculum include time scheduling of classes and other school activities; facilities provided; materials, such as textbooks and computer software; examinations; required courses; special programs, such as speech therapy or advanced placement; extracurricular activities and services; and grading and grouping policies.

Cultural aspects of hidden curriculum include school norms or ethos; décor and wall decorations; roles and relationships, including intergroup relations (within and between teachers and students); student cliques, rituals, and celebrations; and teacher expectations of various groups of students.

Mediation and Effects

While considerable attention has been paid to the messages of hidden curriculum, relatively little has been directed to whether they are received, how they are interpreted, and what effects they have on individuals or groups. Messages sent are not necessarily received or interpreted as intended by the sender. Particularly when a school's hidden curriculum offers varied or contradictory messages, as all but the smallest and most homogeneous tend to do, students have choices regarding which messages to act on and how to do so. Most students appear to neither totally accept nor completely reject the various messages of schooling. Numerous students become adept at "playing school," that is, keeping up appearances and seeming to go along in order to gain advantage, such as good grades, without internalizing the school's values or views of the world.

While the incorporation or Americanization of generations of immigrants and their children attests to the effectiveness of hidden curriculum, evidence of specific effects on individuals or groups of students remains sketchy. Illustrative evidence comes from the political socialization and citizenship education literature. For example, according to a 1980 article by Lee Ehman, a classroom setting in which controversial issues are freely discussed and students believe that they can influence classroom events shows a consistently strong relationship with political and participatory attitudes, including higher political efficacy and trust and lower political cynicism and alienation.

In sum, the primary value of the concept of hidden curriculum is that it calls attention to aspects of schooling that are only occasionally acknowledged and remain largely unexamined. Messages communicated by schools' organization and culture can support or undermine their stated purposes and official curricula.

BIBLIOGRAPHY

ANYON, JEAN. 1979. "Ideology and United States History Textbooks." *Harvard Educational Review* 49:361–386.

APPLE, MICHAEL W. 1971. "The Hidden Curriculum and the Nature of Conflict." *Interchange* 2(4):27–40.

CORNBLETH, CATHERINE. 1984. "Beyond Hidden Curriculum." *Journal of Curriculum Studies* 16(1):29–36.

EHMAN, LEE H. 1980. "The American School in the Political Socialization Process." *Review of Educational Research* 50(1):99–119.

HEMMINGS, ANNETTE. 1999–2000. "The 'Hidden Corridor' Curriculum." *The High School Journal* 83(2):1–10.

JACKSON, PHILIP W. 1968. *Life in Classrooms.* New York: Holt, Rinehart and Winston.

VALLANCE, ELIZABETH. 1977. "Hiding the Hidden Curriculum: An Interpretation of the Language of Justification in Nineteenth-Century Educational Reform." In *Curriculum and Evaluation,* eds. Arno A. Bellack and Herbert M. Kliebard. Berkeley, CA: McCutchan.

CATHERINE CORNBLETH

CURTI, MERLE (1897–1996)

A leading U.S. historian, Merle Curti studied the complex relationship of education to democratic values and to capitalist institutions. Born in Nebraska, he went to Harvard for his B.A. and stayed to complete his Ph.D. He worked with both Frederick Jackson Turner and Arthur M. Schlesinger, Sr. During Curti's years as a graduate student, he became acquainted with Charles Beard, the most influential American historian between 1910 and the 1940s. Around 1910 Beard had joined with James Harvey Robinson and Carl Becker to call for a "New History." These three believed that historians should be aware of the ways in which they constructed narratives: they should be aware that their narratives either protected the status quo or worked to create a better future.

Curti was an enthusiastic practitioner of the "New History." He rapidly published three books—*The American Peace Crusade, 1815–1860* (1929), *Bryan and World Peace* (1931), and *Peace or War: The American Struggle, 1636–1936* (1936)—that were designed to strengthen the peace movement in the United States. Beard admired Curti's scholarship

and enlisted him to participate in the Commission on the Social Sciences created by the American Historical Association. The purpose of this commission was to improve the teaching of history at the high school and college levels. Curti was asked to write volume ten of the Report of the American Historical Association's Committee on the Social Studies in the School. This book, *The Social Ideas of American Educators* (1935), analyzed the educational philosophy of a group of men from the colonial period onward, concluding with John Dewey. Curti focused on whether the educational ideas of these men encouraged or discouraged the development of democracy. Like his mentors, Charles Beard and John Dewey, Curti argued that capitalism, with its emphasis on competition and with its hierarchical organization, was a threat to democracy. He shared Dewey's hope that schools could provide an alternative environment of cooperation and equality that would strengthen democracy in the United States. Curti's next book, *The Great Mr. Locke: America's Philosopher, 1783–1861* (1937), was another expression of his interest in educational philosophy.

Beard also enlisted Curti to provide leadership for a project of the Social Science Research Council of the American Historical Association. This project resulted in a group of essays called *Theory and Practice in Historical Study: A Report of the Committee on Historiography* (1946). Known in the history profession as *Bulletin 54*, this volume would, in the minds of Beard and Curti, help create a consensus among historians in the 1940s that accepted the outlook of the "New History." During this decade, however, the report received more criticism than support. Beard, Dewey, and Curti were isolationists. Many intellectuals believed in 1918 that American participation in World War I had been a mistake. By the end of the 1930s, numerous scholars were embracing internationalism and wanted the United States to participate in World War II. These pro-war historians believed that the "New History" encouraged a position of moral relativism that made it difficult to condemn the evils of totalitarianism and to support the traditions of liberty in the United States and England. The pro-war historians also argued that Beard, Dewey, and Curti were representatives for a "conflict" school of historical writing. Their emphasis on a conflict between capitalism and democracy would, according to a new school of "consensus" historians, divide the nation in wartime. The "consensus" historians who became dominant in the

1950s argued that there was no conflict between capitalism and democracy.

At the same time Curti experienced this professional political defeat, he experienced success in helping to establish intellectual history as a topic to be taught in history departments. In 1943 he had published an intellectual history of the United States and its colonial past, *The Growth of American Thought.* This book won a Pulitzer Prize, and a poll of historians in 1950 voted it the most important contribution to history between 1936 and 1950. It expressed Curti's belief that ideas should be rooted in social history. It was a challenge to the approach to the history of ideas represented by Arthur Lovejoy and the *Journal of the History of Ideas.* Curti criticized Lovejoy for discussing ideas as if they were autonomous.

After teaching at Smith College, Curti moved to Teachers College of Columbia University and then to the University of Wisconsin in 1942. At Columbia he had directed the work of Richard Hofstadter, who became a leader in the new field of intellectual history. Under Curti's leadership, the University of Wisconsin was probably the most important center in the 1940s and 1950s for the study of the intellectual history of the United States. Several of Curti's first students at Wisconsin—John Higham, Warren Susman, and David W. Noble—became, like Hofstadter, leaders in the new field.

Curti continued to publish steadily, producing eight more books after 1946. The most important of these was *The Making of an American Community: A Case Study of Democracy in a Frontier County* (1959). Here he tested the frontier thesis of Frederick Jackson Turner by a detailed analysis of census materials.

BIBLIOGRAPHY

CURTI, MERLE. 1943. *The Growth of American Thought.* New York and London: Harper and Brothers.

CURTI, MERLE. 1946. *The Roots of American Loyalty.* New York: Columbia University Press.

CURTI, MERLE. 1954. *Prelude to Point Four: American Technical Missions Overseas, 1838–1938.* Madison: University of Wisconsin Press.

CURTI, MERLE. 1955. *Probing Our Past.* New York: Harper.

CURTI, MERLE. 1956. *American Paradox: The Conflict Between Thought and Action.* New Brunswick, NJ: Rutgers University Press.

CURTI, MERLE. 1959. *The Making of an American Community: A Case Study of Democracy in a Frontier Society.* Stanford, CA: Stanford University Press.

CURTI, MERLE. 1963. *American Philanthropy Abroad: A History.* New Brunswick, NJ: Rutgers University Press.

CURTI, MERLE. 1980. *Human Nature in American Thought: A History.* Madison: University of Wisconsin Press.

CURTI, MERLE. Collected Papers. Madison: State Historical Society of Wisconsin.

CURTI, MERLE, and CARSTENSEN, VERSON. 1949. *The University of Wisconsin: A History.* Madison: University of Wisconsin Press.

CURTI, MERLE, and NASH, RODERICK. 1965. *Philanthropy in the Shaping of American Higher Education.* New Brunswick, NJ: Rutgers University Press.

NOVICK, PETER. 1988. *That Noble Dream: The "Objectivity Question" and the American Historical Profession.* Cambridge, Eng.: Cambridge University Press.

SKOTHEIM, ROBERT A. 1966. *American Intellectual Histories and Historians.* Princeton, NJ: Princeton University Press.

DAVID W. NOBLE

D

DALTON SCHOOL

The Dalton School, founded by Helen Parkhurst in New York City in 1919, was one of the important Progressive schools created in the early part of the twentieth century and the home of the internationally famous Dalton Plan. In the early twenty-first century it is a competitive, elite, coeducational K–12 independent day school located on Manhattan's Upper East Side.

Parkhurst opened her school in New York City, naming it after the hometown of her benefactress, Mrs. Murray Crane, of Dalton, Massachusetts. The Dalton School followed Parkhurst's particular philosophy, "education on the Dalton Plan," an innovative synthesis of the ideas of the American educator and philosopher John Dewey and Progressive school superintendent (Winnetka, Illinois) Carleton W. Washburne, which featured House, Laboratory, and Assignment, designed to individualize instruction and, concurrently, create community.

Parkhurst's Dalton Plan reflected the child-centered Progressive movement of its time: often chaotic and disorganized, but also intimate, caring, nurturing, and familial. It focused on child growth and development, community and social service, and it strove to effect a synthesis between the affective and cognitive domains of the child.

In 1942 Parkhurst was forced to resign due to financial irregularities. By the time she did so, the Dalton Plan was firmly established from the nursery school through the high school. In addition, the Dalton Plan was internationally accepted as an important model for schooling and Parkhurst's ideas had been implemented in such places as Japan, the former Soviet Union, and the Netherlands.

Charlotte Durham, a teacher and administrator under Parkhurst since 1922, was headmistress from 1942 to 1960. She inherited an innovative, experimental, but financially troubled institution. Under Durham, Dalton was able to retain its child-centered pedagogy and its caring and familial orientation, while placing more emphasis on academic rigor. It was also administered in a more orderly and rational fashion and became perhaps less experimental and more a part of the traditional New York City independent school community. In essence, Durham's genius was to create a tradition out of a Progressive experiment, using the Dalton Plan as its guiding ritual.

Donald Barr served as Dalton's headmaster from 1964 to 1974. His educational background included attending the Progressive Lincoln School in New York City. He came to Dalton having been assistant dean of the Engineering School at Columbia University. Although a product of Progressive education, Barr had developed an educational philosophy closer to that of such conservative critics of Progressivism as Arthur Bestor. He thought Progressive education anti-intellectual and permissive and he sought to inject a rigorous and traditional curriculum into the Dalton Plan.

Under Barr, the parent constituency began to change, including a greater proportion of the recently affluent. The curriculum and physical plant expanded, enrollment more than doubled, the high school became coeducational, and the emphasis on academic rigor and achievement intensified still more. Reflecting an actual antipathy for Progressive education, Barr began the transformation of Dalton into a large, academically competitive, fashionable—and even trendy—institution. Although Barr created a desirable school, his administration was rife with controversy, and in the end, he resigned under a cloud.

Gardner Dunnan served as Dalton's headmaster from 1975 to 1997. He came to Dalton in 1975 after a career as a public school administrator in a number of affluent suburban school districts—the first head to come from the public sector, rather than from the independent school world, or in Barr's case, the university. Dunnan continued Dalton's transformation into an organized, efficient, selective, and academically rigorous institution. He enlarged the physical plant and initiated the Dalton Technology Plan, which he promoted as the link between the Progressivism of Helen Parkhurst and the Dalton of modernity. The school's graduates continued to enter prestigious colleges and universities, reflecting the goals of its parent body. By the time Dunnan resigned amid financial and personal problems in 1997, the Dalton School had become a traditional, elite college preparatory school with only vestiges of its Progressive past.

After four years of uninspired leadership, in which certain members of the board of trustees filled the leadership vacuum, Ellen Stein, a former Dalton student, became head in 2001. Although the school continues to pay lip service to the Dalton Plan, and the school is more progressive than most public schools, it is a far cry from the school Helen Parkhurst founded.

See also: ELEMENTARY EDUCATION, *subentry on* HISTORY OF; INSTRUCTIONAL STRATEGIES; PROGRESSIVE EDUCATION.

BIBLIOGRAPHY

SEMEL, SUSAN F. 1992. *The Dalton School: The Transformation of a Progressive School.* New York: Lang.

SEMEL, SUSAN F. 2002. "Helen Parkhurst." In *Founding Mothers and Others: Women Educational Leaders During the Progressive Era,* ed. Susan F. Semel and Alan R. Sadovnik. New York: Palgrave.

SUSAN F. SEMEL

DEAF STUDENTS

See: HEARING IMPAIRMENT, EDUCATION OF INDIVIDUALS WITH.

DECENTRALIZATION AND EDUCATION

The ways in which public primary and secondary education is financed and delivered varies greatly throughout the world. In France, education is highly centralized at the level of the national government, whereas in Canada the national government does not even have an education ministry, and in the United States education is mainly the responsibility of local school districts. Many developing countries and countries in transition to market economies have highly centralized government administration of education and other public services. During the 1990s and early twenty-first century, many of these countries began to decentralize education. This phenomenon proceeded fastest in Latin America and eastern Europe, but several countries in Asia and Africa also began initiating decentralization policies.

Definition

Decentralization is defined as the transfer of decision-making authority closer to the consumer or beneficiary. This can take the form of transferring powers to lower levels of an organization, which is called deconcentration or administrative decentralization. A popular form of deconcentration in education is to give additional responsibilities to schools. This is often called school autonomy or school-based management and may take the form of creating elected or appointed school councils and giving them budgets and the authority to make important educational decisions. Deconcentration may also take the form of empowering school directors or directors and teaching faculty to make decisions within the school.

Another form of decentralization, called devolution, entails transferring powers to lower levels of government. Most often, education responsibilities are transferred to general-purpose governments at the regional or local levels. Examples are the decentralization of basic education to local (district) level governments in India and Pakistan. In rare cases additional responsibilities are given to single-purpose governments, such as the local school district in the

United States. When education responsibilities are transferred to general-purpose governments, the elected governing bodies of those governments must make decisions about how much to spend on education versus other local services.

Measurement

The measurement of education decentralization is especially difficult. Economists often measure decentralization to lower levels of government by looking at the percent of educational revenues that come from local (or regional) sources, or, alternatively, by looking at the share of educational resources—whatever their origin—that local governments control. Using these measures, education is highly centralized in countries such as Greece, Italy, and Turkey and highly decentralized in countries such as Canada, Norway, the United Kingdom, and the United States.

However, these measures may be misleading when central governments mandate educational policies or programs that require the local government to allocate its revenues in a certain way. Mandating reductions in class size or the creation of special education programs, for example, reduces the degree of power the local government has to allocate its own revenues or resources. In the United States, the federal and state governments influence local education resource allocation both through unfunded policy and program mandates and through the use of conditional grants-in-aid, which require local governments or school districts to match federal or state funding for certain purposes. The combination of these mandates and conditional grants results in local school districts having discretionary expenditure control over only a small portion of their revenues and budgets.

An alternative means of measuring education decentralization is more subjective and entails (1) identifying the major decisions made regarding the finance and provision of education and (2) answering the question, who makes each decision? The Organisation for Economic Co-operation and Development (OECD) has developed a methodology for measuring the degree of education decentralization. This methodology divides educational functions into four groups: the organization of instruction, personnel management, planning and structures, and resources. The content of each group is given in Table 1.

TABLE 1

Types of decisions that may be decentralized

Organization of instruction	Select school attended by student. Set instruction time. Choose textbooks. Define curriculum content. Determine teaching methods.
Personnel management	Hire and fire school director. Recruit and hire teachers. Set or augment teacher pay scale. Assign teaching responsibilities. Determine provision of in-service training.
Planning and structures	Create or close a school. Select programs offered in a school. Define course content. Set examinations to monitor school performance.
Resources	Develop school improvement plan. Allocate personnel budget. Allocate nonpersonnel budget. Allocate resources for in-service teacher training.

SOURCE: Adapted from the Organisation for Economic Co-operation and Development.

Some educational functions are decentralized even within centralized systems, and others are centralized even within decentralized systems. An OECD survey of its members, for example, shows that, even in centralized systems, schools make most of the decisions about the organization of instruction. On the other hand, in many countries most personnel-management decisions are made at a central level.

Measuring decentralization by answering questions concerning who makes decisions in what areas does not provide an easy answer as to how decentralized one country's education system is relative to another's. Not all decisions are equally important. Indeed, one decision-making area is far more important than the others. Teachers and other school staff represent about 80 percent of total recurrent education spending in developed countries and more than 90 percent of total recurrent education spending in many developing countries. Research on learning also demonstrates that teachers and their ability to teach are the single most important factor in the school that affects learning. Thus, a shortcut for determining whether one country is more decentralized than another is to compare the countries' policies in personnel management. Countries that allow school councils to select school directors and allow schools to recruit, hire, and evaluate teachers have already achieved a significant degree of decentralization even though school finance may still be highly centralized and teachers may be paid according to a national pay scale.

Rationale

The rationale for education decentralization tends to be associated with four distinct objectives: democratization, regional and/or ethnic pressures, improved efficiency, and enhanced quality of schooling. Several countries with a history of authoritarian government have decentralized government in the name of democratization. More specifically, decentralization in these countries is designed to increase the voice of the local citizen and to empower the citizen to more fully participate in decision-making at the local level. Democratization has been the rationale for transferring education responsibilities to local governments in countries as diverse as Poland and Brazil.

In other countries, there have been pressures from regionally based ethnic and language groups to develop their own curriculum, teach in their own languages, and manage their own schools. A good example of this is Spain, where initially the Basque and Catalan regions gained the right to manage their own educational systems, followed later by other regions.

One of the potential benefits of decentralization is increased accountability to the citizen/beneficiary, resulting in improved efficiency in the use of school resources. The improved efficiency results from two effects. One effect is the better match between services provided and the preferences of citizens. The other effect is increased output relative to resources or expenditures. Chile is an example of a country where education was decentralized to local governments primarily in the pursuit of greater efficiency.

When education is decentralized in pursuit of democratization, or in response to regional/ethnic pressures, it is usually just one of several services being transferred to local or regional governments. In addition, educators often resist decentralization for these purposes, fearing greater inequality in spending and educational outcomes. On the other hand, when education is decentralized in pursuit of greater quality, it is usually done as part of a larger reform promoted by educators themselves. An example of this can be found in several large U.S. cities where school councils and school directors have been given greater decision-making autonomy. At

the same time, however, the performance of schools is carefully monitored, and schools are held accountable for improved performance to both parents and system administrators.

These four objectives account for most, but not all, of the reasons for education decentralization. Some countries have transferred the finance and delivery of education to lower levels of government to help solve the central government's own fiscal problems. Argentina, for example, transferred education from the national to the regional governments in order to reduce central government fiscal deficits. Since the education sector employs more personnel than other sectors and also requires large recurrent salary expenditures, it is a tempting target to decentralize for fiscal reasons. Other countries have given local governments the authority to run their own schools as a means of circumventing central government bureaucracies in order to rapidly increase enrollments in remote areas. El Salvador provides an example of decentralization to remote rural communities for this purpose.

Implementation

Like other education reforms, decentralization can result in political winners and losers. The potential winners are those gaining new decision-making powers, while the potential losers are those losing those powers. Two of the potential losers—civil servants and teacher unions—are sufficiently powerful that that they can effectively stop decentralization processes. The civil servants working in education ministries have perhaps the most to lose, because some of their jobs become redundant and their power to influence the allocation of resources may be diminished. In countries where corruption in government is a serious problem, reduced power will be also reflected in a reduced ability of civil servants to extract financial or in-kind rents. The leaders of national teacher unions also lose power to the extent that salary negotiations, teacher recruitment, and teacher promotion are moved from national to lower levels of government. Union members may also fear lower salaries if the funding of education is moved to local governments with fewer sources of government revenues. In countries where being elected head of a teacher union is an important stepping-stone to a political career, decentralization of labor negotiations is likely to reduce the political importance of leading the national union.

The implementation of education decentralization reforms can either be rapid or slow. Legislative or constitutional changes that immediately transfer responsibilities from the national to lower levels of government run the risk that lower levels of government will lack the required administrative capacity required to manage the system well. The result may be disruption in the delivery of schooling to children that adversely affects their learning, at least for a time. A more gradual decentralization can allow powers to be transferred to lower levels of government as those governments gain administrative capacity. The difficulty with gradual decentralization is that it may never occur at all, as the potential losers marshal their forces to fight the policy change.

In some countries with serious problems of internal conflict, weak public bureaucracies, or very weak government finances, one finds de facto decentralization of education. In these cases, the central government abdicates its responsibility for financing and providing public education, especially in remote areas, so local communities organize and finance their own schools and recruit and hire their own teachers. In Africa, the countries of Benin and Togo provide examples of community control and finance of schools resulting from the lack of central government supply. In other cases, the central government finances an inadequate number of teachers and other school resources to ensure schooling of adequate quality. In these cases, parents may form school councils to raise revenues to hire additional teachers, construct and equip school buildings, and provide other school resources. By virtue of their important role in funding education, parents and school councils may exercise significant decision-making power.

School Finance

The financing of decentralized education can be very complicated in systems where two or three levels of government share financing responsibilities. The choices for financing education in such systems can be framed as follows: (1) central versus local funding, (2) conditional versus unconditional grants, and (3) negotiated versus formula-driven grants. The choices made concerning education finance are extremely important as they determine both the degree of effective control local governments have as well as the implications for efficiency and equity.

The single most important choice is whether the level of government providing education (in most cases, the local government) is expected to generate its own revenues for education from its own tax and other revenues sources or if it will receive the bulk of the required educational revenues from a higher level government. Local government capacity to generate revenues (i.e., its tax base, or its fiscal capacity) tends to vary widely across local governments within regions or countries. Thus, requiring local governments to raise all their own revenues for education ensures an unacceptably high degree of inequality in spending per child. Countries where local governments finance education from their own source revenues (e.g., Brazil, the United States) have adopted intergovernmental grants to help even out spending inequalities. In the case of Brazil, the central government provides additional financing to ensure each jurisdiction spends a minimum amount per student. In the case of the United States, school finance policies vary by state, but in general they, too, ensure a minimum level of spending and, in some cases, put a cap on the maximum amount a local school district can spend.

Most countries have made the choice to fund a large portion of primary and secondary education spending from either the regional or national government budgets. This funding can be provided in one of two ways. Monies can be transferred from the central government to either the general fund of the local (or regional) government or to a special education fund of the local (or regional) government. In the former case, the local or regional government receives funding sufficient to cover a large portion of expected education expenditures, but the local or regional government makes the decision of how much to spend on education. In the latter case, the local or regional government is required to spend the grant monies on education only. Requiring grant monies to be spent on education ensures adequate education spending but reduces the expenditure autonomy of the local (or regional) government.

Once a decision is made to transfer monies to lower levels of government, a further decision needs to be made as to how to determine what amount of money should be transferred to each receiving government. The basic choice is whether to negotiate that amount between governments or to determine the amount using a capitation formula. Negotiation has political advantages in that it allows central governments to reward their political allies, and thus it is often popular. Capitation formulas, however, are more equitable and may also provide incentives for educational performance. Chile, for example, determines how much it provides to each local government based on a formula that includes indicators of educational cost, educational need, and student average daily attendance. Since local governments receive more revenues if more students are enrolled and attending regularly, the formula has encouraged those governments to undertake campaigns to keep children in school.

Effects of Decentralization

It is extremely difficult to disentangle the effects of education decentralization policies from other variables simultaneously affecting educational outcomes, and there have been few rigorous attempts to do so. Two studies that did attempt to isolate the effects of devolution in Central America concluded that it increased parental participation, reduced teacher and student absenteeism, and increased student learning by a significant, but small, amount.

See also: GOVERNMENT AND EDUCATION, THE CHANGING ROLE OF; SCHOOL-BASED DECISION-MAKING.

BIBLIOGRAPHY

FISZBEIN, ARIEL, ed. 2001. *Decentralizing Education in Transition Societies: Case Studies from Central and Eastern Europe.* Washington, DC: World Bank.

HALASZ, GABOR. 1996. "Changes in the Management and Financing of Educational Systems." *European Journal of Education* 31(1):57–71.

HANNAWAY, JANE, and CARNOY, MARTIN, eds. 1993. *Decentralization and School Improvement: Can We Fulfill the Promise?* San Francisco: Jossey-Bass.

ODDEN, ALLAN, and CLUNE, WILLIAM H. 1998. "School Finance Systems: Aging Structures in Need of Renovation." *Educational Evaluation and Policy Analysis* 20(3):157–177.

ORGANISATION FOR ECONOMIC CO-OPERATION AND DEVELOPMENT. 1998. *Education at a Glance: OECD Indicators.* Paris: Organisation for Economic Co-operation and Development.

WINKLER, DONALD, and GERSHBERG, ALEC IAN. 2000. "Education Decentralization in Latin America: The Effects on the Quality of Schooling." In *Decentralization and Accountability of the Public Sector,* ed. Shahid Javed Burki et al. Washington, DC: World Bank.

WOHLSTETTER, PRISCILLA, and ODDEN, ALLAN. 1992. "Rethinking School-Based Management, Policy, and Research." *Educational Administration Quarterly* 28:529–542.

DONALD WINKLER

DECISION-MAKING IN DEVELOPING NATIONS, APPLYING ECONOMIC ANALYSIS TO

In mainstream economic analysis, education is seen as a production process in which *inputs* (e.g., students, teachers, and textbooks) are combined to yield desired *outputs* (e.g., student learning) within the education sector, and larger societal outcomes outside the sector (e.g., increased earnings in the workplace or greater social equality), under the prevailing educational technology (encompassing pedagogy, curriculum, and school organization) and input prices. A major application of economic analysis is to inform decision-making in education in order to improve efficiency in educational production; that is, producing more desired education outputs and outcomes given educational resources. Analytically, educational efficiency can be distinguished as internal efficiency and external efficiency. Internal efficiency relates educational outputs to educational inputs, while external efficiency relates educational outcomes to educational inputs. Analysis of educational efficiency is not confined to economic concerns only, since educational outputs and outcomes also pertain to social and political dimensions of national development.

A substantial literature exists concerning the economic analysis of educational development in developing nations. Developing nations are not a homogenous group; there are substantial differences between them in terms of the level of socioeconomic development, extent of ethnic and religious diversity, history, and cultural values.

Internal Efficiency of Education

The internal efficiency of education is improved when more education outputs are produced at given education resources or fewer education resources are used in producing the same amount of education outputs. Thus educational economic analysis is centrally concerned with the production of education outputs and with education costs.

An educational production function is a mathematical construct that mainstream economists and researchers from other disciplines often use to study educational production. It relates some measure of education output (e.g., student achievement) to various inputs used in education (e.g., student characteristics and family background, teacher characteristics and other school-related factors). An early application in developing nations is the 1975 study by Leigh Alexander and John Simmons that found that family backgrounds and socioeconomic factors, not school factors, were the most important determinants of student achievement. But a 1983 study by Stephen Heyneman and William Loxley countered that school factors could also affect student achievement, and that such factors had stronger effects in low-income nations than in high-income nations. Other studies also tried to identify school factors that could boost student learning and to show that spending on school quality could have a good return. These studies argued that it is not enough to focus on quantitative development of the education system, and that the government and the donor community should pay more attention to improving school quality. Patrick McEwan and Martin Carnoy's 2000 study and Emmanuel Jimenez and Marlaine Lockheed's 1995 study of educational production include data that compare the effectiveness of public versus private schools and that employ more sophisticated statistical techniques.

The costs of education refer to resources utilized in the education production process; they include not only government expenditure on education, but also household spending on education and the foregone opportunities of schooling (e.g., gainful employment). Education cost studies range from macroanalysis of national educational expenditures across nations to microanalysis of educational decision-making by individuals and households. Cross-national studies have found that government spending on education (as a percentage of national output) has declined in the developing nations since the 1980s, after a rising trend in the 1960s and 1970s. Studies in a number of developing nations have shown that private spending on education is a significant part of the total spending on education, and that private costs are an important source of educational inequality and inequity in these nations. In addition, household education costs could be a

heavy economic burden on poor and rural households, resulting in negative educational consequences such as dropping out. Financial assistance targeted at poor and rural populations should be part of the overall strategy to improve school attendance for marginalized population groups. There is a need to carefully estimate the costs of educational inclusion of marginalized groups because such costs tend to be quite different from those for nonmarginalized groups.

Privatization of schooling has been proposed as a strategy for improving the effectiveness and cost-effectiveness of education in developing nations. Proponents of privatization argue that private schools are more effective and are more likely to be less costly than public schools. Competition in the education market could also lead to improvement of public schools. Critics of privatization point out that there is no conclusive evidence to show that private schools are more effective than public schools. For example, in 2000 McEwan and Carnoy found that Chile shows different types of private schools—some more effective; others, less effective than government schools. An unpublished review by Mun C. Tsang of the costs of public and private schools in developing nations finds that most studies tend to underestimate the costs (thus overestimate the internal efficiency) of private schools relative to public schools. Controversy remains as privatization is concerned not only with cost-effectiveness, but also with opposing ideologies and competing goals of schooling.

A subject of sustained interest in developing nations is the economic analysis of new educational technology because of the need to provide educational services in remote and sparsely populated areas, to reduce unit cost and meet educational demand under very tight government education budgets, and more generally to improve educational quality through more cost-effective alternatives to traditional schooling. Studies found that small media (e.g., radio) were less costly and more cost-effective than large media (e.g, television). Distance education is an effective way to reach learners in remote and sparsely populated areas. Cost analysis indicates that programs using educational media demonstrate economies of scale. But since they require large start-up costs, these programs have to have large enrollments and a long period of operation in order to be comparable to traditional schooling in terms of unit costs. The use of computers in the school context has had mixed success. Of particular current interest is the use of the Internet in education. It is necessary to ascertain the potential of the Internet in developing nations and to address the concern of some observers that there is an increasing digital divide between developing nations and advanced industrialized nations. A mindful introduction of new technology into education, informed by a careful analysis of the education problems to be addressed and the range of technological alternatives available, is highly desirable.

Teachers are a key input in educational production, and an adequate supply of skilled teachers is a prominent policy concern in many nations, including developing ones. Not unexpectedly, teacher supply is influenced by such factors as teachers' salaries and working conditions relative to those in other occupations, and the costs of teacher preparation relative to those for other occupations. The harsh working conditions in rural areas in developing nations often lead to a shortage of skilled teachers in these areas. In some developing nations, low educational quality is related to the existence of a significant proportion of untrained teachers, an uneven distribution of teachers across schools, and teacher absenteeism. There is a lack of published studies of teachers' markets and the utilization of teachers in the developing world.

Educational finance is an important domain in education economics since it deals with the mobilization and allocation of resources in the production of education. For many nations in the developing world, especially poor ones, external resources, in terms of bilateral or multilateral assistance, are a key source of funding for educational development. However, international funding is becoming more problematic over time because of a combination of factors, including declining financial support from advanced industrialized nations, the increasing demand and competition among receiving nations, and the imposition of more stringent conditions for receiving aid. Economic reforms pushed by the International Monetary Fund in developing nations often impose strong limits on government spending. Such a policy was associated with negative effects on the education sector in much of the 1970s and 1980s. Since the 1990s international development agencies have become more vocal in calling for more spending on the social sectors, including education. The ability of developing nations to finance educational development has also been hampered by the need of each government to make interest payments on international and domestic debts. Increasingly, there is a call that debt relief for developing nations and for international development agencies be in the form of grants instead of loans to these nations, especially in the social sectors. As the leadership of the World Bank pointed out in 1995, however, debt relief is only part of the solution; what is also needed is the opening up of agricultural and other markets in advanced industrialized nations to products from developing nations.

It would be misguided to focus only on central government and external sources for financing education. In many developing nations, the community has been an important source, in cash and/or in kind, for educational development. Community involvement is useful not only for financial reasons, but also for educational and accountability purposes. Participation from parents and community members can discourage teacher and student absenteeism. In addition, fiscal and administrative decentralization in education have the potential for not only mobilizing additional resources to education from various levels, but also enabling more informed and more efficient decision-making about education matters at the local level. To mitigate the disequalizing and inequity effects that often accompany decentralization, however, central and regional governments need to provide equalization aid to poor and rural areas. Moreover, nongovernmental organizations (NGOs) could have an important role to play in raising additional resources for education and/or in implementing educational programs, particularly for marginalized populations. Finally, there is an increasing emphasis on cost recovery in education, especially at the higher-education level, so that the financing responsibility is shifted more from the government to households.

External Efficiency of Education

The external efficiency of education is improved when more education outcomes are produced at given education resources or fewer education resources are used in producing the same amount of education outcomes. During the closing decades of the twentieth century, emphasis in developing nations regarding educational development has been placed on three broad outcomes of education: contribution to economic growth and competitiveness, improvement in social equity, and poverty alleviation.

According to human capital theory, education is a form of human capital that could raise the productive capacity of individuals in economic production. Empirical studies in agriculture found a positive and significant relationship between productivity and education. At the macro level, education was also associated with economic growth. Spending on education can be seen as an investment activity with both costs and benefits, and thus subject to a cost–benefit analysis. A review of rate of returns studies, such as the 1994 study of George Psacharopoulos, found that in developing nations education had a high rate of return and that the return was higher at lower education levels. Paul Bennell, however, has criticized these studies, in terms of appropriateness of method and quality of data. Some analysts, such as Ronald Dore, point out that educational expansion in a depressed economy could lead to unemployment of the educated or overeducation. Nevertheless, there is increasing consensus across nations that human capital, particularly in terms of problem-solving skills, communication skills in a diverse setting, and the ability to adapt to change, can enhance economic competitiveness in the global economy of the twenty-first century. There is also increasing attention to investment in preschool education and in education for sustainable development.

Growth with Social Equity?

There have been different views on whether increased economic growth and improved social equity could coexist. Using the experience of eight East Asian economies, the World Bank concluded in a 1993 publication that growth with equity was possible. This study made a guarded but positive assessment of the role of education: education was only one of many contributing factors to growth with equity but appropriate education policy did matter, especially in terms of adequate investment in education and the focus of government policy on lower levels of education. The financial crisis that began in 1997, however, underscored the importance of noneducation factors that could affect the health of the economy in these nations.

Earlier efforts in promoting education for poverty reduction have been accompanied by high hope and disillusionment. The urgent need for poverty reduction in the developing world is reflected by the World Bank's redefining itself as a poverty-reduction organization. There is common under-standing in the early twenty-first century that "quality basic education for all" is an important part of the overall strategy for poverty reduction. But education alone is not sufficient; rather a multisectoral approach involving related interventions in agriculture, education, health (including addressing the AIDS epidemic), credit market for small producers, and other social sectors, is needed. Poverty reduction also requires targeted interventions. Women are one of the most important targeted groups because they are often subject to multiple disadvantages in the developing world. Increasing educational access and improving quality for girls could have profound economic, social, and political benefits for women and for society.

See also: DECISION-MAKING IN SCHOOLS, APPLYING ECONOMIC ANALYSIS TO; SOCIAL CAPITAL AND EDUCATION.

BIBLIOGRAPHY

ALEXANDER, LEIGH, and SIMMONS, JOHN. 1975. *The Determinants of School Achievement in Developing Countries: The Educational Production Function.* Washington, DC: World Bank.

ANKHARA-DOVE, LINDA. 1982. "The Deployment and Training of Teachers for Remote Rural Schools in Less-Developed Nations." *International Review of Education* 28(1):3–27.

BECKER, GARY. 1975. *Human Capital,* 2nd edition. Chicago: University of Chicago Press.

BEHRMAN, JEREMY R., and KING, ELIZABETH M. 2001. "Household Schooling Behaviors and Decentralization." *Economics of Education Review* 20(4):321–341.

BENNELL, PAUL. 1998. "Rates of Return to Education in Asia: A Review of the Evidence." *Education Economics* 6(2):107–120.

BRAY, MARK, and LILLIS, KELVIN, eds. 1988. *Community Financing of Education: Issues and Policy Implications in Less-Developed Nations.* Oxford: Pergamon.

DE MOURA CASTRO, CLAUDIO, ed. 1998. *Education in the Information Age.* Washington, DC: Inter-American Development Bank.

DORE, RONALD. 1976. *The Diploma Disease.* Berkeley: University of California Press.

HEYNEMAN, STEPHEN, and LOXLEY, WILLIAM. 1983. "The Effect of School Quality on Academic

Achievement across Twenty-Nine High- and Low-Income Nations." *American Journal of Sociology* 88:1162–1194.

INTER-AGENCY COMMISSION. 1990. *Meeting Basic Learning Needs: A New Vision for the 1990s.* New York: United Nations.

JAMISON, DEAN, and ORIVEL, FRANCIS. 1982. "The Cost-Effectiveness of Distance Education for School Equivalency." In *Alternative Routes to Formal Education: Distance Education for School Equivalency,* ed. Hillary Perraton. Baltimore: Johns Hopkins University Press.

JIMENEZ, EMMANUEL, and LOCKHEED, MARLAINE. 1995. *Public and Private Secondary Education in Developing Nations: A Comparative Study.* Washington, DC: World Bank.

KING, ELIZABETH M., and HILL, M. ANNE, eds. 1993. *Women's Education in Developing Nations: Barriers, Benefits, and Policies.* Baltimore and London: Johns Hopkins University Press.

LEVIN, HENRY. 2000. *A Comprehensive Framework for Evaluating Educational Vouchers.* New York: National Center for the Study of Privatization in Education, Teachers College, Columbia University.

MCEWAN, PATRICK, and CARNOY, MARTIN. 2000. "The Effectiveness and Efficiency of Private Schools in Chile's Voucher System." *Educational Evaluation and Policy Analysis* 22(3):213–239.

NARVARRO, JUAN CARLOS, ed. 1994. *Community Organizations in Latin America.* Baltimore: Johns Hopkins University Press.

NETTLETON, GRETA. 1991. "Uses and Costs of Educational Technology for Distance Education in Developing Countries." In *Education Technology: Sustainable and Effective Use,* ed. Marlaine E. Lockheed, John Middleton, and Greta Nettleton. Washington, DC: World Bank.

PARRY, TARYN R. 1997. "Decentralization and Privatization: Education Policy in Chile." *Journal of Public Policy* 17:107–133.

PSACHAROPOULOS, GEORGE. 1994. "Returns to Investment in Education: A Global Update." *World Development* 22:1325–1343.

SCHULTZ, THEODORE. 1971. *Investment in Human Capital.* New York: The Free Press.

STROMQUIST, NELLY. 1996. "Gender Delusions and Exclusions in the Democratization of Schooling in Latin America." *Comparative Education Review* 40(4):404–425.

TSANG, MUN C. 1988. "Cost Analysis for Educational Policymaking: A Review of Cost Studies in Education in Developing Countries" *Review of Educational Research* 58(2):181–230.

TSANG, MUN C. 1994. *Cost Analysis of Educational Inclusion of Marginalized Population.* Paris: International Institute for Educational Research, United Nations Educational, Scientific and Cultural Organization.

WOLFENSOHN, JAMES, and FISCHER, STANLEY. 2000. *The Comprehensive Development Framework and Poverty Reduction Strategy Papers.* Washington, DC: World Bank and International Monetary Fund.

WORLD BANK. 1993. *The East Asian Miracle.* New York: Oxford University Press.

WORLD BANK. 1995. *Priorities and Strategies for Education: A World Bank Review.* Washington, DC: World Bank.

MUN C. TSANG

DECISION-MAKING IN SCHOOLS, APPLYING ECONOMIC ANALYSIS TO

In the 1999 through 2000 school year, spending for all levels of education amounted to $646.8 billion. According to the National Center for Education Statistics, of this total, $389 billion was spent for K–12 education and the remaining $257.8 billion was expended by postsecondary institutions. Despite the substantial financial commitment to education, the impact of economics on the way educational institutions allocate and use their resources has been remarkably limited. Economics is concerned with obtaining the best possible outcome from a limited budget, and thus seems an ideal approach for dealing with how to allocate resources within schools. Although economists are beginning to analyze educational problems in increasing numbers, they have yet to make major inroads in improving educational productivity. This article describes ways in which economic analysis could be used to improve decision-making in educational institutions, and to inform the allocation and use of educational resources.

Even though virtually all educators believe that additional resources will lead to higher student performance, it remains unclear how best to spend dollars to achieve that goal. As a result, demands for more money, absent a well-reasoned description of how the money will be used, does not build confidence that money—by itself—will make a difference.

Researchers have used production functions—a statistical approach linking outcomes with specific inputs—to understand how money matters. To date, this research has been inconclusive with some arguing that money matters and others suggesting a systematic link between higher levels of resources and more money does not appear to exist. This stems in part from disagreement over the proper outcome of schooling.

Traditional allocation tools like cost–benefit analysis are infrequently applied in educational settings due largely to the difficulty of placing a monetary value on the outcomes or benefits of education. Henry M. Levin and Patrick McEwan suggest that linking costs to some measure of performance, or effectiveness, is a better approach for education. Under this model, the cost per unit gain of achievement is estimated so that programs that are more efficient, or cost effective, can be identified and chosen.

Eric Hanushek argues that the proper incentives for better performance and efficient use of educational resources are not in place, and that holding schools accountable for student performance is essential to use more effectively existing and new money. Improvement of student performance, with or without new funds, requires improved decision-making in the following four areas.

- Reallocation of existing resources
- Incentives for improved performance
- Development of the concept of *venture capital* for schools and school systems
- A more market-based budgeting environment

Reallocation of Existing Resources

Regardless of what impact additional funds might have, it is important that existing resources be used as efficiently as possible. In many districts it may be possible to reduce class size through different assignments of teachers throughout the district. To the extent that smaller class size improves student performance, these changes would offer an improvement in student performance at little or no cost.

Before seeking additional funds, schools may investigate other ways to restructure what is done with current funds. Allan Odden and Carolyn Busch argue that schools can find additional resources through a combination of creative use of categorical funds, elimination of classroom aides, and reallocation of resources, such as the elimination of one or two teaching positions. Although some of these options may result in larger classes, or fewer teachers, the more intensive use of staff and greater professional development activities available have resulted in improved student performance in many of the schools that have adopted this approach.

Incentives

The use of incentives to encourage schools or school districts to allocate resources in ways that lead to improved student performance is not a new idea. Unfortunately, the incentives that seem to have the most success have been sanctions. Schools faced with threats of intervention often act quickly to improve performance rather than risk the stigma of a sanction. Conversely, many positive incentives have been less successful. For example, high-performing schools are often granted waivers from state regulation in exchange for success. In this case, the regulatory system loosened constraints that may have made the organization successful. Perhaps the more appropriate incentive would be to provide such waivers to under-performing schools with the hope that increased flexibility would lead to improvements.

Hanushek argues that the incentives currently in place in schools do not encourage teachers to work towards improving student performance and therefore need to be changed. He suggests that there is not sufficient awareness of positive performance incentives, and that more experimentation and research is needed.

Venture Capital (Equity)

One problem of education in the early twenty-first century is that once funds are appropriated to a school or program, they become the possession of that entity. In a study of the costs of implementing California's "Caught in the Middle" reforms for middle schools, published in 1992, David Marsh and Jennifer Sevilla found that the annual costs of restructuring schools to meet the requirements of this program were between 3 and 6 percent higher than current average expenditures per pupil in California schools. However, they also concluded that the first year start-up costs amounted to approximately 25 percent of annual costs. The problem schools face is finding those start-up funds. Often such funds are not available for all schools in a district, and schools receiving such funds treat them as a continuous source of revenue. Yet if such funds were rotated among schools, it would be possible to institute new programs in all schools over a few years.

Related to the concept of venture capital is the concept of revolving funds. This notion offers a way for school districts to deal with large purchases, like computers, that occur on a regular but nonannual basis. Budget procedures in school districts do not reward schools for saving resources in one year to make large purchases the next year. A school that receives a sum of discretionary money in one year is likely to lose any of the funds it has not expended by the end of the fiscal year. As a result, schools are often unable to make a large coordinated purchase.

A solution to this would be a revolving fund in the district to pay for such purchases. Schools would receive large appropriations of funds for such purchases once every few years. Finding a way to use the money in a revolving fashion would facilitate continued improvements in educational programs. The major problem is determining who gets the venture capital funds first and who has to wait. In many large districts, the superintendent publishes lists of the best- and worst-performing schools, and such lists could be used to prioritize the allocation of these funds. Another issue is the equity of the distribution. Although some schools will get more funds one year than others, over the established time period, all schools will receive an equal amount—one simply has to accept the idea that equity is measured over some time frame, and not on an annual basis.

Market Approaches

Many reformers call for market-based changes in the organization of schools. There are many ways to introduce the market into the educational arena, but most of these fall under the heading of school choice. Public school choice can be considered as either an intradistrict or interdistrict choice, and these can be broken down further into the various types of programs in each category. Two other types of choice involve the blurring of the line between public and private education: private school vouchers and privatization of former public schools.

Intradistrict choice programs, by definition confined to one school district, grew largely out of

an attempt to desegregate schools, rather than to provide competition or parent choice. The first of these programs is called controlled choice, where districts created models for assigning students to schools outside of the traditional neighborhood school model as a way of reducing segregation. A second type of intradistrict choice program is the magnet school. Magnet schools were designed to attract white students to schools with high minority populations, often located in heavily minority communities.

The newest model of intradistrict choice is the charter school. With the development of the charter school, the purpose of the choice models shifted away from desegregation to a focus on providing parents with the choice to send their children to schools that may be less regulated than their traditional neighborhood school. These schools operate under a charter between those who organize the school (typically teachers and parents) and a sponsor (typically the local school board or state board of education).

Interdistrict choice programs allow the transfer of students between school districts. Although interdistrict choice programs also grew out of attempts to desegregate, they always had the goal of increasing parental choice as well. Many states allow interdistrict choice through open enrollment policies, which vary from state to state; some states mandate that all districts have open enrollment while others allow districts to choose whether they wish to be open or closed.

Perhaps the most talked-about form of choice program is the voucher program. Voucher programs can be organized in different ways, but the basic idea is to give some children access to private schools by issuing vouchers to their families, which the families then give to the school in lieu of a tuition payment. Often these programs have the intention of allowing low-income students to go to schools they could not otherwise afford to attend, although vouchers are not necessarily limited to those in poverty.

A final market-based approach is the privatization of schools that were formerly public. This is also a relatively new approach, and one that arose largely out of a demand for strategies that could save failing schools. The argument is that if public education functions like a monopoly (a firm that has control over its price and product) because it is not subject to competition, it has little incentive to function efficiently. By introducing some competition through privatization, schools would be forced to provide higher-quality education at a lower price.

Recent efforts to collect resource data at the school site and even student level may lead to enhanced knowledge of how resources impact student outcomes. To the extent that such knowledge is applied to decisions about how schools are operated, the long-term impact may be improved educational productivity through enhanced and informed decision-making.

See also: PUBLIC SCHOOL BUDGETING, ACCOUNTING, AND AUDITING.

BIBLIOGRAPHY

HANUSHEK, ERIC A. 1994. *Making Schools Work: Improving Performance and Controlling Costs.* Washington, DC: The Brookings Institution.

HANUSHEK, ERIC A. 1997. "Assessing the Effects of School Resources on Student Performance: An Update." *Educational Evaluation and Policy Analysis* 19(2):141–164.

LEVIN, HENRY M., and McEWAN, PATRICK. 2000. *Cost Effectiveness Analysis: Methods and Applications.* Thousand Oaks, CA: Sage.

MARSH, DAVID, and SEVILLA, JENNIFER. 1991. *Goals and Costs of Middle School Reform.* USC Center for Research on Education Finance Policy Brief. Los Angeles: University of Southern California, Center for Research on Education Finance.

ODDEN, ALLAN, and BUSCH, CAROLYN. 1998. *Financing Schools for High Performance.* San Francisco: Jossey-Bass.

INTERNET RESOURCE

NATIONAL CENTER FOR EDUCATION STATISTICS. 2001. "Digest of Education Statistics: Table 31." <http://nces.ed.gov/pubs2001/digest/dt031.html>.

LAWRENCE O. PICUS

DE LIMA, AGNES (1887–1974)

Journalist, educator, and activist, Agnes de Lima wrote significant books and articles about Progressive education. She was born in Holywood, New Jersey, and grew up in Larchmont, New York, and New York City in a prosperous, conservative banking family that had emigrated from Curacao. De Lima attended private school and entered Vassar College in 1904 at the age of seventeen. At Vassar, de Lima received an excellent liberal education and majored in English. Through such teachers as feminist Lucy Salmon she encountered some of the liberal reformist thinking of the Progressive period. She worked with the College Settlement Association and was active in a campus organization that tried to improve the pay and working conditions of college maids. Her Vassar experience led her away from her family's conservative values, and she became active in socialist, feminist, labor, educational, and other reform movements.

After graduating from Vassar in 1908, de Lima moved to New York City, where she lived in a settlement house and worked as a writer for the Russell Sage Foundation and the Bureau of Municipal Research. She continued her education at the New York School of Social Work from which she received a master's degree in 1912. In 1917 there was a major political struggle over the efforts of reformist mayor John Mitchel to begin a "platoon school" innovation in New York City. In these schools students moved through a variety of workshops, assemblies, and libraries in platoons or groups, rather than remaining in one classroom. Willard Wirt, who had created a platoon system in Gary, Indiana, was hired to develop the program in New York. De Lima worked with Randolph Bourne and other young activists to promote the innovation, which was dropped in 1918 after voters rejected the reformist mayor.

These activities led to de Lima's more intense involvement with education and liberal journalism. Randolph Bourne had been the major education writer for the *New Republic* after the founding of that journal in 1914. Following his death in 1918, de Lima became the leading writer on education both for that journal and for the *Nation,* the other influential liberal periodical. She wrote for these journals a series of articles on Progressive education, which she then collected into a 1924 book titled *Our Enemy the Child.* This was one of the earliest books to describe and interpret what was actually happening in Progressive classrooms, and it has since been widely cited by scholars in educational history. It was the first study to identify clearly the three figures of Progressive education that Lawrence Cremin, in his influential 1960s book *The Transformation of the School,* labeled "scientists, sentimentalists, and radicals." De Lima's parallel groups were the "technicians," who focused on testing and methods; the "child-centered" educators; and the "visionaries," who hoped to reform society through the schools. De Lima was particularly supportive of the child-centered educators, believing that the best learning began with the needs and interests of children. She was most critical of the behaviorist "technicians" whom she described as "socializers, habit makers, and standardizers." As a socially concerned reformer, she encouraged the extension of successful Progressive experiments from private to public schools.

De Lima's brief marriage to Arthur McFarlane in the 1920s ended in divorce. During the 1930s de Lima continued her career as an education writer, publishing articles and reviews in the *Nation,* the *New Republic, Progressive Education,* the *New York Times,* the *New York Herald Tribune,* and other periodicals. She also wrote publicity materials for Progressive schools, including the Lincoln School and the Bank Street School.

De Lima's own teaching career was brief, but the experience of running her own small Progressive school helped her to understand and write about education and related social issues from the perspective of teachers. De Lima worked effectively with Progressive school faculties to help them report on and evaluate their work. She and the elementary teachers of the Lincoln School produced *A School for the World of Tomorrow* in 1939. With the secondary faculty of the same school two years later she wrote *Democracy's High School.* In 1942, with the same group of high school teachers, she published *South of the Rio Grande: An Experiment in International Understanding.* That same year she published *The Little Red Schoolhouse,* written in collaboration with the faculty of the school by that name. John Dewey, the leading figure in Progressive education, wrote an enthusiastic introduction to the book.

From 1940 to 1960, de Lima was director of public relations for the New School for Social Research in New York City. The New School, led by economist Alvin Johnson, was one of America's leading Progressive experiments in higher education, and de Lima contributed to its success and reputation by publicizing its innovative programs and activities. De Lima retired from the New School in 1960 and lived quietly in Greenwich Village until her death in 1974. De Lima is remembered chiefly for her role in describing and interpreting Progressive education and for promoting it as an essential element in broader movements of social and political reform.

See also: EDUCATION REFORM; PROGRESSIVE EDUCATION.

BIBLIOGRAPHY

DE LIMA, AGNES A. 1925. *Our Enemy the Child.* New York: New Republic.

DE LIMA, AGNES A. 1939. *A School for the World of Tomorrow.* New York: Lincoln School of Teachers College.

DE LIMA, AGNES A. 1941. *Democracy's High School.* New York: Lincoln School of Teachers College.

DE LIMA, AGNES A. 1942. *The Little Red Schoolhouse.* New York: Macmillan.

WALLACE, JAMES M. 1991. *Liberal Journalism and American Education, 1914–1941.* New Brunswick, NJ: Rutgers University Press.

JAMES M. WALLACE

DENTAL HEALTH AND CHILDREN

The oral health of children is important to their overall well-being. Just as the mouth cannot be separated from the rest of the body, oral health cannot be considered separate from the rest of children's health. Often thought to be only the presence or absence of tooth decay, oral health actually includes all the sensory, digestive, respiratory, structural, and emotional functions of the teeth, the mouth, and associated facial structures.

Like other aspects of children's health, oral health must be considered in the context of social, cultural, and environmental factors. Dental and oral disorders can have a profound impact on children, and the burden of untreated dental health problems is substantial. Untreated dental decay (cavities) can result in pain, infection, tooth loss, difficulty eating or speaking, and poor appearance, all of which present challenges for maintaining self-esteem and attentiveness to learning. Chronic pain can alter a child's ability to sleep and play, and it hinders efforts to show them that their personal actions can make a difference in their own health.

Tooth decay is one of the most common chronic childhood diseases—it is five times more common than asthma. By the first grade, more than 50 percent of children in the United States have dental caries (decay) in their primary teeth, and more than 80 percent of U.S. adolescents have dental decay by age seventeen. Despite the availability of cost-effective preventive measures and improvements in children's oral health in the United States, many children still lack needed dental care—more, in fact, than lack medical care. There are significant and important disparities in oral health and access to dental care for poor and minority children, and for those with unusual health care needs. Hispanic, African-American and Native American children have more severe disease and greater levels of untreated disease than other children. In addition, children from low-income families are much less likely to have access to dental care than their peers, and their disease is almost twice as likely to remain untreated. Sadly, the children at greatest risk for problems resulting from tooth decay are also those least likely to receive dental care. In fact, dental care has become the most frequently reported unmet health need of children.

Prevention of Dental Diseases

Fortunately, most dental diseases can be prevented. The most common oral health problem for children is dental decay, which is preventable by a combination of community, professional, and individual measures, including water fluoridation, professionally applied topical fluorides and dental sealants (protective plastic coatings), regular use of fluoride toothpastes, and healthful dietary practices. Childhood is also a time to form healthful habits to reduce injury to the mouth or face, especially during sporting and recreational activities. Use of protective devices in schools may help young athletes recognize the hazards posed by their athletic interests and as they attain adulthood they may be more comfortable using the devices than if they had not used them at a younger age. A significant proportion of other oral problems, such as destructive gum disease and mouth and throat cancer, do not commonly arise until adulthood, and much of this burden can be attributed to the use of tobacco. Most daily smokers started smoking before age eighteen, and more than 3,000 young persons in the United States begin smoking each day. School programs to prevent tobacco use could become one of the most effective strategies to reduce tobacco use in the United States.

Community water fluoridation is the most effective way to prevent dental caries in all children, regardless of socioeconomic status, race, or ethnicity; and it can reduce cavities in children by up to 40 percent. Yet, more than 100 million people in the United States do not have fluoridated water. Where children do not have fluoridated water and dental screenings have identified them to be at high risk for dental caries, fluoride can be provided through school programs that offer supplemental tablets or rinses, and the importance of brushing with fluoride toothpaste at home every day can be reinforced.

Unfortunately, fluoride has somewhat limited effectiveness on the chewing surfaces of teeth. Not surprisingly, more than 80 percent of tooth decay in schoolchildren is on the chewing surfaces of molar (back) teeth. The use of dental sealants applied to the chewing surfaces can prevent 60 percent of decay on these surfaces, but only about one in four children have at least one sealed tooth. Among poor minority children, less than 5 percent have received dental sealants, except those who attend schools that have programs to assure access to this service.

School-Based Health Care Services

The school is a good setting for programs to assure that children have an opportunity to receive protective dental sealants in a timely manner to prevent tooth decay. Although such programs can be a component of more comprehensive dental programs, it is far more common for school programs to be more narrowly focused on these effective preventive services. Dental sealants can be provided at school or through active referral to participating dentists in the community. Although these programs have been found to be effective among children of varying socioeconomic status and risk of decay, most such programs in the United States target those vulnerable populations less likely to receive private dental care, such as children eligible for free or reduced-cost lunch programs. Accordingly, these programs can not only increase the prevalence of dental sealants, but also reduce disparities in sealant use by race or income.

Health education programs in schools can stress the importance of oral health, increase understanding of the disease process, promote healthful behaviors, and reinforce the value of regular professional care for prevention. Such a role for professional care may not be consistent with the experiences of children who have not received dental care or who only associate it with treatment of toothaches. Instruction of the children and their parents—through educational materials that are taken home—can help alleviate the consequences of some parents' own experiences and dental fears, which may impede their seeking care for their children.

When preventive measures fail to completely stop disease, schools can assure that tooth decay is treated early so that it does not negatively affect learning and quality of life. Some schools have programs of screening and referral, which are not only helpful to the individual children referred for care, but also provide information that enables the public health system to target, organize, and evaluate programs. In addition, some schools have health centers on the grounds, which have been critical providers of health services for young people, particularly those who are uninsured. Central to the effectiveness of these centers are partnerships with community-based providers and collaboration with parents and school administrators.

Through the initiatives described here, schools can make important contributions to the quality of life of low-income, minority, migrant, and immigrant children, who frequently have difficulty accessing information and services for both the prevention of disease and dental care. When these children do not get the dental care they need, their already difficult lives can become even more stressful, and they may be less likely to overcome obstacles, achieve their dreams, and contribute to society.

Dental-Health Education Curriculum for Schoolchildren

The ideal dental-health education curriculum would encourage students to think about the relationships between knowledge, choice, behavior, and enhanced human health. Knowledge and choice equals power, and having power and engaging in appropriate behavior can lead to enhanced human health. In addition to acquiring knowledge, students need to develop the skills to incorporate healthful behaviors into their lives. Behaviors that promote oral health and prevent disease include brushing teeth with fluoride toothpaste, reducing the number of times sugar-rich foods are eaten, and resisting tobacco use. Curricula should be age-appropriate for both children's cognitive abilities and the main health risks they face at each stage of development.

During the preschool years, development of the habit of using fluoride toothpaste twice per day and acquisition of a positive attitude about visiting the dentist are the most important outcomes of education about oral health. Parental participation may be particularly important for children from disadvantaged homes, where parents may not otherwise appreciate the importance of these behaviors.

During the primary school years, the dental-health education curriculum can support the type of learning that frames experiences for children in a way that builds on their prior knowledge and encourages them to explore and seek answers to new concepts by themselves. Ideally, such a curriculum should link lessons with the National Science Education Standards developed by the National Academy of Sciences for grades K–4. Children at this age can learn to brush plaque from their teeth, and to protect their teeth with a toothpaste containing fluoride. In addition, these children should receive dental care within a year after the eruption of their first permanent molars (age six or seven), so that protective sealants can be placed on the chewing surfaces. These children are old enough to understand that eating several times during the day can create as many problems as eating too many sugary or starchy foods, especially if they eat those foods as between-meal snacks. Curricula should help students see that choices they make can affect their overall oral health.

During adolescence, when children increasingly make their own decisions regarding both self-care and diet, the health education curriculum should reinforce oral hygiene, prevention of tobacco use, and healthful dietary practices. Interest in the social advantages of a healthy mouth can make students more receptive to information about oral hygiene techniques, as they can be shown that appropriate use of the toothbrush and dental floss can make their teeth more attractive, prevent bleeding gums, and reduce halitosis (bad breath). These are the years to reinforce healthful lifestyle behaviors that will have important consequences for maintaining oral health with minimal need for expensive dental care repair—behaviors that will provide benefits for a lifetime.

Summary

The oral health of children is essential to their overall well-being. Education in schools prepares girls and boys to accept responsibility for their own health and to engage in personal care that will maintain and improve health. The use of precious classroom time to teach personal self-care skills, using the classroom to deliver fluoride products, and using the school setting to screen and refer children for needed dental services can be justified by the impact on children's health and welfare. Dental health problems can profoundly affect children, impairing their performance as students, lowering self-esteem, and slowing personal development. In addition, failure to prevent dental diseases has a large effect on school attendance. It is estimated that more than 50 million school hours are lost nationally each year due to dental-related illness or care, a loss that could be sharply reduced with more timely receipt of preventive services.

See also: HEALTH EDUCATION, SCHOOL; HEALTH SERVICES, *subentry on* SCHOOL.

BIBLIOGRAPHY

BIOLOGICAL SCIENCES CURRICULUM STUDY AND VIDEODISCOVERY, INC. 2002. *Open Wide and Trek Inside.* NIH Publication No. 00-4869. Bethesda, MD: National Institutes of Health.

CENTERS FOR DISEASE CONTROL AND PREVENTION. 1994. "Guidelines for School Health Programs to Prevent Tobacco Use and Addiction." *Morbidity and Mortality Weekly Report* 43(RR-2):1–18.

CENTERS FOR DISEASE CONTROL AND PREVENTION. 2001. "Impact of Targeted, School-Based Dental Sealant Programs in Reducing Racial and Economic Disparities in Sealant Prevalence Among Schoolchildren—Ohio, 1998–1999." *Morbidity and Mortality Weekly Report* 45(34):736—738.

CENTERS FOR DISEASE CONTROL AND PREVENTION. 2001. "Promoting Oral Health: Interventions for Preventing Dental Caries, Oral and Pharyngeal Cancers, and Sports-Related Craniofacial Injuries: A Report on the Recommendations of the Task Force on Community Preventive Services." *Morbidity and Mortality Weekly Report* 50(RR-21):1–13.

MOURADIAN, WENDY I.; WEHR, ELIZABETH; and CRALL, JAMES J. 2000. "Disparities in Children's Oral Health and Access to Care." *Journal of the American Medical Association* 284(20):2625–2631.

NEWACHECK, PAUL W.; HUGHES, DANA C.; HUNG, YUN Y.; WONG, S.; and STODDARD, JEFFREY J. 2000. "The Unmet Health Needs of America's Children." *Pediatrics* 105(4):989–997.

U.S. DEPARTMENT OF HEALTH AND HUMAN SERVICES. 2000. *Oral Health in America: A Report of the Surgeon General.* Rockville, MD: U.S. Department of Health and Human Services, National Institute of Dental and Craniofacial Research, National Institutes of Health.

INTERNET RESOURCE

RHODE ISLAND DEPARTMENT OF EDUCATION. 2002. "Oral Health Education Tools and Resources." <www.health.state.ri.us/disease/primarycare/oralhealth/resource-list-schools.htm>.

WILLIAM R. MAAS

DENTISTRY EDUCATION

There are fifty-four dental schools in the United States as of 2001. These schools share the goal of producing graduates who are dedicated to the highest standards of health involving the teeth, gums, and other hard and soft tissues of the mouth. Dentists are educated in the basic and clinical sciences and are capable of providing quality dental care in several specialty areas.

More than 17,000 students were enrolled in U.S. dental schools during the 1998–1999 academic year; 4,268 of them were first-year students. The first-year enrollees were selected from 9,477 individuals who applied for admission to dental schools. The process of applying to dental school involves several defined steps, including completion of specific undergraduate college courses, earning an acceptable score on the Dental Admissions Test (DAT), and submitting formal applications to selected schools.

Undergraduate Requirements

The minimum requirement for admission to dental school is two years of undergraduate or predental education. Most dental schools, however, accept students who have three or four years of undergraduate education. Science courses are the mainstay of the predental education. Most dental schools require courses with laboratory experience in inorganic and organic chemistry, biology, and physics for admission to their degree-granting programs. In addition to these nearly universally required courses, some schools also require courses in mathematics, English composition, zoology, psychology, a foreign language, social sciences, biochemistry, microbiology, and physiology. Because requirements vary from school to school, applicants should obtain specific information about required undergraduate courses from the individual dental schools.

The majority of applicants to dental schools major in science, predentistry, or premedicine; however, majoring in a science is not a prerequisite for admission. The most important consideration at the majority of schools is whether the applicant has met the minimum course requirements. Most dental schools have established a minimum undergraduate grade point average (GPA) for admission. The lowest acceptable GPA for admission to a dental school is 2.0 (on a 4.0 scale). The preferred GPA for most dental schools is 3.0 or above.

The Dental Admissions Test

The single mandatory requirement for admission to all U.S. dental schools is the DAT. Dental schools view the DAT, along with the undergraduate GPA, as a predictor of performance in dental education. This standardized test has been administered on a national basis since 1950. The test is designed to assess general academic ability, comprehension of scientific information, and perceptual ability. The DAT consists of four separate examinations of 100 multiple-choice questions, which test knowledge of the natural sciences, reading comprehension, quantitative reasoning, and perceptual ability. Most students who sit for the DAT have completed two or more years of undergraduate education. The American Association of Dental Schools (AADS) recommends taking the DAT one year prior to entering dental school. As of 1999 the DAT is administered only on the computer. The DAT can be taken on almost any day of the year at designated testing centers. Scoring of the DAT, which ranges from 1 to 30, is based on the number of correct answers. Nationally a score of 17 on the examination is considered average.

The Application Process

The American Association of Dental Schools sponsors a centralized application service. Applicants to U.S. dental schools complete one application form, which (for a fee) is distributed in a standardized format to the schools designated by the applicant. Most participants in the AADS Application Service (AADSAS) complete and submit the application using the Internet.

Upon receiving the AADSAS application, admission committees at each school may ask appli-

cants to submit an institution-specific application form, letters of recommendation, and academic transcripts. The admission committee, generally composed of dental school faculty members, review the academic and biographical information provided by applicants. Results of the DAT, the GPA, and letters of recommendation are evaluated by the committee. Students who meet requirements for admission are invited for personal interviews. Some dental schools have special programs for underrepresented minority students, which are designed to enhance the diversity of the student population and increase racial and ethnic diversity within the profession. Admissions committees strive to select applicants whose academic and personal qualities appear to mesh with their school's program objectives and suggest the candidate has the potential to successfully complete the academic program.

Choosing and applying to dental school requires careful consideration of one's career goals, personal interests, and family circumstances. Applicants may choose to apply to traditional four-year dental programs that award the Doctor of Dental Surgery (D.D.S.) or Doctor of Dental Medicine (D.M.D.), which are equivalent degrees, or to combined-degree programs. Twenty-seven schools offer formal combined bachelor's and dental degree programs. Thirty-seven schools offer combined dental and graduate degrees. Although deadlines for submitting applications vary among dental schools, most range from October to March. Most schools fill their entering class for the next academic year by December.

Cost is also a major consideration for some applicants. Applicants to dental schools are encouraged to apply for financial assistance at the same time they apply for admission. Federal student financial aid programs, mostly loan programs, are the primary sources of support for dental education. Other sources of support include scholarships and grants, research fellowships, commitment service scholarships, and loan repayment programs. Applicants are advised to contact schools individually to obtain information about financial assistance.

Licensing and Certification

Most students who enroll in dental schools participate in a traditional four-year academic program. During the first two years, dental students study the biological sciences to learn the function and structure of the human body. Courses offered during this phase of education include oral anatomy, oral pathology, oral histology, and principles of oral diagnosis and treatment. The third and fourth years of study provide clinical training. During clinical training, students learn basic techniques for oral diagnosis, restorative dentistry, periodontics, oral surgery, orthodontics, pediatric dentistry, prosthodontics, endodontics, and other areas of treatment. Students acquire these skills by rotating through various dental clinics under the supervision of a clinical instructor.

To fulfill the requirements for licensure to practice dentistry, dental students take Part 1 and Part 2 of the National Board Dental Examination (NBDE) while in dental school. Part 1 is usually taken after the second year, following completion of all biological science courses. Part 1 assesses knowledge in four areas: anatomic sciences, biochemistry/physiology, microbiology/pathology, and dental anatomy and occlusion. Part 2 is usually taken during the last year of dental school and tests for knowledge in the dental sciences. Students are eligible to sit for Part 1 and Part 2 when the dean of the dental school or a designee of the dean certifies the student has successfully completed all subjects covered by the examinations. The minimum standard passing score on each part is 75. Licensure boards in all fifty states, the District of Columbia, and Puerto Rico and the U.S. Virgin Islands use the NBDE as a major portion of their requirements for licensure. All states also require a performance-based clinical examination for licensing.

Upon graduation from dental school, graduates may pursue licensure in general dentistry or one of nine recognized specialties: dental public health, endodontics, oral and maxillofacial pathology, oral and maxillofacial radiology, oral and maxillofacial surgery, orthodontics and dentofacial orthopedics, pediatric dentistry, periodontics, or prosthodontics. Dentists who pursue postdoctoral training through residencies and advanced education programs are encouraged to obtain certification from dental specialty boards.

See also: MEDICAL EDUCATION.

BIBLIOGRAPHY

AMERICAN ASSOCIATION OF DENTAL SCHOOLS. 2000. *Admission Requirements of United States and Canadian Dental Schools: Entering Class of 2001,* 38th edition. Washington, DC: American Association of Dental Schools.

WEAVER, RICHARD G.; HADEN, N. KARL; and VALACHOVIC, RICHARD W. 2000. "U.S. Dental School Applicants and Enrollees: A Ten Year Perspective." *Journal of Dental Education* 64:867–874.

INTERNET RESOURCES

AMERICAN DENTAL ASSOCIATION. 2000. "Dental Admission Testing Program." <www.ada.org/prof/ed/testing/dat.asp>.

AMERICAN DENTAL ASSOCIATION. 2001. "National Board Dental Examination Program." <www.ada.org/prof/prac/licensure/lic-natbd.html>.

JUANITA F. BUFORD

DEPARTMENT CHAIRPERSON, THE

Over time, the profile of academic department chairpersons, often referred to as chairs, has remained fairly constant. They are tenured faculty, primarily male, and between the ages of forty and sixty. For the most part, chairs are internal appointees, either selected by their deans or elected by their departments and then appointed by their deans for terms of usually three to five years.

In some colleges, faculty become chairs out of a sense of duty with little enthusiasm for the job. Many times these chairs see themselves as scholars who temporarily accept responsibility for administrative tasks so other professors can continue their teaching and scholarly pursuits. In fact, few department chairs view themselves as administrators, and less than one-third of them will seek a higher administrative position. Their primary function is to champion their faculty. They work for and with faculty, providing protection from central administrative intrusion and support for faculty academic endeavors.

In the first instance, department chairs guard faculty autonomy and academic freedom by filtering and interpreting demands placed on faculty and departments by college deans. In the second, they foster collegiality, honor specialized expertise, and promote excellence in teaching, research, and service to the department, college, and university by ensuring that department work gets shared equitably, that a collaborative work environment exists, and that requisite resources are allocated properly.

The dilemma for many department chairs arises from their treatment as faculty in some venues, such as evaluation for promotion and merit, and as administrators in others, where eleven- or twelve-month contracts preclude research time. In addition, the task of carrying out administrative mandates can often pit them against their faculty peers.

Chairperson Roles

Chairs engage in four primary categories of tasks: faculty development, management, scholarship, and leadership. Each role is important to success as a department chair.

Faculty development. As faculty developers, chairs are responsible for supervising the recruitment, selection, and evaluation of faculty and for enhancing faculty teaching, research, and morale through development and support. Certain behaviors help build and monitor an environment that prizes effective teaching, research excellence, and service to the community of scholars in which they reside. These actions fall into several categories that include, but are not limited to, selection, support, development, networking, recognition, rewarding, and reinforcement.

Selection refers to the establishment of deliberate and well thought out faculty hiring policies, which are in accord with departmental practices and governing procedures and clearly delineate what the department values. Chairs *support* faculty in their academic endeavors by encouraging faculty to attend learned societies and professional meetings, and by sponsoring activities such as team teaching, collaborative research efforts, and peer mentoring.

Development of faculty is closely related to providing support. Here, the chair shows concern for each faculty member's growth as both an instructional leader and an academic expert. Providing departmental reimbursement of the expenses that faculty incur while attending workshops and seminars on effective teaching or professional conferences where they present their research to peers outside their departments sends the message that excellence counts. So does creating individual development plans annually with faculty members.

When a department chair promotes *networking*, faculty can engage in dialogue with each other and debate about effective practice. Mentoring also occurs, with veteran faculty teaching new colleagues the bureaucratic ropes of a department and an institution.

Recognition and *rewarding* go hand-in-hand. The first refers to such intangibles as praise, verbal communication, and expressions of appreciation. The second denotes tangible benefits, such as merit increases, promotions, better teaching assignments, and release time for pursuing research agendas that accrue to a faculty member as a result of good teaching, research, and departmental citizenship.

Finally, *reinforcement* is used to provide for continued success of the department. An effective chair builds on a foundation set by the development of sound plans for achieving teaching and research effectiveness and engaging in institutional service where progress gets monitored, recognized, and rewarded regularly.

Management. As managers, chairs oversee the day-to-day fiduciary requirements of the department. They assign duties to faculty, plan meetings, plan and evaluate curriculum, keep faculty informed of college priorities, and coordinate department activities. In addition, they manage the department's fiscal resources and non-academic staff, prepare budgets, keep accurate records, and serve as the department's representative to the administration. In some instances, chairs also select and supervise graduate students and attempt to obtain external funding for departmental projects.

Scholarship. The chair's role as a scholar is perhaps the most comfortable one and at the same time most frustrating. It is comfortable because it encompasses one's academic identity; it can be frustrating because time previously devoted to academic endeavors is now siphoned off by managerial and other duties. In order to retain stature as scholars, department chairs must maintain research plans, obtain resources for personal research, and remain current in their academic discipline.

Leadership. Leadership may well be considered by many academic department chairs the most elusive of their roles. Tasks related to leadership focus on either faculty or the department as a whole. The first group includes encouraging faculty research, publication, and professional development. Departmental leadership tasks aim at maintaining a conducive work environment and setting long-range departmental goals. An important part of this second leadership role involves soliciting ideas from faculty to improve the department.

Leadership tasks are often summarily ignored by otherwise well-meaning department chairs. Many surmise that this occurs because chairs come to the position without leadership training or prior administrative experience, and without a clear understanding of the complexity of the role or the cost to their academic careers and personal lives that it can exact. Typically, chairs are not prepared or equipped to deal with increasing legal and organizational demands, and they harbor only vague notions of what it means to be entrepreneurial or responsive to changes in institutional direction. As a result, they misconstrue leadership to mean management, and in doing so, immerse themselves in a process of maintenance rather than one based on creativity and innovation.

A Challenging, Important Position

Interestingly, experts estimate that more than 80 percent of all administrative decisions in universities take place at the department level. In the early twenty-first century, department chairs face a complex, changing environment. The success of a department chair depends upon department members acting with integrity; engaging in open communication; exhibiting a willingness to accept criticism; valuing human potential, growth, and accomplishment; and manifesting a collective spirit. Strong institutional cultures or governance policies and practices can prove strong inhibitors to any such efforts. Subcultures built on a tradition of mistrust may also render chairs powerless.

Proactive chairs undertake their tasks with the determination to develop faculty as researchers and teachers, the will to persevere as a scholar, a concern for the fiscal viability of the department, and the administrative savvy and foresight to ensure departmental regeneration. As such, department chairs fill one of the most important, yet most challenging, administrative positions in the academy.

See also: ACADEMIC DEAN, THE; BOARD OF TRUSTEES, COLLEGE AND UNIVERSITY; CHIEF ACADEMIC OFFICERS, COLLEGE AND UNIVERSITY; COLLEGES AND UNIVERSITIES, ORGANIZATIONAL STRUCTURE OF; FACULTY SENATES, COLLEGE AND UNIVERSITY; GOVERNANCE AND DECISION-MAKING IN COLLEGES AND UNIVERSITIES; PRESIDENCY, COLLEGE AND UNIVERSITY.

BIBLIOGRAPHY

GMELCH, WALTER H., and MISKIN, VAL D. 1995. *Chairing an Academic Department.* Thousand Oaks, CA: Sage.

HECHT, IRENE W. D.; HIGGERSON, MARY LOU; GMELCH, WALTER H.; and TUCKER, ALLAN. 1999. *The Department Chair as Academic Leader.* Phoenix, AZ: Oryx Press/American Council on Education.

LUCAS, ANN F., et al. 2000. *Leading Academic Change: Essential Roles for Department Chairs.* San Francisco: Jossey Bass.

MIMI WOLVERTON

DEPARTMENT OF EDUCATION
See: U.S. DEPARTMENT OF EDUCATION.

DEPRESSION
See: STRESS AND DEPRESSION.

DEVELOPING NATIONS, APPLYING ECONOMIC ANALYSIS TO DECISION-MAKING IN
See: DECISION-MAKING IN DEVELOPING NATIONS, APPLYING ECONOMIC ANALYSIS TO.

DEVELOPMENTAL THEORY

HISTORICAL OVERVIEW
Maureen Kessenich
Frederick J. Morrison
COGNITIVE AND INFORMATION PROCESSING
Jeffrey Bisanz
Elaine Ho
Melissa Kachan
Carmen Rasmussen
Jody Sherman
EVOLUTIONARY APPROACH
David C. Geary
VYGOTSKIAN THEORY
M. Susan Burns
Elena Bodrova
Deborah J. Leong

HISTORICAL OVERVIEW

Developmental psychology attempts to understand the nature and sources of growth in children's cognitive, language, and social skills. Within that context, there are four central themes that are unique to a developmental perspective and that bear on issues in childhood education. The first is the role of *nature versus nurture* in shaping development. Specifically, developmentalists want to know the contribution of genetic or maturational influences on development as well as the role played by environmental experiences. One important educational issue related to this topic is the question of whether a child's entrance age, or maturational level, is important for school success. For this and other important educational questions, nature and nurture interact in complex ways to shape a child's academic growth.

The second question focuses on whether children's growth proceeds in a continuous or more stage-like fashion. Stage theories, such as those proposed by Jean Piaget, Erik Erikson, and Sigmund Freud, contend that development progresses through maturationally determined stages. While this perspective underscores the contributions of both biology and the environment, a greater emphasis is placed on a maturationally predetermined progression through a fixed developmental sequence. Many researchers and theorists dispute such a rigid, step-like theory of development, emphasizing instead a more continuous, gradual process influenced equally by both brain maturation and environmental stimulation. Two important educational questions relevant to this issue are the extent to which children can be taught particular concepts or skills prior to entering a given developmental stage, and whether concepts learned in one domain are automatically transferred to other similar domains as a child reaches a new developmental stage.

A distinct but related theme centers on the existence of critical or sensitive periods in human development. A critical or sensitive period is defined as a time of growth during which an organism is maximally responsive to certain environmental or biological events. Critical periods emphasize the interaction of both nature and nurture, with environmental experiences (nurture) activating biologically programmed (nature) developmental changes, or, conversely, biologically determined changes enabling an organism to assimilate certain environmental experiences. In terms of language development, educators often wonder whether there is a critical or sensitive period during which children should learn a second language. While certain components of language, such as phonological process-

ing, are believed to be constrained by sensitive periods in development, other elements of language, such as vocabulary, clearly evolve over the lifespan.

The final theme concerns the importance of early experience in shaping later growth and development. Developmental scientists such as Mary Ainsworth, Alan Sroufe, and Freud emphasize the significance of early attachment and emotional conflict in predicting later psychological adjustment. It is argued that early risk factors have a more permanent influence on the course of development than later experiences. Early negative circumstances such as family conflict and social disadvantage have been linked to later delinquent behavior and school failure. Nevertheless, many children display resilience in the face of such early adverse social and environmental conditions. Thus, it is the cumulative impact of both early and later experiences that determines a child's developmental outcome. Children's literacy development, for example, is a product of both early experiences, such as parent–child book reading, as well as later experiences, such as reading instruction in school.

Modern developmental theory centers on these four central issues. An in-depth examination of these topics within a historical context will provide a more comprehensive understanding of developmental theory and its relevance for educational policies and practices.

Nature Versus Nurture

Philosophers and psychologists have debated the relative roles of nature and nurture in human development for centuries. The seventeenth-century English philosopher John Locke described a young child's mind as a *tabula rasa* (blank slate) upon which the child's experiences are written. Jean-Jacques Rosseau, an eighteenth-century French philosopher, also argued that human development was primarily a function of experience. He believed in the existence of a *natural,* unspoiled state of humankind that is altered and corrupted by modern civilization. In contrast, nineteenth-century scientists such as Gregor Mendel, Charles Darwin, and Sir Francis Galton highlighted the importance of heredity in shaping development. While all of these scientists provided meaningful insights into the role of heredity and the environment, modern researchers have sought to further explore the dynamic interactions between nature and nurture that shape human development.

The twentieth century saw the evolution of various theories of development that differentially emphasized the role of biological versus environmental factors. These theories can be classified according to four major developmental frameworks: (1) environmental learning (empiricism), (2) biological maturation (nativism), (3) cultural context, and (4) constructivist.

The environmental-learning framework, best exemplified by the behaviorist theories of John B. Watson and B. F. Skinner, underscores the paramount importance of empirical learning in development. According to behaviorist theories, learning is characterized as the process by which an organism's behavior is shaped by experience. While environmental-learning theorists do not completely discount the role of innate factors, they argue that it is the external environment that has the greatest influence on development.

Biological-maturationist theories represent the opposing swing of the theoretical pendulum. This framework posits that biologically and genetically predetermined patterns of change have a greater impact on development than environmental influences. During the early twentieth century, theorists such as Freud and Arnold Gessell proposed that experiential influences were secondary to innate maturational mechanisms. This perspective regained popularity in the late twentieth and early twenty-first centuries as a result of major advances in genetic research, as well as the introduction of twin studies and behavioral genetics. Researchers such as Robert Plomin, Noam Chomsky, and Steven Pinker assert that human characteristics such as personality, intelligence, and language acquisition are, to a great extent, genetically grounded and maturationally controlled.

The cultural-context perspective of psychologists such as Lev Vygotsky and Barbara Rogoff contends that while both biological and experiential factors exert important influences on development, such factors are filtered through an individual's social and cultural context. Lev Vygotsky believed that the activities, symbols, and customs of particular social groups are formed by the collective social, cultural, and historical experiences of their ancestors. Through influences on social customs and practices, parenting, and the environment, culture shapes children's cognitive, language, and social development. For example, children's academic performance has been found to vary cross-culturally, as demonstrated

by studies showing that Asian immigrant children outperform their white peers in the United States, as well as the black-white test score gap.

Finally, the constructivist, or interactionist, approach stresses the balanced interaction of nature and nurture in forming the foundation for developmental change. In such a framework, both genetics and environment play an important role, and it is the dynamic relations among such internal and external influences that ultimately shape development. Piaget's theory of cognitive development asserts that children *construct* their knowledge based on the combination of input received from both maturational and environmental sources. Theorists such as Richard Lerner, Gilbert Gottlieb, Esther Thelen, and Linda Smith have taken this conceptualization one step further with the introduction of dynamic systems theories, which emphasize that the source of developmental change is in the process of bidirectional interaction among complex environmental and biological systems.

Frederick Morrison and colleagues have explored one facet of the nature-nurture question relevant to education by examining the importance of entrance age, or maturation level, on school readiness and academic growth. They found that younger first graders benefited as much from instruction in reading and math as older first graders, and that the younger students made significantly more progress than older kindergarteners of essentially the same age. Thus, entrance age—or maturation level—is not an important indicator of learning or academic risk.

The dispute over the relative importance of nature and nurture in children's development has endured for several centuries, and will no doubt continue to divide theorists for a long time to come. Increasingly, however, developmental scientists are concluding that, for most human characteristics, nature and nurture are inextricably linked and interact in complex ways to shape human growth.

Stages in Development

According to Piaget's stage theory, children progress through a sequence of qualitative transformations, advancing from simple to more complex levels of thought. Piaget believed these transformations to be universal, innately programmed shifts in a child's perception and understanding of the world. He proposed four main stages of cognitive development:

sensorimotor, preoperational, concrete operational, and formal operational.

The transition from preoperational to concrete operational thought, at about five to seven years of age, corresponds with entry into formal schooling. While children in the preoperational stage are able to internally represent reality through the use of symbols such as language and mental images, concrete-operational children move beyond this simple mental representation of objects and actions and are able to logically integrate, order, and transform these objects and actions. For instance, because preoperational children cannot integrate information about height and width simultaneously, they are unable to recognize that water poured from a short, wide container into a tall, narrow container represents the same volume of water. Yet once they reach the *age of reason,* their maturational level converges with their accumulated experiences to facilitate a qualitative shift toward concrete operational thinking.

In addition to Piaget's stage theory of cognitive development, several others have proposed stage theories of psychosexual/personality development (Freud), psychosocial/identity development (Erikson), moral reasoning (Lawrence Kohlberg), and social development (Theory of Mind). These theories claim that children proceed through universal, age-specific stages of growth. Yet not all psychologists agree with such a rigid, step-like representation of development. Recently, neo-Piagetian theorists such as Kurt Fischer, Robbie Case, Annette Karmiloff-Smith, and others have attempted to reconcile the variability and domain-specificity observed in children's cognitive growth with Piaget's static stage theory.

In general, the neo-Piagetian perspective expands upon Piagetian theory by asserting that, while some general constraints or core capacities are hard-wired at birth, learning and experience lead to variation and domain-specificity in the acquisition of knowledge and skills. Cross-cultural studies have shown that varying cultural experiences result in the acquisition of different, contextually relevant skills. For example, children from a Mexican village known for its pottery-making learn conservation of solids (e.g., the fact that a ball of clay has the same mass even when it is molded into a long, thin roll) before conservation of number, which is generally mastered first in formally schooled children. Thus, most neo-Piagetians believe that while learning is constrained by innate mechanisms or information processing ca-pacities, it proceeds in an individualized, domain-specific manner.

The question of whether certain knowledge or skills can be acquired before a child has reached a specified stage of development has also been addressed by neo-Piagetians. Renee Baillargeon conducted experiments with young infants and found that they recognize properties of object permanence prior to reaching that designated Piagetian stage of development. In addition, researchers have demonstrated that children can be taught concrete-operational concepts even before they have formally reached that stage of cognitive understanding—though these children are unable to transfer such knowledge outside the context of the testing situation.

Other theorists construe development as a constructive web (Kurt Fischer) or as a series of overlapping waves (Robert Siegler), rather than a sequence of qualitatively distinct steps. They recognize that cognitive development is the result of gradually acquired skills and abilities that build upon each other. Siegler, in particular, emphasizes the overlapping use of progressively more advanced strategies in the acquisition of skills such as addition. He found that children learning addition use various strategies in "overlapping waves," such as finger counting, verbal counting in their head, the Min strategy (taking the larger of two numbers as a base and adding the smaller number to it) and, eventually, retrieval from memory. They gradually move from using easier, less efficient strategies to more difficult, but more efficient, strategies.

The neo-Piagetian view resembles the information-processing perspective in that both contend that cognitive development is limited by general constraints that are hard-wired at birth. Information-processing researchers such as Robert Kail, Wolfgang Schneider, and David Bjorklund argue that children's learning is restricted by the broad processing capacities of the brain, which improve with age. This perspective regards development as a more gradual, continuous process that evolves as children's processing speed or capacity for holding information increases. Thus, the step-like progression of development is rejected for a more linear representation.

Critical Periods

A *critical,* or *sensitive* period is defined as a period of time in development when a particular environmental experience or biological event has its greatest influence. Evidence demonstrates that some physiological and psychological processes are constrained by critical periods.

The existence of sensitive periods in children's psychological development has been noted in aspects of language acquisition. Children deprived of verbal stimulation during the first few years of life are severely impaired in their capacity to learn language and have great difficulty acquiring normal language later on. In addition, while young infants are able to distinguish among the variety of phonemes present in all human languages, after about six months of age the infant's knowledge becomes more focused, and they are only able to discriminate between the various phonemes in their own native language. Consequently, infants can learn any language that they are exposed to, yet it is more difficult for an older child or adult to completely master a non-native or secondary language.

Taken together, such information lends support to the argument that the first few years of life represent a sensitive period for certain aspects of language development. However, the fact that children continue to benefit from exposure to new vocabulary, semantics, and grammatical rules well into elementary school and beyond leads researchers to question whether all language learning is restricted by a sensitive period. During the first few years of life, children's brains grow and become more organized, specialized, and efficient. Yet brain growth and development does not end at three years of age, but rather continues throughout childhood, benefiting from the effects of schooling and other environmental stimulation. Thus, the question of when educators should teach children a second language depends on the components of language being considered (e.g., phonology, semantics, vocabulary, grammar) and the level of proficiency desired.

Another area of development believed to be constrained by a sensitive period is attachment. Psychologists such as John Bowlby, Ainsworth, Sroufe, Erikson, and Freud contend that children's early attachment to their primary caregiver (e.g., mother, father) during the first few years of life sets the foundation for their later socioemotional development. Research conducted by Harry Harlow on infant monkeys found that those deprived of maternal attachment prior to six months of age had a more difficult time recovering socially than those deprived of maternal contact after six months of age, thus lend-

ing support to the existence of a critical period for social development in monkeys. Yet many "natural experiments" looking at orphan children who have been deprived of adequate affection and sensitivity from a primary caregiver have found that, if removed from such a socioemotionally impoverished environment and placed in a loving adoptive home, most children are able to recover socially, emotionally, and cognitively. Thus, while early experiences can and do have an impact on later development, children often demonstrate resilience in response to adverse early experiences.

Early Experience

Early experience is the consummate critical period. During the broad social reform of the late 1800s, scientists in the newly evolving field of developmental psychology brought attention to the harmful effects of child industrial labor and validated the importance of a healthy and nurturing environment for promotion of normal development. Throughout the twentieth century, psychologists such as Bowlby, Freud, Erikson, and Sroufe have stressed the profound importance of early socioemotional experiences on later psychological outcomes. In addition, scientists and policymakers have recognized the importance of early intervention programs, such as Head Start, that seek to enrich the cognitive development of socially disadvantaged children. During the late twentieth and early twenty-first centuries, public interest and government policy has advocated even earlier interventions, focusing on *zero to three* as the most important age range on which to concentrate resources. Yet, as theorists such as John Bruer argue, the importance of the first three years of life has reached "mythical" proportions. According to Bruer, it is important to recognize the cumulative nature of development, emphasizing both early and later experiences in shaping children's growth.

Evidence from researchers such as Baillargeon and Susan Rose has demonstrated that cognitive skills begin to develop very early in life, and that these skills follow rather stable trajectories over time. Such findings suggest that children's developmental course begins to solidify before they enter formal schooling, and even before they utter their first words.

A problem of particular interest is the poor state of literacy in America, and the impact of early experiences on literacy development. The amount of cognitive enrichment, verbal stimulation, and book reading, for example, that children are exposed to at an early age is predictive of later literacy skills. Research conducted by Betty Hart and Todd Risley (1995) found a wide range of variability in young children's vocabulary skills as early as two years of age, and this variability was highly correlated with the number of words spoken by their parents. Socioeconomically disadvantaged toddlers were exposed to a substantially lower number of words per day as compared to toddlers from professional families. It is clear from such research that children's early experiences can lead to striking differences among children from enriching versus impoverished environments. Furthermore, studies have shown that the achievement gap between low- and high-performing children widens once children enter school.

With respect to socioemotional development, psychologists such as Freud, Sroufe, Bowlby, Erikson, and Mary Main have claimed that children's early attachment relationships with their primary caregivers lay the foundation for later social functioning. Researchers have found that securely attached children are more cooperative with their mothers, achieve higher cognitive and academic scores, are more curious, and maintain better relationships with teachers and peers, as compared to insecurely attached children. Taken together, such research affirms the impact of early attachment and socioemotional experiences on later psychosocial and cognitive development.

While early risk factors such as poor attachment and socioeconomic disadvantage can have long-term effects on children's cognitive, academic, social, and emotional development, children do demonstrate varying levels of vulnerability and resilience toward such early conditions. Differences in temperament and coping abilities, for example, can moderate the degree to which a child's early experiences forecast their later developmental outcomes. Furthermore, while there is ample evidence that early experiences have a substantial effect on later cognitive and social outcomes, the real question is whether early experiences are any more important than later experiences. Growing evidence suggests that it is the cumulative effects of both early and later experiences that define an individual's trajectories later in life.

In summary, developmental theory pursues four central themes: (1) the importance of nature versus nurture, (2) stages in development, (3) the existence of critical or sensitive periods, and (4) the impact of early experience. Significant progress has been made over the last thirty years on each of these topics, resulting in a more complex view of human psychological growth and the forces that shape it. With regard to educational practice, modern developmental theory stresses that rigid notions of genetic determinism, stages, critical periods, or the lasting impact of early experience are being replaced by more flexible views that emphasize the malleability of human nature and its potential for change.

See also: DEVELOPMENTAL THEORY, *subentries on* COGNITIVE AND INFORMATION PROCESSING, EVOLUTIONARY APPROACH, VYGOTSKIAN THEORY.

BIBLIOGRAPHY

AINSWORTH, MARY. 1985. "Patterns of Attachment." *Clinical Psychologist* 38(2):27–29.

BOLBY, JOHN. 1988. *A Secure Base: Parent-Child Attachment and Healthy Human Development.* New York: Basic Books.

BRUER, JOHN T. 1999. *The Myth of the First Three Years: A New Understanding of Early Brain Development and Lifelong Learning.* New York: Free Press.

COLE, MICHAEL, and COLE, SHEILA R. 1996. *The Development of Children,* 3rd edition. New York: W. H. Freeman.

DEMETRIOU, ANDREAS; SHAYER, MICHAEL; and EFKLIDES, ANASTASIA. 1992. *Neo-Piagetian Theories of Cognitive Development: Implications and Applications for Education.* London: Routledge.

GOTTLIEB, GILBERT; WAHLSTEN, DOUGLAS; and LICKLITER, ROBERT. 1998. "The Significance of Biology for Human Development: A Developmental Psychobiological Systems View." In *Handbook of Child Psychology* Vol. 1: *Theoretical Models of Human Development,* 5th edition, ed. William Damon and Richard M. Lerner. New York: Wiley.

HART, BETTY, and RISLEY, TODD R. 1995. *Meaningful Individual Differences in the Everyday Experience of Young American Children.* Baltimore: Paul H. Brookes.

KAIL, ROBERT. 1991. "Development of Processing Speed in Childhood and Adolescence." In *Advances in Child Development and Behavior* Vol. 23, ed. Hayne W. Reese. San Diego, CA: Academic Press.

KARMILOFF-SMITH, ANNETTE. 1992. *Beyond Modularity: A Developmental Perspective on Cognitive Science.* Cambridge, MA: MIT Press.

LERNER, RICHARD M. 1998. "Theories of Human Development: Contemporary Perspectives." In *Handbook of Child Psychology* Vol. 1: *Theoretical Models of Human Development,* 5th edition, ed. William Damon and Richard M. Lerner. New York: Wiley.

PIAGET, JEAN. 1983. "Piaget's Theory." In *Handbook of Child Psychology* Vol. 1: *History, Theory, and Methods,* 4th edition, ed. William Kessen. New York: Wiley.

PLOMIN, ROBERT. 1990. *Nature and Nurture: An Introduction to Human Behavior Genetics.* Pacific Grove, CA: Brooks/Cole.

ROGOFF, BARBARA. 1998. "Cognition as a Collaborative Process." In *Handbook of Child Psychology* Vol. 2: *Cognition, Perception, and Language,* 5th edition, ed. William Damon and Richard M. Lerner. New York: Wiley.

SIEGLER, ROBERT S. 1998. *Emerging Minds: The Process of Change in Children's Thinking.* New York: Oxford University Press.

SINGER, DOROTHY G., and REVENSON, TRACY. 1997. *A Piaget Primer: How a Child Thinks.* Madison, CT: International Universities Press.

THELEN, ESTHER, and SMITH, LINDA. 1998. "Dynamic Systems Theories." In *Handbook of Child Psychology* Vol. 1: *Theoretical Models of Human Development,* 5th edition, ed. William Damon and Richard M. Lerner. New York: Wiley.

VYGOTSKY, LEV. 1978. *Mind in Society: The Development of Higher Psychological Processes.* Cambridge, MA: Harvard University Press.

MAUREEN KESSENICH
FREDERICK J. MORRISON

COGNITIVE AND INFORMATION PROCESSING

Cognitive development typically refers to age-related changes in knowledge and acts of knowing, such as perceiving, remembering, problem solving, reasoning, and understanding. The development of cognition is studied most frequently in infants, children, and adolescents, where changes often are relatively rapid and striking. Many researchers also study cognitive development in aging adults, in children and adults during recovery of function following brain damage, and in a variety of species other than humans. Since the 1890s, when researchers such as James Mark Baldwin and Alfred Binet established cognitive development as a substantive area of inquiry, two overlapping goals have been evident. One goal is to provide insights into how complex, organized knowledge systems develop, an issue with a long history in philosophy and science. The other goal is to provide insights into optimizing human development, especially with respect to education. Researchers have adopted many different theoretical approaches to the study of cognitive development over the past 100 years, and they continue to do so. During the latter part of the twentieth century a relatively new approach, information processing, gained a degree of ascendancy because of its potential for providing rich insights into how cognition develops and how instruction might be improved.

Assumptions and Findings

In the 1950s and 1960s researchers began to notice similarities between human thinking and the new computers of that era, which could manipulate not only numbers but also a variety of nonnumeric symbols. Allen Newell and Herbert Simon were among the first to suggest that humans and computers could both be viewed as general symbol manipulators, and that knowledge of computers could be used as a metaphor for exploring human cognition. The argument that emerged was not that humans are computers, but rather that computers could be used as a source of ideas about how human cognition works and also as a tool for expressing ideas about how humans process information mentally. Information-processing studies of cognition and its development began to flourish in the 1960s and 1970s.

Information processing is not a theory of cognition but rather a general framework that comprises a family of theories sharing certain core assumptions. One assumption is that all cognitive activities involve mental processes that operate over real time on internal, symbolic representations of information. That is, information of all sorts—including the words on this page, memories of past events, knowledge about friends or world events, and abstract concepts such as "justice"—are all coded as mental representations with certain structural properties.

When one sees a painting for the first time, for example, perceptual processes code new sensory information and may also create more elaborate representations of what is seen. Memory processes store these representations and also retrieve previously developed representations that can be useful for interpreting the painting. Problem-solving and reasoning processes operate to help understand the artist's intent in creating the painting. From an information-processing view, one does not simply *experience* the painting. Instead, one is engaged in a series of events in which mental representations are created and manipulated by processes operating over time. Information-processing researchers seek to identify these processes and representations and to understand their properties. Researchers therefore focus less on *whether* children solve problems correctly and more on *how* problems are solved. This approach has led to a rich set of findings about the skills and knowledge children acquire on specific tasks in such domains as reading, mathematics, and scientific thinking.

A second assumption is that these processes and representations exist within an organized system with definable properties and constraints. An important goal of research is to define the *cognitive architecture,* that is, the general structural characteristics of the information-processing system. For example, the amount of information that can be activated at any one time is limited, as is often evident when people try to remember new telephone numbers or solve difficult problems. This phenomenon is often interpreted in terms of *working memory,* an important, limited capacity system for manipulating information. Research on working memory has revealed the operation of three interacting components: a *phonological loop* for storing speech-based information; a *visual-spatial sketchpad* for storing visual information; and an *executive system* for combining information from various sources to solve problems and create plans. New research, such as that reported in 2000 by Susan E. Gathercole and Susan J. Pickering, is beginning to link developmental change and individual differences in cognitive performance to changes in these components of working memory. Another constraint on cognitive processing is the speed at which processes operate. In general, faster processing speed should enable more competent performance on particular tasks. Not only does general processing speed increase from early childhood through adolescence, but as researcher Robert Kail reported in 1991, it does so at a consistent and well-defined rate of change. The

reasons for this phenomenon still are not understood.

A third assumption is that cognitive development occurs via self-modification of the information-processing system. Although environmental events critically influence development, the mechanisms by which the information-processing system changes over time are assumed to be internal to the system itself. A number of such mechanisms have been proposed. For example, as children develop some processes become *automatized* in the sense that they are executed more rapidly and with less demand on limited attentional capacity than earlier in development. According to some theories, increasing automatization allows children to operate at higher levels of complexity and flexibility. Knowledge modification processes, such as *generalization* and *discrimination,* operate to create more powerful and accurate processes and representations. A critical task for developmental theorists is defining a cognitive architecture and self-modification mechanisms that, together, can account for the striking changes in thinking that emerge as children develop.

Information-processing theories of development differ significantly from other approaches in fundamental ways. They are not *phenomenological* because they are not limited to conscious experience, and they are not *neurological* in that they do not rely on neural or biochemical mechanisms as explanations. They differ from traditional stimulus-responses theories because of their emphasis on detailed descriptions of mental processes and representations that interact over time. Unlike *structural* theories, such as that of Jean Piaget, the focus is on very specific processes and representations that underlie performance. Information-processing theories often can be amalgamated to some extent with these other approaches, however. In contemporary neuroscience research, for example, information-processing concepts, such as working memory and processing speed, are often used to explore relations between brain and behavior.

Methods

The assumptions of information processing have led researchers to adapt or create methods appropriate for identifying processes, representations, and characteristics of cognitive architecture. Given the emphasis on temporal properties of processes, researchers have developed highly specialized, *chronometric methods* for measuring the speed of particular mental processes. With *rule assessment,* tasks are structured so that patterns of responses can be used to identify particular processes and decision rules. *Protocol analysis* is used to examine verbal self-reports, provided by participants as they solve problems, for evidence about solution procedures, internal representations, and processing constraints. When applied to the study of development, these methods need to be used carefully so that they are equally sensitive to important aspects of performance at different developmental levels.

Information-processing researchers also have adopted a number of distinctive methods for illustrating or representing their theories. Because of the emphasis on specific processes and their organization, flow charts and diagrams often are used to indicate how processing is structured. Some researchers take a more formal approach: They implement their theories of cognitive development as computer programs. To the extent that the programs mimic children's behavior and development, researchers receive some support for the veridicality of their theory. If, however, the program crashes, then clearly the theory is lacking.

Educational Implications

Ideally, educational assessment would provide specific insights about how to adapt instruction to individual children so as to optimize learning. In principle, information processing should provide a basis for assessing specific strengths and weaknesses and for identifying specific processes and representations that can be targeted for instruction. Teachers want their students to answer problems correctly, but measuring achievement only in terms of correct answers can be misleading: Often children can answer a problem correctly but for the wrong reasons, or incorrectly but for reasons that make sense. More important than answering correctly, in terms of educational goals, are whether students use appropriate solution strategies and whether they understand what they are doing. The value of information-processing research for education lies in its inherent distinction between the *products* of children's thinking (i.e., *whether* children solve problems correctly) and the *processes* (i.e., *how* problems are solved). Research on the development of school-related knowledge and skills is beginning to yield impressive advances.

In studies of young children's arithmetic, for example, researchers have identified a wide range of solution procedures, correct and incorrect, that children use to solve problems. To account for how children select among these procedures, how procedures change as children gain experience, and how some new procedures arise, Robert S. Siegler and Christopher Shipley (1995) developed an information-processing model that includes assumptions about an associative memory for number facts, a memory system for recording the results of past solutions, and a system for deciding whether and how to apply particular procedures. This model accounts extremely well for some aspects of children's development in arithmetic, and it has some specific instructional implications. For example, according to this model, associating problems and correct solutions is critical for later development of efficient solution procedures. Discouraging children from counting accurately with their fingers may increase the chance of incorrect associations developing and thus delay the use of more advanced procedures. The model is far from complete, but it provides a coherent basis for analyzing how children solve arithmetic problems, how and why change occurs, and how instruction might be adapted to the needs of individual children.

Similar progress has been made in other areas. Reading, for example, is a complex skill consisting of numerous components, and information-processing methods have been useful for identifying and measuring these components. One such component is phonological awareness, which includes the ability to identify and manipulate phonemes. Lynette Bradley and Peter E. Bryant (1983) found that instruction designed to enhance phonological awareness in young children strongly and positively influences the rate at which they become effective readers. Problem solving is critical to success in many academic domains. Amarjit S. Dhillon (1998) studied the behavior of experts and novices as they solved physics problems and found that their strategies could be analyzed in terms of fourteen processes or activities. Experts and novices differed systematically in the use and sequence of these activities, a finding that provides insights into understanding students' knowledge in terms of specific concepts and procedures. The results of this research were used to develop problem-solving instruction for high school and university students.

Aside from its use in specific academic domains, information processing also has provided a basis for assessing broad intellectual skills. A new generation of tests is emerging that are constructed so that children's performance can be interpreted in terms of relatively specific processing skills that, in principle, may be amenable to targeted instruction. One example is the Cognitive Assessment System (CAS), developed by Jagannath P. Das and Jack A. Naglieri, in which tasks from information-processing research have been adapted to measure four aspects of processing (planning, attention, simultaneous processing, and successive processing) that are emphasized in a comprehensive theory developed by the neuropsychologist Aleksandr Luria. Because of the links between theory and measures, the CAS has proved useful in interpreting performance for children with or without learning disabilities and for developing specific instructional interventions.

Prospects

Information processing is by no means the only approach for studying cognitive development, but its assumptions and methods have proved helpful in exploring the many ways in which children's thinking changes with development. Its greatest utility to date has been in studying task-specific or domain-specific processes and representations. It has been applied with somewhat less success to domain-general characteristics of development, as well as to topics such as motivation and affect that are critical to understanding development and optimizing education. At this point, it is not clear whether these apparent deficiencies are inherent to information processing or whether they are simply a result of how information-processing concepts and methods have been applied to date. The information-processing approach is challenged by connectionist and dynamic systems theories that do not share the assumptions about symbolic representations and discrete processes; by ecological theories that focus on environmental factors and their structure; by neuroscientific theories that provide explanations in terms of neural functioning and neuroanatomy; and by traditional theories, such as those of Jean Piaget and Lev Vygotsky, in which a more general level of analysis and explanation is emphasized. The extent to which information processing succeeds will depend, in part, on the extent to which its practitioners can adapt to accommodate these challenges and contribute to research that enriches educational assessment and instruction.

See also: LEARNING; TAXONOMIES OF EDUCATIONAL OBJECTIVES.

BIBLIOGRAPHY

BRADLEY, LYNETTE, and BRYANT, PETER E. 1983. "Categorizing Sounds and Learning to Read—A Causal Connection." *Nature* 301:419–421.

CAIRNS, ROBERT B. 1998. "The Making of Developmental Psychology." In *Handbook of Child Psychology,* ed. William Damon, Vol. 1: *Theoretical Models of Human Development,* ed. Richard M. Lerner. New York: John Wiley and Sons.

DAS, JAGANNATH P., and NAGLIERI, JACK A. 1997. *The Cognitive Assessment System.* Itasca, IL: Riverside Publishing.

DHILLON, AMARJIT S. 1998. "Individual Differences Within Problem-Solving Strategies Used in Physics." *Science Education* 82:379–405.

GATHERCOLE, SUSAN E., and PICKERING, SUSAN J. 2000. "Working Memory Deficits in Children with Low Achievements in the National Curriculum at 7 Years of Age." *British Journal of Educational Psychology* 70:177–194.

KAIL, ROBERT. 1991. "Developmental Change in Speed of Processing During Childhood and Adolescence." *Psychological Bulletin* 109:490–501.

KAIL, ROBERT, and BISANZ, JEFFREY. 1982. "Cognitive Strategies." In *Handbook of Research Methods in Human Memory and Cognition,* ed. C. Richard Puff. New York: Academic Press.

KAIL, ROBERT, and BISANZ, JEFFREY. 1992. "The Information-processing Perspective on Cognitive Development in Childhood and Adolescence." In *Intellectual Development,* ed. Robert J. Sternberg and Cynthia A. Berg. New York: Cambridge University Press.

KLAHR, DAVID, and MacWHINNEY, BRIAN. 1998. "Information Processing." In *Handbook of Child Psychology,* ed. William Damon, Vol. 2, *Cognition, Perception, and Language,* eds. Deanna Kuhn and Robert S. Siegler. New York: John Wiley and Sons.

SIEGLER, ROBERT S. 1998. *Children's Thinking.* Upper Saddle River, NJ: Prentice-Hall.

SIEGLER, ROBERT S., and SHIPLEY, CHRISTOPHER. 1995. "Variation, Selection, and Cognitive Change." In *Developing Cognitive Competence: New Approaches to Process Modeling,* ed. Tony J. Simon and Graeme S. Halford. Hillsdale, NJ: Erlbaum.

SIMON, HERBERT A. 1962. "An Information Processing Theory of Intellectual Development."

Monographs of the Society for Research on Child Development 6(2, Serial No. 27).

JEFFREY BISANZ
ELAINE HO
MELISSA KACHAN
CARMEN RASMUSSEN
JODY SHERMAN

EVOLUTIONARY APPROACH

The English naturalist Charles Darwin's principles of natural selection provide the theoretical foundation for the biological sciences and are frequently used to address issues in the medical and social sciences. Evolutionary theory can also be used to understand human development in general and children's academic development in particular.

Life History

Biologists study development by documenting species' life history. Life history refers to the typical ages associated with developmental milestones, such as length of gestation, age of weaning, and life span. Certain life history patterns have been found in many different species. For instance, a long developmental period is common for species that have large brains and sophisticated cognitive skills, and live in complex social groups. The implication is that the demands of living in a complex social world resulted in evolutionary expansions of the developmental period and brain size, and resulted in more complex social-cognitive abilities. The larger brain supports complex social-cognitive abilities, such as language in humans. The long developmental period allows the individual to engage in activities that refine social and other (e.g., foraging) skills.

Human life history. The same life history perspective has been applied to human development and is understood in the context of hunter-gatherer societies, that is, societies that are similar to those in which humans evolved. In these societies, there are five distinct periods in the human life cycle. *Infancy* is the time of breast-feeding, and lasts until the age of three years. *Childhood* begins with weaning and lasts until age seven. During this four-year span, children are still heavily dependent on parents, but are becoming increasingly independent. *Juvenility* ranges from seven years until the onset of puberty, which often does not occur until the mid-teens in hunter-gatherer societies. *Adolescence* is the time of

physical maturation, and *adulthood* is the period of mature reproductive activities. These include finding a mate and providing for the well-being of children. Each of these periods is characterized by different social relationships and degree of cognitive maturity.

Social development. Social relationships in infancy and childhood function to allow normal physical development (e.g., rapid brain development) and to reduce mortality risks. In hunter-gatherer societies, a high percentage (50%) of children die before reaching juvenility. Social relationships and other activities during juvenility involve a preparation for later survival-related (e.g., hunting) and reproductive activities. Social relationships in adolescence and adulthood are focused more directly on survival and reproduction.

The primary relationship during infancy and childhood is between the child and his mother, although the father is also heavily involved in some cultures. The nature of this relationship is termed *attachment*. Attachment-related behaviors, such as separation anxiety, keep the child close to his parents and thus safe. Play becomes an important activity during childhood, and models adult activities, as in play parenting. During juvenility, the focus of social relationships shifts from parents to peers. Peer relationships mirror and thus provide a context for practicing adult social activities. As an example, boys engage in play fighting and organize themselves into large groups that then compete against other groups of boys. These activities result in the practice and refinement of the social and cognitive skills associated with primitive warfare.

Adolescence is defined by the physical changes that prepare the individual for reproductive activities, such as bearing children or competing for mates. During this time, juvenile play activities become increasingly adult-like. Early adulthood is the reproductive period and in hunter-gatherer societies usually begins in the late teens for girls and a few years later (sometimes much later) for boys. In hunter-gatherer societies, many men will have more than one wife and thus continue to reproduce into old age. Older women, in contrast, focus their activities on raising their later-borne children and investing in the well-being of grandchildren.

Cognitive development. In hunter-gatherer societies, people have to learn how to deal with other people; use the local ecology to find food and medicine;

navigate from one place to another; and use tools. The cognitive skills that allow people to engage in social activities and maintain relationships are called *folk psychology*. These skills include language, understanding body language and facial expressions, as well as theory of mind. Theory of mind is the ability to make inferences about what other people are thinking or feeling and predicting their later behavior. The cognitive skills that allow people to understand the behavior, growth patterns, and potential uses of plants and animals for food and medicine are called *folk biology*. *Folk physics* includes the ability to move about in the physical environment, remember the location of things in the environment, and know how to use objects as tools.

The basic skeletal knowledge that supports these cognitive abilities appears to be innate, but must be fleshed out during development. Infants, for instance, automatically attend to human voices and faces, and toddlers easily learn human language through innate brain and cognitive systems that guide children's attention to other people and process social information (e.g., language sounds). However, these brain and cognitive systems are immature, and require extended exposure to language, human faces, and so forth to develop appropriately. Children's play and other activities, such as exploration of the environment and objects, provide the experiences needed to flesh out these innate skeletal systems. The result is an elaboration of the systems that support folk psychology, folk biology, and folk physics. The elaboration results in the adaptation of these brain and cognitive systems to local conditions, such as the local language and the plants and animals in the local ecology.

Implications for Education

The folk psychological, biological, and physical knowledge that emerges through an interaction between innate brain and cognitive systems on the one hand and children's play and exploration on the other is not sufficient for living in industrial societies. In industrial societies, schools exist to facilitate the acquisition of competencies, such as reading, that are essential for living in these societies, but are not part of our evolutionary heritage. Several educational issues arise from this perspective.

Academic development. The evolved cognitive competencies that comprise folk psychology, biology, and physics are called *biologically primary abilities*, and skills that build upon these primary abilities

but are principally cultural inventions, such as reading, are *biologically secondary abilities*. The mechanisms by which evolved systems are adapted to produce secondary competencies are not yet fully understood, but involve, in part, co-opting primary systems for secondary learning, and access to knowledge built into primary systems.

As an example of co-opting, consider the relation between language, a primary ability, and reading, a secondary ability. The acquisition of reading-related abilities, such as word decoding, involves co-opting language and language-related systems, among others (e.g., visual scanning). The result is that these systems can be used for purposes for which they were not designed. For instance, individual differences in the sensitivity of kindergarten children's phonological processing systems, which are part of the language domain, are strongly predictive of the ease with which basic reading skills are acquired in first grade. In other words, the evolutionary pressures that selected for phonological processing, such as the ability to segment language sounds, were unrelated to reading, but these systems are used, or co-opted, when children learn how to read.

As an example of using implicit knowledge for secondary learning, consider that the development of geometry may have been initially based on access to knowledge built into the primary navigation system. In cataloging the basic principles of classical geometry, Euclid started with self-evident truths—implicit navigational knowledge—and then proceeded to prove the rest by logic, that is, by means of fundamental theorems. For example, the implicit understanding that the fastest way to get from one place to another is to go "as the crow flies," was made explicit in the formal Euclidean postulate, "a line can be drawn from any point to any point," that is, a line is a straight line. The former reflects an evolved but implicit understanding of how to quickly get from one place to another and is knowledge that is built into the brain and cognitive systems that support navigation. The latter was discovered, that is, made explicit, by Euclid. Once explicit, this knowledge was integrated into the formal discipline of geometry and became socially transmittable and teachable.

Motivation to learn. Another implication of the evolutionary perspective is that the motivation to acquire school-taught secondary abilities is based on the requirements of the wider society and not on the inherent interests of children. Given the relatively recent advent of near-universal schooling in contemporary societies, there is no reason to believe that all children are inherently motivated to acquire the skills that are taught in school, nor is school learning likely to be inherently interesting or enjoyable. Stated differently, an important difference between primary and secondary abilities is the level and source of motivation to engage in the activities needed for their acquisition.

This does not preclude the self-motivated engagement in some secondary activities. Many children and adults are motivated to read. The motivation to read, however, is driven by the content of what is being read rather than by the process itself. In fact, the content of many stories and other secondary activities (e.g., video games) appears to reflect evolutionarily relevant themes that motivate engagement in these activities, such as social relationships and social competition. Furthermore, the finding that intellectual curiosity is a basic dimension of human personality suggests that there will be many intellectually curious individuals who will pursue secondary activities. Euclid's investment in formalizing the principles of geometry is one example. However, this type of discovery typically reflects the activities and insights of only a few individuals, and the associated advances spread through the larger society only by means of informal (e.g., newspapers) and formal education. The point is, the motivation to engage in the activities that will promote the acquisition of secondary abilities is not likely to be universal.

Instructional activities. The basic brain and cognitive systems that support the acquisition of primary abilities are inherent, and children are inherently motivated to seek out experiences, through social play, for example, that ensure the appropriate fleshing out and development of these systems. In contrast, there is no inherent structure supporting the acquisition of secondary abilities, nor are most children inherently motivated to engage in the activities that are necessary for secondary learning. Although this conclusion might seem self-evident, it runs counter to many assumptions about children's learning in contemporary education; for example, that children are inherently motivated to learn secondary abilities and will do so through activities that involve play and social discourse.

Thus, from the evolutionary perspective, one essential goal of schooling is to provide content, organization, and structure to the teaching of secondary abilities, features that have been provided by evolution to primary abilities. It cannot be assumed that children's inherent interests (e.g., social relationships) and preferred learning activities (e.g., play) will be sufficient for the acquisition of secondary abilities. Instruction must often involve engaging children in activities that facilitate the acquisition of secondary abilities, whether or not children would naturally engage in these activities. This does not mean that play and social activities cannot be used to engage children in some forms of secondary learning. It does, however, mean that it is very unlikely that the mastery of many secondary domains (e.g., reading or algebra) will occur with only these types of primary activities. In fact, research in cognitive and educational psychology indicates that some forms of secondary learning will require activities that differ from those associated with fleshing out primary abilities. These would include, among others, direct instruction, where teachers provide the goals, organization, and structure to instructional activities and explicitly teach basic competencies, such as how to sound out unfamiliar words or manipulate algebraic equations. In closing, the evolution of brain, cognition, behavior, and motivation has profound but largely unrecognized implications for educational theory and practice.

See also: CHILD DEVELOPMENT, STAGES OF GROWTH.

BIBLIOGRAPHY

ATRAN, SCOTT. 1998. "Folk Biology and the Anthropology of Science: Cognitive Universals and Cultural Particulars." *Behavioral and Brain Sciences* 21:547–609.

BOGIN, BARRY. 1997. "Evolutionary Hypotheses for Human Childhood." *Yearbook of Physical Anthropology* 40:63–89.

COSMIDES, LEDA, and TOOBY, JOHN. 1994. "Origins of Domain Specificity: The Evolution of Functional Organization." In *Mapping the Mind: Domain Specificity in Cognition and Culture*, eds. Lawrence A. Hirschfeld and Susan A. Gelman. New York: Cambridge University Press.

DARWIN, CHARLES. 1859. *On the Origin of Species by Means of Natural Selection.* London: John Murray.

GEARY, DAVID C. 1995. "Reflections of Evolution and Culture in Children's Cognition: Implications for Mathematical Development and Instruction." *American Psychologist* 50:24–37.

GEARY, DAVID C. 1998. *Male, Female: The Evolution of Human Sex Differences.* Washington, DC: American Psychological Association.

GEARY, DAVID C., and BJORKLUND, DAVID F. 2000. "Evolutionary Developmental Psychology." *Child Development* 71:57–65.

GELMAN, ROCHEL. 1990. "First Principles Organize Attention to and Learning about Relevant Data: Number and Animate-Inanimate Distinction as Examples." *Cognitive Science* 14:79–106.

JOFFE, TRACEY H. 1997. "Social Pressures Have Selected for an Extended Juvenile Period in Primates." *Journal of Human Evolution* 32:593–605.

KEIL, FRANK C. 1992. "The Origins of an Autonomous Biology." In *Modularity and Constraints in Language and Cognition: The Minnesota Symposia on Child Psychology*, Vol. 25, ed. Megan R. Gunnar and Michael Maratsos. Hillsdale, NJ: Erlbaum.

ROZIN, PAUL. 1976. "The Evolution of Intelligence and Access to the Cognitive Unconscious." In *Progress in Psychobiology and Physiological Psychology*, ed. James M. Sprague and Alan N. Epstein. New York: Academic Press.

SHEPARD, ROGER N. 1994. "Perceptual-Cognitive Universals as Reflections of the World." *Psychonomic Bulletin and Review* 1:2–28.

WAGNER, RICHARD K.; TORGESEN, JOSEPH K.; and RASHOTTE, CAROL A. 1994. "Development of Reading-Related Phonological Processing Abilities: New evidence of Bi-Directional Causality from a Latent Variable Longitudinal Study." *Developmental Psychology* 30:73–87.

DAVID C. GEARY

VYGOTSKIAN THEORY

Lev Semenovich Vygotsky was born 1896 in Orsha (in what is now Belarus), and grew up in Gomel in a prosperous Jewish family in the western provinces of the Russian Empire. His higher education was at Moscow University, despite the fact that in Russia under Czar Nicholas II there were strict laws limiting how many Jewish people could receive advanced degrees. His university studies focused on medicine, and later law. In addition, he studied in an independent university majoring in philosophy and history. After working as a schoolteacher and then as an instructor in a teacher training college, Vygotsky turned to psychology. His career as a psychologist spanned just ten years, ending with his death in 1934. In that time Lev Vygotsky produced about one hundred books and papers, many of which have only recently been published and translated into English. At the time of his death, Lev Vygotsky's work included numerous powerful ideas, however, many were not fully developed and some were even speculative. His students, including most notably Alexander Luria, Alexei Leontiev, Daniel Elkonin, and Alexander Zapororzhets, and others (in Russia and throughout the world) have been responsible for further elaborating many of the ideas of his initial papers.

In the last decade, the intellectual climate of educational theory in the United States has had been dramatically influenced by the work of Lev Vygotsky. His work was first introduced to the West in 1962 through the translation of *Thought and Language*. Many Westerners learned about the basic ideas of cultural-historical theory from *Mind in Society*, edited by James Wertsch and published in 1978. This brief entry presents the major ideas pioneered by Vygotsky and successors, along with an overview of contemporary Vygotskian educational efforts taking place in Russia and the United States.

Vygotsky's theory is known in the West as sociocultural, although Vygotsky himself and his close colleagues preferred to describe it as *cultural-historical*, emphasizing the dual focus of this theory: the history of human development and the cultural tools that shape this development. At the core of this theory is Vygotsky's belief that human development—child development as well as the development of all humankind—is the result of interactions between people and their social environment. These interactions are not limited to actual people but also involve cultural artifacts, mainly language-based (written languages, number systems, various signs, and symbols). Many of these cultural artifacts serve a dual purpose: not only do they make possible the integration of a growing child into the culture but they also transform the very way the child's mind is being formed. Vygotsky refers to these as special cultural tools, acquisition of which extends one's mental capacities, making individuals the master of their own behavior. In the course of child development, a child typically learns how to use these cultural tools through interactions with parents, teachers, or more experienced peers. As a result of using these tools—first in cooperation with others and later independently—the child develops higher mental functions: complex mental processes that are intentional, self-regulated, and mediated by language and other sign systems. Examples of these higher mental functions include focused attention, deliberate memory, and verbal thinking. According to Vygotsky, although all human beings are capable of developing these functions, the particular structure and content of higher mental functions depend on specific social interactions, as determined by culture in general and by each person's unique social situation of development.

Of all the processes involved in acquisition of mental tools, Vygotsky focused primarily on the use of language (it was through the work of his colleagues and students that acquisition of non-verbal mental tools was studied). For him, language is both the most important mental tool and a medium facilitating the acquisition of other mental tools. One of the best-known concepts that illustrates Vygotsky's view of language is the concept of *private speech*. Private speech, or self-talk, originates in social speech, the initial form of speech that is directed to other people. Although it retains the audible characteristic of social speech, private speech changes its function. It now becomes speech directed to oneself rather than speech that is regulated or directed by a more capable person. Noticing that children tend to increase the amount of self-talk when facing more challenging tasks, Vygotsky hypothesized that at some point, they start using private speech to organize (plan, direct, or evaluate) their behaviors. The use of private speech peaks during preschool years and then decreases. Vygotsky associates this decrease with private speech turning first into inner speech and then into verbal thinking. This evolution of speech—from social to self-directed to internalized—exemplifies the path of all higher mental functions, which was described by Vygotsky in his "law of the development of higher mental functions." According to this law, each higher mental function appears twice in the course of child development: first as shared or carried out by an individual jointly with other people—*intersubjective*—and then as appropriated or internalized by this individual and used independently—*intrasubjective*.

Vygotsky's view of child development and education is an extension of his general approach to the development of higher mental functions. Consistent with his definition of development as socially determined, Vygotsky introduced a new relationship between education, learning, and development. Vygotsky argued against the theorists who believed that child development occurs spontaneously and is driven by the processes of maturation and cannot be affected by education. Neither did he agree with those who claimed that instruction could alter development at any time regardless of a child's age or capacities. Instead, he proposed a more complex and dynamic relationship between learning and development that is determined by what he termed a child's *zone of proximal development* (ZPD).

Vygotsky's theory is based on the idea that learning can lead development, and development can lead learning, and this process takes place through a dynamic interrelationship. The ZPD is the area between a learner's level of independent performance (often called developmental level) and the level of assisted performance—what the child can do with support. Independent performance is the best the learner can do without help, and assisted performance is the maximum the learner can achieve with help. By observing assisted performance one can investigate a learner's potential for current highest level of functioning. ZPD reveals the learner's potential and is realized in interactions with knowledgeable others or in other supportive contexts (such as make-believe play for preschool children). By providing assistance to learners within their ZPD we are supporting their growth.

Through identification of a learner's ZPD, teachers find out what knowledge, skills, and understandings have not yet surfaced for the learner but are on the edge of emergence. Teachers also study ways to engage the learner in shared or co-operative learning experience through participation in the learner's ZPD. This involves doing more than completing a task in a combined fashion; it involves developing the learner's higher mental functions, such as the ability to plan, evaluate, memorize, and reason. In *How Children Think and Learn* (1998), David Wood points out: "By *reminding* children we are helping them to bring to mind and exploit those aspects of their past experience that we (as experts) but not they (as novices) know to be *relevant* to what they are currently trying to do" (p. 97).

Applications in Contemporary Russia

Examples of work being done in contemporary Russia within Vygotsky's cultural-historical paradigm are too numerous to be listed in a short article. One could say that most of Vygotsky's ideas, suppositions, and insights were further elaborated upon, verified in empirical studies, and often implemented into practical applications. Some of these ideas became starting points to new theories such as the theory of periods in child development developed by Daniel Elkonin, based on Vygotsky's ideas of psychological age and leading activity. Other theories developed by Vygotsky's colleagues and students can be better described as Vygotsky-inspired in a broader sense rather then purely Vygotskian. Among these are Alexei Leont'ev's activity theory and Piotr Gal'perin's theory of step-by-step formation of mental actions. Common features of most of these theories can be traced back to Vygotsky; these include beliefs in social and cultural determination of child development and in the power of education to shape this development. Because of these assumptions, post-Vygotskians were generally successful in implementing their theoretical principles in classroom practice to create innovative educational programs. Examples of those include a number of preschool and kindergarten curricula based on theories of Alexander Zaporozhets and his student Leonid Venger and the system of "developmental education" based on the work of Daniel Elkonin and his student Vasili Davidov, which has been implemented in curricula for school-aged children from primary grades through high school.

Applications in the United States

As mentioned above, this entry focuses on just a couple of examples of Vygotsky-inspired educational work in the United States. For more perspectives, see the work of Michael Cole and colleagues in *The Construction Zone: Working for Cognitive Change in School*, and Roland G. Tharp and Ronald Gallimore's 1988 book, *Rousing Minds to Life: Teaching, Learning and Schooling in Social Context*. The following are descriptions of two examples: Tools of the Mind, which is an early childhood education program, and Reciprocal Reading, used with older children.

Tools of the mind. This first example might be considered a transitional model. Though the work is being developed in the United States, one of the lead authors is Russian and has worked at the Institute of Preschool Education with Lev Vygotsky's student Alexander Zaporozhets. Elena Bodrova and Deborah Leong have developed an early childhood education model titled, *Tools of the Mind* (1996, 2001). The model has a Vygotskian theoretical basis: development cannot be separated from its social context; learning can lead development; language plays a central role in mental development; teaching should provide organized experiences that are in advance of a child's independent functioning but still remain within the child's ZPD; and teachers should encourage (and even create) opportunities for problem-solving. Implemented in Head Start, preschools, and kindergartens, the program focuses on play, the leading activity of this age. In addition, there are a number of activities designed to promote symbolic representation and self-regulation, such as play planning using Scaffolded Writing, and specially designed artifacts or tools, including the Sound Map, the purpose of which is to support young children in their beginning efforts to spell.

Reciprocal listening/reading. A second program motivated by the work of Lev Vygotsky and developed in the United States is *reciprocal listening/reading,* which was introduced in the mid-1980s by Annemarie Sullivan Palincsar and Ann Brown. It is a strategy for teaching reading comprehension that addresses children's need to examine the background of a text and particular words while learning to monitor their own reading process. Children are taught to interact with text and as a result to regulate their own thinking about the text as they read and listen (when being read to).

The ties of this program to Vygotsky lie in the belief that development of complex comprehension strategies has to start in a cooperative activity (intersubjective) and then move inward for use by a student (intrasubjective). Reciprocal teaching provides guided practice in the use of four strategies—predicting, question generating, summarizing, and clarifying—that are designed to enhance children's ability to construct the meaning of text. These strategies for interacting with the text are most often used automatically and soundlessly by readers and listeners. In reciprocal reading and listening, the strategies are vocalized and made available to other learners. To engage in reciprocal teaching dialogues, the children and their teacher read a piece of common text. This reading may be done as a read-along, a silent reading, or an oral reading, depending on the decoding abilities of the children and the level of the text.

The children and the teacher take turns leading the discussion of segments of the text, using strategies to support their discussion. The teacher uses the strategies and the children are encouraged to play the "teacher role" and to interact with the text. Children then learn new ways of interacting with the text by implementing these previously unobserved strategies and being an integral part of what is being taught in their role as "teacher." Following Vygotskian theory, the children begin to internalize the processes until they become an automatic part of their internal reading and listening comprehension activities. An ultimate purpose of the discussion is the application of the strategies for the purpose of coming to a shared sense of the meaning of the text at hand.

See also: LEARNING; VYGOTSKY, LEV.

BIBLIOGRAPHY

BODROVA, ELENA, and LEONG, DEBORAH J. 1996. *Tools of the Mind: The Vygotskian Approach to Early Childhood Education.* Englewood Cliffs, NJ: Merrill.

BODROVA, ELENA, and LEONG, DEBORAH J. 2001. *Tools of the Mind: A Case Study of Implementing the Vygotskian Approach in American Early Childhood and Primary Classrooms.* Geneva, Switzerland: International Bureau of Education, United Nations Educational, Scientific and Cultural Organization.

ELKONIN, DANIEL. 1977. "Toward the Problem of Stages in the Mental Development of the Child." In *Soviet Developmental Psychology* (1971), ed. Michael Cole. White Plains, NY: M. E. Sharpe.

GAL'PERIN, PIOTR YAKOVLEVICH. 1969. "Stages of Development of Mental Acts." In *A Handbook of Contemporary Soviet Psychology,* ed. Michael Cole and Irving Maltzman. New York: Basic Books.

LEONT'EV, ALEXEI. 1977. *Activity, Consciousness, and Personality.* Englewood Cliffs, NJ: Prentice-Hall.

NEWMAN, DENIS; GRIFFIN, PEG; and COLE, MICHAEL. 1989. *The Construction Zone: Working for Cognitive Change in School.* Cambridge, Eng.: Cambridge University Press.

PALINCSAR, ANNEMARIE SULLIVAN, and BROWN, ANN L. 1984. "Reciprocal Teaching of Comprehension Fostering and Monitoring Activities." *Cognition and Instruction* 1(2):117–175.

PALINCSAR, ANNEMARIE SULLIVAN; BROWN, ANN L.; and CAMPIONE, JOSEPH C. 1993. "First-Grade Dialogues for Knowledge Acquisition and Use." In *Contexts for Learning: Sociocultural Dynamics in Children's Development,* ed. Ellice Forman, Norris Minick, and C. Addison Stone. New York: Oxford University Press.

THARP, ROLAND G., and GALLIMORE, RONALD. 1988. *Rousing Minds to Life: Teaching, Learning and Schooling in Social Context.* New York: Cambridge University Press.

VYGOTSKY, LEV SEMENOVICH. 1962. *Thought and Language* (1934), trans. Eugenia Hanfmann and Gertrude Vokar. Cambridge, MA: MIT Press.

VYGOTSKY, LEV SEMENOVICH. 1978. *Mind in Society: The Development of Higher Psychological Processes,* ed. James V. Wertsch. Cambridge: Harvard University Press.

VYGOTSKY, LEV SEMENOVICH. 1983. *Sobranie sochinenii: Tom tretif. Problemy razvitya psikhiki* (Collected works: Vol. 3. Problems of mental development). Moscow: Izdatel'stvo Pedagogika.

VYGOTSKY, LEV SEMENOVICH. 1993. *The Collected Works of L. S. Vygotsky,* Vols. 1 and 2. New York: Plenum Press.

WERTSCH, JAMES V., ed. 1984. *Culture, Communication and Cognition: Vygotskian Perspectives.* New York: Cambridge University Press.

WOOD, DAVID. 1998. *How Children Think and Learn: The Social Contexts of Cognitive Development,* 2nd edition. Malden, MA: Blackwell Publishers.

M. SUSAN BURNS
ELENA BODROVA
DEBORAH J. LEONG

DEWEY, JOHN (1859–1952)

Throughout the United States and the world at large, the name of John Dewey has become synonymous with the Progressive education movement. Dewey has been generally recognized as the most renowned and influential American philosopher of education.

He was born in 1859 in Burlington, Vermont, and he died in New York City in 1952. During his lifetime the United States developed from a simple frontier-agricultural society to a complex urban-industrial nation, and Dewey developed his educational ideas largely in response to this rapid and wrenching period of cultural change. His father, whose ancestors came to America in 1630, was the proprietor of Burlington's general store, and his mother was the daughter of a local judge. John, the third of their four sons, was a shy boy and an average student. He delivered newspapers, did his chores, and enjoyed exploring the woodlands and waterways around Burlington. His father hoped that John might become a mechanic, and it is quite possible that John might not have gone to college if the University of Vermont had not been located just down the street. There, after two years of average work, he graduated first in a class of 18 in 1879.

There were few jobs for college graduates in Burlington, and Dewey spent three anxious months searching for work. Finally, a cousin who was the principal of a high school in South Oil City, Pennsylvania, offered him a teaching position which paid $40 a month. After two years of teaching high school Latin, algebra, and science, Dewey returned to Burlington to teach in a rural school closer to home.

With the encouragement of H. A. P. Torrey, his former philosophy professor at the University of Vermont, Dewey wrote three philosophical essays (1882a; 1882b; 1883) which were accepted for publication in the *Journal of Speculative Philosophy,* whose editor, William Torrey Harris, hailed them as the products of a first-rate philosophical mind. With this taste of success and a $500 loan from his aunt, Dewey left teaching to do graduate work at Johns Hopkins University. There he studied philosophy—which at that time and place primarily meant Hegelian philosophy and German idealism—and wrote his dissertation on the psychology of Kant.

After he received the doctorate in 1884, Dewey was offered a $900-a-year instructorship in philosophy and psychology at the University of Michigan. In his first year at Michigan, Dewey not only taught but also produced his first major book, *Psychology* (1887). In addition, he met, wooed, and married Alice Chipman, a student at Michigan who was herself a former schoolteacher. Fatherhood and ten years' teaching experience helped his interest in psychology and philosophy to merge with his growing interest in education.

In 1894 the University of Chicago offered Dewey the chairmanship of the department of phi-

losophy, psychology, and pedagogy. At Chicago he established the now-famous laboratory school (commonly known as the Dewey School), where he scientifically tested, modified, and developed his psychological and educational ideas.

An early statement of his philosophical position in education, *My Pedagogic Creed* (1897), appeared three years after his arrival at Chicago. Four other major educational writings came out of Dewey's Chicago experience. The first two, *The School and Society* (1956), which was first published in 1899, and *The Child and the Curriculum* (1902), were lectures which he delivered to raise money and gain support for the laboratory school. Although the books were brief, they were clear and direct statements of the basic elements of Dewey's educational philosophy and his psychology of learning. Both works stressed the functional relationship between classroom learning activities and real life experiences and analyzed the social and psychological nature of the learning process. Two later volumes, *How We Think* (1910) and *Democracy and Education* (1916), elaborated these themes in greater and more systematic detail.

Dewey's work at Chicago was cut short when, without consulting Dewey, Chicago's president, William Rainey Harper, arranged to merge the laboratory school with the university training school for teachers. The merger not only took control of the school from Dewey's hands but changed it from an experimental laboratory to an institution for teacher-training. Dewey felt that he had no recourse but to resign and wrote to William James at Harvard and to James M. Cattell at Columbia University, informing them of his decision. Dewey's reputation in philosophy had grown considerably by this time, and Cattell had little difficulty in persuading the department of philosophy and psychology at Columbia to offer him a position. Because the salary offer was quite low for a man with six children (three more had been born during his ten years at Chicago), arrangements were made for Dewey to teach an additional two hours a week at Columbia Teachers College for extra compensation. For the next twenty-six years at Columbia, Dewey continued his illustrious career as a philosopher and witnessed the dispersion of his educational ideas throughout the world by many of his disciples at Teachers College, not the least of whom was William Heard Kilpatrick.

Dewey retired in 1930 but was immediately appointed professor emeritus of philosophy in residence at Columbia and held that post until his eightieth birthday in 1939. The previous year he had published his last major educational work, *Experience and Education* (1938). In this series of lectures he clearly restated his basic philosophy of education and recognized and rebuked the many excesses he thought the Progressive education movement had committed. He chastised the Progressives for casting out traditional educational practices and content without offering something positive and worthwhile to take their place. He offered a reformulation of his views on the intimate connection between learning and experience and challenged those who would call themselves Progressives to work toward the realization of the educational program he had carefully outlined a generation before.

At the age of ninety he published his last large-scale original philosophical work, *Knowing and the Known* (1949), in collaboration with Arthur F. Bentley.

Experience and Reflective Thinking

The starting place in Dewey's philosophy and educational theory is the world of everyday life. Unlike many philosophers, Dewey did not search beyond the realm of ordinary experience to find some more fundamental and enduring reality. For Dewey, the everyday world of common experience was all the reality that man had access to or needed. Dewey was greatly impressed with the success of the physical sciences in solving practical problems and in explaining, predicting, and controlling man's environment. He considered the scientific mode of inquiry and the scientific systematization of human experience the highest attainment in the evolution of the mind of man, and this way of thinking and approaching the world became a major feature of his philosophy. In fact, he defined the educational process as a "continual reorganization, reconstruction and transformation of experience" (1916, p. 50), for he believed that it is only through experience that man learns about the world and only by the use of his experience that man can maintain and better himself in the world.

Dewey was careful in his writings to make clear what kinds of experiences were most valuable and useful. Some experiences are merely passive affairs, pleasant or painful but not educative. An educative experience, according to Dewey, is an experience in which we make a connection between what we do to things and what happens to them or us in conse-

quence; the value of an experience lies in the perception of relationships or continuities among events. Thus, if a child reaches for a candle flame and burns his hand, he experiences pain, but this is not an educative experience unless he realizes that touching the flame resulted in a burn and, moreover, formulates the general expectation that flames will produce burns if touched. In just this way, before we are formally instructed, we learn much about the world, ourselves, and others. It is this natural form of learning from experience, by doing and then reflecting on what happened, which Dewey made central in his approach to schooling.

Reflective thinking and the perception of relationships arise only in problematical situations. As long as our interaction with our environment is a fairly smooth affair we may think of nothing or merely daydream, but when this untroubled state of affairs is disrupted we have a problem which must be solved before the untroubled state can be restored. For example, a man walking in a forest is suddenly stopped short by a stream which blocks his path, and his desire to continue walking in the same direction is thwarted. He considers possible solutions to his problem—finding or producing a set of stepping-stones, finding and jumping across a narrow part, using something to bridge the stream, and so forth—and looks for materials or conditions to fit one of the proposed solutions. He finds an abundance of stones in the area and decides that the first suggestion is most worth testing. Then he places the stones in the water, steps across to the other side, and is off again on his hike. Such an example illustrates all the elements of Dewey's theoretical description of reflective thinking: A real problem arises out of present experiences, suggestions for a solution come to mind, relevant data are observed, and a hypothesis is formed, acted upon, and finally tested.

Learning

For Dewey, learning was primarily an activity which arises from the personal experience of grappling with a problem. This concept of learning implied a theory of education far different from the dominant school practice of his day, when students passively received information that had been packaged and predigested by teachers and textbooks. Thus, Dewey argued, the schools did not provide genuine learning experiences but only an endless amassing of facts, which were fed to the students, who gave them back and soon forgot them.

Dewey distinguished between the psychological and the logical organization of subject matter by comparing the learner to an explorer who maps an unknown territory. The explorer, like the learner, does not know what terrain and adventures his journey holds in store for him. He has yet to discover mountains, deserts, and water holes and to suffer fever, starvation, and other hardships. Finally, when the explorer returns from his journey, he will have a hard-won knowledge of the country he has traversed. Then, and only then, can he produce a map of the region. The map, like a textbook, is an abstraction which omits his thirst, his courage, his despairs and triumphs—the experiences which made his journey personally meaningful. The map records only the relationships between landmarks and terrain, the logic of the features without the psychological revelations of the journey itself.

To give the map to others (as a teacher might) is to give the results of an experience, not the experience by which the map was produced and became personally meaningful to the producer. Although the logical organization of subject matter is the proper goal of learning, the logic of the subject cannot be truly meaningful to the learner without his psychological and personal involvement in exploration. Only by wrestling with the conditions of the problem at hand, "seeking and finding his own way out, does he think . . . . If he cannot devise his own solution (not, of course, in isolation but in correspondence with the teacher and other pupils) and find his own way out he will not learn, not even if he can recite some correct answer with one hundred percent accuracy" (Dewey 1916, p. 160).

Although learning experiences may be described in isolation, education for Dewey consisted in the cumulative and unending acquisition, combination, and reordering of such experiences. Just as a tree does not grow by having new branches and leaves wired to it each spring, so educational growth does not consist in mechanically adding information, skills, or even educative experiences to students in grade after grade. Rather, educational growth consists in combining past experiences with present experiences in order to receive and understand future experiences. To grow, the individual must continually reorganize and reformulate past experiences in the light of new experiences in a cohesive fashion.

School and Life

Ideas and experiences which are not woven into the fabric of growing experience and knowledge but remain isolated seemed to Dewey a waste of precious natural resources. The dichotomy of in-school and out-of-school experiences he considered especially wasteful, as he indicated as early as 1899 in *The School and Society:*

> From the standpoint of the child, the great waste in the school comes from his inability to utilize the experiences he gets outside the school in any complete and free way within the school itself; while on the other hand, he is unable to apply in daily life what he is learning in school. That is the isolation of the school—its isolation from life. When the child gets into the schoolroom he has to put out of his mind a large part of the ideas, interests and activities that predominate in his home and neighborhood. So the school being unable to utilize this everyday experience, sets painfully to work on another tack and by a variety of [artificial] means, to arouse in the child an interest in school studies . . . . [Thus there remains a] gap existing between the everyday experiences of the child and the isolated material supplied in such large measure in the school. (1956, pp. 75–76)

To bridge this chasm between school and life, Dewey advocated a method of teaching which began with the everyday experience of the child. Dewey maintained that unless the initial connection was made between school activities and the life experiences of the child, genuine learning and growth would be impossible. Nevertheless, he was careful to point out that while the experiential familiar was the natural and meaningful place to begin learning, it was more importantly the "intellectual starting point for moving out into the unknown and not an end in itself" (1916, p. 212).

To further reduce the distance between school and life, Dewey urged that the school be made into an embryonic social community which simplified but resembled the social life of the community at large. A society, he reasoned, "is a number of people held together because they are working along common lines, in a common spirit, and with reference to common aims. The common needs and aims demand a growing interchange of thought and growing unity of sympathetic feeling." The tragic weakness of the schools of his time was that they were endeavoring "to prepare future members of the social order in a medium in which the conditions of the social spirit [were] eminently wanting" (1956, pp. 14–15).

Thus Dewey affirmed his fundamental belief in the two-sidedness of the educational process. Neither the psychological nor the sociological purpose of education could be neglected if evil results were not to follow. To isolate the school from life was to cut students off from the psychological ties which make learning meaningful; not to provide a school environment which prepared students for life in society was to waste the resources of the school as a socializing institution.

Democracy and Education

Dewey recognized that the major instrument of human learning is language, which is itself a social product and is learned through social experiences. He saw that in providing a pool of common meanings for communication, the language of each society becomes the repository of the society's ideals, values, beliefs, and accumulated knowledge. To transmit the contents of the language to the young and to initiate the young in the ways of civilized life was for Dewey the primary function of the school as an institution of society. But, he argued, a way of life cannot be transmitted by words alone. Essential to acquiring the spirit of a way of life is immersion in ways of living.

More specifically, Dewey thought that in a democratic society the school should provide students with the opportunity to experience democracy in action. For Dewey, democracy was more than a form of government; it was a way of living which went beyond politics, votes, and laws to pervade all aspects of society. Dewey recognized that every social group, even a band of thieves, is held together by certain common interests, goals, values, and meanings, and he knew that every such group also comes into contact with other groups. He believed, however, that the extent to which democracy has been attained in any society can be measured by the extent to which differing groups share similar values, goals, and interests and interact freely and fruitfully with each other.

A democratic society, therefore, is one in which barriers of any kind—class, race, religion, color, pol-

itics, or nationality—among groups are minimized, and numerous meanings, values, interests, and goals are held in common. In a democracy, according to Dewey, the schools must act to ensure that each individual gets an opportunity to escape from the limitations of the social group in which he was born, to come into contact with a broader environment, and to be freed from the effects of economic inequalities. The schools must also provide an environment in which individuals may share in determining and achieving their common purposes in learning so that in contact with each other the students may recognize their common humanity: "The emphasis must be put upon whatever binds people together in cooperative human pursuits . . . and the fuller, freer, intercourse of all human beings with one another . . . . [This] ideal may seem remote of execution, but the democratic ideal of education is a farcical yet tragic delusion except as the ideal more and more dominates our public system of education" (Dewey, 1916, p. 98).

Dewey's belief in democracy and in the schools' ability to provide a staging platform for social progress pervades all his work but is perhaps most clearly stated in his early *Pedagogic Creed:*

> I believe that education is the fundamental method of social progress and reform. All reforms which rest simply upon the enactment of law, or the threatening of certain penalties, or upon changes in mechanical or outward arrangements, are transitory and futile . . . . By law and punishment, by social agitation and discussion, society can regulateand form itself in a more or less haphazard and chance way. But through education society can formulate its own purposes, can organize its own means and resources, and thus shape itself with definiteness and economy in the direction in which it wishes to move . . . . Education thus conceived marks the most perfect and intimate union of science and art conceivable in human experience. (1964, pp. 437–438)

Perhaps it was with these ideas in mind that Dewey was prompted to equate education with philosophy, for he felt that a deep knowledge of man and nature was not only the proper goal of education but the eternal quest of the philosopher: "If we are willing to conceive of education as the process of forming fundamental dispositions, intellectual and emotional, toward nature and fellow men, philosophy may even be defined as the general theory of education" (1916, p. 328).

See also: PROGRESSIVE EDUCATION.

BIBLIOGRAPHY

ARCHAMBAULT, REGINALD D., ed. 1964. *John Dewey on Education.* New York: Modern Library.

ARCHAMBAULT, REGINALD D., ed. 1966. *Dewey on Education: Appraisals of Dewey's Influence on American Education.* New York: Random House.

CREMIN, LAWRENCE A. 1961. *The Transformation of the School: Progressivism in American Education, 1876–1957.* New York: Knopf.

DEWEY, JOHN. 1882a. "The Metaphysical Assumptions of Materialism." *Journal of Speculative Philosophy* 16:208–213.

DEWEY, JOHN. 1882b. "The Pantheism of Spinoza." *Journal of Speculative Philosophy* 16:249–257.

DEWEY, JOHN. 1883. "Knowledge and the Relativity of Feeling." *Journal of Speculative Philosophy* 17:56–70.

DEWEY, JOHN. 1887. *Psychology.* New York: Harper.

DEWEY, JOHN. 1902. *The Child and the Curriculum.* Chicago: University of Chicago Press.

DEWEY, JOHN. 1929. *My Pedagogic Creed* (1897). Washington, DC: Progressive Education Association.

DEWEY, JOHN. 1933. *How We Think: A Restatement of the Relation of Reflective Thinking to the Educative Process* (1910), revised edition. Boston: Heath.

DEWEY, JOHN. 1938. *Experience and Education.* New York: Macmillan.

DEWEY, JOHN. 1961. *Democracy and Education* (1916). New York: Macmillan.

DEWEY, JOHN. 1956. *The Child and the Curriculum and The School and Society.* Chicago: Phoenix.

DEWEY, JOHN. 1960. "From Absolutism to Experimentalism." *On Experience, Nature, and Freedom.* Indianapolis, IN: Bobbs-Merrill.

DEWEY, JOHN, and BENTLEY, ARTHUR F. 1949. *Knowing and the Known.* Boston: Beacon.

THOMAS, MILTON H. 1962. *John Dewey: A Centennial Bibliography.* Chicago: University of Chicago Press.

JONAS F. SOLTIS

DISABILITIES

See: ADAPTED PHYSICAL EDUCATION; ASSISSTIVE TECHNOLOGY; AUTISM, EDUCATION OF INDIVIDUALS WITH; COLLEGE STUDENTS WITH DISABILITIES; COUNCIL FOR EXCEPTIONAL STUDENTS; EMOTIONALLY DISTURBED, EDUCATION OF; LEARNING DISABILITIES, EDUCATION OF INDIVIDUALS WITH; MENTAL RETARDATION, EDUCATION OF INDIVIDUALS WITH; PEOPLE WITH DISABILITIES, FEDERAL PROGRAMS TO ASSIST; PHYSICAL DISABILITIES, EDUCATION OF INDIVIDUALS WITH; READING DISABILITIES; SEVERE AND MULTIPLE DISABILITIES, EDUCATION OF INDIVIDUALS WITH; SPECIAL EDUCATION; SPEECH AND LANGUAGE IMPAIRMENT, EDUCATION OF INDIVIDUALS WITH; VISUAL IMPAIRMENT, EDUCATION OF INDIVIDUALS WITH.

DISCIPLINE

See: CLASSROOM MANAGEMENT.

DISCOURSE

CLASSROOM DISCOURSE
Graham Nuthall
COGNITIVE PERSPECTIVE
Arthur Graesser
Natalie Person

CLASSROOM DISCOURSE

The term *classroom discourse* refers to the language that teachers and students use to communicate with each other in the classroom. Talking, or conversation, is the medium through which most teaching takes place, so the study of classroom discourse is the study of the process of face-to-face classroom teaching.

The earliest systematic study of classroom discourse was reported in 1910 and used stenographers to make a continuous record of teacher and student talk in high school classrooms. The first use of audiotape recorders in classrooms was reported in the 1930s, and during the 1960s there was a rapid growth in the number of studies based on analysis of transcripts of classroom discourse. In 1973, Barak Rosenshine and Norma Furst described seventy-six different published systems for analysing classroom discourse.

It soon became clear from these early studies that the verbal interaction between teachers and students had an underlying structure that was much the same in all classrooms, and at all grade levels, in English-speaking countries. Essentially, a teacher asks a question, one or two students answer, the teacher comments on the students' answers (sometimes summarizing what has been said), and then asks a further question. This cyclic pattern repeats itself, with interesting variations, throughout the course of a lesson.

The following excerpt from a whole-class discussion in a fifth-grade science class illustrates the nature of this typical participation structure. The teacher was reviewing what the students learned earlier in the day during a science activity on light.

Teacher. What's transparent? Something is transparent. What does that mean? We did that this morning, didn't we? What does transparent mean?

Valerie. Ah, it doesn't . . . It goes through.

Teacher. Can you explain that a little more? What goes through?

Valerie. Well it goes through like, um . . . You can, like, you shine a torch on and you can see.

Teacher. What goes through?

Valerie. The light.

Teacher. The light. Light can pass through something if it's transparent. What's the next one? Translucent. What does it mean? Jordan?

Jordan. Um, just some light can get through.

Teacher. Absolutely. Some light can get through. Can you look around the room and see an example of something that might be translucent? Well, you all can tell me something in here that's translucent because you discovered something this morning that would let some light through. What was it?

Clarice. Paper.

Teacher. Right. Some paper is translucent. It will allow some light to pass through it. Think of something else that's translucent.

Morgan. Oh, um, the curtains over there, you can see right through them.

Teacher. OK. Yes that's interesting. They do let some light through don't they. Another

example? Think about light bulbs. Do you think some light bulbs would be translucent?

Pupils. Yes.

Teacher. They would allow some light through?

Pupil. No. Transparent.

Teacher. You think they're transparent. They let all the light through. I'm not too sure about that one either. So we might investigate that one.

This excerpt contains two episodes, each initiated by a question ("What does transparent mean?" and "Translucent. What does it mean?"). Within each episode the teacher directed the discussion by commenting on student answers and asking further questions. Each question set off a question-answer-comment cycle. At the beginning of the first episode, the teacher set the context by repeating the question several times and reminding the students that they had learned the answer during the morning's activity. This focused the students' attention and let them know (from their previous experiences with this teacher) that they were expected to know the answer.

The first answer (from Valerie) was not in the appropriate language of a definition. Through two further questions the teacher elicited the missing information and, through a summary, modelled the form of a scientific definition ("Light can pass through something if it's transparent.").

In the next episode, after Jordon copied this model to define translucent, the teacher asked a question to find out if the students understood the term well enough to identify an example ("Can you look around the room and see an example?"). After two answers (paper, curtains) the teacher provided additional help by suggesting an example (light bulb) and asking if the students agreed.

This excerpt illustrates how teachers use questions and student answers to progressively create the curriculum, to engage the students' minds, and to evaluate what the students know and can do. Underlying this exchange are the implicit rules and expectations that determine what, and how, teachers and students communicate. Each statement depends for its meaning on the context in which it occurs and, in turn, adds to the context that determines the meaning of subsequent statements.

Analysis of the patterns of interaction characteristic of most classrooms has shown that, on average, teachers talk for more than two-thirds of the time, a few students contribute most of the answers, boys talk more than girls, and those sitting in the front and center of the class are more likely to contribute than those sitting at the back and sides. Bracha Alpert has identified three different patterns of classroom discourse: (1) silent (the teacher talks almost all the time and asks only an occasional question), (2) controlled (as in the excerpt above), and (3) active (the teacher facilitates while the students talk primarily to each other). Recent attempts to reform teaching based on constructivist views of learning have called for teachers to ask fewer questions and for students to learn to state and justify their beliefs and argue constructively about reasons and evidence.

Earlier research on classroom discourse tended to focus on specific teacher or student behaviors, and, because of the key role that they play, teacher questions have been most frequently studied. Questions that challenge students to think deeply about the curriculum are more likely to develop students' knowledge and intellectual skills than questions that require recall of facts. In the excerpt above, the first question required simple recall ("what does transparent mean?) while the last question ("do you think some light bulbs would be transparent?") required the students to apply their understanding of *transparent* to their own experience.

The results of this early research were often equivocal, and researchers have argued more recently that specific utterances cannot be separated from the context in which they occur. Greater attention is now being paid to the ways in which meanings evolve as teachers and students mutually construct the unique discourse (with its roles, rules, and expectations) that characterizes each classroom.

An entirely different form of classroom discourse occurs when students are working together in small groups. The following excerpt is from a sixth-grade class studying Antarctica. The teacher organized the students to work in groups of two or three and instructed the students to "write down all the different types of jobs that you think people might do down in Antarctica." Ben, Paul, and Jim worked together, and Ben wrote down the list that they created. A nearby group consisted of Tilly, Koa, and Nell.

Ben. Most of the people there are scientists. In fact, just about all of them are.

Jim. Even the cooks would be scientists?

Ben. Not necessarily. OK.

Jim. Some of them?

Ben. Pilots.

Jim. Yeah, they'd need pilots.

Ben. All the things that need to be done to keep you living. You know, you need to have food, you need to have shelter.

Jim. I know, a driver. But you could have a scientist to be a driver.

Ben. What else would they do? A-ah, what are they called? I don't know.

Jim. Maintenance man. Maintenance man.

Tilly (overhearing). Thank you. Maintenance person!

Jim. Or lady. Maintenance person.

Paul. I'll tell you what. Um, explorer.

Jim. Um, expedition leader.

Ben (aware that the next group is listening). Just whisper, will you?

(to next group) Stop copying, you lot. Can't you use your own brain?

Jim. Yeah, they haven't got any brain to use.

Ben. Exactly.

Tilly. How many have you got [on your list]?

Jim. Twenty-eight thousand.

Ben. You'll have a job to beat that.

Jim (whispering to Ben). Mm. Builder?

Ben (to teacher passing group). They're copying.

Tilly and Nell. We are not.

Jim. Yeah, they are too.

Teacher. Oh, you don't need that sort of carry on.

Jim. Let's see, um . . . um . . . a guide.

Ben. Isn't that kind of like a leader?

Jim. No, 'cause the expedition leader is a leader. He just, the guide knows where everything is. The expedition leader doesn't.

Ben. An expedition leader has to know where everything is as well, or else he wouldn't be an expedition leader 'cause he's supposed to guide them all around the place and tell 'em where to go. He's the most experienced and therefore he should be the guide.

Jim. Yeah, but first of all they'd need a guide that's been there. While he's learning.

Ben. Well, he wouldn't be the leader while he was learning.

Jim. Yeah.

Unlike the teacher-led discussions, the structure of this excerpt is determined by the social relationships between the students. Paul and Jim thought Ben knew a lot and encouraged him to assume a leadership role. Mimicking the role of a teacher, he evaluated Jim's contributions ("Not necessarily. OK."), and provided guidance about how to think about the problem ("All the things that need to be done to keep you living."). When Jim suggested "guide," Ben questioned whether this was different from "expedition leader." Jim tried to defend his suggestion but, in the face of Ben's reasons and authority, he agreed with Ben. Researchers have noted that students are more likely to have their thinking changed by their peers than by their teacher, and that resolving differences is simultaneously about negotiating social relationships and consideration of reasons and evidence.

In this classroom there was an underlying competitiveness, and the teacher had previously talked with the students about the gender bias in their texts and personal experiences. These two agendas combined in the conflict that erupted between Ben's and Tilly's groups. When Tilly overheard Jim use a sexist title ("maintenance man"), she corrected him. This alerted Ben to the possibility that Tilly's group was listening and copying his group's ideas. He told his own group to whisper and told the other group they had no brains. Jim followed Ben's lead ("Yeah, they haven't got any brain to use") and challenged Tilly's group by claiming they had a list of "twenty-eight thousand" items. Clearly, the structure and function of this discourse reflects both the requirements of the task and the evolving social relationships and culture (e.g., about gender and ability differences) of this class.

Classroom Discourse and Learning

There have been two distinct approaches to explaining how classroom discourse relates to what students learn. Since the 1960s a large number of studies have been carried out in which frequencies of teacher and student verbal behaviors and interaction patterns (such as asking higher-order questions, providing structuring information, praising student answers) have been correlated with student achievement. These developed into experimental studies in which

teachers were scripted to talk in specific predetermined ways. Such studies came to be criticized for their impersonal empiricism and lack of theory. They failed to consider the contextual nature of classroom discourse, particularly the meanings that participants attributed to what was being said.

As interest in the constructivist nature of language developed, researchers argued that the learning process was contained in the process of participating in classroom discourse. As students engage in the discourse they acquire ways of talking and thinking that characterize a particular curriculum area. For example, to learn science is to become an increasingly expert participant in classroom discourse about the procedures, concepts, and use of evidence and argument that constitutes science. This approach is supported by the theories of the Russian psychologist Lev Vygotsky who argued that the higher mental processes are acquired through the internalization of the structures of social discourse. There is still a need, however, for these detailed linguistic and ethnographic analyses of classroom discourse to include independent evidence of how students' knowledge and beliefs are changed by their participation in the discourse.

See also: CLASSROOM MANAGEMENT; CLASSROOM QUESTIONS; DISCOURSE, *subentry on* COGNITIVE PERSPECTIVE; LANGUAGE AND EDUCATION.

BIBLIOGRAPHY

ALPERT, BRACHA R. 1987. "Active, Silent, and Controlled Discussions: Explaining Variations in Classroom Conversation." *Teaching and Teacher Education* 3(1):29–40.

BROPHY, JERE E., and GOOD, TOM. 1986. "Teacher Behavior and Student Achievement." In *Handbook of Research on Teaching,* 3rd edition, ed. Merle C. Wittrock. New York: Macmillan.

CAZDEN, COURTNEY B. 1986. "Classroom Discourse." In *Handbook of Research on Teaching,* 3rd edition, ed. Merle C. Wittrock. New York: Macmillan.

HICKS, DEBORAH, ed. 1996. *Discourse, Learning, and Schooling.* Cambridge, Eng.: Cambridge University Press.

LEMKE, JAY L. 1990. *Talking Science: Language, Learning, and Values.* Norwood, NJ: Ablex.

NUTHALL, GRAHAM A., and CHURCH, R. JOHN. 1973. "Experimental Studies of Teaching Behaviour."

In *Towards a Science of Teaching,* ed. Gabriel Chanan. Windsor, Eng.: National Foundation for Educational Research.

ROSENSHINE, BARAK, and FURST, NORMA 1973. "The Use of Direct Observation to Study Teaching." In *Second Handbook of Research on Teaching,* ed. Robert M. W. Travers. Chicago: Rand McNally.

VYGOTSKY, LEV S. 1987. "Thinking and Speech." In *The Collected Works of L. S. Vygotsky,* Volume 1: *Problems of General Psychology,* trans. Norris Minick, ed. Robert W. Rieber and Aaron S. Carton. New York: Plenum Press.

GRAHAM NUTHALL

COGNITIVE PERSPECTIVE

The field of *discourse processing* investigates the structures, patterns, mental representations, and processes that underlie written and spoken discourse. It is a multidisciplinary field that includes psychology, rhetoric, sociolinguistics, conversation analysis, education, sociology, anthropology, computational linguistics, and computer science.

Researchers in discourse processing have identified a number of mechanisms that promote learning. The practical mission of the field is to improve the comprehension and production of discourse in textbooks, tutoring sessions, classrooms, computer-based training, and other learning environments. While focused primarily on cognitive mechanisms, it is clear that cognitive, social, emotional, and cultural foundations are tightly intertwined in contemporary theories of discourse processing.

Levels of Discourse Processing

Discourse researchers have identified five levels of cognitive representation that are constructed during comprehension. These include the *surface code,* the *textbase,* the *situation model, pragmatic communication,* and the *discourse genre.* In order to illustrate these five levels, suppose that a high school student had a broken door lock and was reading the following excerpt from the book *The Way Things Work*:

> Inserting the key raises the pins and frees the cylinder. When the key is turned, the cylinder rotates, making the cam draw back the bolt against the spring. (Macaulay, p. 17)

The *surface code* is a record of the exact wording and syntax of the sentences. This code is preserved in memory for only a few seconds when technical text is read. The *textbase* contains explicit propositions in the text in a stripped-down form that captures the semantic meaning but loses details of the surface code. For example, the textbase of the first part of the second sentence includes the following: (1) someone turns a key, and (2) the cylinder rotates when the key is turned. The textbase is preserved in memory for several minutes or longer.

The *situation model* (sometimes called the *mental model*) is the referential mental world of what the text is about. In the above example, the situation model contains causal chains of events that unfold as the key unlocks the door, a visual spatial image of the parts of the lock, and the goals of the person who uses the lock. The construction of an adequate situation model requires a sufficient amount of relevant world knowledge, such as general knowledge about locks and mechanical equipment. *Deep comprehension* consists of the construction of this referential situation model, whereas *shallow comprehension* is limited to the surface code and textbase. The situation model is retained in memory much longer than the textbase and the surface code, assuming that the comprehender has adequate world knowledge to build a situation model.

The *pragmatic communication* level refers to the information exchange between speech participants. In a two-party oral conversation, the two speech participants take turns speaking while pursuing conversational goals. There may be additional participants in a conversation, such as side participants in the circle of conversation and bystanders who are outside of the circle. Speech acts are crafted in a fashion that is sensitive to the common ground (shared knowledge) between speech participants, and linguistic cues differentiate given (old) information in the dialog history from new information. The cognitive representation of a spoken utterance can be quite complex when there are several communication channels between multiple participants (sometimes called *agents*) in a conversation. When printed text is read and comprehended, the pragmatic communication is somewhat simplified, although there are vestiges of oral communication and multiple communication channels in textual matter. For example, there is communication between the reader and writer, between the narrator and audience, and between agents in embedded dialogues within the text content. Text comprehension improves when readers are sensitive to the communication channel between author and reader.

Discourse genre is the type of discourse—such as narration (stories), exposition, persuasion, and so on. Discourse analysts have proposed several different discourse classification schemes, which are organized in a multilevel hierarchical taxonomy or in a multidimensional space (a set of features or levels of representation that are potentially uncorrelated). The Macaulay excerpt above would be classified as *expository text. Narrative text* is normally much easier to comprehend than expository text because narrative has a closer affinity to everyday experiences.

Deep comprehenders construct rich representations at the levels of the situation model, pragmatic communication, and discourse genre, whereas the textbase and surface code have a secondary status. Paradoxically, the examinations that students normally receive tap the surface code and textbase rather than the deeper levels. Teachers generally ask students to recall explicit content or to answer multiple-choice questions that tap word recognition, definitions, or attributes of concepts. One way of promoting deep comprehension is to compose exams with questions that emphasize the situation model, inferences, reasoning, and other aspects of the deeper levels. Since the late 1980s, researchers have advocated a shift in assessment standards to encourage deep comprehension.

Discourse Coherence

Coherence is achieved both *within* and *between* the levels of representation when comprehension occurs. This means that there should be no serious coherence gaps within a particular level and there should be harmony between the levels of representation. A coherence gap occurs within the situation model, for example, when an incoming clause (the clause currently being read) in the text cannot be linked to the previous content on any conceptual dimension, such as causality, temporality, spatiality, or motives of characters. Simply put, a coherence gap occurs when information is mentioned out of the blue. Similarly, there may be coherence gaps at the levels of the surface code, textbase, pragmatic communication, and discourse genre. Regarding coherence between levels, the elements of the representation at one level need to be systematically related to the elements at another level. Comprehension suffers, for example, when there is a clash between the textbase and situation model. If the text stated,

"The key is turned after the cylinder rotates," there would be a discrepancy between the order of events in the correct situation model (the key is, in fact, turned before the cylinder rotates) and the explicit textbase, which reverses the correct order.

Comprehension breaks down when there are deficits in world knowledge or processing skills at particular levels of representation. When there is a deficit at one level of representation, the problems can propagate to other levels. For example, non-native speakers of English may have trouble processing the words and syntax of English, so they may also have trouble constructing the deeper levels of representation. Readers have trouble comprehending technical texts on arcane topics because they lack world knowledge about the topic. A barrier in constructing the situation model ends up confining the processing to the surface code and textbase levels, so the material will soon be forgotten.

While studying a test about heart function, Mc-Namara et al. (1996) documented an intriguing interaction among readers' knowledge about a topic, coherence of the textbase, and the level of representation that was being tapped in a test. The readers varied in the amount of prior knowledge they had about the topic covered in the text. In the study, half of the readers read a text with a coherent textbase. That is, clauses were linked by appropriate connectives (e.g., therefore, so, and), and the topic sentences, headings, and subheadings were inserted at appropriate locations. The other texts had low coherence due to violations in the insertion of connectives, topic sentences, headings, and subheadings. The tests tapped either the textbase level of representation (which included recall tests) or the situation level (which included tests of inferences and answers to deep-reasoning questions).

The results of the McNamara study were not particularly surprising for low-knowledge readers. For these readers, texts with high coherence consistently produced higher performance scores than texts with low coherence. The results were more complex for the readers with a high amount of prior knowledge about the heart. A coherent textbase slightly enhanced recall, but actually lowered performance on tasks that tapped the situation model. The gaps, or breaks in temporality, spatiality, and causality, in text coherence forced the high-knowledge reader to draw inferences, construct rich elaborations, and compensate by allocating more processing effort to the situation model. In essence, deep comprehension was a positive compensatory result of coherence gaps at the shallow levels of representation.

Comprehension Calibration

One counterintuitive finding in comprehension research is that most children and adult readers have a poor ability to calibrate the success of their comprehension. *Comprehension calibration* can be measured by asking readers to rate how well they comprehend a text, and then correlating such ratings with comprehension scores on objective tests. These correlations are always either low or modest (r = .2 to .4), which suggests that college students have disappointing comprehension calibration. Another method of calibrating comprehension is to plant contradictions in a text and observe whether readers detect them. Such contradictions are not detected by a surprising number of adult readers. Instead, there is a strong tendency for readers to have an illusion of comprehension by adjusting their expectations at handling the surface code and textbase. Readers need to be trained to adjust their metacognitive expectations and strategies to focus on the deeper levels.

Classroom discourse is too often skewed to the shallow rather than the deep end of the comprehension continuum. Teachers typically follow a curriculum script that covers definitions, facts, concepts, attributes of concepts, and examples. This content is at the lower levels of Benjamin Bloom's taxonomy of cognitive objectives. Teachers rarely attempt to encourage Bloom's higher levels of inference, synthesis, integration, and the application of knowledge to practical problems.

Discourse Mechanisms that Promote Deep Comprehension

There are some methods of improving deep comprehension and learning by invoking discourse processing mechanisms, including: (1) constructing explanations, (2) asking questions, (3) challenging a learner's beliefs and knowledge, and (4) tutoring.

Constructing explanations. Good comprehenders generate explanations as they read text or listen to lectures. These explanations trace the causes and consequences of events, the plans and goals of agents (humans, animals or organizations), and the logical derivations of assertions. The questions that drive explanations are *why, how, what-if,* and *what-if-not* questions. For example, a deep comprehender might implicitly ask the following questions while reading

the cylinder lock text: Why would the person turn the key to the right? How does the bolt move back? What causes the cam to rotate? What if the pins don't rise? Students learn much more when they construct these explanations on their own (self-explanations) than when they merely read or listen to explanations.

Asking questions. Students should be encouraged to ask and answer deep-reasoning questions to help them construct explanations. Unfortunately, students are not in the habit of asking many questions, and most of their questions are shallow. A typical student asks only .11 questions per hour in a classroom, and less than 10 percent of student questions involve deep reasoning. When students are trained how to ask good questions while reading or listening to lectures, their comprehension scores increase on objective tests. Teachers rarely ask deep-reasoning questions in classroom settings, so it would be prudent to improve the questioning skills of teachers.

Challenging the learner's beliefs and knowledge. One of the easiest ways to get students to ask questions is to challenge one of their entrenched beliefs, and thereby put them in *cognitive disequilibrium.* Suppose, for example, that a teacher expresses the claim that overpopulation is not a significant problem to worry about. This will normally stimulate a large number of student questions and counterarguments. Research on question asking has revealed that genuine information-seeking questions are inspired by contradictions, anomalies, incompatibilities, obstacles to goals, salient contrasts, uncertainty, and obvious gaps in knowledge. Therefore, one secret to eliciting student questions is to create cognitive disequilibrium and then provide useful information when students ask questions.

Tutoring. One-to-one human tutoring is superior to normal learning experiences in traditional classroom environments. This advantage cannot entirely be attributed to the possibility that tutors are more accomplished pedagogical experts than teachers. Peers often do an excellent job serving as tutors. Normal tutors rarely implement sophisticated pedagogical strategies, such as the Socratic method, building on prerequisites, error diagnosis and repair, or modeling-scaffolding-fading. It is the discourse patterns in normal tutoring that explain much of the advantages of tutoring over the classroom. The discourse in tutoring emphasizes collaborative problem solving, question asking and answering, and explanation building in the context of specific problems, cases, and examples. There is a turn-by-turn collaborative exchange (speakers take turns talking) in tutoring that would be impractical to implement in the classroom.

In summary, research in discourse processing can help solve some of the pressing challenges in education. Discourse plays an important role in helping the learner shift from shallow to deep comprehension, and from being a fact collector to being an inquisitive explainer.

See also: CLASSROOM QUESTIONS; DEVELOPMENTAL THEORY, *subentry on* COGNITIVE AND INFORMATION PROCESSING; DISCOURSE, *subentry on* CLASSROOM DISCOURSE; SCIENCE LEARNING, *subentry on* EXPLORATION AND ARGUMENTATION.

BIBLIOGRAPHY

BECK, ISABEL L.; MCKEOWN, MARGARET G.; HAMILTON, REBECCA L.; and KUCAN, LINDA. 1997. *Questioning the Author: An Approach for Enhancing Student Engagement with Text.* Newark, DE: International Reading Association.

BIBER, DOUGLAS. 1988. *Variations Across Speech and Writing.* Cambridge, Eng.: Cambridge University Press.

BLOOM, BENJAMIN S. 1956. *Taxonomy of Educational Objectives: The Classification of Educational Goals. Handbook I: Cognitive Domain.* New York: McKay.

CHI, MICKI T. H.; DE LEEUW, N.; CHIU, M.; and LAVANCHER, C. 1994. "Eliciting Self-explanations Improves Understanding." *Cognitive Science* 18:439–477.

CLARK, HERBERT H. 1996. *Using Language.* Cambridge, Eng.: Cambridge University Press.

GERNSBACHER, MORTON A. 1997. "Two Decades of Structure Building." *Discourse Processes* 23:265–304.

GRAESSER, ARTHUR C.; GERNSBACHER, MORTON A.; and GOLDMAN, SUSAN B., eds. 2002. *Handbook of Discourse Processes.* Mahwah, NJ: Erlbaum.

GRAESSER, ARTHUR C., and MCMAHEN, CATHY L. 1993. "Anomalous Information Triggers Questions when Adults Solve Problems and Comprehend Stories." *Journal of Educational Psychology* 85:136–151.

GRAESSER, ARTHUR C.; MILLIS, KEITH K.; and ZWAAN, ROLF A. 1997. "Discourse Comprehension." *Annual Review of Psychology* 48:163–189.

GRAESSER, ARTHUR C., and PERSON, NATALIE K. 1994. "Question Asking during Tutoring." *American Educational Research Journal* 31:104–137.

HACKER, DOUGLAS J.; DUNLOSKY, JOHN; and GRAESSER, ARTHUR C., eds. 1998. *Metacognition in Educational Theory and Practice.* Mahwah, NJ: Erlbaum.

KING, ALISON. 1994. "Guiding Knowledge Construction in the Classroom: Effects of Teaching Children How to Question and How to Explain." *American Educational Research Journal* 31:338–368.

KINTSCH, WALTER. 1998. *Comprehension: A Paradigm for Cognition.* Cambridge, Eng.: Cambridge University Press.

MACAULAY, DAVID. 1988. *The Way Things Work.* Boston: Houghton Mifflin.

MCNAMARA, DANIELLE; KINTSCH, EILENE; SONGER, NANCY B.; and KINTSCH, WALTER. 1996. "Are Good Texts Always Better? Interactions of Text Coherence, Background Knowledge, and Levels of Understanding in Learning From Text." *Cognition and Instruction* 14:1–43.

ROSENSHINE, BARAK; MEISTER, CARLA; and CHAPMAN, SAUL. 1996. "Teaching Students to Generate Questions: A Review of the Intervention Studies." *Review of Educational Research* 66:181–221.

TRABASSO, TOM, and MAGIANO, JOSEPH P. 1996. "Conscious Understanding during Comprehension." *Discourse Processes* 22:255–287.

ZWAAN, ROLF A., and RADVANSKY, GABRIEL A. 1998. "Situation Models in Language Comprehension and Memory." *Psychological Bulletin* 123:162–185.

ARTHUR GRAESSER
NATALIE PERSON

DISTANCE LEARNING IN HIGHER EDUCATION

For more than a century, distance learning in higher education has constantly evolved—both in practice and in the definition of the term. As in many academic pursuits that are still in a state of development, there have been debates not only about the definition, but also about the words *distance* and *learning* themselves. While there is no one authority to arbitrate this issue, reviewing some well-researched definitions yields some common concepts.

In the mid-1990s, the U.S. Department of Education undertook two studies that tallied the number of U.S. institutions offering distance-learning courses, the number of courses that they offered, and the number of students served by the courses. The studies defined *distance education* as "education or training courses delivered to remote (off-campus) location(s) via audio, video (live or prerecorded), or computer technologies" (Lewis, Farris, and Levin, p. 2). To gain a precise count, the Department of Education listed what should and should not be counted as distance education. For example, they asked that courses taught by faculty traveling to a remote site not be included.

In the late 1990s the American Association of University Professors addressed the rapid adoption of distance learning in their *Statement on Distance Education*. This document defined distance education (or distance learning) as education in which "the teacher and the student are separated geographically so that face-to-face communication is absent; communication is accomplished instead by one or more technological media, most often electronic (interactive television, satellite television, computers, and the like)" (American Association of University Professors website).

Also late in the 1990s, the Western Cooperative for Educational Telecommunications (WCET) developed a publication entitled *The Distance Learner's Guide* to assist learners in successfully finding and taking courses at a distance. The authors sought a definition that did not focus on technology and would be easy for anyone to understand: "Perhaps the simplest definition is that distance learning takes place when the instructor and student are not in the same room, but instead are separated by physical distance" (Connick, p. 3).

Three main concepts are common to these definitions:

- **Education.** A course of study is being undertaken involving both teaching and learning.

- **Overcoming barriers of place and/or time.** Teachers and learners traditionally meet at an appointed place at an appointed time to pursue a course of study. Distance learning originally

developed to overcome the difficulties of teachers and learners who were not in the same geographic location. More recently, distance learning may also serve those who might be at the same location, but choose not to meet at the same time.

- **A tool is used to facilitate learning.** To overcome the distance of place or time, some form of technology is used to communicate between the teacher and learner. Originally, the technologies of pen, paper, and the postal service were used to connect them. As electronic communication technologies (audio, video, and data) became readily accessible to learners, these have been increasingly used.

Related Terms and Concepts

While the term *distance learning* is widely used, the rapid development of communications technologies in the late 1990s and early 2000s created many variations on the theme. To understand distance learning, it is helpful to examine other closely related terms and concepts.

Correspondence study. The original form of distance learning, correspondence study involves the exchange of the written word, on paper, between teacher and learner. Improvements in transportation technologies (i.e., trains, trucks, planes) have assisted the postal service in making this an increasingly more viable method of study.

Distance education. Those wishing to focus on the learner as the center of the instructional process favor using the word *learning*. Others insist that the higher education institution cannot force someone to learn, and that the activity undertaken by the institution is *education*, not *learning*.

Distributed education. As electronic technologies provided more assistance to overcome the barriers of time, instead of just distance, some felt that the focus on *distance* had outlived its usefulness. In distributed education, education is available (or "distributed") to any location at any time. Often a mix of technologies is proposed, including face-to-face instruction.

Hybrid classes. These courses use a mixture of distance learning and face-to-face techniques. For example, a group of learners in a biology class may meet face-to-face for their laboratory work, but the remainder of the instruction may be offered via television or computer.

Open learning. This is a term for distance learning commonly used in the British Commonwealth countries. The term derives from the Open University of the United Kingdom. To assist those not privileged to attend Britain's selective universities, the Open University began offering classes in the 1960s via a combination of written materials, televised programs, and local tutors. Open universities have spread throughout the Commonwealth countries and serve millions of students throughout the world.

Online learning. Distance learning where the bulk of instruction is offered via computer and the Internet is called online learning.

E-learning. Gaining popularity in the early 2000s, the term *e-learning* refers to any electronically assisted instruction, but is most often associated with instruction offered via computer and the Internet.

Goals of Distance Learning

Educational opportunities are numerous: There are colleges and universities throughout the world, and there are specialty colleges that teach trades of every kind. Why then is distance learning needed?

The main goal of distance learning is to overcome barriers of place and time. Learners may live in isolated, rural areas and have no access to education. Other learners may have ready access to a college, but that college might not offer the course of study needed by that learner. Distance learning allows education to reach those who are not able to physically attend courses on a campus. Further, as learners attempt to balance family, work, and education, time becomes a precious commodity. Driving to campus, parking, and spending time in class at an appointed (and probably inconvenient) time may not fit into the learner's overall schedule. Distance learning courses increasingly allow learners to participate at a time that is most suitable for their schedule.

Distance learning can also overcome barriers of learning styles. "We now know that people learn in different ways, and that because some students do not absorb information well from a lecture style of instruction does not mean they are stupid. . . . But research won't change things until its findings are put to use" (Hull, p. 7). The common complaint about distance learning is that "it is not for everyone." While this complaint could also be made of the lecture method of teaching, it still predominates on campus. Electronic education tools, formerly used only in distance learning, are increasingly being used in both on- and off-campus courses. "Almost two-thirds (64.1%) of all college courses now utilize electronic mail, up from . . . 20.1 percent in 1995" (Green, p. 7). Using video, audio, active learning, simulations, and electronic advances can overcome problems encountered by learners who do not adapt to just one learning style.

Other educational barriers can also be overcome by distance learning. Learners with physical or mental handicaps have attained degrees without going to a campus. Distance learning allows those with physical handicaps that prevent or hamper their attendance in person to pursue an education. Distance learning allows those with mental handicaps to follow the instructional materials at their own pace.

Workers may find that they are in need of additional skills to maintain a job or advance in the workplace. Distance learning allows these workers to obtain these skills without quitting their jobs, uprooting their families, and moving to a campus.

Distance learning can help students advance toward a degree more quickly. Utah has made a statewide strategic plan to use distance learning to allow high school students to take college courses while still in high school. Distance learning allows students to enter college with credits and obtain a higher education degree in less time.

Learners already enrolled on a campus may seek specialized courses not available on that campus. Distance learning has allowed some learners to transfer courses into their program that are only available at other campuses.

There is also a cost avoidance, or cost saving, factor. Some countries and U.S. states have avoided or delayed investments in campus buildings by serving some learners via distance or open learning. Sometimes erroneously labeled a *cost savings,* the investments in distance learning assist the government in avoiding the higher costs of building new campuses or campus buildings.

Technologies Used in Distance Learning

Various technologies have been used to overcome the distance between the teacher and the learner. Using these technologies, the teacher prepares the lesson and sends it to the learner, and the learner then interacts with the lesson and sends feedback (questions, assignments, tests) to the teacher. As technologies have improved, so has the quality of this interaction.

An important concept to understand is the difference between two distinct forms of communications: synchronous and asynchronous. "*Synchronous communication* is communication in which all parties participate at the same time. Synchronous communication in distance learning emphasizes a simultaneous group learning experience. Teachers and students communicate in 'real time'" (Connick, p. 8). An example of synchronous (happening at the same time) communication is a conversation. Whether face-to-face or on the telephone, to have a conversation both parties in the conversation must participate at the same time.

"*Asynchronous communication* is communication in which the parties participate at different times. Asynchronous communication offers a choice of where and, above all, when you will access learning . . . you may read or view these materials at your own convenience" (Connick, p. 8). Examples of asynchronous (not at the same time) communication include letters and e-mails. To communicate by letter does not require both parties to communicate at the same time. One person composes a letter and mails it. The other reads the letter upon receiving it and then responds.

Most teachers and learners are much more familiar with synchronous communication in education. All teacher and learners come to the classroom at the same time, make presentations, and hold discussions. As communication technologies have developed, distance-learning teachers have experimented with them to find ways to improve teacher-learner and learner-learner interactions.

Advances in printing, writing, and transportation led to correspondence study, the first major form of distance learning. Teachers would identify books, prepare lessons, and mail them to the learner. Initially, these materials were completely in printed or written form, and the learner would study the lessons, complete the assignments, and mail them back to the teacher. Communication depended on the speed of the postal service. Given the long lag time between lessons, learners often failed to complete the courses.

In the first half of the twentieth century, *broadcast technologies,* such as radio and television, became staples in every home, and colleges experimented with offering lectures via radio as a way to supplement correspondence courses. "The advent of television brought *Sunrise Semester* and its relatives: the first telecourses. Professor Frank Baxter introduced Shakespeare to millions . . . there was a heavy instructional component in the schedules of America's first educational television stations in the 50's and 60's, well before the creation of PBS" (Witerspoon, p. 5). In the early twenty-first century, open universities (in the United Kingdom and throughout the British Commonwealth) and the Public Broadcasting System in the United States still broadcast many courses via television. The increasingly high production values and use of experts of world-renown have increased the educational effectiveness of these courses. With the advent of cable television, federal regulations in the United States required that a few channels be set aside for public, education, and government use. Some colleges broadcast classes to cable television subscribers.

Recording and playback technologies are asynchronous technologies that have also found their ways into the homes of learners. Colleges in metropolitan areas have used audiotapes of lectures to reach learners who spend a considerable amount of time commuting to work. Videotapes of lectures and classroom interaction have been used to supplement correspondence course materials. Some colleges have also created highly produced courses that rival those made by PBS. CD-ROMs have increased in popularity as a recording medium as they can contain audio, video, and data files. CD-ROMs are durable, easy to reproduce, and inexpensive to mail.

All of these technologies have relied on consumer products that are available in many homes. There is also experimentation and widespread use of *closed-circuit technologies* that require special equipment and often require the learner to travel to a local college, library, or other learning center to access the instruction. "In 1959 . . . two DC-6 aircraft became high-altitude TV stations, operating from Purdue University and flying figure eights over Indiana to serve K–12 schools in portions of six Midwestern states" (Witerspoon, p. 5). That experiment was the precursor of satellite transmissions of courses. National Technological University still transmits engineering courses via satellite from its member colleges to corporate sites throughout the world. Students may participate synchronously, or they may tape the courses and view them later. In the United States, the federal government has set aside a portion of the microwave broadcast spectrum for educational use only. Colleges use the resulting Instructional Television Fixed Services (ITFS) to transmit courses to sites and homes that have special receivers. In the late 1980s and into the mid-1990s, two-way video was adopted by a large number of colleges. This synchronous technology employs cameras and monitors at geographically dispersed sites, allowing teachers and learners to both see and hear each other.

The most recent advances in technologies have focused on computers and the Internet. The popularity of these technologies has grown as an increasing number of personal computers entered homes, and as an increasing amount of data could be transmitted over regular telephone lines. The 1960s and 1970s saw experiments using computer-assisted instruction, which were self-contained computer programs that led the learner through the lessons. Given the speed of the computers, many of these programs were originally text-based, and they were greatly improved in later years when graphics, pictures, animation, video, and audio could be added. The Internet created a boom in online learning at the end of the twentieth century. The choice of either synchronous or asynchronous communications options, the ability to add audio and video, as well as a variety of new teaching techniques has made the online learning environment more attractive to both teachers and learners.

In the future, computer processing power should continue to increase at the same great rate that it did during the 1890s and 1990s. *Internet 2,* a high-speed Internet focused on education and research, is one of many high-speed communications options that are under development. Such advances will allow distance learners to have more access to both synchronous and asynchronous audio, video, and computer simulations. As teachers become more familiar with these technologies, they will continue to become part of nearly every class, both on and off campus.

See also: CONTINUING PROFESSIONAL EDUCATION; CORPORATE COLLEGES; OPEN EDUCATION; TECHNOLOGY IN EDUCATION, *subentry on* HIGHER EDUCATION.

BIBLIOGRAPHY

CONNICK, GEORGE P., ed. 1999. *The Distance Learner's Guide.* Upper Saddle River, NJ: Prentice Hall.

GREEN, KENNETH C. 2001. *Campus Computing 2001.* Encino, CA: Campus Computing Project.

HULL, DAN. 1995. *Who Are You Calling Stupid?* Waco, TX: Cord.

LEWIS, LAURIE; SNOW, KYLE; FARRIS, ELIZABETH; and LEVIN, DOUGLAS. 1999. *Distance Education at Postsecondary Education Institutions: 1997–98.* Washington, DC: U.S. Department of Education, National Center for Education Statistics.

WITERSPOON, JOHN P. 1997. *Distance Education: A Planner's Casebook,* revised edition. Boulder, CO: Western Cooperative for Educational Telecommunications—Western Interstate Commission for Higher Education Publications.

INTERNET RESOURCE

AMERICAN ASSOCIATION OF UNIVERSITY PROFESSORS. "Statement on Distance Education," <www.aaup.org/govrel/distlern/spcdistn.htm>

RUSSELL POULIN

DIVINITY STUDIES

The nature of divinity schools' programs of study and admissions policies, procedures, and qualifications differ greatly from institution to institution. Some generalizations can be made, however. The Association of Theological Schools—the central accrediting agency for divinity schools and seminaries—is a good source for more specific information regarding individual schools or programs.

Admission to Divinity School

The admissions processes at divinity schools in the United States are typically less strenuous than those of many other graduate programs. Generally, with a few notable exceptions, standardized tests are not required, though they may be used when considering students for scholarships and other kinds of financial aid. Most programs implement a rolling admissions process (admissions is ongoing until a certain number of students is attained) and require submission of all postsecondary transcripts, multiple essays, recommendations, and a consideration fee. Some may also request an interview. Despite the lack of a required standardized test, however, gaining admission to some divinity schools can be a highly competitive endeavor. Most programs require applicants to have completed a minimum of a bachelor's degree from an accredited four-year institution of higher education, and others mandate certain minimum grade point averages.

Significant financial aid awards usually accompany admission to a divinity school, compensating the student for the reality that most persons who graduate from one of these programs do not find themselves in monetarily lucrative fields.

Degrees Conferred

Divinity school programs of study are diverse, and their respective foci are even more numerous. Generally, however, there are roughly a dozen or so degrees that are most common to divinity schools.

The master of divinity (M.Div.) is considered a professional degree and is probably the most common one awarded by divinity schools. The aim of this program is generally to prepare an individual to move in the direction of ordained ministry, although this is not always the case. Many such programs do, in fact, allow for significant elective credit hours to be spent in other areas of study. However, most M.Div. degrees consist of anywhere from seventy-two to ninety semester hours of study, comprising a mostly Christian-centered curriculum, and require a significant emphasis on practicum. Potential areas of focus include pastoral counseling, missionary work, parish ministry, youth ministry, and social justice ministry. Also, the vast majority of M.Div. programs have a mandatory thesis or "senior project" that must be completed for graduation.

The master of theological studies (M.T.S) tends to be more of an academically focused degree, although it would still fall under the classification of professional degree. It rarely has a practicum component and is generally thought of as a degree that serves as a broad introduction to theological study. The potential fields of study tend to include a more diverse curriculum, including non-Christian religions, social ethics, and philosophy. This program may also allow individual students the opportunity to design (usually under the guidance of professors and the academic dean) their own program of study. The M.T.S. degree is often sought out by those interested in various kinds of social reform, or by persons looking to go on to pursue another degree. The length of this program generally varies anywhere from thirty to fifty-four semester hours of study, and may or may not require a thesis to be written at its culmination.

Usually understood as an academic degree, the master of arts (M.A.) is a program more often found within the graduate school at a university. Even so, many divinity schools that are not affiliated with universities also offer the degree. It is seen as a program of study that will probably lead to another degree, possibly a Ph.D. The master of arts degree usually spans twenty-four to thirty-six semester hours and requires a thesis, but does not have a practicum component. Areas of concentration may include New Testament, Hebrew Bible, ethics, church history, homiletics, and theology.

The master of theology (Th.M., M.Th.) generally requires that a student already hold the M.Div. or equivalent degree. It affords an opportunity for students to pursue advanced theological studies for one year or roughly twenty-four semester hours. The program is especially recommended for students who seek to gain additional competence for the ministry beyond that provided by the master of divinity degree.

A professional degree, the master of religious education (M.R.E.) centers on the process of education as it relates to understanding the Christian faith and its implications for human existence. Areas such as creativity, imagination, spirituality, and pedagogy are often fused to create a holistic process whereby individuals learn to educate the entire person. The length of the degree may last anywhere from twenty-four to fifty-four semester hours, and usually requires a practicum component.

Quite similar to the Th.M. and M.T.S. in terms of degree requirements, the master of sacred theology (S.T.M.) tends to focus primarily on Christian theology, texts, and history.

The master of sacred music (M.S.M) is also a professional degree and generally consists of a series of required courses in three categories: theology, music, and the ministry of music. It requires the successful completion of anywhere from thirty to sixty credit hours, and a final project is generally mandatory. Proficiency in music theory and history as well as choral conducting is usually required to graduate. In addition to the other general requirements for admission to this program, an audition is sometimes also expected.

Those who wish to enhance their knowledge and their ministerial or teaching competence in certain advanced areas of theology and ministry obtain the doctor of theology degree (Th.D.). It has a stronger academic specialization than the D.Min, but also differs from the Ph.D. in its integrative character and clear connection to the church. Admission to this program generally requires the M.Div or equivalent degree and superior performance in the respective master's program. The Th.D. program consists of thirty-six to fifty-four hours of credit and a major project, thesis, or dissertation.

A terminal academic degree, the doctor of philosophy (Ph.D.) is usually sought by those with the aim of research and teaching. And like the M.A., this is a degree that is generally offered through the graduate school in cases where a divinity school is part of a greater university. Whatever the case may be, admission to the program is generally very difficult and requires at least one master's degree in a related field, usually accompanied by a significant research paper or thesis. Areas of concentration may include New Testament, Hebrew Bible, ethics, church history, homiletics, and theology.

The Doctor of Ministry (D.Min) is a professional degree that generally has a prerequisite of the M.Div., and serves as a more advanced ministerial degree. Often it allows for more in-depth study in a specific area of Christian ministry than is generally possible in the M.Div. program. A thesis or dissertation is almost always required.

Other degrees that are conferred by divinity schools in the United States may include doctor of educational ministry (D.Ed.Min.), doctor of musical arts (D.M.A.), doctor of missiology (D.Miss.), doctor of education (Ed.D.), master of church music (M.C.M.), master of Christian studies (M.C.S.), master of religion (M. Rel.), master of ministry (M.Min.), and master of pastoral studies (M.P.S.). In addition, there are a few divinity schools that have dual degree programs with other schools at either their own university or those of nearby institutions (i.e., J.D./M.Div., M.D./M.T.S, M.B.A./Th.M.).

INTERNET RESOURCES

BOSTON UNIVERSITY SCHOOL OF THEOLOGY. 2002. <www.bu.edu/sth/>.

CANDLER SCHOOL OF THEOLOGY AT EMORY UNIVERSITY. 2002. <http://candler.emory.edu>.

HARVARD UNIVERSITY DIVINITY SCHOOL. 2002. <www.hds.harvard.edu>.

VANDERBILT UNIVERSITY DIVINITY SCHOOL. 2002. <http://divinity.library.vanderbilt.edu/div/index.html>.

YALE UNIVERSITY DIVINITY SCHOOL. 2002. <www.yale.edu/divinity/>.

BRIAN LLOYD HEUSER

DOCTORAL DEGREE, THE

Advanced education culminates with the awarding of the doctoral degree. Allen R. Sanderson and Bernard Dugoni, in the 1997 edition of their annual survey of new doctoral recipients from U.S. universities, identified fifty-two different research doctorates. Traditionally, the nonprofessional doctoral degree most often awarded is the doctor of philosophy (Ph.D.), although other degrees such as the doctor of education (Ed.D.), doctor of arts (D.A.), and the doctor of science (D.Sc./Sc.D.) are being offered in greater numbers. Professional doctoral degrees such as the doctor of jurisprudence (J.D.) and the doctor of medicine (M.D.) also indicate the ending of advanced education, but the requirements for these doctoral degrees differ from those of the Ph.D. and its equivalents.

Requirements for doctoral degrees are generally established within the United States. While there are differences with course requirements and completion rates, the basic doctoral degree begins with one to two years of course work and ends with the oral defense of the dissertation. Credit hours generally range from sixty to seventy-five points beyond a master's degree, and course work is most often individually tailored based on the student's background, interests, and professional goals. In addition to completing class work prior to the dissertation, doctoral students are required to take comprehensive exams. Depending on the program, a student may be required to take more than one comprehensive exam throughout the course of study. Typically, a comprehensive exam is administered immediately following completion of course work, and the exam itself may take various forms such as a daylong session where students answer questions based on knowledge obtained in their studies. In most circumstances this is a closed-book exam and, after faculty have had the opportunity to grade the exam, doctoral students must defend their responses orally before a faculty panel.

The Dissertation

The dissertation is an original topic of research investigated by the student in his final years as a doctoral student. A typical dissertation completed by a Ph.D. candidate will include five chapters: the first is a general introduction, the second is a thorough literature review of the subject, the third chapter contains the methodology or how the research is to be conducted, the fourth chapter shows the findings from research, and the final chapter is a discussion of the findings with suggestions for possible future research.

Prior to conducting the dissertation research, the graduate student must defend her proposal to her dissertation committee, which is generally made up of three to five members. The proposal is typically the first three chapters of the dissertation. After the proposal is approved the doctoral student may begin her research and work to complete the dissertation. After the research has been conducted and data analyzed, the doctoral student must again orally defend the dissertation before her committee. Each Ph.D. candidate must show a thorough knowledge of the subject being studied and present original research and findings that add to the body of knowledge for her discipline.

Ph.D.'s, M.D.'s, and J.D.'s

The Ph.D. is the typical doctoral degree awarded at universities, although the areas of study range from the basic humanities to the sciences and education. Those receiving Ph.D.'s have traditionally gone on to faculty positions at colleges or universities. It is not uncommon, however, for Ph.D. recipients to go immediately into careers outside of academe.

Professional doctoral education, as previously mentioned, is postbaccalaureate study in the professions. Two of the most established professional education fields are medicine and law. The requirements for obtaining an M.D. or J.D. are rigid and do not vary greatly at different universities. In contrast, students in research doctoral programs have more flexibility in their individual courses of study. Professional doctoral students enter their graduate program as a cohort, take the same classes, and graduate within the recommended time period unless serious circumstances delay their progress. The curriculum focuses on more applied areas of study. Unlike a Ph.D. where the dissertation is the culmination of study, often after the professional education is completed, the graduate is required to take state-regulated exams in order to practice their profession such as medicine, law, or nursing.

Trends

Sanderson and Dugoni's 1997 doctoral survey shows several trends that are expected to continue. One is an upward trend of Ph.D.'s awarded. While the number of doctorates awarded annually is typically the greatest for the life sciences, the largest growth during the 1990s came in engineering. Doctorates granted to women have been on an upward trend since the late 1960s, but women continue to receive the fewest doctorates in the physical sciences and engineering. Racial/ethnic minority groups also have seen increases in the numbers of Ph.D.'s awarded.

See also: GRADUATE SCHOOL TRAINING.

BIBLIOGRAPHY

SANDERSON, ALLEN R., and DUGONI, BERNARD. 1999. "Doctorate Recipients from United States Universities: Survey of Earned Doctorates. Summary Report." Chicago: National Opinion Research Center.

PATRICIA A. HELLAND

DRIVER EDUCATION

Driver and traffic safety education began as a concept in 1928 as part of a doctoral thesis by Albert W. Whitney. Whitney argued that since so many high school students were learning to drive cars, schools had a responsibility to include driver education and safety instruction in the curriculum. Driver and traffic safety education was developed as a method for persons to gain licensure to use an automobile on public roadways. Prior to this period, state licensure to operate an automobile was not required in all states and localities. As automobiles became less costly and more available, the need to control the interaction of trucks, cars, trains, horse-drawn vehicles, ridden horses, bicyclists, and pedestrians became evident as death rates became an issue in larger cities. Public agencies such as the American Automobile Association (AAA), the Highway Users Federation for Safety and Mobility, and the Association of Casualty and Surety Companies called on government agencies to provide better roadway surfaces, roadway signs, roadway controls, driver evaluation, and driver licensing.

Government agencies responded to these lobbying efforts with roadway building projects and driver licensing programs. Legislative actions provided funding for roadways and licensing agencies. Minimum requirements for licensure established a need to train novice automobile drivers to operate a vehicle effectively. Some local school districts in Pennsylvania and Michigan conducted training programs to help novice drivers as early as 1929. Amos Neyhart, a professor at Pennsylvania State University, established the first recognized driver education curriculum program in 1934. He worked with the State College School District to develop a curriculum for driver education at the high school level. Neyhart became known throughout the United States as the father of high school driver education. His efforts to train high school driver education instructors—efforts that were supported by AAA—have long been recognized as the start of driver education for high-school-age youth. Herbert J. Stack developed the Center for Safety Education at New York University in 1938 and is remembered as the father of safety education in the United States.

Goals and Purposes

The American Driver and Traffic Safety Education Association (ADTSEA) developed a comprehensive driver education plan to provide an effective educational component for graduated licensing efforts. The goals of such a program would include:

- ensuring that novice drivers are trained for practice driving and capable of entering the restricted licensing process, through the use of a competency-based training and assessment process

- instituting a competency-based training and assessment process for drivers moving from a restricted licensing stage to an unrestricted licensing stage

- ensuring that trained novice drivers qualify for appropriate reductions in insurance premiums

- ensuring that novice drivers are trained to recognize risk and potential consequences in order to make reduced-risk choices

- ensuring that novice drivers make choices to eliminate alcohol or other drug use while using a motor vehicle

- ensuring that novice drivers will use occupant protection as a crash countermeasure

- ensuring that novice drivers are capable of using anger management skills to avoid aggressive driving

- ensuring that novice drivers are capable of recognizing fatigue factors that contribute to crashes

- ensuring that novice drivers are trained to deal successfully with new vehicle technologies

- ensuring that novice drivers and mentors work together as a team in practicing risk-reduction driving strategies as a component of the lifelong driver development process

Course Offerings in the School Curriculum

Course offerings in the public school curriculum vary in each state, commonwealth, or territory as a result of licensing efforts controlled by state agencies and institutions not under direct federal government control. The course offerings, when offered in the public setting, are often conducted outside the school day or as a summer course. The courses are usually minimum requirement courses consisting of thirty to thirty-five hours of classroom instruction combined with four to eight hours of in-car training. The school curriculum includes traffic safety programs from kindergarten through senior high school in the scope and sequence of the school district program. These programs are usually not coordinated efforts but develop on the expertise and interest of the instructor, students, or parents.

Student Enrollment

Student enrollment in driver education varies as a result of state requirements, but studies funded by AAA and ADTSEA indicated that 30 percent of the nation's driving population had enrolled in a driver education program prior to licensing. Nearly 40 percent of novice drivers had completed a driver education program for licensing or insurance requirements. These figures are significantly lower than those for the period from 1965 through 1980 when more than 60 percent were enrolled prior to licensing and up to 70 percent of novice drivers completed a state-approved program for licensing or insurance requirements.

Issues and Trends

Trends in driver and traffic safety education include the shifting of training responsibility from public agencies to private agencies in larger cities. Rural areas are continuing to provide training in the public agencies often because of the lack of an appropriate private agency to provide the training.

The advancement of new vehicle technology has provided a challenge for driver and traffic safety instructors. The technology development is moving forward at a rapid pace while instruction techniques are slow to be released by agencies developing the technologies. Instructors and novice drivers often use vehicles with the new technologies and therefore have to teach/learn new driving techniques even though the vehicles that novice drivers often use do not have the new features and technology.

Public financing of driver education continues to decline, so parents and novice drivers are increasingly bearing most of the costs associated with driver and traffic safety education. Parents are beginning to assume new roles because the instructor needs to work with both student and parent regarding new technology and techniques for vehicle control. Parents are assuming more responsibility under graduated licensing programs for training novice drivers and for developing them into responsible roadway users.

Effectiveness of the Program

Program effectiveness has been considered by many agencies and been the subject of a number of reports throughout the period of federal involvement in crash reduction that began with the passage of the Federal Highway Safety Act of 1966. This act required that states provide comprehensive highway safety programs, including driver education. Unfortunately, the state of knowledge regarding the effectiveness of driver education in the early twenty-first century provides no certainty, and much doubt, that the return on this enormous effort will be commensurate with the investment. The National Highway Traffic Safety Administration (NHTSA) has supported training efforts for drivers in a number of ways. NHTSA supported a study of driver training techniques over a period of five years in De Kalb County, Georgia, and found that elaborate training programs were no more effective than more basic instruction in crash reduction. The study found that a more comprehensive program resulted in a reduction in crashes for a six-month period but that the effects diminished as time increased. The comparisons in this study involving education methods were misconstrued by the public and media to mean that driver education did not work. The Insurance Institute for Highway Safety continues to support driver education as an adequate program for prelicensing efforts in a graduated licensing system, but not as a crash reduction program.

Driver education has been criticized as a program that does not reduce young driver crashes. To their credit, driver and traffic safety education efforts have long been designed to aid the driver in gaining a license to meet minimum standards designed by state agencies. The driver education programs designed in states that require driver education for state licensure have demonstrated a reduced crash rate for fifteen-, sixteen-, and seventeen-year-old drivers when compared to states that do not require driver education for licensure. Michigan developed a graduated licensing program involving two phases of driver education for novice drivers and has demonstrated a reduced crash rate for teen drivers. North Carolina provides driver education as the first stage of a graduated license and has demonstrated a reduction in crash rates. Kentucky, however, does not require driver education as part of its initial phase of graduated licensing and has not demonstrated a reduced crash rate for teen drivers. Such research may indicate that driver and traffic safety education needs to be part of a graduated licensing program as well as the lifelong learning process.

See also: SCHOOL-LINKED SERVICES.

BIBLIOGRAPHY

AGENT, KENNETH R.; PIGMAN, JERRY G.; STEENBERGEN, L. C.; POLLACK, SUSAN H.; KIDD, PAMELA S.; and McCOY, C. 2002. "Evaluation of the Kentucky Graduated Driver Licensing System." Lexington: University of Kentucky Highway Safety Research Center.

ASSOCIATION OF CASUALTY AND SURETY COMPANIES. DEPARTMENT OF PUBLIC SAFETY. 1949. *Man and the Motor Car,* 4th edition. New York: Peter Mallon.

ROBINSON, ALLEN R., and KLINE, TERRY L. 2000. "Traffic Safety Education Driver Development Outcomes for the Life Long Learning Process: Restricted Licensure Qualification Segment I and Unrestricted Licensure Qualification Segment II." Indiana: American Driver and Traffic Safety Education Association, Indiana University of Pennsylvania.

SEATON, DON CASH; STACK, HERBERT J.; and LOFT, BERNARD I. 1969. *Administration and Supervision of Safety Education.* New York: Macmillan.

U.S. DEPARTMENT OF HEALTH, EDUCATION, AND WELFARE. SECRETARY'S ADVISORY COMMITTEE

ON TRAFFIC SAFETY. 1968. *Report of the Secretary's Advisory Committee, U.S. Department of Health, Education, and Welfare.* Washington, DC: U.S. Government Printing Office.

WEAVER, J. A. 1987. "Follow-up Evaluation of the Safe Performance Curriculum Driver Education Project." Presentation to Research Division of the American Driver and Traffic Safety Education Association, Spokane, Washington.

TERRY L. KLINE
VANESSA WIGAND

DROPOUTS, SCHOOL

Individuals who leave school prior to high school graduation can be defined as school dropouts. From the early 1960s into the twenty-first century, as universal secondary school attendance became the norm, such individuals were the subject of study by educators, educational researchers, and concerned policymakers in the United States. With some variation in local circumstances, they are of increasing concern around the world as the educational requirements for full participation in modern societies continue to increase.

Extent of the Problem

Dropout rates have been examined from several perspectives. Event dropout rates measure the proportion of students who drop out of school in a single year without completing a certain level of schooling. Status dropout rates measure the proportion of the entire population of a given age who have not completed a certain level of schooling and are not currently enrolled. Cohort dropout rates measure dropping out among a single group or cohort of students over a given period. High school completion rates measure the proportion of an entire population of a given age who have left high school and earned a high school diploma or its equivalent.

The U.S. National Center for Education Statistics (NCES) reports annual event dropout rates that describe the proportion of young adults ages fifteen through twenty-four who dropped out during the school year prior to the data collection. Between 1972 and 2000 this annual event dropout rate ranged between 4 and 6.7 percent. This rate decreased from 1972 through 1987. From 1987 to 2000 there were year-to-year fluctuations, but the overall pattern was one of stable rates ranging from 4 to 5.7 percent.

Status dropout rates are reported by the NCES as the proportion of young adults ages sixteen through twenty-four not currently enrolled in school who have not completed a high school diploma or the equivalent. Between 1972 and 2000 the annual status dropout rate declined from 14.6 percent to 10.9 percent.

Cohort dropout rates are calculated for various cohorts studied as they make their way through secondary school. The most recent large-scale secondary school cohort is found in the National Educational Longitudinal Study of 1988. That study examined the cohort dropout rates for the eighth-grade class of 1988 followed up at two-year intervals through 1994. For this national sample of U.S. secondary school students, the cohort dropout rate in the spring of 1992, when they were scheduled to complete high school, was 10.8 percent. The rate declined to 10.1 percent by August 1992 after some of the students completed high school in the summer. The rate declined further to 7.2 percent by August 1994, two years following their scheduled completion of high school.

High school completion rates reported by the NCES are the proportions of those aged eighteen to twenty-four not in high school who have earned a diploma or the equivalent. Between 1972 and 2000 this rate ranged from 82.8 percent to 86.5 percent.

Dropout rates differ by various demographic factors, including gender, race and ethnicity, immigration status, and geographic location. In the United States dropout rates are higher for males than for females. Hispanics have the highest dropout rates by far, followed by African Americans, non-Hispanic whites, and Asian Americans. For example, in 2000 the status dropout rate for Hispanics was 27.8 percent, while the corresponding rates for African Americans, non-Hispanic whites, and Asian Americans were 13.1 percent, 6.9 percent, and 3.8 percent, respectively. Individuals born outside the United States have a higher dropout rate than those born in the United States. There are also regional differences in the United States, with the South and West having higher dropout rates than the Northeast and Midwest. Students in urban areas are more likely to drop out of school than students in suburban areas.

Internationally, there is considerable variation in dropout rates, because different nations are in different stages of extending universal secondary education. Among developed countries the high school completion rates are generally as high as or higher than in the United States, though the nature of the secondary programs varies considerably. Rates in other countries lag behind those in developed countries, but secondary enrollments and graduation rates have been increasing worldwide. There are also differences in dropout rates associated with socioeconomic and demographic factors. One notable demographic difference concerns the dropout rates for males and females. Females are less likely to drop out in developed countries and in Latin American and the Caribbean, but females are more likely to drop out prior to high school completion in the rest of the world.

Factors Associated with Early School Leaving

In searching for the reasons that students drop out of school prior to graduation, researchers have focused on three different types of factors. The earliest line of work in this area examined the characteristics of students and their immediate circumstances. This work has been joined by research examining the role of school characteristics. Another set of investigations concerns the impact of broader factors outside of schools, including policies governing the overall educational system.

Student and family factors. In view of the pronounced associations between easily recognized student characteristics and dropout rates, it is not surprising that investigators have devoted attention to the potential impact of such characteristics. Among the student characteristics identified as contributing to dropping out have been gender, racial and ethnic minority status, low socioeconomic status, poor school performance, low self-esteem, delinquency, substance abuse, and pregnancy. In addition to these individual characteristics, research has also examined the impact of certain family characteristics, including single-parent families, non-English-speaking families, and families that are less involved in the educational process.

School factors. Noting differences in dropout rates among schools, researchers have investigated the characteristics of schools and their programs that appear to be associated with early school leaving. These investigations have considered the academic and social dimensions of schooling as well as the issue of the availability of schooling.

Schools in which students have limited opportunities for academic success appear to have higher dropout rates. One of the strongest correlates of early school leaving in studies of students is the lack of academic success. Students who more often get low grades, fail subjects, and are retained in grade are more likely to leave school prior to graduation. Students experiencing difficulty meeting the academic demands of the school tend to leave rather than continue in the face of the frustration of failing to achieve good grades. The lack of opportunities for success can be viewed as an imbalance between the academic demands of the school and the resources students have to meet those demands. The availability of such resources appears to be related to the structure and organization of schools. In 2000 Russell W. Rumberger and S. L. Thomas found that public, urban, and large schools and those with higher student–teacher ratios tended to have higher dropout rates.

The failure of students to find positive social relationships in schools and the lack of a climate of caring and support also appear to be related to increased rates of dropping out. Positive relationships between teachers and students and among students and a climate of shared purpose and concern have been cited as key elements in schools that hold students until graduation. In 1994 Nettie Legters and Edward L. McDill pointed to organizational features of schools conducive to positive social relations including small school size, teacher and student contacts focused on a limited number people within the school, and teachers who have been prepared to focus on the needs of students and their families and communities. In 2001 Robert Croninger and Valerie E. Lee found lower dropout rates in schools where students report receiving more support from teachers for their academic work and where teachers report that students receive more guidance about both school and personal matters.

In addition to issues of access to academic success and social acceptance within schools, in some contexts there is an issue of the availability of schooling at all. This is primarily an issue in areas of the world where secondary schooling is not widely available. Although this situation tends to be more prevalent in the developing world, there are areas within developed countries, such as sparsely populated or geographically isolated areas, where access to schooling is not readily available. Completing high school in such circumstances often takes students far from home and from family and community support and so makes dropping out more likely.

Outside factors. Factors outside of schools have also been considered for their impact on dropping out. Examinations of these outside factors typically concern the degree to which they are supportive of schooling or the degree to which schooling is perceived as relevant to the current or future lives of students. In both cases external factors can be the natural consequence of broader social forces or the result of deliberate educational policies.

Support for schooling in general or for the continued enrollment of students through graduation can vary from community to community and society to society. For example, in the United States the long-held view that schooling is essential for a democratic society was reinforced in the late twentieth century by the notion that schooling is essential to meeting the increasing technical requirements of the U.S. economy. These ideologies of support for schooling are reflected in specific policies, such as educational requirements for jobs, and in media campaigns emphasizing the importance of staying in school.

The relevance of schooling and school completion as perceived by students also has an impact on dropping out. When conditions outside of school indicate to students that school completion is important for their current and future success, students are more likely to remain in school. These conditions can be structured by indirect processes as when high school diplomas become so common that they lose their value and are replaced by university graduation as a mark of distinction. Such conditions can also be structured directly through policies such as those requiring students to remain in school to obtain a driver's license.

Dropout Prevention Programs and Their Effects

The major approaches to dropout prevention seek to use knowledge of the factors associated with dropping out to craft interventions to increase the chances that students will remain in school through high school graduation. The various prevention efforts fall into three major categories: school-based approaches, environmental approaches, and system-building approaches.

School-based approaches have included both programs and practices designed to enhance the prospects for student academic success and those de-

signed to strengthen the positive social relationships and climate of support and concern students find in school. Approaches to the former have included improved diagnosis of student abilities and tailoring of instruction to individual students, altering evaluation processes to recognize student effort, restructuring school tasks to draw on a wider range of abilities, enhancing remediation programs to make use of more time for instruction during the school year and during the summer, and increasing the use of tutoring and technology to deliver instruction to students whose needs are not met by regular classroom instruction. Efforts to improve social relationships and create a shared climate of concern for students have included mentoring programs linking adults and students, house plans in large schools to create smaller environments in which a limited number of students and teachers work on the entire academic program, and the use of older students as peer mentors for younger students.

Environmental approaches have included strategies to address unsupportive outside conditions by developing new relationships between families and schools and the integration of educational and human services to address the social and economic problems that impede progress through school. Attempts to reduce the problem of the lack of relevance of school to the current and future lives of students have involved revised curricula that more clearly relate to real-world experiences, updated vocational education programs that integrate academic and vocational skills and make clear links to the world of work, multicultural curricula that include materials and role models from students' own ethnic or cultural backgrounds, and programs that make more salient the link between schooling and work.

System-building approaches include all those activities entailed in continuing to expand secondary education in those societies in which secondary schooling is not widely available. Included are things such as establishing schools closer to the local communities of students and enhancing the quality of the teaching force and the curriculum.

The evaluation evidence on the effectiveness of the various dropout prevention efforts is limited, with most programs subjected to little in the way of rigorous study. Attempts at evaluation are complicated by the long lead time between early interventions and on-time high school completion and by the complex and multifaceted approaches often attempted with students in secondary schools.

See also: GENERAL EDUCATIONAL DEVELOPMENT TEST; SECONDARY EDUCATION, *subentry on* CURRENT TRENDS.

BIBLIOGRAPHY

ALEXANDER, KARL L.; ENTWISLE, DORIS R.; and KABBANI, NADER S. 2001. "The Dropout Process in Life Course Perspective: Early Risk Factors at Home and School." *Teachers College Record* 103:760–822.

BEDARD, KELLY. 2001. "Human Capital versus Signaling Models: University Access and High School Dropouts." *Journal of Political Economy* 109:749–775.

CATERALL, JAMES S. 1998. "Risk and Resilience in Student Transition to High Schools." *American Journal of Education* 106:302–333.

CRONINGER, ROBERT, and LEE, VALERIE E. 2001. "Social Capital and Dropping out of High School: Benefits to At-Risk Students of Teachers' Support and Guidance." *Teachers College Record* 103:548–581.

KAUFMAN, PHILLIP; ALT, MARTHA NAOMI; and CHAPMAN, CHRISTOPHER D. 2001. *Dropout Rates in the United States, 2000.* Washington, DC: U.S. Department of Education, National Center for Education Statistics.

LEGTERS, NETTIE, and McDILL, EDWARD L. 1994. "Rising to the Challenge: Emerging Strategies for Educating Youth at Risk." In *Schools and Students at Risk: Context and Framework for Positive Change*, ed. Robert J. Rossi. New York: Teachers College Press.

LIPPMAN, LAURA. 2001. *Cross-National Variation in Educational Preparation for Adulthood: From Early Adolescence to Young Adulthood.* Washington, DC: U.S. Department of Education, National Center for Education Statistics.

McMILLEN, MARILYN, and KAUFMAN, PHILLIP. 1997. *Dropout Rates in the United States, 1996.* Washington, DC: U.S. Department of Education, National Center for Education Statistics.

McPARTLAND, JAMES M. 1994. "Dropout Prevention in Theory and Practice." In *Schools and Students at Risk: Context and Framework for Positive Change*, ed. Robert J. Rossi. New York: Teachers College Press.

NATRIELLO, GARY; McDILL, EDWARD L.; and PALLAS, AARON M. 1990. *Schooling Disadvantaged Students: Racing against Catastrophe.* New York: Teachers College Press.

RUMBERGER, RUSSELL W. 1987. "High School Dropouts: A Review of Issues and Evidence." *Review of Educational Research* 57:101–121.

RUMBERGER, RUSSELL W., and THOMAS, S. L. 2000. "The Distribution of Dropout and Turnover Rates among Urban and Suburban High Schools." *Sociology of Education* 73(1):39–67.

UNITED NATIONS. 2000. *The World's Women, 2000: Trends and Statistics.* New York: United Nations.

U.S. DEPARTMENT OF EDUCATION. NATIONAL CENTER FOR EDUCATION STATISTICS. 2000. *The Condition of Education, 2000.* Washington, DC: U.S. Government Printing Office.

U.S. DEPARTMENT OF EDUCATION. NATIONAL CENTER FOR EDUCATION STATISTICS. 2001. *Digest of Education Statistics, 2000.* Washington, DC: U.S. Government Printing Office.

WAGENAAR, THEODORE. 1987. "What Do We Know about Dropping Out of High School?" In *Research in the Sociology of Education and Socialization*, Vol. 7, ed. Ronald Corwin. Greenwich, CT: JAI Press.

GARY NATRIELLO

DRUG ABUSE

See: DRUG AND ALCOHOL ABUSE; FAMILY COMPOSITION AND CIRCUMSTANCE, *subentry on* ALCOHOL, TOBACCO, AND OTHER DRUGS; PERSONAL AND PSYCHOLOGICAL PROBLEMS OF COLLEGE STUDENTS; RISK BEHAVIORS, *subentry on* DRUG USE AMONG TEENS.

DRUG AND ALCOHOL ABUSE

SCHOOL
    Gilbert J. Botvin
    Kenneth W. Griffin
COLLEGE
    Leigh Z. Gilchrist

SCHOOL

Drug and alcohol abuse are important problems that affect school-age youth at earlier ages than in the past. Young people frequently begin to experiment with alcohol, tobacco, and other drugs during the middle school years, with a smaller number starting during elementary school. By the time students are in high school, rates of substance use are remarkably high. According to national survey data, about one in three twelfth graders reports being drunk or binge drinking (i.e., five or more drinks in a row) in the past thirty days; furthermore, almost half of high school students report ever using marijuana and more than one-fourth report using marijuana in the past thirty days. Marijuana is the most commonly used illicit drug among high school students. However, use of the drug ecstasy (MDMA) has seen a sharp increase among American teenagers at the end of the twentieth century, from 6 percent in 1996 up to 11 percent reporting having tried ecstasy in 2000. Indeed, at the beginning of the twenty-first century, ecstasy was used by more American teenagers than cocaine.

Many educators recognize that drug and alcohol abuse among students are significant barriers to the achievement of educational objectives. Furthermore, federal and state agencies and local school districts frequently mandate that schools provide health education classes to students, including content on drug and alcohol abuse. The Safe and Drug-Free Schools Program is a comprehensive federal initiative funded by the U.S. Department of Education, which is designed to strengthen programs that prevent the use of alcohol, tobacco, drugs, and violence in and around the nation's schools. In order to receive federal funding under this program, school districts are expected to develop a comprehensive education and prevention plan, which involves students, teachers, parents, and other members of the community. Thus it is clear that schools have become the major focus of drug and alcohol abuse education and prevention activities for youth. This makes sense from a practical standpoint because schools offer efficient access to large numbers of youth during the years that they typically begin to use drugs and alcohol.

Since the 1970s several approaches to drug and alcohol abuse education and prevention have been implemented in school settings. Traditionally, drug and alcohol abuse education has involved the dissemination of information on drug abuse and the negative health, social, and legal consequences of abuse. Contemporary approaches include social resistance and competence-enhancement programs, which focus less on didactic instruction and more on interactive-skills training techniques. The most promising contemporary approaches are conceptualized within a theoretical framework based on the etiology of drug abuse and have been subjected to empirical testing using appropriate research methods. Contemporary programs are typically categorized into one of three types: (1) *universal* programs focus on the general population, such as all students in a particular school; (2) *selective* programs target high-risk groups, such as poor school achievers; and (3) *indicated* programs are designed for youth already experimenting with drugs or engaging in other high-risk behaviors.

Traditional Educational Approach

Information dissemination. The most commonly used approach to drug and alcohol abuse education involves simply providing students with factual information about drugs and alcohol. Some information-dissemination approaches attempt to dramatize the dangers of drug abuse by using fear-arousal techniques designed to attract attention and frighten individuals into not using drugs, accompanied by vivid portrayals of the severe adverse consequences of drug abuse.

Methods. Informational approaches may include classroom lectures about the dangers of abuse, as well as educational pamphlets and other printed materials, and short films that impart information to students about different types of drugs and the negative consequences of use. Some programs have police officers come into the classroom and discuss law-enforcement issues, including drug-related crime and penalties for buying or possessing illegal drugs. Other programs use doctors or other health professionals to talk about the severe, often irreversible, health effects of drug use.

Effectiveness. Evaluation studies of informational approaches to drug and alcohol abuse prevention have shown that in some cases a temporary impact on knowledge and antidrug attitudes can occur. However, 1997 meta-analytic studies by Nancy Tobler and Howard Stratton consistently fail to show any impact on drug use behavior or intentions to use drugs in the future. It has become increasingly clear that the etiology of drug and alcohol abuse is complex, and prevention strategies that rely primarily on information dissemination are not effective in changing behavior.

Contemporary Educational Approaches

Social resistance approach. There has been a growing recognition since the 1970s that social and psychological factors are central in promoting the onset of cigarette smoking and, later, drug and alcohol abuse. Drug abuse education and prevention approaches are increasingly more closely tied to psychological theories of human behavior. The social resistance approach is based on a conceptualization of adolescent drug abuse as resulting from pro-drug social influences from peers, persuasive advertising appeals, and media portrayals encouraging drug use, along with exposure to drug-using role models. Therefore, social influence programs focus extensively on teaching students how to recognize and deal with social influences to use drugs from peers and the media. These resistance-skills programs focus on skills training to increase students' resistance to negative social influences to engage in drug use, particularly peer pressure.

Methods. The goal of resistance-skills training approaches is to have students learn ways to avoid high-risk situations where they are likely to experience peer pressure to smoke, drink, or use drugs, and/or acquire the knowledge, confidence, and skills needed to handle peer pressure in these and other situations. These programs frequently include a component that makes students aware of pro-smoking influences from the media, with an emphasis on the techniques used by advertisers to influence consumer behavior. Also, because adolescents tend to overestimate the prevalence of tobacco, alcohol, and drug use, social resistance programs often attempt to correct normative expectations that nearly everybody smokes, drinks alcohol, or uses drugs. In fact, it has been proposed that resistance skills training may be ineffective in the absence of conservative social norms against drug use, since if the norm is to use drugs, adolescents will be less likely to resist offers of drugs.

Effectiveness. Resistance skills programs as a whole have generally been successful. A comprehensive review of resistance skills studies published from 1980 to 1990 reported that the majority of prevention studies (63%) had positive effects on drug use behavior, with fewer studies having neutral (26%) or negative effects on behavior (11%)—with several in the neutral category having inadequate statistical power to detect program effects. Furthermore, several follow-up studies of resistance skills interventions have reported positive behavioral effects lasting for up to three years, although longer term follow-up studies have shown that these effects gradually decay over time, suggesting the need for ongoing intervention or booster sessions.

The most popular school-based drug education program based on the social influence model is Drug Abuse Resistance Education, or Project DARE. The core DARE curriculum is typically provided to children in the fifth or sixth grades and contains elements of information dissemination and social influence approaches to drug abuse prevention. DARE uses trained, uniformed police officers in the classroom to teach the drug prevention curriculum. Despite the popularity of DARE, 1998 evaluation studies of DARE by Dennis Rosenbaum and Gordon Hanson examined the most scientifically rigorous published evaluations of DARE and concluded that DARE has little or no impact on drug use behavior, particularly beyond the initial posttest assessment. Some of the possible reasons why DARE is ineffective may be that the program is targeting the wrong mediating processes, that the instructional methods are less interactive than more successful prevention programs, and that teenagers may simply "tune out" what may be perceived as an expected message from an ultimate authority figure.

Competence enhancement approach. A limitation of the social influence approach is that it assumes that young people do not want to use drugs but lack the skills or confidence to refuse. For some youth, however, using drugs may not be a matter of yielding to peer pressure but may have instrumental value; it may, for example, help them deal with anxiety, low self-esteem, or a lack of comfort in social situations. According to the competence-enhancement approach, drug use behavior is learned through a process of modeling, imitation, and reinforcement and is influenced by an adolescent's pro-drug cognitions, attitudes, and beliefs. These factors, in combination with poor personal and social skills, are believed to increase an adolescent's susceptibility to social influences in favor of drug use.

Methods. Although these approaches have several features that they share with resistance-skills training approaches, a distinctive feature of competence-enhancement approaches is an emphasis on the teaching of generic personal self-management skills and social coping skills. Examples of the kind of generic personal and social skills typically included in this prevention approach are decision-making and problem-solving skills, cognitive skills for resisting interpersonal and media influences, skills for enhancing self-esteem (goal-setting and self-directed behavior change techniques), adaptive coping strategies for dealing with stress and anxiety, general social skills (complimenting, conversational skills, and skills for forming new friendships), and general assertiveness skills. These skills are best taught using proven cognitive-behavioral skills training methods: instruction and demonstration, role playing, group feedback and reinforcement, behavioral rehearsal (in-class practice) and extended (out-of-class) practice through behavioral homework assignments.

Effectiveness. Over the years, a number of evaluation studies have been conducted, testing the efficacy of competence-enhancement approaches to drug abuse prevention. These studies have consistently demonstrated behavioral effects as well as effects on hypothesized mediating variables. More important, the magnitude of reported effects of these approaches has typically been relatively large, with studies reporting reductions in drug use behavior in the range of 40 to 80 percent. Long-term follow-up data indicate that the prevention effects of these approaches can last for up to six years. In summary, drug abuse prevention programs that emphasize resistance skills and general life skills (i.e., competence-enhancement approaches) appear to show the most promise of all school-based prevention approaches.

Challenges for School-Based Drug Abuse Prevention

In the final analysis, research-based prevention programs proven to be successful are unlikely to have any real public health impact unless they are used in a large number of schools. However, programs with proven effectiveness are not widely used. Drug prevention programs most commonly used in real-world settings are those that have not shown evidence of effectiveness or have not been evaluated properly. Thus an important area that deserves further attention is how effective school-based drug abuse prevention programs can be widely disseminated, adopted, and institutionalized. Furthermore, once effective programs are disseminated, steps must be taken to ensure that programs are implemented with sufficient fidelity. Regardless of how effective a prevention program may be, it is not likely to produce the desired results unless it is provided in full and by qualified and motivated staff.

See also: FAMILY COMPOSITION AND CIRCUMSTANCE, **subentry on** ALCOHOL, TOBACCO, AND OTHER DRUGS; HEALTH EDUCATION, SCHOOL.

BIBLIOGRAPHY

BOTVIN, GILBERT J. 2000. "Preventing Drug Abuse in Schools: Social and Competence Enhancement Approaches Targeting Individual-Level Etiological Factors." *Addictive Behaviors* 25:887–897.

BOTVIN, GILBERT J.; BAKER, ELI; DUSENBURY, LINDA; BOTVIN, ELIZABETH M.; and DIAZ, TRACY. 1995. "Long-Term Follow-Up Results of a Randomized Drug Abuse Prevention Trial in a White Middle-Class Population." *Journal of the American Medical Association* 273:1106–1112.

BOTVIN, GILBERT J.; GRIFFIN, KENNETH W.; DIAZ, TRACY; SCHEIER, LAWRENCE M., et al. 2000. "Preventing Illicit Drug Use in Adolescents: Long-Term Follow-Up Data from a Randomized Control Trial of a School Population." *Addictive Behaviors* 5:769–774.

DONALDSON, STEWARD I.; SUSSMAN, STEVE; MacKINNON, DAVID P.; SEVERSON, HERBERT H., et al. 1996. "Drug Abuse Prevention Programming: Do We Know What Content Works?" *American Behavioral Scientist* 39:868–883.

HANSEN, WILLIAM B. 1992. "School-Based Substance Abuse Prevention: A Review of the State of the Art in Curriculum, 1980–1990." *Health Education Research: Theory and Practice* 7:403–430.

JOHNSTON, LLOYD D.; O'MALLEY, PATRICK M.; and BACHMAN, JERALD G. 2000. *Monitoring the Future National Survey Results on Drug Use, 1975–1999, Vol. 1: Secondary School Students.* Rockville, MD: National Institute on Drug Abuse.

ROSENBAUM, DENNIS P., and HANSON, GORDON S. 1998. "Assessing the Effects of School-Based Drug Education: A Six-Year Multilevel Analysis of Project D.A.R.E." *Journal of Research in Crime and Delinquency* 35:381–412.

TOBLER, NANCY S., and STRATTON, HOWARD H. 1997. "Effectiveness of School-Based Drug Prevention Programs: A Meta-Analysis of the Research." *Journal of Primary Prevention* 18:71–128.

GILBERT J. BOTVIN
KENNETH W. GRIFFIN

COLLEGE

Alcohol, tobacco, and other drugs used in American colleges and universities represents a public health problem of critical proportions. Institutions of higher education are under increased scrutiny due to policy developments from the public health, governmental, and higher education sectors in the 1990s that place revised importance on initiatives addressing student substance use. Despite variation in campus use rates, no institution of higher education is immune to substance use and its related adverse consequences. The negative effects reach beyond the parameters of the campus, catapulting this issue into the forefront of the national agenda. It is in the interest of society to design and implement policies and programs that aim to curb college student substance use and abuse.

Extent of Use

Alcohol, tobacco, and other drug use represents a ubiquitous problem for American colleges. Alcohol and other drug use on college campuses radically increased between 1993 and 1997, then stabilized between 1997 and 1999. This trend produces great concern as college student use rates are expected to climb due to a radical increase in drug use among those aged twelve to seventeen.

Alcohol, tobacco, and marijuana represent the most frequently used drugs on college campuses. Nationwide, 84 percent of college students report having drunk alcohol within the last year, 68 percent within the previous month, and 3.6 percent on a daily basis, according to Henry Wechsler (1996). Tobacco use shares a student use rate similar to alcohol. Schools indicate a significant increase of 28 percent in student smoking during the 1990s, with nearly one-third of college students having smoked within the past year. Drug use rates are rising on campuses; Arthur Levine and Jeanette S. Cureton estimated that 25 percent of students indicated that they had used some form of illegal drug within the past year. The prevalence of marijuana use rose 22 percent between 1993 and 1999—an increase that occurred among most student demographic groups and at almost all kinds of colleges. Marijuana is used by 24 percent of college students, cocaine by 4 percent, and hallucinogens by nearly 5 percent.

Alcohol

Alcohol is the number one drug of choice for college students of both two-year and four-year institutions,
and continues to pose tremendous challenges to higher education. On average, college students consume about 4.5 drinks per week and about two in five college students engage in high-risk or binge drinking at least once in an average two-week period. Binge drinking, consuming five or more drinks in succession for men and four for women, is on a substantial increase, affecting about two fifths of the college population. It accounts for the majority of alcohol consumed and is associated with the bulk of problems encountered on campuses, impacting students' social lives, health, and education.

The negative consequences of student alcohol use span well beyond the parameters of the college campus and affect students, the institution, and the community. Alcohol is associated with increased absenteeism from class and poor academic performance, which results in a lower grade point average. The majority of injuries, accidents, vandalism, sexual assaults and rape, fighting, and other crime, on and off college campuses, are linked to alcohol and other drug use. Unplanned and uninhibited sexual behavior may lead to pregnancy and exposure to sexually transmitted diseases and HIV/AIDS. Alcohol use can be associated with injury and death from drinking and driving, alcohol poisoning, and suicide.

Tobacco

Many students perceive the college years as a time of experimentation, although in fact it is a period heavily shaped by environmental factors, social norms, and peer influences. During these years, it is common for intermittent tobacco use to quickly manifest into a life-long habit. For college students, tobacco in the form of cigarettes, smokeless tobacco, and cigars presents a legal and accessible alternative to other drug use. Its use is linked to various cancers, emphysema, heart disease, and other life-threatening illnesses.

Other Drugs

By their nature, illicit drugs do not carry a legal age for purchase, consumption, or distribution. Therefore, colleges must address the problem somewhat differently than they do alcohol and tobacco. Students are entering higher education with increased exposure to drugs, which predisposes them to substance dependency. Variation exists among college and universities as to the rate and type of substances used. Marijuana, amphetamines, hallucinogens, inhalants, cocaine, steroids, and designer drugs represent but a few general forms entering the higher education arena. Marijuana is reported as the illicit drug of choice on campuses. Illicit drug use factors into tragedies that include rape, overdose, vandalism, violence, and death. Memory loss, diminished concentration and attention, increased absenteeism, impaired academic performance, and physical illness are also associated with drug use.

Secondhand Effects

The secondhand effects of substance use on campus are often overlooked and underappreciated for the deleterious effects they may have on students and the quality of their collegiate experience. Students who abstain, use legally, or in moderation often suffer secondhand effects from the behaviors of students that use substances in excess. Nonbinging and abstaining students may become the targets of insults and arguments, physical assaults, unwanted sexual advances, vandalism, and humiliation. Sleep deprivation and study interruption results when these students find themselves caring for intoxicated students. Passive smoke is associated with life-threatening health risks, and smoking within residence halls places people at risk due to fire.

Campus Environment

Perceptions of campus use, campus climate, substance availability, awareness of campus policies and enforcement, and students' family histories of substance abuse impact the extent of substance use on any given campus. The campus and surrounding community exert profound influence on innumerable facets of student life. Establishments encircling college campuses that cater specifically to college students contribute to the substance use climate by selling to underage or intoxicated students. The social, academic, and cocurricular milieux are often shaped by the social norms and perceptions related to campus alcohol, tobacco, and other drug use.

Students typically overestimate the amount and the extent of high-risk drinking, tobacco use, and illicit drug use on their campus and on college campuses in general. These misconceptions lead students to feel pressured and justified in their increased substance use. By exploring how students perceive substance use, policies, and rule enforcement on campus, college administrators are better able to discern and roughly predict how students will react to the perceptions of social norms.

Social fraternities, sororities, and athletics typify student groups at high risk for substance abuse. Fraternities and sororities often find themselves at the center of growing concern as their mere presence on campus is associated with higher campus-wide levels of substance use, particularly alcohol consumption. Leaders of Greek organizations, particularly male members, accounted for the highest alcohol consumption on many college campuses. Due to the integral social role these organizations occupy on most college campuses, the practices they espouse often advocate the use of alcohol, tobacco, and other drugs.

Intercollegiate athletics represents an important aspect of the college experience. However, the college athlete may experience anxiety associated with the dual roles and conflicting expectations of being both an athlete and a student. Attempting to rectify this discourse, college athletes may become increasingly susceptible to substance dependency. Collegiate athletes are more likely to use alcohol and smokeless tobacco, and experience binge drinking more than nonparticipating students. Colleges and universities compound the problem by sending students mixed messages concerning substance use by endorsing alcohol and tobacco industry advertising at collegiate sporting events.

Policies

Affecting the campus environment relies heavily on the pervasive commitment of the college or university. Focused policy, procedures, prevention strategies, data gathering, counseling, and referral approaches enable schools to effectively address this problem. Institutions often find themselves caught in a legal quagmire when they attempt to combat rising substance use and are confronted with issues of legal responsibility and institutional liability while simultaneously acknowledging the behavioral and health implications related to substance abuse.

Local, state, and federal governments play a central role in assisting and bolstering higher education's efforts to reduce substance use and the resulting problems that plague American college campuses. Federal legislative such as the 1986 amendments to the Higher Education Act of 1965, Drug-Free Schools and Communities Act of 1989, and the Crime Awareness and Campus Security Act of 1990 represent such initiatives. The 1998 Parental Notification law permits schools to inform parents if their child violates the rules or laws governing alcohol or controlled substances. The Drug-Free Schools and Campuses regulations mandate that schools prepare a biennial report, which certifies that the school has implemented and assessed prevention policy and programs and documents the consistency of policy enforcement. This report must be made available to anyone who requests it.

With increasing cost pressures on colleges, it is difficult to assure adequate and continuous funding for substance-related programs and policy enforcement. In 1993, the Higher Education Center for Alcohol and Other Drug Prevention was established by the United States Department of Education to assist in developing and carrying out substance prevention policies and programs. The U.S. Department of Education and other granting organizations provide national funding support in an effort to address this issue. Specialized task forces and advocacy groups, such as the National Institute on Alcoholism and Alcohol Abuse task force on college drinking, illustrate the nation's commitment to this problem.

Substance abuse is not a campus-centered problem but one that impacts the entire community. To effect change, institutions of higher education acknowledge the need to form committees and coalitions, comprised of administration, students, parents, faculty, alumni, campus organizations, governmental and law enforcement agencies, and the community. By activating multiple, campus-wide policy levers, campus leaders ensure that initiatives span all facets of the institution.

Schools are tightening regulations, strengthening academic requirements, adjusting course scheduling, and offering extended hours for library and recreational facilities, while providing alternative alcohol-free campus-sponsored activities. Schools are withdrawing endorsement of alcohol and tobacco industry advertising on campus and establishing substance-free residences. By targeting social groups such as fraternities and sororities for programming and monitoring of policy compliance, schools are attempting to further shape the social climate. Novel disciplinary actions exhibit the decisive consequences of such behavior, provide support services, and offer mandatory alcohol or drug assessment with the possible introduction of counseling, Twelve Step, and treatment services.

Programs

Through a paradigm that conceptualizes students' college experience systemically, substance-related strategies strive to alter the social, physical, intellectual, legal, and economic environment on campus and in surrounding communities. Effective initiatives offer diversified programs that account for students' developmental level year in school, age, and level of readiness to change behavior with special attention to the first-year experience.

A variety of creative and versatile approaches are available to institutions of higher education to address issues related to substance use. Education, prevention, counseling, and treatment programs are the most commonly utilized. Approaches that promote increased understanding about substance use and the related effects, provide suggestions for alternative substance-free activities, and attempt to counter misconceptions around social norms comprise the foundation to effective program initiatives.

Standardized programs, developed and distributed by external vendors, offer schools an alternative method for educating students. Many schools find these programs beneficial because of the variety of issues targeted. With the advent of novel technology, innovative and interactive computer programs add to the program arsenal. Often expensive, standardized programming may not to be a viable option for institutions with limited resources.

Campus-initiated programming offers another option for colleges and universities. These efforts may include programming such as alcohol awareness month, safe spring break, and substance-free social activities. The formation of substance use task forces, student organizations, and committees corrals the campus community around efforts to devise strategies and initiate change in campus norms, perceptions, and climate. Typically cheaper than standardized initiatives, these methods are readily utilized.

Higher education must recognize that alcohol and other drug use and the problems that result from substance abuse are never entirely going to go away. Nevertheless, through continued commitment, campus communities significantly impact the problem through policy and program initiatives that are directed at altering social norms, climate, and practices. To initiate and maintain change in higher education with respect to alcohol, tobacco, and other drugs, programs, policies, and partnerships must become permanent and pervasive fixtures on college and university campuses.

See also: ADJUSTMENT TO COLLEGE; DRUG AND AL-
COHOL ABUSE, *subentry on* SCHOOL; FAMILY COM-
POSITION AND CIRCUMSTANCE, *subentry on*
ALCOHOL, TOBACCO, AND OTHER DRUGS; SOCIAL
FRATERNITIES AND SORORITIES.

BIBLIOGRAPHY

BACHMAN, JERALD G., et al. 1997. *Smoking, Drinking, and Drug Use in Young Adulthood: The Impacts of New Freedoms and New Responsibilities.*
Mahwah, NJ: Erlbaum.

CLAPP, JOHN D., and McDONNELL, ANITA LYN.
2000. "The Relationship of Perceptions of Alcohol Problems Reported by College Students."
Journal of College Student Development
41(1):19–26.

LEVINE, ARTHUR, and CURETON, JEANETTE S. 1998.
*When Hope and Fear Collide: A Portrait of
Today's College Student.* San Francisco: Jossey-
Bass.

THOMBS, DENNIS L., and BRIDDICK, WILLIAM C.
2000. "Readiness to Change among At-Risk
Greek Student Drinkers." *Journal of College Student Development* 41(3):313–322.

WECHSLER, HENRY. 1996. "Alcohol and the American College Campus: A Report from the Harvard School of Public Health." *Change* 28(4):20.

WECHSLER, HENRY; DOWDALL, GEORGE W.; MAEN-
NER, GRETCHEN; and GLENHILL-HOYT, JEANA.
1998. "Changes in Binge Drinking and Related
Problems among American College Students
between 1993 and 1997: Results of the Harvard
School of Public Health College Alcohol Study."
Journal of American College Health 47:57–68.

INTERNET RESOURCES

CORE INSTITUTE. 2001. "Core Institute, Center for
Alcohol and Other Drug Studies."
<www.siu.edu/departments/coreinst/public_
html>.

HIGHER EDUCATION CENTER. 2001. "Alcohol and
Other Drug Prevention on College Campuses."
<www.edc.org/hec/pubs/model.html>.

LEIGH Z. GILCHRIST

DU BOIS, W. E. B. (1868–1963)

Scholar, educator, philosopher, and social activist,
William Edward Burghardt Du Bois is among the
most influential public intellectuals of the twentieth
century. A pioneer of the civil rights movement, Du
Bois dedicated his life to ending colonialism, exploitation, and racism worldwide. Experiencing many
changes in the nation's political history, he served as
a voice for generations of African Americans seeking
social justice.

The Formative Years

Du Bois was born the only child of Alfred and Mary
Burghardt Du Bois in Great Barrington, Massachusetts. In the period following the Civil War, Great
Barrington was a small town with fewer than 50 African Americans among its 5,000 residents. Du Bois's
father, of French and African descent, left home
soon after William was born. His mother, of Dutch
and African descent, encouraged Du Bois in his educational studies. Aunts, uncles, and close friends
gave poverty-stricken Du Bois adequate clothing,
food, and finances for schooling.

Attending an integrated grammar school, Du
Bois had little direct experience with color discrimination; much of what he did learn came from the
visible social divisions within his community as he
discovered the hindrances that African Americans
faced. Du Bois, however, was quite aware of his intellectual acuity. He excelled and outperformed his
white contemporaries, receiving a number of promotions throughout his public schooling.

By the age of seventeen, Du Bois had already
served as a correspondent for newspapers in both
Great Barrington and New York. He was the first African American to graduate as valedictorian from
Great Barrington High School. Influential community members arranged for Du Bois to attend Fisk
University in Nashville, Tennessee, where he began
studies in 1885. While on a partial scholarship at
Fisk University, Du Bois had far greater exposure to
African-American culture. In the white South, Du
Bois encountered firsthand the oppression faced by
the sons and daughters of former slaves, whom he
taught in country schools during the summer. As Du
Bois witnessed politicians and businessmen destroy
the gains of Reconstruction, and African Americans
struggle against social, political, and economic injustice, he formed his stance on race relations in America. He began to speak out against the atrocities of

racism as a writer and chief editor of the *Fisk Herald,* until his graduation in 1888.

After receiving his first baccalaureate, Du Bois entered Harvard University in 1888 as a junior. Two years later, he earned a second B.A. in a class of 300 and was one of six commencement speakers. In the fall of 1890, Du Bois began graduate work at Harvard. He studied under legendary professors William James, Josiah Royce, George Santayana, and Albert Bushnell Hart. His studies focused primarily on the subjects of philosophy and history and then gradually shifted into the areas of economics and sociology.

Du Bois acquired his master's degree in the spring of 1891 and chose to further his studies at the University of Berlin (1892–1894), observing and comparing race problems in Africa, Asia, and America. After two years in Berlin, Du Bois became the first African American to earn a Ph.D. from Harvard. His doctoral thesis, approved in 1895, was published in the first volume of the Harvard Historical Studies series as *The Suppression of the African Slave-Trade to the United States of America, 1638 to 1870.*

Early Scholarship

In 1896 Du Bois married Nina Gomer; they had two children, Yolande and Burghardt (who died at the age of three). After teaching Greek and Latin at Wilberforce University (1894–1896), Du Bois accepted an assistant professorship at the University of Pennsylvania to conduct a research project in Philadelphia. For two years, Du Bois and his wife lived in the heart of Philadelphia's seventh ward, where the notable work *The Philadelphia Negro, A Social Study* (1899) took form.

The Philadelphia Negro marked the first major study of American empirical sociology and represented Du Bois's quest to expose racism as a problem of ignorance. DuBois personally interviewed several thousand residents, and his study documented the living conditions of poor African Americans enduring dilapidated housing, inadequate health care, disease, and violence. In this body of work, Du Bois contended that crime and poverty were manifestations of institutional and structural racism.

In 1897 Du Bois and his family moved to Atlanta, where he taught economics and history at Atlanta University. Here Du Bois witnessed racism, lynching, Ku Klux Klan cross burnings, race riots, and disfranchisement. To challenge these acts, he published papers in the *Atlantic Monthly* and other journals that explored and confronted discriminatory southern society.

A compilation of unpublished papers led to what many consider Du Bois's greatest work, *The Souls of Black Folk* (1903). In it Du Bois wrote, "The problem of the twentieth century is the problem of the color-line" (p. 54). *The Souls of Black Folk* provided a philosophical framework by which Du Bois addressed the problem of race and the distressing realities of African-American life in America. Within its pages, he challenged the prominent African-American leader, Booker T. Washington. Du Bois firmly opposed Washington's policies of accommodation, calling instead for more social agitation to break the bonds of racial oppression. In addition to his writings, publications, teachings and public speeches, Du Bois served as secretary for the first pan-African congress in London in 1900. He would later go on to organize subsequent sessions in 1919, 1921, 1923, and 1945.

In 1905, Du Bois took on the leadership role in organizing a group of African-American leaders and scholars in what became known as the Niagara Movement. The group was opposed to the conservative platform of Booker T. Washington and the Tuskegee Machine. Despite the failure of the Niagara Movement, it would later serve as a model for another of Du Bois's initiatives in 1909, the National Association for the Advancement of Colored People (NAACP).

The *Crisis* Years

Upon leaving his professorship at Atlanta University, Du Bois joined the central staff of the NAACP in November 1910. Having been instrumental in that group's formation, he became the only African American on its executive board, and, more importantly, director of publications and research. In that position, he assumed control of the *Crisis,* the official journal of the NAACP.

While the expanding economy provided former slaves with moderate economic and educational gains, discrimination, violence, and lynching were rampant. Black anger, impatience, and heightened consciousness, combined with expanding literacy, provided a growing audience for the *Crisis.* This journal expanded Du Bois's influence and audience beyond academia to the public. By 1913 its regular circulation reached 30,000.

The *Crisis* informed people about important events, offered analysis, and sowed themes of uplift and civil rights. Du Bois's voice dominated as though it were his own personal journal. His authoritative editorials spoke against injustice, discriminatory practices, lynching, miseducation, and the widespread mistreatment of African Americans. Du Bois was not hesitant to confront those whom he believed misled his people.

World War I was significant for Du Bois. He believed the enthusiastic participation of black soldiers would lead to returned favors from white America. He traveled to France in 1919 reporting the heroism of black soldiers to the *Crisis* directly from the front.

Du Bois was optimistic that the new generations of African Americans would advance the struggles for civil rights and racial justice. His magazine produced articles and pictures about young people. In 1920 he launched the short-lived *Brownies Book,* a *Crisis*-type publication for children.

Crisis came to be seen as an authoritative and informative resource by many in black America. Beyond ideological commentary, it published and supported black artistic expression. Langston Hughes, Countee Cullen, Jean Toomer, Claude McKay, and Alain Locke were among the core group of the "Harlem Renaissance" supported by the *Crisis*. Columbus Salley (1999) asserts that Du Bois deserves as much credit as anyone in giving birth to the Harlem Renaissance.

While editing the *Crisis,* Du Bois continued to write books and essays that explained his theories and fueled antagonism. In 1920 he examined global race issues and conflict in *Darkwater: Voices from within the Veil.* Over the years the internationalist and radical Du Bois clashed regularly with the leadership of the NAACP who were committed to gradualism and legalism. In 1934, under fierce pressure, Du Bois retired from the executive board and the *Crisis.*

After the *Crisis*

Du Bois lost his national platform in the midst of economic depression, international fascism, and political uncertainty. With no resources or base from which to operate, in 1934 he accepted and invitation to return to Atlanta University as chair of the sociology department.

Since his study of the *Philadelphia Negro* (1899), Du Bois was drawn to big research projects. He adhered to the new school of social science, arguing that knowledge of social problems could lead to social change. He proposed that his university along with others undertake large studies of black life including employment, education, family life, and so forth. Additionally, he was hopeful for the eventual publication of an *Encyclopedia Africana.* Lack of funds, changes in university administration, and a changing political climate all worked against Du Bois.

This period found Du Bois refining his views on pan-Africanism and Marxian socialism. He wrote *Black Reconstruction in America* (1935), *Black Folk Then and Now* (1939), *Dusk of Dawn* (1940), and *Color and Democracy* (1945). In 1940 he began *Phylon,* a journal of social science, published at Atlanta University.

Undermined by the new school administration, Du Bois retired from the faculty of Atlanta University in 1943. Declining offers at Howard and Fisk universities, he would never return to academia. As the nation's largest and most recognized civil rights organization, the integrationist NAACP was increasingly drawn into public dialogue. Its leaders, believing that Du Bois could be useful in their research activities, offered him the position of director of special research. Du Bois, fiercely independent and outspoken, challenged American capitalism, imperialism, racial inequality, and the legal system that supported privilege. His linking of pan-Africanism to socialism, and then to democracy, offered an interesting and provocative position. He was denounced by some as a bourgeois intellectual, and by others as a radical extremist.

Although pan-Africanists had gathered since the turn of the century, until 1945 those meetings did little more than unleash indignation from middle-class intellectuals. The 1945 fifth pan-African congress held in Manchester, England, was different. Revolutionary students and activists from throughout colonized sub-Saharan Africa gathered to confront the colonial masters. They resolved to "control their own destiny. . . . All colonies must be free from imperialist control whether political or economic. . . . We say to the peoples of the colonies that they must fight for these ends by all means at their disposal" (Lemelle and Kelley, p. 352). A "third world" movement for independence and social justice now accompanied the modern civil rights movement slowly emerging in the United States. By 1948, Du Bois's support of the Soviet Union, revolution in

Africa, strident criticism of American apartheid, and support of Progressive candidate Henry Wallace in the United States alienated him from the NAACP leadership, especially its moderate chairperson, Walter White. He was dismissed from his position in 1948 leading to a final break with the organization.

The Final Years

Once again without funds or an organizational base, Du Bois continued his critique of American capitalism and racial inequality. At the end of World War II and the beginning of the cold war, the nation's political climate moved decidedly to the right. Du Bois's Africanist and prosocialist sentiment placed him at odds with the unfolding hysteria. His social circle now consisted of avant-garde intellectuals, internationalists, and left-leaning cultural workers such as Paul Robeson and Shirley Graham. Amid the new jingoism, Du Bois was drawn to the "peace" community. By 1950 he was chair of the Peace Information Center, drawing the antagonism of federal authorities.

In July 1950 Du Bois's first wife, Nina, died, and later that year he ran for the U.S. Senate in New York on the ticket of the American Labor Party. Surprisingly he received 210,000 votes—equivalent to 4 percent of the vote. In early 1951 Du Bois and his Peace Information Center were ordered by the Justice Department to register as foreign agents. Refusing, Du Bois was indicted and jailed but soon exonerated.

Now remarried to Shirley Graham, Du Bois was both vilified and celebrated during the difficult McCarthy period. He watched as friends, associates, and notables such as poet Langston Hughes, actress Lena Horne, Africanist Alphaeus Hunton, actor William Marshall, black professors Forrest Wiggins and Ira Reid, Harlem politician Benjamin Davis, and black Marxists Claude Lightfoot, Claudia Jones, and Henry Winston and others were discredited. Du Bois and his wife were also frequent targets of communist-baiters. As the hysteria escalated, so did Du Bois's defense of those victimized.

Du Bois continued to speak out against the cold war, capitalist exploitation, colonialism, and the international mistreatment of African people. He foresaw a new period of socialistic pan-Africanism, writing in 1955, "American Negroes, freed of their baseless fear of communism, will again begin to turn their attention and aim their activity toward Africa" (p. 5). Denounced at home, Du Bois was regarded as a champion of human rights around the world.

As the civil rights movement began, Du Bois attended the Stockholm Peace Conference where he delivered an address. After visiting Czechoslovakia and Germany, the Du Boises spent five months in the Soviet Union. Having visited the Soviet Union on several previous occasions, Du Bois marveled at the country's continued progress in employment, housing, education, the status of women, and race relations. During this visit, he lobbied endlessly for increased Soviet interactions with Africans and for more research on that continent. Du Bois's visit to the People's Republic of China profoundly influenced him since China served as a reminder that people of color could successfully engage socialism. He noted that a majority of the world's people lived under socialism and declared that egalitarian socialism was the economic system of the future. He believed that African Americans, given their history of mistreatment, could benefit from this type of social system.

Upon returning to America, Du Bois expressed grave pessimism that black Americans could ever achieve economic and political justice under corporate monopoly capitalism, and continued to advocate connection with Africa. He now had a special relationship with Kwame Nkrumah and the revolution in Ghana.

In 1960 Du Bois had one longstanding unfilled objective, to publish his *Encyclopedia Africana*, which would explore every aspect of black life. He had contacted scholars, funding agencies, and anyone who would listen to him to accomplish this project. On October 1, 1961, Du Bois joined the U.S. Communist Party and made a statement that began "Capitalism cannot reform itself; it is doomed to self-destruction. No universal selfishness can bring social good to all. . . . this is the only way of human life. . . . In the end communism will triumph." (Manning, p. 212). Four days later he and his wife moved to Ghana. Working on his encyclopedia to the very end, Du Bois died one day before the famous March on Washington.

See also: MULTICULTURAL EDUCATION; RACE, ETHNICITY, AND CULTURE.

BIBLIOGRAPHY

DU BOIS, W. E. B. 1899. *The Philadelphia Negro: A Social Study.* Boston: Ginn.

DU BOIS, W. E. B. 1935. *Black Reconstruction in America: An Essay toward a History of the Part*

Which Black Folk Played in the Attempt to Reconstruct Democracy in America, 1860–1880. Philadelphia: Saifer.

DU BOIS, W. E. B. 1939. *Black Folk Then and Now: An Essay in the History and Sociology of the Negro Race.* New York: Holt.

DU BOIS, W. E. B. 1940. *Dusk of Dawn: An Essay toward an Autobiography of a Race Concept.* New York: Harcourt Brace.

DU BOIS, W. E. B. 1945. *Color and Democracy: Colonies and Peace.* New York: Harcourt Brace.

DU BOIS, W. E. B. 1955. "American Negroes and Africa." *National Guardian* February 14.

DU BOIS, W. E. B. 1968. *The Autobiography of W. E. B. Du Bois: A Soliloquy on Viewing My Life from the Last Decade of its First Century.* New York: International.

DU BOIS, W. E. B. 1969. *Darkwater: Voices from within the Veil* (1920). New York: AMS.

DU BOIS, W. E. B. 1995. *The Souls of Black Folks: Essays and Sketches* (1903). New York: Signet Classic.

LEMELLE, SIDNEY J., and KELLEY ROBIN D. G. 1994. *Imagining Home: Class, Culture and Nationalism in the African Diaspora.* London: Verso.

MARABLE, MANNING. 1986. *W. E. B. Du Bois: Black Radical Democrat.* Boston: Hall.

PATRICK, JOHN J. 1969. *The Progress of the Afro-American.* Winchester, IL: Benefic.

SALLEY, COLUMBUS. 1999. *The Black 100: A Ranking of the Most Influential African Americans, Past and Present.* Secaucus, NJ: Citadel.

WILLIAM H. WATKINS
HORACE R. HALL

E

EARLY CHILDHOOD EDUCATION

OVERVIEW
Janet S. Hansen
PREPARATION OF TEACHERS
Daniel J. Walsh
Betty J. Liebovich
INTERNATIONAL CONTEXT
Robert G. Myers

OVERVIEW

Early childhood education is concerned with the learning experiences of children below the age when compulsory schooling begins (usually age five or six). In terms of organized educational programs, it generally encompasses kindergartens (enrolling mainly five-year-olds) and pre-kindergartens and preschools aimed at children starting at about age three.

Mapping American Early Education

Kindergarten, while not compulsory in most states, became over the course of the twentieth century largely the responsibility of public schools. In the process it became accessible and free to most children, and it came to be administered as part of elementary education. By contrast, preschool at the beginning of the twenty-first century is part of a piecemeal and haphazard "nonsystem" of early care and education in which a wide range of providers offer varying mixtures of structured learning and child care to interested parents who either can afford to enroll their children or receive public subsidies, most of which are targeted to lower income families.

Kindergarten. Margarethe Schurz founded the first American kindergarten in her home in 1855; a cen-

tury later kindergarten education was available as part of public school systems to just over half of children of kindergarten age. By October 2000, 73 percent of five-year-olds were enrolled in kindergarten, along with 4 percent of three- and four-year-olds and 14 percent of six-year-olds. The overwhelming majority of kindergartners (83%) attended public schools—just 17 percent attended private kindergartens.

Although most children attend public kindergarten, attendance is not compulsory in most states and not all states require that public schools offer kindergarten. In 2001, eleven states did not require that districts offer kindergarten, though districts could choose to do so. Only eight states set their compulsory school age at five and required children to attend kindergarten. Several others mandated kindergarten attendance and either permitted parents to hold their children out of kindergarten until the children were six years old or allowed the children to skip kindergarten by demonstrating "readiness" for first grade.

State and district policies about the length of the kindergarten day vary enormously, and the absence of data on and common definitions of "full-day" and "part-day" complicate the task of portraying the availability of different kindergarten offerings. A study of a national sample of about 22,000 kindergartners enrolled in 1998 indicated that 55 percent attended full-day programs and 45 percent attended half-day programs. Some states required districts to offer full-day kindergarten but not necessarily to the exclusion of half-day offerings.

States were slower to assist districts with the funding of kindergarten than with elementary and secondary education, but in 2001 all provided some assistance with kindergarten costs of public schools. Twenty-five states and the District of Columbia financed full-day kindergarten for all districts or schools or those that chose to provide it. The remaining twenty-five states financed half-day programs or provided partial funds for kindergarten.

Preschool. Characterizing the early education experiences of three- to five-year-olds who have not yet entered kindergarten is made difficult by the absence of clear rules defining the offerings of the myriad providers who serve these children in center-based settings (as distinct from services provided to children by relatives or nonrelatives in home-based settings). What is known is that by the late twentieth century, it had become the norm for these children to spend at least part of a week in a center-based program. In 1999, 59 percent of these pre-kindergarten-age children were enrolled in settings variously labeled day care, nursery school, pre-kindergarten, preschool, and Head Start. The older the child, the more likely she was to be enrolled in such a program: 46 percent of three-year-olds were so enrolled, 69 percent of four-year-olds, and 76 percent of five-year-olds.

Center providers operate under a variety of auspices. Nonprofit groups, including religious organizations, operate some of the centers. Some centers are profit-making businesses, in the form of both single centers and large corporate chains. In some places the public school system offers pre-kindergarten classes, often targeted to children who are at risk of not being ready to succeed in school because of poverty, limited ability to speak English, disabilities, or other factors.

It is not known precisely how many centers serve children age three and over who have not yet entered kindergarten, but in 2001 there were well over 100,000 licensed child-care centers. States differ, however, in the extent to which they include or exclude educationally oriented preschool programs in their child-care licensing requirements. Some states, for example, exclude pre-kindergartens operated by public schools, which may be regulated by different agencies. Some states exclude religiously affiliated centers from licensing requirements.

While precise information on who pays for preschool education is unavailable, it is clear that at the start of the twenty-first century parents bear far more responsibility for preschool costs than they do for kindergarten or elementary and secondary edu-

cation. Federal and state subsidies supplement parent-paid fees through a variety of programs that differ in the extent to which they emphasize educational purposes or custodial care to help working parents.

Federal preschool initiatives. At the start of the twenty-first century, most of the federal funding that subsidized education and care for children under age five came from two programs: Head Start and the Child Care Development Fund (CCDF). The former had its origins in 1960s' efforts to expand educational opportunity by giving disadvantaged children a "head start" in school. The CCDF was created out of several earlier child-care programs as part of the Welfare Reform Act of 1996.

Head Start furnishes grants to local agencies to provide comprehensive early childhood developmental, educational, health, nutritional, social, and other services to low-income children and their families. Most participants must be from families whose income is below the poverty level, and in fiscal year 2000, 94 percent of the enrolled children were ages three to five, with a modal age of four. Head Start programs have traditionally been half-day and part-year programs, and local grantees have had wide flexibility in deciding on program structure. They must comply with federal program standards, which have increasingly put more emphasis on school readiness.

The CCDF provides federal grants to states for subsidizing the child-care costs of eligible families and for improving the overall quality and availability of child-care services. Children up to age thirteen who reside with a family whose income does not exceed 85 percent of the state median income are eligible to participate. States are free to set lower eligibility levels and most do. States also set subsidy levels and fee schedules. Parents share responsibility for paying child-care fees, which states may waive for families below the poverty line. In keeping with the CCDF's link to welfare policy, the law requires parents to be working or in education or training.

Although children benefiting from the CCDF may receive care that helps prepare them for school, school readiness and organized educational instruction are not explicit program goals. As of 2002 there were no national performance standards for services or staff other than a basic requirement that states must have and enforce health and safety rules.

In addition to some smaller child-care subsidy programs, federal aid for children with disabilities included educational assistance for children under age five. Some federal aid for supplemental educational and related services to educationally disadvantaged children in low-income areas went to children under age five, though the bulk of it was used for elementary and secondary students.

State preschool initiatives. As of 1998–1999, forty-one states and the District of Columbia invested in state pre-kindergarten initiatives offering regularly scheduled group experiences to help young children learn and develop before entering elementary school. Only Georgia offered pre-kindergarten to all four-year-olds whose parents wanted them to participate. New York and Oklahoma had launched school-district-based initiatives to open pre-kindergarten to all four-year-olds, regardless of income, but not all districts in these states participated (in New York the state limited district eligibility because of funding constraints). The remaining states tended to target pre-kindergarten services to lower-income children or those considered especially in need of preschool preparation. Some served mainly four-year-olds and others included younger children as well.

Unlike publicly funded elementary and secondary education, which was provided through public schools, pre-kindergarten programs in many states operated in a variety of settings, such as public and private schools, Head Start centers, profit-making and nonprofit child-care centers, and churches. Most state pre-kindergarten programs offered only part-day (two to four hours a day), part-year services, although a few states provided the necessary funding for full-day and/or full-year pre-kindergarten for eligible children and also required that it be offered by at least some percentage of eligible programs. Parental fees were required in these extended programs. Many but not all state pre-kindergarten initiatives required providers to meet quality standards that were higher than the state's child-care licensing standards.

Pressures for Improvement

While educators and other child advocates repeatedly urged the expansion of formal early education opportunities for young children during the twentieth century, what had developed by the dawn of the new century was a fragmented and haphazard early learning "nonsystem" that seemed increasingly inadequate to meet the needs of both children and society.

Changing views of education, work, and welfare. Changing societal perspectives on education, work, and welfare make early education an important public issue and not just a family concern. Efforts in the 1980s and 1990s to improve the quality of elementary and secondary education for all children caused reformers to increasingly realize that student achievement is affected by differences in children's development that are already evident when formal schooling begins.

State courts in New Jersey in 1998 and in North Carolina in 2000 ordered state officials to provide preschool education to children at risk of developing later educational problems. The judicial decisions came in school finance lawsuits challenging the legality of state school funding laws on the grounds that insufficient and inequitable funding denied some students their constitutional rights to an adequate education.

Preschool education also was increasingly seen as a factor helping families balance child-rearing and work responsibilities. Most women are in the labor force; 60 percent of women were working in 2000. This included 73 percent of all women with children under age 17 and 72 percent of women with children aged three to five years.

Reflecting that employment had become the norm for American women, public policy concerning welfare also shifted in its expectations about low-income mothers' participation in the workplace. The major overhaul of welfare policy enacted by the U.S. Congress in 1996 had as key assumptions that all adults, even those with young children, should be self-supporting and that receipt of public income subsidies should be contingent on meeting work or work preparation requirements. This, too, had the effect of shining a brighter spotlight on arrangements for the early care and education of young children.

Untapped capacity for learning. Research provides growing evidence that young children have much greater power to learn than has traditionally been realized or developed. In 2001 the National Research Council (NRC) published a report that claimed to be "the first attempt at a comprehensive, cross-disciplinary examination of the accumulated theory, research, and evaluation literature relevant to early childhood education" (p. 31). The review documented a shift in view about "the major tasks for children during the preschool years" (p. 37). In earlier times, these tasks were seen primarily as ones of "socialization: separating from home, learning how to interact with peers and unfamiliar adults, and experiencing new material in a novel environment. Today we recognize the first five years as a time of enormous growth of linguistic, conceptual, and social competence" as well (p. 37).

The NRC review found that there was no one preschool curriculum that was superior to others in terms of effectiveness. The study panel did not find this surprising in light of the evidence that other aspects of learning in addition to curriculum are important to early learning: the adult-child relationship, temperament, social class, and cultural traditions. The panel did, however, find that "children who attend well-planned, high-quality early childhood programs in which curriculum aims are specified and integrated across domains tend to learn more and are better prepared to master the complex demands of formal schooling" (p. 307). It concluded that, among other factors, incorporating more ambitious learning goals into programs for young children requires teachers who are deeply knowledgeable about how children develop in the early years and about how to teach preschool youngsters.

Such expectations about teachers were quite at odds with the training levels of many of the adults who work with young children. Public school kindergarten teachers generally have college degrees and often have additional degrees and certificates common to elementary school teachers, though they may not have specific backgrounds in early childhood education. In 2000, twenty-nine states required their pre-kindergarten teachers to be certified, which required a college degree.

In other pre-kindergarten and preschool settings, however, training levels were significantly lower. In 2000, thirty-one states set no minimum requirements for teachers in child-care centers, and individuals could often be hired with only a high school diploma and little or no experience. Of states with minimum requirements, only Rhode Island and New York City (which has regulations separate from New York State) required teachers in child-care centers to have bachelor's degrees.

In 2002 the most widely held credential among child-care workers (which also qualified holders to teach in pre-kindergarten programs in some states) was the child development associate (CDA). A nationally recognized credential originally developed for Head Start workers, it certifies that high school graduates with experience working with children and 120 hours of formal child-care education have also passed a performance-based assessment of their care-giving knowledge and skills. Efforts to upgrade preschool teacher qualifications are likely to reduce the importance of the CDA: the Georgia Prekindergarten Program removed it from the list of acceptable credentials for lead teachers for the 2002–2003 school year, and Congress decreed in 1998 that by 2003 half of Head Start teachers must have an associate's degree.

The poor pay of early education teachers makes it difficult to attract a highly qualified and stable workforce. Median annual earnings for those teaching in preschools was $17,310 in 1998, with higher averages for those teachers working in elementary and secondary school systems and lower averages for those classified as working in "child day-care services." Other child-care workers fared even worse. Moreover, preschool teachers and child-care workers frequently do not receive benefits such as paid vacation and health care. Not surprisingly, high levels of turnover have plagued the preschool and child-care industries.

Access to educational opportunities. While kindergarten opportunities are widely available to children from all socioeconomic backgrounds, preschool enrollment patterns in 2000 indicated that children of higher-income and better-educated parents were mostly likely to have the advantage of structured educational programs.

In October 2000 the U.S. Census Bureau found that 52 percent of all three- to five-year-olds not yet enrolled in kindergarten were enrolled in "nursery school"—a group or class organized to provide educational experiences for pre-kindergarten children that included instruction as an important and integral phase of its program. Hispanic children were significantly less likely to be enrolled than non-Hispanic white and African-American children, and only 44 percent of children from the poorest families were enrolled as compared to 71 percent of children from families in the top income level ($75,000 and over). An even wider gap was evident between the enrollment rates of children whose mothers had only an elementary school education and those whose mothers had college degrees. Poorer children were mostly enrolled in public nursery schools, whereas children from wealthier families depended mostly on private schools.

Unequal access to early education is worrisome because learning gaps are developing among children in the preschool years, and children who are behind when they enter school are unlikely to catch up with their peers. In 2000 the National Center for Education Statistics reported initial findings from a longitudinal study of 22,000 kindergartners that documented many differences in what children know and can do when they enter kindergarten that are linked to family income and mother's education. Differences were found not only in knowledge and academic skills but also in noncognitive domains that are important for school success (such as physical health) and in learning-related experiences that children have at home (such as being read to frequently).

Unequal access to early education is also disturbing in light of a growing body of research showing that early education offers long-term benefits that can substantially offset the large costs involved. Evidence from model demonstration programs providing intensive, high-quality educational and related services to young children from disadvantaged backgrounds shows that participation increased enrollee's school success on such measures as reduced referral to special education, lower incidence of retention in grade, reduced dropout rates, and improved test scores.

The most persuasive results were produced by the High/Scope Perry Preschool and the Carolina Abecedarian projects, both of which employed "gold standard" research designs using randomized treatment and control groups and follow-up of participants over many years. Analyses of the age twenty-seven follow-up on the Perry Preschool program, for example, found that benefits exceeded costs by ratios ranging from 2:1 to 7:1, depending on whether benefits included just savings to government or benefits to program participants, their families, and other members of society as well.

Because model programs are typically small and more expensive than "scaled-up" programs are likely to be, there have long been questions about whether investments in more typical and less-expensive early education programs, such as Head Start and pre-kindergarten, would have similar payoffs. The first large-scale, random-assignment research study on Head Start was scheduled to begin data collection in the fall of 2002 and continue through 2006. Prior research suggests that childcare, health and nutrition, and educational benefits

of Head Start partially or perhaps substantially offset the costs of public investment. Methodological concerns (absence of control or comparison groups, short-term perspectives rather than long-term follow-up, and others) have made findings about the size and sustainability of cognitive gains among Head Start participants controversial.

The most persuasive evidence that large-scale programs that run at lower cost than model preschool programs can also generate significant benefits comes from the Chicago Child-Parent Center (CPC) program begun in 1967. CPC provides preschool and other services to three- to five-year-olds as well as extended interventions into the elementary school years to economically disadvantaged minority children. Researchers followed a group of 1,539 children, born in 1980, who received some combination of CPC services or who were enrolled in locally funded full-day kindergarten programs but did not receive preschool services (the comparison group). The follow-up study of participants at age twenty-one showed that each component of CPC had economic benefits that exceeded costs, with the greatest return resulting from the preschool component. Benefits included increased earnings for participants expected from attaining higher education levels, lower crime rates, and reduced need for school remedial services.

Comparatively little research has been done on the costs and benefits of early education programs for children from middle- and upper-income families, because these children historically were not eligible for public subsidies. As early education programs grow through such developments as the adoption by states of universal pre-kindergarten, this situation should change. While the "payoff" to public investments in disadvantaged children will almost certainly be higher, it is reasonable to expect that all children can potentially benefit from early education, especially if findings from research on the learning capacities of young children are translated into high-quality preschool programs.

The need for integrated early education and care. Public policy at the start of the twenty-first century has not caught up with economic and social realities facing parents and society. In fact, "education and care in the early years are two sides of the same coin" (National Research Council, p. 306). Children need early education to develop social competence and exploit their learning potential. Parents, most of whom are employed, need to know that their young children not only are learning but also are being well-cared-for during the working day.

Public programs, however, are not connected by a comprehensive vision that encompasses both the goals of school readiness for children and support of working parents. Programs tend to emphasize one goal or the other. The result is a service delivery system with disparate missions, administrative mechanisms, and objectives. As a consequence, states face a huge challenge in trying to build comprehensive and coordinated systems of services for young children. Service providers must cope with different eligibility requirements for children and families, different methods of delivering federal and state funds, and different requirements and standards for the programs they deliver. Families face barriers trying to understand the public subsidies for which they are eligible and looking for providers who can meet both the educational and child-care needs of their children.

Falling behind internationally. The United States entered the twenty-first century significantly behind other industrialized countries in recognizing the wisdom of investments in young children. European countries in particular have made much progress in providing early learning opportunities available for all with convenient schedules for working parents.

Countries such as Belgium, France, and Italy offer universal, voluntary, and free programs for preschool children age three to six and in 1999–2000 enrolled 95 to 99 percent of this age group. Preschool in these countries lasted for the normal school day, seven or eight hours, with supplemental services (with costs shared by parents) available before and after school and during school holidays. Denmark, Sweden, and Finland enrolled 73 to 83 percent of their three- to six-year-olds in early education programs that integrated education and care, with government paying most of the costs. Austria, the Netherlands, Spain, Germany, and the United Kingdom also had preschool enrollment rates above 70 percent either for children age three and over or those age four and over.

These figures are especially impressive because they apply to education-oriented programs that are required to recruit staff with specialized qualifications in education and exclude day-care centers and similar facilities. Professional staff in Europe who work with children age three and over are generally required to have completed at least three years of postsecondary education (which is the equivalent of a bachelor's degree in many countries).

Public financing is widely accepted as the appropriate way to pay for preschool in the industrialized countries of Europe. Parents share costs on an ability-to-pay basis in some cases, but their share is small and sometimes limited to the wraparound care needed by those who work.

Conclusion

Public investment in education in the United States appears seriously unbalanced. In 2001 governments spent roughly $20 billion to $25 billion annually on early education for children from birth to age five, compared to roughly $400 billion on elementary and secondary education and at least $100 billion on postsecondary education, including student aid. Nobel laureate economist James Heckman argued that at these levels of investment devoting additional funds to improving the basic learning and socialization skills of the very young is the best way to improve the skill levels of American workers. Early education is as vital to both individual and society well-being as the education of older children and young adults and equally worthy of public support.

See also: CHILD CARE; COMPENSATORY EDUCATION; ELEMENTARY EDUCATION, *subentries on* CURRENT TRENDS, HISTORY OF; FROEBEL, FRIEDRICH.

BIBLIOGRAPHY

BARNETT, W. STEVEN. 1996. *Lives in the Balance: Age-Twenty-Seven Benefit-Cost Analysis of the High/Scope Perry Preschool Program.* Ypsilanti, MI: High/Scope Press.

COMMITTEE FOR ECONOMIC DEVELOPMENT. 2002. *Preschool for All: Investing in a Productive and Just Society.* New York: Committee for Economic Development.

CURRIE, JANET. 2001. "Early Childhood Education Programs." *Journal of Economic Perspectives* 15:213–238.

HECKMAN, JAMES J. 2000. "Policies to Foster Human Capital." *Research in Economics* 54:3–56.

KAROLY, LYNN A., et al. 1998. *Investing in Our Children: What We Know and Don't Know about the Costs and Benefits of Early Childhood Interventions.* Santa Monica, CA: RAND.

MITCHELL, ANNE. 2001. *Education for All Young Children: The Role of States and the Federal Gov-*

ernment in Promoting Prekindergarten and Kindergarten. New York: Foundation for Child Development.

NATIONAL RESEARCH COUNCIL. 2001. *Eager to Learn: Educating Our Preschoolers.* Washington, DC: National Academy Press.

"Quality Counts 2002: Building Blocks for Success." 2002. *Education Week* 21(17).

REYNOLDS, ARTHUR J.; TEMPLE, JUDY A.; ROBINSON, DYLAN L.; and MANN, EMILY A. 2001. "Long-Term Effects of an Early Childhood Intervention on Educational Achievement and Juvenile Arrest: A Fifteen-Year Follow-Up on Low-Income Children in Public Schools." *Journal of the American Medical Association* 285:2,339–2,346.

SCHULMAN, KAREN; BLANK, HELEN; and EWEN, DANIELLE. 1999. *Seeds of Success: State Prekindergarten Initiatives, 1998–1999.* Washington, DC: Children's Defense Fund.

U.S. DEPARTMENT OF EDUCATION, NATIONAL CENTER FOR EDUCATION STATISTICS. 2001. *Digest of Education Statistics, 2000.* Washington, DC: U.S. Department of Education, National Center for Education Statistics.

U.S. DEPARTMENT OF LABOR. 2001. *Report on the American Workforce.* Washington, DC: U.S. Department of Labor.

U.S. DEPARTMENT OF LABOR, BUREAU OF LABOR STATISTICS. 2001. *Occupational Outlook Handbook, 2000–2001 Edition.* Washington, DC: U.S. Department of Labor, Bureau of Labor Statistics.

WEST, JERRY; DENTON, KRISTIN; and GERMINO-HAUSKEN, ELVIRA. 2000. *America's Kindergartners.* Washington, DC: U.S. Department of Education, National Center for Education Statistics.

INTERNET RESOURCES

CENTER FOR CAREER DEVELOPMENT IN EARLY CARE AND EDUCATION. 2001. "Child Care Licensing: Qualifications and Training for Roles in Child Care Centers and Family Child Care Homes: 2000 Summary Sheet." <www.nccic.org/cctopics/cclicensing00.pdf>.

CHILDREN'S FOUNDATION. 2002. "Child Care Center Licensing Study Summary Data." <www.childrensfoundation.net/centerssum.htm>.

EDUCATION COMMISSION OF THE STATES. 2001. "StateNotes: Kindergarten." <www.ecs.org>.

REYNOLDS, ARTHUR J.; TEMPLE, JUDY A.; ROBINSON, DYLAN L.; and MANN, EMILY A. 2001. "Age Twenty-One Cost-Benefit Analysis of the Title I Chicago Child-Parent Center Program, Executive Summary, June 2001." Waismann Center. <www.waisman.wisc.edu/index.htmlx>.

JANET S. HANSEN

PREPARATION OF TEACHERS

A major theme endures through the history of early childhood education: Because young children learn differently than older children, their schooling must be different. Thus, their teachers require specialized training.

History

The kindergarten became the first large-scale early childhood program in the United States. With it came the first formal training for teachers of young children.

Kindergartens. Private kindergarten training schools, usually connected to a kindergarten, spread as the kindergarten spread. The first kindergarten training school was begun in Boston in 1868 by German kindergartners Matilda Kriege and her daughter Alma (the term "kindergartner" is used both for a child attending a kindergarten and for a teacher at a kindergarten). Matilda Kriege studied with Baroness von Marenholtz-Buelow, a patroness and disciple of the German educator Friedrich Froebel (1782–1852), the founder of the kindergarten.

Initially kindergartens were German-speaking and were started by German immigrants, many fleeing the failed 1848 Prussian Revolution. Margarethe Schurz started the first in the United States in her home in Watertown, Wisconsin, in 1855. Schurz had worked in the London kindergarten run by her sister Bertha Ronge, immigrating to the United States in 1852. In 1859 Schurz and her young daughter Agathe met Elizabeth Peabody by chance in Boston. Impressed by Agathe, Peabody pressed Schurz to describe the kindergarten. In 1860 Peabody began the first English-language kindergarten in Boston. In 1867, dissatisfied with her kindergarten, Peabody traveled to Europe. She visited many kindergartens, including the training class in Hamburg run by Luise Froebel, Friedrich Froebel's widow. On her return, Peabody advocated tirelessly for kindergartens and for normal-school training for kindergarten teachers.

In 1873 William Torrey Harris, superintendent of the St. Louis Public Schools, opened the first public kindergarten in the United States, with Susan Blow as head teacher. The kindergarten had twenty children and twelve kindergartners in training, who, for a year, assisted Blow in the mornings and studied Froebelian theory in the afternoons. The second year, Blow taught an advanced class on Saturdays. Blow studied in New York with Maria Kraus-Boelte, who had trained in Hamburg for two years with Luise Froebel and then worked at Ronge's London kindergarten. In 1873 Kraus-Boelte opened the New York Seminary for Kindergartners with her husband, John Kraus, a friend of Froebel. The training consisted of one year of course work and one year of practice teaching. She trained kindergartners until her retirement in 1913.

Alice Putnam, an early Chicago kindergartner, studied with Kraus-Boelte and Blow. From 1876 she ran kindergarten-training classes at Hull-House and later at the University of Chicago and Cook County Normal School. Putnam was instrumental in founding the Chicago Free Kindergarten Association and the Chicago Froebel Association, where many kindergartners trained. In 1887 Elizabeth Harrison, a Putnam student, founded the Chicago Kindergarten and Training School, which evolved through many name changes to become National-Louis University. Another Putnam student, Anna Bryan, founded the Louisville Kindergarten and Training School in 1887. Patty Smith Hill, the dominant figure in early childhood education in the early 1900s, was her first student.

Emma Marwedel, a student of Froebel's, came to the United States at Peabody's urging. She ran a training school in Washington, DC, from 1872 to 1876, then founded a training school in Los Angeles. Her first graduate, Kate Douglas Wiggin, began the Silver Street Kindergarten Training School in San Francisco in 1880. Wiggin's student Caroline Dunlap began the first Kindergarten Training School in Oregon in 1881.

As training schools proliferated, educational publications warned of spurious training schools. In 1894 the president of the National Education Association's (NEA) Department of Kindergarten Education decried "'so-called trainers' who were . . . turning out all graduates with enough money to pay for a course" (Hewes, p. 10).

Kindergartens spread rapidly. By 1880, 7,800 children were enrolled in kindergartens in St. Louis.

Milwaukee included kindergartens in the public schools in 1882. In 1884 the NEA established the Department of Kindergarten Education. One year later, the NEA recommended kindergartens in all public schools. In 1892, in Sarasota Springs, New York, the International Kindergarten Union was founded. By 1890, 150 local kindergarten associations had been formed. By 1900, 189 cities had kindergartens, with 250,000 children attending; by 1910, the latter number had increased to 360,000. In 1912 there were 7,557 kindergartens and 8,856 teachers. By 1933 public kindergartens enrolled 723,000 children and private kindergartens, 54,000.

As the kindergarten became part of the public schools, administrators pressed for kindergarten teachers to meet the same licensure standards as other teachers. Training began to move from private kindergarten-training schools to normal schools. The New York Normal School began a short-lived training program in 1870, reopening it in 1874 with a Kraus-Boelte-trained supervisor. By 1880 some kindergarten training was available at the Milwaukee Normal School. In 1892 the Wisconsin State Normal School of Milwaukee added a Department of Kindergarten Education, which required two years of normal school. Students received a kindergarten assistant certificate after one year and a kindergarten director diploma after two.

Between 1880 and 1895 kindergarten training was incorporated into state normal schools in Oshkosh, Wisconsin; Winona, Minnesota; Oswego and Fredonia, New York; Emporia, Kansas; Connecticut; and Michigan; as well as into the city normal schools in New York and Boston, the Cook County (Illinois) Normal School, and the Philadelphia Girls Normal School.

By 1913, 147 institutions offered kindergarten training. As more normal schools offered kindergarten training, kindergarten-training schools declined—a 1916 report of 126 teacher-training programs showed only twenty-four freestanding kindergarten-training schools. During the 1900s normal schools slowly transformed into colleges and universities. As normal schools became colleges, training for kindergarten teachers became four-year degree programs.

Nursery schools. With the nursery school movement, early childhood education became increasingly identified with preschool (pre-kindergarten) education. The nursery school was founded in England by Margaret and Rachel McMillan in 1911. The first American nursery teachers went to England for training, many with the McMillans.

Nursery schools spread rapidly. In 1924 there were twenty-eight nurseries in eleven states; by 1933 the number grew to 1,700. In 1926 Patty Smith Hill invited a select group of early educators to New York. This group formed the National Committee on Nursery Schools, which later became the National Association for Nursery Education, and still later the National Association for the Education of Young Children (NAEYC). Nursery schools also became part of many universities. Between 1924 and 1930, Lawrence Frank, at the Laura Spelman Rockefeller Memorial Fund, directed funding toward the establishment of many university laboratory nursery schools, most often in home economics departments, at, for example, Iowa State University, the Ohio State University, Cornell University, the University of Georgia, Spelman College, and Michigan State University.

The Merrill-Palmer Nursery School in Detroit and the Ruggles Street Nursery in Boston were early nursery-teacher-training institutes. By the mid-1920s teacher training was occurring at nursery laboratory schools at the Iowa Child Welfare Research Station, the University of California–Los Angeles, the University of Minnesota, Columbia University, Yale University, National Kindergarten and Elementary College, Cleveland Kindergarten–Primary Training School of Western Reserve University, and normal schools in Kalamazoo, Michigan, and Milwaukee. In 1927 the National Committee on Nursery Schools Second Conference recommended a four-year college degree for nursery teachers to better enable them to deal with specialists from such fields as nutrition and psychology.

The primary focus at many laboratory schools, however, was research on child development. The training was seen as important for women in general. Edna Noble White, who founded Merrill-Palmer, stated in a letter to Lawrence Frank in 1924 that a "laboratory for training young women in child care . . . should be made part of the training of every young woman since they come in contact with children in many capacities—mothers, teachers, social workers etc." (Braun and Edwards, p. 149).

During the Great Depression of the 1930s, the Works Progress Administration (WPA) set up emergency nursery schools to provide work for unemployed teachers. As many as 2,500 nursery schools appeared in the public and private sector by 1940. WPA nursery funding ended in 1942, the year that the Lanham Act set up about 2,000 day-care centers to enable mothers to enter the work force to support the war effort. Both programs required rapid and large-scale training, often of teachers without experience with young children. A survey in the second year of the WPA nursery schools found that of 3,775 teachers, 158 had nursery experience, 290 had kindergarten experience, and 64 percent had teaching experience. Many groups were involved in the training, including the National Association of Nursery Educators, the Association for Childhood Education, and the National Committee on Parent Education. The training itself is not well documented.

Following World War II, the Lanham Act day care centers closed down. Early schooling returned to the pre-depression level until the summer of 1965 when Head Start began with 652,000 children in 2,500 centers, employing 41,000 teachers and 250,000 other workers, including volunteers. Head Start spawned more federally funded early intervention programs, such as Child Parent Education Centers, which targeted poor young children. In the 1980s and 1990s individual states began funding preschool programs for young children termed "at-risk." At the same time, the day-care industry grew rapidly as more women worked outside of the home.

Current Structure and Organization

The Council for Professional Development reported that almost 1,400 two- and four-year institutions offered early childhood programs in 2000. More than half of these were two-year institutions offering associate degrees. As early schooling and care expands, many teachers of young children receive their training in other than four-year institutions. The 1985 NAEYC guidelines for an early childhood associate degree specified that at least half the program be professional courses. Programs vary greatly across institutions.

Many early childhood teachers earn the Child Development Associate (CDA) degree, which was initiated in 1971 by the U.S. Office of Child Development. The goal was to identify basic competencies and provide training in them, leading to a national credential. Since 1985, NAEYC has administered the program. The program's competency goals emphasize performance rather than prescribed courses or credits. There is considerable local control in interpreting standards and providing training.

Early childhood programs at four-year institutions also vary greatly depending on how early childhood is defined in a given state. In 1997, sixteen states had licensure for teaching ages zero to eight. Seventeen others and the District of Columbia had licensure for ages three to six. Three states defined early childhood as age five to age nine. Five states had an early childhood endorsement to be added to the elementary license, while ten included kindergarten in the elementary license. Increasingly four-year institutions educate early childhood teachers for public school programs requiring state certification, and two-year programs educate teachers for other early childhood programs.

In-Service and Staff Development Programs

NAEYC, the Association for Childhood Education International (ACEI), and Head Start offer guidelines and recommendations for professional development and in-service training. Historically, the goal of in-service and staff development has been to improve weak areas of practice. In the late 1980s the goal shifted to a developmental model that emphasizes growth and collegiality. This model prepares teachers to participate in decision-making and to advance professionally.

NAEYC's 1993 position statement on early childhood professional development specifically addresses "an effective system of early childhood professional development that provides meaningful opportunities for career advancement to ensure a well-qualified and stable work force" (p. 1). NAEYC and ACEI offer publications that support preparation and training, conferences to improve professional preparation and training, and professional preparation and program review. NAEYC stresses the importance of developing a professional development system embedded within the larger system of effective early childhood programs.

Head Start's in-service training approach addresses the needs of teachers, children, and families. From its inception Head Start has been committed to staff development. Educators in Head Start programs have a wide range of early childhood experiences and credentials. Head Start offers a variety of in-service approaches to assist staff in developing their practice and professionalism. Some of the in-service programs include integration of training with exemplary Head Start programs, hands-on participatory activities, mentoring, collaborative learning, training teams, individualized training, goal-setting strategies, and follow-up training.

Trends, Issues, and Controversies

Programs at four-year institutions face the perennial challenges of teacher education: how to balance professional education, general education, and specific areas of academic study; and how to balance university course work and clinical experience. In the 1980s and 1990s, the general trend was to decrease professional education and to increase general education and courses in a noneducation specialization. The amount of clinical experience has generally stayed the same or increased. The tension between the amount of coursework in pedagogy versus child development in the professional education component remains.

The importance of training for early childhood teachers has become increasingly recognized. For example, Head Start has mandated that half of all program staff must have an associate degree by 2003. In 1998 forty-one states and the District of Columbia had early childhood initiatives, many with more stringent requirements for early educators. At least nineteen states require some pre-service training for child-care providers.

Many early childhood educators promote a system of certification by which teachers would move up a career ladder from, for example, a CDA to an AA (Associate in Arts) to a bachelor's degree and state licensure. Although some progress has been made toward such a system, differences in course types and patterns between two-year and four-year institutions remain an obstacle. Arguments for academic credit for work experience further complicate matters.

Both ACEI and NAEYC now define early childhood as birth through age eight (or third grade). It remains to be seen how this shift in emphasis from preschool to preschool through third grade will actually affect teacher training. Early childhood programs in traditional home economics programs and two-year colleges focus on preschools. Preschool education is often regulated by state agencies other than education, usually child-welfare agencies.

A serious teacher shortage is predicted for the first decades of the twenty-first century. A shortage may lead, once again, to abbreviated teacher training and different routes to licensure. It should be noted, however, that discussions of alternative licensure generally focus on high school and elementary teachers, in specified shortage areas, not on early childhood.

The question of who controls teacher credentialing remains. Originally local districts credentialed teachers but soon states took over. Many groups have a stake in credentialing, in particular, state boards of education, professional organizations, teachers unions, and universities; and shifting coalitions across these groups are common. NAEYC's 1996 *Guidelines for Preparation of Early Childhood Professionals,* for example, cites endorsements by the Association of Teacher Educators, the Division of Early Childhood of the Council for Exceptional Children, and the National Council for Accreditation of Teacher Education.

Given the changing and local nature of teacher licensure, generalizing about credentialing is difficult. Nevertheless, the general historical trend has been as follows. Until the early 1900s teachers were credentialed by examination. They were then credentialed based on professional training. In the 1950s states moved from credentialing based on state-specified courses and hours to approved programs, which meet state requirements but vary across colleges and universities. In most states the approved program is accompanied by some form of state competency examination in one or more of the following areas: basic skills, subject matter, and professional knowledge. By the early twenty-first century, the trend was toward performance-based credentialing, often requiring student-produced portfolios as evidence of successful performance.

Conclusion

The major challenge to education of early childhood teachers is the broad and changing nature of the field. The term *teacher-caregiver* has become common, giving some sense of this breadth and change. Across teaching in general and in early childhood teaching in particular, the diversity of roles people take in working with young children makes it difficult to identify a single knowledge base. Early childhood education serves an increasingly diverse population and is expected to provide an increasingly wide range of services to these children and their families. The most pressing, and perennial, challenge is the "widespread misconception that work with young children can be carried out effectively without

the benefit of specialized knowledge" (Powell and Dunn, p. 63).

See also: CHILD CARE; TEACHER EDUCATION; TEACHER EVALUATION.

BIBLIOGRAPHY

ABDAL-HAQQ, ISMAT. 1989. "The Influence of Reform on Inservice Teacher Education." *ERIC Clearinghouse on Education.* ERIC Document Reproduction Service No. ED322147.

BEATTY, BARBARA. 1995. *Preschool Education in America: The Culture of Young Children from the Colonial Era to the Present.* New Haven, CT: Yale University Press.

BRAUN, SAMUEL J., and EDWARDS, ESTHER P. 1972. *History and Theory of Early Childhood Education.* Worthington, OH: Charles A. Jones Publishing.

DEASY, DENNISON. 1978. *Education under Six.* London: Croom Helm.

EPSTEIN, ANN S. 1999. "Pathways to Quality in Head Start, Public School, and Private Nonprofit Early Childhood Programs." *Journal of Research in Childhood Education* 13:101–109.

HEWES, DOROTHY W. 1990. "Historical Foundations of Early Childhood Teacher Training: The Evolution of Kindergarten Teacher Preparation." In *Early Childhood Teacher Preparation,* ed. Bernard Spodek and Olivia Saracho. New York: Teachers College Press.

LASCARIDES, V. CELIA, and HINITZ, BLYTHE F. 2000. *History of Early Childhood Education.* New York: Falmer.

MCCARTHY, JAN; CRUZ, JOSUE; and RATLIFF, NANCY. 1998. "Early Childhood Teacher Licensure Patterns: A State by State Analysis." Paper presented at the annual meeting of the National Association for the Education of Young Children, Toronto.

NATIONAL ASSOCIATION FOR THE EDUCATION OF YOUNG CHILDREN. 1993. *A Conceptual Framework for Early Childhood Professional Development.* Washington, DC: National Association for the Education of Young Children.

NATIONAL ASSOCIATION FOR THE EDUCATION OF YOUNG CHILDREN. 1996. *Guidelines for Preparation of Early Childhood Professionals.* Washington, DC: National Association for the Education of Young Children.

OSBORN, D. KEITH. 1991. *Early Childhood Education in Historical Perspective.* Athens, GA: Daye Press.

OTT, DANIEL J.; ZEICHNER, KENNETH M.; and PRICE, GARY GLEN. 1990. "Research Horizons and the Quest for a Knowledge Base in Early Childhood Teacher Education." In *Early Childhood Teacher Preparation,* ed. Bernard Spodek and Olivia Saracho. New York: Teachers College Press.

POWELL, DOUGLAS R., and DUNN, LORAINE. 1990. "Non-Baccalaureate Teacher Education in Early Childhood Education." In *Early Childhood Teacher Preparation,* ed. Bernard Spodek and Olivia Saracho. New York: Teachers College Press.

SCHULMAN, KAREN; BLANK, HELEN; and EWEN, DANIELLE. 1999. *Seeds of Success: State Pre-kindergarten Initiatives, 1998–1999.* Washington, DC: Children's Defense Fund.

SNYDER, AGNES. 1972. *Dauntless Women in Childhood Education, 1856–1931.* Washington, DC: Association for Childhood Education International.

VANDEWALKER, NINA CATHARINE. 1908. *The Kindergarten in American Education.* New York: Macmillan.

INTERNET RESOURCE

ANGUS, DAVID L. 1998. "Professionalism and the Public Good: A Brief History of Teacher Certification." Thomas B. Fordham Foundation. <www.edexcellence.net/library/angus/angus.html>.

DANIEL J. WALSH
BETTY J. LIEBOVICH

INTERNATIONAL CONTEXT

Early education, sometimes referred to as *early childhood care and development* (ECCD), emerged at the 1990 World Conference on Education for All, held in Jomtien, Thailand, as an important extension of the more traditional approach to basic education, in which "education" begins with entrance into school. According to the Jomtien Declaration, "learning begins at birth. This calls for early childhood care and initial education. These can be provided through arrangements involving families, communities or institutional programs, as appropriate." One of the targets for the 1990s of the Jomtien Framework for Action was an "expansion of early childhood care and development activities, including family and community interventions, especially for poor, disadvantaged and disabled children." The Jomtien Declaration and Framework for Action gave international presence and sanction to early childhood care and development, and to "initial education" in a way that it had not enjoyed previously. Expectations were raised at Jomtien in relation to: (a) the well-being of young children; (b) enrollments; (c) conditions favoring improvement in ECCD programs; and (d) shifts in the type and quality of program being provided.

It is difficult to understand changes in the field of early childhood care and development without paying attention to the broader context in which changes occur. Trends that have important effects on ECCD include: industrialization, urbanization, and internal migration; declining birth rates; technological and scientific developments; globalization; changing social values; the mobilization and emancipation of women; internal strife and civil wars; the ecology movement, the HIV/AIDS pandemic; and moves toward greater administrative decentralization. While space does not allow a detailed description and analysis of these changing contexts, or of their effects on childrearing practices, the welfare and quality of life of young children, and the evolution of ECCD programs, it should be noted that conditions and contexts, as well as the rate at which they are changing, vary widely among and within countries, making it likely that changes in ECCD, for good or ill, may be more closely related to local circumstances than to the influence of the World Conference on Education for All and the ensuing activities.

The Well-Being of Young Children

Health and nutritional status. Despite the fact that millions of children in the world still die from preventable diseases, major advances have been made since the 1980s in reducing infant and child mortality. For example, the positive effect of immunization programs on infant mortality has been widely documented, and polio is on the verge of being eradicated. Micronutrient supplementation programs seem to have had important positive effects; particularly notable are advances related to the provision of vitamin A and iodine.

At the same time, it is important to note the dramatic setback in general well-being related to the HIV/AIDS pandemic, particularly in Africa. Major health advances and remaining challenges are documented in the annual reports of the World Health Organization and United Nations Children's Fund (UNICEF). Relatively high levels of undernourishment and vitamin deficiencies continue in many parts of Asia, Africa, and Latin America. Moreover, feeding programs have not always lived up to expectation. For example, two evaluations carried out in Latin America found that there was little or no improvement in the nutritional status of participants in ECCD programs, despite a relatively high cost of feeding children in the programs. Evaluations suggest that broad approaches, directed to the whole family, need to be promoted if health and nutrition components of ECCD programs are to be effective in improving the well-being of young children—simple supplementary feeding programs are insufficient.

Psychosocial development and learning. Unfortunately, very few countries provide measures of the psychosocial well-being of young children, or of their advances in learning during their early years. It is therefore impossible to judge advances in this area for national populations or to link advances to the many program initiatives that have been undertaken.

Enrollment

The most commonly used indicator for early childhood programs is the percentage of a particular age group who are enrolled in recognized programs, creating a *gross enrollment ratio* (GER). From the evaluation reports presented by countries prior to the World Education Forum held in Dakar in 2000, it is possible to obtain a rough overview of enrollments and changes over the last decade of the twentieth century. Although the data need to be interpreted with caution, a number of conclusions seem to be valid.

General enrollment trends. The general tendency has been for enrollments to increase since 1990. In Latin America and southern and eastern Asia, all of the countries reporting data showed an increase in enrollments, with the exception of Afghanistan. In the Caribbean, all but one country (Grenada) showed increases (or remained steady at more than 100 percent). Cook Islands in the Pacific showed a decrease, but all other countries in the region increased their enrollments. A summary from the Spanish-, Portuguese-, and French-speaking countries in Africa notes a marginal increase for the region during the 1990s (from 0.7% percent to 3.6%), and specifically mentions a decrease only in Togo. The United Nations Educational, Scientific and Cultural Organization (UNESCO) reported in 1999 that "enrollment has grown and access, although small, has improved" (UNESCO 1999b); there is no indication, however, of cases in which there may have been a decrease.

As a major exception to the above, decreases in enrollments were found in all the central Asian countries that were former members of the Soviet Union, and for which data were available. These decreases are a product of the breakup of the former Soviet Union, of economic difficulties associated with independence and the shift to a market-based economy (sometimes accompanied by civil war or territorial battles with neighbors), and of a decentralization process within the countries. With these changes, the centrally supported, extensive, and expensive system of relatively high-quality early-childhood provision broke down. This was particularly significant for rural areas where attention had been provided through rural cooperatives. It appears, however, that enrollments began to recover slightly during the late 1990s, related to somewhat greater stability, financial assistance from abroad, and the emergence of a range of new alternatives.

The most dramatic increases during the 1990s appeared in the Caribbean, where statistics for the tiny Turks and Caicos Islands show a jump from zero coverage at the beginning of the decade to an enrollment of 99 percent. Cuba showed a major increase over the period (from 29% to 98%), a result of having introduced (and having included in their statistics) a massive parental education program. Honduras, Nicaragua, and Paraguay also showed significant advances, but began from a relatively low baseline. The same is true of the Philippines. China, Thailand, and Vietnam also showed important enrollment increases.

In most cases, however, change has been modest, slogging along at one or two per cent per year. UNESCO reported that "ten years after Jomtien, despite efforts of some governments, very little progress has been made to achieve the set goals" (UNESCO 1999b). It can be concluded, therefore, that a great deal of work is still needed if ECCD programs are to have a significant effect on the lives of children, families, and countries.

In 1998, the variation in enrollment rates was enormous, ranging from almost zero to more than 100 percent:

- In Latin America, Ecuador reported a coverage of 14 percent for children up to age five, contrasting with 98 percent for Cuba.
- In the Caribbean, Belize reported 26 percent of its children three to five years of age were enrolled, contrasted with 100 percent for the Bahamas and Jamaica.
- In the Middle East and North Africa, Yemen reported 1 percent, and Bahrain 36 percent, of children ages three to five were enrolled.
- In southern and eastern Africa, Zambia reported 7 percent of children ages three to six were enrolled, whereas Mauritius report an enrollment of 98 percent for children four and five years of age.
- In central Asia and eastern Europe, Afghanistan reported 0 percent enrolled, Tajikistan reported 4 percent of children ages one to six were enrolled, and Russia reported an enrollment of 54 percent. Seychelles, an island nation in the Indian Ocean, however, had 107 percent enrollment.
- Enrollments in the Pacific Islands vary from 15 percent in Fiji to 73 percent in Papua New Guinea and 100 percent in Tuvalu.

These immense disparities across countries, when added to the obvious cultural and economic differences within countries, reinforces the idea that formulas should be avoided.

Preschool trends. Attention to ECCD continues to be very much focused on preschool, and is concentrated on the age just prior to entry into primary school. This preprimary age may be as young as four (because kindergarten is considered part of the primary-school system and the enrollment at age five is virtually 100 percent, a situation found in various Caribbean countries), or as old as age six. Data from the evaluation reports, when broken down by age, shows the greatest enrollments for age five or ages five to six. In Chile, for instance, 83 percent of children five to six are enrolled, as compared with only 35 percent of children three to four. In Japan, the corresponding figures are 97 percent and 58 percent. These figures support the notion of a strong bias to-

wards preschool education as the main strain of ECCD. In Latin America, at least seven countries (Argentina, Chile, Costa Rica, Cuba, Mexico, Peru, and Uruguay) can point to enrollment figures of more than 80 percent for the year prior to entry into primary school. The general point is reinforced when one takes into account that various countries include in their statistics special programs designed specifically to prepare children for primary schooling.

Coverage is very low, however, in institutionalized ECCD programs for children under two, and even under four, years of age. In most of the world, the tradition of mothers or other family members caring for very young children at home on a full-time basis continues to be the norm. Accordingly, parental support and education programs that will guide parents in helping their young children not only to survive and grow, but also to develop their full potential, are extraordinarily important. Together with the hope that many people can be reached at a relatively low cost, this has led to a spate of *parenting education* programs. These are often mentioned in country reports, but are not usually included in statistics.

Although countries in the Third World, and in eastern Europe and central Asia, are likely to provide families with noninstitutionalized support (e.g., maternity and paternity work leave, sick leave, child payments, housing subsidies), this type of support for families with young children is seldom found in developed nations, where responsibility for the first years falls squarely, and even exclusively in some places, on family and community. Sweden has reported a relatively high proportion of children ages one to two in child-care centers.

Urban versus rural education. Urban children are more likely than rural children to be enrolled in some sort of ECCD program, though in a number of countries there is a suggestion that rural enrollments grew more than urban enrollments during the 1990s. The bias towards urban areas is probably greater for daycare programs, which are usually linked to urban work situations, but this information is not available in reports.

Socioeconomic factors. Children from families that are better off economically and socially are more likely to be enrolled than are children from families with few resources or that are part of groups discriminated against socially. Although this statement is logical and comes from a general literature review, in evaluation reports prepared for the World Education Forum almost no attempt was made to present hard data showing how enrollment is related to economic or social status. The main exception is Chile, which reported a direct relationship between enrollment and income based on household survey data—in 1996, enrollment for children under six years of age was more than twice as high for children from families in the upper fifth of the income distribution (48%) as it was for children from families in the lowest fifth (22%). In the period from 1990 to 1996, enrollment grew 32 percent for the lowest income group and 49 percent for the highest.

Boys versus girls. In most countries, there is virtual parity between boys and girls, but there are exceptions in which girls lag behind. Nepal, Pakistan, India, Maldives, and Iran are cases in point. Several of the countries in the Middle East and North also show lower enrollments for girls, but there is evidence that the gap is slowly narrowing. Gender inequality tends to be magnified in rural areas.

Political factors. The role of the state, of private-sector institutions, and of communities varies widely from region to region and country to country. In nations with a socialist bent (including former members of the Soviet Union, the Lao People's Democratic Republic, Cuba, and Sweden, among others) education has been a major responsibility of the state, including education and care during the preschool years. Accordingly, important efforts were made prior to the 1990s to develop state-funded systems of comprehensive care and early education. During the 1990s, however, the role of the state changed dramatically in many of these countries, sometimes with newfound independence and a shift towards a market economy.

The socialist stance contrasts markedly with that of the United States and the United Kingdom, where ECCD has developed along mixed private and governmental lines, but with a heavy bias towards private and community provision regulated through the market. In Africa, with some exceptions, governments have paid little attention to ECCD, which has been viewed as the responsibility of families and communities. Nongovernmental organizations (NGOs)—which are statistically labeled as private, but might better be considered part of a social sector—have played an important role in the region.

In Latin America, the percentage of enrollments accounted for by nongovernmental programs runs between 10 percent and 15 percent for most countries. In the Caribbean, heavy emphasis is placed on private and community programs. In Southeast Asia, Indonesia reported 19 percent (1996) and Thailand reported 24 percent (1998) of their enrollments were administered by organizations that are not part of the government.

Changes in Conditions Affecting ECCD Programming

The immediate conditions affecting ECCD are changing, including shifts in: (1) knowledge and its dissemination, including the conceptual and scientific bases available to be drawn upon and the formation of communication networks; (2) attitudes and awareness of political leaders, funders, planners, and the population at large about the importance of ECCD and its potential benefits; (3) policies and legal and legislative frameworks for programming, both internationally and nationally; (4) the availability of resources, both financial and human; and (5) organizational bases, both governmental and nongovernmental.

Changes in the knowledge base and conceptual shifts. In a survey carried out by Robert Myers, the most frequently mentioned advance in knowledge related to ECCD during the 1990s was an advance in understanding how the brain develops and functions. To many survey respondents, it was clear that new discoveries in neuroscience—and their dissemination through scientific, professional, and popular channels—have had an important influence on the demand for, and the willingness to consider support for, early childhood education and development programs. An example is the finding that there are "windows of opportunity" for learning during the early years when learning particular practices is most efficient and which, if missed, make subsequent learning very difficult.

Also mentioned with some frequency was a growing body of knowledge from research studies and program evaluations showing long-term benefits of early intervention programs for children at risk. It is now possible to point to longitudinal studies in various countries showing clearly that ECCD programs can have effects on children in primary school. A prime example is the excellent work done in Turkey, in which children cared for in different settings, and whose mothers participated in a parent education program, were shown to benefit in later life from such programs. These studies have helped to convince policymakers and programs of the value of investing in ECCD. They reinforce the Jomtien commitment to including early education within basic education.

These studies, together with the few cases where there has been some agreement on an indicator of psychosocial development and where consistent measurement has occurred over time (e.g., Chile), show that:

- Programs of reasonable quality do have important positive effects on early development, often with longer-term effects.

- The effects can favor rural children who are at a social disadvantage.

- An important improvement in the nutritional status of children does not automatically bring about the anticipated improvement in various dimensions of psychosocial development.

- The area of language development seems to show a consistent lag in development related to socioeconomic conditions, as well as to first-language differences.

Other new avenues of research that are beginning to influence practice include studies of resilience; conditions under which programs can have a negative effect on child development (for example, when the quality of a center is very low); and child-rearing practices and patterns.

A range of conceptual shifts was also noted by survey respondents. For example, although a behaviorist model that is not very "child friendly" still holds sway in some countries, there has been a shift towards active learning and the constructivist ideas of Jean Piaget (1896–1980). Although Piaget has had a strong influence on early childhood curricula and practices, particularly in the developed world and in Latin America, even more of a shift has been noted towards programs based on the thinking of Lev Vygotsky (1896–1934). While not contradicting Piaget, Vygotsky places greater emphasis on social and cultural influences that affect all aspects of children's development (as contrasted with emphasis on individual discovery) giving renewed importance to the role of the teacher and to the place of language in the teaching/learning process.

The influence of ecological and transactional models that gained prominence in the 1980s continues to provide a basis for complementary approaches to ECCD that work towards changing the family, community, and broader institutional and cultural environments with which a child interacts in the process of developing and learning.

The search for *best practices,* which took off in the 1980s, continues, but the chorus of those who question the search for universals and the base for best practices in developmental psychology has grown ever louder. Additional importance is being attached to discovering, respecting, and incorporating cultural differences into thinking about how early childhood education and care should occur. Viewpoints grounded in anthropology, sociology, ethics, and other fields are being brought to bear on ECCD, highlighting the need to begin with the cultural and social definitions of childhood and education held by those who are the participants in early childhood programs rather than with a predetermined set of definitions and models imposed from outside. This tendency is consistent with a strand of thinking about social and economic development that is grounded in local participation, and in "putting the first last," as Robert Chambers aptly subtitles his study.

To try to overcome inevitable tensions between international and local expressions of what "should be," a third path is evolving in which the search for best practices begins by looking for and supporting those practices valued both in terms of traditional wisdom based on experience and their scientific value. Points of difference are handled through dialogue in which underlying values are made explicit.

There are also shifts in the way planning, programming, and implementing organizations are going about moving knowledge into action. For instance, there is a tendency for ECCD programming to be set within broader frameworks such as poverty alleviation. There have also been calls for a "new citizenry" as transitions to democracy occur, and for moderating problems of street children and criminal behavior. Incipient is a tendency to think more in preventive, rather than compensatory, terms.

Related to globalization, there appears to be a conceptual shift in how governments see their role in the provision of ECCD services, with a tendency toward privatization.

Changes in attitudes, awareness, policies, and legal frameworks. The 1980s and 1990s saw an important increase in awareness of the importance of ECCD, sometimes linked to research findings, sometimes to evaluations and the perceived effectiveness of particular programs, and sometimes to discussions of children's rights. In some circles, awareness has grown of the importance of the very early years, not only linked to research on the brain, but also to a new appreciation for the effects of *bonding* and *attachment*.

In some cases, this new awareness has been translated into policies and/or legal and legislative frameworks. Some countries have lowered the age of entrance into primary school, thereby giving what had been one year of preschool a new obligatory status; others have declared one or more years of preschool education to be obligatory. New policy statements have been issued in several countries, India being a prime example. In Africa, new policies appeared in at least ten countries during the 1990s. In the Caribbean, a regional plan of action has been jointly approved and is moving into an operational phase. However, new awareness and new laws do not necessarily translate into greater financial commitment to ECCD, or to major advances in enrollment or quality.

Changes in the availability of financial resources. During the 1990s the availability of financing from international banks and donors for ECCD programs increased significantly, particularly from the World Bank, with important new initiatives financed also by the Inter-American Development Bank and the Asian Development Bank. The picture is less clear, however, with respect to national budgets. Little specific information is available about national financing of ECCD programs, but the general impression is that very small proportions of educational budgets are devoted to early childhood programs. According to a UNESCO report, "governments in general have neither the financial nor administrative capacity to engage in early childhood education in the way they are involved in the provision of primary universal education" (UNESCO 1999b).

Estimates are not available for the financial support that is provided by the private and social sectors. Despite laws in some countries that mandate employers to provide child care, the contributions of the private sector to ECCD seem to be minimal. The low allocations by governments and the private sector suggest that the major burden of financing ECCD continues to fall on families and communities, as well as on civic and religious organizations.

Changes in program strategies and quality. Shifts appear to be occurring, albeit slowly, in the strategies used to foster early childhood development and to improve learning and education during the preschool years. For example:

- Although most attention in the field continues to be focused on the immediate pre-school years, there is more attention being given to children under four years of age—not only through health programs, but also through programs of parental education that include attention to psychosocial development.

- Although fractured and uncoordinated sectoral and monofocal programs still predominate, more attention is being given to multidimensional strategies that seek convergence, coordination, or integration.

- Strategies more often provide for a variety of service models, using a range of different agents, as contrasted with the still prominent strategy that extends the same service and the same model to all families and children, regardless of their culture and circumstances.

- Somewhat greater attention is being given to adjusting curricula to culture, as the idea of "beginning where people are" is gaining ground.

- The presence of nonformal programs has grown.

Unfortunately, very little is known, in a systematic way, about the quality of ECCD programs in the developed world, whether defined in terms of inputs, processes, or results. It has been difficult to arrive at an agreement about the instruments and methods that should be used for measuring quality. Nevertheless, it seems fair to say that program expansion has outrun attention to quality.

Problems and Proposals

Weak political will. In many, even most, countries, the need continues to convince politicians, policymakers, programmers, and education officials of the importance of ECCD. To do so, better strategies of communication, lobbying, and advocacy are needed, together with a better information base related to systematic monitoring efforts.

Weak policy and legal frameworks. In order to formulate and strengthen policy there is a need to: (1) undertake analytical studies of existing policies affecting children, looking beyond narrowly conceived educational policies to (for example) social welfare, health, and labor policies; (2) seek conformity with the Convention on the Rights of the Child; (3) establish norms and standards that are not so rigid or high as to be unworkable, but which will assure positive attention to children; and (4) clarify the roles of the family, state, civil society, and the private sector—as well as forms of partnerships among them.

Lack of, or poor use of, financial resources. ECCD programs generally command a small portion of government budgets. There is a need to increase, and make more permanent allocations to, ECCD in national budgets; strengthen the capacity of states and municipalities to obtain resources for ECCD; and seek cost-effective approaches, including quality community-based nonformal programs. In addition, alternative avenues of funding, such as debt swaps, philanthropic contributions, and private-sector involvement, need to be explored, and local organizations should have access to central pools of money in order to better respond to the needs of local communities.

Uniformity (lack of options). The bureaucratically convenient tendency to extend the same program to all children conflicts with the need to tailor ECCD programs to cultural, geographic, economic, and age differences. There is therefore a need to: (1) think in terms of complementary and varied approaches to ECCD that include family and community-based programs; (2) involve NGOs more actively as partners; (3) decentralize; and (4) construct culturally relevant programs with local communities.

Poor quality. There is a pressing need to reexamine training and supervision, and provide sound training (both pre-service and in-service) at all levels, with respect to a diversity of ECCD approaches, and to reduce the number of children (or families) per education/care agent. Curricula must be improved and reformulated, taking into account local definitions of what constitutes best practices. In addition, existing experience can be drawn upon in a more systematic way, and better systems for monitoring and evaluating children and programs need to be established.

Lack of attention to particular populations. The following "disadvantaged" populations need to be given greater attention: low-income, rural, and indigenous populations; girls; HIV/AIDS patients; children up to three years of age; pregnant and lactating mothers; working mothers; and fathers.

Lack of coordination. If a holistic and integrated notion of learning and development is to be honored, and if resources are to be used more effectively,

greater coordination is needed among governmental programs, within the education sector (especially between ECCD and primary schooling), and between governmental and nongovernmental organizations. There is a need to create intersectoral, interorganizational coordinating bodies; to construct joint programs crossing bureaucratic boundaries; to strengthen the ability of families and communities to call upon and bring together services that are currently offered in an uncoordinated fashion; and to seek agreement on the populations that are most in need of attention, and then direct services to those populations in a converging manner.

Narrow conceptualization. The conceptual frameworks guiding programs intended to improve early childhood care and development and early learning have come primarily from developmental psychology and formal education. There is a need to go beyond the knowledge that these fields provide to incorporate broader views, with cultural, social, and ethical dimensions brought to bear. There is also a need to relate ECCD programming, conceptually and operationally, to other program lines that begin from (for example) analyses of children's rights, poverty, working mothers, rural development, special needs, refugees, adolescents, and gender.

See also: CHILD CARE; EARLY CHILDHOOD EDUCATION, *subentries on* OVERVIEW, PREPARATION OF TEACHERS; HEALTH AND EDUCATION; FROEBEL, FRIEDRICH.

BIBLIOGRAPHY

BARNETT, W. STEVEN, and BOOCOCK, SARANE S. 1998. *Early Care and Education for Children in Poverty: Promises, Programs, and Long-Term Results.* Albany: State University of New York Press.

BEKMAN, SEVDA. 1998. *A Fair Chance: An Evaluation of the Mother-Child Education Program.* Istanbul, Turkey: Mother-Child Foundation.

BERK, L. E., and WINSLER, A. 1995. *Scaffolding Children's Learning: Vygotsky and Early Childhood Education.* Washington, DC: National Association for the Education of Young Children.

CHAMBERS, ROBERT. 1997. *Whose Reality Counts? Putting the First Last.* London: Intermediate Technology Publications.

COA CLEMENTE, RAMIRO. 1996. *Proyecto integral de desarrollo infantil: desnutrición infantil.* La Paz,

Bolivia: Unidad de Analisis de Politicas Sociales UDAPSO.

COCHRANE, MONCRIEFF. 1993. "Public Child Care, Culture and Society: Crosscutting Themes." In *International Handbook of Child Care Policies and Programs,* ed. Moncrieff Cochrane. Westport, CT: Greenwood Press.

COLECTIVO MEXICANO DE APOYO A LA NIÑEZ. 1998. *IV Informe sobre los derechos y la situación de la infancia en México 1994–1997.* Mexico: D.F., Impretei.

COLLETTA, NICOLAS, and REINHOLD, AMY JO. 1997. *Review of Early Childhood Policy and Programs in Sub-Saharan Africa.* Washington, DC: World Bank.

CONSULTATIVE GROUP ON EARLY CHILDHOOD CARE AND DEVELOPMENT. 1994. *Child Rearing* (Issue No. 15).

DAHLBERG, GUNILLA; MOSS, PETER; and PENCE, ALAN. 1999. *Beyond Quality in Early Childhood Education and Care: Post-Modern Perspectives.* London: Falmer.

EUROPEAN COMMISSION NETWORK ON CHILDCARE. 1996. *A Review of Services for Young Children in the European Union, 1990–1995.* London: European Commission Network on Childcare.

EVANS, JUDITH; KARWOWSKA-STRUCZYK, MALGORZATA; KORINTUS, MARTA; HERSENI, IOANA; and KORNAZHEVA, BOYANKA. 1996. *Who Is Caring for the Children? An Exploratory Survey Conducted in Hungary, Poland, Bulgaria and Romania. Main Report and Country Reports.* Haydensville, MA: Consultative Group on Early Childhood Care and Development.

HUNT, JOSEPH, and QUIBRIA, M. G. 1999. *Investing in Child Nutrition in Asia.* Metro Manila, Philippines: Asian Development Bank.

INTER-AMERICAN DEVELOPMENT BANK. 1999. *Breaking the Poverty Cycle: Investing in Early Childhood.* Washington, DC: Inter-American Development Bank.

INTERNATIONAL JOURNAL OF EDUCATIONAL RESEARCH. 2000. "Early Childhood Education and Care." Special Issue. *International Journal of Education Research* 33(1).

KAGAN, SHARON, and COHEN, NANCY. 1997. *Not By Chance: Creating an Early Care and Education System for America's Children.* New Haven, CT: Bush Center, Quality 2000 Initiative.

KAGITÇIBASI, ÇIGDEM. 1996. *Family and Human Development Across Cultures: A View from the Other Side.* Hillsdale, NJ: Erlbaum.

KAHN, ALFRED, and KAMERMAN, SHEILA. 1994. *Social Policy and the Under-3s: Six Country Case Studies. A Resource for Policy Makers, Advocates, and Scholars.* New York: Colombia University School of Social Work.

KAROLY, LYNN A.; GREENWOOD, PETER W; EVERINGHAM, SUSAN S.; HOUBÉ, JILL; KILBURN, M. REBECCA; RYDELL, C. PETER; SANDERS, MATTHEW; and CHIESA, JAMES. 1998. *Investing in Our Children: What We Know and Don't Know about the Costs and Benefits of Early Childhood Interventions.* Santa Monica, CA: Rand Corporation.

KAUL, VENITA. 1999. "Early Childhood Care and Education in the Context of EFA." Paper prepared for the World Bank.

KHATTAB, MOHAMMAD SAILB. 1995. *A Comprehensive Review of the Status of Early Childhood Development in the Middle East and North Africa.* Study prepared for the Education Section of UNICEF/Middle East and North Africa Regional Office, Amman, Jordan.

LUTHAR, SUNIYA; CICCHETTI, DANTE; and BECKER, BRONWYN. 2000. "The Construct of Resilience: A Critical Evaluation and Guidelines for Future Work." *Child Development* 71:543–562.

MALAWI, REPUBLIC OF. MINISTRY OF WOMEN, YOUTH AND COMMUNITY SERVICE. 1998. *National Early Childhood Development Policy.* (Mimeo.)

MYERS, ROBERT G. 1995. *The Twelve Who Survive: Strengthening Programs of Early Childhood Development in the Third World.* Ypsilanti, MI: High/Scope Educational Research Foundation.

MYERS, ROBERT G. 2000. "Early Childhood Care and Development." A thematic study prepared for the World Education Forum, Dakar, Senegal, 26–28 April 2000. Paris: United Nations Educational, Scientific and Cultural Organization.

ORTIZ, NELSON, et al. 1992. *Evaluación de los hogares comunitarios de bienestar. Informe técnico final.* Santafé de Bogotá, Colombia: Instituto Colombiano de Bienestar Familiar.

PENN, HELEN. 1999. "Researching in the Majority World: Is It Feasible or Ethical?" Paper presented to the Thomas Coram Research Institute, Institute of Education, University of London.

PERALTA, MARIA VICTORIA, and FUJIMOTO, GABY. 1998. *La atención integral de la primera infancia en América Latina: Ejes centrales y los desafíos para el siglo XXI.* Washington, DC: Organización de Estados Americanos.

SCHWEINHART, LAWRENCE, et al. 1993. *Significant Benefits: The High/Scope Perry Preschool Study through Age 27.* Ypsilanti, MI: High/Scope Educational Research Foundation.

SHORE, RIMA. 1997. *Rethinking the Brain: New Insights into Early Development.* New York: Families and Work Institute.

SYLVA, KATHY. 1995. "Research on Quality in Early Childhood Centres." Paper presented at the Mother-Child Education Foundation Conference, Istanbul, 19–20 October 1995. London: Institute of Education, University of London.

UNITED NATIONS CHILDREN'S FUND. 2002. *The State of the World's Children.* New York: United Nations Children's Fund.

UNITED NATIONS EDUCATIONAL, SCIENTIFIC AND CULTURAL ORGANIZATION. 1997. *Educating the Young Child in Europe.* Paris: United Nations Educational, Scientific and Cultural Organization.

UNITED NATIONS EDUCATIONAL, SCIENTIFIC AND CULTURAL ORGANIZATION. 1999a. *General Tendencies in Basic Education in Spanish, Portuguese and French Speaking Countries: Insufficient Performances.* Paris: United Nations Educational, Scientific and Cultural Organization.

UNITED NATIONS EDUCATIONAL, SCIENTIFIC AND CULTURAL ORGANIZATION. 1999b. *Report of Commission One: Early Childhood Care and Education* (Report on African Regional Meeting on Education for All, Johannesburg, 6–10 December 1999). Paris: United Nations Educational, Scientific and Cultural Organization.

WOODHEAD, MARTIN. 1996. *In Search of the Rainbow: Pathways to Quality in Large Scale Programs for Young Disadvantaged Children.* The Hague, Netherlands: Bernard van Leer Foundation.

ROBERT G. MYERS

EAST ASIA AND THE PACIFIC

The region of East Asia and the Pacific encompasses some of the richest and poorest nations in the world, as well as the largest (China) and some of the smallest (the island states). It includes states with most successful record of economic development in the late twentieth century—the high-performing Asian economies (HPAEs) of the Republic of Korea, Taiwan, Hong Kong (China), and Singapore—and those where growth has been fragile and disrupted by strife and natural disasters (Vietnam and Cambodia). Cultural, ethnic, and linguistic diversity exists throughout the region, both between and within countries. So also do different historic legacies, which influence the form, content, and future development of education.

There are a number of possible criteria that could be applied to groups of countries in this area that highlight some of these differences. Conventional geographical groupings can be useful, but conceal large variations in educational development, economic conditions, history, and culture. An alternative is to select a set of general indicators, which might include demographic factors (e.g. population size, population growth rates, measures of the rate of urbanization); levels of literacy; and economic status, which is determined by measures such as GNP (gross national product), GDP (PPP) (gross domestic product, based on purchasing power parity estimates), growth rates, and changes in the structure of employment. The Human Resource Development Index (HDI) of the United Nations Development Program (UNDP), based on measures of life expectancy, literacy, and real GDP per capita, is also potentially useful.

Using a combination of these characteristics, five groups of countries can be identified. The first group consists only of China, which stands on its own as a mega-state containing most of the region's population. China itself is very diverse, and includes areas where educational participation and achievement levels are very high (predominantly the coastal provinces), alongside parts where educational disadvantage is widespread and literacy levels are low (in the interior and among national minorities). The HDI is used by the UNDP to rank levels of development using an aggregate measure of life expectancy, literacy, and real GDP per capita. China in the early twenty-first century has an HDI rank of 87, placing it among other medium (49 to 127) human-development countries as does its GDP (PPP) per capita of $5,200. More than 35 percent of its population is urban, and it has a low population growth rate, creating a dependency ratio of less than 40 percent (the dependency ratio reflects the number of 0–14 year olds as a percentage of 15–65 year olds).

The second group includes the HPAEs (Korea, Taiwan, Hong Kong (China), and Singapore). These countries have an HDI rank between 24 and 27 (HDI not available for Taiwan), and more than 80 percent urban populations. GDP (PPP) per capita is more than $15,000, and the largest proportions of their labor force are employed in services. Malaysia shares many characteristics with this group, as does Brunei Darussalam. The former has experienced rapid sustained growth, ranks 56 on the HDI, and has a small (15%) and diminishing proportion of its labor force in agriculture. The latter has a high HDI ranking (32) and high levels of GNP per capita, with a labor force mostly concentrated in the service sector.

The third group comprises a collection of states that have HDI rankings between 50 and 100 (Indonesia, Philippines, and Thailand). These countries have low- to middle-levels of GDP (PPP) per capita, and most have experienced substantial levels of growth, have an average of about 50 percent of the labor force in agriculture, and generally low illiteracy. Thailand is both the richest and fastest growing nation in this group, but also has the lowest level of urbanization. Vietnam is also urbanizing and developing rapidly.

The fourth group of countries have HDI ranks from 120 to about 135, and all have lower GDP (PPP) per capita than those in the third group. On average, they have lower levels of urbanization and industrialization. Included in this group are Myanmar, Cambodia, and the Lao People's Democratic Republic. They are all low-income and low-growth countries, with less than 20 percent urbanization and predominantly agricultural economies—with the great majority of employment in this sector and little industrial production.

The Pacific Islands fall into the last grouping, though they are far from homogeneous. All have populations of less than one million, except Papua New Guinea, which shares historic and cultural links with many of the islands. HDI ranks are between 85 and 125 (for countries where HDI is available) with the exception of Fiji (67). Most of these countries have middle levels of GDP (PPP) per capita and low rates of urbanization. Countries in this group include Kiribati, Samoa, the Solomon Islands, Tonga,

Tuvalu, the Cook Islands, and Vanuatu. Table 1 presents basic data on countries in East Asia and the Pacific Islands and profiles population, national wealth, the length of school cycles, participation, and educational expenditure.

Some Key Issues

The key issues confronting these nations reflect different priorities, historic preferences, expectations about the future, and responses to changing exogenous circumstances. It is therefore difficult to look across East Asia and the Pacific Islands as if they were homogeneous. However, if there is some consensus that the purposes of public investment in education is intended to promote economic growth, improve equity in access to basic education services, enhance quality and internal efficiency, and respond to emerging needs, then several sets of issues suggest themselves as likely to be prominent across groups of countries.

First, educational investment in the region will be conditioned by the resources available and the sociopolitical environment in which choices are made. Macroeconomic conditions are likely to remain difficult in some countries (Cambodia, Laos, Myanmar, and Papua New Guinea and some other Pacific Islands). Growth in real GDP per capita (and hence the ability to invest in educational services) seems likely to be slow and unlikely to release substantial additional resources for educational investment. External assistance may have the biggest role to play in these countries. Indonesia has better prospects of real growth, as do Vietnam and the Philippines—assuming political stability is a reality. In these countries, national resources should be largely sufficient to support educational development if it is prioritized in public expenditure plans. The HPAEs, Malaysia, and Thailand should continue to experience sustained economic growth. This, coupled with falling proportions of school-age children and an increased propensity to invest private resources in education, should lead to rapid growth in higher levels of educational investment.

Second, in those countries where spending is relatively low as a proportion of GNP per capita and public budget, increased allocations may be a priority. This will especially be the case where what is currently delivered is manifestly inadequate. However, increasing spending in already inefficient systems has few attractions, unless the underlying sources of inefficiency are addressed simultaneously with en-

TABLE 1

Basic educational data: East Asia and the Pacific

	Population (thousands)	Population growth (percent)	Dependency 0–14/15–65 (percent)	Urban (percent)	Life expectancy	GNP per capita (U.S. $)	GDP (PPP) (Int. $)	HDI Rank
Asia								
Brunei Darussalam	308	2.6	54	69	76	—	—	32
Cambodia	10,478	2.8	78	20	53	300	1,290	121
China	1,244,202	1.1	38	30	70	860	3,070	87
China Hong Kong	6,511	1.9	26	95	78	25,200	24,350	24
Indonesia	203,380	1.5	50	35	65	1,110	3,390	102
Laos	5,032	2.8	85	21	53	400	1,300	131
Macau	450	2.7	36	99	78	—	—	—
Malaysia	20,983	2.3	58	54	72	4,530	7,730	56
Myanmar	43,936	1.2	46	26	60	—	—	118
Philippines	71,430	2.4	64	54	68	1,200	3,670	70
Korea	45,731	0.9	32	81	72	10,550	13,430	27
Singapore	3,427	1.8	31	100	77	32,810	29,230	26
Thailand	59,736	1.0	39	20	69	2,740	6,490	66
Vietnam	76,387	2.0	60	19	67	310	1,590	101
Oceania								
Cook Islands	19	0.6	—	60	—	—	—	—
Fiji	786	1.1	54	41	73	2,460	3,860	—
Kiribati	80	1.4	—	36	—	910	—	—
Papua New Guinea	4,499	2.3	68	16	58	930	—	122
Samoa	172	1.0	68	21	71	1,140	3,570	—
Solomon Islands	404	3.3	82	17	72	870	2,270	—
Tonga	98	0.3	—	41	—	1,810	—	—
Tuvalu	11	2.9	—	47	—	—	—	—
Vanuatu	177	2.5	80	19	67	1,340	3,230	—

	Primary years	Lower secondary years	Upper secondary years	Primary gross enrollment rate	Secondary gross enrollment rate	Primary pupil-teacher ratio	Secondary pupil-teacher ratio	Higher education students/ 100,000	Education expenditures (percent of GNP)	Education expenditures (percent of government budget)
Asia										
Brunei Darussalam	6	5	2	106	77	15	11	516	—	—
Cambodia	6	3	3	110	24	46	18	85	3	—
China	5	3	2	123	70	24	17	473	2	—
China Hong Kong	6	5	2	94	73	24	20	—	3	—
Indonesia	6	3	3	113	51	22	14	1,157	—	—
Laos	5	3	3	112	28	30	17	260	3	10.3
Macau	6	—	6	—	—	—	—	1,701	—	—
Malaysia	6	3	4	101	64	19	19	1,048	5	15.4
Myanmar	5	4	2	121	30	46	16	590	1	14.4
Philippines	6	—	4	114	77	35	32	2,958	3	17.6
Korea	6	3	3	94	102	31	25	6,106	4	17.5
Singapore	6	4	3	94	74	25	20	2,730	3	23.4
Thailand	6	3	3	87	56	—	—	2,252	5	—
Vietnam	5	4	3	113	47	32	29	678	3	—
Oceania										
Cook Islands	6	3	3	—	—	—	—	—	—	—
Fiji	6	—	6	—	—	—	—	—	—	—
Kiribati	7	—	5	—	—	24	17	—	11	—
Papua New Guinea	6	4	2	—	14	37	24	318	—	—
Samoa	8	3	2	—	62	24	19	—	—	—
Solomon Islands	6	3	2	100	17	24	—	—	—	—
Tonga	6	—	7	97	—	—	—	—	—	—
Tuvalu	8	4	—	—	—	—	—	—	—	—
Vanuatu	6	4	3	—	—	—	—	—	5	—

SOURCE: Based on data from United Nations Educational, Scientific and Cultural Organization, 2000.

hanced resource allocation. Where much less than 3 percent of GNP per capita is allocated (and less than 15 percent of the public budget), some reconsideration would seem desirable.

Third, where primary enrollment rates are significantly below 100 percent, especially where literacy is also low and gender differences are large, investment at the primary level should be a priority. The benefits for equity and economic development should be considerable. This is likely to be the most cost-effective way to improve adult literacy in the medium term, and one of the easiest ways to reduce gender inequity.

Fourth, internal efficiency needs improvement, both to extend the resources available to make increased access affordable, and to ensure better distribution of participation and achievement of valued outcomes. Where student–teacher ratios are high and very uneven across schools, these need to be reduced; where they are low, they may need increasing. Unequal investment that arises from wide differences in actual resource allocation (uneven teacher deployment and utilization, within-school preferences for spending on higher grades, heavy subsidy of some institutions and levels at the expense of others) is likely to suppress retention and on-schedule graduation rates, increase repetition, and enhance social selectivity and regressive subsidy related to household incomes. (A regressive subsidy is one that favors households with high income rather than low income.) Initiatives that decentralize control and finance may have a role to play in increasing efficiency and engaging the energies of stakeholders to improve quality and relevance, but they appear unlikely to be sufficient unless accompanied by appropriate checks and balances to encourage desired outcomes and monitor effects. Decentralization may be least attractive where infrastructure is weakest and incomes lowest.

Fifth, more effective educational management, administration, and monitoring—and steps to reverse regressive subsidies—can help provide better value and contribute to equity. Where it can be demonstrated that new incentive structures would work to improve quality without adverse effects that compromise their value, these should be incorporated into management systems.

Sixth, the public costs of secondary schooling should be limited to a small multiplier (no more than about 2:1) of those for primary education, unless there are strong contraindications. In those countries where primary schooling is not universalized, high secondary-unit costs may represent a poor allocation choice unless restricted to a small number of schools with open and fair selection. Where primary schooling of acceptable quality is becoming widely available, access to, and financing of, secondary schooling will become a dominant policy issue.

Seventh, higher-education policy can encourage more cost recovery from those who benefit. This appears to be the most plausible mechanism for expanding access in the face of growing demand without conceding a growing public subsidy to those most likely to enjoy above-average incomes subsequently. How this is implemented must be context sensitive, since in the poorer countries scope may be extremely limited and some possible mechanisms could result in counter-productive outcomes. Cross-border trading of educational services at the tertiary level is likely to grow rapidly, and may begin to have consequences for national institutions that become uncompetitive in cost and quality with institutions in other countries.

Eighth, education systems should be encouraged to respond to the changing characteristics of labor markets, in which there are an increasing proportion of service and manufacturing sector jobs. As these jobs become more knowledge and skill intensive, curricula, especially at the secondary level and above, need adaptation and redesign to promote outcomes valued in the marketplace. Traditional curricula need to be questioned to establish if they meet new needs and opportunities, and to balance domestic priorities for learning with those derived from educational development at an international level.

Prospects for the Future

It is difficult to predict the educational future of the countries in this region. History provides a reminder of how fragile foresight can be. Predictions of China's economic and educational growth, vocationalization of secondary schools, and increasingly autonomous higher education institutions with large numbers of fee-paying, self-supporting students entering into a burgeoning socialist market economy were conspicuously absent in 1975. Malaysia's rapid and sustained educational development was easier to anticipate. However, the successful contribution of education policy to maintaining stability, redistributing employment opportunities, and generating wealth surprised those critical of its strongly interventionist character under the country's New Economic Policy. Nevertheless, it is worth speculating how things will unfold as a way of drawing attention to some of the issues that will preoccupy future policymakers.

China

In much of China, access to six to nine years of education is assured, and enrollment rates are high, with gross enrollment rates (GERs) at the primary level over 125 percent (GER is the number enrolled over the size of the relevant age group; it can therefore exceed 100% because of overage enrollment and repetition). The main development agendas are improved internal efficiency, greater quality, and higher levels of achievement. Legislation has been in place since the mid-1980s to universalize enrollment, and this has largely been achieved. In the poorest areas and among the national minorities, underenrollment, high dropout rates, and substantial repetition remain a problem, but one manageable with domestic resources. Sustained rates of economic growth and generally low population growth (though not in many national minority areas) should facilitate the extension of the educational franchise. What will be achieved in basic education will depend on the political will to spread social benefits of development to areas that lag behind the coastal provinces and developed parts of central China.

At the secondary level, enrollments will continue to grow rapidly, to the point where most students will complete the lower secondary level in the near future. This will substantially increase rural enrollments. Participation rates at upper secondary schools will continue to expand, and will probably retain an emphasis on technical and vocational education, where the challenge is to maintain relevance to employment and develop a consistent certification system. Tertiary-level enrollments are likely to grow substantially to meet demand from students. Tertiary institutions will be consolidated into fewer and larger institutions, and will progressively take more responsibility for their own funding. It is probable that a core of universities, perhaps twenty or so, will remain directly supported as national institutions, and a similar-sized group will retain provincial government support. Most of the others will move away from the control of specific ministries and will have to seek mixed sources of funding. At the upper secondary and tertiary levels, it can be expected that fee systems will provide a growing proportion of operating costs, and the number of self-financing students will continue to increase.

Competition for access to secondary *key schools* (schools with selective entry for the most able children, and which have additional resources and high-quality teachers) will intensify, as it will for entry to associated primary schools and to prestigious universities. Providing access in ways that are seen as equitable and socially efficient will be an important issue. In many respects, China will probably move towards patterns of participation and access found in several of the HPAEs, while retaining and developing a large range of educational delivery services using the media, adult study programs, and training related to the workplace.

During the early twenty-first century, China will experience the effects of rapid urbanization (which was already well advanced in 2000) and an aging population. The former will concentrate more and more educational services in towns and cities, and may exacerbate the problem of the relative neglect of educational development in rural areas. The aging population will ultimately cause the dependency ratio to rise (in this case, dependency ratio includes those over sixty-five), with possible consequences for the amounts available to subsidize public educational provision.

The HPAEs

Among the high-performing Asian economies, economic growth has been strong, despite temporary setbacks in the late 1990s. Population growth rates are low and declining, enrollments are approaching universal levels at the primary and secondary levels, illiteracy only exists on the margins, and distribution of public expenditure is fairly even. At the primary and lower secondary levels, enrollments are likely to fall for demographic reasons, creating further opportunities to improve quality and enrich curricula offerings. Student–teacher ratios may continue to decline slowly, and at the primary level are likely to converge towards those at the secondary level. Private provision is likely to continue to grow, both in separate schools and in parallel systems providing complementary services. Preschool enrollments will increase rapidly (mostly outside state provision) as a result of available income continuing to rise, parental investments in schooling being concentrated on fewer children, and strong beliefs in the value of a head start in schooling.

At the secondary level, school facilities are often good and will continue to improve, especially in relation to access to new information technologies.

Skill-based and competency-linked curricula are likely to spread, and links with changing patterns of employment, especially the continued growth of the service sector, will have an impact on teaching and learning. Some of these countries appear to have low between-school variations in achievement, while in others the school attended seems to account for much of the variation in performance in particular subjects. Differences between schools may be expected to diminish as resource distribution ceases to be a major constraint and competitive pressures improve the performance of lower-achieving schools.

Competition for access to higher education is likely to intensify, though participation rates will increase to levels where a majority of the population experience some post-school periods of study and training. The competition will center on the most prestigious institutions at home and abroad. The tertiary sector as a whole is likely to become more diversified and accessible to a wide range of students, including those in midcareer and those in nontraditional fields of specialization. Cross-border flows of students will also increase both from HPAEs to richer countries and from other Asian countries to HPAEs. Private financing and mixed systems of support will develop where these are not already dominant, and where they are already substantial they will grow further. The integration of Hong Kong's education system into China may influence the rate of change in Chinese institutions, particularly at the tertiary level.

Middle- and Low-Income Countries

In middle-income countries with industrialization already under way, several scenarios are possible. In Thailand and Indonesia, survival rates up until the fourth grade are high, and enrollment rates are approaching universal levels for all primary grades. Quality remains a problem, as does repetition and the number of dropouts. Uneven resource distribution remains a critical issue, and urbanization will result in more resources being needed for city and town schools. In these countries a demographic transition to low growth is already established, and universal access to a basic education cycle is achievable by 2020. Enrollment rates at the secondary level will increase, especially in Thailand and Indonesia, and it is here that the resource demands are likely to be largest. Malaysia will converge towards the educational characteristics of the HPAEs, with which it now has much in common. Higher education

growth will occur, especially in privately financed institutions, which already enroll large numbers in the Philippines, Indonesia, and Thailand.

Poorer Asian countries with a developing industrial base include Myanmar and Vietnam. Myanmar's development will be partly determined by the extent to which it adopts reforms similar to those in surrounding countries, which would lead to increased resources for education and higher participation rates. Vietnam is rapidly modernizing, and economic growth and industrialization are taking place. Secondary school participation rates will start to rise, and tertiary-level enrollment is likely to begin to grow rapidly.

The poorest agriculturally based countries confront the most difficult conditions. Basic educational infrastructure is impoverished, resources for growth are heavily constrained, and needs are greatest. School provision is predominantly rural, retention is poor, repetition is high, and illiteracy widespread. These fundamental realties will condition educational development (e.g., in Cambodia and Laos) and should focus attention on building basic delivery systems with reasonable coverage and quality. Expansion at higher levels that utilizes public funding should probably be deferred until greater proportions of the population acquire basic skills.

In most of the Pacific Islands, primary enrollment rates are high, except in Papua New Guinea, where there is some way to travel to reach universal access. Fiji stands out as having high levels of enrollment. There are problems associated with small populations in these countries, and most will continue to send students overseas for higher education. Migration will also affect demand in many of these states, and curriculum will remain dependent and derived from larger and richer metropolitan countries, many of which receive high levels of external support for education and have close links with larger countries that sponsor educational development and receive students and migrant labor.

Conclusion

This short review has highlighted some of the main characteristics of education in East Asia and the Pacific Islands. It gives some of the flavor of the diversity of circumstances, current problems, and future developments. In particular, it distinguishes five broad groups of countries at different points in their development. The challenges these groups face are somewhat different. However, across the region there is cause for optimism that educational participation will grow and become more equitable, quality will improve, and labor markets will benefit from more and more investment in the skills and competencies associated with education and training. This will be accelerated by governments that maintain stability, prioritize educational investment, judiciously take advantage of opportunities created by globalization, learn from the experience of the HPAEs, and capitalize on the special characteristics of each national system.

See also: EASTERN EUROPE AND CENTRAL ASIA; INTERNATIONAL EDUCATION; POPULATION AND EDUCATION; SOUTH ASIA.

BIBLIOGRAPHY

BEHRMAN, JERE, and SCHNEIDER, RYAN. 1994. "An International Perspective on Schooling Investments in the Last Quarter Century in Some Fast-Growing East and Southeast Asian Countries." *Asian Development Review* 12(2):1–50.

COLCLOUGH, CHRISTOPHER, and LEWIN, KEITH M. 1993. *Educating All the Children; Strategies for Primary Education in the South.* New York: Oxford University Press.

CUMMINGS, WILLIAM K. 1997. "Private Education in Eastern Asia." In *The Challenge of Eastern Asia Education,* ed. William K. Cummings and Philip G. Altbach. Albany: State University of New York.

LEWIN, KEITH M. 1997. "The Sea of Items Returns to China; Backwash, Selection, and the Diploma Disease Revisited." *Journal of Assessment in Education* 4(1).

LEWIN, KEITH M. 1998. "Education and Development in Asia: Issues in Planning, Policy and Finance." *Asian Development Review* 15(1).

LEWIN, KEITH M. 1998. "Education in Emerging Asia; Patterns, Policies and Futures into the 21st Century." *International Journal of Educational Development* 18(2):81–119.

LEWIN, KEITH M., and WANG, YING JIE. 1994. *Implementing Basic Education in China: Progress and Prospects in Rich, Poor, and National Minority Areas.* Paris: International Institute for Educational Planning.

TAN, JEE-PENG, and MINGAT, ALAIN. 1992. *Education in Asia: A Comparative Study of Costs and Financing.* Washington, DC: World Bank Regional and Sectoral Studies.

UNITED NATIONS DEVELOPMENT PROGRAM. 2001. *Human Development Report 2001.* New York: United Nations Development Program.

UNITED NATIONS EDUCATIONAL, SCIENTIFIC AND CULTURAL ORGANIZATION. 2001. *World Education Report 2000.* Paris: UNESCO.

WOODHALL, MAUREEN. *Turning Point in the Development of Higher Education in Asia: A Comparative Study of Alternative Patterns of Provision, Financing, and Governance, 1960–1990.* Washington, DC: World Bank.

WORLD BANK. 1993. *The East Asian Miracle: Economic Growth and Public Policy.* Washington, DC: World Bank.

KEITH M. LEWIN

EASTERN EUROPE AND CENTRAL ASIA

The Europe and Central Asia (ECA) region includes Central Europe (the Czech Republic, Hungary, Poland, and the Slovak Republic), Southeast Europe (Albania, Bulgaria, and Romania), the Baltic States (Estonia, Latvia, and Lithuania), the western Commonwealth of Independent States (Belarus, Moldova, Russia, and Ukraine), the Caucasus (Armenia, Azerbaijan, and the Republic of Georgia), former Yugoslavia (Slovenia, Croatia, Republic of Macedonia, Bosnia and Herzegovina, and the Federal Republic of Yugoslavia), and the Central Asian republics (Kazakhstan, Kyrgyzstan, Tajikistan, Turkmenistan, and Uzbekistan). In the early 1990s, the countries of the ECA began a transition from command economies to market economies. As the transition began, the countries had reason to take pride in their education systems. They had solved educational problems that still bedeviled several other regions of the world. Adult literacy was generally universal; participation and completion rates for children and youth of both genders were high at all levels of education; teachers came to work; students had textbooks; students in countries that participated in international assessments of mathematics and science performed well; school dropout rates and rates of grade repetition were low.

In the early 1990s, therefore, education seemed so secure that it could safely be ignored as countries faced the staggering problems of collapsing economies, fragile democracies, unproductive state-owned enterprises, and rapidly increasing poverty. Within ten years that reality changed. ECA education systems joined the ranks of the deeply troubled sectors.

New Rules for Education in the ECA Region

The rules for market economies and open political systems differ from those for command economies and authoritarian political systems. For example, the continuous changes characteristic of market economies and the ambiguities of a democracy require such skills as knowing how to learn, problem solving, and evaluating. Most ECA education systems, however, focus on memorized factual and procedural knowledge, which is adequate for the predictability of a planned economy and the dogma of authoritarianism but not for the volatility of a market economy or the choices required of citizens in democracies.

Analyses of the education systems of ECA identified five central problems:

- Alignment: Educational quality is contextual; it is not a constant under all conditions. ECA education systems that were a good fit with planned economies and authoritarian political systems do not fit well with open market economies and open political systems.

- Fairness: Education is an important mechanism for reducing and preventing poverty. Differences in children's learning opportunities are emerging in ECA countries at that very point in the region's history when skills and knowledge increasingly determine a family's poverty status.

- Financing: ECA countries need to realign the financing of their education systems with fiscal realities without jeopardizing the fairness and quality of educational services. Their failure to rationalize education finance is eroding the achievements of the pretransition period.

- Efficiency: Most ECA education systems use inputs inefficiently. These inefficiencies are the legacy of centrally planned economies, where prices and budgets did not affect allocation decisions.

- Governance, management, and accountability: Most ECA education systems do not perform well against standards of transparent and effective governance, efficient management, and vigorous accountability to a range of stakeholders.

The sector is still dominated by governments unchecked by private sector competition and participation of stakeholders.

These problems were found to apply at all levels of education, but they play out in different ways at each level.

The Economic Imperative

Both economic and civic imperatives for ECA countries define how their education systems will have to adapt. In regard to the economic imperative, the region is undergoing three radical economic shifts: (1) from centrally planned to market economies; (2) from protected trade based on politics to global trade based on economic comparative advantage; and (3) from mass production to flexible, or customized, production.

Market economy. The implications of a market economy for education are significantly different from those of a planned economy, but they are fairly easy to see. In market economies wages reflect skills and knowledge; in planned economies, there is little relationship between the two.

Globalization. Integrating into the global economy imposes a discipline on domestic producers by increasing competition and clarifying comparative advantages. It is a stimulus for doing what producers have to do anyway in order to raise productivity, which is the key to higher wages and higher standards of living. Globalization, in conjunction with the flexible production of goods and services and expanded and cheaper communication and transport systems, gives customers more choice. Thus, moving into the global economy raises the standards for goods and services that suppliers have to meet. These higher standards prevail even within suppliers' domestic markets, because standards "leak" back and forth across national boundaries in the form of traded goods and services.

Flexible production. Moving from mass production to the flexible production of goods and services changes the opportunities and ultimately the basis for economic growth. Computerized technologies have revolutionized production by allowing both long and short production runs that can respond to niche or customized markets at the cost savings of mass production.

Employer responses. Globalization and flexible production have combined to change the profile of customer demand for manufactured goods, agricultural products, and services. Customers have come to expect a large, varied, and continuously improving basket of goods and services, fast delivery of orders, high and consistent quality, and low prices. To meet these demands, employers have to change technologies and the organization of work. Mass production of goods and services depended on routinization and a hierarchical specialization of function, where most workers, even middle managers, were order takers. Workers were not expected to exercise judgment, initiative, or problem-solving skills, and most decisions were referred up the chain of command. This productive regime was predicated on slow rates of change that minimized the need for adult learning.

Under flexible production, however, employers broaden job descriptions to give each worker authority over more of the component tasks of production. Employers flatten organizational hierarchies and introduce job rotation and team-based work. These changes save the time lost by referring decisions up and down organizational ladders; they reduce middle management and supervisory jobs. The jobs of less-skilled workers begin to incorporate some of the supervisory, planning, repair, maintenance, and quality-control functions previously reserved for managers or specialists.

Worker skills required. In this context workers need solid literacy or information-processing and interpretive skills, better problem-solving skills, better knowing-how-to-learn skills, and greater initiative. Advanced economies confront increasing unemployment rates and falling wages for those with low educational qualifications.

Status of ECA countries. Evidence from the Organisation for Economic Co-operation and Development (OECD) International Adult Literacy Survey (IALS) suggests that the region's education systems are a poor fit with modern economies. Four ECA countries—Hungary, Slovenia, Poland, and the Czech Republic—have participated in the IALS. Of these four, three—Hungary, Slovenia, and Poland—seriously lag OECD countries in the information-processing and interpretive skills that modern economies require of their citizens.

A comparison of the IALS data for the low-performing ECA countries with those for the strong ECA performer (the Czech Republic) and with participating OECD countries tells an important story. First of all, in Hungary, Slovenia, and Poland, very high percentages of workers aged sixteen to sixty-five tested at levels one and two on the prose, document, and quantitative scales, with about 75 percent of the workers in each of the three countries testing below level three on the prose scale. Scores at or above level three predict the ability of a person to function in a modern workplace.

The differences between the tested skills of adults in Hungary, Poland, and Slovenia and those of Czech adults and adults in participating OECD countries cannot be attributed to the *quantity* of education that low-performing ECA populations complete.

The performances of those still in, or recently graduated from, school reflect most pertinently on the quality of their country's education system. Substantially higher percentages of twenty- to twenty-five-year-olds in Hungary, Poland, and Slovenia tested at lower literacy levels than those of the same age group in the Czech Republic and participating OECD countries, indicating that education systems of the transition countries are not producing the skills that new entrants into the workplace will need as these workplaces modernize.

Multivariate analyses show that parental socioeconomic status has a significantly greater effect on scores in the three low-performing ECA countries than in the Czech Republic and OECD countries. Apparently, education policy in these three ECA countries is not designed to minimize the effect of parental background and may operate to reinforce it via mechanisms such as early tracking.

The Civic Imperative

For decades ECA countries were ruled by authoritarian regimes that controlled their populations through fear and the deliberate creation and manipulation of distrust. In the posttransition era, ECA schools can be important weapons for socializing children to the rights and obligations of citizenship and for developing the trust among groups that leads to a willingness to cooperate across the boundaries that normally divides the groups (e.g., clan, ethnic or religious membership)—provided that the political context supports these values.

Increasing Inequality in Education

In the pretransition period learning opportunities were inequitable, but given the region's wage compression (the lack of variation in wages), unequal access to education had little effect on family income.

Unequal learning opportunities matter more in ECA countries in the early twenty-first century because education matters more. Skills and knowledge affect individuals' earnings, unemployment probabilities, and likelihood of receiving wage-enhancing training from employers. Because the education acquired by parents affects that acquired by their children, lower levels of education in one generation can ignite intergenerational cycles of poverty through the intergenerational transmission of lower levels of skills and knowledge.

Statistical relationships are emerging in the ECA region between educational attainment and such outcomes as employment status, wage level, and poverty. Figures from 1993 to 1998 show that households whose heads had completed only basic education were 20 to 80 percent more likely to be poor than the average household.

Declining enrollment rates. Enrollment rates, the best available measure of learning opportunities in ECA countries, are declining at all levels except at the tertiary level (see Table 1). These enrollment rates indicate that a larger number of young people are building fewer skills and less knowledge and a smaller number are building more. Calculations show a decline in the number of years of full-time education (excluding preschool) that the average six-year-old child in the ECA region can expect to achieve over her lifetime. In 1989 the average full-time school expectancy was 11.2 years; by 1997 it had declined to 10.6 years. In contrast, the average full-time school expectancy for OECD countries in 1998 was 15.4 years.

The secondary vocational/technical track accounts for enrollment losses at the secondary level. Enrollment declines at this level signal emerging educational inequalities of particular significance because a solid upper-secondary education increases the chances of acquiring the skills required in modern workplaces.

Relationships between enrollment rates and family income and education costs. Results of poverty assessments show that youth from poorer and less well-educated families in the ECA region are likely to leave school before completing basic education or at the time of its completion. Because students from poorer families tend to select the technical/vocational track, losses out of upper-secondary education are concentrated among poorer families. As a result, upper-secondary enrollments are becoming increasingly biased in favor of the nonpoor.

TABLE 1

Gross enrollment rates in Europe and Central Asia by level of education, 1989–1997

Level of Education	Year	
	1989	1997
Preschool	51.4	41.0
Basic	94.4	90.6
Upper secondary	71.4	61.3
Academic	26.2	27.4
Vocational/technical	45.2	33.8
Tertiary	13.1	17.8
Expected years of education completed	**11.2**	**10.6**

SOURCE: Based on data from World Bank. 2000. *Making Transition Work for Everyone: Poverty and Inequality in Europe and Central Asia.* Washington, DC: World Bank, Europe and Central Asia Region, Human Development Sector Unit.

ECA countries have substantial poverty overall, and income inequality is growing as a predictable and inevitable consequence of the shift to market economies where demand, not central wage-setting, determines the price for labor. Greater income inequality translates into less-equal abilities to pay the costs of education. Early studies indicate that education is costing families more than before the transition, although costs vary by country and among jurisdictions within countries. These studies also show that poor families are paying a higher percentage of per capita consumption for education than nonpoor families. Not surprisingly, the countries and jurisdictions that are under the greatest fiscal pressures are shifting costs to families more than those that are less fiscally constrained. Unfortunately, it is just these countries and jurisdictions that tend to have higher levels of family poverty.

Problems Stemming from the Financing Structure

Since the transition, the education systems in many ECA countries have been experiencing serious fiscal constraints that will almost certainly persist for the foreseeable future. Governments have yet to reconcile their education sectors with fiscal realities without jeopardizing education outcomes and fairness of educational opportunities.

The resource imbalance in the sector stems from three causes: (1) macroeconomic declines have reduced total public funds available for education; (2) the removal of subsidies and price distortions has led to market-based pricing for inputs, particularly for energy; and (3) major inefficiencies inherited from the pretransition period are pervasive in the sector, a problem discussed in the efficiency section below.

Following the disintegration of the Soviet Union, macroeconomic conditions deteriorated dramatically in all ECA countries. Most countries in Central Europe and the Baltics have subsequently recovered, but the rest of the region continues to face macroeconomic decline or stagnation. Countries experiencing declines in gross domestic product (GDP) have tended to react by reducing public spending on education even more rapidly, causing not only an absolute decline but also a decline in the ratio of public education spending to GDP.

How have education sectors reacted to budget pressures? ECA governments and local education authorities have not yet adjusted effectively to reduced funding (in some cases) or to increased prices (in all cases). Instead, they have tended to take temporary measures that only paper over fiscal shortfalls and that tend to delay genuine adjustment. Such temporary measures, which increase the eventual costs of adjustment and undermine education outcomes and fairness, include:

- continuing to defer building maintenance, thereby borrowing from the future at exorbitant interest rates because it will cost much more to rehabilitate schools in the future than it would to repair them in the present
- cutting the purchase of teaching materials and equipment
- saving on heating bills by closing schools
- allowing teachers' wage rates to fall relative to other wages
- shifting financing responsibilities to local governments that lack adequate taxing authorities to pay schooling costs
- running up arrears in energy bills and teacher wages
- shifting costs of education to families

The Command Economies' Legacy of Inefficiency

Depending on the country, ECA countries may consume at least double the resources employed per basic and secondary student in the West. The most egregious examples of the inefficient use of resources are space norms per student, utility consumption, and labor inputs. Many of the inefficiencies are a legacy of pretransition economies when planners, not market forces, determined wages, subsidies, and prices. There were no mechanisms for determining the total costs of anything and therefore no incentives to contain costs.

Schools in the ECA region were not built to conserve energy and consume, on average, between two and three times as much energy as modern school buildings in OECD countries. For example, the average Danish school consumes about 100 kilowatt-hours per square meter per year, in contrast to Latvia's typical 285 kilowatt-hours per square meter per year. Now that energy is being priced at market levels, the percentage of education budgets devoted to energy has increased from less than 5 percent to between 25 and 40 percent, depending on the severity of the climate.

Staffing norms inherited from the pretransition period mean that the proportion of teachers to students is two or three times as great as in OECD countries. Low at the start of the transition, student/teacher ratios worsened over the next decade for most ECA countries. The ECA practice of using single-subject teachers after the primary grades fuels labor inefficiencies, given that highly specialized resources of any kind are more difficult to allocate efficiently. Although data on nonteaching staff are not generally available, limited data hint at further inefficiencies in the countries that had comprised the Soviet Union. For example, in 1999 Moldova had a ratio for all levels of education of 1.35 nonteaching staff to one teacher.

Total fertility rates for all ECA countries declined dramatically between 1989 and 1997, falling from 2.1 to 1.3 children per family in all ECA countries except Albania and the Central Asian republics. Thus, at least in the short- to medium term, ECA education systems are sized for more children than will be going through them, adding to the need to downsize inputs.

Failures in Governance, Management, and Accountability

Because the state takes actions in education on behalf of its citizens and taxpayers, it must respond to questions about how well it represents their interests. Is the education sector doing the right things? Is it doing the right things right? What mechanisms do stakeholders have to hold the state accountable for its actions?

The answers to these questions lie in the sector's arrangements for governance, management, and accountability. Unfortunately, ECA education systems tend to fail spectacularly on these three key dimensions. Improving these functions seems to be absolutely essential for straightening out other problems of the sector.

Governance—goal setting and monitoring. Major changes in context, such as ECA countries are experiencing, normally force countries to rethink and debate goals for their education systems. The discussion in the ECA region is not well focused, however, and only the most progressive countries in the region have moved toward goals that are practical rather than focusing on vague ideals.

Management. Countries can vary in how they distribute responsibilities and powers among levels of government and still secure reasonably efficient service. In the ECA region's education sector, however, the responsibilities of management tend to be allocated to different levels of government in ways that are contradictory, unclear, or duplicated within or between levels; the responsibilities are often misaligned with the availability of resources, or they may be missing altogether. For example, even in centralized education systems, ministers often do not perform functions that should be centralized, such as leading improvement efforts, setting learning standards and ensuring educational quality, monitoring performance, and ensuring educational fairness.

Even where functions and decision-making powers are complete and sensibly allocated among levels of government, functions may be performed well or poorly. In the ECA region, the performance of functions in the education sector falls woefully short of good international practice.

Accountability. The key to accountability in education is a checks-and-balances relationship among the interests of three groups: the public sector (government and professional educators), the private sector, and the civic society (taxpayers, users, and beneficiaries). Each of these three actors plays according to different rules. The public sector uses rules and standards to establish the framework for service delivery; the private sector uses competition and choice; and the civic society uses participation or "voice."

Analyses show that the state cannot be trusted to supply educational goods and services efficiently without the competitive checks of markets or the exercise of voice by beneficiaries. These same studies, however, also show that efficiency and responsiveness decline if any one of these players dominates. Mechanisms for strengthening accountability carry their own distortions. Thus, it is the checks and balances among the three mechanisms that result in the most efficient and responsive provision of services.

In ECA the state dominates the sector. Competition in the form of private provision and contracting out of services is still in its infancy. Voice is a very weak reed in the region. Several ECA countries impose legal or political constraints on mechanisms for expressing voice—such as constraints on the press.

See also: GLOBALIZATION AND EDUCATION; GOVERNMENT AND EDUCATION, THE CHANGING ROLE OF.

BIBLIOGRAPHY

BERRYMAN, SUE E. 1997. *Preparing for the Global Economy: Focus on Educational Quality.* Washington, DC: World Bank.

BERRYMAN, SUE E., and BAILEY, THOMAS. 1992. *The Double Helix of Education and the Economy.* New York: Institute on Education and the Economy, Teachers College, Columbia University.

COUNCIL OF EUROPE. 2001. *Recent Demographic Developments in Europe.* Strasbourg, France: Council of Europe Publishing.

EUROPEAN BANK FOR RECONSTRUCTION AND DEVELOPMENT. 1994–. *Transition Report.* London: European Bank for Reconstruction and Development.

ISHIDA, HIROSHI; MULLER, WALTER; and RIDGE, JOHN. 1995. "Class Origin, Class Destination, and Education: A Cross-National Study of Ten Industrial Nations." *American Journal of Sociology* 101:145–193.

JOHNSTONE, D. BRUCE; ARORA, ALKA; and EXPERTON, WILLIAM. 1998. *The Financing and Management of Higher Education: A Status Report on Worldwide Reforms.* Washington, DC: World Bank.

KEEFER, PHILIP. 1998. *Contracting Out: An Opportunity for Public Sector Reform and Private Sector Development in Transition Economies.* Washington, DC: World Bank, Development Research Group.

KING, ELIZABETH M. 1995. *Does the Price of Schooling Matter? Fees, Opportunity Costs, and Enrollment in Indonesia.* Washington, DC: World Bank.

KNACK, STEPHEN, and KEEFER, PHILIP. 1997. "Does Social Capital Have an Economic Payoff? A Cross-Country Investigation." *Quarterly Journal of Economics* 112:1251–1288.

MILANOVIC, BRANKO. 1998. *Income, Inequality, and Poverty during the Transition from Planned to Market Economy.* Washington, DC: World Bank.

MINCER, JACOB. 1993. "Job Training, Wage Growth, and Labor Turnover." In *Studies in Human Capital,* ed. Jacob Mincer. Brookfield, VT: Edward Elgar.

ORGANISATION FOR ECONOMIC CO-OPERATION AND DEVELOPMENT. 1992–. *Education at a Glance: OECD Indicators.* Paris: Centre for Educational Research and Innovation.

ORGANISATION FOR ECONOMIC CO-OPERATION AND DEVELOPMENT. 1997. *Literacy Skills for the Knowledge Society.* Paris: Organisation for Economic Co-operation and Development; Ottawa: Human Resources Development Canada.

ORGANISATION FOR ECONOMIC CO-OPERATION AND DEVELOPMENT. 1998. *Human Capital Investment: An International Comparison.* Paris: Centre for Educational Research and Innovation.

ORGANISATION FOR ECONOMIC CO-OPERATION AND DEVELOPMENT. 2000. *Literacy in the Information Age.* Paris: Organisation for Economic Co-operation and Development; Ottawa: Human Resources Development Canada.

PALOMBA, GEREMIA, and VODOPIVEC, MILAN. 2000. *Efficiency, Equity, and Fiscal Impact of Education in Albania.* Washington, DC: World Bank, Europe and Central Asia Region, Human Development Unit and Development Research Group.

PRUD'HOMME, REMY. 1995. "The Dangers of Decentralization." *World Bank Research Observer* 10(2):201–220.

RESNICK, LAUREN B. 1987. *Education and Learning to Think.* Washington, DC: National Academy Press.

RINGOLD, DENA. 2000. *Roma and the Transition in Central and Eastern Europe: Trends and Challenges.* Washington, DC: World Bank, Europe and Central Asia Region, Human Development Unit.

SHORE, RIMA. 1997. *Rethinking the Brain: New Insights into Early Development.* New York: Families and Work Institute.

STATE INSTITUTE OF STATISTICS OF TURKEY. 1995. *The Population of Turkey, 1923–1994: Demographic Structure and Development.* Ankara: Republic of Turkey, Prime Ministry.

STATE INSTITUTE OF STATISTICS OF TURKEY. 1997. *Statistical Yearbook of Turkey.* Ankara: Republic of Turkey, Prime Ministry.

STATE INSTITUTE OF STATISTICS OF TURKEY. 1999. *National Education Statistics, 1996–1997: Formal Education.* Ankara: Republic of Turkey, Prime Ministry.

UNITED NATION'S CHILDREN'S FUND. 1998. *Education for All?* Florence, Italy: UNICEF International Child Development Center.

WILLMS, J. DOUGLAS. 1999. *Literacy Skills in Poland.* Fredericton, New Brunswick, Canada: University of New Brunswick, Atlantic Centre for Policy Research.

WORLD BANK. 1989–. *World Development Indicators.* Washington, DC: World Bank.

WORLD BANK. 1996. *Armenia: Confronting Poverty Issues.* Washington, DC: World Bank.

WORLD BANK. 1996. *Estonia Living Standards during the Transition.* Washington, DC: World Bank.

WORLD BANK. 1997. *Azerbaijan Poverty Assessment.* 2 vols. Washington, DC: World Bank.

WORLD BANK. 1997. *Romania: Poverty and Social Policy.* Washington, DC: World Bank.

WORLD BANK. 1997. *World Development Report, 1997: The State in a Changing World.* New York: Oxford University Press.

WORLD BANK. 1998. *Georgia: Education Sector Strategy Note.* Washington, DC: World Bank, Europe and Central Asia Region, Human Development Sector Unit.

WORLD BANK. 1999. *Bulgaria: Poverty during the Transition.* Washington, DC: World Bank, Europe and Central Asia Region, Human Development Sector Unit.

WORLD BANK. 1999. *Civil Service Reform: A Review of World Bank Assistance.* Washington, DC: World Bank, Operations Evaluation Department.

WORLD BANK. 1999. *Former Yugoslav Republic of Macedonia: Focusing on the Poor.* Washington, DC: World Bank, Europe and Central Asia Region, Human Development Sector Unit.

WORLD BANK. 1999. *Georgia Poverty and Income Distribution.* 2 vols. Washington, DC: World Bank, Europe and Central Asia Region, Poverty Reduction and Economic Management Sector Unit.

WORLD BANK. 1999. *Russia: Regional Education Study.* Washington, DC: World Bank, Europe and Central Asia Region, Human Development Sector Unit.

WORLD BANK. 2000. *Albania's Education Sector: Problems and Promise.* Washington, DC: World Bank, Europe and Central Asia Region, Human Development Sector Unit.

WORLD BANK. 2000. *Making Transition Work for Everyone: Poverty and Inequality in Europe and Central Asia.* Washington, DC: World Bank, Europe and Central Asia Region, Human Development Sector Unit.

SUE BERRYMAN

ECONOMIC BENEFITS OF EDUCATION INVESTMENT, MEASUREMENT

The concept of the rate of return on investment in education is very similar to that for any other investment. It is a summary of the costs and benefits of the investment incurred at different points in time, and it is expressed in an annual (percentage) yield, similar to that quoted for savings accounts or government bonds.

Returns on investment in education based on human capital theory have been estimated since the late 1950s. Human capital theory puts forward the concept that investments in education increase future productivity. There have been thousands of estimates, from a wide variety of countries; some based on studies done over time and some based on new econometric techniques. All reaffirm the importance of human capital theory.

The rise in earnings inequality, and the subsequent increase in the returns on schooling experienced during the 1980s and 1990s in many countries, led to renewed interest in estimates of returns on educational investment. The literature suggests that systematic changes in the production process brought about by changes in technology and the growth of the knowledge-based economy whereby product cycles become shorter and flexibility is needed, led to changes in the demand for skilled labor.

An Illustration

For illustrative purposes, assume that an eighteen-year-old secondary-school graduate is driven only by monetary considerations in deciding whether or not to invest in a four-year university degree. Such a student will have to contemplate and compare the costs and benefits associated with going to college. The cost per year for tuition and other related expenses ($10,000 in this hypothetical case) is the *direct cost.* In addition, the student will incur an indirect (or opportunity) cost because he or she will not be able to work while attending college. This cost is approximated by what the average student with a secondary school diploma earns in the labor market, perhaps $20,000 per year. On the benefits side, the student expects to be making, on average, approximately $15,000 more than a secondary school graduate over his or her lifetime after graduating from college.

A rough way to summarize the above costs and benefits is to divide the annual benefit of $15,000 by the lump-sum cost of $120,000, yielding a 12.5 percent rate of return on investment in education. The logic of this calculation is similar to that of buying a $120,000 bond giving an annual coupon of $15,000. The yield of the bond is 12.5 percent.

Private Versus Social Costs

A very important distinction in rate of return calculations is whether one evaluates the private cost or the social cost of an education. The example given above refers to a private rate of return, where the costs are what the individual actually pays in order to receive an education. A social rate of return calculation includes, on the cost side, the full resource cost of one's education. That is, it includes not only what the individual pays, but also what it really costs society to educate one person. In most countries education is heavily subsidized, so the social cost is much higher than the private cost. The social rate of return, therefore, is typically less than the corresponding private rate of return.

Beyond the above monetary calculations used to arrive at a private rate of return, the social rate of return should ideally include the externalities associated with education. This is, of course, extremely difficult to measure, and the issue of externalities has remained a qualification accompanying rate of return estimates—in the sense that such rates, as conventionally computed on the basis of monetary earnings and costs, must underestimate the true social return on investment in education.

The earnings of educated individuals do not reflect the external benefits that affect society as a whole. Such benefits are known as *externalities* or *spillover benefits,* since they spill over to other members of the community. They are often hard to identify and even harder to measure. In the case of education, some studies have succeeded in identifying positive externalities, but few have been able to quantify them. If one could include externalities, then social rates of return might well be higher than private rates of return on education.

Empirical Findings

Typically, returns on educational investment are higher at lower levels of schooling and also higher for countries at lower levels of economic development. The scarcity of human capital in low-income countries provides a significant premium to investing in education. The high returns on primary education provide an added justification for making education a priority in developing countries.

In low-income countries, the returns are high, as can be seen in Table 1, which presents an illustrative summary of typical rates of return. Estimates of rates of return over a range of country types show the usual pattern most researchers find. For low-income countries, rates of return can be as high as 12 percent or more. In middle-income countries similar estimates can be found. In many eastern European transition economies, returns are relatively low, but rising. In high-income countries, rates of return on education tend to be lower than in lower-income countries. However, during the 1980s and 1990s returns on schooling increased in these countries, especially in the United States.

Private rates of return are higher than social returns. This is because of the public subsidization of education and the fact that typical social rate of return estimates are not able to include social benefits. Nevertheless, the degree of public subsidization increases with the level of education, which has regressive policy implications. Illustrative rates of return for a variety of countries are shown in Table 2. Higher education remains a profitable investment for individuals in high-income countries, as represented by the private rate of return. There is an even greater private incentive to invest in education in middle- and low-income countries. In these countries the social returns on education are particularly high, signaling a priority investment for society.

Overall, women receive higher returns on their schooling investments, though the returns on primary education are much higher for men (20%) than for women (13%). Women experience higher returns on secondary education (18% versus 14%, respectively).

The highest returns on a per-country basis are recorded for low- and middle-income countries. Overall, the average rate of return on another year of schooling is about 10 percent. From 1990 to 2002, average returns on schooling have declined by 0.6 percent. At the same time, average schooling levels have increased. Therefore (and according to human capital theory), everything else being the same, an increase in the supply of education has led to a slight decrease in the returns on schooling. That is, if there are no "shocks,"—such as changes in technology—that increase the demand for schooling, then an increase in overall school levels should lead to a decrease in the returns of schooling. Over the recent decades the returns to schooling have declined in many low income countries, while the technological revolution has increased demand for skilled labor in developed countries and the returns to schooling have increased.

Estimation Issues

Ideally, a rate of return on investment in education should be based on a representative sample of a country's population. But in reality this is the exception rather than the rule. It is problematic when the estimated rates of return are based on a survey of firms (rather than households), because firm-based samples are highly selective. In order to control survey costs, such samples focus on large firms with many employees. Second, the questionnaire is typically filled out by the payroll department rather than by the individual employee. This approach leads to the use of samples concentrated only in urban areas.

Another problem occurs when rate-of-return estimates are based on samples that include civil servants, since public-sector wages, in most cases, do not reflect market wages. Of course, in many countries (although fewer than in the past) the majority of graduates end up in public-sector employment.

The concentration of graduates in public-sector employment is identified as a problem in major growth studies. However, rate-of-return estimates based on civil-service pay are useful in private calculations regarding the incentives set by the state to invest in education.

A less serious problem occurs when wage effects are confused for returns on investment. Jacob Mincer has provided a great service and convenience in estimating returns on educational investment by means of the well-known earnings function he first put forward that explains differences in earnings among individuals according to their differences in schooling attainments and work experience.

Another methodological limitation is that many researchers feel obliged to include in the regression whatever independent variables they seem to have in the data set, including occupation. In effect, this procedure leads to those other variables taking away a significant part of the effect of education on earnings that comes from occupational mobility.

Perhaps the returns on education estimates that stem from the work of Ashenfelter and colleagues using twins, and other natural experiments, are the most reliable of all. According to this work, the overall private rate of return on investment in education in the United States is of the order of 10 percent, and this figure establishes a benchmark for what the social rate of return would be (a couple of percentage points lower, if not adjusted for externalities), or what the rate of return should be in a country with a lower per capita income than the United States (several percentage points higher, as based on the extrapolation of the noncomparable returns on education presented earlier).

Extensions

More research on the social benefits of schooling is needed. For developing countries, there is a need for more evidence on the impact of education on earnings using a quasi-experimental design—for example, looking at the earnings of different groups, say those exposed to a special training program and those who are not; or children who received early interventions such as nutrition and those who did not. There are more opportunities in the early twenty-first century for this type of research. Moreover, this research needs to be used to create programs that promote investment and reform financing mechanisms.

TABLE 1

The overall private rate of return on investment in education

Type of country	Country	Rate of return (percent)
Low-income countries	Ghana	9.7
	India	10.6
	Indonesia	7.0
	Nicaragua	12.1
Middle-income countries	Bolivia	10.7
	China	12.2
	Poland	7.0
	Venezuela	9.4
High-income countries	Denmark	4.5
	Finland	8.2
	Netherlands	6.4
	United States	10.0

SOURCE: Based on Psacharopoulos, George, and Patrinos, Harry Anthony. 2002. *Returns on Investment in Education: A Further Update.* Washington, DC: World Bank.

There is a concern in the literature with social rates of return that include true social benefits, or externalities. Efforts to make such estimates are numerous, but the estimates vary widely. If one could include externalities, then social rates of return may well be higher than private rates. Richard Venniker's 2000 review found that empirical evidence is scarce and inconclusive, providing some support for human capital externalities (though this support is not very strong and has been disputed). These studies estimate externalities in the form of an individual's human capital enhancing the productivity of other factors of production through channels that are not internalized by the individual (similar to Lucas's 1998 theory). As Venniker states, the evidence is not unambiguous. In fact, some estimates give negative values, while others give very high estimates.

A few studies in Africa have focused on estimating external benefits of education in agriculture using the education of neighboring farmers. A one-year rise in the average primary schooling of neighboring farmers is associated with a 4.3 percent rise in output, compared to a 2.8 percent effect of one's own primary education in Uganda. Another study found that neighboring farmers' education raises productivity by 56 percent, while one's own education raises productivity by only 2 percent in Ethiopia; however, the 56 percent figure seems rather high. Overall, the results are inconclusive.

TABLE 2

Rate of return on education by level, type, and country, in percent

Income level	Country	Year	Private Primary	Private Secondary	Private Higher	Social Primary	Social Secondary	Social Higher
High-income	Greece	1993		8.3	8.1		6.5	5.7
	New Zealand	1991		13.8	11.9		12.4	9.5
Middle-income	Bolivia	1990	20.0	6.0	19.0	13.0	6.0	13.0
	China	1993	18.0	13.4	15.1	14.4	12.9	11.3
	Mexico	1992	18.9	20.1	15.7	11.8	14.6	11.1
Low-income	Ethiopia	1996	24.7	24.2	26.6	14.9	14.4	11.9
	Nepal	1999	16.6	8.5	12.0	15.7	8.1	9.1

SOURCE: Based on Psacharopoulos, George, and Patrinos, Harry Anthony. 2002. *Returns on Investment in Education: A Further Update*. Washington, DC: World Bank.

Not only has the academic literature on returns on schooling increased, both in quantity and quality, but the policy implications have changed as well. Returns on education are no longer seen as prescriptive, but rather as indicators, suggesting areas of concentration. A good example is the impact of technology on wage differentials, which has led to a huge literature on changing wage structures.

At the same time, the importance of returns on education is seen in their adoption as a key indicator by the Organisation for Economic Co-operation and Development (OECD) in their annual *Education at a Glance* series and other policy documents. Increasingly, governments and other agencies are funding studies of returns on education, along with other research, to guide macro-policy decisions about the organization and financing of education reforms. This was the case in the United Kingdom higher education reforms as well as the Australian higher-education financing reforms.

Innovative use of rate-of-return studies is being used to both set overall policy guidelines and to evaluate specific programs. Examples include the Indonesia school building program, India's Operation Blackboard project, and Ethiopia's major sector investment program.

Above all, returns on investment in education are a useful indicator of the productivity of education, and they serve as an incentive for individuals to invest in their own human capital. As such, they can play an important role in the design of policies and the crafting of incentives that both promote investment and ensure that low-income families make an investment in education.

See also: DECISION-MAKING IN DEVELOPING NATIONS, APPLYING ECONOMIC ANALYSIS TO; INTERNATIONAL EDUCATION STATISTICS.

BIBLIOGRAPHY

APPLETON, SIMON. 2000. "Education and Health at the Household Level in Sub-Saharan Africa." Center for International Development Working Paper No. 33. Cambridge, MA: Harvard University.

ASHENFELTER, ORLEY, and KRUEGER, ALAN B. 1994. "Estimates of the Economic Return on Schooling from a New Sample of Twins." *American Economic Review* 84(5):1157–1173.

ASHENFELTER, ORLEY, and ROUSE, CECILIA E. 1998. "Income, Schooling, and Ability: Evidence from a New Sample of Twins." *Quarterly Journal of Economics* 113:253–284.

BECKER, GARY S. 1964. *Human Capital: A Theoretical and Empirical Analysis.* New York: National Bureau of Economic Research.

CARD, DAVID. 2001. "Estimating the Return on Schooling: Progress on Some Persistent Econometric Problems." *Econometrica* 69(5):1127–1160.

DUFLO, ESTHER. 2001. "Schooling and Labor Market Consequences of School Construction in Indonesia: Evidence from an Unusual Policy Experiment." *American Economic Review* 91(4):795–813.

HAVEMAN, ROBERT H., and WOLFE, BARBARA. 1984. "Schooling and Economic Well-Being: The Role of Non-Market Effects." *Journal of Human Resources* 19(3):128–140.

Krueger, Alan B. 1993. "How Computers Have Changed the Wage Structure: Evidence from Microdata, 1984–1989." *Quarterly Journal of Economics* 108(1):33–60.

Lucas, Robert E. 1988. "On the Mechanics of Economic Development." *Journal of Monetary Economics* 22:3–22.

Murphy, Kevin, and Welch, Finis. 1992. "The Structure of Wages." *Quarterly Journal of Economics* 107:285–326.

Organisation for Economic Co-operation and Development. 1997. *Human Capital Investment: An International Comparison.* Paris: Organisation for Economic Co-operation and Development.

Organisation for Economic Co-operation and Development. 2001. *Education at a Glance: OECD Indicators 2001.* Paris: Organisation for Economic Co-operation and Development.

Organisation for Economic Co-operation and Development. 2001. *Education Policy Analysis 2001.* Paris: Organisation for Economic Co-operation and Development.

Pissarides, Christopher A. 2000. *Human Capital and Growth: A Synthesis Report.* Paris: OECD Development Centre.

Psacharopoulos, George. 1973. *Returns on Education: An International Comparison.* Amsterdam: Elsevier.

Psacharopoulos, George. 1985. "Returns on Education: A Further International Update and Implications." *Journal of Human Resources* 20(4):583–604.

Psacharopoulos, George. 1994. "Returns on Investment in Education: A Global Update." *World Development* 22(9):1325–1343.

Psacharopoulos, George, and Patrinos, Harry Anthony. 2002. *Returns on Investment in Education: A Further Update.* Washington, DC: World Bank.

Weisbrod, Burton A. 1964. *External Benefits of Education.* Princeton, NJ: Princeton University, Industrial Relations Section.

World Bank. 1998. *Ethiopia: Education Sector Development Program.* Report No. 17739-ET. Washington, DC: World Bank.

INTERNET RESOURCE

Venniker, Richard. 2001. "Social Returns on Education: A Survey of Recent Literature on Human Capital Externalities." A CPB (Netherlands Bureau for Economic Policy Analysis) Report. <www.cpb.nl/eng/cpbreport/2000_1/s3_4.pdf>.

Harry Anthony Patrinos
George Psacharopoulos

EDUCATIONAL ACCOUNTABILITY

Accountability has been an educational issue for as long as people have had to pay for and govern schools. The term covers a diverse array of means by which some broad entity requires some providers of education to give an account of their work and holds them responsible for their performance. These means include, among others:

- "performance by results" schemes used by the English school system in the nineteenth century, and later variations on the theme of merit pay;
- the American pattern of a school board held accountable through a local election, with the school board in turn holding a superintendent and district staff accountable;
- marketizing education through charter schools, vouchers, and the Dutch practice of using the same system for funding what Americans would call both public and private schools;
- the school inspections used in many European countries; and
- the recent rise of state testing of students in which test results are sometimes, but not always, linked to rewards or punishments for students or school staffs.

According to a 1999 article written by Jacob E. Adams and Michael W. Kirst, what these and other examples have in common is a relationship in which a "principal" holds an "agent" responsible for certain kinds of performance. The agent is expected to provide an "account" to the principal. This account describes the performance for which that agent is held responsible. It may be simply descriptive—such as the percent of children in a school passing a particular test—or it may also include an explanation for and/or a justification of the performance achieved. Often the principal sets standards for what constitutes adequate performance. The principal may reward the agent for performance that exceeds the standard or punish the agent for below standard work.

Many ideas about accountability come from the business world and are developed in the fields of economics and political science. Attention paid to accountability waxes and wanes. While it never disappears, it often receives more attention in periods of conservative ascendance. This article briefly describes six approaches to educational accountability: moral, professional, bureaucratic, political, market, and legal. These are described singly, although in practice they are usually combined. It then examines one legal strategy that has received a great deal of attention in the United States: the use of state standards and assessment to promote student, school, and district accountability. Finally, it comments on the interaction among different accountability approaches.

Moral and Professional Accountability

The principal has the least control with moral accountability where the agent's actions depend largely on an internalized obligation, reinforced with a personal sense of remorse or potential social ostracism if the obligation is not met.

Professional accountability also provides the agent with a high degree of autonomy. This form operates on the assumption that the agent on the spot—typically a teacher—has special knowledge either of general principles or of the specific situation. Either way, it is difficult for the principal to specify actions or outcomes in great detail, so the agent has a great deal of discretion. On the other hand, before taking a position, the agent must demonstrate that he or she has the required competence, values, and knowledge by taking a prescribed course of study and/or passing specialized certification examinations. Thus, the primary point of control is more at entry to the profession or the specific position rather than over performance across time. Newer developments related to professional accountability include stronger state licensure requirements and the introduction of new assessments of initial competence. These, however, are usually introduced using the authority of the state, so professional and legal accountability intertwine. The National Board for Professional Teaching Standards, with its advanced certification for experienced teachers, tight connections to the field of teaching, and relatively loose ties to government, is closer to the form of professionally guided licensure found in other fields.

In addition, peer review can provide further oversight for the professional. The individual teacher offers evidence of practice that is reviewed by colleagues to ensure that it meets professional standards. These standards usually refer to the use of appropriate procedures and materials, recognizing that the outcome is usually a joint product of both the teacher and the student. The difficulty with peer review is the tendency for professionals to protect their own. This is especially problematic in education where teaching is usually practiced in isolation. Nevertheless, studies of the formation of professional communities in schools have shown that, under special conditions, teachers can band together to enforce shared and challenging standards and help colleagues improve their practice.

Bureaucratic Accountability

Bureaucratic accountability is based on the superior-subordinate relationship and depends upon the formal definition of the responsibilities of positions within an organization. An educational example might be the relationship between a superintendent and a principal. Where bureaucratic accountability dominates, the superior assigns tasks to subordinates. Rules and procedures for doing the work are specified in advance, and criteria for good performance are established. The supervisor then observes the process and evaluates both the process and the results.

Formal authority alone may be used to enforce compliance, but that authority can be reinforced with incentives that are linked to performance as judged by the superior. These incentives might include promotions, salary increases, and removal from a position. Such incentives work best when agents are held accountable for work processes that are relatively easy to specify in procedures—such as teaching certain content that can be specified in a written curriculum—and that are observable by supervisors. Incentives are more difficult to use when the work is unpredictable and uncertain. There have been several efforts to increase bureaucratic authority through various forms of merit pay and related approaches. While such experimentation continues, for the most part American education has stayed with salary systems that reward experience and formal education and provide few means for superiors to reward subordinates. A major reason for the difficulty in adopting such systems has been the inability to design ones that teachers believe fairly reflect their work rather than reflecting the capricious judgments on the part of higher administrators.

Political Accountability

Political accountability in its purest form is between an elected official—such as a school board member—and the voters. As with professional accountability, the performances expected can be quite variable and hard to specify. They may include curriculum taught, the level of spending on education, or special treatment for a constituent's children. They may also change radically over time so that what the voters want at one point, they reject at another. Political accountability facilitates the lobbying of elected officials to ensure that they act on one's preferences, and it may include rewarding them by helping them get reelected. Political accountability extends to officers appointed (more or less directly) by elected representatives, especially superintendents appointed by elected school boards.

Historically, American schools have primarily used a mix of political, bureaucratic, and professional accountability. The elected school board set policy and appointed the superintendent, who held the highest position in the formal bureaucracy. Still, teachers had considerable autonomy to choose instructional methods, even if licensure standards were rarely challenging and peer accountability was the exception, not the rule.

This older system remains in place in the early twenty-first century, although it has undergone changes as some forms of site-based management have shifted the balance between bureaucratic and political accountability as well as accountability to local principals from more central ones. New approaches to teacher licensure have also increased professional accountability. The major developments, however, have been the extension of two forms of accountability that historically played a lesser role in education: market and legal accountability.

Market Accountability

With market accountability, children or parents are customers who choose schools and can shop for the one that best reflects their preferences. The discipline of competition ensures that educators respond to parent and student preferences. Market accountability has become more popular as confidence in government has waned and the public questions the costs of public provision of services. It is especially prescribed where schools have become excessively bureaucratized, politically nonresponsive, and un-

willing or unable to improve their performance. American cities appear to be a ripe target for marketization because performance is so poor and improvement so slow.

The United States has always provided a small measure of choice through private and parochial schools operating alongside the public schools as well as through the housing market that allows some Americans to choose their schools. Recently, there has been a strong upsurge in interest in two new developments. One is charter schools, which are state funded but started by individuals or groups outside the public system and which then compete with public schools for students (and funding). The other is vouchers whereby tax receipts go to schools indirectly. Fixed amounts are given to parents who then use state funds (sometimes supplemented with their own money) to select the school their child will attend. In other countries, the public-private distinction is more muted or, as in New Zealand, parents are given total freedom of choice of which public school their children will attend.

Many claims have been made for various privatization approaches. It is said that they will be more efficient, increase variation in the kind of education delivered, raise test scores, increase equity, and, through competition, promote improvement of regular public schools. In most cases, it is difficult to tell what the effects of market accountability are. For instance, there have been few well-designed studies clarifying the effects of choice on achievement, at least in the American context, and those that have been conducted are much disputed. There is little evidence to suggest that competition is changing public schools in the United States, perhaps because competition is still so limited. On the other hand, there is evidence that choice programs are inequitable. The clientele of such programs tends to be more white and better off, and there tend to be fewer children with the more severe handicaps attending such schools. This is true even when schools of choice must use lotteries and other systems that preclude selecting more advantaged students and when whole countries have gone to choice systems.

Legal Accountability

Legal accountability occurs when the principal formulates rules and monitors and enforces the agent's compliance with those rules. It differs from bureaucratic accountability where the rules are formulated within an organization in that the principal is usually one level of government, such as the federal or state government, formulating rules for organizations at a lower level. Rules are usually formulated by legislatures but can be elaborated through executive regulation and formulated de novo (over again) by both the executive branch and the courts. Legal accountability often works in conjunction with professional, political, and bureaucratic accountability by establishing the broad framework within which they operate.

Legal accountability structures the inputs and resources teachers receive through funding formulas and teacher licensure regulations. The former have been highly contested and the source of a great deal of school finance litigation. The latter is a central pillar of professional accountability. Legal accountability also defines the structures and processes through which education is delivered by defining forms of governance—for instance, school boards and local control—attendance policies, desegregation orders, and building codes.

What has been new since the 1970s has been the use of legal accountability to specify, monitor, and improve the outcomes of education. Historically, states have specified outcomes indirectly by defining high school graduation requirements. Beginning in the 1970s and more often since the early 1980s, however, state governments took stronger steps. At first, these focused on testing students and increasing high school graduation requirements. More recently, there has been more emphasis on setting standards and assessing performance in light of those standards. By now, almost every American state and many foreign countries take these two linked steps. Because this approach has become so pervasive, it deserves special attention.

Standards and Assessment

A system of state standards might include the following elements:

- Content standards that set out the knowledge and skills children are expected to develop,
- Tests or assessments aligned with those content standards,
- Student performance standards that define proficient performance in terms of those assessments, and
- Rewards provided to students or schools that meet or exceed the standards and punishments or remediation activities for those that do not.

A strong system would have all four elements. The theory of action behind such a system is that the formal sanctions linked to meeting standards motivate educators and students to learn what is tested. A weak system would certainly not have the last two elements and might not have the first—many states began testing without any guidance from standards. The theory then is that the publication of test scores will motivate improvement either by appealing to professional pride or indirectly to the public, which will use political accountability to promote improvement.

While the theory is clear enough at a general level, states face difficult design issues with both technical and political dimensions related to each element of the accountability system. In practice, the politics of state standards and assessment has led to rapid, dramatic changes in state tests and related policies. Each element listed above has been problematic in some instances. For instance, content standards have become a source of frequent disputes. In science, whether or not to teach evolution has been an issue from the Scopes trial to the 1999 deliberations of the Kansas school board. Even more seemingly neutral subjects have been cause for great debate. For instance, while the National Council of Teachers of Mathematics has urged states to develop standards that focus on exploring mathematical ideas, logical reasoning, and the ability to solve nonroutine problems, many people still want state standards to require memorizing mathematical facts and procedures.

The design of tests has created other problems. In the 1970s states relied primarily on multiple-choice tests, which were familiar (thereby ensuring a certain legitimacy), inexpensive, and could obtain reliable scores relatively inexpensively. During the 1990s there was a push for portfolios and performance assessments where students constructed the responses. Such assessments were viewed as more valid measures of higher standards and better guidance, and were believed to encourage teachers to adopt more challenging instructional approaches. It now appears that while performance assessments have many advantages for improving instruction, they often lack the economy and reliability required for public accountability.

Other issues relate to performance standards, including whether and how to take into account the well-known correlation between family background and performance when measuring school performance, whether to develop standards for absolute performance or improvement and—if the latter—how to measure improvement, and whether to use norm-referenced (comparison to some larger group) or criterion-referenced (comparison to an absolute level of performance) standards of performance. Developing criterion-referenced standards has been the subject of much research, but a great deal of art is still involved.

Another major issue concerns the usefulness of rewards and punishments. The theory of action behind accountability systems is that the challenge for the principal is to motivate the agent to perform in ways the principal prefers. A criticism of this theory as it applies to state assessment systems is that strong sanctions, also referred to as high stakes, will lead to "teaching to the test." This term refers to a wide range of behaviors from adjusting the curriculum to ensure that topics tested are taught before the test is given, to cheating. The term implies that something is done to raise test scores without necessarily increasing students' knowledge of the subject tested. Moreover, critics argue that more challenging forms of instruction are less likely to be adopted in high-stakes settings.

An alternative theory for improving teaching and learning in schools is that the major problem is a lack of capacity—that is, the knowledge, skills, funding, and other resources needed to perform in effective ways. Numerous capacities are needed to raise test scores by improving student knowledge. These include understanding the content taught and effective ways to teach it, the ability to analyze tests and know what performances are really called for, and the collective capacity of members of the target school in question to work together to improve itself. Even a weak accountability system can make teachers aware of the need to change practice and provide general guidance about the kinds of changes preferred. Without appropriate internal capacity or capacity-building efforts, however, movement toward more challenging instruction is not likely.

A number of studies have recently pointed to the need to align internal and external accountability. These studies suggest that schools with reasonably strong cultures develop their own internal accountability often based on peer professional accountability. Such cultures can provide strong support for improvement because they combine motivational and capacity-building efforts. Where internal and external accountability are mutually re-

inforcing, it appears that change is powerfully supported. Where the two are not aligned, internal accountability is likely to overwhelm external accountability or external accountability may undermine local capacity.

Coordinating Accountability Mechanisms

For all of the difficulty in designing and implementing individual accountability mechanisms, policy analysts recognize that educators face a variety of interacting mechanisms. The American educational system is highly fragmented, with authority dispersed between political and professional organizations and across local, state, and federal levels of government. Consensus on what constitutes effective education and who should be educated are difficult to achieve.

Moreover, educators are accountable to multiple constituencies. The research on internal accountability illustrates how professional accountability may reinforce or work against state assessment systems. Other work suggests that the public may not understand or support state standards and assessment. When they do not, they may protest at the state level, or local school boards may not give top priority to achieving high standards, thus undermining efforts to achieve them.

In sum, educators and policy analysts will always be concerned about educational accountability. It is hard to imagine an educational system where educators are not accountable to multiple constituencies through a variety of mechanisms. This means that educators will be accountable to different people for different things. It is becoming more and more important to design accountability mechanisms that encourage schools to provide a more effective education for all children and to orchestrate these mechanisms so that they send as consistent a message to educators as possible.

See also: Constitutional Requirements Governing American Education; Educational Policy; Principal, School; School Boards; Superintendent of Schools.

BIBLIOGRAPHY

Adams, Jacob E., and Kirst, Michael W. 1999. "New Demands and Concepts for Educational Accountability: Striving for Results in an Era of Excellence." In *Handbook of Research on Educa-*

tional Administration, 2nd edition, ed. Joseph Murphy and Karen Seashore Louis. San Francisco: Jossey-Bass.

FAIRMAN, JANET, and FIRESTONE, WILLIAM A. 2001. "The District Role in State Assessment Policy: An Exploratory Study." In *From the Capitol to the Classroom: Standards-Based Reform in the States,* ed. Susan H. Fuhrman. Chicago: University of Chicago Press.

FIRESTONE, WILLIAM A. 1994. "Redesigning Teacher Salary Systems for Educational Reform." *American Educational Research Journal* 31:549–574.

FIRESTONE, WILLIAM A., and MAYROWETZ, DAVID. 2000. "Rethinking 'High Stakes': Lessons from the United States and England and Wales." *Teachers College Record* 102:724–749.

FULLER, BRUCE, and ELMORE, RICHARD F. 1996. *Who Chooses? Who Loses? Culture, Institutions, and the Unequal Effects of School Choice.* New York: Teachers College Press.

LEITHWOOD, KENNETH; EDGE, KAREN; and JANTZI, DORIS. 1999. *Educational Accountability: The State of the Art.* Gütersloh, Germany: Bertelsmann Foundation Publishers.

LINN, ROBERT L. 2001. *Reporting School Quality in Standards-Based Accountability Systems.* Los Angeles: National Center for Research on Evaluation, Standards, and Student Testing.

LINN, ROBERT L., and BAKER, EVA L. 1996. "Can Performance-Based Student Assessments Be Psychometrically Sound?" In *Performance-Based Student Assessment: Challenges and Possibilities,* ed. Joan B. Baron and Dennis P. Wolf. Chicago: University of Chicago Press.

MURPHY, JOSEPH. 1996. *The Privatization of Schooling: Problems and Possibilities.* Thousand Oaks, CA: Corwin Press.

NEWMANN, FRED M.; KING, M. BRUCE; and RIGDON, MARL. 1997. "Accountability and School Performance: Implications from Restructuring Schools." *Harvard Education Review* 61:41–69.

SMITH, MARY LEE. 1991. "Meanings of Test Preparation." *American Educational Research Journal* 28:521–542.

SMITH, MARY LEE; HEINECKE, WALTER; and NOBLE, AUDREY J. 1999. "Assessment Policy and Political Spectacle." *Teachers College Record* 101:157–191.

WIRT, FRED, and KIRST, MICHAEL W. 1997. *The Political Dynamics of American Education.* Berkeley: MacCutchan Press.

WILLIAM FIRESTONE

EDUCATIONAL BROADCASTING, FEDERAL SUPPORT

The U.S. federal government has always had a strong interest in broadcasting, but its relationship with the broadcasting industry was not formalized until the enactment of the Communications Act of 1934. The primary objective of this legislation was to clearly and officially assert federal, rather than private, control over all channels of interstate and international communications by wire and radio in the United States. The act created the Federal Communications Commission (FCC), and within a broad range of regulatory power, this body was authorized to grant licenses to eligible persons and organizations for limited periods of time to operate radio (and by subsequent interpretation, television) stations "in the public interest, convenience, and necessity."

Radio, even from its earliest days, incorporated educational and instructional materials in its programming. Nevertheless, both radio and television broadcasting was mainly a commercial endeavor through the 1940s. The first significant action to spur educational television broadcasting on a national level came in 1952 when the FCC, revising its table of frequency allocations, set aside 242 channels for the exclusive use of noncommercial educational television (ETV). FCC actions in 1961 and 1966 increased this number to 329.

The University of Houston became the first institution to establish a noncommercial broadcasting station when it began operation of station KUHT in 1953. Encouraged by grants of $100,000 from the Ford Foundation, other stations came into being in such cities as Miami, Pittsburgh, Chicago, Denver, and Madison, Wisconsin. Nevertheless, the cost of building, equipping, and operating a television station remained prohibitive for many institutions, and by 1962 there were only eighty ETV stations on the air or under construction throughout the United States.

It became obvious that if the channels reserved by the FCC for noncommercial use were to be used as intended, federal funding would be required, and so Congress passed the Educational Television Facilities Act (Pub. L. 87-447) in 1962, which included $32 million in facility construction grants. By June 1967 the number of ETV stations on the air had more than doubled, to 175, with ten more under construction and grants to activate another thirty stations in process. When the ETV Facilities Act expired in 1967, Congress passed the Public Broadcasting Act, which broadened considerably the federal role in noncommercial broadcasting—most notably through the formation of the Corporation for Public Broadcasting (CPB).

CPB was set up as a private, nongovernmental, not-for-profit corporation to provide for the improved quality of "public" broadcasting (previously known as ETV) and for a live network interconnection of educational broadcasting stations. CPB began by establishing entities that would build on the common needs and interests of public broadcasting stations around the country, and create some of the economies of a broadcast network. The Public Broadcast Service (PBS) was incorporated in November 1969 to provide an interconnection, or a means of sharing programs, among public television stations, and a source of production funding. PBS was prohibited, however, from producing programs itself, or from owning and operating any stations. National Public Radio (NPR) plays a similar role in terms of interconnection for radio stations but, unlike PBS, it was chartered as a producing entity as well.

The activities of CPB, PBS, and NPR overlap in terms of their common mission to support public broadcasting, but their operations remain appropriately distinct. CPB receives a federal appropriation for public broadcasting and distributes it to TV and radio stations. The stations, in turn, can choose to become members of PBS or NPR, which in return fund (in the case of PBS) or produce (in the case of NPR) national programming, and both PBS and NPR provide the technical infrastructure necessary to distribute the programming nationally.

Financial Arrangements

Even with such generous support from taxpayers, the public broadcasting system (a $2 billion per year industry by 1997) receives just 17 percent of its revenue from the federal government. In addition to an annual appropriation to CPB, public broadcasting stations may receive federal funding through the National Telecommunications and Information Administration (NTIA) at the Department of Commerce, or through programming grants from various federal agencies such as the Department of Education, the National Science Foundation, the National Endowment for the Arts, and the National Endowment for the Humanities.

NTIA money, funded through the Public Telecommunications Facilities Program (PTFP) has become particularly crucial as public broadcasting moves into the digital age. Massive infrastructure costs are being incurred for the transition to digital broadcasting that will ultimately increase channel capacity by a factor of five or six, and allow for a wide range of new interactive services for the benefit of the public.

Programming dollars from the Department of Education (and its predecessors) have supported children's programming from *Sesame Street* to *Arthur*. The National Endowment for the Humanities has supported extraordinary programming like Ken Burns's documentary *The Civil War* and continuing series such as the *American Experience*. Jazz, classical, and traditional music on the radio, and performance programs on PBS are supported through the National Endowment for the Arts.

Current Scope of Services and Analysis of Impact

The decentralized and inherently local nature of public broadcasting in the United States is intrinsic to its independence and unique brand of public service. At the same time, this structure limits a range of "efficiencies" that might be practiced in a commercial environment. Consequently, debates flare up on Capitol Hill regarding the role of federal funding in public broadcasting. But while there is little in the way of quantitative measures of public broadcasting's impact, the ongoing and overwhelming public support that is demonstrated when funding cuts are considered reflects a significant positive impression and impact on the American people.

The Challenges and Opportunities Ahead

The explosive growth of nonbroadcast (i.e., cable and direct satellite) television has provided a new level of competition to public television. The Discovery Channel, A&E, the History Channel, and Nickelodeon, among others, have built entire channels around particular genres that were previously unique to public broadcasting. Direct satellite radio began broadcasting in 2001, and may prove to be a similar challenge for public radio.

The Internet has also provided competition for public broadcasting, at least in terms of claiming another slice of time from each individual's media viewing. At the same time, however, the Internet has provided great opportunities to extend the impact of public broadcasting.

Both nonbroadcast television and the Internet have pushed public broadcasting to do what it has always done best: innovate. Public broadcasting must clearly demonstrate that it is a vital public service, and at the same time it must achieve a fine balance between sustainable financial practices while retaining an unimpeded, commercial-free environment to the satisfaction of its viewers and listeners. In an era when media outlets have essentially been consolidated into a handful of international conglomerates, the need for unbiased, public-interest broadcasting is as powerful as ever.

BIBLIOGRAPHY

BEHRENS, STEVE, ed. 2000. *A History of Public Broadcasting.* Washington, DC: Current.

CARNEGIE COMMISSION ON EDUCATIONAL TELEVISION. 1962. *Public Television: A Program for Action.* New York: Harper.

INTERNET RESOURCES

CORPORATION FOR PUBLIC BROADCASTING. 2002. <www.cpb.org>.

CURRENT ONLINE. 2002. <www.current.org>.

NATIONAL PUBLIC RADIO. 2002. <www.npr.org>.

PUBLIC BROADCASTING SERVICE. 2002. <www.pbs.org>.

PETER M. NEAL

EDUCATIONAL CHANGE

Education is generally thought to promote social, economic, and cultural transformation during times of fundamental national and global changes. Indeed, educational change has become a common theme in many education systems and in plans for the development of schools. According to Seymour Sarason, the history of educational reform is replete with fail-ure and disappointment in respect to achieving intended goals and implementing new ideas. Since the 1960s, however, thinking about educational change has undergone several phases of development. In the early twenty-first century much more is known about change strategies that typically lead to successful educational reforms.

Phases of Educational Change

The first phase of educational changes was in the 1960s when educational reforms in most Western countries were based on externally mandated large-scale changes that focused on renewing curricula and instruction. The second phase, in the 1970s, was a period of increasing dissatisfaction of the public and government officials with public education and the performance of schools, decreasing financing of change initiatives, and shrinking attention to fundamental reforms. Consequently, in the 1980s the third phase shifted toward granting decision-making power to, and emphasizing the accountability of, local school systems and schools. Educational change gradually became an issue to be managed equally by school authorities and by the local community, including school principals and teachers. The fourth phase started in the 1990s when it became evident that accountability and self-management, in and of themselves, were insufficient to make successful changes in education.

Furthermore, educational change began to place more emphasis on organizational learning, systemic reforms, and large-scale change initiatives rather than restructuring isolated fields of education. In brief, educators' understanding of educational change has developed from linear approaches to nonlinear systems approaches that emphasize the complexity of reform processes, according to Shlomo Sharan and his colleagues. Similarly, the focus of change has shifted from restructuring single components of educational systems towards transforming the organizational cultures that prevail in given schools or school systems, as well as towards transforming large sections of a given school or system rather than distinct components of schooling.

Emerging Theories of Educational Change

In the early twenty-first century it is generally acknowledged that significant educational change cannot be achieved by a linear "recipe-like" process. The consensus among theorists and practitioners is growing that traditional models of thinking about educational change no longer provide sufficient conceptual tools for responding to multidimensional needs and politically contested environments. The major challenge of educational change is how to understand and cope with rapid change in an unpredictably turbulent world. Emerging new theories of educational change are beginning to employ concepts and ideas derived from the sciences of chaos and complexity. The main characteristics of these new theories are nonlinearity of processes, thinking about education as an open system, the interdependency of the various components of the system, and the influence of context on the change process itself.

Although educational change occurs everywhere, it is still not discussed systematically or analyzed by researchers and educators worldwide. Particularly in countries undergoing political and economic transition, educational change remains a political agenda rather than a well-designed engine of social reform. The heart of successful educational change is learning, both at the individual and at the community levels.

See also: EDUCATION REFORM; SCHOOL-BASED DECISION-MAKING; SCHOOL REFORM.

BIBLIOGRAPHY

FULLAN, MICHAEL. 1998. "The Meaning of Educational Change." In *The International Handbook of Educational Change,* ed. Andy Hargreaves, Michael Fullan, Ann Lieberman, and David Hopkins. Dordrecht, The Netherlands: Kluwer.

FULLAN, MICHAEL. 2000. "The Return of Large-Scale Reform." *Journal of Educational Change* 1:5–28.

HARGREAVES, ANDY, ed. 1997. *Rethinking Educational Change with Heart and Mind.* Alexandria, VA: Association for Supervision and Curriculum Development.

HARGREAVES, ANDY. 2000. "Representing Educational Change." *Journal of Educational Change* 1:1–3.

SARASON, SEYMOUR B. 1990. *The Predictable Failure of Educational Reform: Can We Change Course Before It's Too Late?* San Francisco: Jossey-Bass.

SHARAN, SHLOMO, et al. 1999. *The Innovative School: Organization and Instruction.* Westport, CT: Bergin and Garvey.

PASI J. SAHLBERG

EDUCATIONAL EXPENDITURES, PROJECTING

Every responsible educational organization estimates the amount of expenditures necessary to provide services desired by its students, staff, and faculty. Utilizing historical financial data, an analyst can use a variety of statistical methods to project fairly accurately what expenditures will be needed to provide the same level of educational services in future years. Though there are a number of sophisticated and reliable statistical methods used to project expenditures, three methods are prevalent: (1) average annual increases in expenditures; (2) average annual percentage increases in inflation (i.e., the Consumer Price Index); and (3) regression analysis. These methods have been validated and refined by use in a wide variety of economic, political, and social contexts. Moreover, the accuracy of these expenditure projection methods has improved with advances in data definitions, data reporting, generally accepted accounting principles, and data collection methods.

Projections Using Average Annual Increases in Expenditures

Although a variety of methods can be used to project educational expenditures, one of the simplest methods is to survey states and educational institutions (e.g., state departments of education or local district offices) to find out some details about their historical spending patterns for educational dollars (see Table 1). Then, based on this contextual information, one would use an average annual increase in educational expenditures—taken over some period of time—to project an incremental increase to the most recent year's actual data.

Table 2 provides sample state-level projections for educational expenditures over multiple time periods using the average annual increases in expenditures to determine projected expenditures for the 2003 academic year. The ten-year projection using the average annual increase methodology is $5,678; the seven-year projection using the average annual increase is $5,714, the five-year projection using the average annual increase is $5,797; and the three-year projection using the average annual increase is $5,786. Notice that the ten-year and seven-year expenditure projections are substantially lower than the remaining projections due to the inclusion of an unusually low increase in 1997.

TABLE 1

Sample state-level data for educational expenditures and consumer price indices with annual increases

Year	Expenditures	Annual increase in expenditures	CPI	Annual percent increase in CPI
1992	$2,409	–	136.2	–
1993	$2,563	$154	140.3	3.0
1994	$2,784	$221	144.5	3.0
1995	$3,047	$263	148.2	2.6
1996	$3,250	$203	152.4	2.8
1997	$3,300	$50	156.9	3.0
1998	$3,706	$406	160.5	2.3
1999	$4,167	$461	163.0	1.6
2000	$4,526	$359	166.5	2.2
2001	$4,924	$398	172.2	3.4
2002	$5,381	$457	177.1	2.8

SOURCE: Courtesy of author.

TABLE 2

Sample state-level projections of 2003 educational expenditures using average increases in expenditures, average increases in CPI, and OLS regression analysis

Years of data	Average increases in expenditures	Average increases in CPI	OLS regression analysis
Ten-year projection	$5,678	$5,525	$5,541
Seven-year projection	$5,714	$5,520	$5,663
Five-year projection	$5,797	$5,513	$5,656
Three-year projection	$5,786	$5,679	$5,580

SOURCE: Courtesy of author.

Usually, the longer the time period used when computing an average annual increase, the less likely the probability that an atypical yearly increase (i.e., an annual increase, or decrease, that does not fall within the trend over a period of time) will influence negatively the estimated level of expenditure. In the case of an atypical increase (or decrease) in expenditures, due caution should be noted when examining the results.

Projections Using Average Annual Percentage Increases in Inflation

Another method used to project educational expenditures is to use an average annual percentage increase in inflation—taken over some period of time—to project an incremental increase to the most recent year's actual data. Again, the longer the time period used when computing an average annual increase, the less likely the probability that an atypical yearly increase will negatively influence the estimated level of expenditure. Table 2 also provides sample state-level projections for educational expenditures over multiple time periods using the average annual percentage increases in expenditures to estimate a projected expenditure for the 2003 academic year. The ten-year projection using the average annual percentage increase in inflation methodology is $5,525; the seven-year projection using the average annual increase is $5,520, the five-year projection using the average annual increase is $5,513; and the three-year projection using the average annual increase is $5,679. Notice that the five-year expenditure projection is substantially lower than the

remaining projections due to the inclusion of an unusually low increase in 1999.

Projections Using Regression Analysis

This statistical technique for predicting educational expenditures—specifically called Ordinary Least Squares (OLS) Regression Analysis—consists of constructing a line that "best fits the data" over a certain period of time (see Figure 1). The line of best fit (also known as the *regression line*) is the one line—and the only line—that falls as close as possible to every coordinate simultaneously and can be used to make fairly accurate expenditure projections (Because this discussion is limited to linear regression, and does not include non-linear regressions, the mathematical functions discussed will be equations for straight lines). Now the process of expenditure projections using regression analysis involves two steps: (1) determining the mathematical equation for the regression line; and (2) using the mathematical equation to predict scores.

The mathematical equation for the straight line in Figure 1 expresses a direct relationship between time (along the horizontal axis) and expenditures (along the vertical axis). The general form of the equation for a line is $Y = bX + a$, where Y is the predicted expenditure, b is the slope of the line, a is Y-intercept, and X is the year to be predicted. Theoretically, every line extends infinitely in both directions, but for the purposes of this discussion, the line extends along the horizontal axis from the year 1992 to 2003.

For each set of expenditure data analyzed, a specific regression line is fitted onto the graphed data using the mathematical methods of ordinary least squares. The formulas for the slope—referred to as

FIGURE 1

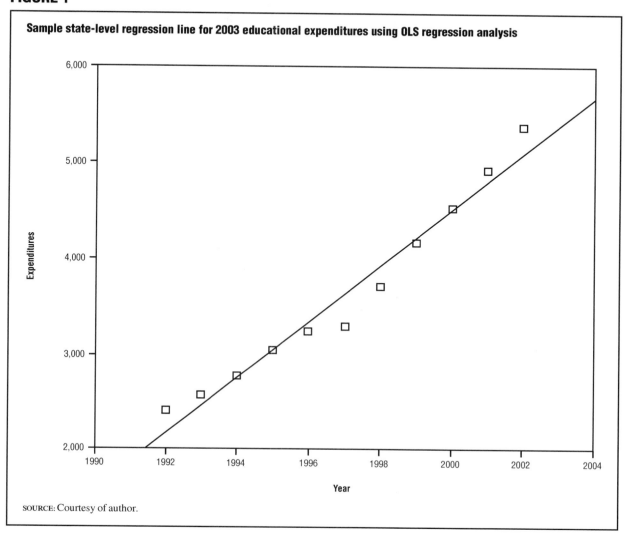

Sample state-level regression line for 2003 educational expenditures using OLS regression analysis

SOURCE: Courtesy of author.

the *regression coefficient*—and the Y-intercept—referred to as the *regression constant*—are derived using calculus and can be found in any statistics book. Once the specific regression equation has been determined, the prediction of educational expenditures is straightforward: Substitute the values of X, a, and b into the equation and solve for Y. For example, the ten-year projection using OLS regression analysis is $5,541; the seven-year projection using regression analysis is $5,663; the five-year projection using regression analysis is $5,656; and the three-year projection using regression analysis is $5,580. Notice that the seven-year and five-year expenditure projections are substantially lower than the remaining projections due to the inclusion of an unusually high increases as a percentage of expenditure in 1998 and 1999.

Summary

Despite the improvements in the precision of expenditure projections methods, it is important to remember that the usefulness of any economic or financial estimate rests upon the strength and validity of the assumptions used to define the context of the analysis. For example, local school districts are expected to provide a broad-based curriculum, fully-equipped classrooms, quality teaching materials, new technologies, qualified teachers, and a wide range of programs, services, and products. Simply investing more money into a school district's total available revenue is not enough to improve educational services or student attainment. However, targeting new expenditures to effective programs that improve the quality of the education system for students, staff, and faculty can improve educational services. And, accurately projecting distributions of revenues and expenditures is key for these types of school improvements.

Two major institutions provide primary resources in the determination of educational expenditures: the National Center for Education Statistics (NCES) and the National Education Association (NEA). The National Center for Educational Statistics is the primary federal institution for collecting, analyzing, and reporting educational data related to education in the United States. Annually, NCES sends surveys to state educational agencies and uses this data to publish reports and develop estimates for publications such as *The Condition of Education, The Digest of Education Statistics,* and *Early Estimates of Public Elementary and Secondary Education Statistics.* The National Education Association presents its expenditure projections in a combined annual report called *Rankings and Estimates.* The *Rankings* portion of the report presents expenditure data useful in determining how states differ from one another on selected demographic, economic, political, and social arenas. The *Estimates* portion of the report provides projections of information about educational expenditures in addition to data on student enrollment, school employment, personnel compensation, and other educational finances. The data elements presented by both of these organizations permit general assessments of trends and should be used with the understanding that specific contextual elements influence their interpretations.

See also: PUBLIC SCHOOL BUDGETING, ACCOUNTING, AND AUDITING.

BIBLIOGRAPHY

MCDOWELL, LENA M. 2001. *Early Estimates of Public Elementary and Secondary Education Statistics: School Year 2000–2001* (NCES 2001–331). U.S. Department of Education. Washington, DC: National Center for Education Statistics.

NATIONAL CENTER FOR EDUCATION STATISTICS. 2001. *The Digest of Education Statistics.* Washington, DC: U.S. Department of Education.

NATIONAL CENTER FOR EDUCATION STATISTICS. 2001. *Projections of Education Statistics to 2011.* Washington, DC: U.S. Department of Education.

NATIONAL EDUCATION ASSOCIATION. 1999. *Investing in Public Education: The Importance of Schooling in the New Global Economy.* Washington, DC: National Education Association.

NATIONAL EDUCATION ASSOCIATION. 2001. *Rankings and Estimates—Rankings of the States 2000 and Estimates of School Statistics 2001.* Washington, DC: National Education Association.

INTERNET RESOURCES

NATIONAL CENTER FOR EDUCATION STATISTICS. 2002. <http://nces.ed.gov/edstats>.

NATIONAL EDUCATION ASSOCIATION. 2002. <www.nea.org>.

R. ANTHONY ROLLE

EDUCATIONAL INTEREST GROUPS

Public schools in the United States operate in a pluralist democracy that enables competing interests to gain access to the decision-making process. Quite frequently, conflicts over educational issues occur. Political leaders and educational professionals formulate policies that attempt to mediate competing views and contending interests. There are, however, three understandings about the interaction between interest groups and the public educational enterprise. One school of thought finds that the school system benefits from interest group activities as it incorporates diverse demands. Another perspective views interest groups as autonomous centers that can undermine the schools' legitimacy. A third perspective observes a reconfiguration of the goals and functions of interest groups in an era in the early twenty-first century of "postmaterialism."

Diversity

Pluralistic representation, according to many researchers, can strengthen public schools. Historically, school responsiveness to its diverse clients is seen in the development of an increasingly professionalized system. In his study of three central-city districts from 1870 to 1940, Paul Peterson observed in 1985 the "politics of institutionalization," where clients who had previously been excluded from school services gradually gained admission to the system. As schools expanded their client base, Peterson saw no single interest as dominant over all school issues. Although the business elites tended to prevail in fiscal issues, working-class organizations exercised substantial influence over compulsory education. Because diverse actors and interests contributed to an expanding school system, the real winners were the school system and its broadening clientele. The urban public school system practiced the politics of nonexclusion, gradually extending services from the middle class to the low-income populations, and from groups with roots in the United States to various immigrant and racial groups.

Conceptually, Peterson's analysis is consistent with the tradition of pluralist scholarship in political science as exemplified by Robert Dahl's classic 1961 work *Who Governs?*. From a policy point of view, interest group competition has encouraged the school bureaucracy to adopt objective, universal criteria in distributing resources to neighborhood schools.

School responsiveness to its diverse clients also improves equal educational opportunity for the disadvantaged since the 1960s. In 1986 Gary Orfield and Susan Eaton discussed "group rights" politics in securing governmental resources for low-income inner-city African Americans in the Atlanta metropolitan area. Further, using data from the U.S. Office of Civil Rights in districts with at least 15,000 students and 1 percent African-American enrollment, Kenneth Meier and colleagues examined in 1989 the practice of second-generation discrimination in the classroom following the implementation of a school desegregation plan. They found that African-American representation on the school board has contributed to the recruitment of African-American administrators, who in turn hired more African-American teachers. African-American teachers, according to the study, are crucial in reducing the assignment of African-American students to classes for the educable mentally retarded. African-American representation in the instructional staff also reduces the number of disciplinary actions against African-American students and increases the latter's participation in classes for the gifted. Luis Fraga and colleagues found a similar situation in 1986 with Hispanic students in thirty-five large urban districts. Thus, "group rights" politics is critical to ensure allocative practices that benefit the disadvantaged.

Autonomous Power Centers

Although interest group politics may facilitate collective concerns, organized interests can become autonomous power centers that undermine the

organizational capacity of the school system. A major interest group is the teacher union. William Grimshaw's 1979 study of Chicago's teacher union suggested that the union had gone through two phases in its relationship with the city and school administration. During the formative years, the union largely cooperated with the administration (and the mayor) in return for a legitimate role in the policy-making process. In the second phase, which Grimshaw characterized as "union rule," the union became independent of both the local political machine and the reform fractions. Instead, it looked to the national union leadership for guidance and engaged in tough bargaining with the administration over better compensation and working conditions. Consequently, Grimshaw argued that policymakers "no longer are able to set policy unless the policy is consistent with the union's objectives" (p. 150).

Organizational growth, in Bruce Cooper's view, has led to problems of "mature institutions," where union leaders have to mediate trade-offs between quality and supply. Seeing a new trend in school competition, Susan Moore Johnson observed the need for replacing "collective bargaining" with "reform bargaining."

Another organized interest is the increasingly well-organized taxpaying public, a substantial portion of which no longer has children in the public schools. The aging population has placed public education in competition with transportation, public safety, community development, and health care over budgetary allocation. Discontent with property taxes became widespread during the time of the much-publicized campaign for Proposition 13 in California. According to Jack Citrin, between 1978 and 1983, of the sixty-seven tax or spending limitation measures on state ballots across the nation, thirty-nine were approved. During the 1990s, business-organized lobbying groups have been successful in pushing for higher academic standards and stronger accountability measures. In districts where public schools fail repeatedly, political leaders tend to seek for alternative ways of delivering schooling services, including privatization or creating charter schools. At the federal level, the No Child Left Behind Act of 2001 that was passed in January 2002 allowed for public school choice as a corrective action to schools that fail repeatedly.

Postmaterialism

A third perspective sees a weakening of the hierarchical structures of organizing interests. In the postmaterialist era, Ronald Inglehard, Terry Clark, Jeffrey Berry, and other social scientists argue that political parties no longer play a key role in mobilizing voter turnout. The union is losing its direct influence over its membership. Ideologically based groups, both left and right, seem to have lost much of their reputation in the nation's capital. Instead, organized interests are realigned in several ways. They have become more focused on "quality of life" issues, less organized along rigid class cleavages, and more pragmatic about governmental and market solutions to educational and social problems. Increasingly, racial and class categories are less predictive of how citizens view and decide on educational policy issues. In short, this early-twenty-first-century reconfiguration of interest group politics is likely to shape the research community's understanding of group-based influence in public education.

See also: EDUCATIONAL ACCOUNTABILITY; SCHOOL-BASED DECISION-MAKING; TEACHER UNIONS.

BIBLIOGRAPHY

CITRIN, JACK. 1984. "Introduction: The Legacy of Proposition 13." In *California and the American Tax Revolt: Proposition 13 Five Years Later,* ed. Terry Schwadron. Berkeley: University of California Press.

CLARK, TERRY N., and HOFFMANN-MARTINOT, VINCENT. 1998. *The New Political Culture.* Boulder, CO: Westview.

COOPER, BRUCE S. 2000. "An International Perspective on Teachers Unions." In *Conflicting Missions? Teachers Unions and Educational Reform,* ed. Tom Loveless. Washington, DC: Brookings Institution Press.

DAHL, ROBERT. 1961. *Who Governs?* New Haven, CT: Yale University Press.

FRAGA, LUIS; MEIER, KENNETH; and ENGLAND, ROBERT. 1986. "Hispanic Americans and Educational Policy: Limits to Equal Access." *Journal of Politics* 48:850–876.

GRIMSHAW, WILLIAM. 1979. *Union Rule in the Schools.* Lexington: Heath.

HILL, PAUL; CAMPBELL, CHRISTINE; and HARVEY, JAMES. 2000. *It Takes A City.* Washington, DC: Brookings Institution Press.

INGLEHART, RONALD. 1990. *Culture Shift.* Princeton, NJ: Princeton University Press.

JOHNSON, SUSAN MOORE. 2001. "Reform Bargaining and Its Promise for School Improvement." In *Conflicting Missions? Teachers Unions and Education Reform,* ed. Tom Loveless. Washington, DC: Brookings Institution Press.

MEIER, KENNETH; STEWART, JOSEPH; and ENGLAND, ROBERT. 1989. *Race, Class, and Education.* Madison: University of Wisconsin Press.

ORFIELD, GARY, and EATON, SUSAN. 1996. *Dismantling Desegregation.* New York: New Press.

PETERSON, PAUL E. 1985. *The Politics of School Reform.* Chicago: University of Chicago Press.

WONG, KENNETH K. 1999. *Funding Public Schools.* Lawrence: University Press of Kansas.

KENNETH K. WONG

EDUCATIONAL LEADERSHIP

Schools are social institutions that play an important role in what is arguably the most complex responsibility of society: the healthy development of children. The people who lead schools must have a deep understanding of the many dimensions of this task, yet the challenges fall within the general category of crafting and carrying out agreements among many stakeholders. Some of these agreements have long timelines and reach into the heart of the enterprise. The bulk of the agreements, however, are short, temporary arrangements that get the various stakeholders—students, teachers, parents, policy makers—from one step in the process to the next. Effective schools are places in which these agreements are fashioned and honored successfully. Effective educational leaders are people who make that happen.

In the United States, the responsibility for public schools falls within the jurisdiction of the states, but from an operational perspective schools are the business of local government. The authority of principals and superintendents derives from that basic structure, and educational leadership is traditionally associated with the people in those positions. Accordingly, principals and superintendents are the parties most responsible for crafting the essential agreements upon which schools either succeed or fail.

The role of these leaders has evolved as society has changed and as schools have been asked to take on responsibilities that far exceed the basic literacy and numeracy skills that were expected in the early days of American public schools. As communities grew and schools increased in size beyond the point where a single teacher could meet the needs of all pupils, and as the amount of schooling required of all children increased, the position of principal—a term that literally implies the first teacher—or headmaster was created to provide instructional leadership to ensure coordination among the teachers. When the continuing growth of communities forced them to create multiple schools, the superintendent position was created to coordinate the system within those schools operated.

Beginning in the early 1960s with the advent of comprehensive high schools and consolidated school districts, and eventually in response to increased demands placed upon schools by the states and the federal government, there was dramatic growth in the number of other administrative positions in the district's central office. These school leaders are more specialized, working, for example, in a single area such as finance or curriculum.

School administration also became differentiated through positions associated with content-area specialists and, in some cases, basic assistance for the principal. During the last decades of the twentieth century, there was steady growth in the number of educators working in districts who did not participate directly in the instruction of students. Pressures throughout the schools and districts, including the supervision of these new administrators, and the steady flow of multiple mandates from state and federal government, began to erode the opportunity principals and superintendents once had to provide real leadership.

In the late 1990s, another notion about educational leadership arose. Recognizing the value of distributing leadership responsibility to those people who were closest to student learning, some educators began to talk about the need for teacher leadership. The concept was unusual in a system that associates leaders with people who have specific titles. Also, the idea that teachers might be expected to provide leadership for their peers, their schools, and their profession while remaining in the primary role as teacher was a radical departure from the norm.

A Challenging Environment

The basic context in which schools operate makes leadership difficult. Everyone, it seems, has a vested interest in schools. Each of the nation's chief executives has regularly tried to identify himself as the "Education President." Governors make similar assertions, and states have a chief school officer, either appointed or elected, who is surrounded by an administrative staff to oversee the proper operation of schools. Money, and who provides that money, gives another road map to lines of authority, and for all but the nation's poorest schools, the combined contributions of state and federal dollars do not equal the dollars provided by local government and local taxpayers. That balance leads to a large amount of authority vested in school boards, typically elected officials, who run for these offices for a variety of reasons, or appointed people who have their own allegiances.

Thrown into this mix are teacher unions, connected with powerful national associations, and other unions serving the needs of support staff. Anyone trying to lead a public school cannot take lightly the contract a district has with a bus company, for example, or with the maintenance staff who have control of very basic parts of the operation. This list of interested parties is far from complete, and the challenges of leadership have outpaced the profession's capacity to recruit, prepare, and sustain those who take on that responsibility.

Recruiting, Preparing, and Sustaining School Leaders

As public schools became larger and more complex, the professional path to becoming a school leader became more prescribed. As with other professions, the responsibility for preparing school leaders came to rest within the universities and particularly in graduate departments of education. In keeping with the traditional patterns of the academic world, preparation was defined by certain courses of study and the successful accumulation of credits. School administration became an actual course and eventually was broken up into a series of courses that included everything from finance to labor relations to organizational behavior. While most graduate degree programs include a practicum or internship, this part of required study has been minimal.

The states have been involved in the formalizing and conceptualizing of what skills and credentials a person must have in order to become a principal or superintendent. States prescribe these skills and credentials within a certification process. Because supply and demand for principals and superintendents varies over time and sometimes puts districts at risk of losing good candidates or not having enough candidates to fill positions, many states have alternative paths to certification and interim permissions that can be granted in lieu of certain requirements or until those requirements can be completed.

This standard approach to preparing principals and superintendents has been questioned during the school reform era that began in the early 1980s. One response, directly related to an increasing concern over the quantity and quality of the candidate pool for principals, was the rise in what are called *aspiring principal programs*. These programs require educators who hope to become principals to spend large amounts of time with successful principals on the job. The belief is that while formal courses can help prepare people to become principals, the more important skills are acquired through apprenticeship.

The principalship has changed significantly since the 1960s. With the growth of strong central offices and increasing unionization of teachers, principals began to be removed from their role as first teacher or headmaster. They lost the authority to hire and fire their own teachers and were no longer in a position to provide leadership for curriculum and instruction. In many cases, principals are not even the highest paid educators within a school building, while they regularly work a longer school year than teachers do.

Principals have a difficult time finding the authority to secure agreements among the key stakeholders, and they seldom have the resources necessary to support such work. These conditions are not conducive to encouraging educators who have passion and vision about teaching and learning to consider moving from the classroom to the principal's office.

One positive development for principals began in 1981 when the first Principals Center was created at the Harvard Graduate School of Education. This center was founded to provide a professional community for principals, who often are the most isolated educators in their schools, and to encourage the kind of lifelong learning that would improve the skills of principals as leaders and managers of their schools. The concept spread rapidly, and within ten years, more than one hundred similar centers had been founded throughout the United States and in other countries. These centers are connected through their own international association.

Superintendents have had similar difficulties. Their domain is connected with local politics, the elected or appointed school boards and mayors and city councils that often play a significant role in approving budgets. These challenges have been exacerbated in large urban districts that saw their tax base decline in the last four decades of the twentieth century, their middle class families depart, and a growing number of special challenges related to rapidly changing populations, high levels of poverty, and a physical infrastructure that was crumbling. Many urban districts also face a disproportionate increase in the number of school-age children and a decreasing amount of money to support them. In many cases, these financial pressures lead to greater state subsidies for these districts and the accompanying demands, all of which only add to the political climate surrounding the work of superintendents.

One measurable result of these increased pressures has been the length of time the average superintendent remains in that position, which by the late 1990s had dropped to under three years. Given the difficulties of leading these complex organizations, such a rapid turnover among superintendents makes it nearly impossible for any meaningful change to take place.

Public school superintendents have responsibility in four basic areas: managing a complex enterprise, managing multilayered politics, building community and public support for schools, and leading a whole systems improvement process. Most superintendents accept inherited agreements made by their predecessors in the first three areas. They come into their jobs with all of those areas in place and little opportunity to refashion agreements. Their vision for the fourth area cannot easily penetrate the existing structure of the district, much of which is already dictated by a variety of contracts with teachers, administrators, and different support staff. The budget, too, is often already established, and given the large percentage of school budgets that is earmarked for salaries, benefits, and maintenance, there are very few financial resources superintendents can deploy to help support their initiatives. As is the case with principal preparation programs, university-based programs leading to advanced degrees and certification have had a difficult time keeping up with the rapid changes in the field and the demands placed on these district leaders.

Leadership in the Twenty-First Century

State standards enacted in the 1990s defined a new goal of helping all students graduate ready for further learning, work and citizenship. States, frustrated by the slow pace of progress in too many schools, began to attach consequences to school failure. Although few could argue with the validity of this new proposition, it challenged the beliefs, assumptions, structures, and practice of the American educational system, and required school leaders to craft new agreements. It also multiplied the complexity and difficulty of educational leadership. By 2000, state assessments regularly were diagnosing the health of schools and were testing the success and strength of the agreements that school leaders either crafted or inherited.

Low-performing schools suffer most from a lack of leadership. The agreements made or tolerated in these schools leave children ill-prepared for the world they will inherit and do a particular disservice to disadvantaged youth. The identification of low-performing schools often results in a variety of district and state interventions. To be effective, these interventions take the shape of new agreements designed to create a clear focus, improve curriculum and assessment of student work, and strengthen staff evaluation and professional development.

While those strategies often find fertile ground in elementary schools, they seldom are enough to improve secondary schools, especially those that are large and comprehensive. In these schools the agreements that exist among stakeholders are simply not conducive to the national goal of leaving no child behind. The first task that the principals of these schools must confront, in concert with their superintendent, is leadership focused on redesigning their large comprehensive high schools into small learning communities.

System Leaders as Agreement Crafters

Least well understood, and central to all of these roles, is the question: how should the system work? With growing diversity, emerging opportunities and challenges of information technology, evolving knowledge about high performance organizations, and the new proposition that all students can and should achieve at high levels, it is often not clear what success at scale looks like. The new proposition of the standards movement—that all students should leave high school prepared for college, work, and citizenship—is easy to accept in theory but much more difficult to actualize. As school districts grapple with standards, high-stakes tests, growing frustration among taxpayers and politicians, and new alternatives to the public schools, the most important agreement that every superintendent and principal must craft is around the basic way that the district and the schools should work.

Given the multiple layers of federal, state, and local bureaucracy in education, and decades of piling layers of programs and policies onto schools, the first challenge of system leaders is to create coherence—making everything work together for students and teachers. Leaders can either attempt to create coherence, or alignment, throughout the system or create a system where schools achieve their own unique form of coherence.

Whatever the answer to the question about how a school or district should work, the system leader must be able to describe the organizational strategy in simple terms and support it with consistent organizational behavior. In order for that vision to take root, the leader must bring many parties to the agreement. Radically changing the way a school system works takes a reshaping of virtually all of the agreements between the district and schools and many of the basic agreements inside schools. Making any answer work requires a sustained effort, perhaps over a period of at least a decade.

The role of agreement crafter implies the need for new experiences and skills for both principals and superintendents. Superintendents and principals need opportunities to study a variety of approaches and the context in which they are being deployed. They need to adopt, modify, or reject the agreements that they inherit based on a deep understanding of the local context and exposure to strategic options.

Agreement crafters must be politically savvy, possess sophisticated consulting skills, and be adept change managers. Principals and superintendents need to be aware of community power structure, key influencers, and political decision makers. The demands of diversity, technology, and standards, particularly at the secondary level, require a set of consulting skills to design and facilitate a series of linked conversations that lead to adult learning and shared vision. As change managers, principals and superintendents must sequence complex tasks in a way that is manageable for the staff to incorporate.

See also: PRINCIPAL, SCHOOL; SUPERINTENDENT OF SCHOOLS.

BIBLIOGRAPHY

BARTH, ROLAND S. 1990. *Improving Schools from Within.* San Francisco: Jossey-Bass.

BOYER, ERNEST L. 1983. *High School: A Report on Secondary Education in America.* New York: Harper and Row.

DEAL, TERRENCE E., and PETERSON, KENT D. 1998. *Shaping School Culture: The Heart of Leadership.* San Francisco: Jossey-Bass.

FULLAN, MICHAEL. 2001. *Leading in a Culture of Change.* New York: John Wiley and Sons.

GARDNER, JOHN W. 1990. *On Leadership.* New York: The Free Press.

SIZER, THEODORE R. 1984. *Horace's Compromise: The Dilemma of the American High School.* Boston: Houghton Mifflin.

THORPE, RONALD D., ed. 1995. *The First Year as Principal: Real World Stories from America's Principals.* Portsmouth, NH: Heinemann.

TYACK, DAVID B. 1974. *The One Best System: A History of American Urban Education.* Cambridge, MA: Harvard University Press.

WAGNER, TONY. 2001. *Making the Grade: Reinventing America's Schools.* New York: Routledge.

TOM VANDER ARK
KATHY KLOCK

EDUCATIONAL POLICY, UNITED STATES

Education is an instrument of the broader social order. When society changes, education, sooner or later, also changes. Few activities or agencies, however, change as slowly, or in such small increments, as formal education—both schools and colleges as well as both public and private institutions. Education's roots are deep and wide, penetrating almost every facet of society. Hence, education is subject to virtually every political force, including those that want change and those that want to protect the status quo.

Public K–12 education—which operates across fifty states, 14,000 local school districts, and 100,000 schools; involves 5 million employees and more than 48 million students; and costs more than $2 billion each day—is too large, too costly, and too enmeshed in political dynamics to change quickly. Postsecondary institutions—colleges and universities—have become equally ponderous. With the advent of post–World War II enrollment increases; the significance of university-based research for preserving the nation's economic, medical, and military preeminence; and the substantial assumption of student financial aid by government, higher education also has become a major feature of the political landscape and become engulfed by much of the inertia that immobilizes lower schools.

For most of American history, the nation's most prestigious elementary and secondary schools and elite colleges have been few in number, and their private charters and religious affiliations have rendered them generally independent of government. But for colleges and universities, nearly all of which, in the early twenty-first century, are accepting student financial-aid subsidies from government and engaging in government-sponsored research, this situation has changed. Government now is a major constituent for higher education, both public and private.

Even for private preparatory and religious elementary and secondary schools, the condition of independence from government could change. If the U.S. Supreme Court approves allocation of public funds for private and religious institutions, private schools could come under the full umbrella of public policy in the same way as their public institutional counterparts.

Still, even as subjects of increasing politicization, and even if only at a glacial pace, schools and colleges do change. Formal education at the onset of the twenty-first century exhibited many differences from that of even thirty years previous, and it certainly was different from what children and parents experienced in the early part of the twentieth century.

The Basics of Educational Policy

Societies rely upon the informal socialization of youth and immigrants and the formal education of citizens to preserve the polity and facilitate pursuit of individuals' collective and personal preferences. Because of this mediating role in maintaining a society, formal education systems, and those who steer them, are unusually sensitive to alterations in citizens' will or shifts in decision makers' views. When a society perceives itself subjected to threat or is engrossed in a major economic, technological, demographic, or ecological transformation, the education system is a principal instrument to which it turns in order to adjust to change and seek a new social equilibrium.

The larger and more democratic a society, the less linear and less transparent its education system alterations will be. In a dictatorship or narrow oligarchy, it is relatively easy to change an education system. In the booming, buzzing cacophony of the open, modern information age and a globally interdependent society, education reform is episodic, conflict prone, inconsistent, and, sometimes painful.

Indeed, the more porous and dynamic a society, the more inconsistent and conflictual its efforts to change its education system will appear. Interests deeply rooted in spheres such as economics, religion, ideology, institutions, geography, race, and ethnicity will vie to have their worldview represented most forcefully in whatever education system emerges. These are the centrifugal forces that threaten the momentum and unity of any society. Countering these are centripetal (unifying) forces, mostly institutions, ideologies, and influential individuals that seek consensus and cohesion. It is the tension between these dynamics that eventually shapes changes to a democracy's education system.

The Pressure for Reform in American Education

The twentieth century, particularly its last two decades, represented a period of remarkably intense change. A brief review of what took place globally during this period suggests the reason why America's education system has been under such intense pressure to reform.

The post–World War II cold war rivalry between East and West ended in the early 1990s. Democratic capitalism generally surmounted totalitarian socialism to become the world's dominant political economy. Modern communication and transportation technologies contributed to globally oriented, highly mobile, and rapidly paced societies. Economic developments created a heretofore-unknown degree of individual, organizational, and international interdependence. The United States emerged as the leading economic and political power in the world. This condition, coupled with globalization, generat-

ed added diplomatic, military, and humanitarian responsibilities for the nation and its citizens.

The United States is fortunate in having vast resources. It has become expected, however, to deploy these riches not only for the protection and promotion of its citizens but also for the well-being of the world. Issues of health in Africa, overpopulation in Asia, political instability in Latin America, religious conflict in the Middle East, trade restrictions in Europe, ozone depletion in Antarctica, overfishing in the North Atlantic, or ice cap reductions in the Arctic are no longer remote issues. The eventual outcome of these conditions now matters as much for a child being raised on a productive family farm in South Dakota as to an apartheid-liberated farm family in South Africa.

This new and fast-paced world has dampened some old issues. Widespread fears of nuclear annihilation, pestilence, and global famine have become ameliorated. But age-old concerns regarding religious and racial intolerance, social injustice, economic inequality, and discouraging instances of inhumanity have by no means been eliminated. Even a few new issues have evolved, for example, fear of widespread environmental degradation and uneven economic development between nations in the northern and southern hemispheres.

In making its adjustments to the new global world, American education policy is moving on two fronts simultaneously. First, the new world order necessitates that everyone be educated. Hence, issues of access and equality remain important. Second, it is no longer sufficient that individuals simply be exposed to schooling, it is increasingly important that they actually learn. Hence, the additional policy pressure is to render education institutions effective, both in achieving their objectives and in the use of the vast resources they command. The upshot is that both equality and efficiency are paramount issues on the education policy agenda. When pressures emerge, however, for maximization of these two ends, then, inevitably, counterforces arise out of reaction to protect and extend the other policy objective, liberty.

Defining Policy

Policy is one of the principal vectors through which influence flows between the larger society and education institutions. The term *policy* refers to the decisions and rules enacted by the three branches of government at all levels—national, state, and local. The policy pipeline is capable of reciprocal transmission. Whereas society's preferences shape and continually reshape education, the outcomes of education continually influence the values and preferences of the broader society.

The word *policy* is derived from the Greek *polis,* referring to city or citizen. Subsequent Roman usage led to the term *polity,* meaning government, government organization, regime, or nation. In modern parlance, policy refers to a uniform decision rule, a regulation, or a set of prescriptions that applies in all similar circumstances. The term *public policy* refers to a government-specified or -enacted decision rule. Of course, when people speak of education policy, or at least public education policy, they are referring to government decision rules regarding education, schools, colleges, or related matters.

Government rules regarding school attendance, graduation, college entry, what will be studied, who will teach, who will be paid, and who will pay are all illustrations of education policies. Policies are enacted by all three branches of government in the form of executive orders from the president, governors, and mayors; statutes and ordinances enacted by legislative bodies such as the U.S. Congress, state legislatures, and city councils; and judicial decisions issued by courts.

The Public Values Underlying Education Policy

American culture contains three strongly held values that significantly influence public policy in general and education policy specifically. They are equality, efficiency, and liberty. Government actions regarding national defense, housing, taxation, antitrust regulation, racial desegregation, and literally hundreds of other policy dimensions, including education, are motivated and molded by one or more of these three values.

The overwhelming majority of the public views equality, liberty, and efficiency as conditions that government should attempt to maximize. The historical roots of these values are deeply embedded in the cultural streams that comprise the common heritage of the United States. These values permeate the ideologies promulgated by political parties, religions, schools, and other social institutions.

Despite widespread public devotion to equality, efficiency, and liberty as abstract goals, it is almost impossible to pursue these values to their ultimate practical fulfillment. At their roots, the three desired conditions are inconsistent and antithetical. Exclusive or concentrated pursuit of equality restricts or eliminates liberty and efficiency. Similarly, one-sided attention to either one of the other values reduces the remaining two. Consequently, efforts to rearrange society so as to maximize fulfillment of one of the three values are constrained by forces desiring to enhance or preserve the status quo of one or both of the others.

The three values are always suspended in dynamic equilibrium. The practical relationships among them constantly shift; the balance at any particular point in time is fixed as a consequence of a complicated series of compromises made within the political and economic systems.

It can be argued that liberty or freedom is the highest of the three values. Efficiency for its own sake is absent much meaning. The justification for desiring that an endeavor be undertaken efficiently is to conserve resources that then can be used for other endeavors, thus achieving greater equality or expanding choice. Similarly, equality as an end in itself appears hollow. Few if any persons desire absolute parity with their peers. Rather, equality of wealth, power, and circumstance can be viewed as desirable means to the end of greater opportunity or choice. Education is one of the prime instruments through which American society attempts to promote fulfillment of all three values.

Education as Policy Instrument in the Pursuit of Equality, Efficiency, and Liberty

Various large-scale social movements have, over time, contributed to formal education's place among society's major institutions. For example, the sixteenth-century Protestant Reformation encouraged education as a means to facilitate individual interpretation of religious scriptures. Similarly, among eighteenth-century leaders of the new republic, the United States, education was viewed as a means to enable one to participate as an equal in the affairs of government. Under these circumstances, education was important to ensure political liberty. It was not until the nineteenth century, however, that formal education began to assume significance for economic purposes in Western societies.

The increasing technical complexity of nineteenth-century industrialization necessitated a more highly educated workforce. This condition provoked widespread provision of public schooling, and, in subsequent periods, schooling has been taken as an important contributor to economic efficiency.

In the opening of one of his famous mid-nineteenth-century annual reports as secretary for the Massachusetts Board of Education, Horace Mann said "Education prevents being poor." Here was one of the first highly visible expressions of the new nineteenth-century relationship between education and economic well-being. By the twentieth century, and even more so in the early twenty-first century, schooling has been rendered crucial for an individual's economic and social success. Consequently, schooling has assumed new importance for fulfilling the practical expression of individual equality.

Beginning with the 1954 U.S. Supreme Court decision in *Brown v. Board of Education of Topeka, Kansas,* and continuing with the vast increase in federal government education programs of the 1960s and the education finance reform efforts of the 1970s, a major portion of mid- and late twentieth-century education policy was directed at achieving greater equality.

Equality in and Access to Education

In the latter half of the twentieth century, courts began to apply the U.S. Constitution's equal protection clause to a spectrum of social conditions, such as voting rights, housing, employment, and education. This Civil War–era constitutional provision stretched the mantle of federally protected civil liberties to include state government. Hence, the 1950s and several decades thereafter marked a period of intense judicial activism by which courts began to ensure that federally guaranteed civil rights were not overridden by state or local policies. A long-heralded era of "local control" regarding schools was now about to be substantially restricted.

Racial desegregation. It is possible that the topic of racial desegregation provoked greater controversy in the United States than any other public policy issue in the last half of the twentieth century. National guard mobilization, massive public demonstrations, civil disobedience, heated political campaigns, acrimonious school board elections, and movements aiming to recall state officials are but a few illustrations of the intensity of the conflict.

The initial U.S. Supreme Court decision in *Brown v. Board of Education* incorporated social

science evidence in support of the view that legally enforced segregation of schools violated the Fourteenth Amendment and was damaging to minority students. In subsequent years, researchers, primarily sociologists, conducted numerous analytic studies to assess the effects of desegregated schooling. For the most part, results proved ambiguous. No clear path of direct evidentiary proof exists as to whether minority students benefit from desegregated school settings. Even the original social science research cited by the U.S. Supreme Court is disputed in the early twenty-first century. There are those who contend that the entire school desegregation movement, on balance, is a social experiment that has failed. They cite as evidence for their position the following: more African-American children attended racially isolated classes in 2000 than was the case twenty-five years before. Conversely, there is aggregate evidence that suggests racial desegregation is beneficial for so-called minority families and children. For example 2000 census results show that middle-income African-American students more often than their lower income counterparts attend schools in desegregated suburban communities. In such communities, African-American students' academic achievement and economic performance measures are higher. Such studies are unable to control for a host of competing hypotheses such as that those who flourish economically, and who choose a suburban lifestyle, are possibly more motivated personally. The confounding of conditions renders a solid answer difficult.

Despite the ambiguity of social science desegregation results and the mixed success of northern school desegregation efforts, one facet of the issue emerges with relative clarity. The de jure segregated school systems of southern states, with few exceptions, have been successfully dismantled. This is the case not because of the dramatic findings of policy analysts and researchers, but because of the construction of successful legal strategies and judicial enforcement.

Education finance. In 1967 Arthur E. Wise questioned the constitutionality of state school financing arrangements. Wise, then a doctoral student in school administration at the University of Chicago, contributed to the effort to eliminate inequality, not a new set of fiscal analyses, but, rather, the suggestion of a new legal theory. He published his ideas in a 1968 book titled *Rich Schools, Poor Schools.*

Other legal scholars were quick to follow. Subsequently, John E. Coons, William H. Clune III, and

Stephen D. Sugarman wrote *Private Wealth and Public Education,* which, in a lucid fashion, dissected the operation of state school finance statutes and described a strategy whereby they could be challenged legally. Wise, as well as Coons and his colleagues, formulated the principle of fiscal neutrality, that is, the principle that the quality of a child's schooling should not be a function of wealth, other than the wealth of the state as a whole. By providing a negatively phrased decision rule, permitting courts to strike down existing schemes while allowing legislatures to construct a statutory redress of the inequity, Wise and Coons and his colleagues rescued the fledgling "equal protection" school finance movement from judicial oblivion. Prior to that time, courts were deciding against plaintiffs on grounds that no judicially manageable solutions were apparent.

By the close of the twentieth century, most gross fiscal disparities had been mitigated. Only a few egregious inequities remained. Indeed, a study by Sheila Murray, David Evans, and Robert Schwab demonstrated that most school spending differences were between states, not within states.

In the latter years of the twentieth century, proponents of greater equality of education financing began to alter conventional "equal protection" arguments. They took their cue from the Kentucky Supreme Court in its 1989 *Rose v. Council for Better Education* decision. Here the court held the state accountable not only for equal financing but also for equal educational opportunity. The Kentucky decision gave rise to a subsequent genre of what has come to be known as "adequacy" suits. In these suits, the distribution of school dollars has not been the consideration as much as the consequences of school dollars. The contention of plaintiffs is that education is a state constitutional responsibility, and, thus, states must ensure that local districts and schools deliver an education adequate for a student to succeed in the workforce and as a democratic citizen.

Special education. Special education was the latest school population category to be the focus for substantial reform. The reform proceeded on two dimensions: the provision of appropriate school services to students with physical and mental disabilities and the provision of bilingual instruction to non- or limited-English-speaking students.

The historic inability or unwillingness of school districts to serve adequately the needs of students with disabilities had long been recognized. As was the case historically with school finance inequities, however, there appeared no easy means by which the situation could be altered. Specialized services can be extraordinarily expensive; school officials claimed that their budgets simply were too stretched to provide them. When state categorical funds were provided for special education, local school districts all too frequently diverted all or a portion of such moneys to subsidize the regular school program. The mid-1960s innovation aimed at rectifying these conditions was the construction of a successful legal theory to mandate change.

The landmark cases are *Mills v. Board of Education* and *Pennsylvania Association of Retarded Children v. Commonwealth of Pennsylvania* for students with disabilities and *Lau v. Nichols* for the non-English speaking. These cases both altered the special education practices of states and local school districts and influenced Congress in enacting the Education for All Handicapped Children Act of 1975. The consequence of these movements has been to increase dollar spending for special education by billions. At the beginning of the twenty-first century, American public schools were spending 20 percent of their operating budgets on the education of students with disabilities. No claim is made that all problems have disappeared in the schooling of students with disabilities. At the turn of the twenty-first century, however, the landscape was powerfully different than even a quarter of a century before.

Collective bargaining. Concerns for equity have not concentrated upon students exclusively. Professional educators have also sought means by which they could be treated more equally.

Beginning in the 1950s, teachers began to expand their unions to engage more effectively in collective bargaining with school boards. This development was initiated in large cities and subsequently spread to almost every school district in the United States. To a large degree, increases in organizational size, bureaucratization, and the expansion of administrative levels probably accounted for teachers' feelings of inefficacy and alienation and prompted them to unionize.

Although it frequently is the case that teacher representatives come to the bargaining table with concerns for the welfare of students and respect for the interests of the broader public, their primary allegiance is to teachers' welfare. They cannot legitimately claim to represent the larger public. Nevertheless, duly elected public representatives— school board members—must share decision-making authority with them. The outcome is to further centralize school policymaking and to erode the ability of the general public to participate in the process. It is conditions such as these that prompt critics of public education to demand yet other changes.

Higher education. The pursuit of greater equality has also left an imprint on the nation's colleges. For example, Title IX of the Higher Education Act decrees parity in athletics for males and females at postsecondary institutions. In addition the Higher Education Act requires colleges to pledge themselves not to discriminate racially or in other ways if they use federal funding to subsidize student financial aid, promote research, or construct dormitories.

The Pursuit of Efficiency in Education

Efficiency advocates, usually overlooking the substantial expansion in functions expected of America's public schools, claim that per-pupil expenditures nationwide have escalated in a troublesome manner. They argue that even when inflation is discounted, the per-pupil increase in school spending between 1950 and 2000 was 500 percent. The additional funds have been used to purchase items that, according to conventional education wisdom, will facilitate production. For example, class sizes have been reduced, and many categories of instructional and administrative specialists have been added. Despite such added resources, there appear to be no dramatic increases in output. Indeed, to the extent that standardized test scores are valid indicators of school production, output has diminished.

Efficiency has always been a major concern for educational policymakers and school administrators. There have existed points in history, however, at which particular attention has been accorded the topic. The mid-1920s was a time of such intense interest. This period coincided with the expansion of school administration as a specialized field. In an effort to enhance their professionalism, education officials attempted to adopt for schools many of the efficiency techniques then popular in industry. Raymond E. Callahan, in his 1960 book *Education and the Cult of Efficiency,* described this movement.

School district consolidation was another strategic arrow in the quiver of pre–World War II education efficiency proponents. By 1930 the number of

local school districts in the United States had reached its high point—in excess of 125,000 separate units. By 1976 this number had been reduced to approximately 16,000. The number of districts hovered around 14,000 at the beginning of the twenty-first century. This drastic reduction in the number of units of a specialized local government took place in a manner so subtle as virtually to escape the notice of policy analysts. It also took place without a shred of persuasive evidence that it would indeed save money. Nevertheless, it constitutes one of the most dramatic of all changes in America's patterns of government.

In the 1960s, sociologists dominated school efficiency research. The premier study of this period was the *Coleman Report,* named after its principal author, James S. Coleman. The Coleman team concluded that school quality had little effect on student achievement independent of the social background of students. This finding, even though not so intended, was widely interpreted by the media and other lay sources as meaning that dollars for schools made little difference in student learning. This misunderstood assertion was widely publicized by efficiency advocates, and the Coleman finding served as justification during the 1970s for reducing the trajectory of school spending increases.

At various points in U.S. education history, the term *accountability* appears as a symbol. It represents a policy effort to control escalating school costs and insufficient student achievement by employing techniques that advocates suggest will improve school productivity. The efficiency movement of the late twentieth and early twenty-first centuries, operating under the episodically popular label of accountability, was launched by the 1983 appearance of *A Nation at Risk,* a highly visible national report by the National Commission on Excellence in Education. Seldom has an elite panel issued a document whose thesis was more inaccurate. Paradoxically, seldom has a blue-ribbon report had such a widespread and long-lasting consequence and had such a profound and lasting impact on public opinion and policy.

The report asserted that America's preeminence in defense, technology, economics, science, and industry was threatened by the mediocrity of its public education system. The report left the impression that the United States was about to succumb to a deluge of foreign dominance, unless its schools were rapidly rendered more rigorous. But twenty years later, it became plain to see that the economic slump in which the United States found itself at the report's 1983 issuance was far more a consequence of inefficient management practices than it was the nation's ineffective education system. Also in the intervening period, the Japanese economy plummeted, and its once vaunted education system was unable to protect it from its inefficient financial practices and protectionist trade policies. Indeed, beginning in 2000, Japan took steps to pattern its education system more after the United States. Rightly or wrongly, however, *A Nation at Risk* launched two decades of education reform in America, and the call for change shows no signs of subsiding.

Illustrating the Changes

The early twenty-first century mantra of educational accountability has an accompanying lexicon. This includes terms and ideas such as high performance schools, high-stakes testing, academic accountability, school effectiveness, organizational efficiency, teacher productivity, performance financing, charter schools, alternative schools, break-the-mold schools, privatizing, outsourcing, and pay for results. These and similar terms are illustrative of the slogans, issues, and topics that dominate American education policy and practice at the onset of the twenty-first century.

Underneath the slogans, two major change strategies have evolved. One is called the standards movement. The other travels under the banner of "competition" or "privatization." The two strategies are not mutually incompatible. Each necessitates government specification of learning standards or curricular goals that schools are expected to meet.

In the standards movement, textbooks and other instructional materials, teacher training, professional licensing, financial arrangements, statewide achievement testing, and performance awards and penalties are expected to be aligned and made consistent with these purposes. Advocates for the second strategy, competition, contend that American automobiles improved in the 1970s only under the threat of foreign competition, and schools are no different. Only when the current public school monopoly is severed, the argument goes, will professional educators be motivated to try harder and teach better. Competition or privatization advocates seek magnet schools, charter schools, voucher plans, parent choice plans, and smaller schools and school districts.

At the beginning of the twenty-first century, the standards movement held the upper hand. Literally thousands of legislative enactments, commission reports, gubernatorial campaigns, and regulatory activities had been constructed in its support. It was too early, however, to judge its effects.

Competition or choice has not yet seen a full day. Proposals for greater privatization of schooling have not come to dominate either the marketplace of policy ideas nor the practical arena of school operation. Union leaders speak in substantial opposition to privatization. Other critics fear the prospect of religious and ideological extremists being the recipients of government support. There are yet other critics who fear that greater privatization will further impede achieving a vision of a more fully integrated society, both racially and economically.

The U.S. Supreme Court was expected to rule in 2002 on the constitutionality of an Ohio law permitting public funds to be used in support of students' private schooling. Should the court rule favorably on the plan, privatization and competition might receive a substantial boost. An unfavorable decision might slow or substantially stall competition.

The Pursuit of Liberty

A third deeply held value that frequently influences the direction of American education policy is liberty. This value provided a major ideological justification for the revolution that gave birth to the United States as a nation. In an essay on the new Constitution published in the *National Gazette* on January 17, 1792, James Madison wrote: "In Europe, charters of liberty have been granted by power. America has set the example, and France has followed it on charters of power granted by liberty."

For Americans, liberty has meant the freedom to choose, to be able to select from among different courses of action. The desire for choice fueled the historical American affection for a market economy. Competition among producers, along with other benefits, is held to expand the range of items from which consumers can choose. In the public sector, responsive governmental institutions are taken to be a crucial element for the expressions and preservation of choice and liberty.

In the view of those who initially designed the structures of American government, authority was vested in the citizenry, who then delegated the power to govern to selected representatives. A measure of representatives' effectiveness was the degree to which they were responsive to the will of those they governed. Lack of responsiveness eroded power of the citizenry and, thus, constituted grounds for removal from office.

A second means for preserving liberty was to dispense governmental authority widely. This accounts for the separation of powers between three branches and over various levels of government. Efforts to inhibit accumulation of power also account for the deliberate fragmentation of decision-making authority, with some specific powers accorded to the federal government, some accorded to the states, and some reserved for the people themselves. Historically, the power to make educational decisions was structured in the same fashion. Centralized authority was viewed as perilous because of the prospect of exerting widespread control and uniformity. Formation of literally thousands of small local school districts, portending both inefficiency and inequality, was intended as an antidote to the accumulation of power. Proximity to constituents, coupled with the electoral process, was taken as a means to enhance governmental responsiveness and preserve liberty.

The federal constitution provides the state governments with ultimate legal responsibility for school decision-making. Historically states delegated substantial policy discretion to local units of government. In the period since World War II, however, factors such as increasing school costs, the politicization of school decisions, and intensified efforts to achieve greater equality of educational opportunity and more efficient use of school resources have heightened state-level participation.

A consequence of this increased state participation has been to remove a large measure of decision-making discretion from local education authorities. For example, state specifications on accountability dimensions such as the school curriculum, teacher salaries and working conditions, graduation requirements, and school architecture have increased markedly. Fewer persons now determine more decisions regarding schools. Choice is restricted, the ability of local officials to respond to constituent preferences is constrained, and, at least in a legal sense, local autonomy, liberty, and probably efficiency have been diminished.

By the latter half of the 1960s, a reaction to the diminished status of representativeness had begun.

Requests for change stemmed initially from ethnic enclaves in large cities, which perceived themselves as relatively impotent in affecting the operation of their children's schools. They demanded what was then labeled "community control." For example, several community-control experiments were attempted in the New York City schools. The state legislature ultimately recognized the growing political tide by dividing New York City into thirty-two elementary school districts. Given that each of the thirty-two averaged 30,000 students, approximately the size of the entire school system of the city of Syracuse, this could not realistically be characterized as community control. Nevertheless, each of New York's local districts was authorized to elect a nine-member local board of education. Thus, New York's elected school policymakers grew from 9 to 297.

Reaction to the dilution of representativeness also reached Congress. Federal education acts were amended in the early 1970s to mandate parent participation in the making of decisions about the use of federal program funds. Also, by the mid-1970s several state legislatures were requiring formation of parent advisory councils at school sites. Numerous local school districts were voluntarily implementing plans for wider involvement of citizens in school decision-making.

By the 1990s, and extending into the twenty-first century, liberty advocates were pursuing more powerful strategies than simply enhanced parent advisory councils. The new expressions of liberty were charter schools and voucher plans.

Charter schools in effect are local schools free to operate outside the restraint of a school district. Their operating charter can be granted either by state authority or, in some instances, by a local school board. They can be private or public. They derive their financial support from public sources. They are the equivalent of so-called grant-maintained schools in Great Britain. They are required to have a board of directors and to be fiscally responsible. In most states, charter schools are also required to adhere to a minimal state curriculum and to administer state standardized achievement tests. Students are free to attend charter schools or to select their regularly assigned public school.

Voucher plans involve public education funds flowing to households that then choose the school for their children. Vouchers are the subject of experimentation in Milwaukee, Wisconsin; Cleveland,

Ohio; and San Antonio, Texas. They are unusually controversial because their subsidy may pierce the conventional First Amendment prohibition of public funding in support of religious causes. In June 2000 the U.S. Supreme Court ruled that students in Cleveland may use state-funded vouchers to pay tuition at private schools, including schools with a religious affiliation. The decision in this case is likely to have a significant policy impact for years to come.

Conclusion

Will accountability efforts succeed in elevating U.S. school performance? Will colleges and universities eventually be subjected to the same kind of efficiency requirements experienced by public schools? Will the achievement gap between middle- and lower income students be narrowed? Will public funding of private and religious schools eventually be approved, and, if so, will such arrangements prove the undoing of the great American socialization engine, public schooling?

There is no effort here at predicting the outcome of such queries. The answers will come in time and, no doubt, will be the subject of future analysis and comment. What is predictable, however, is that the significance of education for society will only increase and that government will continue to be challenged by continually having to strike a new balance among the advocates of greater equality, efficiency, and liberty.

See also: EDUCATION REFORM; EFFICIENCY IN EDUCATION; FINANCIAL SUPPORT OF SCHOOLS; GOVERNMENT AND EDUCATION, THE CHANGING ROLE OF; MULTICULTURAL EDUCATION; SCHOOL REFORM; SPECIAL EDUCATION.

BIBLIOGRAPHY

BAILYN, BERNARD. 1967. *The Ideological Origins of the American Revolution.* Cambridge, MA: Harvard University Press.

BARKER, ROGER G., and GUMP, PAUL V. 1964. *Big School, Small School.* Palo Alto, CA: Stanford University Press.

CALLAHAN, RAYMOND E. 1960. *Education and the Cult of Efficiency.* Chicago: University of Chicago Press.

COLEMAN, JAMES S., et al. 1966. *Equality of Educational Opportunity.* Washington, DC: National Center for Educational Statistics.

CONANT, JAMES BRYANT. 1959. *The American High School Today.* New York: McGraw-Hill.

COONS, JOHN E.; CLUNE, WILLIAM H., III; and SUGARMAN, STEPHEN D. 1970. *Private Wealth and Public Education.* Cambridge, MA: Harvard University Press.

GARDNER, JOHN W. 1961. *Excellence: Can We Be Equal and Excellent Too?* New York: Harper and Row.

HAYEK, FRIEDRICH A. VON. 1960. *The Constitution of Liberty.* Chicago: University of Chicago Press.

KAUFMAN, HERBERT. 1963. *Politics and Policies in State and Local Governments.* Englewood Cliffs, NJ: Prentice-Hall.

NATIONAL COMMISSION ON EXCELLENCE IN EDUCATION. 1983. *A Nation at Risk: The Imperative for Educational Reform.* Washington, DC: U.S. Government Printing Office.

RUDOLF, FREDERICK, ed. 1969. *Essays on Education in the New Republic.* Cambridge, MA: Harvard University Press.

WISE, ARTHUR E. 1968. *Rich Schools, Poor Schools: The Promise of Equal Educational Opportunity.* Chicago: University of Chicago Press.

YUDOF, MARK. 1973. "Equal Educational Opportunity and the Courts." *Texas Law Review* 51:411–437.

JAMES W. GUTHRIE

EDUCATIONAL PSYCHOLOGY

Educational psychologists "study what people think and do as they teach and learn a particular curriculum in a particular environment where education and training are intended to take place" (Berliner, p. 145). The work of educational psychologists focuses "on the rich and significant everyday problems of education" (Wittrock, pp. 132–133).

History

Long before educational psychology became a formal discipline, scholars were concerned about what people think and do as they teach and learn. The Greek philosophers Plato and Aristotle discussed topics still studied by educational psychologists—the role of the teacher, the relationship between teacher and student, methods of teaching, the nature and order of learning, the role of affect in learning. In the 1500s the Spanish humanist Juan Luis Vives emphasized the value of practice, the need to tap student interests and adapt instruction to individual differences, and the advantages of using self-comparisons rather than competitive social comparisons in evaluating students' work. In the 1600s the Czech theologian and educator Johann Amos Comenius introduced visual aids and proclaimed that understanding, not memorizing, was the goal of teaching. Writings of European philosophers and reformers such as Jean-Jacques Rousseau (1712–1778), Johann Heinrich Pestalozzi (1746–1827), Johann Friedrich Herbart (1776–1841), and Friedrich Wilhelm August Froebel (1782–1852) stressed the value of activity, prior experience, and interest. All these ideas are consistent with current work in educational psychology.

In the United States, psychology was linked to education and teachers from its inception. In 1890 the American philosopher William James founded psychology in America and then followed with a lecture series for teachers titled "Talks to Teachers about Psychology." These lectures were given in summer schools for teachers around the country and then published in 1899 both as a book and in the *Atlantic Monthly* magazine. Again, some of James's ideas were quite modern—he supported the use of discussion, projects and activities, laboratory experiments, writing, drawing, and concrete materials in teaching.

James's student, G. Stanley Hall, founded the American Psychological Association and was its first president. Teachers helped him collect data for his dissertation about children's understandings of the world. Hall founded the child-study movement in the United States and wrote extensively about children and adolescents. He encouraged teachers to make detailed observations and keep careful records to study their students' development—as his mother had done when she was a teacher. Hall's ideas influenced education through courses in child study introduced into normal schools beginning around 1863.

Hall's student, John Dewey, founded the Laboratory School at the University of Chicago and is considered the father of the Progressive education movement. Another of William James's students, Edward Lee Thorndike, wrote the first educational psychology text in 1903 and founded the *Journal of Educational Psychology* in 1910.

Psychology and key ideas in education. Developments in education continued to be closely tied to psychologists in the first half of the twentieth century. In fact, in 1919, Ellwood Cubberly dubbed educational psychology a "guiding science of the school" (p. 755). It was not uncommon for psychologists such as Thorndike, Charles H. Judd, or their students to be both presidents of the American Psychological Association and authors of materials for teaching school subjects or measuring achievement in reading, mathematics, or even handwriting. The work of Thorndike, Alfred Binet, Jean Piaget, and Benjamin Bloom illustrate earlier connections between psychology and education.

Thorndike, teaching, and transfer. Although Thorndike is most well known in psychology for his research on learning that paved the way for B. F. Skinner's later studies of operant conditioning, his impact in education went beyond his studies of learning. He developed methods for teaching reading and arithmetic that were widely adopted, as well as scales to measure ability in reading, arithmetic, handwriting, drawing, spelling, and English composition. He supported the scientific movement in education—an effort to base teaching practice on empirical evidence and sound measurement. His view proved narrow as he sought laws of learning in laboratories that could be applied to teaching without actually evaluating the applications in real classrooms. It took fifty years to return to the psychological study of learning in the classroom, when the Soviet Union's successful launch of *Sputnik* in 1957 startled the United States and precipitated funding for basic and applied research on teaching and learning. Thorndike also had a lasting effect on education by demonstrating that learning Greek, Latin, and mathematics did not "exercise the mind" to improve general thinking abilities. Partly because of his research, required study of the classics decreased.

Binet and assessments of intelligence. About the time that Thorndike was developing measures of reading and arithmetic abilities, Alfred Binet was working on the assessment of intelligence in France. Binet, a psychologist and political activist in Paris in the early 1900s, was charged with developing a procedure for identifying students who would need special education classes. He believed that having an objective measure of learning ability could protect students of poor families who might be forced to leave school because they were assumed to be slow learners. Binet and his collaborator Théodore Simon identified fifty-eight tests, several for each age group from three to thirteen, that allowed the examiner to determine a mental age for a child. A child who succeeded on the items passed by most six-year-olds, for example, was considered to have a mental age of six, whether the child was actually four, six, or eight years old. The concept of intelligence quotient, or IQ, was added after Binet's procedure was brought to the United States and revised at Stanford University to become the Stanford-Binet test. The early Stanford-Binet has been revised four times as of 2002, most recently in 1986. The success of the Stanford-Binet has led to the development of several other modern intelligence tests.

Piaget and the development of thinking.

As a new Ph.D. working in Binet's laboratory, Jean Piaget became intrigued with children's wrong answers to Binet's tasks. Over the next several decades, Piaget devised a model to describe the thinking behind these wrong answers and to explain how humans gather and organize information. Piaget's theory of cognitive development is based on the assumption that people try to make sense of the world and actively create their knowledge through direct experience with objects, people, and ideas. Maturation, activity, social interaction, and equilibration (the constant testing of the adequacy of understanding) influence the way thinking and knowledge develop. Piaget believed that young people pass through four stages in their cognitive development: sensorimotor, preoperational, concrete-operational, and formal-operational. Piaget's theory transformed education in mathematics and science and is still a force in the early twenty-first century in constructivist approaches to teaching.

Bloom and the goals of instruction.

Also during the 1950s and 1960s, results of a project directed by Benjamin Bloom touched education at all levels around the world. Bloom and his colleagues developed a taxonomy, or classification system, of educational objectives. Objectives were divided into three domains: cognitive, affective, and psychomotor. A handbook describing the objectives in each area was eventually published. These taxonomies have been included in hundreds of books and articles about teaching and testing. Teachers, test developers, and curriculum designers use the taxonomies to develop instructional objectives and test questions. It would be difficult to find an educator trained in the past thirty years who had not heard of Bloom's taxonomy

in some form. The cognitive domain taxonomy was revised in 2001 by Lorin W. Anderson and David R. Krathwohl.

Moving toward contemporary educational psychology. In the 1960s a number of educational psychologists developed approaches to teaching that foreshadowed some of the contemporary applications and arguments. Jerome Bruner's early research on thinking stirred his interest in education. Bruner's work emphasized the importance of understanding the structure of a subject being studied, the need for active learning as the basis for true understanding, and the value of inductive reasoning in learning. Bruner believed students must actively identify key principles for themselves rather than relying on teachers' explanations. Teachers should provide problem situations stimulating students to question, explore, and experiment—a process called discovery learning. Thus, Bruner believed that classroom learning should take place through inductive reasoning, that is, by using specific examples to formulate a general principle.

David Ausubel disagreed. He believed that people acquire knowledge primarily through reception rather than discovery; thus learning should progress not inductively from examples to rules as Bruner recommended, but deductively: from the general to the specific, or from the rule to examples. Ausubel's strategy always began with an advance organizer—a technique still popular in the twenty-first century—which is a kind of conceptual bridge between new material and students' current knowledge.

Contemporary Views of Learning and Motivation

Educational psychologists have studied cognition, instruction, learning, motivation, individual differences, and the measurement of human abilities, to name just a few areas that relate to education and schooling. Of all these, perhaps the study of learning is the most closely associated with education. Different theories of learning have had different impacts on education and have supported different practices.

Behavioral views of learning. The behavioral approach to learning developed out of work by Skinner, whose research in operant conditioning showed that voluntary behavior can be altered by changes in the antecedents of the behavior, the consequences, or both. Early work focused on consequences and demonstrated that consequences following an action may serve as reinforcement or punishment. Skinner's theories have been used extensively in education, by applying principles of reinforcement and punishment to change behaviors, often called applied behavior analysis. For much of the 1960s Skinner's ideas and those of behaviorists who followed him shaped teaching in regular and special education, training in the military, coaching, and many other aspects of education. Principles of reinforcement continue to be important for all teachers, particularly in classroom management and in decisions about grades and incentives for learning.

In the 1970s and 1980s a number of educational psychologists turned their attention from research on learning to research on teaching. Their findings shaped educational policy and practice during those years and since. Much of the research that focused on effective teaching during that time period pointed toward a model of teaching that is related to improved student learning called direct instruction or explicit teaching.

Cognitive views of learning. Behaviorists define learning as a change in behavior brought about by experience with little concern for the mental or internal aspects of learning. The cognitive view, in contrast, sees people as active learners who initiate experiences, seek out information to solve problems, and reorganize what they already know to achieve new insights. In fact, learning within this perspective is seen as "transforming significant understanding we already have, rather than simple acquisitions written on blank slates" (Greeno, Collins, and Resnick, p. 18). Much of the work on behavioral learning principles has been with animals in controlled laboratory settings. The goal is to identify a few general laws of learning that apply to all higher organisms (including humans, regardless of age, intelligence, or other individual differences). Cognitive psychologists, on the other hand, focus on individual and developmental differences in cognition; they have not sought general laws of learning. Cognitive views of learning are consistent with the educational theories of Bruner and Ausubel and with approaches that teach learning strategies, such as summarizing, organizing, planning, and note taking.

Constructivist theories of learning. Constructivist perspectives on learning and teaching are increasingly influential today. These views are grounded in the research of Piaget, Lev Vygotsky, the Gestalt psychologists, Fredric Bartlett, and Bruner as well as the Progressive educational philosophy of Dewey. There are constructivist approaches in science and mathematics education, in educational psychology and anthropology, and in computer-based education. Some constructivist views emphasize the shared, social construction of knowledge; others see social forces as less important.

Even though there is no single constructivist theory, many constructivist teaching approaches recommend the following:

- Complex, challenging learning environments and authentic tasks
- Social negotiation and shared responsibility as a part of learning
- Multiple representations of content
- Understanding that knowledge is constructed
- Student-centered instruction

Inquiry is an example of constructivist teaching. Dewey described the basic inquiry learning format in 1910. There have been many adaptations of this strategy, but the teacher usually presents a puzzling event, question, or problem. The students formulate hypotheses to explain the event or solve the problem, collect data to test the hypotheses, draw conclusions, and reflect on the original problem and on the thinking processes needed to solve it. Like discovery learning, inquiry methods require great preparation, organization, and monitoring to be sure everyone is engaged and challenged.

A second example of constructivist teaching influenced by Vygotsky's theories of assisted learning is called cognitive apprenticeships. There are many models, but most share six features:

1. Students observe an expert (usually the teacher) model the performance.

2. Students get external support through coaching or tutoring (including hints, feedback, models, reminders).

3. Conceptual scaffolding (in the form of outlines, explanations, notes, definitions, formulas, procedures, etc.) is provided and then gradually faded as the student becomes more competent and proficient.

4. Students continually articulate their knowledge—putting into words their understanding of the processes and content being learned.

5. Students reflect on their progress, comparing their problem solving to an expert's performance and to their own earlier performances.

6. Students are required to explore new ways to apply what they are learning—ways that they have not practiced at the professional's side.

Motivation in education. Much work in educational psychology has focused on student motivation: the engine that fuels learning and the steering wheel that guides its progress. Just as there are many theories of learning, there are quite a few explanations of motivation. Behaviorists explain motivation with concepts such as "reward" and "incentive." Rewards are desirable consequences for appropriate behavior; incentives provide the prospect for future rewards. Giving grades, stars, and so on for learning—or demerits for misbehavior—is an attempt to motivate students by extrinsic (external) means of incentives, rewards, and punishments. Humanistic views of motivation emphasize such intrinsic (internal) forces as a person's needs for "self-actualization," the inborn "actualizing tendency," or the need for "self-determination." From the humanistic perspective, motivation of students means to encourage their inner resources—their sense of competence, self-esteem, autonomy, and self-actualization.

Cognitive theorists believe that behavior is determined by thinking, not simply by whether one has been rewarded or punished for the behavior in the past. From this perspective, behavior is initiated and regulated by plans, goals, schemas (generalized knowledge), expectations, and attributions (the causes we see for our own and other people's behavior). Social learning theories of motivation are integrations of behavioral and cognitive approaches: They take into account both the behaviorists' concern with the effects or outcomes of behavior and the cognitivists' interest in the impact of individual beliefs and expectations. Many influential social learning explanations of motivation can be characterized as expectancy and value theories that view motivation as the product of two main forces: (1) the individual's expectation of reaching a goal and (2) the value of that goal to the individual. Attempts to build a sense of efficacy for classroom learning are educational applications of this approach.

Issues and Controversies

The application of psychology to education has seen many controversies. The psychological content of teacher preparation moved from Hall's emphasis on child study to Thorndike's connectionist approach to learning; to educational psychology texts for teachers in the 1920s that included measurement and the psychology of school subjects; to an emphasis in the 1950s on mental hygiene, child development, personality, and motivation; to a greater emphasis on learning theories and programmed instruction in the 1960s; to research on teaching in the 1970s; to the dominance of Piagetian theories and the resurgence of cognitive approaches in the 1980s; to current texts that emphasize Vygotskian influences and constructivism along with a return to the instructional psychology of school subjects. Once a requirement in virtually all teacher preparation programs, educational courses have been replaced, renamed, redesigned, and integrated into other education courses. As examples of two issues in educational psychology and schooling, consider conceptions of intelligence and approaches to the teaching of reading.

What does intelligence mean? The idea of intelligence has been with us for a long time. Plato discussed similar variations more than 2,000 years ago. Most early theories about the nature of intelligence involved one or more of the following three themes: (1) the capacity to learn; (2) the total knowledge a person has acquired; and (3) the ability to adapt successfully to new situations and to the environment in general.

In the twentieth century there was considerable controversy over the meaning of intelligence. In 1986 at a symposium on intelligence, twenty-four psychologists each offered a different view about the nature of intelligence. More than half of the experts mentioned higher-level thinking processes such as abstract reasoning, problem solving, and decision-making as important aspects of intelligence, but they disagreed about the structure of intelligence: Is it a single ability or many separate abilities? Evidence that intelligence is a single basic ability affecting performance on all cognitively oriented tasks comes from consistent correlations among scores on most tests of specific mental abilities. In spite of these correlations, however, some psychologists insist that there several separate "primary mental abilities." In 1938 Louis Leon Thurstone listed verbal comprehension, memory, reasoning, ability to visualize spatial relationships, numerical ability, word fluency, and perceptual speed as the major mental abilities underlying intellectual tasks. Joy Paul Guilford and Howard Gardner are the most prominent modern proponents of the concept of multiple cognitive abilities. Gardner's theory of multiple intelligences has had the greatest impact on education. According to

Gardner there are at least eight separate kinds of intelligences: linguistic, musical, spatial, logical-mathematical, bodily-kinesthetic, interpersonal, intrapersonal, and environmental.

Ability differences in schools. In the early 1900s, before group intelligence tests were readily available, teachers dealt with student achievement differences by promoting students who performed adequately and holding back others. This worked well for those who were promoted, but not for those who failed. The idea of social promotion was introduced to keep age-mates together, but then teaching had to change. When intelligence test became available, one solution was to promote all students, but group them by ability within their grade level. Ability grouping was the basis of many studies in the 1930s, but fell from favor until 1957 and the era of *Sputnik,* when concern grew about developing talent in mathematics and science. Again, in the 1960s and 1970s, ability grouping was criticized. In the early twenty-first century, teachers are encouraged to use forms of cooperative learning and heterogeneous grouping to deal with ability differences in their classes.

Learning to read. Educational psychologists have made great progress understanding how students learn different subjects. Based on these findings, approaches have been developed to teach reading, writing, science, mathematics, social studies, and other subjects. Reading instruction has been the focus of great controversy. Educators have debated whether students should be taught to read and write through code-based (phonics, skills) approaches that relate letters to sounds and sounds to words or through meaning-based (whole-language, literature-based, emergent literacy) approaches that focus on the meaning of the text.

Research in educational psychology demonstrates that whole language approaches to reading and writing are most effective in preschool and kindergarten because they improve students' motivation and interest and help them understand the nature and purposes of reading and writing. Phonemic awareness—the sense that words are composed of separate sounds and that sounds are combined to say words—in kindergarten and first grade predicts literacy in later grades. If children do not have phonemic awareness in the early grades, direct teaching can dramatically improve their chances of long-term achievement in literacy. Excellent primary school teachers use a balance of explicit decoding-skills teaching and whole language instruction.

Testing in education. By 1925 Charles Judd proclaimed that "tests and measures are to be found in every progressive school in the land" (p. 807). In fact, psychology has had a profound impact on education through the adoption of testing. On the average, more than 1 million standardized tests are given per school day in classes throughout the United States. But tests are not without controversy. Critics of standardized testing state that these tests measure disjointed facts and skills that have no use or meaning in the real world. Often test questions do not match the curriculum of the schools, so the tests cannot measure how well students have learned the curriculum. Supporters assert that tests provide useful information. As Joseph Rice suggested more than a century ago, a good way to judge if teaching has been effective might be to test what the students learned. The test, however, does not tell all. Also more than 100 years ago, William James suggested that with test results must be combined with observations made "upon the total demeanor of the measured individual, by teachers with eyes in their heads and common sense and some feeling for the concrete facts of human nature in their hearts" (p. 84).

Expectations of the profession. Increasingly technology offers an alternative or addition to traditional materials in teaching and learning. For example, the Cognition and Technology Group at Vanderbilt University has developed a problem-based learning environment called anchored instruction. The anchor is the rich, authentic, and interesting situation presented via videodisk or computer that provides a focus—a reason for setting goals, planning, and using mathematical tools to solve problems. Anchored instruction is an example of cognitive apprenticeships described above.

It is likely that educational psychologists will continue to contribute to education as they learn more about the brain and how learning occurs; the development of intellect, affect, personality, character, and motivation; ways of assessing learning; and the creation of multifaceted learning environments. It also is likely that some issues will spiral through these contributions. What is a useful and appropriate balance of discovery and direct instruction? How can teachers, who must work with groups, adapt instruction to individual variations? What should be the role of testing and grading in education? What are the goals of education and how do instructors balance cognitive, affective, and psychomotor objectives? How can learning technologies be used to best advantage for students? How can teachers help students understand, remember, and apply knowledge? These questions may not be as new as they seem upon attendance to the history of psychology and its applications to education.

See also: DEVELOPMENTAL THEORY; INDIVIDUAL DIFFERENCES; INSTRUCTIONAL DESIGN; LEARNING THEORY.

BIBLIOGRAPHY

ALEXANDER, PATRICIA A. 1996. "The Past, Present, and Future of Knowledge Research: A Reexamination of the Role of Knowledge in Learning and Instruction." *Educational Psychologist* 31:89–92.

ALEXANDER, PATRICIA A., and MURPHY, P. KAREN. 1998. "The Research Base for APA's Learner-Centered Psychological Principles." In *How Students Learn: Reforming Schools through Learner-Centered Education,* ed. Nadine M. Lambert and Barbara L. McCombs. Washington, DC: American Psychological Association.

ANDERSON, LORIN W., and KRATHWOHL, DAVID R. 2001. *A Taxonomy for Learning, Teaching, and Assessing: A Revision of Bloom's Taxonomy of Educational Objectives.* New York: Longman.

ANDERSON, LORIN W., and SOSNIAK, LAUREN A., eds. 1994. *Bloom's Taxonomy: A Forty-Year Retrospective.* Chicago: University of Chicago Press.

AUSUBEL, DAVID PAUL. 1963. *The Psychology of Meaningful Verbal Learning.* New York: Grune and Stratton.

BERLINER, DAVID C. 1992. "Telling the Stories of Educational Psychology." *Educational Psychologist* 27:143–152.

BERLINER, DAVID C. 1993. "The 100-Year Journey of Educational Psychology: From Interest, to Disdain, to Respect for Practice." In *Exploring Applied Psychology: Origins and Critical Analyses,* ed. Thomas K. Fagan and Gary R. VandenBos. Washington, DC: American Psychological Association.

BRUNER, JEROME S. 1966. *Toward a Theory of Instruction.* New York: Norton.

CUBBERLEY, ELLWOOD PATTERSON. 1919. *Public Education in the United States.* Boston: Houghton Mifflin.

DE CORTE, ERIK; GREER, BRIAN; and VERSCHAFFEL, LIEVEN. 1996. "Mathematics Learning and Teaching." In *Handbook of Educational Psychology,* ed. David C. Berliner and Robert C. Calfee. New York: Macmillan.

DRISCOLL, MARCY P. 1994. *Psychology of Learning for Instruction.* Boston: Allyn and Bacon.

GRAHAM, STEVE, and HARRIS, KAREN R. 1994. "The Effects of Whole Language on Children's Writing: A Review of the Literature." *Educational Psychologist* 29:187–192.

GREENO, JAMES G.; COLLINS, ALLEN M.; and RESNICK, LAUREN B. 1996. "Cognition and Learning." In *Handbook of Educational Psychology,* ed. David C. Berliner and Robert C. Calfee. New York: Macmillan.

HILGARD, ERNEST R. 1996. "History of Educational Psychology." In *Handbook of Educational Psychology,* ed. David C. Berliner and Robert C. Calfee. New York: Macmillan.

JAMES, WILLIAM. 1899. *Talks to Teachers on Psychology: And to Students on Some of Life's Ideals.* New York: Holt.

JUDD, CHARLES H. 1925. "The Curriculum: A Paramount Issue." In *Addresses and Proceedings.* Washington, DC: National Education Association.

MAYER, RICHARD E. 1992. "Cognition and Instruction: Their Historic Meeting within Educational Psychology." *Journal of Educational Psychology* 84:405–412.

NEISSER, ULRICH, et al. 1996. "Intelligence: Knowns and Unknowns." *American Psychologist* 51:77–101.

PIAGET, JEAN. 1970. "Piaget's Theory." In *Handbook of Child Psychology,* 3rd edition, ed. P. Mussen. New York: Wiley.

ROSS, DOROTHY. 1972. *G. Stanley Hall: The Psychologist as Prophet.* Chicago: University of Chicago Press.

SKINNER, B. F. 1953. *Science and Human Behavior.* New York: Macmillan.

THURSTONE, LOUIS LEON. 1938. *Primary Mental Abilities.* Chicago: University of Chicago Press.

VYGOTSKY, LEV SEMENOVICH. 1978. *Mind in Society: The Development of Higher Mental Process,* ed. Michael Cole et al. Cambridge, MA: Harvard University Press.

WHARTON-MCDONALD, RUTH; PRESSLEY, MICHAEL; and MISTRETTA, JENNIFER. 1996. *Out-*

standing Literacy Instruction in First Grade: Teacher Practices and Student Achievement. Albany, NY: National Reading Research Center.

WITTROCK, MERLIN C. 1992. "An Empowering Conception of Educational Psychology." *Educational Psychologist* 27:129–142.

WOOLFOLK HOY, ANITA. 2000. "Educational Psychology and Teacher Education." *Educational Psychologist* 35:257–270.

WOOLFOLK HOY, ANITA. 2001. *Educational Psychology,* 8th edition. Boston, MA: Allyn and Bacon.

ANITA WOOLFOLK HOY

EDUCATIONAL RESOURCES INFORMATION CENTER

The Educational Resources Information Center (ERIC) is a federally funded nationwide information system established to provide easy access to information about education research. ERIC offers educators and researchers a single source through which they can identify and obtain copies of education-related documents, articles, books, monographs, tests, manuals and handbooks, bibliographies, statistical reports, conference papers, dissertations and theses, historical materials, yearbooks, and translations. ERIC's mission is to improve American learning, teaching, and educational decision making by facilitating access to helpful educational research and information.

Program

The massive ERIC database contains more than 1 million abstracts of education-related documents and articles, making it the world's largest repository of education information. The database is updated monthly, and more than 30,000 items are added each year. Interested parties can access the database via the Internet or through commercial vendors. Access to the ERIC database is also available at more than 1,000 libraries and education resource centers around the world. Many of these sites maintain an ERIC microfiche collection and can provide electronic copies of ERIC documents. In addition, ERIC abstracts are available in the print publications *Resources in Education,* ERIC's main announcement bulletin, and *Current Index to Journals in Education,* a monthly comprehensive index to periodical literature in education research.

Anyone interested in education can obtain copies of the full text of many ERIC documents at any library that owns the ERIC microfiche collection. Full-text microfiche or paper copies can also be ordered from ERIC's Document Reproduction Service. The full texts of some documents are also available online. ERIC does not supply full-text copies of journal articles abstracted in the ERIC database; these can be obtained from many library periodical collections or from the journal publisher.

During the 1990s ERIC implemented several invaluable electronic services. One of the most popular is AskERIC, an Internet-based service begun in 1992. AskERIC provides access to a web-based version of the ERIC database that includes document and journal citations from 1966 to the present. AskERIC also offers education-related question-and-answer services, a question archive, lesson plans, mailing lists, internet links, and listings of educational organizations, meetings, and conferences.

ERIC publications include popular two-page research syntheses called *ERIC Digest.* The digests are short reports that give an overview of a current topic of interest in education. ERIC produces approximately one hundred new digests each year. By 2001 there were nearly 2,500 *ERIC Digests,* most available online. Another publication, the *ERIC Review,* features information about emerging education issues, as well as announcements about ERIC products, services, and developments. ERIC also issues Parent Brochures, produces an online journal called *Parent News,* and sponsors the National Parent Information Network for parents who are interested in their children's education.

Organization

ERIC is supported by the U.S. Department of Education's Office of Educational Research and Improvement, and is administered by the National Library of Education. Unlike most federal information systems, in which all activities are conducted under one roof with centralized control, ERIC conducts much of it its document processing and dissemination activities at decentralized and relatively autonomous clearinghouses. The ERIC network consists of sixteen main clearinghouses, nine adjunct clearinghouses, one affiliate clearinghouse, and three support components. ERIC's clearinghouses and components are located at various sites around the country. Most clearinghouses are associated with a college or university.

Each of ERIC's sixteen main clearinghouses is responsible for the collection, processing, and dissemination of documents in a specific topic or field of education research. ERIC clearinghouses include, for example, the Clearinghouse on Adult, Career, and Vocational Education at the Ohio State University; the Clearinghouse on Information and Technology at Syracuse University in New York; the Clearinghouse on Elementary and Early Childhood Education at the University of Illinois in Champaign-Urbana; and the Clearinghouse for Social Studies/Social Science Education at Indiana University. ERIC clearinghouses also respond to requests for information and produce publications on current research and practices in their designated subject area. The nine adjunct clearinghouses are associated with one of the sixteen larger ERIC clearinghouses and have similar responsibilities.

Support components include the online service AskERIC; the ERIC Document Reproduction Service in Springfield, Virginia; and the ERIC Processing and Reference Facility in Lanham, Maryland. The three ERIC support components are responsible for producing, publishing, and disseminating systemwide products and services.

History

ERIC was created in 1966 as the Educational Research Information Center by the United States Office of Education; a year later its name was changed by substituting "Resources" for "Research" (the acronym remained ERIC) because ERIC had grown into a national education information system of service to educators and researchers.

See also: FEDERAL EDUCATIONAL ACTIVITIES; U.S. DEPARTMENT OF EDUCATION.

INTERNET RESOURCES

ASKERIC. 2002. <www.askeric.org>.

ERIC: THE EDUCATIONAL RESOURCES INFORMATION CENTER. 2002. <www.eric.ed.gov>.

LEE G. BURCHINAL
Revised by
JUDITH J. CULLIGAN

EDUCATIONAL TESTING SERVICE

Educational Testing Service (ETS) is a nonprofit organization whose mission is to help advance quality and equity in education by providing fair and valid assessments, research, and related services. Its products and services measure knowledge and skills, promote learning and performance, and support education and professional development worldwide. Founded in 1947 as an independent organization by the American Council on Education, the Carnegie Foundation for the Advancement of Teaching, and the College Entrance Examination Board, ETS has grown to become the world's largest private educational testing and measurement organization, annually administering more than 11 million tests in 181 countries. Helping ETS carry out its mission are the following key divisions.

The ETS Statistics and Research Division is a group of innovative, internationally respected measurement experts who specialize in research and development in psychometrics, equitable testing, and assessment technology. More than 250 division staff, including some of the nation's most distinguished scientists in the fields of psychometrics and statistics, engage in research and analysis to support existing assessments and generate ideas for future assessment products and services. At the same time, they contribute to the field of educational measurement and policy research more broadly, providing objective data to inform current discussions about policy affecting the national education debates.

The School and College Services Division manages testing and nontesting programs, develops tests and ancillary services, prepares a number of publications, and offers a variety of products and services to the education market.

The division carries out work for a number of clients as well as for ETS. It serves ETS's largest client, The College Board, by providing the development and delivery of programs such as the SAT, the Preliminary SAT/National Merit Scholarship Qualifying Test (PSAT/NMSQT), and Advanced Placement tests (AP).

The School and College Services Division also serves the National Center for Education Statistics through the development and delivery of the National Assessment of Educational Progress (NAEP) tests. Its other clients are the Educational Records

Bureau (ERB), the Southern Regional Education Board (SREB), Johns Hopkins University Institute for the Academic Advancement of Youth (IAAY), the New York City Board of Education, the National Association of Independent Schools (NAIS), the University of California, and the California State University System.

The mission of the Graduate and Professional Education Division is to provide leadership and continuous improvement in fair and equitable assessments and services that serve students, institutions, and society in graduate and professional education. It offers the majority of its testing through computers, and its major programs are the Graduate Record Examinations (GRE), the Graduate Management Admission Test (GMAT) and the Test of English as a Foreign Language (TOEFL).

The division also houses the Fairness, Access, Multiculturalism, and Equity (FAME) Initiative, a research-based effort to help ETS address the concerns of its increasingly diverse graduate and professional school education constituencies. FAME is an ethics-based effort designed to examine the connections between the expressed values underlying the company's assessments, products, and services and actual outcomes.

The purpose of the Information Systems and Technology Division is to deliver business value through information technology. Business value is defined as increasing revenue, decreasing costs, improving productivity, and supporting strategic initiatives and directives. Within Information Systems and Technology is the Advanced Assessment and Delivery Technologies (AADT) Division that is responsible for all enterprisewide systems associated with test creation, scoring, analysis, and delivery of assessments, collecting the candidate results. This includes paper-and-pencil tests as well as computer-based tests.

The Teaching and Learning Division is committed to supporting learning and advancing good teaching through a coherent approach to the licensing, advanced certification, and professional development of teachers and school leaders. Its major assessment programs include the Praxis Series: Professional Assessments for Beginning Teachers, the School Leadership Series, and working as the primary contractor to provide certification for the National Board for Professional Teaching Standards. The division also is responsible for the Pathwise Series

that offers a variety of professional development programs tied to research-based standards to help teachers at all levels (student, beginning, and experienced teachers) improve their teaching practices.

The Communications and Public Affairs Division has the responsibility to meet the communication and information needs of ETS employees and key external constituents to support the company's strategic direction. It aids management to project the public voice of ETS, articulating the philosophy, policy, and position of the organization as a leader in education reform.

See also: TESTING, *subentries on* IMPACT OF TEST PREPARATION PROGRAMS, STANDARDIZED TESTS AND HIGH-STAKES ASSESSMENT.

INTERNET RESOURCE

EDUCATIONAL TESTING SERVICE. 2002. <www.ets.org>.

KURT LANDGRAF

EDUCATION COMMISSION OF THE STATES

The Education Commission of the States (ECS) is an interstate compact created in 1965 to improve education by facilitating the exchange of information, ideas, experiences, and innovations among state policymakers and education leaders.

Forty-nine states, three territories, and the District of Columbia constitute the commission's membership, each represented by the governor and six other individuals: legislators, chief state school officers, state and local school board members, higher-education officials, superintendents, teachers, and business leaders. The ECS chairmanship and vice chairmanship are held by a governor and a legislator, respectively, alternating between the two major political parties.

The Education Commission of the States' status as a nonpartisan organization, involving key leaders from all levels of the education system, creates unique opportunities to build partnerships, share information and promote the development of policy based on the best available research and strategies. ECS obtains financial support through a combination of state fees and contracts, sponsorships, and grants from foundations, corporations and the federal government.

ECS, which is headquartered in Denver, Colorado, has three operating divisions that work together to provide state policymakers with the services and products they need to make informed policy decisions about education. The Information Clearinghouse gathers, analyzes, disseminates, and serves as a repository of information on a broad range of education topics, from a wide variety of sources—including state legislation, research studies, reports, journals, and news articles. ECS provides access to this extensive collection of material through its website, through various print publications, and through customized, quick turnaround searches by Clearinghouse staff.

Through its Policy Studies and Programs Division, ECS identifies, studies, and provides heightened visibility for education trends and issues that are of greatest concern to its constituents. The organization's current areas of focus are accountability, finance, governance, leadership, and teaching quality.

State Services provides a range of customized technical assistance to states: consultation and advice, testimony at legislative hearings, policy audits and analysis, meeting facilitation, and support for partnerships and networks.

ECS sponsors state, regional, and national conferences (including the annual National Forum on Education Policy), all of which provide policymakers, educators, and other interested parties with an opportunity to share ideas and learn from one another.

See also: STATES AND EDUCATION.

INTERNET RESOURCE

EDUCATION COMMISSION OF THE STATES. 2002. <www.ecs.org>.

TED SANDERS

EDUCATION DEVELOPMENT PROJECTS

Contemporary education development projects can trace their origins to the programs of bilateral and multilateral official development assistance offered to newly independent and developing countries after World War II. The goals and purposes, content, format, actors, financing, and delivery of education development projects have undergone many changes throughout the last half of the twentieth century.

History

Official development assistance (hereafter, *aid*) for education expanded rapidly during the 1950s and 1960s when many previously colonized countries became independent. Industrialized countries were seen as partly responsible for the development of poorer and newly independent countries, through the provision of both financial resources and technical skills. Many multilateral institutions were founded to deliver development assistance, including the International Bank for Reconstruction and Development (IBRD), and the United Nations Development Program (UNDP). Foundations such as the Rockefeller and Ford Foundations became early players in the delivery of education development projects. Bilateral development assistance institutions, such as the United States Agency for International Development (USAID), were also established, and came to deliver both the largest share of international funding for development, and for educational development.

Ideas about modernization and progress dominated the work of these organizations. Development was generally defined as linear progress toward the kinds of economic and political systems existing in the Western industrialized world. Education, which was associated in industrialized countries with economic progress and national development through the creation of human resources, quickly became an important component of their development agenda.

Initially, educational aid was primarily used to provide tertiary or graduate training to foreign nationals in donor countries, to bring trained educators to developing countries, or to help establish international professional organizations. However, in the 1960s, the focus of educational aid shifted somewhat as concerns about "brain drain" and continued developing country dependency on external institutions led donor governments and organizations to support vocational programs and the construction of tertiary and secondary institutions in developing countries. Donors began to invest in discrete education projects, which often focused on training for education providers (for example, teachers), provided technical support to education ministries, or constructed schools. Projects tended to fund capital as opposed to recurrent costs (like teacher salaries), and were small in scale, and staffed and monitored by the donor organization. Individual donors often specialized in a specific type of educational intervention or level of education, thus dominating that field and the pattern of its development in the recipient country.

The Project Model

The project model for delivering aid had several advantages over the initial focus on high level training. It often kept developing country personnel in country for training, trained lower-level personnel, built infrastructure, and offered a greater variety of technical services and training. It allowed for variation and experimentation—leading, for example, to innovative efforts to focus on grassroots educational development and literacy by Scandinavian donors. Joel Samoff (1997) outlines some of the project model's weaknesses. Project aid often fragmented educational development and planning into a set of mismatched and uncoordinated donor-led interventions. It tended to emphasize short-term goals over longer-term needs, and to focus the resources of many of the countries' ministries of education on short term project management and evaluation, rather than on systemwide development. Donor resources were often tied—provided only to finance goods and services from donor nationals. Finally, the choice and implementation paths of education development projects were often highly politicized. Education development projects produced complex donor/recipient government interactions, often colored by the ideological or institutional experience with education in the donor country and by the donor's control over resources. For this reason, education development projects never functioned as the simple transfer of technical and financial resources originally envisaged in modernization theory.

Aid for Education

Hans Weiler notes that in the late 1970s, even as donor organizations reconfirmed the benefits of education for national development, education aid budgets began to stagnate or decline. Although there is a lack of comparable data before 1973, it appears that overall aid for education from Organisation for Economic Co-operation and Development (OECD) member countries barely kept pace with inflation

after 1980. Ever fewer resources came from Eastern European, Soviet, and OPEC states and greater numbers of newly independent states vied for shrinking aid dollars. At the same time, the balance of influence among donors active in educational development projects shifted, with the World Bank emerging as the most significant single lender to education both in terms of technical and financial capacities.

Throughout the 1980s and 1990s, many developing countries faced a serious crisis in national education spending, caused both by widespread scale economic collapse and by subsequent structural adjustment programs. Financial tensions fueled debates among donors about the merits of educational expansion versus qualitative improvement, basic versus postprimary expansion of education, and academic versus technical/vocational or adult education. In the early 1980s, commentators such as Paul Hurst questioned the assumption that investment in education would yield economic growth, since two decades of large growth in educational investment in developing countries had not convincingly supported this claim. Soon after, new economic studies, such as Maraline Lockheed and Adriaan Verspoor's World Bank–sponsored study claimed that a focus on basic education (particularly for girls) was the most cost-effective and developmentally effective form of educational investment. An era of economic austerity also fueled the introduction of new components in educational development projects, including an emphasis on cost recovery mechanisms, the decentralization of educational systems, the introduction of national testing programs, and support for nongovernmental provision of educational services.

The 1990s saw a new convergence of donor activities, perhaps in part because of the ideological convergence that followed the collapse of state socialism. The 1990 World Conference on Education for All, sponsored by the United Nations Educational, Scientific and Cultural Organization (UNESCO), the World Bank, the United Nations Childrens' Fund (UNICEF), and others, brought donors and developing countries together around a more unified aid agenda focused on the revitalization of primary education in the poorest developing countries. Many donors subsequently reoriented their educational development efforts to focus on primary education. However, despite strong rhetoric, overall levels of donor aid did not increased substantially during the last decade of the twentieth century.

Donors also began to debate the merits of sectorwide or systemwide approaches in education during the 1990s. Sectorwide approaches differ from project-based approaches in a number of ways. One of the most obvious is that sectorwide aid provides money directly to the developing country government's budget, on the basis of a long-term education development plan. There is debate about whether the effect of this mechanism is to give the recipient government greater control over how money is spent, or whether this shift actually amounts to greater restrictions on the government. First, sectorwide aid is often heavily conditioned, and second, donors now can expect recipient governments' entire sectoral approach to align with their increasingly convergent notion of what kind of education is best for development. Furthermore, instead of providing small-scale aid to many countries, the sectorwide model is highly selective, targeting the few countries able to provide a rational sector plan for educational change. Lastly, sectorwide aid is increasingly linked to wider acceptance of reforms in the areas of governance and economic policy.

Another important shift in educational development projects has been the growth of funding to support nongovernmental organizations (NGOs) as direct providers of educational services. There remains considerable debate about the sustainability of such strategies. Several of the largest international nongovernmental organizations active in educational development believe that NGOs should act more as policy advocates that service providers, and have launched an international campaign to this effect.

There have been tremendous changes in the putative focus of educational development projects—towards basic education, and a greater commitment to donor coordination, systemwide planning and local control. However, many scholars question the depth of such changes. In many countries, education development continues to receive limited external funding. A lack of coordination among donors and a lack of government control over the direction of educational development are commonplace. As in the past, the longer term sustainability of such efforts remains open to question.

See also: DECISION-MAKING IN DEVELOPING NATIONS, APPLYING ECONOMIC ANALYSIS TO; INTERNATIONAL DEVELOPMENT AGENCIES AND EDUCATION; NONGOVERNMENTAL ORGANIZATIONS AND FOUNDATIONS.

BIBLIOGRAPHY

ARCHER, DAVID. 1994. "The Changing Roles of Non-Governmental Organisations in the Field of Education (in the Context of Changing Relationships with the State)." *International Journal of Educational Development* 14(3):223–232.

BENNELL, PAUL, and FURLONG, DOMINIC. 1997. *Has Jomtien Made Any Difference? Trends in Donor Funding for Education and Basic Education Since the Late 1980s.* Brighton, UK: University of Sussex Institute for Development Studies.

BERMAN, EDWARD. 1992. "Donor Agencies and Third World Educational Development, 1945–1985." In *Emergent Issues in Education: Comparative Perspectives,* ed. Robert Arnove, Phillip Altbach, and Gail Kelly. Albany: State University of New York Press.

BUCHERT, LENE. 1998. *Education Reform in the South in the 1990s.* Paris: United Nations Educational, Scientific, and Cultural Organization.

CARNOY, MARTIN. 1995. "Structural Adjustment and the Changing Face of Education." *International Labour Review* 134(6):653–673.

CHABBOTT, COLETTE. 1998. "Constructing Educational Consensus: International Development Professionals and the World Conference on Education for All." *International Journal of Educational Development* 18(3):207–208.

COCLOUGH, CHRISTOPHER. 1991. "Who Should Learn to Pay? An Assessment of Neo-Liberal Approaches to Education Policy." In *States or Markets? Neo-Liberalism and the Development Policy Debate,* ed. Christopher Colclough and James Manor. Oxford: Clarendon Press.

FULLER, BRUCE, and HABTE, AKLILU, eds. 1992. *Adjusting Education Policies: Conserving Resources while Raising School Quality.* World Bank Discussion Paper No. 132. Washington, DC: World Bank.

HARROLD, PETER. 1995. *The Broad Sector Approach to Investment Lending: Sector Investment Programs.* World Bank Discussion Papers, Africa Technical Department Series No. 302. Washington, DC: World Bank.

HURST, PAUL. 1981. "Aid and Educational Development: Rhetoric and Reality." *Comparative Education* 17(2):117–125.

KING, KENNETH. 1992. *Aid and Education.* Harlow, Essex: Longman.

KING, KENNETH, and BUCHERT, LENE, eds. 1999. *Changing International Aid to Education: Global Patterns and National Contexts.* Paris: UNESCO Publishing/NORRAG.

LOCKHEED, MARLAINE E., and VERSPOOR, ADRIAAN M. 1991. *Improving Primary Education in Developing Countries.* Washington, DC: Oxford University Press, for the World Bank.

LUMSDAINE, DAVID H. 1993. *Moral Vision in International Politics: The Foreign Aid Regime, 1949–1989.* Princeton, NJ: Princeton University Press.

MUNDY, KAREN. 1998. "Educational Multilateralism and World (Dis)Order." *Comparative Education Review* 42(4):448–478.

MUNDY, KAREN, and MURPHY, LYNN. 2001. "Transnational Advocacy, Global Civil Society: Emerging Evidence from the Field of Education." *Comparative Education Review* 45(1):85–126.

NAGEL, JOANE, and SNYDER, CONRAD, JR. 1989. "International Funding of Educational Development: External Agendas and Internal Adaptation—The Case of Liberia." *Comparative Education Review* 33(1):3–20.

ORGANISATION FOR ECONOMIC CO-OPERATION AND DEVELOPMENT. 1996. *Shaping the Twenty-First Century: The Contribution of Development Cooperation.* Paris: OECD Development Assistance Committee.

SAMOFF, JOEL. 1999. "Institutionalizing International Influence." In *Comparative Education: The Dialectic of the Global and the Local,* ed. Robert F. Arnove and Carlos Alberto Torres. Lanham, MD: Rowman and Littlefield.

SAMOFF, JOEL, ed. 1994. *Coping with Crisis: Austerity, Adjustment and Human Resources.* London: Cassell, with the United Nations Educational, Scientific and Cultural Organization.

UNSICKER, JEFFREY G. 1987. "Adult Education, Socialism and International Aid in Tanzania: The Political Economy of the Folk Development Colleges." Ph.D diss., Stanford University School of Education.

WEILER, HANS N. 1983. *Aid for Education: The Political Economy of International Cooperation in Educational Development.* International Development Research Centre Manuscript Report No. MR84e. Ottawa: International Development Research Centre.

KAREN MUNDY
NANCY KENDALL

EDUCATION REFORM

OVERVIEW
 Jacob E. Adams Jr.
REPORTS OF HISTORICAL SIGNIFICANCE
 Rick Ginsberg

OVERVIEW

In 1983 American education reform entered a new era. It was in that year that the federal government published a report of the National Commission on Excellence in Education entitled *A Nation at Risk: The Imperative for Educational Reform.* Commissioned in August 1981 by President Ronald Reagan's secretary of education, Terrel H. Bell, and chaired by David P. Gardner, then president of the University of Utah, this eighteen-member blue-ribbon panel of educators and elected officials examined the quality of elementary and secondary public education in the United States and found a "rising tide of mediocrity" that threatened the nation's future. In inflammatory tones, the commissioners reported that the United States had engaged in unthinking, unilateral educational disarmament, asserting that if an unfriendly foreign power had attempted to impose on America the mediocre educational performance the commissioners found, the nation might well have viewed it as an "act of war."

In support of their conclusions, the commissioners presented numerous indicators of risk, including Americans' poor academic performance relative to students overseas, high levels of functional illiteracy among U.S. adults and seventeen-year-olds, and declining achievement-test scores. The commissioners also cited increasing enrollments in college remedial courses, increasing business and military expenditures on remedial education, and a diluted curriculum in the schools. They detailed low expectations for student performance and college admissions, less time devoted to instruction and homework, and poor-quality teaching and teacher preparation. According to the commission's analysis, the nation's schools narrowly emphasized basic reading and computational skills at the expense of other essential talents, such as comprehension, analysis, problem solving, and the ability to draw conclusions. For the first time in U.S. history, the report concluded, the educational skills of one generation would not surpass, nor would they even equal, those of its predecessors. This development was particularly striking as it would occur during a period of increasing business demand for highly trained workers.

The commission called for a new public commitment to excellence and education reform anchored in higher expectations for all students. It encouraged students to work harder and elected officials to encourage and support students' efforts. The rhetoric of reform proclaimed that all children can learn and that public policies should do everything possible to fully develop the talents of America's youth.

Specifically, the commission recommended tougher high school graduation requirements, more rigorous and measurable standards of student performance and conduct, more time devoted to learning, better teaching and teacher preparation, more effective school leadership, and greater fiscal support. The report struck a national nerve, defining the public dialog about school quality and sparking state action in education reform. California acted first, adopting omnibus education reform legislation that increased high school graduation requirements, lengthened the school day and year, raised expectations for homework and student conduct, expanded student testing, and increased education funding. Other states followed California's lead, adopting education reforms of varying magnitude. The *excellence era* in education reform was launched, ushering in more than two decades of federal, state, and local initiatives to improve America's public schools.

Reform Groundswell

Why was *A Nation at Risk* such a successful catalyst for U.S. education reform? Arriving against a backdrop of widespread concern regarding the health of the U.S. economy, the report reflected contemporary misgivings that America was losing its "once unchallenged preeminence" in commerce and technology. Confronted by economic recession at home and declining market share abroad, government and business leaders looked to public schools to assign blame and to seek solutions. In fact, one of the fundamental assumptions of education reform in the

mid-1980s was that the quality of K–12 education would determine the nation's economic success. While the booming U.S. economy of the 1990s proved this assumption false in the aggregate, the relationship between improved education and an individual worker's success in the new marketplace remained compelling. According to analysts, the business-related skills needed to earn a middle-class income had changed radically.

In the mid-1990s the economists Richard Murnane and Frank Levy described three elements to these *new basic skills:* (1) basic mathematics, problem-solving, and reading abilities at levels much higher than high school graduates typically attain; (2) the ability to work in groups and to make effective oral and written presentations, skills many schools do not even teach; and (3) the ability to use personal computers to carry out simple tasks such as word processing. To secure these skills, they concluded, schools must help teachers learn to teach new material, devise better tests of student knowledge and understanding, raise expectations, and engage students' attention and energy. Education reform promised an avenue to such changes.

Further reinforcing *A Nation at Risk*'s call for education reform, the mid-1980s saw publication of book-length, unflattering critiques of American high schools written by leading academic researchers. All told, philanthropic foundations, business groups, academic researchers, education organizations, political associations, and government agencies produced more than two dozen influential reports on public education between 1983 and the end of the twentieth century. All of these reports found deficiencies in American schools, and all called for education reforms of one kind or another.

The impetus for reform gained additional energy from growing social and political discontent. Social service agencies reported increasing incidences of poverty, drug abuse, unwanted pregnancy, and violence; while citizens, through property-tax revolts and consideration of privatization proposals, demonstrated a declining confidence in public institutions. Could changes in American education address these social and political ills in the same way that they might better prepare students for productive careers? Advocates thought so, and the call for reform broadened.

Buttressing the imperative for education reform, the nation's top political leaders added their support. In 1989 President George Bush convened an education summit of corporate leaders and the nation's governors. This elite group crafted the first-ever national goals for public education. Subsequently, Presidents Bill Clinton and George W. Bush similarly sponsored national education summits (in 1996 and 2001, respectively), symbolizing the continued importance of public education reform to the nation.

In the 1990s education reform benefited still further from a broad social demand to improve government efficiency. Operating under the moniker *reinventing government,* advocates argued that bureaucratic government had become inefficient, or even bankrupt, and they promoted new forms of government organization and activity that emphasized dispersed authority, competition, flexibility, customer service, community empowerment, performance incentives, and oversight based on results. Many excellence-era education reforms substantially reflected this reinventing government agenda.

Finally, national commissions on teaching and education governance issued reports in the 1990s, the former crafting a blueprint for recruiting, preparing, and supporting excellent teaching; the latter defining options for infusing greater adaptability, flexibility, and accountability into public school governance.

This groundswell for public-education reform was not without critics, however. Contesting the evidence of public education's demise, these critics argued that Americans were being misled about school accomplishments, even to the extent of confronting a "manufactured crisis." The ensuing debate contested the interpretation of student test scores and other performance indicators, while the tone of the debate reflected alternative political claims that conservatives wished to discredit public education and that liberals undercut a legitimate need for education reform. While neither side claimed that public education was satisfactory, they scuffled over which problems deserved attention and which solutions held the key to fundamental school improvement.

This debate was not surprising. As historians David Tyack and Larry Cuban have noted, disagreements about progress and regress in American public education are characteristic of the landscape, and political arguments have often been used to mobilize and direct education reform.

Reform Policies

During the excellence era two strands of activity have dominated the nation's education reform efforts. The more visible strand involved federal, state, and local initiatives to improve educational programs and governance. Designed to influence what students know and are able to do, program and governance reforms divide into three overlapping periods, which are distinguished by their predominant reform strategy and relative reliance on governmental, professional, citizen, and market mechanisms of education reform.

Intensification period initiatives (1983–1987) tightened existing education regulations and raised student requirements. Examples include increased high school graduation requirements, a longer school day and year, and skills tests for beginning teachers. *Restructuring period* initiatives (1986–1995) altered the way education was organized and governed, devolving authority to schools (particularly teachers) and to parents. Examples include school-based management and school choice. So-called whole-school designs emerged during this period as well, representing ambitious attempts to restructure American education. The New American Schools, the Coalition of Essential Schools, Core Knowledge schools, Accelerated Schools, Success for All, and the Edison Project represent these research-based, result-driven comprehensive plans to reorganize entire schools. Restructuring reforms also reached beyond the schoolhouse, linking education and social services in an effort to address poverty, pregnancy, and other nonschool circumstances that inhibit students' learning.

Standards period initiatives (beginning in 1992) established content standards for student knowledge, performance standards regarding levels of student mastery, and opportunity-to-learn standards governing conditions of learning. States reinforced the new standards through equally new performance accountability systems composed variously of public reporting requirements and performance tests, some tied to school rewards, sanctions, or state interventions to assist failing schools.

Standards-based reforms adopted a systemic perspective on education change, pursuing greater coherence across the gamut of learning goals, curriculum changes, professional development, accountability assessment, and governance arrangements. Simultaneously, other governance concerns spawned unrelated experiments with charter schools, contracting, and forms of privatization.

A second strand of education reform activity during the post-1983 period originated in legal challenges to state school-finance systems. Based on equal protection claims, judicially mandated finance changes attempted to ensure the equitable provision of educational resources. In arguing that unequal resources unfairly preclude groups of students from the educational services they need to have even a chance at academic success, equity proponents conceived the problem of poor student performance as an issue of relative, even minimal, educational opportunity.

On the whole, the program-governance and finance reforms developed separately. Program-governance reforms arose as a remedy to the nation's poor showing on international comparisons of economic and educational performance; they sought changes in student achievement, promoted excellence, involved multiple levels of government, mandated changes in educational practice, and promised difficult implementation. In contrast, school finance reforms arose as a remedy to unequal educational resources; they sought a different distribution of dollars, promoted equity, primarily involved state government, and mandated only technical changes in school funding formulas, which were relatively simple to implement.

In the 1990s the two strands began to converge. Fourteen state supreme courts decided school finance cases on the unique basis of education clauses in state constitutions, finding a new obligation that public education must be adequate, not just equitable. Adequacy combines equity concerns regarding resource distribution with attention to what those resources accomplish. Though the future of adequacy as an important impetus to education reform remains uncertain, adequacy does link school finance to the core purposes of public education in ways that equity does not.

Reform Dynamics

While finance, intensification, restructuring, and standards-based reform strategies all sought improvements in student learning, they operated from different conceptions of the problems that hamper school success. Finance reforms attempted to remedy inequitable resource allocations. Intensification policies targeted low expectations. Restructuring ad-

dressed outmoded forms of school organization. Systemic initiatives combated fragmented and uncoordinated state education policies, and standards redressed unspecified student learning goals and measures of success.

Within the excellence era, the transition from one period of reform to another resulted from judgments that current initiatives were not improving student achievement, primarily because they were not addressing the right problem. The transitions signaled the continued search for a sound theory of education reform.

Analysts working from different disciplinary perspectives have identified other dynamics that shape the promise of reform. Political scientists, for instance, have highlighted fundamental value conflicts in education reform proposals. Because values conflict, reform goals and resources shift as often as their supporting political coalitions shift, or as issues gain and lose salience in legislative deliberations.

Policy analysts have depicted the incomplete design of many education reform policies. Researchers Paul T. Hill and Mary Beth Celio coined the phrase *zones of wishful thinking* to describe the situation that occurs when reform initiatives do not cause all of the changes in public education that are necessary to achieve the results they seek, leaving school improvements, in part, to chance. Implementation scholars have noted, at the local level, the lack of motivation or capacity to undertake reform, inspiring Milbrey McLaughlin's conclusion that it is incredibly hard to make something happen, especially across levels of government and institutional settings.

Sociologists have discussed how the organization of schooling shields teaching from education policymaking, protecting classrooms from the turmoil of shifting reform agendas but also fostering a teaching culture of isolated and idiosyncratic practice, rendering uniform changes problematic. This loose coupling of education policy and practice helps explain how constancy and change coexist in public schools. Educators have targeted weak instruction, proposing improvements in teacher preparation, initial licensing, and advanced certification, thus pinning reform hopes on a re-created infrastructure for professional learning and accountability.

While these dynamics influence parts of the education system, political economists have assailed the whole system, arguing that the prevailing bureaucratic organization of public schooling, with its regulatory and compliance mentality and reliance on collective bargaining, precludes serious change. Their remedies would alter education's incentives and governance arrangements.

Psychologists studying adolescent behavior have added a further dimension to the debate, demonstrating how students' home environments, peer culture, and part-time work explain more differences in student achievement than teacher quality or other school factors. From this perspective, education reforms must extend beyond the boundaries of schools.

While demonstrating the complexity of education reform, these analyses also signal how the search for excellence in education has opened the entire educational enterprise to review.

Reform Results

What are the results so far, in the early twenty-first century, of excellence-era education reforms? First, reform produced policy changes at all levels of government. At the national level, elected officials and business leaders articulated national education goals. Three presidents, George Bush, Bill Clinton, and George W. Bush, launched and touted education reform initiatives, while national education organizations adopted new professional standards for teacher education and administrator licensure.

At the state level, all states developed tests to measure student performance, and forty-nine states developed academic standards. Twenty-seven states began to hold schools accountable for results, promoting performance-based accountability but also inspiring debates about the scope and quality of standards, the adequacy of tests, and needed supports for change. Many states, California and Kentucky notably, legislated substantial programs of reform. Eighteen state courts overturned school finance systems, opening the door to greater equity in educational opportunity or adequacy in school funding.

Locally, with varying degrees of success, school districts and schools either adapted to these reforms or launched their own improvement initiatives. School spending increased approximately 36 percent in real terms, and education agencies grappled with how best to intervene in persistently low-performing schools. Throughout this period, education reform remained on legislative agendas, reflecting the public

commitment to reform envisioned by the National Commission on Excellence in Education.

Second, education reform introduced new structures to the institutional landscape of public education. Notable governance additions included school site councils, charter schools, service contracts, and vouchers. The new National Board for Professional Teaching Standards institutionalized professional teaching certification, while experiments with teacher compensation systems and with labor-management relations challenged teacher pay and work arrangements. At the school level, whole-school designs offered ready-made reform structures, and family resource centers integrated educational and social services.

Third, reform's policies and institutions wrought shifts in authority over education's goals and work. Among key actors, control shifted from educators and education interest groups to state policymakers, business leaders, mayors, and parents—the latter two, respectively, through mayoral takeovers of school districts and the introduction of school councils, charter schools, and school choice. At the organizational level, authority shifted simultaneously from school districts upward to state agencies and downward to schools. The shifts resulted from diminished public confidence in educators and education bureaucracies to accomplish school improvements and from the new focus on performance accountability, which enhanced state-school connections.

Fourth, in contrast to the level of reform activity, academic performance remained essentially flat. A gap persisted between test scores of white and minority students, though some gaps narrowed for some age groups in some subjects. More high school graduates made an immediate transition to college, from 53 percent in 1983 to 63 percent in 1999. Dropout trends were erratic but lower overall. In percentage terms, twice as many students took advanced courses in math, science, English, and foreign languages, though the overall numbers remained low—less than a third in English and language, less than half in math and science. In international comparisons of student performance, fourth and eighth graders in the United States scored above international averages in math and science, while twelfth graders scored below international averages in both subjects. On another dimension, Americans failed to attain even one of the six national education goals by the target year 2000.

Fifth, flat achievement notwithstanding, public support for public schools reached a new high in 2001. For the first time, a majority of Americans (51 percent) graded public schools either A or B, with 68 percent of public school parents grading their child's school A or B. Moreover, when asked to choose between reforming the existing school system and seeking alternatives to it, 72 percent of Americans chose education reform.

Finally, lessons learned from extensive school reform efforts in Kentucky and in Houston, Texas, demonstrated that bold education reform is possible but difficult. Observers credited success in these locations to a common vision of success, high expectations for all students, focus on results, strong leadership and teacher competence grounded in coherent curriculum and professional development, and business involvement. In short, education reform in these locations required incentives for performance, investments in organizational and individual capacity, and greater school autonomy.

Enduring Issue

Americans have long translated their social ambitions into demands for education reform. In the excellence era, these ambitions primarily addressed economic and civic vitality. The compelling argument behind excellence-era education reform was that persistent, low levels of student achievement failed to equip students for success in the emerging economy and polity. That challenge remains. History's lesson is that, of all education reforms, changes in teaching and student achievement come slowly.

See also: EDUCATIONAL ACCOUNTABILITY; SCHOOL REFORM.

BIBLIOGRAPHY

BERLINER, DAVID C., and BIDDLE, BRUCE J. 1995. *The Manufactured Crisis: Myths, Fraud, and the Attack on America's Public Schools.* Reading, MA: Addison-Wesley.

BOYER, ERNEST L. 1983. *High School.* New York: Harper and Row.

CHUBB, JOHN E., and MOE, TERRY M. 1988. *Politics, Markets, and America's Schools.* Washington, DC: Brookings Institution.

GOODLAD, JOHN I. 1984. *A Place Called School: Prospects for the Future.* New York: McGraw-Hill.

HILL, PAUL T., and CELIO, MARY BETH. 1998. *Fixing Urban Schools.* Washington, DC: Brookings Institution Press.

HILL, PAUL T.; PIERCE, LAWRENCE C.; and GUTHRIE, JAMES W. 1997. *Reinventing Public Education: How Contracting Can Transform America's Schools.* Chicago: University of Chicago Press.

LADD, HELEN F.; CHALK, ROSEMARY; and HANSEN, JANET S., eds. 1999. *Equity and Adequacy in Education Finance.* Washington, DC: National Academy Press.

MCADAMS, DONALD R. 2000. *Fighting to Save Our Urban Schools . . . and Winning! Lessons from Houston.* New York: Teachers College Press.

MCLAUGHLIN, MILBREY WALLIN. 1987. "Learning from Experience: Lessons from Policy Implementation." *Educational Evaluation and Policy Analysis* 9:171–178.

MURNANE, RICHARD J., and LEVY, FRANK. 1996. *Teaching the New Basic Skills: Principles for Educating Children to Thrive in a Changing Economy.* New York: The Free Press.

MURPHY, JOSEPH, ed. 1990. *The Educational Reform Movement of the 1980s: Perspectives and Cases.* Berkeley: McCutchan.

MURPHY, JOSEPH. 1991. *Restructuring Schools: Capturing and Assessing the Phenomena.* New York: Teachers College Press.

NATIONAL COMMISSION ON EXCELLENCE IN EDUCATION. 1983. *A Nation at Risk: The Imperative for Educational Reform.* Washington, DC: U.S. Government Printing Office.

NATIONAL COMMISSION ON GOVERNING AMERICA'S SCHOOLS. 1999. *Governing America's Schools: Changing the Rules.* Denver, CO: Education Commission of the States.

NATIONAL COMMISSION ON TEACHING AND AMERICA'S FUTURE. 1996. *What Matters Most: Teaching for America's Future.* New York: Teachers College, Columbia University.

OSBORNE, DAVID, and GAEBLER, TED. 1992. *Reinventing Government: How the Entrepreneurial Spirit Is Transforming the Public Sector.* Reading, MA: Addison-Wesley.

PANKRATZ, ROGER S., and PETROSKO, JOSEPH M., eds. 2000. *All Children Can Learn: Lessons from the Kentucky Reform Experience.* San Francisco: Jossey-Bass.

POWELL, ARTHUR G.; FARRAR, ELEANOR; and COHEN, DAVID K. 1984. *The Shopping Mall High*

School: Winners and Losers in the Educational Marketplace. Boston: Houghton Mifflin.

SIZER, THEODORE R. 1984. *Horace's Compromise: The Dilemma of the American High School.* Boston: Houghton Mifflin.

SMITH, MARSHALL S., and O'DAY, JENNIFER. 1990. "Systemic School Reform." In *The Politics of Curriculum and Testing,* ed. Susan H. Fuhrman and Betty Malen. New York: Falmer.

STEDMAN, LAWRENCE C. 1998. "An Assessment of the Contemporary Debate over U.S. Achievement." In *Brookings Papers on Education Policy 1998,* ed. Diane Ravitch. Washington, DC: Brookings Institution Press.

STEINBERG, LAURENCE. 1996. *Beyond the Classroom: Why School Reform Has Failed and What Parents Need To Do.* New York: Simon and Schuster.

TYACK, DAVID, and CUBAN, LARRY. 1995. *Tinkering Toward Utopia: A Century of Public School Reform.* Cambridge, MA: Harvard University Press.

U.S. DEPARTMENT OF EDUCATION. 1991. *America 2000: An Education Strategy,* revised edition. Washington, DC: U.S. Government Printing Office.

U.S. DEPARTMENT OF EDUCATION, NATIONAL CENTER FOR EDUCATION STATISTICS. 2001. *The Condition of Education 2001.* Washington, DC: U.S. Government Printing Office.

JACOB E. ADAMS JR.

REPORTS OF HISTORICAL SIGNIFICANCE

Reports compiled by individuals or commissions suggesting reforms for public education have appeared throughout America's postcolonial history. Beginning in the late nineteenth century, committees and commissions of prominent individuals became popular for suggesting innovations to cure some educational ills. Since the 1983 release of the National Commission on Excellence in Education's landmark report, *A Nation at Risk,* reform reports have peppered the landscape on a wide array of topics affecting K–12 and higher education. Most of the waves of reform since the 1980s have been spearheaded by a high-profile study of schooling containing a clarion call regarding the need for improvements. Indeed, reform-by-commission has

become a mainstay in the arsenal of those hoping to change schools.

Those specifically examining the reform-by-commission process have come to a series of conclusions about these reports: (1) they have been around for a long time; (2) they tend to suggest changes in a very general manner; (3) they rarely attend to the significant issues in the implementation of reforms; and (4) their specific recommendation have had little direct impact on schools. That said, it is also clear that reform reports provide the rhetorical and symbolic context for reforms to be considered, as they denounce perceived problems and attempt to incite a sense of urgency demanding resolution.

Educational reform reports can be separated into three distinct periods. The first period, the period of early reform-report activity, includes the few reports generated in the United States up until the late nineteenth century. The second period, the era of Progressive reforms, roughly covers the late nineteenth century up until the 1980s. The final period, the era of the modern reform report, began in the early 1980s.

Early Reform-Report Activity

A number of reports of Prussian and French educational innovations heightened interest in improving America's schools. For example, the German professor Johann Friederich Herbart published a volume on the psychology of the art of teaching in 1831, while a Frenchman, Victor Cousin, published a report on the Prussian system of preparing teachers that was reprinted in English in 1835. The first U.S. educational reform reports were generally conducted by prominent individuals driven to foster the development of the nation's universal, free, public, and compulsory system of common schools. Leaders such as Henry Barnard of Connecticut, Calvin Stowe of Ohio, Caleb Mills of Indiana, Calvin Whiley of North Carolina, and John Pierce of Michigan advocated reforms for schools. Most significant among these were the reports of Horace Mann, the secretary of the State Board of Massachusetts in the late 1830s and 1840s. Mann's twelve annual reports covered a broad range of topics and decried the poor efficiency of the public schools. His reports analyzed topics including the moral purposes of schooling, the curriculum, libraries, pedagogical methods, the quality and training of teachers, discipline, school facilities, and church-state relations regarding public schools. Mann urged the standardization of the schools.

Toward the end of the early reform period, the analyses of Joseph M. Rice, the editor of *Forum* magazine, were published. Rice, a pediatrician who had studied pedagogy in Germany, visited hundreds of urban classrooms in thirty-six cities during the 1890s. He found the conditions and methods of instruction deplorable. Rice eventually designed a simple method of testing spelling to make more reliable evaluations and reported his findings in a series of articles appearing in *Forum*.

As the design and nature of schooling in the United States unfolded during the nineteenth century, reports emerged that depicted the condition of American education and offered various remedies for reform. The pace of reports about schools intensified as the country expanded west and the American population grew. This pattern was evident in the era of Progressive reforms.

Era of Progressive Reforms

From the 1890s until the 1980s a number of key education reports were published. These ranged from blue-ribbon commissions produced by elite educators and business persons to studies of schools prepared by prominent individual researchers. In this period the practice of conducting surveys of individual school districts was popularized. A 1940 textbook on educational history by John Russell and Charles Judd of the University of Chicago reported an astounding 3,022 educational surveys between 1910 and 1935. Supporters of this burgeoning examination of schools stressed the importance of using scientific techniques to inform policy.

Beginning in the 1890s the National Education Association (NEA), the leading professional education organization, produced a number of reports, the first and most notable being the 1893 report of the Committee on Secondary School Studies (chaired by Harvard president Charles Eliot), the *Report of the Committee of Ten*. The report identified the lack of uniformity in secondary programs and college admission requirements and sought to formulate curriculum and admissions requirements that would bring some harmony to secondary and higher education. Though scholars differ in their interpretation of the impact of this report's findings, the report did force high schools to work towards greater uniformity in curriculum.

In response to the tremendous growth in secondary school enrollment during the early decades of the twentieth century, the NEA established the Committee on the Reorganization of Secondary Education, which produced *The Cardinal Principles of Secondary Education* in 1918. Published by the U.S. Department of Education, the document identified several means of preparing students for their duties as citizens, workers, and family members. The bulk of the report dealt with the goals of education in a democracy, the main objectives of education (seven were identified), and the role of secondary education in achieving these objectives. Key recommendations included compulsory schooling for at least eight hours a week until age eighteen and the creation of junior and senior high schools—with a comprehensive high school being one with a core curriculum, variables depending on vocation, and electives to accommodate special interests. The report reflected much of the thinking on education at the time, though its release during World War I no doubt affected its impact.

Other NEA-sponsored reports were released in the 1930s by the Commission on the Orientation of Secondary Education. *Issues of Secondary Education* (1936) and *Functions of Secondary Education* (1937) produced recommendations and key functions for secondary schools, including the idea of universal secondary school; curriculum beyond college preparatory, which was differentiated to meet specific needs; greater articulation between elementary and secondary schools; and, most controversially, that students should be eliminated from school once it was apparent that they would no longer benefit from being there.

Reports produced by the NEA-related Educational Policies Commission (EPC) included *The Unique Functions of Education in American Democracy* (1937) and *The Purposes of Education in American Democracy* (1938). In the first document, *schooling* was characterized as an institution that should be run by professionals with great academic freedom. Schools were to be run in a climate protective of democratic and scientific principles. The *Purposes* document amplified the key aims laid out in the *Cardinal Principles*. Some argued, however, that these recommendations were out of step with burgeoning issues related to the control of American youth.

The Progressive Education Association undertook several studies, the most prominent of which was the Eight-Year Study, the findings of which were released in 1942. This landmark evaluation project included twenty-nine secondary schools with Progressive curricula whose students were studied for eight years. Several colleges agreed to accept students from these programs who didn't meet usual entrance requirements. The evaluation matched 1,475 pairs of students from Progressive and conventional high schools across an array of variables in college. Much of the impact of the study was clearly blunted by its release during World War II, and although little remained of the programs in the Progressive schools years after the study, the evaluation design served as the model for studies for decades.

Toward the end of World War II, the EPC released *Education for All American Youth* (1944). Re-released in 1952 to account for postwar changes, this report made suggestions for improving secondary education. At that time, more than half of all students never completed high school, yet the growing population and an increased faith in the power of schooling were swelling enrollments. Later in the 1950s, the Carnegie Corporation sponsored James Conant's *The American High School Today,* which involved visitations to fifty-five schools in eighteen states. Schools were evaluated, and it was determined that academically talented students were not being challenged. Key ingredients of successful schools were found to include strong school board members, superintendents, and principals; twenty-one specific recommendations for curriculum were included.

Probably the most significant report of the 1960s was the federally funded research study *Equality of Educational Opportunity,* published in 1966. Authored by James Coleman and associates, the report examined data from 600,000 students in 4,000 schools. The educational and socioeconomic backgrounds of students' families were found to be the most important variables explaining achievement, far outweighing the impact of school or teacher variables. These findings inspired several decades of debate, affecting a variety of school-related policies.

In the 1970s the Kettering Foundation created the National Commission on the Reform of Secondary Education, which worked on updating the Conant findings. Its 1973 report, *The Reform of Secondary Education,* focused primarily on alternatives to the traditional high school curriculum and a general definition for all American high schools.

Most of the reports in this period were driven by the push for scientific inquiry and the expanding role of schooling in American culture. In the early 1980s, highly visible reports underscored perceived problems and offered solutions for change.

Era of the Modern Reform Report

The 1980s became the decade of the reform report starting with the publication of Mortimer Adler's *The Paideia Proposal* in 1982. With the 1983 release of *A Nation at Risk,* the most widely acclaimed report of this genre, an unprecedented period of reform report activity began. It stated that a "rising tide of mediocrity" had overcome America's schools, and that if another nation had tried to impose such mediocrity on U.S. schools it would be considered "an act of war." Its many recommendations included strengthening the curriculum, lengthening the school day and the school year, paying teachers based on performance, and increasing homework. These recommendations were debated from statehouse to statehouse across the country. Though the recommendations may not have been followed exactly, the atmosphere for reform generated by the report ushered in a reform period unlike any other in the nation's history.

Other reports soon followed. In 1983 alone, major reports that were released included: Ernest Boyer's *High School;* the Business-Higher Education Forum's *America's Competitive Challenge;* the College Entrance Examination Board's *Academic Preparation for College;* John Goodlad's *A Place Called School;* the National Science Board Commission on Precollege Education in Mathematics, Science and Technology's *Educating Americans for the 21st Century;* the Southern Regional Education Board's *Meeting the Need for Quality Action in the South;* the Task Force on Education for Economic Growth's *Action for Excellence;* and the Twentieth Century Fund's *Making the Grade.* In 1984 Theodore Sizer's influential *Horace's Compromise: The Dilemma of the American High School* was published. Obviously, diverse entities focused on education, and no reforms could be promulgated without a commission-style report.

This reliance on reform reports continued unabated throughout the 1980s. Key areas for scrutiny included teacher education (*A Nation Prepared* [1986], *Tomorrow's Teachers* [1986]), educational administration (*Leader's for America's Schools* [1987]), improving school performance (*Time for Results* [1986]), and strengthening the economy through schooling (*Investing in Our Children* [1985],

Children in Need [1987]). The pace of reform-report activity continued in the 1990s and the early part of the twenty-first century. Examples of such reports include government-sponsored documents, such as *Does School Quality Matter, Beyond Rhetoric: A New American Agenda for Children and Families,* and *Prisoners of Time;* reports from business groups, such as *Investing in Teaching;* and privately financed reports from think tanks and interest groups, such as *The Teachers We Want and How to Get More of Them* and *The Essential Profession.* It appears that any government agency or interest group wishing to propose a series of educational reforms often launch their initiative with a reform report. With the growth of the Internet and its ability to deliver information quickly and cheaply, reports continue to emerge and are readily available to anyone with access to a computer.

Conclusion

What can be said of reform reports across America's history? Clearly, such reports have been a mainstay of those interested in schools, though their use grew dramatically towards the latter part of the twentieth century. This history suggests that they will continue as a means of examining aspects of schooling and promoting particular solutions. Whether being merely symbolic or ceremonial in terms of creating a climate for considering change, or more directly functional in promoting specific policies into practice, they operate as a form of *trickle-down* reform, where some government agency or other body sets out policy recommendations for policymakers or those close to schools to consider. The policies that ultimately appear may not be as initially intended, but the reform reports help set the tone for the educational reform agenda that policymakers consider.

See also: EDUCATIONAL ACCOUNTABILITY; SCHOOL REFORM.

BIBLIOGRAPHY

ADLER, MORTIMER J. 1982. *The Paideia Proposal.* New York: Macmillan.

BOYER, ERNEST L. 1983. *High School: A Report on Secondary Education in America.* New York: Harper and Row.

BUSINESS-HIGHER EDUCATION FORUM. 1983. *America's Competitive Challenge: The Need for a National Response.* Washington, DC: Business-Higher Education Forum.

CARD, DAVID, and KRUEGER, ALAN B. 1990. *Does School Quality Matter? Returns to Education and the Characteristics of Public Schools in the United States.* Washington, DC: Bureau of Economic Research.

CARNEGIE FORUM ON EDUCATION AND THE ECONOMY, TASK FORCE ON TEACHING AS A PROFESSION. 1986. *A Nation Prepared: Teachers for the 21st Century.* New York: Carnegie Forum on Education and the Economy.

CASWELL, HOLLIS L. 1929. *City School Surveys.* New York: Teachers College Press.

COLEMAN, JAMES S., et al. 1966. *Equality of Educational Opportunity.* Washington, DC: U.S. Government Printing Office.

COLLEGE ENTRANCE EXAMINATION BOARD. 1983. *Academic Preparation for College: What Students Need to Know and Be Able to Do.* New York: College Entrance Examination Board.

COMMISSION ON THE REORGANIZATION OF SECONDARY EDUCATION. 1918. *Cardinal Principles of Secondary Education.* Washington, DC: Government Printing Office.

COMMISSION ON THE REORIENTATION OF SECONDARY EDUCATION. 1936. *Issues of Secondary Education.* Washington, DC: National Education Association.

COMMISSION ON THE REORIENTATION OF SECONDARY EDUCATION. 1937. *Functions of Secondary Education.* Washington, DC: National Education Association.

COMMITTEE FOR ECONOMIC DEVELOPMENT. 1985. *Investing in Our Children.* New York: Committee for Economic Development.

COMMITTEE FOR ECONOMIC DEVELOPMENT. 1987. *Children in Need.* New York: Committee for Economic Development.

COMMITTEE ON SECONDARY SCHOOL STUDIES (COMMITTEE OF TEN). 1893. *Report of the Committee on Secondary School Studies.* Washington, DC: National Education Association.

CONANT, JAMES B. 1959. *The American High School Today.* New York: McGraw-Hill.

CREMIN, LAWRENCE A. 1957. *The Republic and the School: Horace Mann On the Education of Free Men.* New York: Teachers College Press.

DEAL, TERRY E. 1985. "National Commissions: Blueprints for Remodeling or Ceremonies for Revitalizing Public Schools?" *Education and Urban Society* 17:145–156.

EDUCATIONAL POLICIES COMMISSION. 1937. *Unique Functions of Education in American Democracy.* Washington, DC: National Education Association.

EDUCATIONAL POLICIES COMMISSION. 1938. *The Purposes of Education in American Democracy.* Washington, DC: National Education Association.

EDUCATIONAL POLICIES COMMISSION. 1944. *Education for All American Youth.* Washington, DC: National Education Association.

EDUCATIONAL POLICIES COMMISSION. 1952. *Education for All American Youth: A Further Look.* Washington, DC: National Education Association.

FORDHAM FOUNDATION. 1999. *The Teachers We Want and How to Get More of Them.* Washington, DC: Fordham Foundation.

GINSBERG, RICK, and PLANK, DAVID N., eds. 1995. *Commissions, Reports, Reforms, and Educational Policy.* Westport, CT: Praeger.

GINSBERG, RICK, and WIMPELBERG, ROBERT K. 1987. "Educational Change by Commission: Attempting 'Trickle-Down' Reform." *Educational Evaluation and Policy Analysis* 10:344–360.

GINSBERG, RICK, and WIMPELBERG, ROBERT. 1988. "An Assessment of Twentieth Century Commission Reports on Educational Reform." In *Social Goals and Educational Reform,* ed. C. V. Willie and I. Miller. New York: Greenwood Press.

GOODLAD, JOHN I. 1983. *A Place Called School: Prospects for the Future.* St. Louis, MO: McGraw-Hill.

HASELKORN, DAVID, and HARRIS, LOUIS. 1998. *The Essential Profession.* Belmont, MA: Recruiting New Teachers.

HOLMES GROUP. 1986. *Tomorrow's Teachers.* East Lansing, MI: Holmes Group.

KRUG, EDWARD A. 1964. *The Shaping of the American High School, 1880–1920,* Vol. 1. New York: Praeger.

KRUG, EDWARD A. 1972. *The Shaping of the American High School, 1920–1941,* Vol. 2. Madison: University of Wisconsin Press.

MURPHY, JOSEPH, ed. 1990. *The Educational Reform Movement of the 1980s.* Berkeley, CA: McCutchan.

NATIONAL ALLIANCE OF BUSINESS. 2001. *Investing in Teaching.* Washington, DC: National Alliance of Business.

NATIONAL COMMISSION ON CHILDREN. 1991. *Beyond Rhetoric: A New American Agenda for Children and Families.* Washington, DC: National Commission on Children.

NATIONAL COMMISSION ON EXCELLENCE IN EDUCATION. 1983. *A Nation at Risk: The Imperative for Educational Reform.* Washington, DC: U.S. Government Printing Office.

NATIONAL COMMISSION ON EXCELLENCE IN EDUCATIONAL ADMINISTRATION. 1987. *Leaders for Tomorrow's Schools.* Tempe, AZ: University Council on Educational Administration.

NATIONAL COMMISSION ON THE REFORM OF SECONDARY EDUCATION. 1973. *The Reform of Secondary Education: A Report to the Public and the Profession.* New York: McGraw-Hill.

NATIONAL EDUCATION COMMISSION ON TIME AND LEARNING. 1994. *Prisoners of Time.* Washington, DC: National Commission on Time and Learning.

NATIONAL GOVERNORS ASSOCIATION. 1986. *Time for Results: The Governors' 1991 Report on Education.* Washington, DC: National Governors Association.

NATIONAL SCIENCE BOARD COMMISSION ON PRE-COLLEGE EDUCATION IN MATHEMATICS, SCIENCE AND TECHNOLOGY. 1983. *Educating Americans for the 21st Century.* Washington, DC: National Science Foundation.

PASSOW, HARRY. 1984. *Reforming Schools in the 1980s: A Critical Review of the National Reports.* New York: Teachers College Press.

PASSOW, HARRY A. 1984. "Tackling the Reform Reports of the 1980s." *Phi Delta Kappan* 65:674–683.

PETERSON, PAUL E. 1983. "Did the Educational Commissions Say Anything?" *Brookings Review* 1:3–11.

PLANK, DAVID N., and GINSBERG, RICK. 1990. "Catch the Wave: Reform Commissions and School Reform." In *The Educational Reform Movement of the 1980s,* ed. J. Murphy. Berkeley, CA: McCutchan.

PROGRESSIVE EDUCATION ASSOCIATION. 1942. *The Eight Year Study.* Washington, DC: Progressive Education Association.

Russell, John D., and Judd, Charles H. 1940. *The American Educational System.* Cambridge, MA: Riverside Press.

Sizer, Theodore. 1984. *Horace's Compromise: The Dilemma of the American High School.* Boston: Houghton Mifflin.

Southern Regional Education Board. 1983. *Meeting the Need for Quality: Action in the South.* Atlanta, GA: Southern Regional Educational Board.

Task Force on Education for Economic Growth. 1983. *Action for Excellence: A Comprehensive Plan to Improve Our Nation's Schools.* Denver, CO: Education Commission of the States.

Twentieth Century Fund. 1983. *Report of the Twentieth Century Fund Task Force on Federal Elementary and Secondary Education Policy.* New York: Twentieth Century Fund.

Tyack, David B. 1974. *The One Best System: A History of American Urban Education.* Cambridge, MA: Harvard University Press.

Tyack, David B.; Kirst, Michael; and Hansot, Elizabeth. 1980. "Educational Reform: Retrospect and Prospect." *Teachers College Record* 81:253–269.

Wimpelberg, Robert K., and Ginsberg, Rick. 1988. "The National Commission Approach to Educational Reform." In *The Politics of Education Yearbook,* ed. R. Crowson and J. Hannaway. London: Falmer.

Rick Ginsberg

EFFICIENCY IN EDUCATION

Educators often feel ambivalent about the pursuit of efficiency in education. On the one hand, there is a basic belief that efficiency is a good and worthy goal; on the other hand, there is sense of worry that efforts to improve efficiency will ultimately undermine what lies at the heart of high-quality education. Part of the difficulty stems from a misunderstanding about the meaning of efficiency as well as from the legacy of past, sometimes misguided, efforts to improve the efficiency of educational systems. It is therefore useful to begin with a basic discussion of the efficiency concept.

The notion of efficiency applies to a remarkably large number of fields, including education. It is a disarmingly simple idea that presupposes a transformation of some kind. One can think in terms of what was in hand before the transformation, what was in hand after the transformation, and one can also think about the transformation process itself. The *before* elements are commonly referred to as ingredients, inputs, or resources while the *after* elements are called results, outputs, or outcomes. The transformation process is sometimes less obvious and can become confused with ingredients. For example, in an educational setting, a teacher can be thought of as an ingredient while teaching is an important part of the actual transformation process.

The concept of efficiency is often connected to a moral imperative to obtain more desired results from fewer resources. Efficiency needs to be thought of as a matter of degree. Efficiency is not a "yes/no" kind of phenomenon. It is instead better thought of in relative or comparative terms. One operation may be more efficient than another. This said, the more efficient of the two operations could become even more efficient. The quest for greater efficiency is never over, and this sense of a perennially unfinished agenda is one source of the generalized sense of anxiety that tends to surround the efficiency concept.

The Choice of Outcomes

If the goal is to obtain more desired results from fewer resources, then it is important to be clear about what is being sought. Society might have a very efficient system because a large amount of outcome is being obtained relative to the resources being spent or invested, but if the outcomes are out of sync with what is truly desired, there is a real sense in which the system is not very efficient. Of course, this invites important questions about who gets to decide what counts as a desirable outcome, and in education there are longstanding and ongoing debates over what the educational system ought to be accomplishing.

In the United States, education is viewed as a responsibility of the individual states rather than the national government, and the states have made efforts to define the outcomes they seek from their educational systems. These efforts have come to be known as *standards-driven initiatives,* where the standards constitute pronouncements from the states about the collective expectations for what the schools need to accomplish. The idea has been for each state to articulate the desired outcomes and then provide flexibility to the districts, schools, administrators, teachers, and students to meet the standards in ways that make the most sense given local circumstances.

States have handled this in different ways and there are interesting deeper questions about how to balance state judgments with judgments that are made at more localized levels. How, for example, should a disagreement between a duly constituted local school board and the state be settled? Going further, how should the views of local boards be considered as the state sets its standards? What is the proper role for minority views? And how should revisions be handled as time passes?

It is customary to think of the state's setting minimum standards that can be exceeded by individual localities if a locality resolves to do so and can muster the necessary resources. This thinking presupposes a hierarchical view of educational outcomes in the sense that outcome "C" builds upon outcome "B" while outcome "B" builds upon outcome "A." A problem is that outcomes may not always have this kind of hierarchical nature. Suppose a school wants to provide a high degree of personalized attention as part of its program. Is this an input or an outcome? Let us suppose that this is a costly thing to do. The school that pursues this strategy is going to consume more ingredients and if only the standard outcomes are looked at, this school is going to look like costs are high relative to the outcomes that are realized. Hence, the school could look inefficient for the simple reason that it has chosen to pursue a different set of educational goals. There is also the possibility that a locally selected goal can interfere with or undermine one of the state selected goals.

In addition to reaching agreement about the mix of outcomes to pursue, there are important measurement issues to consider. An interest in efficiency is frequently accompanied by an interest in measuring magnitudes. If one is seeking more out of less, one frequently wants to know "how much more," and the result has been a boom in the efforts by educational psychologists and others to develop valid and reliable measures of the learning gains of students. Critics of efficiency analysis in education worry that ease of measurement can unduly influence the selection of the outcomes that the system will be structured to achieve. In other words, the worry is that the drive for efficiency will lead, perhaps inadvertently, toward the use of educational outcomes that are chosen more because they are easy

to measure than because of their intrinsic long-term value for either individual students or the larger society. Standardized tests of various kinds have been relied upon as measures of the outcomes of schooling and have been criticized on these grounds.

Sometimes there is interest in the economic consequences of schooling, and this interest has prompted analysts to use earnings as a measure of schooling outcomes. A rich literature has developed in the economics of education where efforts have been made to estimate the economic rate of return to different levels and types of schooling. This is a challenging area of research because earnings are influenced by many factors and it is difficult to isolate the effects of schooling. The goal of this research is to capture the value added by schooling activities.

The relevance of the *value-added* concept is not limited to economists' studies of rates of return. Even in cases where the focus is on learning outcomes as measured by tests or other psychometric instruments, there are questions to answer about the effects of schooling activities relative to the effects of other potentially quite significant influences on gains in students' capabilities. Serious studies of the efficiency of educational systems measure educational outcomes in value-added terms.

Measurement issues also arise from the collective nature of schooling. The results gained from schooling experiences are likely to vary among individual students and this prompts questions about how best to examine the result for the group in contrast to an individual student. Is one primarily interested in, say, the average performance level, or is there a parallel and perhaps even more important concern with what is happening to the level of variation that exists across all of the students within the unit, be it a classroom, grade level within a school, a school, a district, a state, or a nation? The early research on educational efficiency in the 1960s placed a heavy emphasis on average test score results for relatively large units like school districts. More recent work demonstrates greater interest in measures of inequality among students. The standards-driven reform movement includes a considerable amount of rhetoric about all students reaching high standards; the analysis of efficiency presupposes an ability to move beyond the easy rhetoric to make clear decisions about how uniform performance expectations are for students.

In addition, there is an important distinction to maintain between the level at which a system operates and the rate at which inputs are being transformed into outcomes. One can "get the outputs right" so that the desired items are being taught/learned in the correct proportion to one another. In such a case, gains in the understanding of mathematics are occurring in the correct proportion to, say, gains in language capabilities. But this says nothing about the absolute level at which the system is operating. The naive view might be that the system should operate at 100 percent of its capacity, but this overlooks the fact that scarce resources are needed to operate at this level and that education is not the only worthy use of these precious resources. Policymakers must make often difficult trade-off decisions about the level at which the educational system will operate relative to the level of other competing social services. The early twenty-first century is witnessing a considerable amount of debate over the proper level at which to set the educational system, often as part of an effort to define what counts as an "adequate" education.

With respect to outcomes, the goal is to reach agreement about (1) the relative mix of performance outcomes to realize; (2) the degree of uniformity of performance across students; and (3) the level of capacity at which the system should operate. In addition, there needs to be an ability to measure what is being accomplished.

The Choice of Inputs

The outcomes that are selected drive the entire system. Input issues, in contrast, are more straightforward and almost mechanical in nature. Once what is to be accomplished is known, at what level, and for whom, society can then turn to the challenge of doing so in as economical a way that is possible. In other words the goal is to accomplish the desired results for as little cost as possible, and this involves making the best possible use of whatever ingredients or resources that are available.

Although this seems straightforward, there are a number of complexities that need to be considered. First, there is the dynamic nature of the process. As time passes, more is learned about how to make better and better use of the available resources and new resources may also become available. A good example of a new resource lies in the area of telecommunication and computing technology. These advances have great potential to affect the day-to-day life of educational practice. It is also important to keep in mind that the nature of how technology develops is not external to the system. Technology does not develop in a vacuum. Instead, there are sometimes powerful forces that shape the nature of how technology develops. For example, many existing instructional computing technologies are designed to supplement rather than to supplant existing classroom activities. This tendency for computing to be treated as the handmaiden of the traditional classroom structure may not be in the best long-term interest of the larger society.

Second, there is the technical versus cost dimension to consider. A particular resource or input might be highly productive in the sense that a small amount could make a significant difference, but this same highly productive resource might be extraordinarily costly. For example, suppose having one hour per week of a Nobel prize winning physicist's time turns out to be an extraordinarily productive input for high school students who are learning physics. Suppose further that such a resource is quite costly. In contrast, an hour per week of a local Ph.D. in physics might be less costly but let us also say that it is less productive. From an efficiency perspective, the question is: How do the ratios of benefit relative to cost compare? It is quite conceivable that the benefit/cost ratio for the Nobel prize winner is smaller than the comparable ratio for the local Ph.D., even though the absolute measure of the Nobel prize winner's effectiveness (i.e., the result per unit of input) is higher.

Third, in addition to making sense of benefits relative to costs, there is also the challenge of making the best possible use of whatever resource is being employed. For example, just because a Nobel prize winner has the potential to be a very productive input does not preclude the possibility of that resource being squandered in a particular setting, and the same can be said of the local Ph.D. in physics, or an artist who is hired to spend some time in a school. The quest for greater efficiency requires the parties to make the best possible use of whatever resources come into their possession.

Finally, there is the potential for the costs of inputs to influence the selection of outcomes. Some outcomes are more costly to produce than others. For example, a student who finds it difficult to learn will, by definition, be relatively costly to educate, and these extra costs could influence decisions that are made about how uniform to make the learning outcome standards. And thus, the distinction between outcomes and inputs begins to break down.

The Transformation Process and Implications for Policy

Policymakers are very interested in assessing the degree of efficiency in educational systems. One difficulty arises when indicators are used that fail to provide accurate information. For example, a widely available statistic is the level of spending on education expressed on a per pupil basis. At first glance, this looks like an efficiency indicator since it provides insight into the commitment of resources (the expenditure figure) and the result (the number of students being served by the system). Critics note that this statistic has been rising over time and conclude that the system is becoming less efficient. There are many reasons to be wary of using an expenditure per pupil statistic and its changes over time to reach such a conclusion. Even with a control for the effects of inflation, there remains a fundamental problem on the outcome side of the analysis since there is no direct measure of what the schools are accomplishing and how this might have changed over the period.

Even if accurate, noncontroversial measures of efficiency and its changes over time can be obtained, it is difficult to obtain clear insight into what policies should be developed to ensure gains in efficiency without undermining other key social goals like fairness and freedom of choice. Much of the challenge here depends on the fundamental nature of the transformation process that is presupposed as part of the efficiency concept. The efficiency concept derives from the field of economics where it was initially applied to industrial production processes such as the manufacture of automobiles. These industrial manufacturing processes involve the combination of numerous nonhuman ingredients such as lengths of steel, aluminum, glass, chrome, and so forth. These ingredients are transformed thanks to various physical and chemical processes whose scientific properties are relatively well understood, making the results quite predictable.

For a manager whose goal is to improve efficiency, this kind of information is invaluable. With this information the manager can compare higher performing units with lower performing units and make a diagnosis about the source of the inefficiency in the underperforming units. There may be problems with a unit's ability to get the most out of the inputs it is using; there may be a less than optimal mix of inputs being used; and/or the mix of outputs being produced may be misaligned. The "efficiency expert" in such a situation is able to pinpoint the source of the difficulty and can prescribe steps for improvements.

In contrast, the educational process is heavily committed to the use of human resources and the various inputs are brought together and transformed in ways that are sometimes difficult to predict. Without denying the significance of the human dimension within industrial manufacturing processes, it stands to reason that the production or transformation process that lies at the center of educational systems is fundamentally more complex and less well-understood than production in the industrial sector. A better comparison comes from studies of efficiency in crop production in the field of agricultural economics. But even here, the production process for growing a particular plant is better understood than is the process through which human minds mature and acquire knowledge and understanding. Indeed, it is possible to question whether the educational process really lends itself to the input-output, mechanical formulation that lies at the heart of the efficiency concept. According to this view, educational growth is inherently unpredictable, and the teacher is better thought of as a creative artist than as a productive input whose impact can be measured and predicted in a rigorous and scientific way.

While it is clear that knowledge of the technical properties of the educational process is more limited than what exists, say, in the area of automobile manufacturing, it does not follow that the educational process is inherently unknowable in this sense. In other words, the lack of progress to date in coming to grips with the technical properties of the education transformation process does not mean the process is inherently unpredictable and unmanageable. A more prudent conclusion is that care needs to be exercised in efforts to assess the efficiency of educational systems. It also follows that care needs to be exercised in the use of the efficiency assessment data that are gathered.

Consider the following example of how the results of an efficiency analysis in education can be misapplied. Suppose an analysis goes forward that suggests that a particular school or school district is less efficient than most others. Suppose the response is to penalize the less efficient unit by reducing the flow of state or federal resources. A byproduct of such a policy is a reduction in the funding of the education being provided to students who through no fault of their own find themselves located within an inefficient educational system. Those who work to improve the efficiency of educational systems must guard against this potential to "blame the ultimate victim" of the situation. Similarly, the use of incentives to encourage greater efficiency runs the risk of rewarding those who are already enjoying considerable success. If the problem lies with the unknown nature of the production process, it is perverse to be implicitly penalizing the underperforming districts because they do not have knowledge that is lacking elsewhere. Penalizing underperformers makes sense only if the knowledge is available and the penalties are meant to provide greater incentive to find it. States sometimes handle this by providing technical assistance but technical assistance really works only when it is based on bona fide knowledge, something which is not always possible, given the continued limited understanding of the properties of educational production under a wide range of circumstances.

At this stage of development in efforts to apply the efficiency concept to the field of education several conclusions can be reached.

1. It is important to make sure that the comparative information suggesting that one educational unit is more or less efficient than another is accurate.

2. This accurate comparative information needs to be used as a set of guidelines/suggestions and needs to stop short of becoming overly rigid and prescriptive.

3. Efforts need to be made to monitor very carefully the results of attempts to improve the efficiency of educational systems that are perceived to be below expectations.

4. Additional research efforts need to be made to better understand the technical properties of the transformation process that gives rise to desired educational results.

The results of this continuing research will be instrumental in future efforts to make further efficiency improvements in education and can go far toward reducing the ambivalence that historically has characterized educators' reaction to the efficiency concept and its application to the field of education.

See also: EDUCATIONAL ACCOUNTABILITY; EDUCATION REFORM.

BIBLIOGRAPHY

BECKER, GARY S. 1975. *Human Capital,* 2nd edition. New York: Columbia University Press.

FUHRMAN, SUSAN H. 1999. "The New Accountability." *CPRE Policy Briefs* RB–27 January. Consortium for Policy Research in Education, Graduate School of Education, University of Pennsylvania.

LADD, HELEN F., ed. 1996. *Holding Schools Accountable.* Washington, DC: The Brookings Institution.

LEVIN, HENRY M., and McEWAN, PATRICK J. 2001. *Cost-Effectiveness Analysis,* 2nd edition. Thousand Oaks, CA: Sage.

MONK, DAVID H. 1992. "Education Productivity Research: An Update and Assessment of its Role in Education Finance Reform." *Educational Evaluation and Policy Analysis* 14(4):307–332.

MONK, DAVID H., and WALBERG, HERBERT J., eds. 2001. *Improving Educational Productivity.* Greenwich, CT: Information Age.

MURNANE, RICHARD J., and LEVY, FRANK. 1996. *Teaching the New Basic Skills: Principles of Educating Children to Thrive in a Challenging Economy.* New York: Martin Kessler Books, The Free Press.

DAVID H. MONK

EFFORT AND INTEREST

The research literature provides support for John Dewey's observation that effort and interest in education can be understood as being both oppositional and complementary. Five minutes of work on a task may feel like hours to a student who does not know what the next steps need to be, or even what the longer-range goals for the work are—especially if the student does not have a developed interest for the task. Similarly, a student with a well-developed individual interest for Latin may be able to briefly glance at the third declension adjective endings and decide he knows them, while another, equally able student with a less-developed interest for Latin, has to work after school to learn these endings.

Effort

Effort usually refers to whether a student tries hard, asks for help, and/or participates in class. Studies of student effort suggest that the more difficult a task appears—in the sense of the task's difficulty and the likelihood that the student can complete it successfully—the less likely it is that the student will be motivated to take the task on. On the other hand, studies of student effort also suggest that effort is associated with the possibility of doing well on a task. Thus, students might be expected to figure out what they need to study, study it, and be successful—if they have the *ability* to do the assigned task, confidence in this ability, and no anxiety about the task.

Whether students exert effort or not is typically described as a choice or decision that is made by the student about whether success is possible. Students' *expectancy value* is influenced by their previous success, their perceptions about teachers' beliefs and practices, their goals, and by their self-concept. Students' beliefs about both their own abilities, and about the relation between ability and effort, influence the likelihood that they will exert effort. As Carol Dweck points out, students' beliefs develop over time in conjunction with experience. She also notes that students are increasingly influenced by the feedback they receive, meaning that some change in students' beliefs and motivation is possible.

Deborah Stipek's research, for example, suggests that students are engaged and learning takes place when teachers promote effort in the classroom by emphasizing participation, setting high expectations, and encouraging students to support each other as learners. If students have a clear understanding of the goals of the tasks they are assigned, they also might be expected to be better able to effectively regulate the possibility of their success. In fact, students who have a sense of efficacy, who both value and experience feelings of enjoyment for the task, can also be expected to expend effort to master the task.

Interest

Interest describes the cognitive and affective relationship between a student and particular classes of subject matter. However, one student's effort to master Latin, mathematics, or lacrosse is not likely to be the same as another student's efforts. Moreover, how a student approaches different subjects can be expected to vary, just as the background and basic abilities that each student brings to each subject will vary.

Interest can hold a student's attention, encourage effort, and support learning. It also has been found to enhance strategic processing. Furthermore,

students can experience more than one type of interest concurrently.

Three types of interest can be identified, each of which reflects differing amounts of knowledge, value, and feelings. These are: (1) situational interest, (2) individual interest (sometimes referred to as *topic interest*), and (3) well-developed individual interest. *Situational interest* refers to the short-lived or momentary attention to, or curiosity about, particular subject matter, and can be accompanied by either positive or negative feelings. *Individual interest* is a relatively enduring predisposition to experience enjoyment in working with particular subject matter. An individual interest may or may not provide a student with the support to put forth effort when faced with a difficult task, presumably because the identification of individual interest in terms of enjoyment provides no information about the depth of a student's knowledge about the topic. *Well-developed individual interest* is a relatively enduring predisposition to re-engage particular classes of subject matter over time. A student with a well-developed individual interest for a subject has more stored knowledge and stored value for that subject than he or she has for other subjects. With more stored knowledge and stored value for a given subject matter, the student is positioned to begin asking curiosity questions that drive knowledge acquisition, consolidation, and elaboration, and that leads the student to persist in the face of frustration or difficulty.

Well-developed interest is the type of student interest to which most people are referring when they talk about interest and its impact on learning. For example, students who immerse themselves in a task they have been assigned, or who are willing to expend a lot of effort to master a skill that will allow them to begin work on some future project, are likely to have a well-developed interest for the subject of that project. Importantly, the student who has a well-developed interest for a subject area may not seem to be aware that he or she is exerting effort. Instead, it appears that interest may free up possibilities for students to push themselves, just as it frees up their ability to process interesting stories.

A student does not simply decide to have a well-developed interest for a subject about which he or she has previously had either little knowledge or value. Nor is a well-developed interest a set of beliefs about utility or value. In fact, a student who has a well-developed interest for mathematics may or may not be aware that he or she has begun to think and question in ways that are similar to a mathematician.

A student could, however, make a decision to learn about a subject, and in so doing move rather rapidly from having a situational interest to having an individual interest for it. In this instance, the student's decision to work on developing his or her knowledge is a choice and would involve effort, and would probably be identified as an individual interest. Once the student began to generate his or her own questions about the subject, worked to understand these, and did not find major investments of time effortful, the student might then be considered to have a well-developed individual interest for the subject matter.

All types of interest require conditions that allow the interest to be maintained, to continue to deepen, and to merge with other content. A number of studies have suggested the importance of providing students with meaningful choices, well-organized texts that promote interest, and the background knowledge necessary to fully understand a topic. Even students with a well-developed interest for a particular subject need to be supported to continue challenging what they know and assume in order for their interest to be sustained.

Effort and Interest

The research reviewed here suggests that effort needs to be understood as involving choice, as being rooted in beliefs, and as being influenced by feedback. In addition, interest needs to be understood as a cognitive and affective relationship between a student and a particular subject that varies depending on the type of interest being described. As Andreas Krapp has observed, students who want to be doing what they are supposed to be doing because of a well-developed interest are not a problem for educators. The challenge for education could be understood as one that involves figuring out how to get students to want to do what teachers want them to do. However this interpretation sets effort and interest at cross purposes and is not productive. Instead, the research suggests that educators should focus on the complementarity qualities of effort and interest. Providing students with conditions that will involve them in deepening their knowledge should position them to begin asking their own questions about a particular subject matter; recognize that they both have the ability to work on developing their understanding of, as well as their confidence about their ability to

work with, the subject matter; and provide support for developing interest and effort that includes trying hard, asking for help, and/or participating. In fact, as John Dewey anticipated, it appears that when conditions to support student interest are in place, effort will follow.

See also: MOTIVATION.

BIBLIOGRAPHY

BECK, ISABEL L., and McKEOWN, M. G. 2001. "Inviting Students into the Pursuit of Meaning." *Educational Psychology Review* 13(3):225–242.

BERGIN, DAVID A. 1999. "Influences on Classroom Interest." *Educational Psychologist* 34:87–98.

DEWEY, JOHN. 1913. *Interest and Effort in Education.* New York: Houghton Mifflin.

DWECK, CAROL. 2002. "The Development of Ability Conceptions." In *Development of Achievement Motivation,* ed. Allan Wigfield and Jacquelynne S. Eccles. New York: Academic Press.

GUTHERIE, JOHN T., and COX, KATHLEEN E. 2001. "Classroom Conditions for Motivation and Engagement in Reading." *Educational Psychology Review* 13(3):283–302.

HIDI, SUZANNE, and BERNDORFF, DAGMAR. 1998. "Situational Interest and Learning." In *Interest and Learning,* ed. Lore Hoffmann, Andreas Krapp, K. Ann Renninger, and Jürgen Baumert. Kiel, Germany: Institute for Science Education (IPN).

HIDI, SUZANNE, and HARACKIEWICZ, JUDITH M. 2000. "Motivating the Academically Unmotivated: A Critical Issue for the 21st Century." *Review of Educational Research* 70:151–179.

HIDI, SUZANNE; WEISS, JOEL; BERNDORFF, DAGMAR; and NOLAN, JASON. 1998. "The Role of Gender, Instruction, and a Cooperative Learning Technique in Science Education across Formal and Informal Settings." In *Interest and Learning,* ed. Lore Hoffmann, Andreas Krapp, K. Ann Renninger, and Jürgen Baumert. Kiel, Germany: Institute for Science Education (IPN).

HOFFMANN, LORE. 2001. "Promoting Girls' Learning and Achievement in Physics Classes for Beginners." *Learning and Instruction* 12.

KRAPP, ANDREAS. 1999. "Interest, Motivation, and Learning: An Educational-Psychological Perspective." *Learning and Information* 14(1):23–40.

KRAPP, ANDREAS; HIDI, SUZANNE; and RENNINGER, K. ANN. 1992. "Interest, Learning, and Development." In *The Role of Interest in Learning and Development,* ed. K. Ann Renninger, Suzanne Hidi, and Andreas Krapp. Hillsdale, NJ: Erlbaum.

KRAPP, ANDREAS; RENNINGER, K. ANN; and HOFFMANN, LORE. 1998. "Some Thoughts about the Development of a Unifying Framework for the Study of Individual Interest." In *Interest and Learning,* ed. Lore Hoffmann, Andreas Krapp, K. Anne Renninger, and Jürgen Baumert. Kiel, Germany: Institute for Science Education (IPN).

McDANIEL, MARK A.; FINSTAD, KRAIG; WADDILL, PAULA J.; and BOURG, TAMMY. 2000. "The Effects of Text-Based Interest on Attention and Recall." *Journal of Educational Psychology* 92(3):492–502.

PRENZEL, MANFRED. 1992. "The Selective Persistence of Interest." In *The Role of Interest in Learning and Development,* ed. K. Ann Renninger, Suzanne Hidi, and Andreas Krapp. Hillsdale, NJ: Lawrence Erlbaum.

RENNINGER, K. ANN. 2000. "Individual Interest and Its Implications for Understanding Intrinsic Motivation." In *Intrinsic and Extrinsic Motivation: The Search for Optimal Motivation and Performance,* ed. Carol Sansone and Judith M. Harackiewicz. New York: Academic Press.

RENNINGER, K. ANN; EWEN, LIZA; and LASHER, A. K. 2001. "Individual Interest As Context in Expository Text and Mathematical Word Problems." *Learning and Instruction* 12:467–491.

SANSONE, CAROL, and SMITH, JESSI L. 2000. "Interest and Self-Regulation: The Relation between Having To and Wanting To." In *Intrinsic and Extrinsic Motivation: The Search for Optimal Motivation and Performance,* ed. Carol Sansone and Judith M. Harackiewicz. New York: Academic Press.

SCHRAW, GREGG; FLOWERDAY, TERRI; and LEHMAN, STEVE. 2001. "Increasing Situational Interest in the Classroom." *Educational Psychology Review* 13(3):211–225.

SILVIA, PAUL J. 2001. "Interest and Interests: The Psychology of Constructive Capriciousness." *Review of General Psychology* 5:270–290.

STIPEK, DEBORAH. 2002. "Good Instruction Is Motivating." In *Development of Achievement Motivation,* ed. Allan Wigfield and Jacquelynne S. Eccles. New York: Academic Press.

WADE, SUZANNE E. 2001. "Research on Importance and Interest: Implications for Curriculum Development and Future Research." *Educational Psychology Review* 13(3):243–262.

K. ANN RENNINGER

EIGHT-YEAR STUDY

The Eight-Year Study (also known as the Thirty-School Study) was an experimental project conducted between 1930 to 1942 by the Progressive Education Association (PEA), in which thirty high schools redesigned their curriculum while initiating innovative practices in student testing, program assessment, student guidance, curriculum design, and staff development.

Purpose

By the late 1920s the members of PEA acknowledged that only one out of six American high school students continued on to college, yet conventional college preparation programs still dominated the basic course of study at the secondary school level. Seeking to address the needs of non-college-bound students while also providing better coordination between high schools and colleges for those students who continued their postsecondary education, the PEA initiated in 1930 the first of three Eight-Year Study commissions, the Commission on the Relation of School and College (also known as the Aikin Commission), chaired by Wilford Aikin. The purpose of the commission was to foster relations between schools and colleges that would permit experimentation of the secondary school curriculum and would address how the high school could serve youth more effectively.

The Aikin Commission proceeded to select approximately thirty schools (including some school systems) that were freed to revise their secondary curriculum. Over 250 colleges agreed to suspend their admissions requirements for graduates of the participating high schools, and alternative forms of documentation were provided by the secondary schools for college admission. All of these secondary schools did not embrace Progressive Education practices, however. While some of the most progressive schools in the country participated, including Denver's public high schools, Chicago's Parker School, New York's Lincoln School, Ohio State University's Laboratory School, Des Moines's Roosevelt High School, and Tulsa's Central High School, other participating secondary schools displayed few progressive practices and little interest in experimenting with their curriculum.

Method

During the initial years of the study, each school staff developed its own curricular program—core curriculum—which sought to integrate and unify the separate academic subjects. A series of innovative staff-development workshops were scheduled beginning in 1936 to assist teachers in reconsidering the basic goals and philosophy of their specific school and to support the development of their own teaching materials. The Aikin Commission coordinated the Follow-Up (evaluation) Study and selected 1,475 students to follow from high school into college. These Progressive school graduates were matched with graduates from traditional secondary school programs, and the pairs of students were evaluated as they proceeded through college. In comparison to their counterparts, the Progressive school graduates performed comparably well academically and were substantially more involved and successful in cultural and artistic activities. The Follow-Up Study also concluded that graduates from these thirty experimental schools did not experience any impairment in their college preparation. The Eight-Year Study confirmed that schools could experiment with the curriculum while attending to the needs of all students, and in so doing, those college-bound graduates would not be ill-prepared. The Commission on the Relation of School and College released a five-volume report in 1942, titled *Adventures in Learning,* which described the curriculum and evaluation of the schools.

As the Aikin Commission worked with school and college staff, the Commission on Secondary School Curriculum (also known as the Thayer Commission), chaired by V. T. Thayer, was formed in 1932 to develop curriculum materials for the participating schools. The Thayer Commission recognized that further study of youth needed to be undertaken, and within the auspices of this PEA commission, the Study of Adolescents was conducted. Between 1937 and 1940, five volumes of curriculum materials aligned to the traditional subject areas of general ed-

ucation (science, mathematics, social studies, arts, and language) and an additional six volumes encompassing the study of adolescence were published. A third PEA commission, the Commission on Human Relations (also known as the Keliher Commission) formed in 1935, prepared social-science-related curriculum materials—incorporating the then-innovative use of motion pictures—and examined those human problems faced by youth. Six volumes were released by the Keliher Commission between 1938 and 1943, some written directly for high school students and others written for professional educators who sought to integrate the school curriculum around the needs, interests, and problems of youth. Membership among these three commissions overlapped greatly and are now viewed as integral components of the Eight-Year Study.

Results

To correct a general misconception, the Aikin Commission's Follow-Up Study was not the sole purpose of the Eight-Year Study. Important outcomes of the Eight-Year Study included developing more sophisticated student tests and forms of assessment; innovative adolescent study techniques; and novel programs of curriculum design, instruction, teacher education, and staff development. Moreover, the Eight-Year Study proved that many different forms of secondary curricular design can ensure college success and that the high school need not be chained to a college preparatory curriculum. In fact, students from the most experimental, nonstandard schools earned markedly higher academic achievement rates than their traditional school counterparts and other Progressive-prepared students.

See also: ALBERTY, H. B.; INSTRUCTIONAL STRATEGIES; PROGRESSIVE EDUCATION; SECONDARY EDUCATION, *subentry on* HISTORY OF; THAYER, V. T.

BIBLIOGRAPHY

AIKIN, WILFORD. 1942. *The Story of the Eight-Year Study.* New York: Harper.

AMERICAN EDUCATION FELLOWSHIP. 1938. *Science in General Education.* New York: Appleton-Century.

BLOS, PETER. 1941. *The Adolescent Personality.* New York: Appleton-Century.

CHAMBERLIN, DEAN; CHAMBERLIN, ENID S.; DROUGHT, NEAL E.; and SCOTT, WILLIAM E.

1942. *Did They Succeed in College?* New York: Harper.

COMMISSION ON RELATION OF SCHOOL AND COLLEGE. 1942. *Thirty Schools Tell Their Story.* New York: Harper.

COMMISSION ON SECONDARY SCHOOL CURRICULUM. 1940. *Language in General Education.* New York: Appleton-Century.

COMMISSION ON SECONDARY SCHOOL CURRICULUM. 1940. *Mathematics in General Education.* New York: Appleton-Century.

COMMISSION ON SECONDARY SCHOOL CURRICULUM. 1940. *The Social Studies in General Education.* New York: Appleton-Century.

COMMISSION ON SECONDARY SCHOOL CURRICULUM. 1940. *The Visual Arts in General Education.* New York: Appleton-Century.

CONRAD, LAWRENCE H. 1937. *Teaching Creative Writing.* New York: Appleton-Century.

GILES, H. H.; MCCUTCHEN, S. P.; and ZECHIEL, A. N. 1942. *Exploring the Curriculum.* New York: Harper.

LANGER, WALTER C. 1943. *Psychology and Human Living.* New York: Appleton-Century.

LENROW, ELBERT. 1940. *Reader's Guide to Prose Fiction.* New York: Appleton-Century.

MEEK, LOIS H. 1940. *The Personal-Social Development of Boys and Girls with Implications for Secondary Education.* New York: Appleton-Century.

ROSENBLATT, LOUISE M. 1938. *Literature as Exploration.* New York: Appleton-Century.

SMITH, EUGENE R.; TYLER, RALPH W.; and EVALUATION STAFF. 1942. *Appraising and Recording Student Progress.* New York: Harper.

STERN, BERNHARD J. 1938. *The Family, Past and Present.* New York: Appleton-Century.

TAYLOR, KATHERINE WHITESIDE. 1938. *Do Adolescents Need Parents?* New York: Appleton-Century.

THAYER, VIVIAN T.; ZACHRY, CAROLINE B.; and KOTINSKY, RUTH. 1939. *Reorganizing Secondary Education.* New York: Appleton-Century.

WUNSCH, W. ROBERT, and ALBERS, EDWIN, eds. 1939. *Thicker Than Water.* New York: Appleton-Century.

ZACHRY, CAROLINE B., and LIGHTY, MARGARET E. 1940. *Emotion and Conduct in Adolescence.* New York: Appleton-Century.

CRAIG KRIDEL

ELEMENTARY AND SECONDARY EDUCATION ACT OF 2001

See: NO CHILD LEFT BEHIND ACT OF 2001.

ELEMENTARY EDUCATION

HISTORY OF
   Gerald L. Gutek
CURRENT TRENDS
   Jane McCarthy
   Linda F. Quinn
PREPARATION OF TEACHERS
   Kenneth R. Howey
   Linda M. Post

HISTORY OF

Elementary schools exist worldwide as the basic foundational institution in the formal educational structure. Elementary schooling, which prepares children in fundamental skills and knowledge areas, can be defined as the early stages of formal, or organized, education that are prior to secondary school. The age range of pupils who attend elementary schools in the United States is from six to twelve, thirteen, or fourteen, depending on the organizational pattern of the particular state or school district. While a few, mainly small rural, districts retain the traditional pattern of grades one through eight, a more common pattern is grades one through six. In most school districts as well as in many teacher preparation programs, elementary education is organized into the following levels: primary, which includes kindergarten and grades one, two, and three; intermediate, which includes grades four, five, and six; and upper, which includes grades seven and eight. A commonly found organizational pattern places grades seven and eight, and sometimes grade six and nine, into middle or junior high schools. When the middle school and junior high school pattern is followed, these institutions are usually linked into secondary education, encompassing grades six through twelve.

In comparing elementary schools in the United States with those of other countries, some distinctions in terminology are necessary. In the United States, *elementary* education refers to children's first formal schooling prior to secondary school. (Although kindergartens, enrolling children at age five, are part of public schools, attendance is not compulsory.) In school systems in many other countries, the term *primary* covers what in the United States is designated as elementary schooling. In American elementary schools, the term *primary* refers to the first level, namely kindergarten through grades one, two, and three.

The elementary school curriculum provides work in the educational basics—reading, writing, arithmetic, an introduction to natural and social sciences, health, arts and crafts, and physical education. An important part of elementary schooling is socialization with peers and the creating of an identification of the child with the community and nation.

History of Elementary Education in the United States

The European settlers in the North American colonies, in the sixteenth and seventeenth centuries, initially re-created the school systems of their homelands. They established a two-track school system in which the lower socioeconomic classes attended primary vernacular schools and upper class males attended separate preparatory schools and colleges. The primary schools—elementary institutions under church control—offered a basic curriculum of reading, writing, arithmetic, and religion.

Colonial period. While many similarities existed in the colonial schools, there were some important differences between New England, the Mid-Atlantic, and the South. The New England colonies of Massachusetts, Connecticut, and New Hampshire, which were settled primarily by Puritans, were characterized by a strong sense of religious and social conformity. Because of their Calvinistic emphasis on reading the Bible and other religious literature, the Puritans quickly established elementary schools. In 1642 the Massachusetts General Court, the colony's legislative body, made parents and guardians responsible for making sure that children were taught reading and religion. In 1647 the General Court enacted the Old Deluder Satan Act, which virtually established elementary education by requiring every town of fifty or more families to appoint a reading and writing teacher. Massachusetts and the other New England colonies developed the town school, a locally controlled, usually coeducational elementary school, attended by pupils ranging in age from six to thirteen or fourteen. The school's curriculum included reading, writing, arithmetic, catechism, and religious hymns. The model of the town school, governed by its local trustees or board, became an important feature of later U.S. elementary schooling.

The Middle Atlantic colonies of New York, New Jersey, Delaware, and Pennsylvania were settled by diverse ethnic and religious groups. In addition to English, Scots, and Scotch-Irish, there were Dutch in New York, Swedes in Delaware, and Germans in Pennsylvania. The Middle Atlantic colonies' religious and language diversity had important educational implications. Elementary schools were usually parochial institutions, supported and governed by the various churches.

In the southern colonies—Maryland, Virginia, the Carolinas, and Georgia—enslaved Africans were used as forced labor on the plantations. Wealthy families employed private teachers or tutors to educate their children. Enslaved Africans were trained to be agricultural workers, field hands, craftspeople, or domestic servants, but they were legally forbidden to learn to read or write. There were some notable exceptions who learned to read secretly.

Early national period. After the establishment of the United States as an independent nation, the earliest U.S. federal legislation relating to education was included in the Northwest Ordinance of 1785. The ordinance divided the Northwest Territory into townships of thirty-six square miles, and each township was subdivided into thirty-six 640-acre sections. Each township's sixteenth section was to be used to support education. Unlike constitutions or basic laws in other nations, the U.S. Constitution, ratified as the law of the land in 1789, did not refer specifically to education. The Tenth Amendment's "reserved powers" clause (which reserved to the states all powers not specifically delegated to the federal government or prohibited to the states by the Constitution) left education as a responsibility of each individual state.

During the early national period, the first half of the nineteenth century, American leaders, such as Thomas Jefferson (1743–1826), argued that the United States needed to develop republican schools that were different from those found in the European monarchies. Jefferson's "Bill for the More General Diffusion of Knowledge," introduced in the Virginia legislature in 1779, would have made the state responsible for providing both girls and boys with a basic elementary education, in a local ward school, at public expense. Although not enacted, Jefferson's bill had an important influence on later developments.

The movement to establish an American version of elementary education was promoted by Noah Webster (1758–1843), who sought to create an American version of the English language and instill an American identity into the young through language instruction. Webster's *American Spelling Book* and *American Dictionary* were widely used in schools.

The movement to common or public schools. In the 1830s and 1840s, several Western nations began to develop national elementary or primary school systems that were intended to augment or replace the existing church-controlled institutions. In France, Francois Guizot, the Minister of Education in the regime of Louis Philippe, promoted national elementary schools. In the United States, with its historic tradition of local and state control, the movement to establish public elementary schools was not national but carried on in the various states.

Before public elementary schools were established, attempts were made in the United States to establish various kinds of philanthropic elementary schools, such as the Sunday and monitorial schools. The United Kingdom, a leading industrial nation, also experimented with these approaches to primary education. The Sunday school, developed by Robert Raikes, an English religious leader, sought to provide children with basic literacy and religious instruction on the one day that factories were closed. In both the United States and the United Kingdom, Sunday schools were established in the larger cities.

Monitorialism, also known as mutual instruction, was a popular method of elementary education in the early nineteenth century in the United Kingdom, the United States, and other countries. Two rival English educators, Andrew Bell, an Anglican churchman, and Joseph Lancaster, a Quaker teacher, promoted monitorialism independently. The monitorial method relied heavily on *monitors*—more advanced pupils, trained by a master teacher—to teach younger children. Monitors aided teachers in conducting classes, taking attendance, and maintaining order. In using this method, the master teacher trained a selected group of older students as monitors in a particular skill, such as adding single-digit

numbers or reading simple words. These monitors then taught that particular skill to subgroups of less advanced pupils. Since the monitorial method promised to teach large numbers of pupils basic literacy and numeracy skills, it gained the support of those who wanted to provide basic elementary education at limited costs.

Initially, monitorial schools were popular in the larger American cities such as New York and Philadelphia, where they were typically supported by private philanthropists and occasionally received some public funds. In the early 1840s monitorial schooling experienced a rapid decline and virtually disappeared. By the time that the New York Free School Society, which had operated monitorial schools, turned them over to the public school system in 1853, more than 600,000 children had attended its schools.

The common school. The common school movement refers to the establishment of state elementary school systems in the first half of the nineteenth century. The term *common* meant that these state-supported public elementary schools, exalted as the school that "educated the children of all the people," were open to children of all socioeconomic classes and ethnic and racial groups. Nevertheless, many children, particularly enslaved African Americans, did not attend.

Not a selective academic institution, the common school sought to develop the literacy and numeracy needed in everyday life and work. Its basic curriculum stressed reading, writing, spelling, arithmetic, history, and geography. Emphasizing American patriotism and Christian piety, it was regarded as the educational agency that would assimilate and Americanize the children of immigrants.

The common school movement in the United States paralleled some trends taking place in western Europe in the first half of the nineteenth century. In the 1830s the British parliament, though not creating a state school system, began to provide grants to educational societies for primary schooling. In France, under Guizot, a primary school system, too, was established during the regime of Louis Philippe. These transnational trends, found in Europe and America, indicated that governments were beginning to take the responsibility for providing some kind of elementary schooling. Unlike in France, which was beginning to create a highly centralized national educational system, U.S. public schools were decentralized. The U.S. Constitution's Tenth Amendment reserved education to each state. The states, in turn, delegated considerable responsibility for providing and maintaining schools to local districts. Even within a particular state, especially on the frontier where many small school districts were created, resources available for schooling varied considerably from district to district.

The common school movement scored its initial successes in New England, particularly in Massachusetts and Connecticut. Massachusetts, in 1826, required every town to elect a school committee to provide and set policy for the local schools. The Massachusetts legislature established the first state board of education in 1837. It named Horace Mann (1796–1859), an eloquent spokesman for common schooling, as its secretary. Mann, as editor of the *Common School Journal* and a popular orator, gained considerable support for public schools.

Other northern states emulated New England's common school model. As the frontier moved westward and new states joined the Union, they, too, followed the model and passed laws to create public elementary school systems. In the South, with a few exceptions, common schools were rare until the post–Civil War Reconstruction.

A unique feature in the United States was the small one-room school, found in rural areas and small towns across the country. These schools served local school districts, governed by elected boards. Although small one-room village schools existed in other countries, the American ones were local creations rather than impositions of a national government. The American school's immediacy to its people made the local school a trusted institution rather than an alien intruder into small town life. In contrast, the teacher in France might be suspected as an outsider, a representative of the intrusive central government. Similarly, in tsarist Russia, the zemstvo school, established in the villages, was often extraneous to the needs of life in the countryside. The zemstvo teachers often were not accepted by the peasants whose children they tried to teach or were regarded as rivals of the village priest. In America's one-room schools, the elected school board determined the tax levy and hired and supervised the teacher. This pattern of local control contrasted with the visiting school inspectors sent to inspect teachers and schools in France or even with the royal inspectors in the United Kingdom.

The pupils enrolled in the local one-room schools, often ranging in age from five to seventeen, studied a basic curriculum of reading, writing, arithmetic, history, geography, grammar, spelling, and hygiene. They were instructed by the recitation method in which each pupil stood and recited a previously assigned lesson. Group work might include writing exercises, arithmetic problems, and grammar lessons that stressed diagramming sentences. The values of punctuality, honesty, and hard work were given high priority.

African-American and Native American elementary education. The Civil War, Reconstruction, and the Thirteenth Amendment ended slavery in the United States. Although a small number of free blacks had attended elementary school in some northern states before the war, southern slave states had prohibited instruction of African-American children. After the Civil War, the U.S. Congress, in 1865, established the Freedmen's Bureau, which established elementary schools for the children of former slaves. By 1869 more than 114,000 students were attending bureau schools. Many bureau schools functioned until 1872 when the bureau ceased operations.

In the late nineteenth century, the federal government, assisted by well-intentioned but often misguided reformers, sought to "civilize" Native Americans by assimilating them into white society. From 1890 to the 1930s the Bureau of Indian Affairs, in a policy of forced assimilation, relied heavily on boarding schools, many of which contained elementary divisions. Seeking to remove Native American youngsters from their tribal cultures, the students, forbidden to speak their native languages, were forced to use English. The boarding schools stressed a basic curriculum of reading, writing, arithmetic, and vocational training.

Nonpublic elementary schools. In addition to the public elementary school, the United States also has private elementary schools, many of which are church-related. Today, nonpublic schools enroll about 11 percent of the pupils in U.S. schools. Roman Catholic parochial schools, serving the children of a particular parish, represent the largest number of private elementary schools. Evangelical and fundamentalist Christian schools are the fastest growing sector in nonpublic elementary education.

Goals of Elementary Schools

Elementary schools in the United States, as in other countries, have the goals of providing children with fundamental academic skills, basic knowledge, and socialization strategies. They are key institutions in instilling a sense of national identity and citizenship in children.

In the United States, elementary schools prepare children to use language by teaching reading, writing, comprehension, and computation. Elementary schools worldwide devote considerable time and resources to teaching reading, decoding, and comprehending the written and spoken word. The stories and narratives children learn to read are key elements in political and cultural socialization, the forming of civic character, and the shaping of civility and behavior. Throughout the history of American education, the materials used to teach reading exemplified the nation's dominant values. For example, the New England Primer, used in colonial schools, stressed Puritanism's religious and ethical values. Noah Webster's spelling books and readers emphasized American national identity and patriotism. The McGuffey Readers, widely used in late nineteenth century schools, portrayed boys and girls who always told the truth, who worked diligently, and who honored their fathers and mothers and their country. McGuffey values were reinforced by the American flag, which hung at the front of elementary classrooms, flanked by portraits of Presidents Washington and Lincoln. The "Dick and Jane" readers of the 1930s and 1940s depicted the lifestyle and behaviors of the dominant white middle class. Contemporary reading books and materials portray a much more multicultural view of life and society.

The language of instruction in elementary or primary schools is often highly controversial in many countries, especially in multilingual ones. The ability to use the "official" language provides access to secondary and higher education and entry into professions. In such multilanguage nations as India, Canada, and Belgium, protracted controversies have occurred over which language should be the official one. In the United States, the dominant language of instruction in public schools has been English. The children of non-English-speaking immigrants were assimilated into American culture by the imposition of English through the elementary school curriculum. The later entry of bilingual education in the United States was an often controversial educational

development, and remains so in the early twenty-first century.

Along with the development of language competencies, elementary education prepares children in the fundamental mathematical skills—in counting, using number systems, measuring, and performing the basic operations of adding, subtracting, multiplying, and dividing. Further, the foundations of science, social science, health, art, music, and physical education are also taught.

Curriculum and Organization

In the United States at the primary level, the first level of organization, the curriculum is highly generalized into broad areas such as language arts or life sciences. It gradually becomes more specialized at the intermediate and upper grade levels into more specific subjects. Because of the generality of the elementary curriculum, especially at the primary and intermediate levels, there is likely to be a greater emphasis on methods and styles of teaching in elementary schools in the United States than in primary schools in other countries. For example, U.S. teachers, in their professional preparation and classroom practices, are more likely to emphasize the process of learning, inquiry skills, and social participation than teachers in other countries. Instruction in many other countries tends to be more oriented to specific skills and subjects. While elementary or primary classrooms in the United States and in other countries are likely to be self-contained, the American teacher generally has more autonomy and is not concerned with visitations by outside government inspectors.

The typical U.S. elementary school curriculum is organized around broad fields such as language arts, social studies, mathematics, and the sciences. The essential strategy in this approach is to integrate and correlate rather than departmentalize areas of knowledge. Curricular departmentalization often begins earlier in some other countries such as Japan, China, and India than in the United States.

The language arts, a crucial curricular area, includes reading, handwriting, spelling, listening, and speaking. It includes the reading and discussing of stories, biographies, and other forms of children's literature. Here, the U.S. emphasis on reading and writing is replicated in other countries. The methods of teaching language, however, vary. In the United States, the teaching of reading is often controversial.

Some teachers and school districts prefer phonics; others use the whole language approach or a combination of several methods such as phonics and guided oral reading.

Social studies, as a component of the U.S. elementary curriculum, represents a fusion and integration of selected elements of history, geography, economics, sociology, and anthropology. It often uses a gradual, step-by-step method of leading children from their immediate home, family, and neighborhood to the larger social and political world. While the U.S. approach to social education has been subject to frequent redefinition and reformulation, its defenders argue that the integration of elements of the various social sciences is a more appropriate way to introduce children to society than a strictly disciplinary approach. Critics, some of them educators from other countries, argue that American students lack the structured knowledge of place that comes from the systematic teaching of geography as a separate discipline or the sense of chronology that comes from the study of history.

Like social studies, science in the elementary curriculum consists of the teaching of selected and integrated concepts and materials from the various natural and physical sciences rather than a focus on the specific sciences. Frequently, science teaching will stress the life and earth sciences by way of field trips, demonstrations, and hands-on experiments. Critics contend that the elementary science curriculum in the United States is too unstructured and does not provide an adequate foundational base of knowledge. Defenders contend, however, that it is more important for students to develop a sense of science as a process and mode of inquiry than to amass scientific facts.

The main part of the elementary curriculum is completed by mathematics, with an emphasis on basic computational skills—addition, subtraction, multiplication, division, measuring, and graphing. The curriculum also includes health concepts and practices, games, safety, music, art, and physical education and fitness, which involves the development of motor skills.

As children in the United States progress from the primary to the intermediate grades, the emphasis on reading continues but changes from stories to more informational narratives. The goal is to develop students' interpretive skills as well as to continue to polish the basic decoding skills related to mechan-ics and comprehension that were stressed in the primary grades. The broad fields of the curriculum—social studies, mathematics, and science—are pursued but now become more disciplinary.

Depending on the particular organizational pattern being followed, the upper grades—six, seven, and eight—offer a more specialized and differentiated curriculum. Subject matters such as English, literature, social studies, history, natural and physical sciences, and mathematics are taught in a more differentiated way. In addition to the more conventional academic subjects, areas such as vocational, industrial, home arts, career, sex, and drug abuse prevention education appear, especially in the upper grades and in junior high and middle schools.

At the beginning of the twenty-first century, curriculum is being shaped by an emphasis on subject-matter competencies in English, mathematics, and basic sciences. Computer literacy, computer-assisted instruction, and other technologies in school programs reflect the nation's transition to a high-tech information society.

The Standards Movement

The standards movement, which gained momentum in the late 1990s, has required more standardized testing in U.S. elementary education. Standards advocates argue that academic achievement can be best assessed by using standardized tests to determine whether students are performing at prescribed levels in key areas such as reading and mathematics. Most of the states have established standards and require testing in these areas. Strongly endorsed by U.S. President George W. Bush, the standards approach was infused into the federal No Child Left Behind Act of 2001. The act requires that, in order to receive Title I funds, states and school districts must develop and conduct annual assessments in reading and mathematics in grades three through eight. Opponents of the standards movement argue that it is based on a narrow definition of education that encourages teachers to teach for the test rather than for the development of the whole child.

See also: COMMON SCHOOL MOVEMENT; CURRICULUM, SCHOOL; NO CHILD LEFT BEHIND ACT OF 2001; PRIVATE SCHOOLING.

BIBLIOGRAPHY

ANDERSON, JAMES D. 1988. *The Education of Blacks in the South, 1860–1935.* Chapel Hill: University of North Carolina Press.

BINDER, FREDERICK M. 1974. *The Age of the Common School, 1830–1865.* New York: Wiley.

CAMPBELL, ROALD F.; CUNNINGHAM, LUVERN L.; NYSTRAND, RAPHAEL O.; and USDAN, MICHAEL D. 1990. *The Organization and Control of American Schools.* Columbus, OH: Merrill.

CREMIN, LAWRENCE A. 1951. *The American Common School.* New York: Teachers College Press.

CREMIN, LAWRENCE A. 1970. *American Education: The Colonial Experience, 1607–1783.* New York: Harper and Row.

CREMIN, LAWRENCE A. 1980. *American Education: The National Experience, 1783–1876.* New York: Harper and Row.

CREMIN, LAWRENCE A. 1988. *American Education: The Metropolitan Experience, 1876–1980.* New York: Harper and Row.

FINKELSTEIN, BARBARA. 1989. *Governing the Young: Teacher Behavior in Popular Primary Schools in Nineteenth Century United States.* London: Falmer Press.

FULLER, WAYNE E. 1982. *The Old Country School: The Story of Rural Education in the Middle West.* Chicago: University of Chicago Press.

KAESTLE, CARL, et al. 1991. *Literacy in the United States: Readers and Reading Since 1880.* New Haven, CT: Yale University Press.

GERALD L. GUTEK

CURRENT TRENDS

Reform of elementary education in the United States, which began in the latter part of the twentieth century and intensified after the publication of *A Nation at Risk* in 1983, has been aimed at improving the academic performance of all children, with accountability for student achievement being placed on the schools, districts, and states. The federal government is also playing a larger role in elementary education through the funding provided to states under the Elementary and Secondary Education Act. There is concern that the U.S. educational system is not enabling its students to perform as well academically as students in other nations, although some critics disagree with this assessment. Though the elementary curriculum is constantly in a state of reform and refinement, some common threads exist.

Goals and Purposes of Elementary Education

Democratization of education is the evolution of education away from models intended to support ideological, social, or industrial systems toward open, universal public education. Great Britain demonstrates the evolution of open, democratic systems of European education since the Renaissance. Japan in Asia has redesigned its public education system since World War II to reflect those same open democratic values. Chile in South America is currently undergoing an aggressive democratization of public education. The similarities of the reforms in these nations parallels similar reforms underway in the United States.

United States. Throughout the history of the United States, Americans have expressed a desire for an educated citizenry. Efforts to establish or reform education in this country include the Old Deluder Satan Act, enacted in Massachusetts in 1647, Thomas Jefferson's 1779 Bill for the More General Diffusion of Knowledge, The Common School Movement of the 1800s, the Education for All American Youth initiative of 1944, and George W. Bush's No Child Left Behind Act of 2001. The existence of a cumulative and consecutive system of universal public education for young children is a part of the national heritage of the United States, and it is expected that elementary education will play a major role in preparing future citizens to live in a modern, industrialized, global society.

Control over elementary education is reserved to the states; however, in 1979 the U.S. Department of Education was created by President Jimmy Carter to coordinate, manage, and account for federal support of educational programs. National and local attention continues to be directed at elementary education in the twenty-first century, as leaders, teachers, and parents seek ways to make the first step in the American education system educative, meaningful, and positive.

While current educational reforms reflect a myriad of societal changes, elementary education at the beginning of the new millennium still resembles the vernacular schools of colonial America. The essential skills of reading, writing, spelling, and arithmetic occupy center stage, and the "common school" moral themes of honesty, hard work, diligence, and application prevail.

Europe. Elementary education in the United States has roots in European models of education, and, in fact, elementary education systems around the world share many common characteristics. Efforts to create public elementary school systems in Europe (mostly in the nineteenth century) were initiated by leaders in the national or central governments. Dominant political, social, and economic classes used elementary schools to encourage conformity with the ideas and values that perpetuated the status quo and provided little opportunity for upward socioeconomic mobility. In the twentieth century the requirement for a more educated workforce has enhanced the place of elementary education within the continuum of formerly hierarchical European education systems.

The compulsory age for children to begin elementary school is five or six and elementary education may last for six years. Typical subjects include reading, writing, arithmetic, art, geography, history, physical education, fine arts, and foreign languages. In some countries, noncompulsory religion classes may be offered. Since the fall of Communism, most eastern European elementary school systems follow the western European education model. Elementary schools in Europe experience many of the same issues related to student achievement, diversity, poverty, and violence that face their U.S. counterparts, and standardized testing has become increasingly important in many countries, such as Great Britain.

Asia (Japan). Elementary education in Japan is built on a model of communities of people working together to become healthy in mind, body, and spirit. Students are educated to respect the value of individuals, and to love truth and justice. Elementary education begins at age six in Japan and ends at age eleven or twelve. The structure of Japan's 6-3-3-4 school system was established by the School Education Law of 1947. The educational reforms resulting from this law, carried out under the direction of the American Occupation, decentralized control of education, authorized autonomous private schools, and encouraged the development of community education. The authority to establish schools is limited to the Ministry of Education, local governments, and private organizations that fulfill the requirements of becoming a school corporation. Municipalities are responsible for establishing elementary schools. Parents, especially mothers, take an active role in their children's education and reinforce the school curriculum through teaching their children at home or enrolling them in *Jukus,* which are privately run "cram" schools.

South America (Chile). Children in Chile attend primary (elementary) school for eight years. They study a curriculum and use textbooks approved by the government's Ministry of Education, though following the 1980 educational reforms the oversight of elementary education in Chile was transferred to municipal governments. The typical primary school curriculum includes reading, writing, mathematics, social studies, music, physical education, and art. A national program of school breakfasts and lunches recognizes the importance of nutrition in the education of children. Chilean elementary education is faced with inequities in access to education among the rich and poor and a high dropout rate among the nation's poorest children. The National Council for School Aid and Grants is charged with making scholarships available to all children. Since 1988, the national government of Chile has provided support for private schools, and this has caused a downturn in public primary school enrollments.

The Importance of Elementary Education

In America, children normally enroll in elementary schools at age five or six and exit elementary school at age eleven or twelve. In 2002 approximately 25 million children attended elementary schools in the United States. Readiness for elementary school is viewed as highly important. Through Head Start programs, the government provides educational opportunities for children from disadvantaged circumstances in order for them to be prepared for elementary school. Parents of the children who may not qualify for government-supported programs often enroll their children in privately run preschools in hopes of setting their children on a successful path to elementary school. Although school attendance is not mandatory in most states until first grade, national surveys of parents of early elementary pupils show that 98 percent of primary school children attend kindergarten before entering first grade.

The rapid changes in cognitive, social, and moral growth of an elementary school student makes the elementary classroom an ideal setting for shaping individual attitudes and behaviors. The elementary classroom may provide the best opportunity to set in place moral and ethical characteristics and understandings that have the potential to improve society. Children in the elementary schools are still malleable, and this emphasis on character education is seen as a particularly urgent matter in American classrooms. In fact, the socialization of children in America is no longer viewed as the sole responsibility of their parents.

The view of using the elementary classroom as a stage for molding future citizens of a democratic society is not new, but it does give rise to controversy regarding programs and methods, as parents may disagree with specific curriculum being promoted by local, state, or national agencies. For example, sex education at the elementary school level has been the object of much debate among religious and special interest groups. One result of the disagreements over such controversial curricula may be the large number of children home schooled in 1999–2001 (estimated to be more than 1.3 million). Even so, support may still be offered to home-schooled students through curriculum, books, and materials provided by local schools or districts, as well as access to extracurricular activities and special classes in areas such as technology.

The Curriculum of the Elementary School

Unlike many other nations, the United States does not have a national curriculum. As mentioned previously, control of the schools is reserved to the states, which in turn give local school districts some control over what is taught and how it is taught. Curriculum may be looked at as a negotiated set of beliefs about what students should know or be able to do. A curriculum framework includes these beliefs, and then specifies by what point students should have mastered specific skills and performances. This is known as the *scope and sequence* of curriculum. Until recently, states and local districts had significant latitude in the development of elementary curriculum. The advent of the standards movement, however, has mitigated this freedom—for the better according to some, and for the worse according to others.

Do standards-based curriculum frameworks and standardized tests prepare children for the twenty-first century workplace where problem solving, creativity, and teamwork are necessary tools? Some people in the business world do not think so. Others argue that it is necessary to insure that all children master at least the basic essentials of reading, mathematics and writing in order to be able to perform at higher levels of performance and thinking. At any

rate, the standards movement has had a definite impact on the curriculum of the elementary school. In the early twenty-first century, forty-nine states have curriculum standards. Recent studies indicate that 87 percent of U.S. teachers believe the standards movement is a step in the right direction, and that the curriculum is more demanding and teacher expectations of students are higher as a result of standards. Many teachers also express frustration that they are not provided with the resources necessary to align the standards to the curriculum.

Prior to the standards movement, curriculum development was impacted by the notion of *cultural literacy* advocated by E. D. Hirsch. Hirsch began a national debate with the 1987 publication of what he considered essential common knowledge that all school children need to possess in order to be literate members of their society. His argument was that students could not be successful at understanding the world around them without a grounding in geography, history, literature, politics, and democratic principles. Hirsch then went on to develop a grade-by-grade outline of the knowledge students should master at each grade level. His book stimulated much national debate, especially with regard to whose cultural knowledge should be included in the curriculum—Western civilization only, or a more inclusive body of knowledge. His theories have had a definite impact on the elementary curriculum in many districts and states.

The current elementary school curriculum is influenced by societal needs and political influence. President George H. W. Bush endorsed the *America 2000* goals for American schooling, several of which have had a particular influence on the elementary curriculum. Basically, the goals stipulated that students would demonstrate mastery in five areas: English, mathematics, science, history and geography. President Clinton's *Goals 2000* program continued in the same vein. Societal concerns resulted in federal attention to the national curriculum, which has resulted in state accountability standards.

The state standards and curriculum are also influenced by the professional societies and their development of standards and benchmarks in their subject areas. The National Council of Teachers of Mathematics (NCTM), for example, developed an extensive set of standards that are centered on the need to develop problem-solving skills in addition to basic skills in math. The NCTM stresses conceptual knowledge as a framework for all mathematics learning and provides standards and expectations for each grade level. Other societies have provided similar frameworks that are used by the states in the development of standards.

Elementary curriculum is dynamic, changing as the needs and conditions of society evolve and change. While it cannot be said that there will ever be consensus on the content of the curriculum, the negotiated curriculum serves as a framework for the national agenda for education.

Issues, Trends, and Controversies

The United States has engaged in a national debate over the purposes of schooling since the inception of the public school system. Such debate has resulted in numerous reforms and change efforts over the years. Some reforms have made lasting changes in elementary schooling, while others have gone away as quickly as they arrived. There are a number of burning issues that currently engage the public in discourse and negotiation.

Poor student performance is seen as a failure of the education system and numerous state and national mandates have been put in place to assure equal access to a quality education for all children. In 1983, the National Commission on Excellence in Education's *A Nation at Risk* outlined the decline of American education. This report heralded a revival of academic-driven curricula and resulted in an emphasis on standardized testing and accountability. The No Child Left Behind Act of 2001 requires each state to implement a system of accountability that will identify low-performing schools. It also requires that all students in grades three through eight must be assessed annually in at least reading and mathematics. Parents may also, under certain circumstances, receive governmental support to secure tutoring for children who attend low-performing schools. Such legislation gives rise to controversies surrounding charter schools and school vouchers.

Immigration in the United States has been an issue in elementary education since the advent of public schooling. Immigration patterns shifted dramatically at the beginning of the twentieth century, and continue to shift as children from Southeast Asia, Central America, and eastern European countries enroll in elementary schools. In 2000, 18 percent of the American populace spoke a language other than English at home. In 1990, 15 percent of the total child population was African American, 12

percent Hispanic, 3 percent Asian, and 1 percent Native American. It is projected that, by 2010, Hispanic children will surpass African-American children as the largest child minority. In addition, by 2020, more than one in five American children are expected to be of Hispanic descent. Immigrant children have special needs that must be addressed by the public elementary school. The debate over what form of English education children of immigrants should take has attracted much attention. At the beginning of the twenty-first century, programs for English learners in elementary schools are striving to focus on a holistic approach to educating transcultural/transnational peoples in a global context.

Incidences of school violence and drug use erupted on the school landscape during the late twentieth century. More than half of the nation's schools experienced criminal incidents in 1996–1997, and school security personnel have employed metal detectors to help assure the safety of students. The National Education Association supplies information and tools to help school administrators, teachers, and parents create safe schools. Conflict resolution and counseling have become a part of the elementary education curriculum, as have programs to teach children the dangers of drug use. The Drug Abuse Resistance Education (DARE) program, designed to give kids the life skills they need to avoid involvement with drugs, gangs, and violence, is seen as most influential when delivered to students attending elementary school.

The condition of children living in poverty is an issue of importance to elementary education. Poor children are more likely than more affluent children to experience difficulties in school. The strategies found to be most effective in teaching children of poverty may require special training for teachers, administrators, and school staff. Communication with parents is critical to student success in elementary schools, especially with parents of children of poverty. Many elementary schools in the United States incorporate programs that invite parents to participate in school activities and to feel welcome within the school environment, thereby supporting the families of their students.

The United States has firmly entered the information age. Computers are a common sight in most elementary schools, and school districts employ specialists in instructing students in the use of technology. An important issue that technology brings to elementary education is equal and controlled access.

Questions arise concerning frequent use of computers in schools, supervision of students' access to the Internet, and whether computer use has any impact at all on student learning. National standards have been established to direct the use of technology in schools, and federal funding has been made available to facilitate the widespread use of technology in classrooms. One remarkable problem regarding the use of technology in classrooms stems from the fact that most elementary children have learned technology skills faster than their teachers.

The Education for All Handicapped Children Act of 1975 was designed to assure an "appropriate public education" to meet the unique needs of all students with disabilities. Attached to this bill was a list of provisions for mainstreaming children with disabilities within the public school system. In order to comply with these provisions, elementary schools are faced with the problems of inclusion inherent in making their programs and facilities user-friendly for students with physical, mental, and behavioral disabilities of all sorts.

These issues are just a few of the current challenges faced by elementary education in the early twenty-first century. In spite of the debate, the basic framework of curriculum has survived.

The Evaluation of the Elementary Curriculum

Evaluation of the curriculum has become a focus of concern and disagreement. The use of standardized tests, some argue, drives the curriculum. The importance placed on these tests by local, state, and national entities all but defines what will be taught in schools, thus negating local control of schools and, in fact, creating a form of national curriculum. Teachers who "teach to the test" are neglecting the development of powerful thinking skills and creativity. In fact, the tests are said to penalize those children who are creative thinkers. This limitation was noted by Hilda Taba in 1962, and remains a relevant concern. Some standardized tests, for example, have writing portions that consist solely of multiple-choice questions.

Others insist, however, that standardized tests are a vital tool for measuring the effectiveness of schooling and for holding schools and districts accountable for the education of children. They note that newer versions of these tests include questions to evaluate problem solving and higher-order thinking skills. Yet only a handful of states currently have tests that directly measure student achievement with regard to mastery of state standards.

Standardized test scores of elementary schools are published and are public record. States maintain Internet sites where anyone can find the test scores of a particular school or district. Schools that consistently fall below state averages may be placed in a special category of *at-risk schools,* and in some instances they may actually be taken over by committees appointed by the state department of education if test scores do not rise within a certain probationary period.

National measures of achievement (e.g., the National Assessment of Educational Progress) are also reported to provide information at a national level about the achievement of all students. These national assessments have found that achievement levels of all children have risen annually, including the achievement of minority children. The gap between the scores of minority students and white students still exists, however, and the latest data show that it actually increased during the 1990s. This information has informed the federal government's educational policies of accountability. Federal legislation now requires that all children in grades three through eight to be assessed annually in mathematics and reading. As of 2002, however, only thirteen states and the District of Columbia met this requirement.

School districts often administer their own criterion-referenced tests to measure the effectiveness of the district curriculum framework. These tests attempt to measure the mastery of skills in the district framework at each grade level. The information provided by these tests is designed to give schools and teachers information about the effectiveness of the delivery of the district curriculum.

State, federal, and district assessments are conducted, in addition to the ongoing assessment performed in individual classrooms. Teachers utilize performance assessments, teacher-developed tests, tests that accompany textbooks, and other measures to monitor student progress. Students of the early twenty-first century are becoming the most frequently evaluated students in history. Whether more frequent testing leads to higher achievement in academic skills has yet to be determined, however.

Conclusion

Elementary education is in an exciting period of reform. Technological advances and improved knowledge about how children learn are being infused into the curriculum and instructional practices in schools. The national debate over the purposes and governance of elementary schools continues in the same historical tradition. Educators and policy-makers throughout the world are grappling with the determination of the skills and knowledge necessary for effective citizenship in the twenty-first century.

See also: Character Development; Curriculum, School; Drug and Alcohol Abuse, *subentry on* School; Immigrant Education; Knowledge Building; School Reform; Special Education; Standards for Student Learning; Technology in Education.

BIBLIOGRAPHY

Bracey, Gerald W. 2001. "The Condition of Public Education." *Phi Delta Kappan* 83(2):157–169.

Doherty, Kathryn. 2001. "Poll: Teachers Support Standards—with Hesitation." *Education Week* 20(17):20.

Gutek, Gerald L. 1986. *Education in the United States: An Historical Perspective.* Englewood Cliffs, NJ: Prentice-Hall.

Hirsch, E. D., Jr. 1987. *Cultural Literacy: What Every American Needs to Know.* Boston: Houghton Mifflin.

Meyer, Lori; Orlofsky, Greg F.; Skinner, Ronald A.; and Spicer, Scott. 2002. "The State of the States: Quality Counts 2002." *Education Week* 21(17):68–70.

National Center for Education Statistics. 2000. *The Condition of Education, 2000.* Washington, DC: National Center for Education Statistics.

National Commission on Excellence in Education. 1983. *A Nation at Risk: The Imperative for Educational Reform.* Washington, DC: National Commission on Excellence in Education, U.S. Department of Education.

National Council for Teachers of Mathematics. 2000. *Principles and Standards for School Mathematics.* Reston, VA: National Council for Teachers of Mathematics.

Passe, Jeff. 1999. *Elementary School Curriculum.* Boston: McGraw-Hill.

Reich, Robert B. 2001. "Standards for What?" *Education Week* 20(41):48, 64.

Taba, Hilda. 1962. *Curriculum Development: Theory and Practice.* New York: Harcourt, Brace and World.

Jane McCarthy
Linda F. Quinn

PREPARATION OF TEACHERS

During the first two centuries following the settlement of the American colonies the education of youngsters was a shared endeavor, with the family assuming major responsibility and the church typically taking on a prominent role as well. Various agencies and businesses in the community also contributed as children early on served in apprenticeships and indentures. Certain individuals did formally teach youngsters. However, in his major history of colonial education (1970), Lawrence Cremin noted that usually these individuals did not view teaching as their primary occupation nor were they formally prepared to do so. Some tutored the youngsters of the upper class. Others, typically women, taught the basics of reading, writing, and ciphering in their homes in what were known as dame schools. This rather informal and shared approach to educating youngsters continued well into the nineteenth century.

When the common school evolved in the early decades of the nineteenth century, the principles of free tuition, universal attendance, and hence tax support also became more prevalent. Correspondingly, the need for qualified teachers spread and the first public normal school was established in Massachusetts in 1839. These teacher preparation institutions spread quickly throughout New England and by the end of the nineteenth century to the rest of the country.

The curriculum in these normal schools focused on the subjects these prospective teachers were eventually to teach. Jesse May Pangburn's 1932 review of normal schools revealed, "students needed to show a mastery of reading, writing, spelling, geography, grammar, and arithmetic for admission to the regular professional courses" (p. 14). Examples of these "professional" courses were thirteen weeks devoted to the history of education, twenty-seven weeks in the science of education, and thirty-one weeks in methods in the elementary branches. Observation in elementary schools followed by practice teaching was a culminating feature of the normal school curriculum and the curriculum was spread out over one or two years.

As late as 1898 there were approximately 250 normal schools; however, these institutions graduated only about a fourth of the total number of elementary teachers needed. Most elementary teachers were simply graduates of elementary schools. These teachers were nearly always women who could be recruited for lower salaries than men and who were believed to possess the nurturing qualities needed to interact effectively with younger children.

With the advent of the twentieth century departments of education in universities evolved. Wayne Urban (1990) reported that the motivation for universities to incorporate teacher preparation into the curriculum stemmed from their need for increased enrollment and the positive public relations that came from addressing the needs of the expanding public school systems. The creation of specific departments of education would "also allow women to enroll but not spread their presence or influence across the campuses" (p. 63).

The normal schools now had to transform themselves in order to compete with the universities. Many of these normal schools became teachers colleges. Some of the teachers colleges eventually included other majors, and in the last half of the twentieth century some even became universities. Bachelor's degrees were now offered in both universities and teachers colleges. This resulted in adding general education requirements to the more technical teacher education curriculum. In the late 1920s and throughout the 1930s the foundations movement, guided by the social and philosophical ideas of John Dewey, took place in teacher education. The disciplines of history, philosophy, and psychology were brought to bear more directly on both the problems of teaching and the role of school in addressing broader societal issues. Thus, by World War II, the general structure of the preparation of elementary teachers was shaped much as it remains at the beginning of the twenty-first century: academic study, foundational study, professional study, and practice teaching.

Current Structure and Organization

In the early twenty-first century, teacher preparation in the United States is a huge enterprise. There are more than 3 million teachers in public schools in the United States and more than 1,400 institutions of higher education of various types that offer programs preparing teachers. The preparation of teachers is also increasingly undertaken as a partnership endeavor with elementary and secondary personnel assuming an expanded role, especially in the clinical aspects of this endeavor. A distinctive trend in the 1980s and 1990s was the formulation of professional development, professional practice, or partner schools specifically designed to assist in the preparation of prospective teachers.

The Research About Teacher Education (RATE) Study (1989) was a national survey of the organizational and structural properties of programs preparing elementary teachers in the United States. This study reported that the typical distribution of college credits for an elementary education program consisted of approximately 132 semester hours accordingly: general studies (58 credits), professional studies (42 credits), an area of concentration (20 credits), and student teaching (12 credits). About a third of the programs required an academic major averaging 32 credits, and another fourth required an academic minor averaging 20 credits.

A typical professional sequence for prospective elementary teachers includes six hours in the methods of teaching reading and approximately three hours each in the methods of teaching social studies, math, science, and language arts. Student teaching is usually completed in one setting and lasts about twelve weeks. Many programs preparing elementary teachers are organized into "blocks" of courses so that related subjects can be studied in an integrated fashion.

At the baccalaureate level, one can find preparation programs in relatively equal numbers that begin at the freshman, sophomore, junior, and senior year. However, elementary teacher preparation increasingly has taken on a postbaccalaureate flavor. History shows a pattern of teacher preparation from no formal preparation to two years, then four years, and at the turn of the twenty-first century, often five years and more. Some five-year programs combine undergraduate and graduate credits. Others result in a master's degree along with the baccalaureate award. In addition there are teacher preparation programs offered solely at the masters level, often designed to attract prospective teachers whose undergraduate degree is in another field. Finally, there are also many alternative licensure programs usually intended to accommodate the "nontraditional" student and to recruit teachers for "high need" schools.

The Continuing Education of Elementary Teachers

In addition to the trend towards extended programs of preparation, many states and school districts are offering what are referred to as induction or entry year programs wherein novice teachers in the critical first years of teaching are provided assistance by veteran teachers. Novice teachers also come together periodically to continue their education. Some of these programs are sponsored by the district, others by teachers' unions, and still others in partnership with universities.

The education of teachers hardly stops at this point. Licensing requirements mandate that teachers continue their education, and the rapidly changing student demography, new technologies, and ever-expanding information underscore why they continually need to do so. While many teachers return to universities for further coursework (the majority of elementary teachers now complete at least a master's degree), they also regularly engage in educational activities sponsored by their school districts and teachers' unions. Although summer and after-school workshops remain a staple of this continuing education, increasingly forms of continuing professional development are built into teachers' ongoing daily activities with an emphasis on inquiry into and reflection upon how they are impacting student learning. During the 1990s professional development guidelines and accountability measures were put in place so that veteran teachers could be certified by a national board as accomplished teachers.

Unresolved Issues and Problems

Although inroads generally have been made in the recruitment, preparation, and induction of elementary teachers, problems remain and several issues can be raised as well. First, studies of teaching effectiveness underscore the essentiality of knowing the subject one teaches in considerable depth and having a repertoire of teaching strategies indigenous to that subject. Thus a strong argument can be made that most elementary teachers simply are not adequately prepared to teach five or six subjects well. Rather, what is needed are schools where elementary teachers work in teams assuming collective responsibilities for a group of youngsters but with each teacher on the team teaching only one or two subjects. This suggests quite a different pattern of preparing elementary teachers with an emphasis on effective collaboration among other needed changes. Second, the plurality of cultures and languages that is now represented in many classrooms calls for teaching that is sensitive and responsive to pluralism and youngsters who live in very different neighborhoods; a daunting challenge indeed. Third, the pervasive presence and massive potential of the computer as a teaching tool and vehicle for learning presents particular challenges in preparing teachers. Fourth and finally, while the preparation of elementary teachers has generally been improved and extended over time and entry-year programs are becoming more common, these endeavors tend to be uncoupled and not aligned with one another.

Although partnerships in the preparation of teachers are evolving and outstanding veteran teachers are contributing in expanded ways, these partnerships tend to be ad hoc in nature and tenuous, involving a few individuals rather than interinstitutional arrangements. Reform in teacher preparation tends not to proceed in an aligned and simultaneous manner with needed reforms in elementary schools.

See also: EARLY CHILDHOOD EDUCATION, *subentry on* PREPARATION OF TEACHERS; TEACHER EDUCATION; TEACHER PREPARATION, INTERNATIONAL PERSPECTIVE.

BIBLIOGRAPHY

CREMIN, LAWRENCE A. 1970. *American Education: The Colonial Experience 1607–1783.* New York: Harper and Row.

PANGBURN, JESSE MAY. 1932. *The Evolution of the American Teacher College.* New York: Columbia University, Teachers College, Bureau of Publications.

URBAN, WAYNE J. 1990. "Historical Studies of Teacher Education." In *Handbook of Research on Teacher Education,* ed. W. Robert Houston. New York: Macmillan.

KENNETH R. HOWEY
LINDA M. POST

ELIOT, CHARLES (1834–1926)

During Charles Eliot's forty-year tenure as president of Harvard, he helped transform the relatively small college into a modern university and became a leading spokesman for Progressive educational reform in America.

The son of a prominent Bostonian business-man, Charles Eliot entered Harvard in 1849. After graduating second in his class, Eliot became a tutor and was then promoted to assistant professor of mathematics and chemistry. When Harvard did not renew Eliot's appointment in 1863, he traveled to Europe to study. He returned home to accept a professorship at the new Massachusetts Institute of Technology. In 1869 Eliot published a two-part essay in the *Atlantic Monthly* entitled "The New Education," which solidified his position as an educational reformer and helped him secure a nomination for the presidency of Harvard.

Harvard: From College to University

While Eliot's ideas concerning education brought him the nomination for Harvard's presidency, it also brought great criticism of his possible selection. Clergy dominated the leadership of American higher education, and the college curriculum generally centered on classical studies. Eliot, a thirty-five-year-old scientist, threatened these traditions. Even though his election as president in 1869 was not unanimous, he did not shirk from delineating a reform agenda during his inaugural address. He recommended that Harvard reject the notion of antagonism between classical and scientific studies and proposed, among other things, expanding the curriculum, reforming teaching methods, implementing higher standards, and recognizing individual differences and preferences in education. In short, Eliot presented an outline for Harvard's metamorphosis from college to university.

Eliot understood that graduate and professional education provided an integral part of any true university, and in 1872 his administration created a graduate department. The department, however, failed to have any impact as it did not offer any courses designed specifically for graduate students. In contrast, Johns Hopkins and Cornell provided clear examples of institutions devoted to the university ideal by emphasizing specialization and research. Eliot assimilated many of the philosophies espoused by these universities and used Harvard's resources to develop a stronger graduate program. In 1890 Harvard dropped its graduate department in favor of a graduate school, and offered courses designed specifically for graduate students. At the same time Eliot proposed that professional programs, such as law and medicine, become the arbiters of professional standards. With this in mind, Harvard

required a bachelor's degree to enter its top professional schools. This reform encouraged greater scholarship among faculty and students and prompted other institutions to do the same.

Recruiting a Superior Faculty

High-quality graduate education would not be possible without scholars possessing advanced knowledge in their specific fields, so Eliot provided incentives to lure leading professors to Cambridge. During his first year as president Harvard increased faculty salaries from $3,000 to $4,000. Eliot also ignored theological issues when hiring faculty. The opening of Johns Hopkins provided Harvard with a new school from which to hire American Ph.D.'s. Eliot, however, did not stop with hiring the graduates of new universities; he also raided other institutions' faculties, a standard practice in American higher education. In 1880 Eliot promoted the creation of a pension system to encourage the retirement of unproductive employees. Eventually this system expanded to include all faculty members at Harvard. Then, Eliot helped secure a sabbatical year for Harvard professors wishing to focus on scholarship. All of these practices and innovations allowed Harvard to recruit a superior faculty.

The Elective System

Of all the reforms Eliot implemented at Harvard, none brought more renown than the elective system. Ironically, student freedom in choosing classes was not a new controversy. Thomas Jefferson encouraged the practice when founding the University of Virginia, as did other reformers during the 1840s. While the rationale against student choice as expressed in the Yale Report of 1828 still held sway at Northeastern colleges, even Harvard allowed limited student choice when Eliot took office. The university prescribed all freshmen courses, but some options existed for upperclassmen. Eliot, to the dismay of many colleges, proposed a much more radical version of the elective system. He allowed Harvard seniors to choose all their courses, and gradually loosened restrictions on younger students. By 1884 Harvard granted freshmen some choice in course offerings.

Eliot's primary defense of the elective system emphasized the liberty expressed in both the Protestant Reformation and in American political theory. Freedom, he argued, allowed students to develop true growth of character. Individuals possessed God-given propensities that students needed to cultivate in order to fulfill their mission of service after leaving Harvard. In addition, allowing students to choose classes helped expand the curriculum and graduate programs. Electives promoted specialization and encouraged professors to work closely with students in order to push the boundaries of knowledge in their specific field. Finally, by providing students with options Eliot could determine which professors were no longer inspiring students with their subject matter or teaching methods.

Closely related to Eliot's philosophy of freedom in academics was his policy of increased student freedom outside the classroom. Eliot delegated responsibility of student conduct to the dean, and he encouraged relaxing restrictions on pupils. During his tenure as president the student rulebook shrank from forty pages down to five. Eliot also lobbied to remove conduct as a factor in deciphering class rank. Finally, the in loco parentis attitude was challenged with the ending of mandatory class attendance. All these changes signaled the transformation from college to university.

As an Undenominational Institution

In attempting to end the parental role of Harvard, Eliot diminished the school's religious traditions, and he encouraged other institutions to do the same. The president classified Harvard as "undenominational" and contrasted the institution in Cambridge with smaller denominational liberal arts colleges across the country. The analysis, as his detractors complained, carried a condescending tone, yet Eliot continued to advocate a liberal compatibility between science and religion. At the same time, Eliot derided denominational competition, which spawned large numbers of poorly funded and academically questionable sectarian institutions. As he argued for religious reform nationally, he had more difficulty actually implementing his ideas at Harvard. Eventually the institution followed Eliot's recommendations by abolishing compulsory attendance at daily prayers and emphasizing scientific and intellectual pursuits in the Harvard Divinity School. By doing so, Harvard continued to shed its old-time college image in favor of university status.

Admission Practices

Eliot also sought to raise entrance requirements and to provide standardization for admissions practices. He convinced Harvard to accept the College En-

trance Examination Board's test for admission. This test provided students across the country with the opportunity to apply to Harvard. A more geographically diverse student population, argued Eliot, gave the school another opportunity to shed its historically provincial recruiting practices.

Eliot's ambivalent statements concerning education for minorities mitigated his reforms in admissions. During a tour of the south in 1909 Eliot publicly supported the region's laws prohibiting miscegenation and also opposed relationships between different ethnic groups of European-Americans. Apparently the influx of Irish in Massachusetts convinced him that the proper way to assimilate minorities was through education alone. At the same time Eliot advocated an appeasement approach toward the acceptance of African Americans and failed to condemn Jim Crow laws in the South. Although Harvard accepted a small minority of African Americans, Eliot conceded that a larger black population in the Northeast would precipitate segregated education. Finally, Eliot proved ambivalent on the question of higher education for women. He supported the teaching activities for women at the "Harvard Annex," and he celebrated the creation of Radcliffe College. This system of coordinate education allowed him to argue that Harvard had not become truly coeducational, while he also advanced the notion that Harvard had accepted its role in educating American women. Still, the Harvard president made numerous comments about the possible dangers of educating women, while advocating further inquiry as to the subjects best suited for women to study. These assertions reveal that Eliot's progressivism, like many other reform efforts at the time, did not include the concept of social justice that developed later in the twentieth century.

Harvard's Democratic Ideals

Harvard had always been charged by its critics as elitist and relatively useless to the common man. Eliot used a number of strategies to change this perception and restore the close relationship Harvard once had with the commonwealth and the nation. First, he modified the mission of "practical" higher education advocated by new state universities. He emphasized the progressive reliance on expert scholars who trained other professionals to function in democratic leadership positions. This elitist attitude offended many, but Eliot sought to assuage that tendency. He understood the growing importance of public image and began distributing literature about Harvard to alumni who worked in the media. He also traveled across the nation to speak on behalf of his institution.

While emphasizing Harvard's "democratic" ideals, Eliot also sought the support of wealthy individuals in order to expand Harvard's offerings. His cordial relations with J. P. Morgan and John D. Rockefeller led to donations that funded the building of the medical school. At the same time, other contributions made the creation of the Graduate School of Business Administration possible. Though funded by the elite, these schools exemplified Eliot's assimilationist tendencies by providing education that would help society at large while avoiding overtly vocational activities. His connections with these "robber barons" and the creation of professional schools offended traditionalists, but allowed Harvard to maintain its status as a leading institution of higher education. Eliot also convinced many of Boston's elite that financial support of Harvard's attempts to become a national university also promoted the status and well-being of their city.

Eliot as a National Figure

As president of America's leading institution of higher education, Charles Eliot implicitly wielded national influence in educational reform. Success of his agenda in Cambridge gave him more freedom as an ambassador of the university to the rest of the nation. As the years of his tenure increased so did his travel and speaking engagements. During his educational speeches Eliot did not limit himself to collegiate reform. He became increasingly interested in secondary education and its relationship to higher education. He and John Tetlow, a secondary educator, formed the New England Association of Colleges and Preparatory Schools. The organization regulated primary and secondary education in the region and became a model for other regional accreditation agencies. He also expanded his leadership role in the National Education Association. In 1892 he chaired the Committee of Ten, a group of scholars who sought to provide guidelines for high school curricula and admissions standards for colleges. The report of the committee helped solidify Eliot's position as a leading educator in America and also coerced reluctant Harvard administrators to accept the standardization of admissions. In this way Eliot's public role in American education provided reciprocal benefit to himself, his institution, and education in general. He remained active in this capacity after he retired as Harvard's president in 1909 until his death in 1926. His nomination as the honorary president of the Progressive Education Association revealed his importance to educational professionals and the general public.

Eliot's reforms at Harvard were not offered in a vacuum. He was part of a much larger reform movement in higher education that included such individuals as Andrew D. White of Cornell, James Angell of Michigan, and Daniel Coit Gilman of Johns Hopkins. Eliot provided an example of a leader willing to modify his views in light of changing evidence. He adjusted his stance on such issues as his advocacy of graduate teaching and research, curriculum matters, and the government's role in education. Although Eliot often appeared condescending to those who opposed his ideas, he provided opportunity for dissent. Occasionally his dissenters won, as evidenced by the failure of his three-year plan for a bachelor's degree, his attempts to merge Massachusetts Institute of Technology with Harvard, and early failures with entrance requirements. As president of the nation's oldest institution of higher education, he implemented reforms at Harvard that eventually became commonplace in educational institutions across the country. As he defended his reforms to the nation he became a well-respected public figure whom many considered the most important educational reformer of his time. Opposing factions often criticized Eliot's actions, but his reforms proved to be lasting changes that continue to shape American education in the twenty-first century.

See also: CURRICULUM, HIGHER EDUCATION, *subentries on* INNOVATIONS IN THE UNDERGRADUATE CURRICULUM, TRADITIONAL AND CONTEMPORARY PERSPECTIVES; HARVARD UNIVERSITY; HIGHER EDUCATION IN THE UNITED STATES, *subentry on* HISTORICAL DEVELOPMENT.

BIBLIOGRAPHY

ELIOT, CHARLES W. 1910a. *The Conflict Between Individualism and Collectivism in a Democracy: Three Lectures by Charles W. Eliot.* New York: Scribners.

ELIOT, CHARLES W. 1910b. *The Durable Satisfactions of Life.* New York: Crowell.

ELIOT, CHARLES W. 1924. *A Late Harvest; Miscellaneous Papers Written between Eighty and Ninety.* Boston: Atlantic Monthly.

ELIOT, CHARLES W. 1971. *Charles Eliot: Landscape Architect* (1902). New York: Books for Libraries.

ELIOT, CHARLES W., and NEILSON, WILLIAM ALLEN, eds. 1926. *Charles W. Eliot, the Man and His Beliefs,* 2 Vols. New York: Harper.

HAWKINS, HUGH. 1972. *Between Harvard and America: The Educational Leadership of Charles W. Eliot.* New York: Oxford University Press.

JAMES, HENRY. 1930. *Charles W. Eliot: President of Harvard University, 1969–1909,* 2 Vols. Boston: Houghton Mifflin.

MORISON, SAMUEL ELIOT, ed. 1930. *The Development of Harvard University since the Inauguration of President Eliot, 1869–1929.* Cambridge, MA: Harvard University Press.

MORISON, SAMUEL ELIOT. 1942. *Three Centuries of Harvard, 1636–1936.* Cambridge, MA: Harvard University Press.

ERIC MOYEN
JASON R. EDWARDS
JOHN R. THELIN

EMOTIONAL DEVELOPMENT

See: AFFECT AND EMOTIONAL DEVELOPMENT.

EMOTIONALLY DISTURBED, EDUCATION OF

Since enactment of the Education of All Handicapped Children Act of 1975, under 1 percent of school children have been identified for special education and related services as having *serious emotional disturbance* (SED); since 1997, the term *emotional disturbance* (ED) has been applied under the Individuals with Disabilities Education Act (IDEA). Although the percentage has remained stable for decades, professional estimates suggest the true prevalence is probably three to six times greater. An early twenty-first century report by the U.S. Surgeon General noted that only about one in five children and youth with ED receive mental health services or special education. Reasons for underidentification include economic factors, concern about a stigmatizing label, confusion among professionals, and a vague definition.

Federal legislation incorporates almost verbatim a definition proposed by Eli M. Bower in 1960, which includes five characteristics, one or more of which a student displays to a marked degree and over a long period of time: (1) an inability to learn, which cannot be explained by intellectual, sensory, or health factors; (2) an inability to build or maintain satisfactory interpersonal relationships with peers and teachers; (3) inappropriate types of behavior or feelings under normal circumstances; (4) a general, pervasive mood of unhappiness or depression; and (5) a tendency to develop physical symptoms or fears associated with personal or school problems. Federal language specifies that ED must adversely affect educational performance but does not specifically include social learning or behavior as "educational performance." The definition has been criticized as vague and highly subjective (e.g., what is "a marked extent," or a "long period of time"?), and an additional federal clause makes the definition self-contradictory. The addition is an exclusionary statement that the category "does not include children who are socially maladjusted, unless it is also determined that they are seriously emotionally disturbed" (45 C.F.R. 121a.5[b][8][1978]). Nevertheless, the federal definition remains unchanged.

In the 1990s an alternative definition and the term *emotional or behavioral disorder* (EBD) were proposed by the National Mental Health and Special Education Coalition. The coalition consisted of more than thirty professional organizations serving children's mental health needs. The proposed definition and terminology are thought to be less stigmatizing, to emphasize disorders of emotions and behavior, and they include disabling disorders excluded in the federal definition. Notwithstanding widespread support from coalition members, federal language has not changed. Administrators of special education oppose the alternative definition and terminology, fearing significant increases in the number of students qualifying for special education and related services.

The problems of students with ED are severe and chronic. Only those with the most severe disorders receive services, and appropriate educational services have remained a persistent challenge. Students with ED tend to be served in more restrictive settings (e.g., separate classrooms or schools instead of regular classrooms or schools) than their peers with other disabilities, and student outcomes (school completion, later employment, successful community adjustment) are poorer for students with ED. Research suggests that for children not receiving effective services before the age of eight years, ED should be viewed as a chronic, lifelong condition requiring continuing support services.

In the late twentieth century and into the twenty-first century, controversies surrounded the full inclusion of students with disabilities in regular schools and classrooms. ED students were generally ignored, although serious questions arose about the advisability and feasibility of including all students with ED in general education. Even as other students with disabilities were increasingly included in regular classrooms, those with ED were more likely to be educated in separate classes.

In 1990 Jane Knitzer, Zina Steinberg, and Brahm Fleisch highlighted the overemphasis in many programs on controlling acting-out behavior at the expense of a focus on instruction in academic skills and social behavior. Subsequently, others emphasized design and delivery of effective academic and social instruction.

Controversy continues about placement and programming. Growing evidence that early intervention and prevention are effective has not resulted in widespread prevention. A particular obstacle to truly effective services is the extreme difficulty in coordinating services from multiple agencies and fostering collaboration among schools and numerous community, family, and adult service providers. Awareness of the cultural differences in behavior is increasing. The complexity of the relationship between behavior and culture is underscored by simultaneous calls for increased attention to the mental health needs of students of minority ethnicity and complaints that students of color with ED are overrepresented in special education.

See also: COUNCIL FOR EXCEPTIONAL CHILDREN; SPECIAL EDUCATION, *subentries on* CURRENT TRENDS, HISTORY OF.

BIBLIOGRAPHY

BOWER, ELI M. 1981. *Early Identification of Emotionally Handicapped Children in School,* 3rd edition. Springfield, IL: Thomas.

FORNESS, STEVEN R., and KNITZER, JANE. 1992. "A New Proposed Definition and Terminology to Replace 'Serious Emotional Disturbance' in Individuals with Disabilities Education Act." *School Psychology Review* 21:12–20.

KAUFFMAN, JAMES M. 1999. "How We Prevent the Prevention of Emotional and Behavioral Disorders." *Exceptional Children* 65:448–468.

KAUFFMAN, JAMES M. 2001. *Characteristics of Emotional and Behavioral Disorders of Children and Youth,* 7th edition. Upper Saddle River, NJ: Prentice-Hall.

KAUFFMAN, JAMES M.; LLOYD, JOHN W.; BAKER, JOHN; and RIEDEL, TERESA M. 1995. "Inclusion of All Students with Emotional or Behavioral Disorders? Let's Think Again." *Phi Delta Kappan* 76:542–546.

KAUFFMAN, JAMES M.; LLOYD, JOHN W.; HALLAHAN, DANIEL P.; and ASTUTO, TERRY A., eds. 1995. *Issues in Educational Placement: Students with Emotional and Behavioral Disorders.* Mahwah, NJ: Erlbaum.

KAUFFMAN, JAMES M.; MOSTERT, MARK P.; TRENT, STANLEY C.; and HALLAHAN, DANIEL P. 2002. *Managing Classroom Behavior: A Reflective Case-Based Approach,* 3rd edition. Boston: Allyn and Bacon.

KNITZER, JANE; STEINBERG, ZINA; and FLEISCH, BRAHM. 1990. *At the Schoolhouse Door: An Examination of Programs and Policies for Children's Behavioral and Emotional Problems.* New York: Bank Street College of Education.

PEACOCK HILL WORKING GROUP. 1991. "Problems and Promises in Special Education and Related Services for Children and Youth with Emotional or Behavioral Disorders." *Behavioral Disorders* 16:299–313.

STRAIN, PHILLIP S., and TIMM, MATTHEW A. 2001. "Remediation and Prevention of Aggression: An Evaluation of the Regional Intervention Program Over a Quarter Century." *Behavioral Disorders* 26:297–313.

U.S. DEPARTMENT OF HEALTH AND HUMAN SERVICES. 2001. *Report of the Surgeon General's Conference on Children's Mental Health: A National Action Agenda.* Washington, DC: U.S. Department of Health and Human Services.

WALKER, HILL M.; COLVIN, GEOFF; and RAMSEY, ELIZABETH. 1995. *Antisocial Behavior in School: Strategies and Best Practices.* Pacific Grove, CA: Brooks/Cole.

WALKER, HILL M.; FORNESS, STEVEN R.; KAUFFMAN, JAMES M.; EPSTEIN, MICHAEL H.; GRESHAM, FRANK M.; NELSON, C. MICHAEL; and STRAIN,

PHILLIP S. 1998. "Macro-Social Validation: Referencing Outcomes in Behavioral Disorders to Societal Issues and Problems." *Behavioral Disorders* 24:7–18.

TIMOTHY J. LANDRUM
JAMES M. KAUFFMAN

EMPLOYMENT

GENERAL IMPACT ON STUDENTS

Paid employment begins at a relatively young age in the United States. While exact figures vary, depending on the means of measurement, a survey published in 2000 by the U.S. Department of Labor found that half of American twelve-year-olds have had some kind of work experience. While at such young ages work experiences tend to be informal and short-term, as American youth progress through their teenage years their work becomes more formal and more time-consuming. Researchers have been paying increasing attention to the effects on youth of working. In general, the results from this body of research lead to neither a blanket endorsement nor a condemnation of school-aged youth working for pay.

There have been several phases of research on youth and work. Before 1970, researchers paid almost no attention to students' paid work. The influential report of the Coleman commission of the President's Science Advisory Committee (1974) blamed schooling—because it isolates young people from adults and from productive work—for actually retarding youth's transition to adulthood. The report called for placing young people into work situations earlier, as a tool for social development. Presumably, work would provide a valuable educational experience, even if the work took place in an occupation not related to the eventual employment.

As national surveys in the 1970s and 1980s were demonstrating that paid youth work was very com-

mon, Ellen Greenberger and Laurence Steinberg's *When Teenagers Work,* which reported the results of research on primarily middle-class youth in California, brought attention to some negative consequences of work. This spurred a lively debate and further study among academics. In particular, some feared that work could have negative consequences on school engagement and performance. While youths tend to work more during the summer than during the school months, some data show that the majority of high school juniors and seniors do work during the academic year. At the start of the twenty-first century, researchers have been turning their focus to the quality of young people's jobs and proposing to increase jobs' learning content through formal linkages with school curricula.

In contrast to the concern over too much working, some find access to work for minority and low socioeconomic status youth to be a greater problem. Working during high school does reduce the risk of unemployment later. Racial and ethnic disparities in teenage job-holding and in the number of hours worked are well-established. Multiple studies indicate that minority teenagers, and teens in poor families and families receiving public assistance, are less likely to work than white or higher socioeconomic status youth. As Jeylan T. Mortimer and her colleagues reported in 1990, "employment is very much a middle-class phenomenon" (p. 208). In one study of several hundred youth in Baltimore, African-American youth reported equal or greater job-seeking as white youth but lower rates of obtaining jobs. Hence African-American youth started working later, and were less often employed. The U.S. Department of Labor reported in 2000 that African-American and Hispanic youth have much higher unemployment rates than do white youth. However, when they do work, Hispanic youth work more hours during the school year than do other youth.

Young people's first paid jobs tend to be informal (or "freelance jobs," as the U.S. Department of Labor refers to them), such as child care and lawn work. According to Mortimer and associates (1990), girls tend to start paid work earlier, yet their first jobs are more likely than those of boys to be of the informal type and concentrated within a smaller number of areas. Of the ninth-graders in this study, most of the girls were working in private households while the boys were more divided among informal work, sales work, and restaurant work.

Research has established that there are sex differences in industry and occupation of young workers. Male and female youth are about equally likely to work in eating and drinking places, with about 27 percent of fifteen-year-old boys and 31 percent of fifteen-year-old girls working in such establishments, but males are more likely to be employed in the agriculture, mining, construction, and manufacturing industries. Boys fifteen to seventeen years of age are much more likely to work in farm, forestry, and fishing occupations, as well as blue-collar occupations, while girls of the same ages tend to work in sales occupations such as cashier (this is true for the school year *and* the summer months).

Youth tend to give the reason for working as "to buy things," noted the Mortimer study in 1990. Katherine S. Newman makes the point that teenagers from poor families in particular need to work so that they have money with which to participate in youth culture, yet Doris R. Entwhistle and associates reported that lower-status youth are more likely than other youth to share their earnings with their family. The young fast-food workers in Harlem that Newman studied also sought work as a place to escape from violence in their own neighborhoods.

Earnings for teenage workers are generally just above minimum wage; in 1998 median earnings of fifteen- to seventeen-year-olds were $5.57 per hour, while minimum wage was $5.15. Hourly earnings do increase with age. White and Hispanic males tend to have the highest median hourly earnings while Hispanic and African-American females have the lowest. Mortimer's 1990 report found significant wage differences between boys and girls overall, with boys reporting a higher mean wage.

Employment after School and Effects on Academic Outcomes

The propensity of American youth to work (and often to work a significant number of hours) during the school year has led to debate among researchers and policymakers about the effect of this work on young people, particularly on their academic engagement and achievement.

According to the U.S. Department of Labor, during the 1996–1998 school months, 39 percent of seventeen-year-olds were employed during the average month. This method of measurement, tabulating the percentage of young people employed at a particular point in time, minimizes the extent of youth

work; when students are asked if they have *ever* worked during their high school years, figures are significantly higher. An analysis of National Longitudinal Survey of Youth (NLSY) data in 1995 by Michael Pergamit found that about 64 percent of juniors and 73 percent of seniors said that they had worked at least one week during the school year.

The concern over youth working while in school emanates from two perspectives. One focuses on the amount of time spent at the workplace, reasoning that time spent at work is likely to be time taken away from academic pursuits such as homework. While young people work longer hours during the summer than they do during the school year, the number of hours spent on the job in the academic months, about 17 per week according to the Department of Labor, is still significant. Another concern is about the low quality of the jobs youth tend to hold. As noted above, young people tend to start with informal jobs, such as child care and lawn work, with the majority then moving into the retail trade industry, which includes eating and drinking places such as fast-food outlets. There is the question of whether youth gain developmentally at all on the job, given the low-level positions they tend to have. Young people themselves say they work to earn money to buy things and save for college, rather than to add to their knowledge or skills.

In general, an examination of the literature on youth working while in high school finds costs and benefits, and some of the literature is conflicting. In terms of effects on academic achievement, some researchers have found a negative relationship between the number of hours worked during the school year and both high school and postsecondary school attainment measures. However, David Stern and Derek Briggs reviewed the literature and concluded that the relationship between hours of work and performance in school actually follows an inverted-U pattern, meaning that students who work more moderate hours perform at a higher level in high school than students who work more heavily or not at all. This pattern appears to extend to postsecondary achievement as well; Department of Labor analysis of NLSY data shows that teenagers who worked twenty or fewer hours per week while in high school were more likely to have achieved at least some college education by age thirty than those who had worked more than twenty hours or not at all.

However, some researchers contend that the observed effects are spurious because they do not take into account preexisting differences between students who work and those who do not. And some of the research is not able to fully sort out the direction of causality. For example, students who are not already performing well in school may seek more hours at their paid jobs, rather than spending long hours studying. Researchers have also questioned the zero-sum assumption that hours on the job are hours not spent in study. An analysis of longitudinal data by Mark Schoenhals, Marta Tienda, and Barbara Schneider found that youth employment lowered the amount of time spent in watching television, not the time spent reading or doing homework.

Employment during the Summer

Youth are more likely to work during the summer than during the school year, and according to the Department of Labor, 20 percent of employed youth aged fifteen to seventeen work full-time over the summer months, compared with 6 percent during the rest of the year. Mihaly Csikszentmihalyi and Barbara Schneider report that youth from higher-income families generally have more work experience and are particularly more likely to work solely in the summer.

Employed youth aged fifteen to seventeen tend to work in similar industries in the summer as they do during the school year, with the majority working in retail, which includes eating and drinking establishments. However, in the summer the proportion in retail declines somewhat as teens take more jobs in agriculture, construction, and service industries. Csikszentmihalyi and Schneider note that affluent teenagers tend to have jobs such as camp counselor and lifeguard, likely reflecting their tendency to work only during the summer and the opportunities available in their communities, while working-class youth were found more likely to hold positions in fast-food outlets. Hourly earnings for youth working during the summer versus the school months are about the same.

In the research literature there is much less concern about, and hence much less attention given to, paid work that students perform during the summer months. One study that did attempt to measure the costs and benefits of summer work to youth found that summer employment had positive effects on post–high school employment status and other outcomes. According to Herbert W. Marsh, no negative effects were found. Thus the summer employment problem may be better redefined as the difficulty

that minority and low socioeconomic status youth face in gaining access to valuable paid positions. As noted above, there are racial and ethnic disparities in teenage job-holding and in the number of hours worked. While the federal government has long funded summer job programs aimed at youth with serious barriers to employment, the 1998 Workforce Investment Act changed the focus to year-round services, eliminating the separate appropriation for summer activities.

Effects on Psychosocial Outcomes

There is no doubt about the importance of the work role in adulthood, thus most recognize that for an adolescent, taking on a new social role as worker can be a formative experience. Yet there is considerable debate about whether the experience affects the development of youth positively or negatively. In addition, there may be sex differences with regard to developmental impact, as girls and boys tend to have different types of jobs, particularly in their early teens.

Some researchers question whether youth gain any skills at all on the job, given the positions youth have and the workplaces they are in, and argue, as do Greenberger and Steinberg, that youth work can lead to stress as well as to adult behaviors such as alcohol use. Studies do report that working is associated with "problem behaviors" such as substance abuse and other delinquent activities; Mortimer, Carolyn Harley, and Pamela Aronson provided a review of a number of these studies in 1999. Again, however, the direction of causality is difficult to determine.

Most research finds that the general public regards youth work positively, believing it to have developmental benefits. For example, a study by Mortimer and associates published in 1999 examined parents' retrospective views of their early jobs, as well as their attitudes toward their children's work. The parents were enthusiastic about working during adolescence, listing a variety of competencies they believed they had acquired as a result, such as gaining a sense of responsibility, money management skills, discipline, and so on. Not surprisingly, then, the parents had favorable attitudes about their children's employment. The children reported benefits of working quite similar to those their parents had reported.

With regard to skills learned on the job, a study of youth working in fast food argues that these positions do yield skills, as they require much in the way of information processing, coordination, and responding to unpredictable events. Youth also must learn to handle customers, which can help them to develop what Newman characterizes as "people skills." Other research has found that even positions such as child care can develop innovative thinking skills in and provide challenge to young people. Mortimer and Catherine Yamoor (1987) pointed out that the opportunity for self-direction in a work setting can have positive consequences for a worker's self-concept and interest in work. Thus research has examined not only the types of specific skills youth workers might gain on the job, but also psychological effects that might influence attitudes and behaviors.

An important point brought out in the research is that the influence of a particular job on a young person likely depends on the nature of the job. One study finds that "the quality of the work (i.e., its stressful or rewarding character) is a more important determinant of adolescent psychological functioning than either work status or its intensity" (Finch et al., p. 606). However, young people actually report little stress from their jobs alone; it is combining or juggling being both a worker and a student that can be stressful.

Connecting Work and School

Several researchers have observed that youth perceive school and the workplace as conflicting, not complementary, and argue that more efforts should be made to integrate the two. A study by Barbara Schneider and David Stevenson found that youth enjoy working more than they enjoy being in school.

There seems little chance that students will cease working. Thus researchers and policymakers are increasingly turning to a focus on building and strengthening connections between work and school, which should help to improve the nature of some youth work. While school-arranged work placements such as co-op and internships have been in place for years, the 1990s saw a renewed emphasis on school-sponsored work-based learning, particularly through the 1994 School-to-Work Opportunities Act. Research by Alan M. Hershey, Marsha K. Silverberg, and Joshua Haimson evaluating the effectiveness of the legislation included surveys of 1998 high school seniors, who reported that work opportunities offered through the schools had important advantages over the workplace activities students re-

ported finding on their own. School-developed positions tended to be in a wider range of industries, and tended to more closely match students' career goals. Students with school-arranged paid jobs were more likely than other students to spend at least half their time in training on the job. They were also more likely to report discussing possible careers with adults at their workplace, and were more likely to receive a performance evaluation from school or employer staff. Students who had obtained positions through school more often reported using academic or technical skills learned in school at the workplace, and were more likely to draw on their work experience in school assignments or discussions, thus experiencing more substantive connections between their studies and work experience.

Despite the challenges of coordinating work activities through school, advocates of these arrangements hope to expand them. While there is no definitive answer to the question of whether working during the school year negatively affects students' school work, it is certainly desirable to help youth perceive school and the workplace as complementary, rather than conflicting. Since it is unlikely that young people will stop working, the idea is to help youth gain as much as possible from their employment experiences.

See also: OUT-OF-SCHOOL INFLUENCES AND ACADEMIC SUCCESS; VOCATIONAL AND TECHNICAL EDUCATION.

BIBLIOGRAPHY

BROWN, BRETT. 2001. "Teens, Jobs, and Welfare: Implications for Social Policy." *Child Trends Research Brief.* Washington, DC: Child Trends.

COLEMAN, JAMES S. 1974. *Youth: Transition to Adulthood.* Report of the Panel on Youth of the President's Science Advisory Committee. Chicago: University of Chicago Press.

CSIKSZENTMIHALYI, MIHALY, and SCHNEIDER, BARBARA. 2000. *Becoming Adult: How Teenagers Prepare for the World of Work.* New York: Basic Books.

ENTWISLE, DORIS R.; ALEXANDER, KARL L.; and OLSON, LINDA STEFFEL. 2000. "Early Work Histories of Urban Youth." *American Sociological Review* 65:279–297.

FINCH, MICHAEL D., et al. 1991. "Work Experience and Control Orientation in Adolescence." *American Sociological Review* 56:597–611.

GREENBERGER, ELLEN, and STEINBERG, LAURENCE. 1986. *When Teenagers Work: The Psychological and Social Costs of Adolescent Employment.* New York: Basic Books.

HERSHEY, ALAN M.; SILVERBERG, MARSHA K.; and HAIMSON, JOSHUA. 1999. *Expanding Options for Students: Report to Congress on the National Evaluation of School-to-Work Implementation.* Princeton, NJ: Mathematica Policy Research, Inc.

LOUGHLIN, CATHERINE, and BARLING, JULIAN. 1999. "The Nature of Youth Employment." In *Young Workers: Varieties of Experience,* ed. Julian Barling and E. Kevin Kelloway. Washington, DC: American Psychological Association.

MARSH, HERBERT W. 1991. "Employment during High School: Character Building or a Subversion of Academic Goals?" *Sociology of Education* 64:172–189.

MORTIMER, JEYLAN T., et al. 1990. "Gender and Work in Adolescence." *Youth and Society* 22(2):201–224.

MORTIMER, JEYLAN T., et al. 1994. "Work Experience in Adolescence." *Journal of Vocational Education Research* 19(1):39–70.

MORTIMER, JEYLAN T.; HARLEY, CAROLYN; and ARONSON, PAMELA. 1999. "How Do Prior Experiences in the Workplace Set the Stage for Transitions to Adulthood?" In *Transitions to Adulthood in a Changing Economy—No Work, No Family, No Future?* ed. Alan Booth, Ann C. Crouter, and Michael J. Shanahan. Westport, CT: Praeger.

MORTIMER, JEYLAN T., and YAMOOR, CATHERINE. 1987. "Interrelations and Parallels of School and Work as Sources of Psychological Development." In *Research in the Sociology of Education and Socialization,* ed. Ronald G. Corwin. Greenwich, CT: JAI Press.

NEWMAN, KATHERINE S. 1999. *No Shame in My Game: The Working Poor in the Inner City.* New York: Alfred A. Knopf and the Russell Sage Foundation.

PERGAMIT, MICHAEL R. 1995, June. *Assessing School-to-Work Transitions in the United States.* National Longitudinal Surveys Discussion Paper. NLS 96–32. Washington, DC: U.S. Department of Labor, Bureau of Labor Statistics.

SCHNEIDER, BARBARA and STEVENSON, DAVID. 1999. *The Ambitious Generation.* New Haven, CT: Yale University Press.

SCHOENHALS, M.; TIENDA, MARTA; and SCHNEIDER, BARBARA. 1998. "The Educational and Personal Consequences of Adolescent Employment." *Social Forces* 77(2):723–762.

STERN, DAVID, and BRIGGS, DEREK. 2001. "Does Paid Employment Help or Hinder Performance in Secondary School? Insights from U.S. High School Students." *Journal of Education and Work* 14(3):355–372.

STONE, JAMES R., III, and MORTIMER, JEYLAN T. 1998. "The Effect of Adolescent Employment on Vocational Development: Public and Educational Policy Implications." *Journal of Vocational Behavior* 53:184–214.

U.S. DEPARTMENT OF LABOR. 2000. *Report on the Youth Labor Force.* Washington, DC: U.S. Department of Labor.

KATHERINE L. HUGHES

EMPLOYERS' PERCEPTIONS OF EMPLOYMENT READINESS

Employers in the business community are getting into the education business. From companies like Cisco Systems and Manpower to the Bill and Melinda Gates Foundation, American businesses and business leaders are spending millions of dollars to address what they perceive to be a deficiency in the ability of the American education system to adequately prepare students to meet the demands of the workplace of the early twenty-first century. From funding for inner city computer centers to school-to-work participation, their interest is driven by the belief that high school and college graduates are not ready to adequately contribute in the workplace. This article addresses employer perceptions of employee readiness by outlining what employers need from employees, followed by their perceptions of the readiness of new employees to contribute to the organization's ability to meet these challenges.

Concern about readiness for work is not new. There is a history of government initiatives on this topic, perhaps most notably the Secretary's Commission on Achieving Necessary Skills (SCANS) in 1991. Readiness for work entails preparedness to learn and perform on the job, the ability to continue to learn, and the personal characteristics that contribute to successful accomplishment of work. According to Harold F. O'Neil Jr., Keith Allred, and Eva L. Baker, general categories of readiness skills consist of basic academic skills, higher order thinking or problem solving skills, interpersonal and teamwork skills, and attitudes or other characteristics such as the willingness and ability to take initiative and responsibility.

Organizational Needs and the Employment Environment

Perceptions of readiness are based on a framework of organizational needs that have been influenced significantly in recent years by changes in the competitive environment, in technology, and in theories of managerial best practices. Intense competition has forced organizations to become more customer-focused, with greater emphasis on understanding and quickly satisfying customer needs and on responding rapidly to changing customer preferences. Whereas Harry Braverman argued in 1974 that the technologies of the future would reduce workers to button-pushing automatons, the opposite has been the case. Workers at low levels of the organization are often expected to perform across a range of roles and responsibilities and must take initiative and use judgment in determining how to best satisfy customer needs and keep their team running smoothly. Whether responding to customer needs, competitor activities, or rapidly changing technology, the organizational imperatives are clear: speed, agility, and adaptability are crucial. Traditional command-and-control hierarchies with narrow, highly structured, routine jobs and tightly supervised workers are poorly suited to this kind of environment. Instead, organizations today are often more flexible, utilizing team-oriented, decentralized structures that empower lower-level workers to make decisions and take initiative.

Employer perceptions of employee readiness are influenced by a dynamic interplay among evolving organizational needs, educational institutions' practices, and the preparation of the students who enroll in educational institutions. These factors have changed the employers' needs and expectations of employees on all fronts. First, to function effectively in the twenty-first century workplace, employees need greater ability in the basics such as reading, writing, and arithmetic. Thus, employers desire workers with more formal education. In fact, where-

as jobs requiring at least a bachelor's degree constituted 21 percent of jobs in 2000, they are forecast to comprise 29 percent of jobs by 2010. Employers expect employees to have the interpersonal skills necessary to communicate, solve problems, coordinate activities, and resolve conflict. Employees also need to possess the ability to self-manage, take initiative, and engage in self-directed learning. Moreover, employers want employees who are ethical and flexible. Research by Kristy Lauver and Huy Le shows a relationship between higher levels of emotional stability, agreeableness, and conscientiousness and lower numbers of workplace accidents.

Perceptions of Readiness

Employers tend to expect schools to build general skills such as basic knowledge, discipline, professionalism, good work habits, the ability to communicate, openness, perseverance, problem-solving ability, and well roundedness. Employers have not seen schools as being effective in producing specific, job-related skills, and employers do not view schooling as the sole or even primary source for developing such skills. For example, Madelyn Schulman's 1999 study of high school interns in school-to-work transition across various occupations revealed that, once at work, interns found themselves in an environment of which they had little or no understanding. Furthermore, 73 percent of managers in one survey described in *The Lessons of Experience* (1988) indicated that they used the skills taught in their master's of business administration (MBA) programs either "marginally or not at all" in their initial managerial assignments. Lynne Leveson reports that despite the efforts invested in building general competencies, the essential differences in the educational environment and the work environment create the inevitability of certain discontinuities between the two. Thus, many employers believe that job-related skills are company-specific and best acquired on the job and see the schools' role as making people trainable.

Daniela Gabric and Kathleen L. McFadden reported in 2001 that both employers' and students' judgment of the value of general skills such as working in teams, problem solving, and effective communication was significantly higher than the value of technical skills (which were still important but to a lesser degree). This approach is consistent with an ability to address the ever-changing demands from the competitive environment. However, despite the fact that both students and employers see great value in these general skills, employers still see schools as falling short. As noted above, this can be inferred from the actions taken and expenses incurred by employers to increase the readiness of individuals before, and as, they reach the workplace. In addition, anecdotal comments from employers suggest that many people in the early twenty-first century are coming out of school with a genuine lack of basic skills. Such comments are supported by empirical data from a variety of organizations. For example, Donald F. Treadwell and Jill B. Treadwell studied employers of communications graduates from multiple business sectors. They found that only 18.5 percent of the employers reported that new hires could perform the duties for which they were hired without additional time investment in training. The most critical weaknesses cited were the ability to write effectively for multiple audiences, to write persuasively, to engage in logical or critical thinking, and to work responsibly without supervision. In this area alone, problems resulting from poor written communication have been estimated to cost U.S. businesses more than $1 billion annually.

Employer and Employee Agreement

In order to address employee readiness, it is important for employers, employees, and educational institutions to recognize that there is, in fact, a problem. Are the perceptions of employers and new employees similar regarding employees' readiness for work?

John Arnold and Kate Mackenzie Davey examined whether new employees rated themselves comparably with their new managers on various work place competencies, including company know-how, interpersonal skills, product and service knowledge, specialist skills and knowledge, and achieving results; their findings indicated that perceptions varied between the two groups. Overall new employees rated themselves higher in skill level than did their managers. However, both new employees and their managers were least confident about the new employees' knowledge of the products and services of their organization and its competitors.

Similarly, differences have been found in the skills or traits deemed to be most important by employers and students about to enter the workforce. Gabric and McFadden noted that one of the major differences between employers' and students' ratings was in how highly they ranked the skill of conscientiousness. In a ranking of 34 personality traits, "being conscientious" was ranked sixth most important by employers but eighteenth by students, suggesting that students may not realize how important employers consider conscientiousness to be in employees.

Reducing the gap between new employee abilities and employer expectations may be facilitated by providing students with a better understanding of what qualities and characteristics employers value most and an accurate assessment of where students currently rank on these competencies and traits. Both schools and employers can assist in this process. Teachers may need to learn more about what employers want, do a better job of conveying this information to students, give students feedback, and encourage students to learn in applied settings as well as in the classroom. Employers may assist by providing internships and summer jobs that expose students to employer expectations, and by providing feedback to the students.

Conclusion

In sum, employers see schools as responsible for preparing students for productive work. Changes in technology, managerial practices, and the competitive environment have raised the level and breadth of knowledge, skills, and abilities that employers require from employees. This has further widened the already significant gap between employer needs and the actual skill levels and abilities of the graduates who enter the labor pool. Employers recognize that some forms of training are best conducted on the job and do not expect schools to produce students with specific job skills. However, employers expect schools to produce students with the ability to use general knowledge and with traditional academic skills such as reading, mathematics, writing, oral communication, and problem solving. Employers would also like schools to prepare students with general characteristics that enhance work performance, such as the ability to work productively with others and demonstrate initiative and responsibility.

See also: OUT-OF-SCHOOL INFLUENCES AND ACADEMIC SUCCESS; VOCATIONAL AND TECHNICAL EDUCATION.

BIBLIOGRAPHY

ARNOLD, JOHN, and MACKENZIE DAVEY, KATE. 1992. "Self-Ratings and Supervisor Ratings of

Graduate Employees' Competencies During Early Career." *Journal of Occupational and Organizational Psychology* 65: 235–250.

ASSOCIATION FOR CAREER AND TECHNICAL EDUCATION. 1997. "Interview with Business and Industry: What Do Employers Want?" *Techniques* 72(5):22–25.

BAILEY, THOMAS. 1997. "Changes in the Nature of Work: Implications for Skills and Assessment." In *Workforce Readiness: Competencies and Assessments,* ed. Harold F. O'Neil, Jr. Mahwah, NJ: Erlbaum.

BILLS, DAVID B. 1998. "Credentials and Capacities: Employers' Perceptions of the Acquisition of Skills." *The Sociological Quarterly* 29(3):439–449.

BRAVERMAN, HARRY. 1974. *Labor and Monopoly Capital: The Degradation of Work in the Twentieth Century.* New York: Monthly Review Press.

CANNON-BOWERS, JANIS A., and SALAS, EDUARDO. 1997. "Teamwork Competencies: The Interaction of Team Member Knowledge, Skills, and Attitudes." In *Workforce Readiness: Competencies and Assessments,* ed. Harold F. O'Neil Jr. Mahwah, NJ: Erlbaum.

GABRIC, DANIELA, and McFADDEN, KATHLEEN L. 2001. "Student and Employer Perceptions of Desirable Entry-Level Operations Management Skills." *Mid-American Journal of Business* 16(1):51–59.

HANSEN, RANDALL S. 1993. "Clear, Concise Writing Is Especially Important for Marketers." *Marketing News* Sept. 13, p. 20.

LAUVER, KRISTY, and LE, HUY. 2001. "Personality Factors as Predictors of Workplace Injuries: A Meta-Analysis." Paper presented at the Annual Meeting of the Academy of Management, Washington, DC.

LEVESON, LYNNE. 2000. "Disparities in Perceptions of Generic Skills: Academics and Employers." *Industry and Higher Education* 14(3):157–164.

LYNN, BARRY. 2001. "Getting Into the Education Business" *American Way* 78–85.

McCALL, MORGAN W., JR.; LOMBARDO, MICHAEL L.; and MORRISON, ANN M. 1988. *The Lessons of Experience: How Successful Executives Develop On the Job.* Lexington, MA: Lexington Books.

O'NEIL, HAROLD F., JR.; ALLRED, KEITH; and BAKER, EVA L. 1997. "Review of Workforce Readiness and Theoretical Frameworks." In *Workforce Readiness: Competencies and Assessments,* ed. Harold F. O'Neil Jr. Mahwah, NJ: Erlbaum.

SCHULMAN, MADELYN L. 1999. "Fitting In: The Acculturation Experiences of Entry-Level High School Interns in School-to Work Transition." *Dissertation Abstracts International* 60(1–A):0051.

STEVENS, MICHAEL J., and CAMPION, MICHAEL A. 1994. "The Knowledge, Skill, and Ability Requirements for Teamwork: Implications for Human Resource Management." *Journal of Management* 20(2):503–530.

TREADWELL, DONALD F., and TREADWELL, JILL B. 1999. "Employer Expectations of Newly-Hired Communication Graduates." *Journal of the Association for Communication Administration* 28:87–99.

TSCHIRGI, HARVEY D. 1972. "What Do Recruiters Really Look For in Candidates?" *Journal of College Placement* 33:75–79.

VAN DER WERF, DIRK. 1990. "Work Competencies and Learning Scenarios for the Future." *Applied Psychology, An International Review* 39:237–250.

INTERNET RESOURCE

HECKER, DANIEL E. 2001. "Occupational Employment Projections to 2010." *Monthly Labor Review, U.S. Department of Labor, Bureau of Labor Statistics.* <www.bls.gov/emp>.

JOHN MASLYN
MARK CANNON

REASONS STUDENTS WORK

Most American teenagers work for pay; figures vary depending on whether labor force participation is measured at a particular point in time or over the course of several years. A U.S. Department of Education survey published in 2000 found two-thirds of twelfth graders saying that they worked for pay; other research asking high school students if they have ever worked has yielded even higher figures.

Beginning in the 1980s, researchers have increasingly paid attention to this phenomenon. Yet rather than exploring the reasons for the high incidence of youth employment, for the most part researchers have engaged in a study and debate of the costs and benefits to American youth of their working. Much of the literature has focused on whether working has detrimental effects on young people's engagement in school and academic outcomes, as well as youth's social and psychological development. While some studies have found a negative relationship between the number of hours worked during the school year and school attainment measures, David Stern and Derek Briggs's review of the literature concluded that students who work moderate hours perform better in school than students who work extensively or not at all.

In addition, some of the research is not able to fully sort out the direction of causality, for example, whether students with lower grade point averages tend to work more hours or whether working lowers the grades. Thus negative effects could be due to selection, that is, the possibility that students who are already not engaged in school choose to work more. In *The Ambitious Generation,* Barbara Schneider and David Stevenson report their findings that youth generally enjoy working more than they enjoy being in school.

There has been surprisingly little research examining why youth work, or why many work quite long hours. Youth employment has tended to be studied after the fact, rather than examining reasons or motivations leading to employment. That high school students have part-time jobs has come to be seen as the norm, likely due to the American cultural emphasis on occupation as a primary component of identity, and appreciation for work ethic and entrepreneurship. American youth do tend to start working earlier and work more than youth in other countries. And research has found that adults have quite positive retrospective views of their own early jobs, as well as favorable attitudes about their children's employment.

Some researchers speculate that the motivation for working is entirely financial, as it has been estimated that 54 percent of American youth receive no allowance, as reported by James R. Stone III and Jeylan T. Mortimer in 1998. Certainly American youth require money to participate in the automobile culture and buy the consumer goods that are significant parts of society. Hence, youth do tend to give the reason for working as "to buy things," according to Mortimer and colleagues in a report published in 1990. Teenagers from poor families in particular need to work so that they have money with which to participate in youth culture. Poor and immigrant

youth also tend to share their earnings with their families. And some teenagers work primarily to save money for college, which appears to have positive effects on several outcome measures such as the likelihood of attending college and educational aspirations.

There are other reasons for working aside from monetary gain. Researchers have found that some young people seem to have an internal drive towards working; they like to be occupied by productive activity. In 2000 Mihaly Csikszentmihalyi and Barbara Schneider reported that the young people they studied who spent the most time working perceived work more positively than young people who worked less, and saw work as important to themselves and to their future. Finally, the young fast-food workers in Harlem that Katherine S. Newman reported about in *No Shame in My Game: The Working Poor in the Inner City* needed income but also sought work in order to have a safe, structured place to go, away from the pressures of street violence.

In keeping with the idea that paid employment is the norm for American youth, researchers have examined why some youth do not work. It is well-established that work experience is more common among upper socioeconomic status and white teenagers. Most experts believe that this is due to a lack of employment opportunities for poorer youth, rather than less desire for work. According to Csikszentmihalyi and Schneider's *Becoming Adult: How Teenagers Prepare for the World of Work* (2000), upper class youth are more likely to work during the summer than during the school year, however, likely reflecting a concern about work interfering with studies. However, the minority youth in this study had a more positive view of work than the other young people.

Based on the types of jobs American youth tend to hold, it is unlikely that they are working in order to learn about possible adult career fields. Young people's first paid jobs tend to be informal (or "freelance jobs," as the U.S. Department of Labor refers to them), such as child care and lawn work. As youth progress into their mid-teens, the majority work in retail, which includes eating and drinking establishments such as fast-food restaurants. Even affluent teenagers tend to hold jobs, such as camp counseling and life guarding, that they are not likely to pursue as career fields. To remedy this situation, the 1990s saw a renewed emphasis on school-sponsored work-based learning, particularly through the 1994

School-to-Work Opportunities Act. Research on work opportunities offered through school has found that those positions tend to be in a wider range of industries and tend to more closely match students' career goals. Advocates hope that youth can gain more than money from their employment experiences.

See also: OUT-OF-SCHOOL INFLUENCES AND ACADEMIC SUCCESS; VOCATIONAL AND TECHNICAL EDUCATION.

BIBLIOGRAPHY

BROWN, BRETT. 2001. "Teens, Jobs, and Welfare: Implications for Social Policy." *Child Trends Research Brief.* Washington, DC: Child Trends.

CSIKSZENTMIHALYI, MIHALY, and SCHNEIDER, BARBARA. 2000. *Becoming Adult: How Teenagers Prepare for the World of Work.* New York: Basic Books.

ENTWISLE, DORIS R.; ALEXANDER, KARL L.; and OLSON, LINDA STEFFEL. 2000. "Early Work Histories of Urban Youth." *American Sociological Review* 65:279–297.

HERSHEY, ALAN M.; SILVERBERG, MARSHA K.; and HAIMSON, JOSHUA. 1999. *Expanding Options for Students: Report to Congress on the National Evaluation of School-to-Work Implementation.* Princeton, NJ: Mathematica Policy Research.

MARSH, HERBERT W. 1991. "Employment During High School: Character Building or a Subversion of Academic Goals?" *Sociology of Education* 64:172–189.

MORTIMER, JEYLAN T.; FINCH, MICHAEL D.; OWENS, TIMOTHY J.; and SHANAHAN, MICHAEL. 1990. "Gender and Work in Adolescence." *Youth and Society* 22(2):201–224.

MORTIMER, JEYLAN T.; HARLEY, CAROLYN; and ARONSON, PAMELA. 1999. "How Do Prior Experiences in the Workplace Set the Stage for Transitions to Adulthood?" In *Transitions to Adulthood in a Changing Economy—No Work, No Family, No Future?* ed. Alan Booth, Ann C. Crouter, and Michael J. Shanahan. Westport, CT: Praeger.

NEWMAN, KATHERINE S. 1999. *No Shame in My Game: The Working Poor in the Inner City.* New York: Alfred A. Knopf and the Russell Sage Foundation.

PERGAMIT, MICHAEL R. 1995. *Assessing School-to-Work Transitions in the United States. National Longitudinal Surveys Discussion Paper.* NLS 96–32. Washington, DC: U.S. Department of Labor, Bureau of Labor Statistics.

SCHNEIDER, BARBARA, and STEVENSON, DAVID. 1999. *The Ambitious Generation.* New Haven, CT: Yale University Press.

STERN, DAVID, and BRIGGS, DEREK. 2001. "Does Paid Employment Help or Hinder Performance in Secondary School? Insights from US High School Students." *Journal of Education and Work* 14(3):355–372.

STONE, JAMES R., III, and MORTIMER, JEYLAN T. 1998. "The Effect of Adolescent Employment on Vocational Development: Public and Educational Policy Implications." *Journal of Vocational Behavior* 53:184–214.

U.S. DEPARTMENT OF EDUCATION, NATIONAL CENTER FOR EDUCATION STATISTICS. 2000. *NAEP 1998 Civics: Report Card Highlights.* (NCES 2000–460). Washington, DC: U.S. Government Printing Office.

U.S. DEPARTMENT OF LABOR. 2000. *Report on the Youth Labor Force.* Washington, DC: U.S. Department of Labor.

KATHERINE L. HUGHES

ENGINEERING EDUCATION

As of 1997, 315 institutions housed 1,516 accredited engineering programs within the United States. To receive accreditation for their engineering programs, university departments comply with the standards established by the Accreditation Board of Engineering and Technology (ABET). ABET is an organization that consists of twenty-six professional engineering societies and six other affiliating professional organizations. The twenty-five accredited engineering specializations in the United States include the following: aerospace engineering, agricultural engineering, bio-engineering, ceramic engineering, chemical engineering, civil engineering, computer engineering, construction engineering, electrical engineering, engineering management, engineering mechanics, environmental engineering, geological engineering, industrial engineering, manufacturing engineering, materials engineering, mechanical engineering, metallurgical engineering, mining engineering, naval architecture and marine engineering, nuclear engineering, ocean engineering, petroleum engineering, survey engineering, and nontraditional programs.

Despite the existence of an accreditation board, however, not all engineering schools and engineering programs within the United States are accredited. Therefore, prospective students are responsible for investigating the accreditation status of the department to which they apply. Accredited degrees are especially significant for undergraduate students who wish to pursue advanced degrees in engineering.

In addition to investigating the accreditation status of their proposed schools, engineering students must decide where they will pursue their engineering degrees. Engineering programs within research universities target both undergraduate and graduate engineering scholars. These departments are usually large and sometimes have undergraduate classes that are taught by graduate students pursuing a degree in the department. Schools with a majority of students whose primary area of study is engineering are often called *institutes of technology*. State universities house departments that usually produce the greatest number of engineers in the country because of the increased affordability of an engineering education at these schools and because of the larger number of students who enroll in state universities.

Undergraduate Curricula

The curricula of undergraduate engineering programs may be completed within four years, although most engineering students take longer to complete their bachelor of science (B.S.) degree requirements. Typically, engineering students begin classes within their major during their sophomore year. By their junior year, students continue to fulfill their major's requirements with an increased emphasis on laboratory assignments. Within their senior year design courses, students are expected to use their cumulative knowledge of engineering, writing, and the humanities to solve a problem within their major area of study.

General undergraduate engineering requirements as established by ABET mandate that each student's curriculum includes mathematics, engineering topics, and humanities. Because the entering level of mathematics varies depending upon a stu-

dent's beginning knowledge of the subject, the amount of time required to complete mathematics requirements also varies. Once engineering students meet necessary mathematics prerequisites, they are required to complete differential and integral calculus, differential equations, and one or more upper-level mathematics classes successfully.

Students are also required to complete general engineering courses on topics such as mechanics, thermodynamics, electrical and engineering circuits, transport phenomena, and computer science. Students fulfill the third requirement, humanities, they complete classes in subjects such as literature, art, foreign languages, and social sciences.

In addition to the three requirements established by ABET, all engineering students must take core classes in physics and chemistry, as well as free and technical electives. Within the undergraduate engineering curriculum, electives may be classified as either free electives or technical electives. Free electives are classes that students can take in any department of the university if they meet prerequisites for that class. Technical electives are electives that are a part of a student's major course of study. In the process of fulfilling technical electives and major requirements, students might also fulfill minor area requirements and therefore obtain engineering knowledge across disciplines.

Graduate Curricula

Compared to the undergraduate engineering program, graduate study in engineering is more research intensive and flexible. In addition, the class requirements for graduate students are not as restrictive as the requirements for the undergraduate degree. Because of the variation of specialization in graduate engineering courses across the United States, defining a standard program of study for a particular discipline is difficult. By working closely with an adviser in their major, however, students may create a program of study with classes that not only interest them but also will prepare them to specialize in an area within their field of engineering.

Admission requirements to U.S. graduate engineering departments vary. Students are generally admitted to a program, however, if they have a "B" average in their undergraduate classes. Once admitted into a program, students typically fulfill course requirements within one to two years, depending upon any deficiencies that a student might have prior to beginning a program of study.

Upon completion of a graduate engineering program, students may obtain one of two types of master's degrees within their discipline, the master of science (M.S.) or the master of engineering (M.Eng.). The master of science degree requires the writing of a thesis, whereas the master of engineering degree requires the completion of course work. Two types of degrees also exist for doctoral students of engineering, the doctor of philosophy (Ph.D.) and the doctor of science (Sc.D.). The doctor of philosophy degree is more research oriented than the doctor of science degree and obtaining it requires a student to write and defend a dissertation successfully. A student can typically complete an engineering doctorate two to four years after the completion of the master's degree.

Traditional Degree Areas

The five largest and most traditional areas of engineering study in United States colleges and universities are chemical, civil, electrical, industrial, and mechanical engineering. Within the United States, approximately 260 departments award these five degrees. Over the years, twenty-five specializations have emerged from the basic fields, and in 2001, eighty-five subdivisions of these fields existed in colleges across the United States. Following are descriptions of the five major types of engineering degrees.

Chemical engineering is a field of engineering that combines the knowledge of chemistry and engineering. Unlike chemists, however, chemical engineers develop new materials and design processes for manufacturing. In an effort to design these processes, chemical engineers must stay abreast of technological advancement in society. Specific curricula requirements for undergraduate chemical engineering students include engineering science, engineering design, communications, and basic life sciences. In addition to general engineering requirements, chemical engineering students are expected to earn course credit for classes in materials science and material and energy balances. Engineering design courses include engineering economics, design of chemical reactors, heating and cooling apparatus, and piping. In addition, chemical engineering students are required to understand computer programming languages and complete a technical writing class.

Civil engineers utilize their knowledge of structural processes in a variety of ways. They often oversee the development of facilities such as buildings and bridges, in addition to the construction of highways, water resource facilities, and environmental projects. Specific course requirements for civil engineering undergraduates include classes in engineering and scientific programming, soil mechanics, engineering geology, strength of materials, analysis of determinate and indeterminate structures, hydraulics, highway geometrics, and surveying. A sample topic within a civil engineering design course might include an investigation of the design of steel and concrete structures.

Electrical engineers design and develop various types of electrical processes. Examples of their contributions include computer chips and systems, radio and television equipment, and power generation and control systems. Specific courses for electrical engineering students include classes in logic, set theory, algorithms, probability and statistics, numerical methods and analysis, and operating systems. Subdivisions of electrical engineering include power generation, control systems, communications, or electronics.

Industrial engineers contribute to the successful integration of processes and people. They look at the broad picture of engineering in an effort to maximize the benefits of a system. Additional courses for industrial engineering students include engineering economics, organizational development, computer simulation, statistical quality control, human factors engineering, and system evaluation. Other suggested classes include biology and psychology. Finally, mechanical engineers examine how mechanical work and various types of energy combine in an effort to design materials and processes for use. In addition to core engineering classes, mechanical engineers may complete several courses in electrical and materials engineering.

Other Engineering Specializations

In addition to the traditional engineering fields, there are several branches of engineering and areas of specialization. Aerospace engineering is the study of aspects of aeronautics and space. Aerospace engineers may select from several divisions of study within their field. They are encouraged, however, to also obtain knowledge about mass transportation, environmental pollution, and medical science within their curricula.

Agricultural engineering is a field of engineering that is most closely related to the environment. Agricultural engineers are concerned about the conservation of natural resources and are required to build new tools that will aid the production and distribution of food and fibers.

Biomedical engineering applies the principles of anatomy and engineering to biological systems. With their knowledge of these systems, biomedical engineers may assist the health care industry through the design and maintenance of medical systems and equipment. In addition, biomedical engineering students often use their engineering training as a foundation for medical school.

Computer engineering mandates that students become knowledgeable in the areas of computer information systems, computer science, computer hardware, and information science. In many schools, computer and electrical engineering is a dual specialization. Next, environmental engineering improves the quality of life through the preservation of the environment. Environmental engineers are interested in reducing pollution, encouraging hygiene, and reducing waste and toxins found in air and water.

Nuclear engineering closely resembles the science of physics, because nuclear engineers study matter, including protons, neutrons, and electrons. They primarily investigate the nature of inanimate objects. Metallurgical engineers study metals and investigate ways to improve the characteristics of metal for society's use. Three areas of specialization within this field include process metallurgy, physical metallurgy, and materials science.

BIBLIOGRAPHY

American Society for Engineering Education. 1992. *Directory of Engineering and Engineering Technology: Undergraduate Programs,* 3rd edition. Piscataway, NJ: American Society for Engineering Education.

Basta, Nicholas. 1996. *Opportunities in Engineering Careers.* Lincolnwood, IL: VGM Career Horizons.

Garner, Geraldine O. 1993. *Careers in Engineering.* Lincolnwood, IL: VGM Career Horizons.

Irwin, J. David. 1997. *On Becoming an Engineer: A Guide to Career Paths.* New York: Institute of Electrical and Electronics Engineers Press.

Monica Farmer Cox

ENGLISH AS A SECOND LANGUAGE

See: Bilingualism, Second Language Learning, and English as a Second Language; Language Minority Students.

ENGLISH EDUCATION

TEACHING OF
  Stephen Tchudi
PREPARATION OF TEACHERS
  Pamela L. Grossman

TEACHING OF

The teaching of the English language has a long history in U.S. education; the practice of teaching a native language can be traced to antiquity. In the Greek and Roman worlds, literacy was encouraged both to foster citizen participation in a democracy as advocated by Plato, Quintilian, and Cicero; much later it was fostered by the emergence of print and print cultures in western Europe.

The History of English in the Schools

In the American colonies, education in literacy was the essence of education, along with arithmetic. Literacy education followed patterns of instruction that could also trace their ancestry to Greek and Roman education, transmitted to the colonies via Great Britain. The tradition in early literacy instruction was one of formalism, which posits that knowledge of the forms of language (as identified in such studies as grammar, logic, rhetoric, and orthography) enables a learner to read and write successfully. Thus such seminal books as the *New England Primer* (1775) concentrated heavily on the basic elements of English: the alphabet, then words of one, two, and more syllables—a pattern of small to large language particles to whole meaning.

In a seminal book written in the late 1960s, *Growth Through English,* John Dixon described this formalist approach as characteristic of the first phase in the development of literacy: an era of basic skills. A second stage is one of enculturation, where the mastery of basic skills opens up a canon of "great books" to young learners. A third stage, Dixon asserted, is concerned with personal growth, where knowledge of culture through literacy allows the learner to move freely and flexibly through the full range of language to enhance his or her personal life, philosophy, and aesthetic.

In the United States, Dixon's first two stages can clearly be seen in the nineteenth century, when first grammar, then composition and literature, became standard features in the emerging curricula of the American elementary schools and, in particular, of that dramatic experiment in democracy: the free public high school. By the end of the nineteenth century, the tripod curriculum of language, literature, and composition was established, taught primarily from a formalist perspective.

In the 1960s and 1970s a shift of perspective away from basic skills and enculturation prompted educators to declare that a paradigm shift of major proportions was taking place, matching trends in American education away from formalism toward student- and child-centered education. Proclamation of this paradigm shift may have been premature, for in fact, English education has been and continues to be subject to contrary and contradictory influences and philosophies.

The alleged paradigm shift was toward a contrary (or possibly contradictory) curriculum that can be called *naturalistic* or *experiential*. Its roots can be found in the European philosophies of such educators as Johann Amos Comenius and Jean-Jacques Rousseau, both of whom argued for engagement in learning practices as opposed to rote study. The experiential movement can also be labeled romantic, traceable to the humanistic and naturalistic philosophies of such writers as William Wordsworth and Samuel Taylor Coleridge. In the United States, John Dewey's Progressive education movement translated the experiential strand of educational thought into curriculum designs, reflected most prominently in two publications of the National Council of Teachers of English in the 1930s: one outlining the essentials of an "experience curriculum in English," the other advocating a "correlated curriculum," with language activities infused throughout the school curriculum in all disciplines.

Yet the formalist tradition persisted, setting the stage for conflict in the final quarter of the twentieth century between formalist and experiential schools of thought. For the general public and the legislators who represent them, the formalist strategy—teach the basics and move on to larger activities—makes common sense. Among English language arts educa-

tors, according to Rodger D. Sell, those favoring a formalist approach have become increasingly sophisticated in their understanding of language structures, arguing for teaching multiple discourse forms and an increasingly broad and inclusive literary canon.

Those from the experiential camp, such as Kenneth Goodman and Frank Smith, on the other hand, have developed philosophies of whole language—hotly contested in both convention halls and legislative chambers. The experiential school argues Dewey's theme that the formal structures of language are mastered, not by study of forms, but through engagement with a wide range of "real world" or purposeful discourse.

Consensus: The National Standards

In the 1990s concern about the quality of American education became centered—in English language arts as in other fields—on a quest for national standards in the subject fields. The concept of *standards* appears to be formalist; that is, it posits that by identifying discrete "learnings" that are to be required of all students, one can systematize curriculum and improve scores on standardized tests of literacy. The tests themselves tend to measure formalist rather than experiential "knowledges" and skills. Thus there has often been ideological conflict between, on the one hand, parents and legislators who favor a standards and testing approach, and, on the other, English teachers, who are moving toward an experiential curriculum.

The task of creating national standards in English fell to the National Council of Teachers of English and the International Reading Association, whose members and their representatives agonized over the challenge of defining and describing what young people ought to be able to know and do with language. The resulting document, *Standards for the English Language Arts,* described a consensus view of what the English studies can, could, and should be. The fourteen standards outlined for K–12 classrooms emphasize growth and development of language use for personal, social, academic, and vocational purposes. The standards present a series of illustrative vignettes showing students who are engaged in extending the range of literature they read; developing increasing competence in a broadening range of forms and genres in speaking and writing; reading and writing for personal and aesthetic pleasure as well as public competence; and increasing their skill at using language within the purposeful settings. Perhaps disappointing to the public and legislators, the national standards did not spell out basic skills and knowledges in grammar, spelling, and the like; nor did they suggest a canon of books that all children should read. In short, the standards tended toward the Progressive/experiential model, while making a genuine effort to accommodate the interests and traditions of formalism. The authors of the standards note very clearly that theirs is a work in progress and that it would indeed be naive to suppose that any group of specialists can define and describe the parameters of language study for the unforeseeable future.

Current Issues in the English Language Arts

The national standards in the English language arts thus provide a platform for the development of curricula in the twenty-first century. Clearly, the coming years will produce new demands on literate people and call for new forms of literacy; in addition, research in human learning can be expected to increase educators' understanding of language acquisition and thus how to establish increasingly successful venues for offering language instruction. Ongoing issues, problems, concerns, and debates over the English language arts include the following topics.

Basic skills, testing, and accountability. The standards movement has been part of an ongoing call for accountability for English language arts teachers (and teachers in all fields). The general public wants concrete evidence that teachers are teaching well and that students are learning. In turn, this pressure has led to increased testing in all fields and disciplines, but in no field more than English, where students experience local or state progress testing virtually every year, standardized testing on nationally normed tests at regular intervals, state or district proficiency examinations for high school diplomas, and national measures such as the National Assessment of Educational Progress. Given pressures for students to perform well on these tests, teachers in the schools find themselves increasingly focusing the curriculum on test preparation or, more broadly, on teaching the kinds of formalist knowledge that is most frequently encountered on those tests.

Literacy and society. Beyond the immediate concerns of test scores, there remains considerable debate over the fundamental aims of literacy education. The English teaching profession is in general agreement with the notion that literacy instruction needs to go beyond the demands for practical skills and must include Dixon's category of language for personal and aesthetic growth. This is not to say that English teachers are committed to an elitist view of "art for art's sake" or falsely elevated notions of "taste" and "culture." Rather, from the experiential philosophy of language education, teachers generally believe that broad language education—teaching students to speak, read, and write articulately on a range of issues and problems—not only encompasses, but moves beyond simple mastery of basic English. The work of Paulo Freire has been especially influential in encouraging educators to consider the social and political implications of what they teach, exploring the possibility that narrow training in literacy fosters citizen subservience, while general literacy arguably leads to independent thinking.

However, such issues are also linked more broadly to issues and trends in education, specifically, the role that the general public perceives for the schools. In the last quarter of the twentieth century, an increasingly global economy and greater demands on the American economic system increased pressures on the schools to be a direct part of the economic engine. The accountability and testing movements, for example, are often linked to the goal of keeping the United States competitive in world markets. Although few would disagree with that expression of need, opinions differ dramatically in how it can be met. Some would have the schools focus primarily on job literacy (in both the immediate and long-range senses), which implies an English curriculum more like that advocated by the formalists. Others insist that schools must resist the push to become employment oriented and should return to the concept of general or liberal education, creating well-educated individuals who are equipped to adapt to changing conditions. Contemporary English theory and research lean in the direction of general/liberal education, but the outcome of this debate is more likely to be determined in the legislatures.

Multiple types of English. If there is a single unifying trend in English education, it is that what has been labeled *the English language arts* is becoming increasingly broad through what can be called *the multiple English curriculum,* including the following.

Multidisciplinary English. In the 1970s through the end of the twentieth century, parallel movements for writing across the curriculum and reading in the content areas moved English language arts outside the immediate confines of the language classroom. English educators proposed that reading and writing skills could not be expected to be developed if they are limited to practice inside the English classroom. Moreover, they claimed that by attending to language, teachers in other disciplines would find student learning improved; that is, by attending to the language skills and needs of their own disciplines, educators would find students improving in their understanding of the processes of inquiry and expression and thus of the discipline itself. These movements toward multidisciplinary English in every classroom have found limited success. Although the concept receives widespread general support, many disciplinary teachers do not feel they have the training to deal with language problems, especially with curricula that are already crowded with concepts, national standards, and parental expectations.

Multicultural English. Due in no small measure to the activism of minority and feminist groups, English language arts teachers have greatly broadened the cultural content of their field. Courses in literature by and about minorities and by about women have led to a realization that the traditional English canon of English and American literature, much of it written by white males, is both culturally biased and intellectually limited. Originally isolated in their own courses or units, these multicultural literatures are increasingly being found throughout the curriculum, and they include not only literatures written by people whose first language is not English, but also world literature translated into English. Like every other trend in English, this one is not without its detractors, particularly those who argue that cultural literacy begins at home, and that the canon of Anglo literatures, not world "Englishes," should be the substance of the curriculum.

Multilingual English. Immediately linked to multicultural teaching are questions concerning the use of multiple languages, both languages other than English (e.g., Spanish), and dialects other than standard English (e.g., African-American English). Much theory and research has argued for teaching methodologies based on the concept of bilingualism: that students should be provided with opportunities to develop and learn in their native language as they receive instruction in English. The counterposition to bilingualism argues for quick introduction into the structures of the target language and mainstreaming of bilingual students into classes where English is used exclusively. The latter position also reflects strong public interest in "English Only," a concept that would legislate English as the official national (or adopted state) language. Opponents of that movement note that the United States is rapidly becoming a bilingual country, that the evolution of language is natural, and that one cannot either limit or prescribe peoples' mastery of language.

Analogous arguments are offered in favor and in opposition to insistence on a single dialect of standard English instead of recognizing that all speakers operate in the a range of dialects. Particularly controversial was a decision in the Oakland, California, schools to include the understanding of "Ebonics," a dialect of African-American English, as a curriculum goal for both teachers and students.

Multigenre and multimedia English. Whether one supports the concept of English as practical in orientation—preparing students for the immediate demands of society, the workplace, and school—or more general and liberal in application, research and practice are responding to the rapidly broadening array of discourse forms and technologies. Computer literacy has been widely adopted as an aim of school curricula, with mastery of basic computer skills seen as necessary for any graduate of public education. For the English teacher, such literacy moves beyond the mechanical operation of machinery. In the twenty-first century, English/computer literacy will also include the critical analysis and evaluation of language and information sources as well as the ability to compose and create in new media forms. Thus as an extension of print literacy, many English classes now commonly include language experiences involving e-mail, chat and discussion groups, the Internet, presentation software, and even video and audio production. It is clear that the traditional English classroom centered on books, pencils, and papers will evolve considerably in the coming years.

Reflective Practice, Teacher Preparation, and In-Service Reeducation

Even as the public and legislators have expressed reservations about the performance of students in the English language, the English profession has made great strides in elaborating and rationalizing English programs. Considerable research in English education conducted since the early 1990s has led to widespread discussion of the research-based curriculum, where teachers operate from known principles of rhetoric, linguistics, psychology, and literary criticism rather than from teacher lore and tradition. Equally important is the concept of *reflective practice,* where teachers consciously articulate the reasons for their instruction and seek ways of assessing whether or not it is succeeding.

Particularly notable in English is the growth of portfolio assessment as an alternative to standardized testing, where students prepare collections of materials that demonstrate their best work and their competencies, engage in self-analysis, and discuss with teachers and community members the success of the work.

Also noteworthy is the great success of the National Writing Project (NWP) in promoting growth in English curricula through the sharing of practices among teachers. Founded in the 1970s in response to the "back to basics" crisis, the NWP has branches in every state and in several other countries. Its methodology features the sharing of best practices by teachers, reading and discussion of theory and research, and systematic in-service education.

The NWP is part of a broader movement toward teacher empowerment, which argues that curriculum decisions are best made by teachers themselves. This movement is understandably in opposition to other approaches, most notably the widespread belief that legislation, standards, accountability, and even "teacher-proof" materials can lead to educational reform. By contrast, some professionals, such as Denny T. Wolfe and Joe Antinarella, present the case that English language arts teachers themselves can and should be leaders in educational reform.

See also: CURRICULUM, SCHOOL; ENGLISH EDUCATION, *subentry on* PREPARATION OF TEACHERS; NATIONAL COUNCIL OF TEACHERS OF ENGLISH; SECONDARY EDUCATION, *subentries on* CURRENT TRENDS, HISTORY OF.

BIBLIOGRAPHY

APPLEBEE, ARTHUR. 1974. *Tradition and Reform in Teaching English.* Urbana, IL: National Council of Teachers of English.

BLOOM, ALAN. 1988. *The Closing of the American Mind.* New York: Simon and Schuster.

COMENIUS, JOHANN AMOS. 1969. *A Reformation of Schooles* (1642), trans. Samuel Hartlib. Menston, Yorkshire, Eng.: Menston.

COURTS, PATRICK. 1997. *Multicultural Literacies: Dialect, Discourse, and Diversity.* New York: Lang.

DAVISON, JOHN, and MOSS, JOHN, eds. 2000. *Issues in English Teaching.* London and New York: Routledge.

DEWEY, JOHN. 1900. *The School and Society.* Chicago: University of Chicago Press.

DIXON, JOHN. 1967. *Growth Through English,* 1st edition. Urbana, IL: National Council of Teachers of English.

GARAY, MARY SUE, and BERNHARDT, STEPHEN, A., eds. 1998. *Expanding Literacies: English and the New Workplace.* Albany: State University of New York Press.

GELB, IGNACE J. 1963. *A Study of Writing.* Chicago: University of Chicago Press.

GLYER, DIANA, and WEEKS, DAVID L., eds. 1998. *The Liberal Arts in Higher Education.* Lanham, MD: University Press of America.

GOODMAN, KENNETH. 1996. *On Reading.* Portsmouth, NH; Heinemann.

HAMILTON, EDITH, and CARIUS, HUNTINGTON, eds. 1961. *Plato: The Collected Dialogues.* Princeton, NJ: Princeton University Press.

HIRSCH, E. D. 1999. *The Schools We Need and Why We Don't Have Them.* New York: Anchor/Doubleday.

MURPHY, JAMES, ed. 1987. *Quintillian as the Teacher of Speaking and Writing.* Carbondale: Southern Illinois University Press.

NATIONAL COUNCIL OF TEACHERS OF ENGLISH. 1935. *An Experience Curriculum in English.* New York: Appleton-Century.

NATIONAL COUNCIL OF TEACHERS OF ENGLISH. 1936. *A Correlated Curriculum.* New York: Appleton-Century.

NATIONAL COUNCIL OF TEACHERS OF ENGLISH and the INTERNATIONAL READING ASSOCIATION. 1996. *Standards for the English Language Arts.* Urbana, IL and Newark, DE: National Council of Teachers of English and the International Reading Association.

ONG, WALTER J. 1982. *Orality and Literacy.* New York: Methuen.

PIAGET, JEAN. 1969. *The Child's Conception of the World* (1926), trans. Joan Tomlinson and Andrew Tomlinson. Totowa, NJ: Littlefield, Adams.

RAJU, NAMBURY S., et al., eds. 2000. *Grading the Nation's Report Card: Research from the Evaluation of NAEP.* Washington, DC: National Academy Press.

ROBERTS, PETER. 2000. *Education, Literacy, and Humanization: Exploring the Work of Paulo Freire.* Westport, CT: Bergin and Garvey.

SELL, ROGER D. 2000. *Literature as Communication.* Philadelphia: Benjamin.

SMITH, FRANK. *Reading Without Nonsense.* New York: Teachers College Press.

WALDO, MARK. 1993. "Wordsworth's 'Preface to the Lyrical Ballads' as Preface to Romantic Rhetoric." *Halcyon* 15(spring):199–211.

WARSCHAUER, MARK. 1999. *Electronic Literacies: Language, Culture, and Power in Online Education.* Mahwah, NJ: Erlbaum.

WOLFE, DENNY T., and ANTINARELLA, JOE. 1997. *Deciding to Lead: The English Teacher as Reformer.* Portsmouth, NH: Boynton/Cook.

STEPHEN TCHUDI

PREPARATION OF TEACHERS

The field of English education includes research and practice related to both the teaching and learning of English/language arts and the preparation of English teachers. As befits a broad and comprehensive subject matter, the field of English education includes a wide range of topics and lines of research. Under the umbrella of English education, one might find research on rhetoric and the teaching of writing, on the literature curriculum and different approaches to the teaching of literature, as well as a range of topics related to communication, visual literacy, drama, journalism, and language more broadly. In fact, one of the persistent challenges facing the field of English has been the difficulty of self-definition, as Peter Elbow (1990) plaintively inquires in the title of his book, *What is English?* Others have asked, equally plaintively, what important topics might not be considered the province of English teachers. This lack of self-definition leads to what Robert Protherough termed "a pervasive uncertainty about the nature of the discipline" (p. 1).

The sheer scope of the subject matter and its blurry definition have its roots in the history of the subject matter. In a definitive history of the field, Arthur Applebee demonstrated the various ways in which the subject has been defined over time, from its first emergence as a major school subject in the 1890s. While earlier battles focused more on the relative centrality of classical versus vernacular texts, more recent skirmishes have tackled the role of literature—and the type of literature—in the English classroom. One of the enduring themes in the history of English education has been the search for a way to unify the subject.

In addition to breadth and lack of clear definition, English education is characterized by a multiplicity of theoretical perspectives regarding the subject. Different versions of English to be found in classrooms might include a basic skills approach, an approach that privileges cultural heritage, a personal growth approach, an apprenticeship into the discipline, and an approach that advocates critical or transformative literacy. Each of these versions implies a different set of assumptions regarding the goals for teaching English, posits a different curriculum, and advocates distinctive approaches to teaching.

Preparation of English Teachers

These features of the subject matter pose challenges to the preparation of English teachers. The sheer breadth of the subject raises questions about how to assure that prospective teachers develop a deep understanding of the field. The existence of multiple, and often competing, versions of English suggests that pre-service teachers will encounter quite different practices during their own experiences in schools. Finally, the inherent complexity of the subject, with its separate domains and subcomponents, offers teachers greater autonomy in developing curriculum. For beginning teachers, however, such autonomy can be daunting as they struggle to decide what exactly to teach.

One critical question concerning the preparation of English teachers has to do with how well prepared they are within the subject matter itself. According to a national survey conducted by Applebee in the early 1990s, approximately 95 percent of English teachers received degrees in English or a related major. However, Richard Ingersoll's 1998 study of out-of-field teaching found that nearly one-fourth of teachers who teach English have neither a major nor a minor in English or related fields. While a major in English does not guarantee the depth of subject matter knowledge required for teaching, the fact that people without English majors are teaching the subject is certainly cause for concern.

English teachers in the United States receive their professional preparation in a wide variety of programs, from undergraduate programs lasting four or five years, to fifth-year programs in which teachers have one year of professional preparation following completion of an undergraduate degree, to alternative route programs. In the early twenty-first century, research has only begun to chart how differences among programs affect the quality of teacher preparation. Michael Andrew's 1990 study, for example, found that graduates of five-year programs reported greater satisfaction with both their teacher preparation and chosen career and were more likely to remain in teaching than graduates of four-year programs. However, much more work needs to explore how structural differences among preparation programs affect the quality of their graduates.

Relatively few studies have looked systematically at teacher education within the field of English. Studies on the preparation of English teachers have focused primarily on teachers' knowledge and beliefs about the subject matter, and on how teachers develop their understandings of how to teach English. A growing body of research suggests that what English teachers know and believe about literature influences both their curricular and instructional choices. How teachers choose to teach a literary text reflects their own understanding of literature and its interpretation. Similarly, teachers' knowledge of the complexity of the writing process affects their approaches to the teaching of writing. The teaching of writing requires knowledge of how the demands of writing vary depending upon the nature of the task, audience, and genre, among other factors. Lack of this knowledge among teachers may help explain why writing instruction too often reduces the writing process to a lock-step series of discrete stages.

Another body of research has focused on the development of pedagogical content knowledge—the knowledge of how to teach English to a wide range of students. A number of studies have looked at how teachers transform their knowledge of the subject, per se, to knowledge of how to teach the subject to diverse learners. In looking at this transformation, a number of studies have focused on the importance of subject-specific methods courses. This line of research suggests that prospective teachers begin the task of rethinking their subject matter from a pedagogical perspective within the context of English methods courses. Such courses often require prospective teachers to confront their implicit assumptions about the subject matter, through assignments such as literacy autobiographies or the examination

of personal metaphors for teaching. Methods courses also provide opportunities to learn more about how students learn to read and write, and some of the predictable struggles they may face. The potential of methods classes to shape prospective teachers' classroom practice is mediated by their experiences in actual classrooms. When they do not have opportunities to observe or try out the practices they are studying in methods classes, they may begin to doubt their feasibility.

Learning to teach English takes longer than the brief period allotted for teacher education. Research conducted by Pamela Grossman and colleagues in 2001 suggests that new teachers are still in the process of learning to teach when they enter the classroom. Given the importance of the first few years of teaching, many districts provide support to beginning teachers through mentoring programs. This also suggests the need for more longitudinal studies of learning to teach, that span teacher education and the first few years of teaching.

Professional Development

Perhaps the best-known professional development opportunities for English teachers are the workshops offered by the National Writing Project (NWP) and its affiliates. The NWP is a national network that began in 1974 at the University of California, Berkeley. Its goal is the improvement of the teaching of writing and the quality of student writing. The NWP has served more than 2 million teachers, across all grades and subjects, since it first came into existence. Some of the basic tenets of the NWP model include the need for writing teachers to become writers themselves; the importance of teacher knowledge and expertise in the teaching of writing; and the value of teachers teaching other teachers. Although relatively little systematic research has investigated the influence of teachers' participation in NWP activities on classroom practice, teachers are generally enthusiastic about their experiences and value the sense of community and professionalism engendered by the writing project activities.

No equivalent large-scale professional development model exists for the teaching of literature or language. The closest equivalents are teachers' book clubs, in which teachers read literature, including memoirs, fiction, and other genres, as way of learning both about their students or about literature and how to teach it. However, these are primarily local innovations. Other models that exist are summer institutes for teachers, run by organizations such as the National Endowment for the Humanities and the Bread Loaf School of English, in which teachers have the opportunity to learn more about the subject matter.

The most common form of professional development for English teachers, however, continues to be the district in-service day. By their very structure, in-service days are generally dedicated to technical issues important to the district, such as learning new assessment schemes, writing objectives for student learning, or implementing a new curriculum or textbook series. Because district in-service programs are designed to appeal to a broad spectrum of teachers, they are generally unlikely to address subject-specific concerns.

If English teachers are to benefit from the growing body of knowledge about effective professional development, those responsible for teacher learning will need to invest more strategically in school-based structures that support ongoing teacher learning, collegial interaction, and experimentation. Critiques of the NWP have suggested that without strong support at the school site and without opportunities to get ongoing help in developing new practices, teachers find it difficult to implement the ideas they encountered in summer workshops. Another body of work suggests that departments may be the locus for professional community and provide the impetus and opportunity for continued learning.

Conclusion

English continues to be a contested field of study. Although recent debates have focused on what literature should be taught in schools, others have questioned whether literature should even continue to occupy the center of the subject. The range of literacy required of students, from print literacy to visual and technological literacy, has again expanded the scope of the English curriculum. Such expansions to the curriculum inevitably pose challenges for the education of teachers, as both teacher education and professional development must prepare teachers to incorporate new content and skills into their teaching. Given the features of the subject matter that make such redefinitions inevitable, prospective English teachers will need opportunities to grapple with the multiple purposes envisioned for the teaching of English and to explore ways of bringing coherence to students' experiences in English classes.

See also: LANGUAGE ARTS, TEACHING OF; MENTORING; TEACHER EDUCATION.

BIBLIOGRAPHY

ANDREW, MICHAEL D. 1990. "Differences between Graduates of Four-Year and Five-Year Teacher Preparation Programs." *Journal of Teacher Education* 41:45–51.

APPLEBEE, ARTHUR N. 1974. *Tradition and Reform in the Teaching of English: A History.* Urbana, IL: National Council of Teachers of English.

APPLEBEE, ARTHUR N. 1986. "Problems in Process Approaches: Toward a Reconceptualization of Process Instruction." In *The Teaching of Writing. Eighty-Fifth Yearbook of the National Society for the Study of Education,* ed. Anthony Petrosky and David Bartholomae. Chicago: University of Chicago Press.

APPLEBEE, ARTHUR N. 1993. *Literature in the Secondary School: Studies of Curriculum and Instruction in the United States.* NCTE Research Report 25. Urbana, IL: National Council of Teachers of English.

BARNES, DOUGLAS; BARNES, DOROTHY; and CLARKE, STEPHEN. 1984. *Versions of English.* London: Heinemann.

CLIFT, RENEE. 1991. "Learning to Teach English-Maybe: A Study of Knowledge Development." *Journal of Teacher Education* 42:357–372.

DIXON, JOHN. 1969. *Growth through English.* Oxford: Oxford University Press.

ELBOW, PETER. 1990. *What is English?* Urbana, IL: National Council of Teachers of English.

FLORIO-RUANE, SUSAN. 1994. "The Future Teachers' Autobiography Club: Preparing Educators to Support Literacy Learning in Culturally Diverse Classrooms." *English Education* 26:52–66.

GOMEZ, MARY LOUISE. 1990. "The National Writing Project: Staff Development in the Teaching of Composition." In *On Literacy and its Teaching,* ed. Gail E. Hawisher and Anna O. Soter. Albany: State University of New York Press.

GRAFF, GERALD. 1992. *Beyond the Culture Wars.* New York: Norton.

GROSSMAN, PAMELA L. 1990. *The Making of a Teacher.* New York: Teachers College Press.

GROSSMAN, PAMELA L., et al. 2000. "Transitions into Teaching: Learning to Teach Writing in Teacher Education and Beyond." *Journal of Literacy Research* 32:631–662.

GROSSMAN, PAMELA L. 2001. "Research on the Teaching of Literature: Finding a Place." In *Handbook of Research on Teaching,* 4th edition, ed. Virginia Richardson. New York: Macmillan.

GROSSMAN, PAMELA L.; VALENCIA, SHEILA W.; and HAMEL, FREDERICK. 1997. "Preparing Language Arts Teachers in a Time of Reform." In *Handbook of Research on Teaching Literacy through the Communicative and Visual Arts,* ed. James Flood, Shirley Brice Heath, and Diane Lapp. New York: Macmillan.

GROSSMAN, PAMELA L.; WINEBURG, SAM; and WOOLWORTH, STEPHEN. 2001. "Toward a Theory of Teacher Community." *Teachers College Record* 103:942–1012.

INGERSOLL, RICHARD. 1998. "The Problem of Out-of-Field Teaching." *Phi Delta Kappan* 79:773–776.

MILLER, BARBARA; LORD, BRIAN; and DORNEY, JUDITH. 1994. *Staff Development for Teachers: A Study of Configurations and Costs in Four Districts.* Newton, MA: Educational Development Center.

PROTHEROUGH, ROBERT. 1989. *Students of English.* London: Routledge.

RITCHIE, JOY, and WILSON, DAVID. 1993. "Dual Apprenticeships: Subverting and Supporting Critical Teaching." *English Education* 25:67–83.

SCHOLES, ROBERT. 1998. *The Rise and Fall of English.* New Haven, CT: Yale University Press.

WILLINSKY, JOHN. 1991. *The Triumph of Literature/ The Fate of Literacy: English in the Secondary School Curriculum.* New York: Teachers College Press.

INTERNET RESOURCE

NATIONAL WRITING PROJECT. 2002. <http:// writingproject.org>.

PAMELA L. GROSSMAN

ENROLLMENT MANAGEMENT IN HIGHER EDUCATION

During the last decades of the twentieth century, the concept of enrollment management emerged as a new organizational structure within two- and four-year colleges and universities. The term *enrollment management* refers to the ability of institutions of higher education to exert more systematic influence over the number and characteristics of new students, as well as influence the persistence of students to continue their enrollment from the time of their matriculation to their graduation. The emergence of enrollment management as a new administrative structure within institutions of higher education originated in North America, but it has also been employed in Europe, Africa, and Asia.

This phenomenon can be explained by shifting public-policy priorities in many countries that are the result governments reducing their subsidies for institutions of higher education, and for students earning a postsecondary degree. Increasingly, attending college is being viewed primarily as a private benefit to individuals rather than as a public benefit to society. Colleges and universities are being asked to fund more of their own budgets through tuition revenues, and students are borrowing increasing amounts of money to pay the rising costs of higher education. As a result of these trends, more and more students have come to view postsecondary education as a consumptive decision, and the increased competition for (and reliance upon) student dollars has caused governmental agencies, university governing boards, and university administrators to pay considerable attention to developing more effective student enrollment strategies.

Defining Enrollment Management

Don Hossler, John P. Bean, and colleagues defined *enrollment management* as "an organizational concept and a systematic set of activities designed to enable educational institutions to exert more influence over their student enrollments. Organized by strategic planning and supported by institutional research, enrollment management activities concern student college choice, transition to college, student attrition and retention, and student outcomes. These processes are studied to guide institutional practices in the areas of new student recruitment and financial aid, student support services, curriculum development, and other academic areas that affect enrollments, student persistence, and student outcomes from college" (p. 5). Enrollment management is an open-systems and synergistic organizational approach that fosters an organizational atmosphere that makes reporting relationships among student-service units more transparent. It also fosters an environment where offices and divisions work collaboratively to enhance the quality of the student experience, thus facilitating the strategic management of enrollments.

Enrollment management can be viewed as a synergistic organizational concept that can be used to link several administrative functions within a college or university in order to optimize institutional enrollment goals. Examples of this approach can be found among the financial strategies of many college campuses, where important linkages have emerged between senior enrollment managers and chief financial administrators. Both private and public colleges use some of their tuition income to fund campus-based scholarships for students. Tuition revenue accounts for millions of dollars, and campus-based financial aid has become a large expenditure at most four-year institutions. Enrollment management efforts have therefore become closely linked to budgeting and campus financial planning. Successful enrollment management strategies and practices must also take into account the growing importance of college and university rankings. For many institutions of higher education, enrollment management has come to involve a combination of student enrollment strategy, budgeting strategy, and institutional positioning strategy.

Key Offices and Tasks in Enrollment Management

A university's office of institutional research should play a major role in successful enrollment management efforts. The more enrollment management professionals know about the characteristics, attitudes, and values of prospective students, the better able they are to design effective recruitment and orientation programs. Persistence studies conducted by institutional researchers can inform strategies to enhance the success of first-year students, and institutional research professionals can examine the impact of various forms of student financial assistance upon matriculation decisions and the academic success. A strong institutional function is a critical element of a sound enrollment management effort.

The office of admissions plays a key role in enrollment management efforts. The first order of business for enrollment managers is to ensure that their university has broad marketing efforts in place to make the institution visible and sufficiently attractive, so that desirable prospective students are motivated to seriously consider them. These marketing efforts should be segmented to appeal to differ-

ent types of students, emphasizing different strengths of the institution. Once prospective students have expressed interest, campuses need to provide the right information at the right time in order to be perceived as a good match, and thereby attract applications.

The office of financial aid has a dual purpose. The first purpose is that of providing federal, state, and campus-based need-based financial aid to enable students to attend the institution of their choice. The second purpose is the growing use of campus-based financial aid to reward academic merit and other special talents to enable colleges and universities to attract a desired number of students with the academic ability and other special talents they are seeking. Historically, institutions of higher education relied primarily upon endowed gifts to fund campus-based scholarships. Toward the close of the twentieth century, however, more and more institutions began using part of the tuition students pay to fund scholarships. This practice is often described as *tuition discounting.*

Orientation programs in the summer and fall bring prospective students (and sometimes their parents) to campus for as little as one or two days and for as long as a week. These programs give students a closer look at an institution, and they also help prospective students to succeed once they decide to attend. Through campus tours, academic advising and registration, and structured academic and social programs, orientation programs help aspiring students to become familiar with the campus culture, the norms, and the values of the faculty and of peers. This is crucial to the anticipatory socialization process and the getting-ready behaviors can facilitate a successful transition to college.

Student retention efforts are an important aspect of enrollment management efforts. Few colleges or universities have formal retention offices. Instead they have retention programs that can be organized by a range of academic and student-life offices. The dean of academic affairs, the dean of student affairs, or an enrollment management division can sponsor academic support programs. A number of institutional interventions are known to exert a positive influence upon student success and persistence during the first year of college. These include enhanced student life and academic initiatives to encourage in-class and out-of-class interaction between first-year students and faculty, staff, and other students; creating more opportunities for students to work on campus; engagement in student activities and events; providing academic and career advising that promotes clear career and academic goals; enacting academic and pedagogical policies and practices that enhance student study habits and promote regular class attendance; a strong orientation program; special support programs for international students and students of color; and family and/or spousal/partner support for degree completion.

Other student-life offices can also be integral to the success of enrollment management offices, including academic advising, academic support and tutoring centers, career planning, student activities, and residence life.

Organizational Models

The literature on enrollment management often addresses different administrative approaches for organizing enrollment management efforts.

The enrollment management coordinator. The enrollment management coordinator is charged with organizing recruitment and retention activities. Usually, a midlevel administrator, such as the dean of admissions or financial aid, is asked to coordinate offices such as admissions, financial aid, and registration and records. An important disadvantage is that the coordinator model provides no formal mechanism for linking enrollment concerns into the decision-making agenda of senior level administrators.

The enrollment management matrix. The enrollment management matrix is a more centralized approach. In the matrix model, an existing senior level administrator, such as the vice president for student affairs, academic affairs, or institutional advancement, directs the activities of the enrollment management matrix. In this model, administrative units such as financial aid or student retention are not formally reassigned to a new vice president. Instead, the administrative heads of these units continue their existing reporting relationships, but they also become part of the enrollment management matrix.

The enrollment management division. The most centralized organizational model is the enrollment management division. In the division model, a vice president or associate vice president is assigned the responsibilities for most or all of the administrative areas that influence student enrollments, housed within one large functional unit. This model requires high levels of administrative support; the

president or a senior vice president generally has to become a strong advocate of this model. One important advantage of this model is that an enrollment management vice president can carry enrollment-related concerns directly to the president and the board of trustees.

There is little empirical evidence to indicate that any particular organizational approach is inherently better than another. Most experienced enrollment managers place more emphasis on strong working relationships with other key administrators on campus than on advocating for a specific organizational model. Another recurring theme is the need for a senior campus administrator, such as the president or provost, to provide visible and consistent support for the institution's enrollment management efforts. In colleges and universities of all sizes, support from the top appears to be more important than a specific administrative structure established to manage enrollments.

Given the current pressures on institutions to maximize revenue, and the attention being given to the characteristics of enrolled students, enrollment management is likely to remain an important administrative focus at most colleges and universities.

See also: College Admissions; College Financial Aid; College Recruitment Practices; College Search and Selection; College Student Retention.

BIBLIOGRAPHY

Black, James. 2001. *Strategic Enrollment Management Revolution.* Washington, DC: American Association of Collegiate Registrars and Admission Officers.

Coomes, Michael. 2000. *The Role Financial Aid Plays in Enrollment Management.* San Francisco: Jossey-Bass.

Gaither, Gerald, ed. 2000. *Promising Practices in Recruitment, Remediation, and Retention.* San Francisco: Jossey-Bass.

Hossler, Don; Bean, John P.; and Associates. 1990. *The Strategic Management of College Enrollments.* San Francisco: Jossey-Bass.

Hossler, Don. 1986. *Creating Effective Enrollment Management Systems.* New York: The College Board.

Tinto, Vincent. 1993. *Leaving College: Rethinking the Causes and Cures of Student Attrition,* 2nd edition. Chicago: University of Chicago Press.

Don Hossler

ERIC

See: Educational Resources Information Center.

ERIKSON, ERIK (1902–1994)

Child psychoanalyst Erik Homburger Erikson focused his research on the effects of society and culture on individual psychological development; he also developed the eight-stage model of human development. Erikson was born in Frankfurt, Germany, of Danish parents who had separated before his birth. His surname for the first four decades of his life, Homburger, was that of his stepfather, a physician. Upon becoming a U.S. citizen in 1939 he adopted the surname Erikson.

Career

Although Erikson graduated from a classical gymnasium where he studied Latin, Greek, German literature, and history, he was not a good student. For the next seven years following his graduation, he was a wandering artist through Europe, sketching, doing woodcuts and etchings, and intermittently studying art. In 1927, at age 25, he received an invitation from a childhood friend in Vienna to teach in a small progressive school for English and American children. While teaching art and history, he became acquainted with the Freud family and was judged an excellent candidate for psychoanalytic training. As Robert Coles observed, at that time candidates did not apply, but were chosen.

He graduated with a diploma from the Vienna Psychoanalytic Society in 1933, where he was viewed as a gifted student. He also was one of two men to graduate from the Montessori teachers association. Upon graduation, he and his wife and young son fled from the encroaching Nazi domination to the United States.

Although Erikson had no formal degree, he became the first child analyst in Boston and a research associate at Harvard Medical School. From 1936 through the 1940s, he served as a research associate at Yale, then at the University of California, finally receiving a professional appointment at the latter institution. During this period, in addition to his analytic work with children, he undertook the in-depth observational study of children in two American Indian tribes, the Sioux of South Dakota and the Yuron of northern California. These studies marked the beginning of his integration of the analytic clinical perspective with the social and economic events that influence child development.

Shortly after Erikson received a professorial appointment at the University of California, the signing of a loyalty oath became a contractual requirement for faculty. Refusing to sign the oath, Erikson resigned in June 1950. Noting that his field, psychoanalysis, included the study of hysteria, he stated he could not participate in this inadequate response to public hysteria. Erikson then returned to the analysis of troubled children by accepting a position at the Austen Riggs Center in Stockbridge, Massachusetts. In 1960 he was appointed professor at Harvard University, where he remained until his retirement in the early 1970s.

Contribution

Although trained as a psychoanalyst, Erikson's scholarship, which included fourteen books, transcended the discipline in his interweaving of culture, history, and the individual across a variety of topics. Specifically, he applied psychoanalysis in addressing anthropological, religious, and historical questions in addition to developing a comprehensive life span model of psychological development.

In his work, Erikson went beyond the Freudian focus on dysfunctional behavior to pursue the ways that the normal self is able to function successfully. His unique contribution to the applications of psychoanalysis, his inclusion of the effects of society and culture on individual psychological development, led to the designation of his perspective as psychosocial. Early examples are the study of the American Indian children, which combined anthropological observation and clinical analysis with tribal history and economic circumstances.

Erikson also applied psychoanalysis to develop richly detailed biographical histories of leaders who made a difference in society. Included are his chapter on Maxim Gorky, his lectures on Thomas Jefferson, and his books on Martin Luther (*Young Man Luther:*

A Study in Psychoanalysis and History, 1962) and Mahatma Gandhi. The latter work, *Gandhi's Truth: On the Origins of Militant Nonviolence* (1969), received both the 1970 Pulitzer Prize and the National Book Award. In these works, Erikson applied clinical analysis to develop an understanding of the ways that leaders faced with untenable situations rose above them to forge new identities for themselves and other citizens.

In education and psychology, Erikson is best known for his eight-stage model of the human life cycle, developed with the assistance of his wife, Joan. This model identifies particular goals, challenges, and concerns at each stage of life. They are the following: (1) Basic Trust versus Basic Mistrust (infancy); (2) Autonomy versus Shame and Doubt (early childhood); (3) Initiative versus Guilt (play age); (4) Industry versus Inferiority (school age); (5) Identity versus Role Confusion (adolescence); (6) Intimacy versus Isolation (young adulthood); (7) Generativity versus Stagnation (adulthood); (8) Ego Identity versus Despair (later adulthood). Further, the stages are interdependent in that unresolved conflicts at one stage influence development at later stages, as in the development of either a loving trusting relationship with a caregiver in infancy or mistrust of others.

Unlike Freud, who focused on early childhood, Erikson emphasized adolescence and adulthood. Erikson introduced the term *identity* and *identity crisis* to explain the psychological and social complexities faced by young people in attempting to find their place in a specific town, nation, and time. Adolescent development, in other words, is a complex answer to the question, "Who am I?" and requires organization of the individual's drives, abilities, beliefs, and history into a view of oneself. This focus reflects Erikson's own youthful wanderings before finding his place as a teacher, analyst, and writer.

In the 1960s Erikson focused on the seventh or "generative" stage of adulthood. In this stage, adults are obligated to care for the next generation, either one's own children or a broader group, through personal deeds and words. In the case of Gandhi, his contribution to the next generation was his militant nonviolence as a means to address social injustice. In addition Erikson described the final stage, late adulthood, as an active period that involves acceptance of self and the development of wisdom.

A third focus in Erikson's writing, ethical and moral responsibility, is reflected most prominently in *Insight and Responsibility* (1964). In this work, he included a set of eight virtues that correspond with his eight life stages (hope, will, purpose, competence, fidelity, love, care, and wisdom). He also introduced the term *pseudospeciation* to describe the destructive mechanism that leads to human conflict, aggression, and war. Specifically, pseudospeciation refers to the "arrogant placing of one's nation, race, culture, and (or) society ahead of others; the failure to recognize that all of humanity was of one species" (Friedman, p. 357). Groups of individuals, in other words, are assigned membership in a not-quite human or pseudo-species. With this concept, as in his other writings, Erikson spoke to human psychological issues within the broader context of history and culture.

See also: EDUCATIONAL PSYCHOLOGY.

BIBLIOGRAPHY

COLES, ROBERT. 1970. *Erik H. Erikson: The Growth of His Work.* Boston: Little, Brown.

COLES, ROBERT, ed. 2000. *The Erik Erikson Reader.* New York: Norton.

ERIKSON, ERIK H. 1950. *Children and Society.* New York: Norton.

ERIKSON, ERIK H. 1962. *Young Man Luther: A Study in Psychoanalysis and History.* New York: Norton.

ERIKSON, ERIK H. 1964. *Insight and Responsibility.* New York: Norton.

ERIKSON, ERIK H. 1969. *Gandhi's Truth: On the Origins of Militant Nonviolence.* New York: Norton.

ERIKSON, ERIK H. 1981 "The Galilean Sayings and the Sense of 'I.'" *Yale Review* 70:321–362.

FRIEDMAN, LAWRENCE J. 1998. "Erik H. Erikson's Critical Themes and Voices: The Task of Synthesis." In *Ideas and Identities: The Life and Work of Erik Erikson,* ed. Robert S. Wallerstein and Leo Goldberger. Madison, CT: International Universities Press.

KOTRE, JOHN. 1984. *Outliving the Self: Generativity and the Interpretation of Lives.* Baltimore: Johns Hopkins University Press.

MARGARET GREDLER

ESL

See: BILINGUALISM, SECOND LANGUAGE LEARNING, AND ENGLISH AS A SECOND LANGUAGE; LANGUAGE MINORITY STUDENTS.

ETHICS

SCHOOL TEACHING
Kenneth A. Strike
HIGHER EDUCATION
Carol J. Auster

SCHOOL TEACHING

Ethical concerns about teachers and teaching occur in a variety of contexts and can be thought of in several ways. This article discusses (1) how ethical issues are represented in the law; (2) how ethical issues are represented in the National Education Association's (NEA's) code of ethics; (3) ethically based comprehensive views of education; (4) the role of ethics in educational policy; and (5) meta-ethical disputes relevant to education.

Ethics and the Law

The education codes of many states require that teachers be persons of good character. Most states also permit teachers to be dismissed for unethical conduct. States also forbid particular forms of misconduct, such as child abuse, sexual harassment, and drug abuse, and their violation may be grounds for dismissal.

What counts as good character or conduct can be a contentious matter. In past decades teachers might have been dismissed not only for drunkenness, homosexuality, unwed pregnancy, or cohabitation, but also for myriad other offenses against the moral code of their community. Some of these may still be gray areas; however, in recent years, courts have been inclined to insist that actionable immoral conduct be job-related, providing some protection for the private lives of teachers. Here a particularly contentious matter is whether being a role model is part of the job of teachers, because this expectation can expand public authority over the lives of teachers. In certain cases, as when teachers discuss controversial matters in class or employ controversial teaching methods, they may be protected by the First Amendment. Teachers, especially those who are tenured, are also likely to have significant due-process rights. Dismissal for immoral conduct is most likely when the teacher has committed a felony, in cases of inappropriate sexual advances toward students, or in cases of child abuse. In this last case, teachers may also have a duty to report suspected misconduct by others.

The kinds of misconduct dealt with by the law are usually acts that are (or can be viewed as) unethical in any context. Teachers, like others, are expected to not steal, kill, commit assault, abuse children, or engage in sexual harassment. Although the definition of immoral conduct in the law has not become coextensive with violations of criminal law, there is little in the meaning of immoral conduct that is distinctive to teachers or teaching.

The NEA Code of Ethics and Ethical Principles Internal to Teaching

The most prominent code of ethics for teachers is the NEA's *Code of Ethics for the Education Profession.* The preamble to this code begins: "The educator, believing in the worth and dignity of each human being, recognizes the supreme importance of the pursuit of truth, devotion to excellence, and the nurture of democratic principles. Essential to these goals is the protection of the freedom to learn and to teach and the guarantee of equal education opportunity for all."

The code has two sections with eight provisions in each. The first section, entitled "Commitment to the Student," promotes the freedom to learn, requires equal opportunity, protects students against disparagement, and protects privacy. The freedom-to-learn provisions prohibit teachers from preventing student inquiry, denying students access to diverse points of view, and distorting subject matter. The code-specific provisions do not assert affirmative duties for teachers to create an inquiry-oriented environment or to pursue educational objectives, which might be associated with the pursuit of truth, individual autonomy, or democratic principles. The prohibition against distortion of subject matter falls short of a prohibition of indoctrination.

The second section of the code begins with the comment that "the educator shall exert every effort to raise professional standards, to promote a climate that encourages the exercise of professional judgment, to achieve conditions which attract persons worthy of the trust to careers in education and to assist in preventing the practice of the profession by unqualified persons."

Among its enumerated provisions are prohibitions against misrepresenting one's own qualifications or those of others, prohibitions against assisting unqualified persons to teach, and prohibitions against the defamation of colleagues. Although the ideals expressed in the introduction of the second section of the code might lead one to expect specific provisions requiring conscientious professional development, the maintaining of qualifications, or the creation of a collegial learning environment, no such provisions are found.

The NEA code implicitly recognizes three sources of ethical ideals and principles. The first is what might be termed the *ethics of inquiry*. The second area might be called the *civic ethic*. That is, the NEA code recognizes those ideals and principles that regulate the public conduct of citizens of liberal democratic states to be ideals and principles that should also regulate the practice of education. A reason for this is that one goal of education is the creation of citizens. The third source of ethical ideals is the ideal of *professionalism*.

There are difficulties and questions associated with such ideals and principles. Consider the following examples:

1. What fundamental values underlie these principles? The NEA code suggests that the value that underlies the ethics of inquiry is truth, but another possibility is autonomy.

2. What is the best construction of these abstract principles? The NEA code indicates that students may not be unfairly excluded, denied a benefit, or given favoritism on the basis of a list of presumptively irrelevant characteristics. The use of the word *unfairly* cloaks a multitude of issues. For example, how do we know when exclusion or inclusion on the basis of race (one of the irrelevant characteristics listed) is unfair? Is affirmative action unfair?

3. Are there values that must be balanced against these principles? In some understandings of professionalism, a core commitment of professionalism is: *Those who know should rule.* If so, professionalism in education needs to be balanced against the expectation that public schools are under the democratic authority of school boards and state legislatures.

4. What is omitted? These three sources of ethical content do not clearly include various conceptions concerning human relations that seem relevant to teaching. Examples might be caring and trust. Nor are ideals such as promoting the growth of the whole child or creating community mentioned.

Ethics and the Philosophy of Education

It has been common in the philosophy of education to begin an inquiry into the aims of education by asking questions such as "What is the nature of the good life?" and "What kinds of societies promote the best lives?" The Greek philosopher Plato's *Republic* is a classical example. Such questions fall within the range of the subject matter of ethics. Answers to these questions can provide part of the framework for building a comprehensive vision of education rooted in what John Rawls has termed a "comprehensive doctrine" (1993, p. 13), and they may guide the professional practice of teachers. In societies characterized by what Rawls calls durable pluralism, there are serious difficulties with such an approach. In such societies, the educational systems cannot be rooted in a single comprehensive doctrine without marginalizing or oppressing those who hold other doctrines and without restricting personal autonomy.

Arguably, societies committed to liberal democratic values may respect pluralism and personal autonomy while also emphasizing creation of citizens. Amy Gutmann in *Democratic Education* (1987) argues that the central aim of the schools of a democratic society must be to develop democratic character. Eamonn Callan in *Creating Citizens* (1997) argues that societies committed to liberal principles of tolerance and reasonableness must provide students with an education enabling them to understand and sympathetically engage a variety of ways of life. It may, however, be argued that such an education is itself intolerant of those who wish to transmit a distinctive way of life to their children. One of the more difficult issues for the schools of liberal democratic societies is how to respect diversity while having common schools that produce good citizens.

Ethics and Educational Policy

The civic ethic provides conceptions that are relevant, not only to teachers' classroom practice, but to wide-ranging areas of educational policy. For example, it has been common in recent years to claim that equality of opportunity should emphasize equal educational outcomes instead of equal access or equal inputs. Assume that achievement can be measured by test scores. What pattern of test scores would be desired, and how should resources be distributed to attain it? Consider three possibilities:

1. Emphasize increasing average test scores.

Possible objections are that this is consistent with considerable disparity in levels of achievement. Moreover, average scores might be increased by focusing resources on the most able at the expense of the least able.

2. Emphasize the achievement of the least advantaged or least able. Possible objections are that such an approach might lead to significant investment in the education of students where there will be only modest return, and resources will be used inefficiently.

3. Emphasize getting all who are able above some threshold that defines minimal ability to participate in our society. This approach may lead to difficulties similar to the previous one.

These are competing principles for distributing educational resources. Although they concern such matters as state or school district budgets, in fact they may also concern the distribution of teacher time. They shed light on such questions as whether teachers should spend disproportionate time with those who are most needful or with those who will make the most progress. These various approaches are analogous to principles of distributive justice that are widely discussed in philosophical literature. The first is a utilitarian principle emphasizing the maximization of good outcomes. The second seeks to maximize the welfare of those who occupy the least advantaged positions in society. The third is a threshold view emphasizing getting everyone above some defined level. These principles illustrate the ways in which moral conceptions can inform policy and practice.

Meta-ethical Issues

The term *meta-ethics* concerns the general nature of ethics instead of specific ethical prescriptions. Two meta-ethical disputes are the justice/caring debate and the postmodern critique of modernity.

The justice/caring dispute grows out of a critique of Lawrence Kohlberg's views of moral development by feminist scholars, principally Carol Gilligan. Kohlberg viewed justice as the central moral conception. Gilligan claimed in *In a Different Voice* that women's thinking about ethics emphasizes care. Other advocates of an ethic of care, such as Nel Noddings, have developed the notion into a robust view of ethics and of education. By the early twenty-first century there was some rapprochement between these views, based on the claim that both justice and caring should be a part of any adequate ethic.

A second meta-ethical perspective is postmodernism. Although understandings of this stance are complex and varied, one useful characterization of postmodernism claims that it is incredulity toward all grand meta-narratives. A grand meta-narrative is a sweeping and general view about human beings and society. Liberalism and socialism are examples. Postmodernists often argue that all such grand stories represent the perspectives of groups or eras and, when viewed as the single truth of the matter, are oppressive. Postmodern critiques often seek to deconstruct such meta-narratives by showing their biased character and how they serve the interests of some over others.

Summary

The following (not mutually exclusive) sources of ethical ideals and principles are relevant to an informed view of the ethics of teaching:

1. The law pertaining to teacher certification and dismissal, which is likely to proscribe only the most egregious behavior.

2. The NEA code of ethics. This code draws on three sources of ethical content.

   a. The ethic of inquiry.

   b. The civic ethic.

   c. An ethic of professionalism.

3. Ethical conceptions that inform educational policy, such as views of distributive justice.

4. Conceptions of human flourishing and the nature of liberal democratic societies.

5. Competing meta-ethical conceptions.

Of these sources, ethical conceptions rooted in the ethics of inquiry and in the civic ethic may have the most salience to teachers because they are associated with the paramount educational goals of advancing knowledge and creating citizens. They are "internal" to the activity of teaching. Other sources apply to schools because they apply broadly to most social institutions or human activities.

See also: NATIONAL EDUCATION ASSOCIATION; PHILOSOPHY OF EDUCATION; TEACHER.

BIBLIOGRAPHY

BULL, BARRY. 1990. "The Limits of Teacher Professionalism." In *The Moral Dimensions of Teaching,* ed. John Goodlad, Roger Soder, and Kenneth Sirotnik. San Francisco: Jossey-Bass.

CALLAN, EAMONN. 1997. *Creating Citizens: Political Education and Liberal Democracy.* Oxford: Oxford University Press.

FEINBERG, WALTER. 1998. *Common Schools: Uncommon Identities.* New Haven, CT: Yale University Press.

FISCHER, LOUIS; SCHIMMEL, DAVID; and KELLY, CYNTHIA. 1999. *Teachers and the Law.* New York: Longman.

GILLIGAN, CAROL. 1982. *In a Different Voice.* Cambridge, MA: Harvard University Press.

GUTMANN, AMY. 1987. *Democratic Education.* Princeton, NJ: Princeton University Press.

KATZ, MICHAEL; NODDINGS, NEL; and STRIKE, KENNETH A., eds. 1999. *Justice and Caring: The Search for Common Ground in Education.* New York: Teachers College Press.

KOHLBERG, LAWRENCE. 1981. *The Philosophy of Moral Development.* New York: Harper and Row.

LYOTARD, JEAN-FRANCOIS. 1993. *The Postmodern Condition: A Report on Knowledge.* Minneapolis: University of Minnesota Press.

NODDINGS, NEL. 1984. *Caring: A Feminine Approach to Ethics and Moral Education.* Berkeley: University of California Press.

PETERS, RICHARD. 1996. *Ethics and Education.* Atlanta, GA: Scott, Foresman.

PLATO. 1964. *The Republic of Plato,* trans. Francis MacDonald Cornford. New York: Oxford University Press.

RAWLS, JOHN. 1971. *A Theory of Justice.* Cambridge, MA: Harvard University Press.

RAWLS, JOHN. 1993. *Political Liberalism.* New York: Columbia University Press.

SOCKETT, HUGH. 1993. *The Moral Base for Teacher Professionalism.* New York: Teachers College Press.

STRIKE, KENNETH A. 1988. "The Ethics of Resource Allocation." In *Microlevel School Finance,* ed. David H. Monk and Julie Underwood. Cambridge, MA: Ballinger.

STRIKE, KENNETH A. 1990. "The Legal and Moral Responsibilities of Teachers." In *The Moral Dimensions of Teaching,* ed. John Goodlad, Roger Soder, and Kenneth Sirotnic. San Francisco: Jossey-Bass.

STRIKE, KENNETH A., and SOLTIS, JONAS F. 1998. *The Ethics of Teaching,* 3rd edition. New York: Teachers College Press.

WHITE, PATRICIA. 1996. *Civic Virtues and Public Schooling.* New York: Teachers College Press.

INTERNET RESOURCE

NATIONAL EDUCATION ASSOCIATION. 2002. "Code of Ethics of the Education Profession." <www.nea.org/aboutnea/code.html>.

KENNETH A. STRIKE

HIGHER EDUCATION

As members of the academic community, faculty and students have a responsibility to abide by ethical principles regarding academic freedom, intellectual integrity, and the fair and respectful treatment of others. The notion of academic freedom lies at the very heart of the academic enterprise. In the "1940 Statement of Principles on Academic Freedom and Tenure," the American Association of University Professors (AAUP) states, "Academic freedom . . . applies to both teaching and research. Freedom in research is fundamental to the advancement of truth. Academic freedom in its teaching aspect is fundamental for the protection of the rights of the teacher in teaching and of the student to freedom in learning" (p. 3). Intellectual integrity involves using sound and ethical methods in the pursuit of knowledge as well as embracing honesty in the dissemination of knowledge. Individuals' expectation of fair and respectful treatment by faculty and students applies not only to interactions with one another, but also to administrators, staff, and others with whom they interact in their role as members of the academic community. Fair and respectful treatment also extends, for example, to the evaluation of students' academic work and colleagues' scholarly work.

The ethical principles that guide the behavior of faculty are reflected in standards of ethics described in the documents of professional associations for faculty in higher education, such as the "Statement on Professional Ethics (1987)" published by the American Association of University Professors, and codes of ethics published by disciplinary associations, such as the American Chemical Society, the American Psychological Association, the American Sociological Association, and the Modern Language Association. In addition, college and university faculty handbooks often include a section that addresses ethical standards or expectations regarding the behavior of faculty. Ethical standards for students may be found in official student handbooks or college and university catalogues, although standards for graduate students are also addressed in some of the professional and disciplinary association codes of ethics. These various documents embody shared beliefs that are intended to guide both the activities and the behavior of those engaged in the academic enterprise.

Faculty

Faculty are guided by ethical principles that address their professional responsibilities as teachers, scholars, and, more generally, members of college and university communities. While some aspects of documents concerning ethical standards describe the behavior to be embraced, other aspects make clear what actions must be avoided.

Plagiarism. Representing the ideas, words, or data of another person or persons as one's own constitutes plagiarism. Thus, a person's words, ideas, or data, whether published or unpublished, must be acknowledged as such. For example, the MLA (Modern Language Association) Style Manual states, "To use another person's ideas or expressions in your writing without acknowledging the source is to plagiarize" (Gibaldi, sec. 1.8). "The most blatant form of plagiarism is reproducing someone else's sentences more or less verbatim, and presenting them as your own" (Achten and Gibaldi, sec. 1.4). Although scholars have long recognized the importance of citing both published and unpublished work, those engaged in teaching or research also recognize that information from electronic resources must be properly credited. Proper citation allows others to trace the origin and development of ideas, theories, and research outcomes and helps support the integrity of the academic enterprise and needed mutual trust between those seeking and those disseminating knowledge.

Acknowledgement of contributions. Acknowledgement of the contributions of others means appropriately recognizing and crediting those who have contributed to a scholarly work whether the work is a manuscript, exhibit, or performance. Both recognition and accountability come with allocations of credit. Depending on their contributions, such others, including students, may be deserving of credit ranging from acknowledgement in a footnote to coauthorship. Regardless of whether faculty members work with students or colleagues, the work of all parties should be equitably acknowledged in a manner appropriate to the norms of their discipline.

Data. Researchers must acknowledge the source(s) of their data and accurately describe the method by which their data was gathered. Moreover, the fabrication or falsification of data or results constitutes a violation of ethical standards. While fabrication is defined as "making up data or results," falsification is "changing or misreporting data or results" (Committee on Science, Engineering, and Public Policy, p. 16). Both of these actions interfere with the search for knowledge and truth and undermine trust both within and outside the academic community.

Conflict of interest. Research funded by corporate sponsors potentially leads to a situation in which a conflict of interest may arise. Researchers may feel pressure, for example, to conduct research in a way that would bias the results toward the desires of the sponsor or to reveal only those results that benefit the sponsor. Biomedical research, in particular, brings forth such concerns. Conflict of interest issues are not limited to corporate-sponsored research projects; conflict of interest situations may occur with government-sponsored research as well. Nonprofit organizations and social advocacy groups also have the potential to place college and university researchers in situations that make it potentially difficult to conduct the sponsored research in an unbiased manner. Researchers must be able to publicly disclose their sources of funding and the intent of the research, as well as conduct their research in a manner consistent with the ethical standards for investigation in their respective disciplines. Scholars must not let the source of their funding nor the sponsors' goals cloud their own professional and scientific judgments regarding their research.

Other research concerns. The prevalence of the discussion of particular ethical concerns varies across disciplines because of the nature of the research process. For example, the American Sociological Association's "Code of Ethics" describes the importance of informed consent for research involving human subjects. That is, human subjects must be aware of the nature of the research as well as voluntarily agree to be a part of such research. The American Psychological Association discusses not only informed consent in their code of ethics, but also the importance of the humane use and care of animals in research. Disciplines that rely more heavily on archival research may say little about informed consent from human subjects, but may focus on the importance of obtaining permission to use archival data. Professional associations in the sciences, such as the American Chemical Society, are additionally concerned with providing safe working conditions for those who work in research laboratories.

Harassment. The most frequently discussed form of harassment is sexual harassment. As the AAUP statement on sexual harassment states, "no member of the academic community may sexually harass another" (p. 209). Such policies are applicable to faculty and students as well as to administrators, staff, other employees, and research subjects. The American Sociological Association notes that "sexual harassment may include sexual solicitation, physical advance, or verbal or non-verbal conduct that is sexual in nature" (p. 7). Some types of sexual harassment are quid pro quo, in which the sexual favors are presumably requested in exchange for a promised or implied future benefit, such as a higher grade or appointment to a position. Other conduct, namely that which creates a hostile or uncomfortable work environment, including the classroom environment, also constitutes sexual harassment. The code of ethics of many professional and disciplinary associations addresses the issue of sexual harassment, and faculty handbooks and other institutional documents typically include a set of procedures for dealing with situations in which alleged sexual harassment has occurred.

In addition, members of the academic community should not harass others on the basis of other personal and demographic characteristics, including race, ethnicity, age, religion, national origin, sexual orientation, and disability. Regardless of the basis of harassing or demeaning behavior, victims of harassment may find it helpful to consult with faculty and administrators for advice on avenues of action in such situations.

Nondiscrimination and fair evaluation. In their work, members of the academic community should not engage in discrimination "based on age, gender, race, ethnicity, national origin, religion, sexual orientation, disability, socioeconomic status, or any basis proscribed by law" (American Psychological Association, sec. 1.10). With regard to employment, members of the academic community should not "discriminate in hiring, promotion, salary, treatment, or any other conditions of employment or career development" (American Sociological Association, sec. 8). Furthermore, professors who have agreed to serve as reviewers of manuscripts, grant proposals, or other scholarly submissions, should evaluate those materials in a fair, objective, professional, and timely manner. These standards are also applicable to the evaluation of students' academic work. In "A Statement of the Association's Council: Freedom and Responsibility" the AAUP further explains, "Students are entitled to an atmosphere conducive to learning and to even-handed treatment in all aspects of the teacher-student relationship" (p. 135). The principle of fair and respectful treatment also applies to interactions with and evaluation of the work of other members of the academic community.

Allegations of ethical misconduct. Alleged ethical violations on the part of faculty are dealt with in a number of ways. A student or faculty member may choose to approach the faculty member thought to have engaged in ethical misconduct. One could also speak with another faculty member, chair of the department, or administrator about the alleged misconduct and seek advice about possible avenues of action. A hearing on the matter is one of the possible outcomes. Faculty members accused of ethical misconduct are entitled to academic due process. That is, the educational institution should follow a set of procedures already in place for dealing with such allegations. For faculty, the AAUP also sets forth a number of parameters related to the allegations of various types and methods for proceeding to pursue such allegations, particularly within the confines of the employing educational institution. Although most incidents of alleged misconduct are handled within such institutional frameworks, many disciplinary and professional associations have provisions for pursuing breaches of ethical conduct through mechanisms within those associations.

Students

Students are guided by the same general ethical principles as faculty regarding their academic work. Academic honesty and intellectual integrity are central in the educational process. These two principles apply to academic work, including, but not limited to, papers, theses, assignments, laboratory reports, exams, quizzes, oral presentations, exhibits, and performances. Students can avoid plagiarism by proper citation of the resources that provide them with the ideas, words, and data that they present in their academic work. Although intellectual theft may not have been intended, careless note taking can also result in inadvertent plagiarism. Students must also not engage in the fabrication or falsification of sources, data, or results. If students work on a project together, the work of those students should be equitably acknowledged. Moreover, students must not engage in unauthorized collaboration nor give or receive inappropriate assistance with their academic work. Violation of ethical standards would be grounds for action against a student. The situational context of the violation along with the institutional norms and regulations affect the path of action. Although some situations involving a student's alleged violation of ethical standards may warrant action on the part of a faculty member or an administrative officer, other situations may warrant a hearing by a duly constituted committee to determine whether the alleged act occurred as well as the appropriate sanctions.

Some institutions of higher education have an honor code that makes clear that cheating and other forms of academic dishonesty are violations of ethical standards. These codes typically obligate students to practice academic integrity and avoid engaging in academic misconduct, but also to take action when they believe others have engaged in academic misconduct. The action taken by a fellow student who witnesses the ethical digression can range from directly confronting the alleged perpetrator to reporting the alleged act to individuals acting on the part of the institution, who may find it appropriate to convene a hearing panel for a judicial process in which students usually play an important role.

Broader Concerns

Some ethical standards apply to members of the academic community in their relationship with wider society. The Committee on Science, Engineering, and Public Policy says, "Society trusts that the results of research reflect an honest attempt by scientists to describe the world accurately and without bias" (preface). Many codes of ethics for professional disciplinary associations specifically recognize the consequences of research beyond its intended goal. For example, the American Chemical Society indicates that, "Chemists should understand and antici-

pate the environmental consequences of their work. Chemists have responsibility to avoid pollution and to protect the environment." Under the heading "Social Responsibility," the American Sociological Association says, "Sociologists are aware of the their professional and scientific responsibility to the communities and societies in which they live and work . . . . When undertaking research, they strive to advance the science of sociology and to serve the public good" (Principle E). Both faculty and students need to be aware that their ideas and implications of their research may reach well beyond their own immediate goal.

Socialization to ethical principles needs to be more explicit and the mechanisms of social control within academic profession need to be strengthened in order to improve adherence to ethical principles. To improve faculty adherence to ethical principles, John M. Braxton and Allen E. Bayer suggest, in particular, that faculty and administrations need to (1) better articulate and codify the norms of professional behavior; (2) more explicitly socialize graduate students about the profession and its ethical obligations; (3) increasingly provide incentives for teaching [and research] behavior that is consistent with the standards of the profession; and (4) when necessary, impose sanctions for violations of those standards. Undergraduate and graduate students need to be made more aware of the expectations for their behavior as well as the consequences of the failure to meet those expectations.

If the ethical standards were more explicit, members of the academic community might be more likely to both act in accordance with such standards and speak out against the ethical misconduct of others in the academic community. In fact, the Committee on Science, Engineering, and Public Policy says, "someone who has witnessed misconduct has an unmistakable obligation to act" (p. 18). Yet, allegations of misconduct may require certain types of confidentiality because of the situations or the parties involved. However, if colleges and universities deal with alleged misconduct in a less clandestine manner, it will be easier for members of the academic community, particularly newcomers, to distinguish between ethical and unethical behavior.

See also: ACADEMIC FREEDOM AND TENURE; FACULTY RESEARCH AND SCHOLARSHIP, ASSESSMENT OF; FACULTY ROLES AND RESPONSIBILITIES; HUMAN SUBJECTS, PROTECTION OF; SCIENTIFIC MISCONDUCT.

BIBLIOGRAPHY

ACHTEN, WALTER S., and GIBALDI, JOSEPH. 1985. *The MLA Style Manual.* New York: Modern Language Association of America.

AMERICAN ASSOCIATION OF UNIVERSITY PROFESSORS (AAUP). 2001. *AAUP Policy Documents and Reports,* 8th edition. Washington, DC: American Association of University Professors.

BRAXTON, JOHN M., and BAYER, ALAN E. 1999. *Faculty Misconduct in Collegiate Teaching.* Baltimore: The Johns Hopkins University Press.

COMMITTEE ON SCIENCE, ENGINEERING, AND PUBLIC POLICY. 1995. *On Being a Scientist: Responsible Conduct in Research.* Washington, DC: National Academy Press.

GIBALDI, JOSEPH. 1999. *MLA Handbook for Writers of Research Papers.* New York: Modern Language Association of America.

MODERN LANGUAGE ASSOCIATION OF AMERICA. 1992. "Statement of Professional Ethics." *Profession* 92:75–79.

INTERNET RESOURCES

AMERICAN CHEMICAL SOCIETY. 1994. "The Chemist's Code of Conduct and ASC Ethical Guidelines." <www.acs.org/membership/conduct.html>.

AMERICAN PSYCHOLOGICAL ASSOCIATION. 1992. "Ethical Principles of Psychologists and Code of Conduct." <www.apa.org>.

AMERICAN SOCIOLOGICAL ASSOCIATION. 1997. "American Sociological Association Code of Ethics." <www.asanet.org>.

CAROL J. AUSTER

EXCEPTIONAL CHILDREN, EDUCATION OF

See: SPECIAL EDUCATION.

EXPERIENTIAL EDUCATION

Although experiential education has come to mean simply "learning by doing" for some, educators utilizing this approach recognize both its distinguished historical and philosophical roots and the complexity of applying what appears to be so elementary. When education is said to be *experiential,* it means that it is structured in a way that allows the learner to explore the phenomenon under study—to form a direct relationship with the subject matter—rather than merely reading about the phenomenon or encountering it indirectly. Experiential learning, then, requires that the learner play an active role in the experience and that the experience is followed by reflection as a method for processing, understanding, and making sense of it.

Experiential education, most generally, occurs in different kinds of programs that have as their goal the construction of knowledge, skills, and dispositions from direct experience. Service learning, adventure education, outdoor and environmental education, and workplace internships are just a few examples.

Brief History of the Role of Experience in Education

The role of experience in education has a history that connects back to philosophical debates between rationalists and empiricists. Rationalists argued that the information that is gained through one's senses is unreliable, and the only reliable knowledge is that which is gained through reason alone. Empiricists argued that knowledge is derived from empirical sense impressions, and abstract concepts that cannot directly be experienced cannot be known. In 1787 the German philosopher Immanuel Kant resolved the debate by arguing that both rationality and experience have a place in the construction of knowledge. Indeed, the human mind imposes order on the experience of the world in the process of perceiving it. Therefore, all experiences are organized by the actively structuring mind.

John Dewey (1859–1952), perhaps the most prominent American philosopher of the early twentieth century, expanded on the relationship between experience and learning in the publication of his well-known book *Experience and Education* (1938). He argued that not all experience is educative, noting:

> The belief that all genuine education comes about through experience does not mean that all experiences are genuinely or equally educative. . . . Any experience is miseducation that has the effect of arresting or distorting the growth of further

experience . . . . A given experience may increase a person's automatic skill in a particular direction and yet tend to land him in a groove or rut; the effect again is to narrow the field of further experience. (Dewey, pp. 25–26)

For Dewey, experiences could be judged to be educative if they led to further growth, intellectually and morally; if there was a benefit to the community; and if the experience resulted in affective qualities that led to continued growth, such as curiosity, initiative, and a sense of purpose. Finally, it is important to emphasize that Dewey saw traditional education as hierarchical and inherently undemocratic, and argued that in order to promote the development of a thoughtful and active democratic citizenry, students in schools needed to be able to participate in aspects of the school program democratically.

Kurt Hahn (1886–1974), considered to be one of the foremost educators of the twentieth century, contributed to experiential education as a practitioner worldwide. Hahn established academic schools, such as Salem in Germany and Gordonstoun in Scotland, and the Outward Bound schools, which total twenty-eight in Europe, the United Kingdom, Africa, Asia, Australia, and North America. In addition he founded the Duke of Edinburgh Award for involvement in voluntary, noncompetitive practical, cultural, and adventurous activities for young people between the ages of fourteen and twenty-five. For Hahn, the entire school day— including curricula, daily routines, social life, and extracurricular activities—could be used to help young people develop social responsibility and high aspirations. Most important, it could also provide education and practice in the fundamental principles of democratic life.

The work of field theorist Kurt Lewin (1890–1947), genetic epistemologist Jean Piaget (1896–1980), and educator and activist Paulo Freire (1921–1997) also provides theoretical grounding for experiential education.

Roles for the Teacher and the Student

Reports by John Goodlad and Theodore Sizer suggest that most teaching, particularly at the high school level, still involves the teacher as the authority and the dispenser of knowledge and the students as passive recipients. Perhaps the most obvious marker of experiential education is the shift in roles required for both teachers and students. Teachers who utilize experiential education become facilitators and, in doing so, engage their students in some of the decision-making and problem solving that have in the past been the sole responsibility of the teacher. In addition, teachers facilitate the transfer of learning from the experiential activity to the real world, structure the process of reflection for the students in order to derive the most learning from the experience, and ensure that the learning outcomes are reached. Some educators call this shift a move toward *student-centered teaching,* or a *child-centered curriculum.* Overall it means that the students are placed at the center and the teacher's role is to develop methods for engaging the students in experiences that provide them with access to knowledge and practice in particular skills and dispositions.

The role of the student is transformed in relation to the role of the teacher. Therefore, the student role becomes more active and involved, with additional responsibility and ownership over the process of learning, whether in an outdoor education program or in a middle school. For example, students, as members of a particular learning community, may be responsible for certain day-to-day activities, may be engaged in some aspects of curriculum development, or may be engaged in service activities in their community as a method for learning about different careers and contributing to their neighborhood. Whether in an outdoor education program or a service-learning program in a school, the student's role is one of engagement and deliberation—a continuous cycle of action and reflection, or *praxis,* as defined by Paulo Freire.

The Assessment of Student Learning

The assessment of learning outcomes for students has reflected ongoing economic and political debates surrounding the definition of learning. Legislators in the United States, looking for efficient ways of quantifying learning, advocate standardized multiple-choice tests, which can be mass-produced and are inexpensive to score. Unfortunately, the kind of learning that is measured by these tests is merely a matter of recognition—recognizing the one right answer from among four or five possible answers. Proponents of experiential education define learning in a manner that is more reflective of the complexity of both cognitive and affective development: Learning is "the process whereby knowledge is created through the transformation of experience" (Kolb, p.

41). Central to the process of transformation is reflection.

Reflection. In 1984 David A. Kolb published *Experiential Learning: Experience as the Source of Learning and Development*, which outlines a cycle for reflection. The cycle begins with concrete experience, moves to reflective observation, then to abstract conceptualization, and finally to the application stage, active experimentation. Reflection typically includes reconstructing the experience, making connections to prior knowledge or skills, testing understanding, and making decisions about how to apply the knowledge or skills in a new situation. In addition, David Boud, Rosemary Keogh, and David Walker (1985) offered examples of various methods for promoting reflection including oral conversations, such as informal debriefing sessions following experiential activities and written responses to experiences through diaries, journals, portfolios, and student exhibits, which may include text, pictures, and photos.

Assessing student learning. Assessing experiential learning is an ongoing process based upon the learning outcomes defined at the beginning of the experience or program. As an example, Norman Evans argues that student assessment is "a matter of making independent judgments about the level and quality of learning which has been reached by an individual at a particular time" (p. 68). He notes a four-stage sequence for compiling evidence in a portfolio assessment: "(1) Systematic reflection on experience for significant learning; (2) Identification of significant learning, expressed in precise statements, constituting claims to the possession of knowledge and skills; (3) Synthesis of evidence to support the claims made to knowledge and skills; (4) Assessment for accreditation" (p. 71).

For K–16 students, and particular to service learning, Kathryn Cumbo and Jennifer Vadeboncoeur note that service and learning goals should be articulated early in the planning process for an experiential activity. Indeed, the discussion surrounding the reason behind the experience and the way it reflects the curriculum goals may be a learning experience in and of itself between the teacher and his or her students. Finally, the definition of the service goals requires input from the community group or organization that provides the experiential site through partnership with the school. Cumbo and Vadeboncoeur offer examples of scoring rubrics and assessment tools to assess curricular knowledge.

Evidence of Effectiveness

It is important to emphasize that different experiential programs have different learning outcomes, all of which may be assessed using some type of measure, though much of what is learned may not be assessable on a standardized multiple-choice test. Research, which provides evidence for the effectiveness of experiential education, tends to be separated by the type of experiential program. For example, Alan W. Ewert demonstrated effects for outdoor adventure programs, including enhanced self-concept, effectiveness in treating chemical dependency, and a reduction in the rate of recidivism for young people. In addition, John Hattie, H. W. March, James T. Neill, and Garry E. Richards reviewed the literature for adventure education and Outward Bound programs and completed a meta-analysis of ninety-six separate studies. Their work highlights continued gains and longevity of the positive follow-up effects, in particular for programs lasting more than twenty days. Finally, with regard to service learning, in a national study of Learn and Serve America programs completed over three years by Brandeis University, key findings included positive short-term impacts for a range of civic and educational attitudes and behaviors for participants and a positive impact on the community in terms of service performed.

Major Issues

There are several issues that stand in the way of increasing access to experiential education in schools, although programs that exist outside of schools, such as Outward Bound and the National Outdoor Leadership schools, are flourishing. For in-school programs, the cost of engaging in experiential education, including transportation, can be prohibitive, not to mention the time it takes to plan and carry out experiential programs. In addition, even after the prominence of Dewey's work and the commitment of so many experiential educators, legislators and some parents seem to prioritize teacher accountability as measured through student achievement on standardized tests, over and above a more complex view of student learning. As long as the definition of learning is narrowed to rote memorization, quantifiable on multiple-choice tests, teachers will be restricted to covering curriculum and teaching to the test. There should be a continued effort to develop and share assessment tools for measuring student learning from experiential education. In addition, the culture as a whole should play a part in rethinking the definition of learning, taking into account a more broadly conceived view of the role of experience and reflection.

See also: Outdoor and Environmental Education; Service Learning, *subentry on* Schools.

BIBLIOGRAPHY

Boud, David; Keogh, Rosemary; and Walker, David, eds. 1985. *Reflection: Turning Experience into Learning.* New York: Kogan Page.

Cumbo, Kathryn B., and Vadeboncoeur, Jennifer A. 1999. "What Are Students Learning? Assessing Service Learning and the Curriculum." *Michigan Journal of Community Service Learning* 6:84–96.

Dewey, John. 1938. *Experience and Education.* New York: Macmillan.

Evans, Norman. 1992. *Experiential Learning: Assessment and Accreditation.* New York: Routledge.

Ewert, Alan W. 1989. *Outdoor Adventure Pursuits: Foundations, Models, and Theories.* Columbus, OH: Publishing Horizons.

Freire, Paulo. 1970. *Pedagogy of the Oppressed.* New York: Continuum.

Goodlad, John I. 1984. *A Place Called School: Prospects for the Future.* New York: McGraw-Hill.

Hattie, John; Marsh, Herbert W.; Neill, James T.; and Richards, Garry E. 1997. "Adventure Education and Outward Bound: Out-of-Class Experiences That Make a Lasting Difference." *Review of Educational Research* 67(1):43–87.

James, Thomas. 1995. "Kurt Hahn and the Aims of Education." In *The Theory of Experiential Education,* ed. Karen Warren, Mitchell S. Sakofs, and Jasper S. Hunt Jr. Dubuque, IA: Kendall/Hunt.

Kolb, David A. 1984. *Experiential Learning: Experience as the Source of Learning and Development.* Englewood Cliffs, NJ: Prentice Hall.

Lewin, Kurt. 1952. *Field Theory in the Social Sciences: Selected Theoretical Papers.* London: Tavistock.

National Evaluation of Learn and Serve America. 1999. Waltham, MA: Center for Human Resources, Brandeis University.

Piaget, Jean. 1967. "The Mental Development of the Child." In *Six Psychological Studies,* ed. David Elkind. New York: Vintage Books.

Priest, Simon, and Gass, Michael A. 1997. *Effective Leadership in Adventure Programming.* Champaign, IL: Human Kinetics.

Sizer, Theodore R. 1984. *Horace's Compromise.* Boston: Houghton Mifflin.

Jennifer A. Vadeboncoeur

EXPERTISE

ADAPTIVE EXPERTISE
  Giyoo Hatano
DOMAIN EXPERTISE
  K. Anders Ericsson
  Robert R. Hoffman

ADAPTIVE EXPERTISE

Investigators on knowledge transfer have almost unanimously concluded that students seldom effectively apply short-term training at school to problem-solving situations outside school. Experts, who have had years of problem-solving experience in a given domain, may not be different—they can solve familiar types of problems quickly and accurately but fail to go beyond procedural efficiency. Even in knowledge-rich domains, experts may be characterized by their possession of problem schemas by which they classify problems and apply one of the solution routines accordingly.

The notion of adaptive experts as against routine experts was proposed by Giyoo Hatano as an ideal of educational researchers looking to find ways to teach students so they can apply learned procedures flexibly or adaptively. Keith Holyoak aptly describes the distinction: "Whereas routine experts are able to solve familiar types of problems quickly and accurately, they have only modest capabilities in dealing with novel types of problems. Adaptive experts, on the other hand, may be able to invent new procedures derived from their expert knowledge" (p. 310). Giyoo Hatano and Kayoko Inagaki, in their 1986 paper, slightly expand the above characterization of adaptive experts: They are able to (1) comprehend why those procedures they know work; (2) modify those procedures flexibly when needed; and (3) invent new procedures when none of the known procedures are effective.

Sources of Adaptiveness

Where does the adaptiveness of adaptive experts come from? Adaptive experts are assumed to possess, as the source of their flexibility and inventiveness, conceptual knowledge of the objects of the procedures (that is, what each of these objects is like). "Flexibility and adaptability seem to be possible only when there is some corresponding conceptual knowledge to give meaning to each step of the skill and provide criteria for selection among possible alternatives for each step within the procedure" (Hatano 1982, p. 15). Such conceptual knowledge enables experts to construct mental models of the major entities of the domain, which can be used in mental simulation. Using Holyoak's expression, the key to adaptive expertise is the development of deeper conceptual understanding of the target domain. Needless to say, such conceptual understanding must be connected to procedural competencies and meta-cognitive awareness and monitoring of one's own understanding.

It is hypothesized that if people ask themselves why a skill works or why each step is needed during its application, this question will tend to lead them to form some conceptual knowledge about the object. This was similar to what Donald Schoen in 1983 called "reflection-in-action" as against technical problem-solving in his attempt to characterize professionals. Although experts are seldom taught conceptual knowledge in the verbalized form, they may construct it in the process of solving problems or performing tasks in the domain.

Motivational and Contextual Conditions

When are people likely to gain adaptive expertise? Identifying particular kinds of learning experiences that develop adaptive expertise is a serious challenge for educational researchers. In 1992 Hatano and Inagaki proposed four conditions that would promote sustained comprehension activity that is likely to lead to adaptive expertise. Their proposal is based on the assumption that *cognitive incongruity* (a state of feeling that current comprehension is inadequate; for example, wondering why a given procedure works) induces enduring comprehension activity, including seeking further information from the outside, retrieving another piece of prior knowledge, generating new inferences, examining the compatibility of inferences more closely, and so forth. The first two of the proposed conditions are concerned with the arousal of cognitive incongruity and the last two with the elicitation of committed and persistent comprehension activity in response to induced incongruity. The four conditions are: (1) encountering

fairly often a novel problem to which prior knowledge is not readily applicable or a phenomenon that disconfirms a prediction based on prior knowledge; (2) engaging in frequent dialogical interaction, such as discussion, controversy, and reciprocal teaching; (3) being free from urgent external need (e.g., material rewards or positive evaluations), and thus able to pursue comprehension even when it is time consuming; and (4) being surrounded by reference group members who value understanding.

These conditions can be rephrased in terms of the nature of the practice in which people participate. For example, when a practice is oriented toward skillfully solving a fixed class of problems (e.g., making the same products for years), participants tend not to encounter novel problems, and thus they are likely to become experts distinguished in terms of speed, accuracy, and automaticity (i.e., routine experts). In contrast, when successful participation in a practice requires meeting varied and changing demands (e.g., making new, fashionable products), participants' prior knowledge must be applied flexibly, and they are likely to acquire adaptive skills. From sociocultural perspectives, adaptive experts may not be characterized only by their domain-specific knowledge; in order to invent new procedures, for example, in addition to deeper conceptual understanding, people have to be able to participate in discourse, offer valuable suggestions, evaluate others' suggestions, and so on.

Educational Implications

At school students are seldom expected to become experts in a particular domain. Rather they are expected to learn in many subject-matter domains. Thus the extent to which school instruction and vocational expertise share similar goals and processes of learning is debatable. Trying to build a classroom as a community of adaptive experts is challenging, but practically it may be too ambitious or require too much effort on the part of educators.

Whatever the ultimate goal for instruction should be, the concept of adaptive expertise "provides an important model of successful learning" (Bransford, Brown, and Cocking, p. 36). It is thus encouraging to see attempts to apply this notion to teaching and learning in mathematics, science, history, and other subjects.

See also: EXPERTISE, *subentry on* DOMAIN EXPERTISE.

BIBLIOGRAPHY

BRANSFORD, JOHN D.; BROWN, ANN L.; and COCKING, RODNEY R. 1999. *How People Learn.* Washington, DC: National Academy Press.

HATANO, GIYOO. 1982. "Cognitive Consequences of Practice in Culture Specific Procedural Skills." *Quarterly Newsletter of the Laboratory of Comparative Human Cognition* 4:15–18.

HATANO, GIYOO, and INAGAKI, KAYOKO. 1986. "Two Courses of Expertise." In *Child Development and Education in Japan,* ed. Harold Stevenson, Hiroshi Azuma, and Kenji Hakuta. New York: Freeman.

HATANO, GIYOO, and INAGAKI, KAYOKO 1992. "Desituating Cognition through the Construction of Conceptual Knowledge." In *Context and Cognition,* ed. Paul Light and George Butterworth. Hemel Hempstead, Eng.: Harvester Wheatsheaf.

HOLYOAK, KEITH. 1991. "Symbolic Connectionism: Toward Third-Generation Theories of Expertise." In *Toward a General Theory of Expertise: Prospects and Limits,* ed. K. Anders Erricsson and Jacqui Smith. Cambridge, Eng.: Cambridge University Press.

SCHOEN, DONALD A. 1983. *The Reflective Practitioner.* New York: Basic Books.

GIYOO HATANO

DOMAIN EXPERTISE

Expertise refers to the psychological mechanisms underlying the superior achievement of an expert and the social forces that designate the status of being an expert, that is, "one who has acquired special skill in or knowledge of a particular subject through professional training and practical experience" (*Webster's Third New International Dictionary,* p. 800). The term expert has been used to describe highly experienced professionals, such as medical doctors, accountants, teachers, and scientists, but has been expanded to include any individual who has attained superior performance by instruction and extended practice, ranging from bird-watchers to pianists, golfers to chess players.

Theoretical Frameworks

Experts' behavior looks so effortless and natural that it is often attributed to special talents, though knowledge and training are necessary. The role of acquired skill for the highest levels of achievement has traditionally been minimized. However, when scientists began measuring the experts' presumed superior powers of speed of thought, memory, and intelligence with psychometric tests, no general superiority was found—the demonstrated superiority was domain specific. For example, the chess experts' vastly superior memory was constrained to regular chess positions and did not generalize to other types of materials. Not even IQ could distinguish the chess masters among chess players nor the most successful and creative among artists and scientists. In K. Anders Ericsson and Andreas C. Lehmann's 1996 review, it was found that (1) measures of general basic capacities do not reliably predict success in a domain; (2) the superior performance of experts is often very domain specific and transfer outside their narrow area of expertise is limited; and (3) systematic differences between experts and less proficient individuals nearly always reflect attributes acquired by the experts during their lengthy training.

Thought processes. In a pioneering empirical study first published in 1946 of the thought processes at the highest levels of performance, Adrian de Groot instructed expert and world-class chess players to think aloud while they selected their next move for an unfamiliar chess position. The world-class players did not differ in the speed of their thoughts or the size of their basic memory capacity, and their ability to recognize promising potential moves was based on their extensive experience and knowledge of patterns in chess. In their influential 1973 theory of expertise, Herbert A. Simon and William G. Chase proposed that experts with extended experience acquire and remember a larger number of complex patterns and use these new patterns to store new knowledge about which actions should be taken in similar situations.

According to this influential theory, expert performance is viewed as the result of skill acquired with gradual improvements of performance during extended experience in a domain. Furthermore, this theory assigned a central role of acquired knowledge and encouraged efforts to elicit experts' knowledge to build computer models of experts, that is, expert systems.

It is tempting to assume that the performance of experts improves as a direct function of increases in knowledge through training and extended experience. However, there are many demonstrations that extensive domain knowledge does not necessarily entail superior performance. For example, the outcome of psychological therapy does not increase as a function of the length of training and professional experience of the therapist. Similarly, the accuracy of decision-making—such as medical diagnosis for common diseases and the quality of investment decisions—does not improve with further professional experience. More generally, the number of years of work and experience in a domain is a poor predictor of attained performance.

The development of expert performance. In a 1985 pioneering study, Benjamin S. Bloom and his colleagues studied the developmental history of scientists, athletes, and artists who had attained international awards for their outstanding achievements. These elite performers did not attain their performance from regular experience in their respective domains but were given access to superior instruction in the best educational environments. Their families provided them substantial financial and emotional support to allow them to focus fully on the development of their performance. Bloom's influential research demonstrated the necessity for extended training in the best training environments to reach the highest levels of performance.

Effects of practice and experience. Subsequent research published in 1993 by Ericsson, Ralf Krampe, and Clemens Tesch-Römer analyzed the effects of different types of experience on the improvement of performance. They found that in activities where individuals had attained an acceptable level of performance, such as recreational golf and many professions, even decades of continued experience was not associated with any improvement of performance. The researchers proposed that in those domains where performance consistently increases, aspiring expert performers seek out particular kinds of experience, that is, deliberate practice—activities designed, typically by a teacher, for the sole purpose of effectively improving specific aspects of an individual's performance. In support of a critical role of deliberate practice, expert musicians differing in the level of attained solo performance also differed in the amounts of time they had spent in solitary practice during their skill development, which totaled around 10,000 hours by age twenty for the best experts, around 5,000 hours for the least accomplished expert musicians, and only 2,000 hours for serious amateur pianists. More generally, the accumulated amount of deliberate practice is closely related to the attained level of performance of many types of experts, such as musicians, chess players, and athletes.

Conclusions

Advances in the understanding of the complex representations, knowledge, and skills that mediate experts' superior performance derive from studies where experts are instructed to think aloud while completing representative tasks and from studies using methods of cognitive task analysis and cognitive field research. These process-tracing studies have shown that the difference between experts and less-skilled individuals is not merely a matter of the amount and complexity of the accumulated knowledge; it also reflects qualitative differences in strategies, the organization of knowledge, and the representation of problems. During the acquisition of their performance, experts acquire domain-specific memory skills that allow them to rely on long-term memory to dramatically expand the amount of information that can be kept accessible during planning and during reasoning about alternative courses of action. The superior quality of the experts' mental representations allows them to adapt to changing circumstances as well as anticipate future events in advance, so the expert performers can respond with impressive speed. The same acquired representations appear to be essential for experts' ability to monitor and evaluate their own performance so they can keep improving by designing their own training and assimilating new knowledge.

See also: EXPERTISE, *subentry on* ADAPTIVE EXPERTISE.

BIBLIOGRAPHY

BLOOM, BENJAMIN S., ed. 1985. *Developing Talent in Young People.* New York: Ballantine Books.

CHI, MICKI T. H.; GLASER, ROBERT; and REES, ERNEST. 1982. "Expertise in Problem Solving." In *Advances in the Psychology of Human Intelligence,* ed. Robert J. Sternberg. Hillsdale, NJ: Erlbaum.

DAWES, ROBIN M. 1994. *House of Cards: Psychology and Psychotherapy Built on Myth.* New York: Free Press.

DE GROOT, ADRIAN. 1978. *Thought and Choice in Chess.* (1946) The Hague, Netherlands: Mouton.

ERICSSON, K. ANDERS, ed. 1996. *The Road to Excellence: The Acquisition of Expert Performance in the Arts and Sciences, Sports, and Games.* Mahwah, NJ: Erlbaum.

ERICSSON, K. ANDERS. 2001. "Attaining Excellence through Deliberate Practice: Insights from the Study of Expert Performance." In *The Pursuit of Excellence in Education,* ed. Michel Ferrari. Hillsdale, NJ: Erlbaum.

ERICSSON, K. ANDERS, and KINTSCH, WALTER. 1995. "Long-Term Working Memory." *Psychological Review* 102:211–245.

ERICSSON, K. ANDERS; KRAMPE, RALF THOMAS; and TESCH-RÖMER, CLEMENS. 1993. "The Role of Deliberate Practice in the Acquisition of Expert Performance." *Psychological Review* 100:363–406.

ERICSSON, K. ANDERS, and LEHMANN, ANDREAS C. 1996. "Expert and Exceptional Performance: Evidence on Maximal Adaptations on Task Constraints." *Annual Review of Psychology* 47:273–305.

HOFFMAN, ROBERT R., ed. 1992. *The Psychology of Expertise: Cognitive Research and Empirical AI.* New York: Springer-Verlag.

PROCTOR, ROBERT W., and DUTTA, ADDIE. 1995. *Skill Acquisition and Human Performance.* Thousand Oaks, CA: Sage.

SIMON, HERBERT A, and CHASE, WILLIAM G. 1973. "Skill in Chess." *American Scientist* 61:394–403.

Webster's Third New International Dictionary. 1976. Springfield, MA: Merriam-Webster.

ZSAMBOK, CAROLINE E., and KLEIN, GARY, ed. 1997. *Naturalistic Decision Making.* Mahwah, NJ: Erlbaum.

K. ANDERS ERICSSON
ROBERT R. HOFFMAN